GROVER CLEVELAND

A Study in Courage

By

ALLAN NEVINS

"Tell the Truth"

GROVER CLEVELAND, 1884

Grover Cleveland, A Study in Courage by Allan Nevins

ISHI PRESS INTERNATIONAL

Grover Cleveland, A Study in Courage
by Allan Nevins

First Published in 1932

Copyright © 1932 by **Allan Nevins**

Reprinted in 2018 by Ishi Press International in New York and Tokyo with a new Introduction by Sam Sloan

ISBN 4-87187-186-X
978-4-87187-186-0
Ishi Press International
1664 Davidson Ave, Suite 1B
Bronx NY 10453
USA
1-917-659-3397
1-917-507-7226
samhsloan@gmail.com

Printed in the United States of America

Grover Cleveland, A Study in Courage
by Allan Nevins
Introduction by Sam Sloan

Grover Cleveland was regarded as one of the greatest presidents ever in his day, but was nearly forgotten except by professional historians and students of history until the current president came along which invites comparisons.

One comparison is the current president is 23 years older than his wife.

However, Grover Cleveland married a girl, Frances Folsom, aged 20, who was 28 years younger, while he was president, even though he was administrator of her father's estate.

This scandal may have caused him to lose the presidential election in 1888. Actually, he won the popular vote but lost the electoral vote, similar to the current situation. He then regained the presidency through the 1892 elections.

Grover Cleveland's marriage was successful. They had five children. Their family line is active today with many descendants. The Baby Ruth candy bar is named after their first daughter, Ruth Cleveland.

Grover Cleveland's presidency is known for two unconnected terms from 1885 to 1889 and then from 1893 to 1897 making him both the 22nd and 24th president of the United States.

After the American Civil War, all the presidents were Republicans up until Cleveland.

His terms of office were known for labor unrest and labor strikes, especially the Pullman Strike of railroad workers. Cleveland established Labor Day as a national holiday, the first Monday in September in honor of workers and to quell labor violence.

A famous baseball player, Grover Cleveland Alexander, was named after him.

Grover Cleveland is also known for the fact that he was accused of having fathered an illegitimate child by a Mrs. Halpin. The child had been placed in an orphanage due to neglect and drinking by the mother. Neither the child nor the mother could be produced. What ever happened to them is not known. He is one of several presidents who have been accused of fathering an illegitimate child.

This book is the most authoritative work on the Cleveland presidency. It is also the longest.

The author, Allan Nevins, was born May 20, 1890. He was an American historian and journalist, known for his extensive work on the history of the Civil War and his biographies of such figures as Grover Cleveland, Hamilton Fish, Henry Ford, and John D. Rockefeller, as well as his public service. He was a leading exponent of business history and oral history. He died March 5, 1971.

Sam Sloan
Bronx New York
USA
September 4, 2018

GROVER CLEVELAND
A STUDY IN COURAGE

Portrait inserted by the Secretary of State of New York in Vol. VII of
"Messages from the Governors"

PREFACE

No excuse is needed for a new biography of that one of our political leaders who most signally illustrates the saying that "a man's best armor is his honest thought, and simple truth his utmost skill." Within the last decade important new materials for this biography have become available. It is difficult to thank the great number of those who have lent assistance during the years of research and writing which this book represents. Among those to whom gratitude is chiefly due are Mr. Cleveland's widow, Mrs. Thomas J. Preston, who threw open his papers and gave invaluable advice; his sister, Mrs. E. L. Yeomans, who contributed unpublished letters; his nephew, Mr. Cleveland Bacon, who furnished much family information; the daughters of his early friend and protector, Lewis F. Allen, who gave papers and information; Mr. Robert L. O'Brien, his confidential secretary in his second Administration, who has been of the utmost assistance in every stage of this work; Mr. William Gorham Rice, who permitted the use of his important Cleveland collection; Mr. Louis L. Babcock, who did the same; Mr. Charles S. Hamlin, who not only furnished letters and advice, but opened his invaluable diary for the period; the heirs of William L. Wilson, who furnished letters and the unpublished diary of their father; Mr. John Finley, who has been unsparing in encouragement and aid; Professor Robert McElroy, who lent his copies of many hundreds of Cleveland's letters; Mrs. Hoke Smith, who made available the Cleveland correspondence in her husband's papers; Mr. Charles H. Armitage of Buffalo, Mr. Edgar L. Murlin of Albany, and other newspaper men of those two cities; Mr. Charles Warren, who furnished memoranda of his father's relations with Mr. Cleveland, and gave much expert advice; Mr. Oscar Underwood, jr., Mr. George B. Cortelyou, and Mr. Oswald Garrison Villard, who gave advice and papers; Mrs. Charles H. Fairchild, who supplied letters in her husband's collection; the family of William F. Vilas; Mr. R. S. Leffingwell, who furnished materials from Edward M. Shepard's papers; and Mr. Erskine Hewitt, who permitted use of Abram S. Hewitt's papers. In response to an appeal for letters made through the two associations devoted to Grover Cleveland's memory, hundreds of men and women have sent in copies or originals. The author owes his thanks to them, and to Columbia University for supplying funds for a systematic collection of such letters. He owes a special debt to Miss Margaret Bassett for assistance in research. Among those who have very kindly read part or all of the proofs are Mrs. Thomas J. Preston; Mr. Rollo Ogden, editor of the New York *Times;* Mr. Robert L. O'Brien; Mr. Charles S. Hamlin; Mr. Frank Hill; and Professor Henry Steele Commager of New York University. Mr. Mark David Hirsch, of Columbia University, has given expert assistance in verifying difficult points and correcting errors of detail. To many others, whom he cannot name here, he makes grateful acknowledgments.

A collected edition of the letters of Grover Cleveland, edited by the author, is in preparation and will shortly be published.

CONTENTS

vii

CONTENTS

CONTENTS

ILLUSTRATIONS

GROVER CLEVELAND

A STUDY IN COURAGE

ON March 4, 1885, the sun rose in Washington upon a city crowded in anticipation of a momentous event—the return of the Democratic party to power for the first time since James Buchanan had quit the White House. At noon Grover Cleveland was to become the twenty-second President of the United States. It was a day as bright as the hopes of the party that he led. A springlike breeze blew down the Potomac from the west, and the warm sunshine rapidly drove the light haze from the sky. Every street in the heart of the capital was gay with flags; at an early hour there began to be heard, first from one quarter and then another, the rattle and blare of brass bands; the pavements were full of spectators, pressing slowly toward Lafayette Square and Pennsylvania Avenue. On thousands of faces there was a light of elation. It was a day of victory, of hopes fulfilled, of consecration renewed, for the hosts of a great party. Where the crowds pressed about the Arlington Hotel, a block from the White House grounds, the note of exultation rose loudest, for there was the President-elect. And when at ten o'clock there drew up at the hotel entrance the White House barouche, and the well-known forms of Senators Sherman and Ransom appeared a moment later escorting Cleveland forth, there arose a roar of cheers, punctuated again and again by the wild rebel yell.[1]

Two hours later all was in readiness for the inauguration ceremony. The crowds had rolled down the Avenue to the Capitol. President Arthur had signed his last bills; in the Senate Chamber the new Vice President, Thomas A. Hendricks, had taken the oath of office. President Arthur and Mr. Cleveland led the way from the chamber to the east front of the Capitol. As they passed through the pillars supporting the pediment they saw a magnificent sight. Beyond the temporary platform on which they stood, and far out to the edge of the grounds fronting the Capitol, extended an audience variously estimated at from thirty thousand to fifty thousand people. From this mass rose Greenough's white statue of Washington seated in Olympian attitude with toga-covered knees—a statue now half-hidden by men and boys. Spectators filled every window and niche of the Capitol, and clung to

---

[1] T. C. Evans, *Of Many Men,* describes the inauguration.

the windows and porches of distant houses. A cheer welled up as Cleveland and Arthur bowed, and seated themselves on red morocco chairs. Near them were placed Chief Justice Waite in his black robes, the historian Bancroft, a hale, impressive figure with his white beard, and Generals Sheridan, Terry, and Hancock in their blue and gold uniforms. Down the Capitol steps in their rear trooped the diplomatic corps, resplendent in gold braid and decorations, taking seats close behind the justices of the Supreme Court. Cleveland chatted with Arthur, smiling, while these officers were disposing themselves. Then, without introduction, he stepped to the front, smoothed his thin brown hair where the breeze had ruffled it, and without notes began in a strong, penetrating voice to deliver his address.

But the event most truly symbolical of the day occurred an hour later—the triumphal march back to the White House. President Cleveland and ex-President Arthur, walking through the Capitol, descended the stone staircases to the presidential carriage, which was at once driven to the Peace Monument at the west entrance of the grounds. The four melancholy female figures of this monument marked the traditional starting-point of all presidential parades. Already mounted police were busy clearing Pennsylvania Avenue, and the stone pavement resounded with the clatter of hooves. Far as the eye could reach the ugly buildings of the thoroughfare were swathed in bunting and blazing with emblems. The crush was tremendous, for several hundred thousand people had swarmed into the city. In the streets radiating from the Capitol, paraders were beginning to deploy. A trooper's bugle sounded the signal for the start. First came the mounted police in a solid line across the Avenue; then Cleveland and Arthur in their open carriage; then the Senatorial committee with Vice President Hendricks; then the grand marshal with his staff. Hats were in the air, handkerchiefs flying; a stiff northwest breeze was whipping the flags. Cleveland lifted his hat and bowed again and again. The steady throb of the bands was at one moment heard above the cheering and the next was lost. Then behind the leaders came the imposing spectacle of the military and political organizations.

Not since the grand review of Grant's and Sherman's troops had such a procession been seen in Washington.[1] Every branch of the regular service was there—infantry, a detachment of marines, cavalry, artillery,

[1] Harry Thurston Peck, *Twenty Years of the Republic*, 2.

and sailors. Well toward the front was a body of colored troops—when the last Democratic President had been inaugurated, a slave-market had stood near the Capitol. Then came an entire division of Pennsylvania militia, 7000 men, under their Democratic governor, Pattison. On their heels appeared the first Southerners. Fitzhugh Lee rode proudly before the Richmond State Guards, and after them marched the Fifth Regiment of Baltimore. There were North Carolina troops, Missouri troops, and a Georgia battalion. Applause greeted the fighting Sixty-ninth of New York. Then, toward the rear, came party organizations from all parts of the country. Many of the Democratic clubs were brave with regalia. Tammany Hall headed the line with more than five hundred men, six of them dressed as Indian braves; the County Democracy of New York had 1600 men in line; a contingent of Samuel J. Randall's Pennsylvanians made a striking appearance. Mingled with paraders from Maine, Kansas, and Ohio, the Buffalo Legion and Albany Phalanx were there to do their fellow-townsman honor.

In the crowds which cheered this procession from the curb were types as distinct as the various units in the military pageant. There were the Irish Democrats of the metropolis, with their shamrocks and brogue. There were Western Democrats who seemed to bring a veritable breath of the Jacksonian spirit. There were unmistakable survivors of the Confederate armies—lean and aging veterans, some with an arm or a leg missing. There were Kentucky and Virginia colonels, their broadcloth cut in old-fashioned lines. There were the keen and aggressive men who represented the reform Democracy of Northern cities: old-line Philadelphians and Bostonians, and the followers of Abram S. Hewitt in New York. All were swayed by the same emotions. Expectations long disappointed were at last satisfied; gibed at for years, cheated once (as they believed) of the presidency when it was within their grasp, they at last held the fruits of victory; long treated as enemies of the republic, they had an opportunity to show that its fortunes were safe in their hands.

And what of the leader of this joyful host? As with his most intimate friends beside him he passed within the doors of the White House, he must have experienced the keenest thrill of emotion. His inauguration typified the peaceful and orderly processes by which political revolutions may be effected in the United States. It typified also the romance inherent in the swift rise of many Americans from obscurity to fame. Four years earlier he had been unknown to most citizens of his own State. Now, by a spectacular series of steps, he had been lifted to the chief magistracy of one of the greatest nations of the world. Where two famous Democratic leaders, Horatio Seymour and Samuel J. Tilden, had failed, he had succeeded in revivifying his party. Pitted against the most magnetic, compelling, and resourceful of American political chieftains, James G. Blaine, he had defeated him in a battle that would long be famous in American political annals. He might well have felt a sense of exultation tinged with wonder.

II

The new Democratic leader had brought to his position a peculiar training and a peculiar balance of traits. In our political leaders we may make a rough distinction between two kinds of greatness. There is the greatness of the highly individualized man, like Pitt or Hamilton, who possesses certain rare and brilliant qualities; and the greatness of the strong man, like Washington or Gladstone, whose qualities are not exceptional in kind but are developed to an exceptional degree and held in exceptional balance. The one is great because some traits stand out high above the rest. The other is great because all his traits are kept in close harmony at an unusual level. Doubtless no shrewd observer ever saw much of Hamilton, or John Quincy Adams, or Lincoln, without saying to himself: "Here is a man of striking originality; he gives me a new idea of human power." Probably many intelligent men, after seeing a good deal of Washington, said hastily: "Here is a rather commonplace man; I find in him no quality of genius at all." What they did not see was that the combination of talents in Washington, and the strength of character behind this combination, the calm wisdom controlling it, made him a leader to tower in history.

In Grover Cleveland the greatness lies in typical rather than unusual qualities. He had no endowments that thousands of men do not have. He possessed honesty, courage, firmness, independence, and common sense. But he possessed them in a degree that others did not. His honesty was of the undeviating type which never compromised an inch; his courage was immense, rugged, unconquerable; his independence was elemental and self-assertive. Beneath all this was a virility or energy which enabled him to impose his qualities upon others in any crisis. Under storms that would have bent any man of lesser strength he ploughed straight forward, never flinching, always following the path that his conscience approved to the end. Walter Bagehot once said that the British Prime Minister ought to be simply a man who has more common sense than anyone else. The definition, while illuminating, is inadequate for the leader of a democracy. He needs at once common sense, more conscience, and more courage. Cleveland, who could by no possible license of phrasing be called brilliant, showed how valuable these qualities may be made to a nation in troubled times.

It is as a strong man, a man of character, that Cleveland will live in history. For all his shrewdness of judgment, he was never in any sense a great intellectual force. It was his personality, not his mind, that made so deep an impress upon his time. As we speak of a Jacksonian and a Roosevelt Era in American politics, so men already speak of a Cleveland Era. A young nation—or an old one—needs in its polity all the character, and all the intellectual ability, that it can get. But at different times one becomes more important than the other. The vast and complex problems of the present day—world organization, finance, unemployment, industrial control, poverty—first of all demand brains, and brains of a technically expert quality. But in the hour in which Cleveland rose to authority, when all the social elements churned up by civil war and by excessively rapid national growth were slowly solidifying, character was the principal desideratum. The nation in 1885 needed a man who would typify Reform, and Cleveland proved to be the man. A few years later, in 1893, it needed a man who could hold the gate against financial error and class and sectional antagonism— hold it with grimly stubborn courage; and again Cleveland was the man.

Character is not made overnight. When it appears in transcendent degree it is usually the product of generations of disciplined ancestry, or a stern environment, or both. Genius is a flower that may rise anywhere, but the steely oak requires a deep and hard-knit soil. So it was with Grover Cleveland. If we ask what type of American nurture in the years of 1840–60 offered an ideal training for character, we should have to define just such a home as that in which Cleveland grew up. He had a Puritan ancestry; a rural birthplace, not too far out toward the uncouth frontier; a professional man—a minister—for father; numerous brothers and sisters to teach him habits of give-and-take; and the stern compulsion of standing up at an early age to fight the world. His home was not ideal for intellectual training, aesthetic interests, or breadth, but it was excellent for fibre. And to these varied blessings Cleveland added an inherited strain of stubbornness that gleamed in his clear blue eyes before he was five years old.

Characteristically, Cleveland always manifested indifference to his remoter ancestry. He once wrote that he had had but little time to study genealogy, having always been "kept very busy in an attempt to fulfill the duties of life without questioning how I got into the scrape." [1] Yet his family history possesses marked importance. On his father's side he came of a long line of Puritan ministers and deacons which had always shown sturdiness, and twice within a century had produced men of real distinction. His early biographers have fostered the impression that he rose from a poor and commonplace stock. On the contrary, his forbears were of the truest aristocracy that America can boast: men who were straitened financially, but who valued education, who made themselves community leaders, and who reared large families in an atmosphere of piety and self-respect. The Clevelands had originated in northeastern England. [2] The first of the name to arrive in America was a Moses Cleveland who in 1635 reached Massachusetts from Ipswich as an apprentice indentured to a joiner. He is less than a shadow, a mere name. But it is not long before we begin to see some of the Clevelands more clearly.

There were two Clevelands of pith and note before the birth of the man who was to make the name famous. The first was Aaron Cleveland, grandson of Moses and great-great-grandfather of the President, who was born in Cambridge in 1715, the son of a tavern-keeper, contractor, and land-speculator, and who was graduated from Harvard in 1735. While in college he made himself noted for his feats of strength, excelling as a swimmer, wrestler and boxer. He was a minister first of the Puritan and later of the Anglican denomination, and became a well-known missionary of the Society for the Propagation of the Gospel. Few American churchmen of his time travelled more widely. Marrying into the aristocratic Sewall family of Boston, he

---

[1] Aug. 23, 1887. Cleveland Papers.
[2] E. J. and H. G. Cleveland, *Genealogy Cleveland and Cleveland Families.*

occupied Congregational pulpits in Connecticut and Massachusetts, and in 1750 went to Halifax to organize the body known as Mather's Church. Converted about 1754 to Episcopalianism, he resigned his charge and, there being no bishop in America, voyaged to England to be ordained by the Bishop of London. Near the close of his life he took charge of parishes at Lewes and Newcastle, Delaware. He was long remembered in the various communities where he preached as a witty, scholarly, and earnest man, of handsome presence and leader-like traits. It is not too much to call him one of the notable colonial divines of his time; and it is evidence of his force of character that he won the friendship of Benjamin Franklin, in whose house in Philadelphia he died in 1757.[1]

The second Cleveland to attain any distinction was his son, Cleveland's great-grandfather, also named Aaron. He was born in Haddam, Conn., in 1744, established a hat manufactory at Norwich in the same State, and prospered. An ardent supporter of the Revolution, he entered the Connecticut legislature in 1779, served there for a single term, and introduced the first bill for the abolition of slavery in the State. He further proved his talents by a copious production of verse and essays, his moral poem "The Philospher and Boy" being much admired in his own time. In middle life he felt called to preach, was ordained in 1797 as a Congregational minister, and filled several pulpits in New York, Vermont, and Connecticut. One of the stock political anecdotes of Jeffersonian days in Connecticut, recorded in Peter Parley's entertaining autobiography, relates that Aaron Cleveland was accosted on the highway by a Democratic horseman. "How are you, priest?" demanded the rider. "How are you, Republican?" returned Cleveland. "I knew you by your dress," explained the Democrat. "And I knew you by your address," replied Cleveland. Evidently he possessed humor. A family chronicle states that he was "a person of naturally brilliant talents, ready wit, and a pleasing social companion, whose society was generally courted by the respectable part of the community."[2] Grover Cleveland knew of his career by family tradition, and during the campaign of 1884 had his gravestone in the New Haven cemetery repaired.

[1] For full sketch, see *Dictionary of American Biography*, IV, 202.
[2] *Memorial of David L. Dodge: Autobiography;* see also Norwich *Bulletin,* June 10, 1888.

The Clevelands became a numerous clan, quickly spreading themselves over the New England and Middle States. Most of them were godly, earnest men and women. One of Aaron's daughters, Sarah, in 1798 married David L. Dodge, who became known in Connecticut and New York as a great merchant-philanthropist, and founded a noted family, the name of Cleveland H. Dodge, Woodrow Wilson's friend and supporter, being a reminder of the union. A great-uncle of Grover Cleveland's named Charles became the venerated "Father Cleveland," an Episcopal city missionary of Boston. From the family there sprang in Cleveland's own time Arthur Cleveland Coxe, who for a long generation after the Civil War was Episcopal bishop of western New York and a prolific writer. Another great-uncle, Stephen Cleveland, was a public-spirited citizen of Salem, Mass., who has a place among the footnotes of history as the man who in 1791 brought a memorable prosecution against two Salem shipowners to punish them for participation in the African slave trade.[1]

These details of the Cleveland line are not important. What is important is the general tendency which they indicate, like the strong surge which, under spume and surface ripple, carries a wave forward across the ocean. Right up to Cleveland himself runs this wave of piety and strength. His grandfather, to be sure, was not a minister. He was a silversmith, watchmaker, and jeweller, living on Beacon Hill in Norwich, Conn. When Cleveland was governor an Albany banker brought him a watch, still in daily use, bearing this William Cleveland's name. But the grandfather was a devout deacon of the Congregational church in Norwich, and he dedicated his son, Cleveland's father, as a new offering to the Christian ministry.

III

When we come to the President's father, Richard Falley Cleveland, we meet the first unhappy note in the family annals; for his was unquestionably a hard and pinched career. The early passages we may pass over rapidly. Born in Norwich on June 19, 1804; growing up "a thin, pale, and intellectual boy"; employed for a time with his cousin

[1] Elizabeth Donnan in *New England Quarterly*, III, 271.

William E. Dodge, destined to become one of the richest and most public-spirited of New York merchants, as a clerk in the Dodges' dry-goods establishment in Norwich; and then sent to Yale—so the chronicle runs. He was graduated with honors in 1824. For a time he taught school in Baltimore, simultaneously studying theology with the Rev. William Nevins, an older alumnus of Yale.[1] During the winter of 1827–28 he took courses in the Princeton Theological Seminary. In the fall of the latter year we find him back in New Haven as a resident licentiate, trying his wings as a preacher and earnestly saving every cent. He had fallen in love in Baltimore with pretty Ann Neal, daughter of a rather wealthy bookseller and publisher of lawbooks, and had become engaged. She was a girl of about twenty when he met her, having been born on February 4, 1806; her father, Abner Neal, was of Anglo-Irish extraction—a Protestant, but driven from Ireland for political activities—while her mother, Barbara Real or Reel, was a German Quakeress from Germantown, Pa. She had a little property of her own. On September 10, 1829, she and Richard Cleveland were married, and on October 15 following he was ordained and installed minister of the Congregational church in Windham, Conn.

It is not difficult to picture the life which Cleveland's parents lived in the eight years between their marriage and his birth. Financially, it was a pinched existence, for Richard Cleveland did not rise rapidly in his profession. He spent three years, till October 1, 1832, as minister in Windham, a narrowly Puritanical village. When he brought his bride there from Baltimore in 1829 her negro maid had begged to accompany her, while she had taken along a considerable wardrobe and some jewelry. The people of Windham quickly made her understand that no woman from a slave State could bring a colored maid into Connecticut without incurring suspicion, and that bright dresses and jewels were forbidden a minister's wife. After leaving Windham, Richard Cleveland spent two years as "stated supply" or acting minister of a Presbyterian church in Portsmouth, Va., a pleasant town which his wife liked; and then in November, 1834, he removed his family to Caldwell, N. J. Here, on a salary that never reached $600 a year, he took charge of the First Presbyterian Church, the only one in the village. Caldwell, now a thriving suburb of New York on the

[1] *Memorial Notices of Yale Graduates 1816–1884.*

Erie Railroad, was then an isolated community, connected by stage, over rough, ill-kept roads, with Newark. It took pride in a rather unusual church—a large boxlike structure, fifty by sixty feet in dimensions, with a fine white steeple which rose 130 feet. It also took pride in the fact that its first minister, whom Richard Cleveland succeeded, had served continuously since 1787: the saintly Stephen Grover, a Dartmouth graduate, now worn out by nearly fifty years of pastoral labor.

Children followed each other rapidly in the Cleveland home. Two had been born in Connecticut and one in Portsmouth. The family had hardly settled itself in Caldwell before another arrived, making two girls and two boys. Then came Stephen Grover, born on March 18, 1837, and named in honor of the former pastor, who had died the previous year. Two additional children were born before the family left Caldwell. One of Richard Cleveland's successors in the village pulpit said many years later that "during his six years' pastorate Mr. Cleveland's father had a child baptized every year," and while this was not true, it is easy to see how the impression arose. The pressure upon the minister's tiny salary grew painful. He had the manse—an old-fashioned two-and-a-half story frame house, with four gables, a front porch, low windows, and a general air of comfort and peace, standing in a large yard with ashes and elms in front; it was the first house on the road entering Caldwell from Montclair, and the most dignified residence in the village. He had his winter's supply of firewood and friendly "donations." But of money there was little.

His record in Caldwell, like the record of all the Clevelands everywhere, was creditable. In the spring of Grover's birth the minister called in an evangelist named Clark, and their labors resulted in an "awakening" and seventy-five new members. That same year three hundred Bibles and Testaments were distributed in the parish. During 1839 the church was thoroughly remodelled and repaired, at the then staggering cost of $22,000.[1] The sanding of the floors was stopped, and the first carpets were laid; coal stoves took the place of wood stoves; and the pews were made more comfortable. During Richard Cleveland's ministry 109 persons were added to the church. Caldwell would gladly have kept him, but in 1841, after considering a position in a girls' seminary in Syracuse, he accepted a call to Fayetteville, a village of central New York.

[1] Rev. C. T. Berry, *An Historical Survey of the First Presbyterian Church, Caldwell.*

IV

Caldwell is popularly associated with Cleveland's childhood, for it was the birthplace and the old manse has been converted into a Cleveland memorial; but Fayetteville was the first home that he remembered with affection. In 1841 it was a mere hamlet of little over a thousand people, some of whom had been there since its founding in 1791. The Presbyterian church drew its strength, however, from a good part of the township of Manlius, with a population of some five thousand, while hopes were entertained for the growth of the village. It was only a mile from the Erie Canal, and eight miles from Syracuse, in a rich grain-growing region. A tannery, a pearl-barley mill, and a lime factory furnished employment, and since the picturesque hills and streams gave it potential waterpower, schemes were on foot for establishing grist mills and textile factories. All upper and western New York, as the country recovered from the panic of 1837, was rapidly filling with settlers. Syracuse, Rome, Lockport, and Buffalo were throbbing with energy. Richard Cleveland had at least taken his family into a more vigorous region. If he had remained in Caldwell Grover would doubtless have gravitated to New York city, while now the attraction to an energetic boy lay westward.

There can be no question that Grover enjoyed his dozen years in Fayetteville. He grew up a chubby Saxon youngster, large for his age, and fond of village sports, the hills, the nut-groves, and the swimming holes along Limestone Creek or the Chittenango River. One of his sisters, Susan, has recalled him [1] as "a little round-faced, blue-eyed boy" vainly trying to rock the latest baby to sleep, while with tears in his eyes he looked out on the snowy slope where his schoolmates were sledding. The villagers testified later that he was "chuck full of fun," and inclined to play pranks. One neighbor remembered that "Grove" and "Will" (his older brother) more than once attached a long cord to the academy bell and rang it madly at dead of night; and when Cleveland returned as President he said in a speech that "if some of the old householders were here I could tell them who it was used to take off their front gates." He early formed his lifelong fondness for fishing. "I recall old Green Lake and the fish I tried to catch and never did," he continued, "and the traditional panther on its shores which

[1] Memorandum by Mrs. E. L. Yeomans. Cleveland Papers.

used to shorten my excursions thitherward." He helped to celebrate holidays, and once organized his schoolmates to collect two cartloads of old iron, with which they paid a foundryman in a neighboring village for making a Fourth of July cannon. But he also had to work hard at odd jobs, and once in running a corn-cutting machine he sliced off the tip of the middle finger on his left hand.

Discipline in the Fayetteville parsonage was strict. Family worship was held every evening. The children were required to memorize the Westminster Catechism and to become familiar with the Bible. The house contained many books, including Greek and Latin classics, theology, some history, and Milton and Shakespeare; but the most entertaining volume in the collection was Bunyan's *Pilgrim's Progress,* which they all knew by heart, while the weekly *Christian Observer* was supposed to supply all contemporary knowledge worth knowing.[1] On Sundays everyone but the babies attended two long church services, Sunday school, and a prayer-meeting. The New England observance of the Sabbath from Saturday at sundown to Sunday at sundown still prevailed, and no avoidable work was done in this period. On Saturday afternoon the house was put in order, playthings were stored away, an early supper was prepared, and in the evening the children received their weekly bath. The next day there was no play or secular reading; nothing but religious devotion, broken in the middle of the afternoon by the bountiful dinner prepared by the one family servant, a Canadian woman—a roast, a peck of potatoes, and a rice pudding.[2] Then came the only real recreation of the day, a walk in the garden and the orchard near the house; for Richard and Ann Cleveland had employed part of the first summer in laying out such a formal garden as Fayetteville had never before seen. Cleveland always remembered the names of the flowers—phlox, larkspurs, China asters, pinks, hollyhocks, and Bouncing Bet.

. Sometimes the family had visitors of importance—Mr. and Mrs. David Dodge, of New York; Dr. Samuel H. Cox, a learned churchman, the father (with fourteen other children) of Bishop Arthur Cleveland Coxe, who changed the spelling of the name; and the "Father" Charles Cleveland of Boston already mentioned. "The learned Dr. Cox," recalls Cleveland's sister Susan, "fascinated his hearers by

---

[1] Some of these books are still owned by Mrs. Yeomans and Mr. Cleveland Bacon.
[2] Memorandum by Mrs. E. L. Yeomans.

his abstruse discourse plentifully interspersed with Greek and Latin quotations, which although not in the least comprehended, made great music for the 'big ears of little pitchers.' " [1] Visiting ministers were numerous. It was plain living with high thinking; high not in the sense of reflecting wide cultivation or marked aesthetic interests, but of being heavily tinged by moral austerity. Grover was taught many forcible ethical lessons, he heard much of duty and self-improvement, and his parents spared no effort to lay a solid foundation for his character. One of the first productions of his pen that has been preserved is a brief essay, composed in the Fayetteville academy at the age of nine, upon the value of time and the necessity of making the most of it in order "to become great and good men"—an essay in which there are only two misspellings.

In the early years of his boyhood Cleveland's father was the principal influence upon him; later, his mother. The father was a handsome man, large of frame and in middle life somewhat portly. Genial blue eyes looked out from under a high baldish brow; he had a prominent Roman nose and firm mouth. Family tradition recalls him as a kindly, expansive man, with much charm of manner. Though studious, he was certainly not a brilliant minister. He failed to make his way to the higher reaches of his profession; he left no writings—not even a pamphlet sermon. But then he never cared to seek promotion, believing it his duty to accept humble burdens.[2] Cleveland's uncle, Lewis F. Allen, once recorded his conviction that Richard Cleveland had ability, "but his modesty killed him. I mean he didn't have push enough." When he died, the obituaries in the religious press were restrained in their eulogy. "The character of our departed brother," declared the New York *Evangelist*,[3] "was distinguished rather for the happy union and equal development of his virtues, than for the marked prominence of any single trait. He combined the tastes and habits of the Christian scholar with practical wisdom and efficiency." In other words, he was not a man of striking talents. "As a preacher he was earnest, instructive, affectionate, and impressive"—the writer does not say eloquent. But there was a general agreement as to his fineness of character, incessant industry, and devotion to duty. "With what diligence he

[1] Idem.
[2] Cleveland Bacon to author, Oct. 20, 1931.
[3] October 27, 1853.

wrought in his Master's vineyard!" exclaimed the *Evangelist;* ". . . with what self-denying and invaluable labors in aid of his brethren in the ministry!"

A number of Richard Cleveland's letters, preserved by his descendants, throw a happier light on his character than any description can do. One written from Caldwell just before he left that village presents the more practical side of an unworldly man.[1] It was addressed to a relative, Dr. A. B. Cleveland, in Baltimore:

My dear Doctor:
I duly received your very kind reply to my request, in reference to the female seminary at Syracuse; but before its reception, I had fallen in with a place for ministerial employment which seemed to be the proper location for me, and thither I expect to remove my family about the last week in the present month; I arrived at home today for the purpose of effecting the change. The place is the village of Fayetteville, in the town of Manlius, Onondaga County, New York. It is 8 miles from Syracuse, on the turnpike road, 4 miles from the western railroad, and 1 mile from the Erie Canal. It contains about 1200 inhabitants, 4 churches, an academy, several stores, mills, and mechanical establishments. The society is for the most part rather a choice grade of New England and Eastern New York population. I expect to be engaged for a year, at first, as I hardly thought the character of the place would warrant my accepting a call to be settled there immediately. At the close of this term it may appear best to fix my residence there more permanently. The congregation are totally unanimous in their regard for me, and their desire for my location among them. And this is a choice circumstance especially, in our church at the present day. The prospect is pleasant there, and although the salary is not large yet, I think the support, as it is for the present year, will be better than I ever received before, considerably so. I am to receive $50 toward the expenses of removing, a house to live in, and $500 in money for current expenses, with a fair expectation of other aid in perquisites and so forth, amounting to another hundred. I expect now to be very busy till I get away. . . .

A letter to a Caldwell friend six months later offers a glimpse of the new life at Fayetteville: [2]

We have had a very busy winter in Fayetteville—more things going on than we have time to attend to. I believe I sent your father one of our Temperance Hotel's advertisements. We have two first-rate Temperance Hotels—and two that are not. Our drunkards are nearly all reformed. We have had, and still

[1] October 12, 1841. Cleveland Papers.
[2] To E. R. Crane, Fayetteville, April 11, 1842. Cleveland Papers.

have, notwithstanding the continual diversion of the public mind by other objects, some pleasing indications of the spirit's presence—but not a general and deep work of grace, such as I long to behold.

Still more revealing is another long letter written from Fayetteville in 1847 to the Dr. A. B. Cleveland just mentioned. In one paragraph Richard refers to the Free Soil activities of that year in Northern New York and expresses his own conservative opinion. "I am not much taken with the new-growth reforms of the present day, and am more disposed to make the best of old and well-tried expedients. Still I hope for the world's reformation, and I trust I may even be ready, according to the measure of my ability and opportunity, to promote it." Another gleam of conservatism occurs in a sentence referring to Dr. Cox's son James, a limb of the law. "I think," writes the Rev. Mr. Cleveland, "he will do well—if not too much absorbed with the fiddle and Abolitionism." There is a pleasant account of the Fayetteville household, for after mentioning his uncle's children he goes on:

My number, 3 times 3, is much nearer the extreme limit of J. Q. Adams' desideratum, "from seven to half a score." Our oldest child completed her seventeenth year yesterday. My next is now fifteen. He is fitted for college, but being too young to enter, he is for the present time in a store in the neighboring village of Manlius. My second boy, a stout, athletic chap of twelve years, is on a farm some 15 miles distant in a community of genuine New England farmers. Our children are (of course) all promising, and afford us the common experience of care and comfort. Strangers are apt to "start" at the annunciation of my patriarchal estate. But these olive plants, threatening to out-top us all around, allow of no mistake, and "feelingly instruct us what we are."

Ann's health is not so good in this climate as formerly, but on the whole, we have the utmost cause of gratitude for health and other abundant mercies. I have more opportunity to study than in my former location, and could not expect and hardly wish for a more agreeable congregation. I have resumed German the past winter. My love for such studies has not much abated.

The letter closes with an indication of Richard's interest in theological questions. His brother Francis, he records, had just been in Fayetteville to visit him:

We do not agree on the most important points; but we so far sympathize on subordinate ones as to render our intercourse mutually pleasant, and I trust profitable. He makes show of no animosity against the truths he does not embrace, and was deeply interested in some works and treatises of which I also have the highest estimation. We spent some time in social visits, which he seemed to enjoy heartily, but he was happiest in my study poring over treatises referring to points which of late years have much occupied his own mind. His wife is a worthy woman. . . .

Such a kindly, studious man made a good father. Indeed, the whole family circle constituted an excellent school for a growing boy. There were two older sisters, Anna and Mary, and two older brothers, William Neal and Richard Cecil. Grover was the fifth child, followed by four others—Margaret Louise, Lewis Frederick, Susan, and Rose. Pennies had to be carefully counted. There is but one known instance of reckless expenditure; when Richard Cleveland reached Fayetteville with his family by a lime-boat on the canal, it was late Saturday night, and the minister offered the captain half a dollar if he would moor the vessel before midnight and avoid desecrating the Sabbath.[1] There was plenty of work to be done. Grover minded the younger children, cut wood, carried water, and hoed the garden. Now and then he found an opportunity to earn "half a shilling." One of the principal exports of Fayetteville at that day was rocklime. It was necessary to hail empty boats as they passed along the Erie Canal, and turn them into the feeder or branch a mile from the village. The shippers used to give a dime to the boy who would bring them a boat when needed; [2] and Grover distinguished himself by getting up before four o'clock to anticipate the other youngsters. In fact, he is credited with breaking up a monopoly created by some older boys. But if there was hard work there was also plenty of wholesome play; for besides the outdoor sports, there were candy-pulls and popcorn parties in the big kitchen, and evening games in the parlor.

At Fayetteville Grover's schooling began in the little red frame district schoolhouse. Then at the age of eleven he entered the "Academy," a substantial stone edifice just across the road, managed under the strictest of rules by a teacher who lived to shake his hand when President. The Clevelands believed in education. William, the oldest son, who was destined for the ministry, shortly went away to Clinton, N. Y., to enter Hamilton College. The second son, Richard Cecil, had a taste

---

[1] James D. Hutchins of Fayetteville in the N. Y. *World*, July 20, 1887.
[2] E. T. Chamberlain, *Life of Cleveland*. This campaign biography of 1884 was revised by Cleveland himself, his Ms. corrections being in the possession of Col. William Gorham Rice of Albany.

THE CLEVELAND BIRTHPLACE IN CALDWELL

for mechanics and planned to become an engineer under the tutelage of an Ohio uncle. It was early decided that Grover should also go to college, but the family reckoned without fate.

As we have said, Richard Cleveland's life had more than a touch of the unhappy, for it was a laborious and impoverished life ended by premature death. After the birth in 1846 of his last child, Rose, the future mistress of the White House for her bachelor brother, he found his means increasingly inadequate. The eldest child, Anna, had begun teaching in the village academy. But to feed a dozen mouths, to house, warm, and clothe a dozen bodies, on an annual income which never rose far above $50 apiece, was a difficult task. One daughter, Margaret Louise, had a deformity of the feet, and the father several times took her to New York to consult specialists.[1] To add the cost of higher education as the children grew up was almost impossible. The minister looked about for better employment. Late in 1850 he was appointed district secretary of the Central New York Agency of the American Home Missionary Society, the great foster-mother of struggling new churches both West and East, at a salary of $1,000 a year—a position of some influence and importance. Forthwith the Cleveland family was removed to Clinton. This town, nestling in the valley of the Oriskany, is one of the most beautiful in all central New York. From the high hills about it are visible the wooded river winding to meet the Mohawk, and Lake Cazenovia gleaming in the sun, while from still higher hills a little distant the easternmost of the Finger Lakes may be descried. Here William was completing his college course, Cecil could find training in engineering, and the older daughters might attend Houghton Seminary.

In the autumn of this removal Grover went to visit his uncle Lewis F. Allen at Black Rock, just outside Buffalo, and a letter he wrote his sister Mary on October 29, 1850, is the first bit of his correspondence that has been preserved: [2]

My dear Mary:
    After so long a time I now seat myself in the dining room to answer your kind letter, which was duly received. You can better imagine than I can describe, how it gladdened my heart. My journey here was a very slow one as

[1] Cleveland Bacon to author, Nov. 30, 1930.
[2] Mrs. Yeomans' Papers.

by many hindrances the boat was much later than usual. And on account of this I had to stay all night at Rochester, and take the morning boat. I did not arrive here till Sabbath morning. I have a great many adventures to tell you when I get home (for you must know my journey has been adventurous). I was glad to hear you arrived safe and sound to your place of destination. I long to be with you there, though I do not feel at all homesick. How could I when all appear to take an interest in my happiness? I have enjoyed myself at a great rate since my stay here. I am very much pleased with the place and people and would like to stay the longest allotted time. I find Cleveland [his cousin] to be a very pleasant companion and Uncle, Aunt, and all appear to aim at my enjoyment. Richard's health has been very good until lately he has been suffering with one of his spells of derangement, but we hope for his speedy restoration. Gertrude is perfectly healthy and as full of fun as ever. She sends her love to you and says: Tell her about my pony. Which is one of the prettiest little creatures I ever saw. Tell Father to say in his next letter whether he would be willing to have me stop to our old home as I return and spend a day or two as it would afford me great pleasure. Tell Fred the stump of Pat O'Dagon is still left and will be with him shortly, for I after the manner of Dagon was laid low before an ox by the introduction of his foot a short time since. Tell Ditcher hunting here is good. Patrick has killed 14 black squirrels during his stay.

I have not yet been to see the falls, but expect to go tomorrow (Thursday). I think if I were to have my own way I should not be ready to come home till the middle of the month. It seems a great while since I saw you, and I long to get home and spend a Sabbath with you. As far as money is concerned my funds are low, but I do not know as I wish for more. I have received a letter from Cecil in which he says he is contented and quite happy. It will seem very queer to leave Fayetteville to go home. Tell Father the captain of the boat upon which I came says he will let me come back for the same price, $2. On my way I was fortunate enough to get a berth each night in which I slept as soundly as if I had been at home. . . . Tell Mother those mittens have lasted first-rate, for on opening my bag I found them, as well as some collars, minus, however I got along very well as everything else was O. K. But my stock of news has nearly run out and as Cleveland will soon be in to have me take a ride with him, and as I have a letter to write to Louisa, I think I must close this interesting epistle with a wish for your contentment and happiness. Pass over in this what perhaps you would notice in others and remember me . . .

Stephen G. Cleveland

At Clinton in the winter of 1850–51 Grover attended the town academy at the foot of College Hill—called the Clinton Liberal Institute—where he studied doggedly but without brilliancy. "He was then, as I remember," his sister Margaret writes,[1] "a lad of rather unusual

---

[1] Memorandum by Mrs. Bacon. Cleveland Papers.

good sense, who did not yield to impulses—he considered well, and was resourceful—but as a student Grover did not shine. The wonderful powers of application and concentration which afterwards distinguished his mental efforts were not conspicuous in his boyhood."

The school was small, with but two teachers. In a class of three Grover struggled through four books of the *Aeneid,* using a battered copy of his father's, without notes, and envying his richer classmates their new editions, with large print and explanatory glosses to help them over the difficult passages. One of the classmates later became a prosperous Buffalo lawyer, and the other a professor in Hamilton College. Grover "honestly longed," as he said later, for the higher education which his father and other forbears had received. He profited somewhat by the intellectual atmosphere of the town. "I might speak of the college faculty," he said in an address at Clinton forty years afterward, "who cast such a pleasing though sober shade of dignity over the place, and who, with other educated and substantial citizens, made up the best of social life. I was a boy then, and slightly felt the atmosphere of this condition; but, notwithstanding, I believe I absorbed a lasting appreciation of the intelligence and refinement which made this a delightful home." [1] At commencement the Cleveland house was crowded with visiting ministers. The boy still loved outdoor sports, and spent much time fishing in the Oriskany, which ran midway between the academy and his home on Utica Street.

v

But the life in Clinton was to prove an idyllic interlude all too short. The college town was the last place where the affectionate family found their hearth uninvaded. "Here it was," Cleveland recalled in his address, "that our family circle entire, parents and children, lived day after day in loving and affectionate intercourse; and here, for the last time, we met around the family altar and thanked God that our household was unbroken by death or separation. We never met together in any other house after leaving this, and Death followed closely our departure." Of the two and a half years in Clinton, Grover was absent more than a year. The keeper of a general store in Fayetteville, Deacon John McVicar, required a clerk; he offered Grover $50 for the first

[1] Speech at Clinton Centennial, July 13, 1887.

year, and $100 for the second, with room and board; and the hard-pressed family needed his small assistance. In the spring of 1852 the boy went back to Fayetteville and his novel duties. In after years he remarked that he had learned business lessons of enduring value in this humble post.

Here there were new touches in the formation of character. He had to rise at five in summer and half-past five in winter. He would hastily wash his face in a basin or in the horse-trough in the village square, open the store and sweep it out, build a fire, dust the goods, and have everything in readiness when Deacon McVicar appeared at seven o'clock. During the day he waited on customers, ran errands, and performed odd jobs. At night he and a fellow-clerk, later a dentist in Fayetteville, named F. C. Tibbetts, slept on a corded bed in a bare un-furnished room, without carpets, wallpaper, pictures, or stove. "In winter we fairly froze sometimes," Tibbetts has testified. Cleveland took his responsibilities seriously, and his sister Susan tells a story which may not be accurate in details but is doubtless true in spirit: [1]

It had been the habit of former clerks to indulge in a ham-and-egg supper at rare intervals, to which comrades from other business houses were invited, and who were expected to return the courtesy at proper seasons. There was an unwritten law that the boss must stand treat, which, being the line of least resistance, he usually did. What was the consternation among Grover's guests at his first feast, to learn that the materials which were taken from the store must be paid for, or every participant be branded as a thief, and he indignantly declared that he would never attend or give a supper where the refreshments were stolen. It is needless to say that Grover became a great favorite with the employers of the town when this became known, although he lost the friendship of some boy grafters. Mrs. McVicar took the greatest interest in his affairs and made him very comfortable in her home. She concluded from his integrity and correctness that it was foreordained that he should follow his father and brother William in the ministry and held the idea constantly before him.

Together with other students and former students at the Fayette-ville academy, Cleveland organized (February 3, 1853) a debating society or "gymnasium," of which he was elected vice-archon. It ar-ranged various lectures and discussions. At one of the debates, where he presided as judge, the topic was "Resolved, that Roman Catholic

[1] Mrs. Yeomans' Memorandum.

institutions are a menace to the interests of the Union," and he decided the issue in the negative; at another the question was whether an attorney is justified in defending a man whom he knows to be guilty, and Cleveland argued that he is not.

The year 1853 was an eventful one in the Cleveland household. Anna, the oldest daughter, was engaged to the Rev. Eurotas P. Hastings, a graduate of Hamilton College in the class of 1842 who had spent some years as a missionary in Ceylon. The wedding was fixed for March 9, after which the couple were to sail immediately for the Orient. During the winter the Presbyterian ladies of Fayetteville and Clinton sewed industriously upon an outfit of clothing that she was to take with her. Grover returned to Fayetteville for the ceremony, and remained during the spring and summer to study in the hope of entering Hamilton that fall, receiving private instruction from a retired clergyman, the Rev. Mr. Hyde. Meanwhile, the health of his father had taken a sharp turn for the worse, the ailment being diagnosed as gastric ulcer. It was thought that the constant travel which his Home Missionary post involved, in all weathers and over all kinds of roads, aggravated the disease, and he sought another pulpit. The best available opening was nothing better than one at the hamlet of Holland Patent, in the same region of central New York, some twelve miles north of Utica on the Black River. He was called here by the united voice of the congregation, which felt itself lucky to secure him. The New York *Evangelist* announced that his work for the Home Missionary Society "has been successful, and much approved by the friends of the said Society," who greatly regretted his resignation.[1]

The family removed to Holland Patent early in September. On the 14th day of that month, in a ceremony of great dignity, with no fewer than seven other ministers taking part in the exercises, Richard Cleveland was installed in the Presbyterian pulpit. The following Sunday he delivered his single sermon as pastor there. Then he was prostrated by his disease, and gradually sank. The second daughter, Mary Allen, was about to be married to Mr. M. E. Hoyt, and on October 1 she and Grover, leaving their father asleep, drove into Utica to make some purchases for her trousseau. As Grover sat waiting in the carriage news reached him that his father, seized by acute peritonitis, had died. The funeral was held a few days later, in the presence of many

[1] N. Y. *Evangelist*, September 22, 1853.

ministers—for Richard Cleveland's work had made him known and beloved throughout that section of the State. Grover's sister Susan has described it:

> On 'the 4th day of October the long procession of relatives, fellow-ministers, and parishioners followed the body to its last resting place. Dr. Vermilye of Clinton spoke the beautiful words, under a soft autumnal sunshine, while the crimson and gold maple leaves fluttered over the pathway and dropped into the open grave. He left his family the greatest assets of a good name, work well done, results achieved for God and humanity, and his "works still follow him." It was a dark outlook for the heroic mother from the shadow of that lonely grave, and the strong arms and courageous hearts of her children were her greatest earthly asset.

There was an almost propertyless family of ten. Mrs. Cleveland still had her private income, but it had remained small, for her father's estate had been dissipated by a dishonest trustee.[1] The eldest son, William, had graduated from Hamilton in the class of 1851, and could support himself while he studied for the ministry; the second son, Richard Cecil, was eighteen; two of the daughters were provided for. But the five others were dependents, and three were below their teens. It must have been with heavy hearts indeed that they laid Richard Cleveland in his grave and raised over his body a simple stone inscribed: "Blessed in the sight of the Lord is the death of his saints."

[1] Cleveland Bacon to author, May 10, 1930.

IN the early Victorian period which furnishes the background of these chapters more emphasis was laid upon youthful self-reliance than today. American families were usually large, and the children were soon pushed from the edge of the nest; while the work of pioneering in every field demanded young men of energy and initiative. The prairies of the West were broken and the battles of the Civil War were fought, in the main, by lads hardly out of their teens. In an age which read Samuel Smiles on self-help, and produced innumerable counterparts of Horatio Alger's self-reliant heroes, the fact that Grover Cleveland was forced to strike out for himself at sixteen could not be regarded as a great misfortune. Were Dick Whittington listening to the London bells ring "Turn again," and runaway Ben Franklin munching his penny-roll as he walked down Market Street, to be pitied? Always we must come back, in studying Cleveland's early years, to the keynote of character; his father's death was tragic, but the necessity of making his own way hardened and deepened the essential stuff of his nature. He had been a boy; now he quickly became a man. "Cast the bantling on the rocks," Emerson was writing—and in Cleveland's case the rocks had their edges somewhat smoothed.

There was no question that he now had to stand upon his own feet. The family was too proud to accept help from its neighbors. The ministers of the district immediately proposed a fund for the care and education of the four youngest children, but Mrs. Cleveland declined the offer.[1] Church-members in Holland Patent, with help from the kindly Presbyterians of Fayetteville, insisted upon their remaining in the parsonage rent-free until some years later Lewis Frederick was able to buy it for his mother.[2] Meanwhile, an income had to be provided to eke out Mrs. Cleveland's small property, and it was imperative that Grover should assist.

For a short time he leaned upon his older brother William. The day after the funeral, October 5, 1853, William was appointed the principal male teacher in the literary department of the New York Institu-

---

[1] Mrs. Yeomans' Memorandum.
[2] Will of Lewis F. Cleveland. Cleveland Papers.

tion for the Blind in New York City,[1] where he meant to combine his work with study for the ministry. He obtained a place as assistant teacher for Grover. The salaries were pittances, but the sons hoped to save a little to send home. For a full year, from the fall of 1853 to the fall of 1854, Grover remained in New York, living and working in the Institution. He then left the city, while William entered the Union Theological Seminary for the two years' course which led to his ordination in Brooklyn in 1856.

II

This year of work in a public asylum was unquestionably the bleakest in Cleveland's whole life. The Institution for the Blind then occupied the entire block between Eighth and Ninth Avenues and Thirty-third and Thirty-fourth Streets. It was a large building of "Sing-Sing marble," three stories high, of the so-called Modern Gothic style, somewhat resembling its equally ugly coeval, the New York University building on Washington Square. Till recently the site had been on the outskirts of the city. But New York was rapidly changing; plans were being discussed for a Central Park, the Crystal Palace had just been built in Reservoir Square at Forty-second Street, and population was sweeping up Murray Hill and all the parallel streets. The Institution was maintained by the State, which had founded it in 1831, and pupils might be sent to it from every county on certificates of the local superintendents of the poor. When Cleveland arrived there were 116 of these pathetic inmates, almost equally divided between the two sexes, and ranging in age between eight and twenty-five, though in this year the lower age-limit was raised to twelve.

The cold halls, strict hours, poor meals, and atmosphere of human affliction made it a depressing place, and Cleveland found it particularly dreary. The superintendent, T. Colden Cooper, was a martinet whom few liked. The staff of teachers was large, ill-assorted, and badly paid. There were six in the musical department, including George F. Root, later noted as a composer of Civil War songs and indifferent religious melodies, and five in the mechanical department; but these gave only part time. In the literary department there were two male teachers, the Clevelands, and three women, Miss Mary

[1] Fifteenth Annual Report of the Institution.

Crofut as principal teacher being assisted by Miss Louisa Morey and the blind hymn-writer, Miss Fanny J. Crosby. The payroll in the literary department for Cleveland's year came to only $1,070.09.[1] Instruction in the liberal branches was supervised by two trustees, Augustus Schell and E. L. Beadle, the former of whom later became a Tammany leader of note. The hours were long, from nine to four-thirty, and rigid discipline had to be maintained; at night the two Clevelands were in charge of the boys' dormitory, and the three women teachers took charge of the girls. The sole amusements were occasional teas, some "musical soirees," and an annual winter sleighing party.

This year in the lusty little metropolis is of importance only as completing in an unsatisfactory way the literary portion of Cleveland's education. For the last time he was in a position which, requiring attention to books and keeping him in close association with students, allowed him to pursue the humane branches of knowledge. The instruction was principally oral, for texts suitable to the blind were not always available, while many of the pupils learned to read only with great difficulty. Grover was occupied in teaching the younger children reading, writing, arithmetic, and geography. His brother taught "intellectual and moral philosophy," logic, a smattering of chemistry and physics, and history. Whether the two youths saw any of the livelier sides of city life we do not know. They might have heard Adelina Patti, then a child prodigy, sing; they might have gone to see "Uncle Tom's Cabin," making a sensation in its first long run at the National Theatre; they might have visited the exhibition at the Crystal Palace. The probabilities are that they were too poor for any but the cheaper forms of sight-seeing. But we know that they were entertained occasionally at the home of their rich relative, William E. Dodge, who was active in the temperance movement and Y.M.C.A., while we have a record of one other influence. When Henry Ward Beecher died, Cleveland wrote the widow that he had repeatedly heard him at Plymouth Church, and had been forcibly impressed by his eloquence. At a meeting in memory of Beecher in Brooklyn in 1903 he paid a more striking tribute to the man: [2]

It is now more than forty-nine years ago that I heard in Plymouth Church a sermon whose impressiveness has remained fresh and bright in my mind

[1] Fifteenth and Sixteenth Annual Reports.
[2] N. Y. *Times, Sun,* March 3, 1903.

during all the time that has since passed. In days of trial and troublous perplexity its remembrance has been an unfailing comfort, and in every time of depression and discouragement the lesson it taught has brought restoration of hope and confidence.

I remember as if it were but yesterday the fervid eloquence of the great preacher as he captivated my youthful understanding and pictured to my aroused imagination the entrance of two young men upon the world's jostling activities—one laden like a beast of burden with avaricious plans and sordid expectations, and the other with a light step and cheerful determination, seeking the way of duty and usefulness and striving for the reward of those who love and serve God, and labor for humanity.

I have never for a moment lost the impression made upon me by the vivid contrast thrillingly painted in words that burned between the two careers; nor have I ever failed to realize the meaning of the solace in death of the one, and the racking disappointments in life and the despair in death of the other.

What this sermon has been to me in all these years I alone know.

Men try to forget what is disagreeable, and Cleveland never said much regarding his year with the institution. Our best direct evidence upon it is furnished by Fanny Crosby, a graduate of the place, who had been a teacher since 1847. She was a quick, intelligent woman, who was later to rank second only to Lowell Mason in the number of her contributions to American hymnody, and to write some religious verse which has a sweet simplicity.

Nearly forty years afterward, when past seventy, she dictated a statement which must naturally be taken with large reservations.[1] She said that Cleveland, a tall, slender, sandy-haired youth of sixteen, had felt keenly the death of his father, of whose fine qualities he talked much; that he was thoughtful, reserved, disinclined to make friends, and a hard student; and that he was already planning to follow law as a profession. All this is doubtless true. Miss Crosby further says that he showed a keen appetite for history, which probably means that he read the old-fashioned texts, Rollin's *Ancient History* and Goodrich's *American History,* used in the school curriculum; and that he had a liking for Byron and Tom Moore. Beyond question Cleveland at this age was fond of poetry. William and he took turns in reading aloud several evenings a week to the blind pupils, and he recited verse with unusual spirit.

Miss Crosby adds that Cleveland did not hesitate to show his re-

[1] *McClure's Magazine,* March, 1909.

sentment of the harsh and dictatorial ways of Superintendent Cooper. When this officer once punished a blind boy with undue severity, Cleveland's anger was plain. When on another occasion Cooper rebuked Miss Crosby for asking a small service of Cleveland, the boy pugnaciously bade her to defy him by repeating the offence the next day, and to tell him to mind his own business—which she did with effect. Miss Crosby exaggerated in calling Grover "a marvel of precocity," for he was never that. She was doubtless right, however, in saying that he did his work well, met the older teachers on their own plane, and resented it when William spoke of "my little brother."

III

There was nothing in the Institution to hold Cleveland more than a year, and he was glad to be released. The winter of 1854–55 found him back in Holland Patent, where he spent some evenings reading Latin with an excellent teacher who chanced to be in the village.[1] He also vainly looked for work, first in Utica and then in Syracuse. Deacon McVicar's wife had a brother in Holland Patent named Ingham Townsend, a wealthy landowner and an elder in the church. She had told Townsend about the boy's fine qualities, and he offered to put Grover through college if he would promise to be a minister later. Cleveland refused. All that he would accept was a loan of $25 for a journey that he had planned to the West. Townsend told him that he need not repay the sum, but could give it at a later date to some other needy young man; however, after a dozen years Cleveland discharged the debt with interest. "The loan you made me was my start in life," he wrote, "and I shall always preserve the note as an interesting reminder of your kindness." [2]

With another Holland Patent boy, Cleveland blithely set out for Ohio. He had an uncle there; moreover, the rising city of Cleveland attracted him. His father had known Moses Cleaveland, the founder, a family connection, and had talked much of him. The name "seemed like an inspiration," he said later. On May 21 the two youths reached Buffalo, and Cleveland went out to the Black Rock section on the Niagara River to see his uncle. This was the Lewis F. Allen whom

[1] Chamberlain, *Grover Cleveland.*
[2] January 23, 1867; letter first published in Albany *Argus,* April 5, 1883.

Grover had visited in 1850. Indeed, the uncle said many years later that Grover had been in Black Rock for several visits, staying for weeks together and becoming much liked by the Allen family for his manly ways.[1] On one occasion he had spent all his pocket money, and worked his way back to Fayetteville on a canal-boat rather than tell his relatives. When he called at the Black Rock house he discovered his uncle in the "office," a little room under a corner of the main structure, entered by a special flight of stairs, poring busily over lists of Shorthorn cattle and their pedigrees.

It was an historic meeting, for it determined Cleveland's destiny. When Allen heard of the vague plans for a trip to Ohio, he protested. To go to a strange city without money, friends, or assured employment was too risky. "I endeavored to dissuade him," he wrote later, "from so precarious an attempt, and advised him to remain five months in my employment, where he would be useful, for which I would compensate him, and meanwhile assist him if possible to a situation with some eminent law firm in this city to prosecute his studies for a profession which he had selected for his future hopes and industry." Specifically, he offered Cleveland room, board, and $50 for five months' labor in correcting and arranging pedigrees for the Shorthorn herdbook which Allen—now one of the first stockmen in America— had in hand. Little persuasion was required. But before Cleveland gave his final word he walked back into the city, explained the situation to his Holland Patent comrade, and obtained his assent.

It was thus decided that Buffalo should be the scene of Cleveland's early career. Americans often suppose that a man who makes a conspicuous success in one city would do equally well in another, failing to perceive that a subtle harmony between a man and his environment is indispensable to many careers. Had Cleveland embarked upon the law in an older city like Boston or New York his lack of intellectual distinction would have militated against his advancement; while if he had begun his work farther west, in a still rough-and-tumble city like the Chicago or Milwaukee of that day, his quintessential traits of character and courage would have counted for less than they did. His swift rise to the presidency was due to his ability to make use of an extraordinary sequence of half-fortuitous opportunities. The first and most important of these was the mayoralty of Buffalo, and

[1] Lewis F. Allen in the Buffalo *Courier*, July 14, 1884.

that office came to Cleveland because he and Buffalo had fundamentally a great deal in common.

In the fifties America possessed few more interesting cities than Buffalo. Where the waters of Lake Erie began their race down the Niagara River into Lake Ontario, and the Erie Canal, a straight slender ribbon bound by towpaths, cut into a rough lake harbor, the town had arisen in a sprawled mass along the shores. Fronting on the lake were jagged rows of high, dusty grain elevators, painted red or yellow. Here and there squat piers ran out into the water. The harbor was dotted with vessels, usually in restless and noisy motion—heavy side-wheel steamers with double or triple decks and a single large funnel; deep-breasted sailing ships for carrying grain, with two, three, or four masts; lighter vessels piled with lumber; and barges, scows, towboats, and other craft. Crowded into the canal basin from spring to autumn were hundreds of barges and boats, entering or leaving the busy canal. Factories and foundries smoked as near the waterfront as they could cluster, and warehouses shouldered in among them. Along the wharves and towpaths swarmed thousands of laborers, noisily loading and unloading. Not one railroad, but three or four, rolled their puffing little locomotives, with big-bellied smokestacks and huge cowcatchers, and their light wooden cars, into the heart of the city. Farther back from the water lay the residential streets, some, like Delaware Avenue, already showing pretentious houses under the quick-growing maples and poplars.

It was a city possessing a rough, elemental vigor, which overlay certain characteristics of a simpler, finer kind. It was a Western city with a New England core; a frontier town which nevertheless had evident bonds with the older civilization of the Atlantic seaboard. Observers were struck first of all by the crude, hurried energy of the place. In a Western region full of boom towns it was already a secure little metropolis, easily the largest on the Great Lakes. Yet at the time of Cleveland's arrival the first white child to be born amid the rocks and brakes of its site was still walking its pavements, a man of barely fifty. It seemed but yesterday that the *Walk-in-the-Water*, the first lake steamboat, had churned its way past the wondering savages who christened it. It was actually only yesterday that the eloquent Red Jacket had been visited by awed admirers on the Seneca reservation hard by, and that the town in 1832 had boldly incorporated itself as a city. Old inhabitants still showed resentment as they re-called the burning of the place in the second war with Great Britain. The reasons for its rapid growth were simple. It was the northern gateway to the West, the portal through which the expanding traffic between the seaboard and Great Lakes necessarily passed. Commerce here had followed the pathway so long before trodden by French hunters striding to the Northwest, and by Richelieu's Jesuit missionaries with the cross. As yet there were no trunk railways running directly between the Mississippi Valley and the coast. Most of the wheat and corn produced in the upper valley for export, and the manufactures bound to it, passed over the Erie Canal. Cargo had to be broken at Buffalo, and that city, taking golden toll of the commerce, was growing by visible strides. There were 42,000 people in 1850, and the next census was to show more than 81,000. It had outstripped Pittsburgh and was close on the heels of the southerly portal of the great valley, Cincinnati. Since the suburb of Black Rock had been included in the city limits, it was nine miles in length and covered forty square miles. The harbor-front was full in summer of English and German emigrants, Canadians, Irish, and most of all New Englanders and New Yorkers, talking of the opportunities of the boundless West; of stores in Toledo, railroads in Illinois, iron and copper mines in Michigan, lumber in Wisconsin, town-lots in Detroit, Madison, Keokuk, and Council Bluffs, and farms everywhere. Others discussed invoices to New York and grain prices on the Liverpool exchange. Buffalo was one of the knots that the Spirit of Commerce had tied in her flashing loom to help fix her American pattern.[1]

Citizens who exultantly watched the factory-smoke float away across the skies, who heard the rumble of the elevators and the musical roar of the steamship whistles, had to admit that Buffalo was one of the roughest and most dangerous towns in America. It was sown with saloons. Along the waterfront were solid rows of dives of the worst order—barrel houses, dens selling Monongahela whiskey at four cents a glass, brothels, and gambling joints. Cutting affrays were a daily affair. There were streets where the police walked at midday only in pairs, for an officer who came alone might shortly be found floating face-down in the canal. The Irish longshoremen and the canal-hands

[1] J. N. Larned's *History of Buffalo* is the best book on the subject, but the publications of the Buffalo Historical Society are invaluable.

loved nothing so much as a fight. The prostitutes numbered hundreds. With bad water and gutters carrying sewage, with little care and less knowledge regarding epidemics, disease ran riot. Typhoid, small-pox, and typhus often slew by wholesale. The town was ugly, bare of parks, statues, or museums, and outwardly quite prosaic. Yet there was much that was solid and substantial behind these surface faults —much even that was fine.

Two distinct human elements furnished the rock from which Buffalo was being built—the granite of New England, and the softer, mellower marble of Germany. The stern Yankee stock, following the law by which our population has moved along parallels of latitude, had given the city its leadership ever since the twenties. Most of the lawyers, ministers, doctors, and driving men of business had been born in New England, or their fathers hailed from there. New England had fur-nished the few Buffalo names yet known to fame: Millard Fillmore, Nathan K. Hall, General Peter B. Porter, and Dr. John Lord. It had furnished the names that were becoming best known in business circles—William G. Fargo, who in the forties had been one of the owners of the first express company west of Buffalo, and who in 1852 helped organize the Wells, Fargo Company, and Joseph Dart, the first man on the Great Lakes to erect a steam-elevator and thus sup-plant the unloading of grain by "Irishmen's backs." His experiment in 1842 had been only less important for the development of the Northwest than Fulton's famous trip. It was the New Englanders who spaced the wide avenues, planted the elms, filled the white churches, and founded the historical society, the library, and the struggling college. But during the forties came a steady inflow of Germans, ref-ugees from oppression and poverty. They were a hardworking race who somehow amassed capital as rapidly as they learned the language. Soon almost half the stores seemed to be German. The Germans es-tablished iron-foundries, flour-mills, tanneries, and breweries; they furnished the bakers, grocers, expert mechanics, and cabinet-makers. Their contribution to cultural life lay in music, fine handicrafts, and an appreciation of the uses of leisure which many New Englanders lacked.

A bustling, uncouth, materialistic little city, growing so fast that its population doubled in the decade, belonging half to the Western frontier and half to the conservative East—such was Buffalo when

Cleveland reached it in 1855. The time was approaching when its growth would be checked by the completion of through railways between East and West, converting it from a great terminal for northern trade into a mere way-station. It was to see half the grain of the Mississippi Valley pass eastward by other routes, the Pennsylvania and the Baltimore & Ohio. It was to watch heavy freight trains on the Erie and New York Central thunder over its viaducts without the breaking of a car-seal. Yet it had other resources at its command. Its lake trade remained important, particularly in iron and coal. So, for another generation, did the Erie Canal. Western ore and Pennsylvania anthracite gave it iron works; brass foundries and machine shops were established. It manufactured furniture, leather, and flour. Placed in the centre of the barley district of New York and Ontario, it soon had some of the largest breweries in America. With plenty of enterprise, capital, and trouble, it offered a good field to a would-be lawyer like Cleveland. But as we have said, it offered something more; this hardworking town, without surface graces or much cultivation, but with plenty of sense, tenacity, and stubborn character, harmonized with his own traits.

IV

If Cleveland was fortunate in the city of his choice, he was equally fortunate in his initial protector, Lewis F. Allen. This versatile man, whom Cleveland's biographers have generally slighted, was one of the most prominent citizens of western New York, and except for Millard Fillmore was the best known resident of Buffalo. He was the very archetype of the hard, driving New Englanders, dexterous at everything, who were moulding so much of the plastic West all the way from Rochester to Kansas. Fundamentally there was not much in common between him and Cleveland. His interests were broad, and Cleveland's narrow; he was bent on money-making and rapid advancement, while Cleveland was of plodding temperament; in the intervals of business Allen liked society, church-going, the work of agricultural, historical, and civic organizations, and activity generally, while Cleveland preferred quieter pursuits. The one had a kinetic and the other a static temperament. But Allen was a man of mark and power, whose influence was valuable. There was something essentially misleading

Richard Falley Cleveland

Anne Neal Cleveland

GROVER CLEVELAND'S PARENTS

about Greeley's famous advice to young men to go west and grow up with the country; the leaders of the West never accepted such a rôle, but made the country grow up with them. Allen had helped Buffalo to do just that.

Born in New England, he had settled in Buffalo in 1827, when it was feeling the first stimulus of the Erie Canal. He had helped establish and manage fire, marine, and life insurance companies, and had invested largely and profitably in real estate.[1] Having acquired a small fortune, he turned, like Ezra Cornell, to farming, and became one of the country's most progressive stockmen. One of his real estate ventures had been the purchase, with some New England capitalists, of the greater part of Grand Island in the Niagara River. As under his management this was sold off in farms, he reserved six hundred acres upon which he began raising cattle and sheep. The place became a passion with him, and he developed it into a nationally important centre for pedigreed Shorthorn and Devon cattle and Southdown sheep. In 1846 he began his Shorthorn herdbook, which he kept up until twenty-four volumes had been issued, registering some 125,000 animals; for he was proud of the history of the fine old stock, so ancient that a Shorthorn cow is sculptured in a niche of Durham Cathedral.[2] In 1848 he had been elected president of the State Agricultural Society, then a post of high honor.

Meanwhile, he maintained his numerous business and civic interests in Buffalo. His neighbors in the late thirties sent him to the legislature, where he was active in promoting agricultural enterprises and the enlargement of the Erie Canal. He wrote books on farming, and was a copious contributor to agricultural journals; took delight in public improvements in the city; helped found the Buffalo Historical Society; and was prominent in the councils of the Whig party. From his Black Rock home, originally the house of General Porter, he conducted a wide correspondence, and the papers preserved by his descendants[3] contain long letters from Clay, Webster, Seward, and Winfield Scott. Having seen Buffalo grow from a town surrounded by almost virgin forests and waters into a city whose industries darkened the air, he could well say *quorum magna pars fui*. He had money,

---

[1] *Dictionary of American Biography*, 1, 201, corrected by material in Buffalo Hist. Soc.
[2] *Cf.* L. F. Allen, "Short-Horn Cattle," *Harper's Magazine*, September, 1886.
[3] Allen Papers, Stockbridge, Mass.

respect, connections; it was something to be his nephew.

For "perhaps a year," according to his uncle, Cleveland lived in the Allen house, at first giving all his time to the herdbook. His home was comfortable though far from luxurious. An extremely large, old-fashioned two-story structure of stone and stucco with wide rooms, tall ceilings, and great shuttered windows, it was placed on a broad tract between Niagara Street and the Niagara River. Its rear piazza commanded fine views of the stream and the Canadian shore. The Niagara at this point is a picturesque river, sweeping by with a current of five or six miles an hour, its green surface flecked by foam and broken by multitudinous eddies. Shade trees covered the front lawn, while at the rear was an orchard of carefully tended fruit, for Allen prided himself on his skill as a pomologist. The business centre of Buffalo lay two miles distant. Allen had two children of almost Grover's age, Gertrude and Cleveland, of whom Grover became fond. More than once in the next few years some of the Cleveland sisters or brothers would come from Holland Patent for a visit, and there would be joyous family chatter at the Allen table. The families were related both by blood and marriage, for Allen had married Margaret Cleveland, an elder sister of Grover's father, and he was her cousin as well.

In bits of reminiscence by different persons we can catch a few glimpses of Grover at this period—picking cherries in the yard while he chatted with a neighbor lad, Timothy Mahoney; attending service in the Presbyterian church with his cousins; making an occasional excursion to the Grand Island farm, where he fished for pike and bass; and trying clumsily to ride a little. He had a marked sense of fun. Once when he accompanied his uncle to the State Fair in Utica he was fascinated by a group of young donkeys with greatly accentuated ears. After observing them for some time he inquired their age, and was told they were only six months old. Quite incredulously, but with utter gravity, he asked, "Are their ears the same age?" [1] Mrs. Allen, with motherly interest, saw that he was as well dressed as her own son Cleveland. It was she who purchased his first dress coat, and there still exists a photograph of the eighteen-year-old boy standing up stiffly in it. It does not show the blueness of the eyes and sandiness of his hair, but it does reveal a powerful frame, a firm jaw,

[1] R. W. Gilder, *Grover Cleveland: A Record of Friendship*, 266.

and something of the earnest, stubborn glint of his countenance. Once in these early years Cleveland almost died of typhoid, but was pulled through by the vigilance of good Dr. King.[1]

It is evidence both of Cleveland's independence and his stolidity that the direct influence of his uncle was never great. A more impressionable boy would have caught many of Allen's interests and ideas, would have joined the Breckinridge Street Church which Mrs. Allen helped support and where Allen sang in the choir, and would have followed Allen into the Republican party. Cleveland did none of these things. The influence of the Allen household upon him was chiefly indirect. His uncle had a large and varied body of friends—stockmen, farmers, business men, and politicians. His dinner table had been graced by Webster, Seward, Gideon Granger, and Thurlow Weed. Because of his realty holdings and interest in the city's growth, he frequently entertained Buffalo men who came to talk of additions, streets, and bridges. Stockmen and agricultural editors were brought out to dinner. Mrs. Allen possessed literary tastes, and new books were regularly bought. In short, at the Allens' Cleveland for the first time saw something of the wide world of affairs. His lot was very different from that of the usual penniless boy in a rough new city; he lived in an atmosphere of refinement, surrounded by people whose talk was serious and who gave him an acquaintance with varied human types. He has left some record of the benefits he derived from watching the stream of his uncle's visitors, for he said long afterward: [2]

Since I came into public life many persons have assumed that I had a fair knowledge of a variety of men and have asked how I obtained it. I could only answer that there is no reason for this at all. It was simply because I had come into actual contact constantly, and early in life, with a various lot of men— buyers, sellers, actual farmers, boys, owners, and drovers. As many of them were only a little older than myself, I kept in touch with them as our common lives were enlarged, and so this knowledge was extended both through friends and associates.

Thus I did not have to make a special study of practical things. It was there before me day by day in my practical work. I could not have escaped it if I had tried. I saw many of these men again and again on their business trips up and down the canal, and still maintained pleasant relations with them. This friendly, open life was so much simpler that it is almost beyond comprehension, especially by city dwellers.

[1] Information from the Allen family, June, 1930.
[2] George F. Parker, *Saturday Evening Post*, Aug. 28, 1920.

But the influence of the Allen family never went deep; his uncle's varied intellectual sympathies and his aunt's concern with books and religion failed to lay hold upon the boy. From the beginning he was possessed by the problem of establishing himself in the law. The herd-book was finished in November, he was paid $60 in all, and he looked about him.

V

At first it was thought that he might study law in the Black Rock section, and at his uncle's suggestion he interviewed Daniel Hibbard, a justice of the peace in the neighborhood. When Hibbard asked some questions which Cleveland thought impertinent, the boy walked out of his office. His uncle then introduced him to the Buffalo firm of Henry W. Rogers, Dennis Bowen, and Sherman Rogers, attorneys who occupied quarters in Spaulding's Exchange. He was to be an office clerk and in spare hours to have a desk and the run of the library. In that period little formal tuition was included in such bargains. On the first morning the elder Rogers threw a copy of Black-stone down on Cleveland's desk with a bang, announcing grimly, "That's where they all begin." With that he was left to his own resources.

Many years later Cleveland recalled that on the first day he was so entirely ignored by the partners and clerks that when they went out for lunch they forgot he was seated in a corner with his Black-stone, and locked him in the office; whereupon he simply said, "Some day I will be better remembered." A little later his uncle asked him how he was getting on. "Pretty well, sir," he replied, "only they won't tell me anything." When Allen repeated this remark to Rogers the latter rejoined: "If the boy has brains, he will find out for himself." A law student then had to read hard, keep his eyes and ears open, and in a more or less unsatisfactory fashion school himself. It was a crude and uncertain way of learning law. But until the case system was introduced at Harvard by Langdell in the sixties, even the colleges furnished no better method.

The moment Cleveland entered the office of Rogers, Bowen, and Rogers he began adjusting himself to a wholly new world.

THIS period of the late fifties and early sixties was preëminently one which inspired youth to action. Many young men of Cleveland's generation—Garfield, Randall, Hayes, McKinley—plunged into the smoke of the Civil War. Others, like Henry James, Howells, and Henry Adams, were enriching their experience amid European scenes, or like Mark Twain and Clarence King, found adventure in the Far West. Cleveland was of almost the same age as John Hay, who throughout the war was with Lincoln in the White House and shortly afterwards went gaily off to a diplomatic post in Spain; as Winslow Homer, who was drawing pictures of battle scenes for *Harper's Weekly,* and later studying art in Paris; as J. Pierpont Morgan, who was carrying out financial operations—some of them decidedly adventurous—on two continents. It was a time when home-keeping youths feared homely wits, and when even the future poets and novelists, like Sidney Lanier and George W. Cable, were drawn by the bright face of danger into the full current of events. But Cleveland's history in these years of civil war and reconstruction, of expansion to the Pacific and the birth of a new industrial age, was brief and simple.

It was simple even compared with that of most able young men in less adventurous periods of national life. Ordinarily a young man's chronicle, while centering about his vocation, his avocations, and his social life, includes a good deal besides: intellectual interests, love affairs, travel, or ambitious missteps. It was not so with Cleveland's. His legal vocation was extremely important to him. His avocation, politics, filled a small but uncertain part of his sphere. His social life was remarkable for its masculinity. But when we have dealt with these three subjects, we have dealt with almost everything. He allowed them, and above all the law, to fill nearly his entire horizon.

Young as Buffalo was, it contained attorneys of talent and eminence, whose renown extended far beyond Erie County. Millard Fillmore had long been at the head of the city bar. Cleveland frequently saw the old gentleman driving through the streets with his wealthy second wife—a hard-headed, stolid, bland man, who had been pronounced

by Queen Victoria the handsomest American she had ever met. Next
to him in reputation had stood Nathan K. Hall, Postmaster-General
under President Fillmore and now a Federal judge. When Cleveland
arrived the place of preëminence had been taken by Solomon G.
Haven, a former mayor and from 1851 to 1857 a Congressman. He
was a man of Falstaffian bulk and wit, whose ponderous figure, as he
moved slowly down the streets or took the platform on public occasions, was familiar to every resident. A high position was also held
by a shrewd Yankee named Albert H. Tracy, who was nearing the
close of a singularly picturesque career. Coming from Norwich, Conn.,
he had reached Buffalo as early as 1815. He was elected to Congress
when barely old enough to take his seat, serving six years in the
House in President Monroe's time; he had declined a Cabinet position offered by John Quincy Adams; and in the State Senate in the
thirties he had helped Seward, Weed, and Fillmore to create the Whig
party in New York. But like other Northern Whigs, he felt outraged
by the course which Tyler pursued when he accidentally became
President, and when in 1841 Webster tried to lure him into the Cabinet
with an offer of the Secretaryship of the Treasury, he rejected it. It
was his last approach to national prominence. Fond of reading and
society, and a delightful conversationalist, he exerted a strong influence upon younger men. Lewis F. Allen and he were intimate friends,
and Cleveland was soon taken to Tracy's house, where later he often
called. Among other prominent attorneys were ex-Mayor Henry K.
Smith, Judge Frederick P. Stevens, and Horatio Seymour, Jr.[1]

It was a bar not surpassed at the time by any between New York
City and Chicago, and its conservative traditions and careful code of
ethics had their influence upon Cleveland. It possessed great *esprit
de corps,* and from beginning to end he was at home in it. Cleveland
took his profession seriously, and later spoke of the reverence he
always felt for such eminent legal scholars as Jeremiah S. Black.[2]

In the general practice of the law the firm of Rogers, Bowen, and
Rogers held a high place. All three partners were native New Yorkers,
and though none of them possessed a college education, they were
well trained. The head of the firm, Henry W. Rogers, was fifty-five
years old when Cleveland entered the office, and had practised in

---

[1] There is much material on these figures in the library of the Buffalo Historical Society.
[2] C. to A. B. Farquhar, Dec. 25, 1885. Cleveland Papers.

Buffalo for almost twenty years. He was a large man, with hearty, boisterous manners; full of anecdote; a witty, incisive talker, who easily said smart things and still easier cutting things. He was the orator of the firm and a strong jury lawyer. The other two were young men, Dennis Bowen being thirty-five when Cleveland first knew him, and Sherman S. Rogers twenty-five. While they refused no business of a reputable kind, they cultivated a civil rather than criminal practice, and preferred a few clients of large interests—banks, manufacturers, shippers, and merchants. One of their principal accounts was with Wells, Fargo, and another with Pratt & Company, ironmasters.

Dennis Bowen in particular exercised a powerful influence upon Cleveland, and his position as attorney was much that which Cleveland later sought for himself.[1] Born near Buffalo, he had been thoroughly trained in Millard Fillmore's office, and had already reached a commanding position. In the sixties and seventies he had the largest personal clientage of any lawyer in the city, there being no one whom banks and business corporations so implicitly trusted. Yet he seldom appeared in court and when he did took no prominent part there. He contented himself with furnishing advice and working up cases which his associates argued from his briefs. He was quiet, unobtrusive, and averse to publicity; a master of detail and a lawyer of dispassionate judgment, with an instinct for business essentials. He was also known as a man of enlarged views and undeviating honesty, who always gave full weight to the question of right or wrong as distinguished from that of mere legal advantage, and who acquired a happy reputation for his ability to compose disputes outside the courtroom on terms just to all the participants. In this, too, we shall see that Cleveland followed him.

II

In accordance with custom at the time, Cleveland was paid nothing during his first month or two in the office. Then the firm allowed him $4 a week, this sum being fixed as the precise amount necessary to pay his board, lodging, and washing in the family of a fellow-student,

---

[1] Louis L. Babcock to author, April 12, 1930. Mr. Babcock's law firm (Locke, Babcock, Hollister, and Brown) is the direct successor of Rogers, Bowen, and Rogers.

for just before or after Christmas of 1855 he left Black Rock. This was at the suggestion of Mr. Bowen, who thought that he should be nearer his work during the severe winter months. The ledger-book of Rogers, Bowen, and Rogers is still preserved,[1] and contains a record of small sums disbursed at irregular intervals to Cleveland, the first being dated December 3, 1855. On June 27, 1856, there is an entry of $146.87 for "services to date." But it is impossible to derive exact information as to his income, for the double reason that many small payments to him covered office supplies and other clerical expenditures, and that he earned occasional unrecorded amounts by copying and odd legal jobs. The important fact is that by 1856 he was completely self-supporting. His earnings at the office were eked out from time to time by fresh work on the Shorthorn herdbook. Sometimes this was done at night, Grover trudging two miles out to Black Rock in the evening, and back next day; while once or twice there was a leave of absence from the office. A ledger entry for 1857 states that Cleveland was away at Black Rock from January 13 to February 28, presumably busy on the herdbook, and that on July 29 he took another leave until September 1. When Lewis F. Allen wrote the preface for the fifth volume of his herdbook in 1861 he acknowledged his debt, in the compilation of the second, third, fourth, and fifth issues, to "the kindness, industry, and ability of my young friend and kinsman, Grover Cleveland, Esq."

Grover shortly left his boarding-house and took rooms with a Fayetteville friend, Dunbar by name, in the cockloft of the old Southern Hotel at the corner of Seneca and Michigan Streets. The hostelry was a great resort for cattle-drovers and farmers, a rough, shrewd, talkative set of men. But the place where he lived made little difference to Cleveland. He spent most of his evening hours at the office, stolidly digging into the lawbooks. In the first Buffalo years there was little time for amusements and less money. Writing of them long afterward in the third person, he declared that: [2]

He had adversity in abundance.

He had plenty of willingness to work, plenty of faith, and a fair stock of perseverance in reserve. He had no misgivings.

After securing a temporary job, he was handed Blackstone's *Commentaries*

[1] In possession of Mr. Louis L. Babcock, Buffalo.
[2] Robert McElroy, *Grover Cleveland, The Man and the Statesman,* I, 17.

and turned loose to browse in the library of a law office . . .

He actually enjoyed his adversities.

Even then he was called stubborn. After he had become President of the United States he was still called stubborn, and he is accused of stubbornness to this day.

Saturday afternoon and Sunday often found him at Black Rock or Grand Island, for temporarily his relations with his uncle's family remained close. He loved to hunt and fish—particularly to fish—with Cleveland Allen, and he occasionally rode.

But the best view of his mode of life, his ideas, and his hopes and fears that we possess for this period is afforded by a series of letters which he wrote between 1855 and 1858 to his sister Mary, now a wife and mother.[1] They are sprightly, good-humored, affectionate epistles, and show the livelier side of Cleveland's nature. In the first, dated October 18, 1855, he says that he has just laid aside his Blackstone for a few minutes, "for I don't feel like study this afternoon":

I suppose by this time you are fairly under way in your new responsibility as a housekeeper. How does it go? I don't doubt but you will make a model housewife. Aunt and Uncle have gone West but we expect them back in a few days. We have had quite a party of "young folks at home." I am trying to find a place to board in the city but am so far unsuccessful. I have to work pretty hard just at present as the senior clerk is absent. But it is better for me as the more I do the more I learn. As you say, I find oftentimes "Jordan a hard road to travel," but for the most part feel pretty well encouraged. I think and hope that I shall have no trouble, that is, any more than is the unavoidable concomitant of poverty. . . .

My employers are very kind to me and promise me promotion again soon. They at present pay my board or an equivalent, which is very satisfactory. How is little—what's-his-name—*the* boy? When I get to be an *old lawyer* and he wants to study the profession I'll take him in my office—then you need not thank me—I'll do it with the greatest pleasure. Consider that a fixed arrangement. If you see "that feller" (you know who) just tell him I've *got my eye on him*—he'd better look out how he performs. But here! I haven't made any wishes in your behalf as housekeeper, have I?

Accept (Mrs. Hoyt) my sincere and heartfelt wishes for entire success in your capacity as housekeeper. May your heart and bread be always light and your purse always heavy. May your tea be always strong, and your butter always mild. May your husband be sociable but your baby be dumb. May rats, company, and trouble be scarce and comfort and quiet plenty. And last and most important, next summer (when I come up there) may you have a spare

[1] Mrs. Yeomans' Papers.

room with an extra bed in it. May you have a big table with an extra plate on it. May you have a nice garden with lots of "stuff" in it. And welcome *your friends* to stay and *enjoy* it. . . .

A month later he wrote that he had taken his "homely, burly face" through all the shops to match a bit of dress-trimming for his sister. "I am very busy nowadays—have just 'moved' to town—health good —heart and pocket light—but all right." As the year closed he complained a little of loneliness. "On this last evening of the year when poor '55 shall be consigned to the shades of reminiscence and the new year shall take its place—when Methodists dolefully sing its requiem and the Dutchmen *fire their guns*—on this evening, I say, I have seated myself at my table and am determined that your last shall be forthwith answered." He went on:

We are having beautiful sleighing and I am reminded that others beside myself inhabit this terrestrial globe by the constant and merry jingle of sleighbells and the explosion of guns—for you know there are a great many Germans in Buffalo, and with them the firing of cannon is a common and delightful manner of celebrating the advent of the New Year. You know that I am such a matter-of-fact bachelorish body that New Year's is almost as good as any other day to me and no better. And here let me by way of parenthesis and conforming to the usual custom in such cases "made and provided," wish you a Happy New Year. . . .

Supposing that my situation, prospects, etc., are at all times interesting to you, I shall proceed to inform you in regard to these items. I am still living alone as I have always done, maintaining life and energies by means of eating, drinking, and sleeping. Indeed, I am so addicted to these habits that I find it impossible to forego them for any length of time. I must have my *provender* three times a day and eat and drink in proportion. It's lamentable, isn't it?

I am boarding at a second-class hotel and paying at the rate of $4 a week. I am not very much pleased with my situation in this respect and contemplate a change soon. My employers are very kind to me and, all things taken into consideration, I try to be happy, though I sometimes find it pretty hard.

This note was repeated. The following February he wrote complaining that he was not getting enough letters from his family, and again hinting that he was lonely:

You are, I believe, already informed that "I still live." I am happy to inform you that I am "doing well"—that is, well *considering*. I flatter myself, and my employers assure me, that if I keep on I'll make a lawyer—"a consummation devoutly to be wished," I assure you. . . . I am leading a very quiet life and tread day after day in the same old track. I have very few "blue" turns but 'tis not for the want of those little trials that induce blueness; but I *strongly* suspect 'tis owing to a fixed determination on my part not to yield to such things. I am anticipating much pleasure from a visit home next summer. May I not add to my other pleasing expectations, the hope that I shall see you then?

And after a long silence he sent his sister on January 1, 1858, a New Year's letter which for the first time expressed a decided discontent with his employers. After relating how he had gone to the theatre the previous evening with a friend, he proceeded:

The holidays are over, and I am glad. They don't amount to anything, so "what's the use?" I didn't get no presents and I am glad of *that*.

I have made a new arrangement with the firm here and have engaged to work for them another year for the enormous sum of $500. "O God! that bread should be so dear, and *work should be so cheap!*" I am so ashamed of myself after allowing such a swindle to be practised upon me. It shows how selfish the men I have to do with are, and how easy it is to fool me. I ought to have a great deal more, and from the bottom of my heart I curse the moment in which I consented to the contract. But it's over now and I don't propose to whine. . . .

I don't know but what I shall go down and help Uncle about his herdbook next month. I want to go for the sake of the pay, and I don't want to go for any other reason. If I knew of any pretty music I'd send it to you, but I never hear of any and so am not posted. If you can suggest anything new and pretty and if I can find it, I'll send it to you.

Thus the months and years passed until in May, 1859, the Supreme Court admitted Cleveland to the bar. Now twenty-two, he had spent three and a half years in study at a time when the requirements were elementary, and it could not be said that he had shown a brilliant celerity. But his outside duties had been heavy and he was doubtless more thoroughly prepared than most legal fledglings. He might at once have hung out his shingle. Instead, with characteristic conservatism he stayed on with the firm. Here his advancement was slow but steady. The $500 he mentions was a minimum increased by special fees, and the old ledger indicates that his income was constantly rising. In a little more than a year and a quarter in 1857–58 he received a total of $913 under the head of "services," which after all deductions would show a fair progress. Shortly after his admission to the bar he was promoted to be managing clerk, and his salary in this position was soon $1,000 a year. Every month he folded some bills into an envelope and mailed them to his mother in Holland Patent; and long after-wards, when President, he boasted to his confidential secretary that he had never lost a dollar in this way.[1]

As Cleveland thus slipped into the position of mainstay of the family, one of the great crises of American history was approaching. The slavery question was setting the country ablaze. Where might an earnest young man, the son of New England Presbyterianism, be expected to take his stand? Though most observers would have said with the Republicans, Cleveland had already firmly aligned himself with the Democratic party. In doing this he grieved his uncle, who, like most of the older Yankees of the city, had been a Whig with pronounced free-soil leanings. Allen's resentment had been aroused by the Fugitive Slave Act of 1850, and he was made still angrier by the Kansas-Nebraska bill of 1854, throwing two great territories open to slave settlement. In 1855, joining the general revolt against the old-line Whigs, he presided over the first Republican convention in Erie County. That fall the Republicans polled fewer than a thousand votes in the city; but next year they did much better, though the Democrats swept Buffalo and sent their nominee to Congress. By 1858 the Republicans had become powerful enough to capture the seat in Congress, and were plainly the party of the future in all upper New York.

And why did Cleveland choose the Democratic standard? His father's dislike for Abolitionism may have counted. In 1901, he told Richard Watson Gilder that he had become a Democrat in 1856 because the party seemed to represent greater solidity and conservatism, and that he was repelled by the Frémont candidacy, which struck him as flamboyant and theatrical.[2] This was characteristic. But there were two other influences at work. Most of Cleveland's acquaintances in Buffalo, which now tended to the hotel-lobby and the bar-room set, were Democrats. Above all, his superiors in the office of Rogers, Bowen, and Rogers were firmly Democratic. The elder Rogers had been a lifelong follower of Jackson, and was proud to recall that Polk had appointed him collector of the port of Buffalo. The younger Rogers was of the same party, though after the outbreak of the Civil War he gravitated into the Republican ranks. And as the decisive factor, Dennis Bowen, whose quiet judgment seemed so weighty to

[1] Robert L. O'Brien to author, April 11, 1930.
[2] Gilder Memoranda, December, 1901. Cleveland Papers.

Cleveland, was scornful of Frémont and the Republicans and attached to the doctrines of Stephen A. Douglas. Cleveland drew in Democratic views as part of the office atmosphere.

III

As he completed the requirements for the bar, Cleveland began to do modest work for the local Democratic organization. In every campaign, beginning with the fall of 1858, when he came of age, he acted as a volunteer ward worker in helping to get out the vote. He went to ward caucuses; in advance of the election he was assigned a list of voters; he saw that these men were "lined up," that they got to the polls, and that they carried the right ticket to the ballot box. Such workers, indispensable then as now, attracted notice if they showed energy, while if they were young lawyers it was understood that they hoped for office. The head of the local Democratic organization when Cleveland thus enlisted was Israel T. Hatch, another of the energetic men of the region, almost a match in his versatile activities for Lewis F. Allen—a graduate of Union College, lawyer, grain-merchant, elevator-builder, bank-president, and an inveterate officeholder. He was elected to Congress by the Democrats in 1856, and when two years later the Republicans defeated him, Buchanan appointed him postmaster of Buffalo. Another leading Democrat was John Ganson, a Harvard man and a lawyer, who during the Civil War was elected to Congress. Eli Cook, Jr., an active Democrat, was mayor in 1853–55; Judge Frederick P. Stevens succeeded him, and he in turn gave way in 1858 to another Democrat, Timothy T. Lockwood. It will be noted that in Cleveland's first years in Buffalo the Democrats controlled the city administration. It was also a fact of importance that in 1855–56 Dennis Bowen was an alderman from the tenth ward.

It is not long before we find Cleveland taking a larger part in politics. The city leaders liked his quiet dependability; Bowen and Rogers told them that he worked as if office clocks and fatigue never existed. He began to appear at city conventions. At one held on October 23, 1862, with ex-Mayor Lockwood presiding, he was a delegate from the second ward—a ward which contained many Germans, with whom Cleveland was popular. At a caucus on the following October 30th, he was nominated for ward supervisor, and in November was elected with 509 votes. His first elective office, which has been strangely overlooked by his early biographers, thus came to him at twenty-five. He had begun at the very foot of the ladder—but he had begun. Moreover, promotion lay just ahead. That same November there was an election for district attorney, and the Democratic candidate, Cyrenius C. Torrance, polled nearly 12,000 votes as against 9,300 for his opponent, who was called a Republican by his own party but described as an "Abolitionist" by the Democratic press. Torrance was an elderly lawyer and grist-mill owner of Gowanda, a village on Cattaraugus Creek not far from Buffalo. Shortly after his election it was announced that Cleveland would be appointed assistant district attorney, and had accepted the place.[1]

The significance of this acceptance has been generally misunderstood; for unquestionably it meant that Cleveland was looking tentatively toward politics as a definite career. The assistant district attorneyship counted for almost nothing. Cleveland could not have afforded to take it in itself, for it meant giving up a $1,000 position with Rogers, Bowen, and Rogers for an office paying only $500 a year. But beyond it lay the district attorneyship, and beyond that the possibility of Congress or some similar prize. Clearly Cleveland was thinking of entering public life and Dennis Bowen was encouraging him.

It was a legitimate though a premature ambition. Already no young attorney in the city was better regarded. "Mr. Cleveland," remarked the Buffalo *Courier* of the appointment,[2] "is one of the most promising of the younger members of the bar, is a thoroughly read lawyer, and possesses talent of a high order. He will soon have an opportunity of demonstrating this and 'more too,' and, our word for it, he will prove himself equal to the occasion." For the next three years Grover labored constantly in the dingy prosecutor's office in the old courthouse of Erie County. Since Torrance was ill and infirm, most of the hard work fell upon his assistant. It was excellent legal training and it gave Cleveland a clear insight, which he needed and used later as mayor, into the seamy side of local government. The district attorney is above everything else the investigating officer of the community. It is his business not only to prosecute common malefactors, but to keep an eye on the administration of the city and county to detect mal-

1 Buffalo *Courier, Commercial Advertiser,* Oct. 24, 30, Nov. 6, 7, 8, 1862.
2 Buffalo *Courier,* Dec. 24, 1862.

feasance and corruption. That is why it is wise in counties like New York and Erie to elect a Republican attorney to watch a Democratic administration, and *vice versa*. Torrance did not distinguish himself in public investigation, but Cleveland nevertheless learned a good deal. The young attorney was justifiably proud of his hard work. As he said in a statement dictated to a campaign biographer in 1884: [1]

He was in attendance at every one of the twelve grand juries which met during each of the three years of his term of office, and presented in full a large majority of the cases. Nearly all the indictments during this period were drawn by him, and perhaps more than half the cases he tried in court. On more than one occasion during these busy months he conducted four cases before a jury, won a favorable verdict in each, sat down at eight o'clock in the evening to make preparations for the next day, and did not rise from his desk until three o'clock in the morning. Eight o'clock found him back again at the office, fresh for a day's contest with some of the best criminal practitioners in the county.

In short, he and not Torrance was the real district attorney. In ordinary times he would probably have received an early promotion to the higher office.

But these were not ordinary times. Smoke and flame overhung the long line from Bermuda Hundred to Vicksburg and Little Rock; every southern wind seemed to bring the mutter of skirmishing or the roar of battle. In Buffalo flags flew over recruiting offices, Fort Porter was the scene of incessant drilling, volunteers were marched down Delaware Street to the railway station with drum and bugle, and after every engagement gloomy crowds clustered about the bulletin boards on which casualties were listed. No part of the Union gave more devotedly of her zeal, money, and sons than up-State New York. There were battles which wiped out the flower of whole townships. A gifted writer whom Cleveland was to know well in Albany, Harold Frederic, has pictured the anguish with which these blows were often sustained by unhappy communities.[2] Once or twice there was a stroke which seemed to stun all western New York, as when Gen. James Wadsworth of Geneseo and hundreds of his brave men were killed at the Wilderness.

And what of Cleveland during these years of the Civil War? No

[1] E. T. Chamberlain, *Grover Cleveland;* in its early pages this book is virtually an autobiography.
[2] Harold Frederic, *In War Time.*

man of his simple but deep feelings, with two brothers and many friends at the front, could help being stirred by it. Family tradition records that he was deeply stirred, and that he was a war Democrat of the sternest views. His brother William in 1860 had married a Georgia girl and was lukewarm, but Cleveland was a staunch Unionist.[1] While he left no formal record of his opinions on the political or constitutional issues of the war, beyond doubt as a patriotic Democrat he shared the views of such leaders of western New York as Dean Richmond. The demand for victory and restoration of the Union gave little room for copperheads of the defeatist type in any up-State community like Buffalo. Cleveland more than once heard speeches made by the shrewd and rugged Richmond, a rich Buffalo shipper and railroad-builder who became president of the New York Central, who in 1861 was chairman of the Democratic State committee, and who with Seymour controlled the party destinies. His untimely death in 1866 robbed the party of one of its most brilliant intellects.[2] Richmond utterly denied the right of secession, demanded the complete restoration of the Union, and favored the vigorous prosecution of the war until this result was fully achieved. At the same time, he was willing to compromise upon other issues between the North and South, and vigorously arraigned some of the methods of the Lincoln Administration in carrying on the war.

When Horatio Seymour was nominated for governor in 1862, a Buffalo lawyer, A. P. Laning, whom Cleveland knew well and who later became his partner, was chairman of the platform committee. In drafting this platform, he pledged the New York Democrats to stand behind the government in using "all legitimate means to suppress rebellion, restore the Union as it was, and maintain the Constitution as it is." In other planks, Laning's platform denounced the illegal and arbitrary arrest of citizens, and declared for full liberty of the press and of speech. Seymour, running against General Wadsworth, carried the State by a majority of more than ten thousand, and Cleveland doubtless rejoiced with other Democrats. The party north of the Harlem held that there must be no peace which did not include the return of all the Southern States, but that the use of the utmost force for that end should be accompanied by the proffer of conciliation, and that it

[1] Cleveland Bacon to author, Nov. 4, 1931.
[2] D. S. Alexander, *Political History of the State of New York*, III, 158.

Dennis Bowen

Henry W. Rogers

Sherman S. Rogers

CLEVELAND'S MENTORS IN THE LAW

was folly to wage a war of utter subjugation. They preferred a negotiated peace to a conquered peace; they desired a reunited but not a revolutionized nation. Because after Gettysburg and Vicksburg the Southerners would not yield, the subjugation and the subsequent revolution—euphemistically termed "reconstruction"—came; and we may be sure that Cleveland deplored both.

Yet one significant fact besides family tradition indicates that he leaned much further than Dean Richmond or Horatio Seymour toward complete support of Lincoln. On the authority of his friend Albert Haight, a young lawyer who later became judge of the Court of Appeals, he strongly endorsed Lincoln's action in September, 1863, in ordering a further suspension of the writ of habeas corpus. This suspension, which was evoked by obstruction of the draft, aroused much feeling in Buffalo and elsewhere. Soon after the order was issued an indiscreet Campbellite minister made an address assailing the Administration, and was thrown into a Buffalo jail. His attorney prepared a writ for the purpose of bringing the offender before a Federal judge who was known to be hostile to Lincoln's policy. The judge recognized the writ, a judicial hearing was held, and the clergyman was temporarily released. When Cleveland heard of it, he was indignant. The writ, he declared, should never have been given a moment's attention: "It seems to me that the government has a right in time of war to resort to every possible method in order to protect itself." It is interesting to find thus early his bold view of the emergency powers of the Executive. Cleveland always admired Lincoln as much as in civil affairs he disliked Grant, and his family believed that in 1864 he probably voted for the war President. Long afterwards he told Gilder of his reverence for Lincoln as "a supremely great and good man." [1]

IV

With his unvarying honesty, Cleveland never claimed that he felt a strong desire to enlist. If he had been seized by such an impulse he could have gratified it, and a Roosevelt in his place would have been in the early battles. But he was completely lacking in martial spirit. He might have enlisted as a matter of duty, for he never turned a deaf

[1] Cleveland Bacon and Mrs. E. L. Yeomans to author, June, 1932; Richard Watson Gilder, *Grover Cleveland: A Record of Friendship*, 191.

ear to duty, but a still heavier claim kept him in civil life. He was always the most affectionate of sons and brothers. After he went to Buffalo, his sister Susan writes, "Every year a two weeks' vacation was devoted to his mother, and his weekly letter seldom failed to reach her, while he constantly shared with the other brothers the financial burden of the remaining family."[1] As a matter of fact, he soon assumed the larger share of this burden. His newly-married brother William was merely the "stated supply" for the Presbyterian church of Southampton, L. I., on a meagre salary,[2] and could contribute little. The other two brothers promptly volunteered for the army, leaving Grover the only son able to furnish any considerable sum for his mother and sisters.

The facts respecting the army service of Cleveland's two brothers have been left so vague by his biographers that they are worth stating explicitly. Some critics, indeed, have even denied that his brothers ever enlisted. While the story of a drawing of slips from the family Bible to decide which should serve is an absurd fiction, army records leave no question as to the enlistments. Lewis Frederick Cleveland enrolled in the Thirty-second New York volunteers on May 15, 1861, in New York city, to serve two years. He saw hard fighting in the Army of the Potomac, rose on June 23, 1862, to be first lieutenant, and was mustered out with his company on June 9, 1863, in New York.[3] Richard Cecil Cleveland joined the Twenty-fourth Indiana at Bedford, Ind., was mustered in at Vincennes on July 31, 1861, took part in heavy fighting under Frémont and Grant, became second lieutenant, and was mustered out on December 4, 1864.[4] Cecil did not have better pay than a private until May 17, 1863; Fred did not have better pay than a second lieutenant until the last twelve months of his army career. Neither could send much money home.

Moreover, the family burden had increased. It is true that there were only two daughters at home, for besides the pair who had married, Louise had departed to become a governess in a Long Island family. This left only Susan, who at the outbreak of the war was eighteen, and Rose, who was fifteen, with the mother. But the cost of

---

[1] Mrs. E. L. Yeomans' Memorandum.
[2] *Alumni Catalogue Union Theological Seminary.*
[3] F. Phisterer, *New York in the War of the Rebellion,* third ed., III, 2108.
[4] *Report of Adjutant-General of Indiana,* II, 231 (1865). The swords of the two brothers are in Mr. Cleveland Bacon's possession.

living increased sharply, and Cleveland wished to provide well for the family. In addition, both Susan and Rose desired a college education. Dr. Samuel H. Cox, Cleveland's great-uncle, was at this time much interested in enlarging the attendance at a girls' college pretentiously called Ingham University, a small Presbyterian institution at Le Roy, N. Y., of which he was head. Grover entered Susan in the college, although this implied a financial responsibility decidedly heavier than his income warranted.

"Not until many years later," according to Susan, "did this sister realize her own indebtedness to this best of brothers, and when later she insisted on refunding the expenditure, she had to fight the most vigorous protests to accomplish it. The letter is still extant, begging her 'not to disturb the situation, as those were the days when we found our greatest pleasure in helping each other, and our greatest reward in appreciation of the assistance rendered.' " We have seen that not until 1867 could Cleveland conveniently spare the $25 necessary to repay Ingham Townsend his loan. Moreover, there was his office; important cases arose from the war, which he was far more competent than Torrance to conduct.

The Conscription Act of March 3, 1863, made all able-bodied male citizens between twenty-five and thirty-five (if unmarried, forty-five) liable to be drafted into the army, but permitted those who were called to furnish a substitute, or to pay a commutation of $300. Enrollment began in May. In July the drawing of names commenced. Cleveland's name was among those called on the first day in Buffalo, and it was necessary for him to take advantage of the substitution or commutation clause. His brother Fred, who had just been discharged, wrote offering to take his place, but Grover replied, "Fred has done enough. I have my man." [1]

The substitute he found was an illiterate but intelligent Pole of thirty-two named George Brinske or Benninsky, who had come to the United States in 1851, and since 1856 had been a sailor on the Great Lakes. There was a large Polish settlement in East Buffalo. During the year 1863 Benninsky was employed on the propeller or tug *Acme*, which frequently called at Buffalo. "Mr. Benninsky," wrote Cleveland when President, "was brought to me by George A. Reinhart, who still lives in Buffalo, I suppose, who told me that Benninsky was a sailor

[1] "Justice" in Buffalo *Courier*, Sept. 3, 1884.

on the Lakes and was willing to enlist as my substitute for one hundred and fifty dollars. The bargain had been made before I saw the proposed substitute, as Mr. Reinhart had known him a long time. The terms, however, were distinctly repeated by me and perfectly understood. There was no hint or suggestion of anything more being paid or of any additional obligation on my part. At this time (whatever the date may be) plenty of substitutes were obtained at the price named and even less. Indeed, being then the assistant district attorney of Erie County, I had abundant opportunity to secure without expense a substitute from discharged convicts and from friendless persons accused of crime if I had wished to do so." [1] Benninsky was sworn in at Fort Porter on July 6, 1863. During Cleveland's presidency sensational newspaper stories were printed detailing the wounds and hardships his substitute had suffered, but his actual history was uneventful. He served briefly with the Seventy-sixth New York on the Rappahannock, injured his back, was then detailed to orderly duty in the military hospitals of Washington, and was never in any important battle as a combatant.

V

The war closed at Appomattox. Lincoln was assassinated, and Andrew Johnson entered the White House. Lines were drawn, as Congress prepared to meet in December, 1865, for a bitter struggle over Reconstruction. Meanwhile, in quiet Buffalo Cleveland's first political venture was coming to an unhappy end.

He received the expected nomination for district attorney, and with it the support of the Democratic press. The *Courier* spoke of him as one "whose close application, gentlemanly deportment, and conceded ability have given him a standing at the bar which has seldom been gained by one of his years." Later it expressed confidence in his reelection. Cleveland, it said, "has discharged his duties with an ability and fidelity which have secured the commendation of men of all parties. He is a young man, who, by his unaided exertions, has gained a high position at the bar, and whose character is above reproach. He will be supported by hundreds of Republicans on these grounds." [2]

[1] To John E. Hale, Hugotown, Kan. September 13, 1887. Cleveland Papers.
[2] Buffalo *Courier*, Oct. 2, Nov. 6, 1865. In the fall of 1864 Cleveland had been narrowly defeated for reëlection as ward supervisor.

But the event was otherwise. His opponent was his roommate, Lyman K. Bass. Cleveland ran well in Buffalo, carrying seven of the thirteen wards, but his rival had the advantage in the towns outside. His defeat in November closed his political career for half a dozen years, though in September, 1868—another fact overlooked by his biographers—he was a delegate to the Democratic State Convention in Albany, and a member of the platform committee.[1] Here he saw Tweed's ally, John T. Hoffman, nominated for Governor.

Actually it was fortunate for Cleveland that he was thus cut off from premature officeholding and thrown back into more profitable employment as a lawyer. In the next half dozen years he practised steadily, first with Major Isaac K. Vanderpoel, who had been State Treasurer in 1858–59, and after Vanderpoel became a police magistrate, with Albert P. Laning and Oscar Folsom. The firm of Laning, Cleveland, and Folsom, which was formed in 1869, deserves more than momentary attention. Laning, its head, had come to Buffalo in the same year that Cleveland arrived, had served in both branches of the legislature, and had become one of the important Democratic leaders of western New York. Partly because of his legal ability, and partly for his political prominence, the New York Central and other railroads employed him as their counsel. He was one of the new race of corporation attorneys just springing into prominence after the war. Oscar Folsom was a very different person—a gay and popular young man. A native of Wyoming County and a graduate of Rochester University, he had studied law in Buffalo and had been admitted to the bar in 1861. While Laning possessed masterful qualities, and was an orator of parts, Folsom was valuable for his genial high spirits, bringing the firm a multitude of friends, and for a certain erratic brilliancy. Cleveland respected Laning, but to Folsom he became bound by ties of the deepest affection.

In these half dozen years Cleveland climbed slowly to a creditable place at the Buffalo bar. All records of him in the sixties and seventies emphasize his abounding energy and immense powers of industry. He worked not with set jaw or tense nerves, but simply as a man who never knew physical or mental exhaustion. He could labor all night over some urgent case, turn out his gas-lamp at dawn, take a bath and some hot coffee, and be fresh for presenting his case in court. He could

[1] Homer A. Stebbins, *Political History of the State of New York*, 1865–69, 362.

take a long and intricate brief, possess himself of its contents, and so memorize his argument that he could deliver it without notes and never falter over a sentence. His friends never credited him with an incisive intellect, a wide interest in ideas, or a captivating personality; they regarded him as a man who would accept opportunities rather than make them. But after they became acquainted with his powers of application, common sense, conscientiousness, and rugged character, they were sure that when he had an opportunity he would wrest some genuine result from it. Professionally, he was becoming just such a lawyer as Dennis Bowen had been. He disliked criminal cases, and would never accept a retainer from a man whom he knew to be crooked; he liked to prepare civil cases in his office, and then let Vanderpoel, Laning, or Folsom carry the forensic burden; and he preferred an equitable adjustment to a showy victory on technical points of law. Everyone expected such a man to succeed. But how dramatic a future, how stormy a career, lay just ahead of him, none could have guessed.

Only two or three of his appearances at the bar in these years ever attracted much public notice. In the late spring of 1866 some 1500 Irish Republicans or Fenians under John O'Neill attempted a foolish raid into Canada, raised their green flag on the north side of the Niagara River, and were defeated there in the "battle of Limestone Ridge." Some were brought back to Buffalo as prisoners on a United States steamer. A rash, youthful, sorry-looking band, they had no counsel, and Cleveland, with other Democratic lawyers, volunteered to defend them. He did so ably and successfully, and when they made up a purse, refused it. In 1871 there was another Fenian movement against Canada. Again some of the excited Irish participants were arrested, and this time were taken to Canandaigua for trial. Cleveland was kept in Buffalo by another case, but he arranged with a friend in Ontario County to defend the Fenians free of charge, and after they had been convicted, he joined in petitioning President Grant for a commutation of sentence.[1]

One of his civil cases also attracted attention—his successful defence of the editor of the Buffalo *Commercial Advertiser* in 1868 in a suit for libel. This editor, with the purpose of breaking up a nefarious

---

[1] Assemblyman Donohue in Buffalo *Courier*, Sept. 8, 1881; Representative John F. Finerty in Buffalo *Courier*, Aug. 15, 1884.

though common practice in certain lake ports, had denounced a wealthy Buffalo grain-dealer named David S. Bennett for obtaining a loan through a friendly Buffalo bank on a fraudulent receipt for stored grain. The accused dealer claimed large damages, and when Cleveland undertook the defence seemed likely to obtain them. It was necessary to prove the truth of the charges, and this was difficult because of the high political and social standing of the man, and the complicated nature of the transaction; yet Cleveland did it, and defeated the suit.

Buffalo in these years continued to grow rapidly. The population, a little over 80,000 on the eve of the war, was shown by the census of 1880 to be 155,000. Though Erie County had sent more than 15,000 men into service, the conflict hardly gave a perceptible check to the city's development, and in some ways accelerated it. New iron works had come in, new breweries had sprung up, and the manufacture of clothing, due in part to the demand for uniforms, had become important; while Buffalo became one of the principal American centres in the manufacture of soap and steam threshers. Cleveland was well content with the city, which promised him scope for a career and in which he had taken a completely independent place. He seldom went out now to the Black Rock home of his uncle, and saw little of his uncle's associates. This was partly because he wished to stand alone, and partly because he had made friends with many "queer people" [1]— that is, a rough set—of whom Mrs. Allen disapproved.

He lived simply, at first in various rooming houses and later, beginning in 1873, in a small suite called Room F in the Weed Block; he ate for several years in a popular boarding-house kept by Mrs. A. B. Ganson, and subsequently in restaurants and cafés. The city contained many places which were half saloon, half restaurant, where whole German families came in for food, beer, music, and pinochle or dominoes. When the first mechanical organ was installed in one of the largest and finest of these resorts, playing selections from *Freischütz*, *William Tell*, and other operas, even the fashion of the town turned out to hear it.[2] Cleveland, always methodical, stayed most of his evenings in his room, but habitually spent one or two a week in these cheerful resorts. His family had never objected to moderate use of

[1] Miss Gertrude Allen to author, Aug. 10, 1931.
[2] Frances M. Wolcott, *Heritage of Years*, 12.

liquor; indeed, his father and brother had quoted the Bible in defence of wine.[1] His best friends, men of brains and in part of college education, met him at the beer-halls, the only clubs open to such young men.

Inwardly he changed but little. He retained his simple religious convictions. In a natural reaction against the incessant observances of a minister's home he never went to church in Buffalo, but on his visits to Holland Patent he always did, and seemed to enjoy it. Partly as a gesture of affection for his mother, he often thumbed the Bible she had given him; and above his bed hung a framed Biblical motto from Holland Patent: "As thy days are, so shall thy strength be." Occasionally he found time to read history and poetry. Having made a small circle of friends, he evinced little disposition to enlarge it. While usually genial and open, he could be harsh and stern, and his mother sometimes remarked with pain that he was the only one of her children who showed rudeness. He still took an interest in politics. After the death of Dean Richmond the leadership of the Democratic organization passed for ten years to Joseph Warren, editor of the *Courier,* who predicted a bright political future for him.[2] But for the most part the young attorney lived in and for the law, and for the easy-going sociability of the hotel-lobbies and saloons.

[1] Cleveland Bacon to author, Nov. 4, 1931.
[2] St. Clair McKelway in *Grover Cleveland Memorial* (1909).

THROUGHOUT the years of early manhood Cleveland presented a dual aspect to the world and was indeed a man of two distinctly different sets of traits—so different that it has been easy for writers to draw two sharply contrasting pictures of him.[1] He was a hard-working young lawyer, spending incredibly long hours at his desk and seeming to those who knew him but slightly to be growing into a stiff, heavy, and stern man. Many hasty observers spoke of his impassivity and dignity. But he was also a roystering blade, who knew the inside of dozens of saloons, led the chorus in lusty drinking songs, and prided himself on feats of conviviality which sometimes, as he put it later, caused him to "lose a day." The picture of Cleveland at 2 A. M. laboring over his law-books is strictly accurate; and so is the picture of Cleveland at 2 A. M. in the back room of Diebold's, or Schwabl's, or Louis Goetz's ("the Dutchman's") cafés, chanting "There's a hole in the bottom of the sea" with cronies as intent as himself on filling it up. There was a Cleveland who was described by the press as one of the most promising young lawyers in the city; there was also a Cleveland—nicknamed "Big Steve"—who cracked jokes in Level's livery stable, gambled mildly at euchre or poker, and in the sixties was even seen in a rough-and-tumble fight with one Mike Falvey on Seneca Street. The fight began over Democratic politics, and Cleveland knocked Falvey into the gutter.[2] Nor was it the only encounter of the sort. His exuberant physical energy found an outlet partly in work, partly in fishing trips, and partly in the most boisterous fun that Buffalo afforded and that he could share with his boon companions—"Shan" Bissell, Oscar Folsom, Charles Goodyear, George Talbot, and Charles McCumber. On hot summer evenings he was fond of the German beer-gardens, with their sawdust, music, pretty girls, and jovial banter.

There were always two Clevelands. To the end of his life his intimates were struck by the gulf which separated the exuberant, jovial

---

[1] See Robert McElroy, *Grover Cleveland, The Man and the Statesman*, I, 18–37, for the picture of the wholly virtuous Cleveland, Denis T. Lynch, *Grover Cleveland, A Man Four-Square*, 34–98, for that of the dissipated Cleveland. The two must be combined to furnish an accurate portrait.

[2] Charles H. Armitage, *Grover Cleveland as Buffalo Knew Him*, 28.

Cleveland of occasional hours of carefree banter, and the stern, unbending Cleveland of work and responsibility, whose life seemed hung
round by a pall of duty. An illustrative story is told by his nephew.
On the evening of inauguration day in 1893 there was a family dinner
at the White House. Cleveland, in his most joyous mood, entertained
the circle by a flow of jests and by mimicking the more ponderous
figures of the parade. With his huge figure and rubicund countenance,
there was something irresistibly amusing in his drollery. The table
rang with laughter. But a few minutes after dinner Secretary Gresham
dropped in. At once the severe and unyielding Cleveland, every faculty
concentrated upon the public business, reëmerged. As he conferred
with his Secretary of State he looked like some grim Titan of affairs,
as humorless as Cromwell. In early life these two Clevelands were
often at war with each other, and the impulse toward heedless good-
fellowship was stronger than in later years.

This dual character of the man accounts in part for his curious and
unfortunate step in 1870 in accepting election as sheriff of Erie County.
By so doing he cut himself off for three years from practice and took
a place that most men well launched in the profession, with a growing
clientele, would have eyed disdainfully. As district attorney or as Congressman he would have held a position of dignity, but the sheriff was
usually a political hack. It was his association with the saloon and
livery-stable set that made him willing to consider such an office. He
offered as an excuse his belief that as sheriff he would have time for
study that he had never found in his law office. Actually his principal
reason for seeking the berth was precisely that which made the shrievalty of New York County attractive to Alfred E. Smith in 1915: the
fees would yield perhaps $40,000 in the three years, which was several
times as much as he could earn at the law.

There is no question that, with this unexalted motive, Cleveland actively pulled wires to secure the nomination and election. Oscar Folsom, who was the leader of the third assembly district and the tenth
ward caucus, assisted him. Before the Democrats of the county held
their convention on September 28, it was conceded that William
Williams, a former banker and the local manager of the Lake Shore
Railroad, would be nominated for Congress, and it was desirable to
balance the ticket by a younger man and a lawyer. Cleveland won
against two rivals on the first ballot, mustering 66 votes to their com-

bined strength of 48, and his name was received with general favor. The *Courier* again praised him:

> Grover Cleveland, the candidate for sheriff, is perhaps the most popular man in the Democratic party of the county. Recognized as *facile princeps* among the younger members of the Bar of Buffalo, he is at the same time so true a gentleman, so generous, modest, and lovable a man, that we have never heard of anybody's envying him. He will rally the utmost strength of the Democracy to the polls, and afterwards make one of the best sheriffs Erie County ever had. His very name is a host.

Though in the ensuing campaign Cleveland won, he did not run well. He made three speeches in Buffalo and two elsewhere in the county, addressing a German Democratic meeting at Tonawanda and a Democratic rally at Williamsville. A campaign banner twenty feet long, inscribed "Grover Cleveland for Sheriff," the gift of an admirer, was unfurled from the party staff at the corner of Eagle and Hickory Streets. The *Courier* made several special appeals in his behalf, and its comments indicated that there was danger of vote-trading at his expense. When all the ballots were counted, it was found that the Democratic nominee for governor, Hoffman, had carried Erie County by 1,384 votes; that Williams, running for Congress, had carried it by 603; and that Cleveland had a majority of only 303.

II

Cleveland's new position was far from a sinecure, for he was now one of the chief law officers of a county that, with its large population of canalhands, sailors, roustabouts, vagabonds, and other riff-raff, was full of rowdyism and crime. Few cities of Buffalo's size had so many groggeries and disorderly houses, or witnessed so many assaults, robberies, and murders. In 1873 the city had 673 saloons for a population of less than 150,000. Now and then the police carried out a raid in the tenderloin or "infected" district, but these spasms had no permanent effect. The Buffalo *Express,* which for several years following 1869 was partly owned by Mark Twain and received editorial attention from him, observed a few months after Cleveland took office that the city was a sink of iniquity, with more "social eyesores" than any other of its population in America. Gambling houses operated seven days in the week, saloons and brothels were always open, and under the name of sacred concerts, Sunday performances of the vilest kind were permitted, at which the audiences were composed of loafers, thieves, and prostitutes. This was the county in which Cleveland had to arrest violators of State laws and take custody of them.

With his usual sense of duty, Cleveland paid vigilant attention to his unsavory office, and his Republican successor, John B. Weber (who represented Buffalo in Congress in Cleveland's first presidential term), later testified that it was "administered with great efficiency." He took over his desk on New Year's Day, 1871, amid scenes of conviviality, for the outgoing sheriff entertained a large body of friends with cigars and liquor. His first act was to reappoint the methodical under-sheriff, W. L. G. Smith, a Democratic attorney and a man of exceptional ability, who had published a refutation of Harriet Beecher Stowe called *Life at the South, or Uncle Tom's Cabin as It Is*, and a voluminous biography of Lewis Cass. Cleveland cared nothing for his literary productions, but a great deal for the fact that he knew every detail of office routine and was so precise that men could set their watches by his movements. Cleveland also reappointed the jailer, Richard Harris, and he had under him, beside turnkeys, janitors, and clerks, eight deputy-sheriffs.

For several reasons, the Erie County jail had been a rich spot for grafters. It received more convicts annually than any other county jail in the State; this being because Buffalo had so many floating criminals and because the authorities preferred the imposition of jail sentences to fines.[1] Jack London in his reminiscences of life as a tramp has described what a sink of brutality and vice it was when he spent a term in it some years later.[2] Discovering that an overcrowded jail had meant pretty pickings in the furnishing of supplies, Cleveland launched an attack upon the thievery that his predecessors had ignored. The story of how he made the Democratic contractors supply the full amount of cordwood specified—measuring it himself—and the proper quality of flour and oatmeal ordered, is familiar. He compelled the Democratic deputy-sheriffs to perform all their duties.[3] Naturally, he became unpopular with certain groups. "He looked down on the ward politicians and they reciprocated," said Weber long afterward.

[1] N. Y. Prison Association, 28th Annual Report, 1873.
[2] See Jack London, *The Road*.
[3] Parker, *Saturday Evening Post*, Aug. 28, 1920.

"It was nearly ten years later, when time had somewhat softened his unpopularity, that the party leaders secured his consent to run for mayor." [1]

But the feature of Cleveland's term as sheriff which attracted the greatest attention when he was a candidate for President was not his war upon the grafters, but his share in putting two murderers to death. The law made it part of the sheriff's duty to serve as hangman. In 1872 occurred the first execution in Cleveland's term, the climax of a sensational case of matricide. A drunkard named Patrick Morrissey, living in a slum section of the waterfront, who had long treated his mother with cruelty, sought her tenement on one of his sprees, demanded money, and when she refused, struck her to the floor. As she struggled to her feet she gasped, "You had better kill your mother and be done with it!" At these words he grasped the knife with which she had been cutting bread, and drove it to her breast. The crime being too horrible to admit of any mercy, he was sentenced to die on September 6, the first execution in Buffalo in more than six years. Such events took place inside the jail walls at high noon. While it is unnecessary to go into the details of the hanging, it may be noted that Sheriff Cleveland took the utmost pains to invest the execution with proper solemnity. He excluded all sensation-seekers, covered the jail-yard with canvas to prevent would-be spectators from using the house-tops, directed the deputy-sheriffs and priests, in taking the condemned man to the scaffold, to act with celerity, and standing at a point where he could not see Morrissey, himself sprung the trap. [2]

The second hanging, early in 1873, was that of Jack Gaffney, a dissipated young Irish saloonkeeper who while playing cards in a low dive on Canal Street quarrelled with a friend over the stakes, and shot him dead. After he was condemned to death his lawyer, Lyman K. Bass, made desperate efforts to save him, which Gaffney abetted by shamming insanity. Cleveland, feeling sympathy for the man's wife and little children, was greatly troubled by the case. Exercising his powers as sheriff, he secured a writ from a justice of the Supreme Court and impanelled a jury to ascertain whether Gaffney was really demented; four of the jurymen, at his suggestion, obtaining from Governor Dix a stay of execution for a week. Cleveland then addressed

[1] Armitage, *Cleveland as Buffalo Knew Him*, 57.
[2] Buffalo *Courier* and other newspapers.

the jury, reading the law applicable to the case, and it was evident that he hoped to be spared another hanging. When the jurors pronounced the man sane, he again surrounded the execution with the strictest precautions, again rigidly limited the number of witnesses, and once more himself pressed the fatal lever.

While Cleveland was never opposed to capital punishment and was the last man in the world to give way to squeamishness, these executions caused him genuine anguish. The noun is not too strong, though his friend Dorsheimer contented himself with saying that they were "grievously distasteful." [1] One of his sisters afterwards recalled that, deeply worried, he visited Holland Patent shortly before the first execution to talk about it with his mother.[2] Against her advice, he refused to delegate the task to a deputy, as by paying a $10 fee he might legally have done; saying that he would not ask another man to accept so hateful a task. To all the details, in his anxiety to ensure a merciful death, he gave meticulous attention; and once he awakened a physician at an early hour, after spending an almost sleepless night, to inquire what he should do if some utterly impossible accident occurred.

In every way Cleveland made a conscientious and effective sheriff. He worked well with the public prosecutors—the successive district attorneys, Lyman K. Bass and B. H. Williams, and the young assistant Federal attorney, George J. Sicard. He was resolute with lawbreakers, kept the jail in excellent order, and served writs promptly. There was plenty of leisure, some of which went to fishing and hunting, some to good-fellowship, and some to study. His friend Dorsheimer, who certainly knew, testified that after these three years "he was a stronger and a broader man than he had ever been before, and he at once took a higher place than he had ever held." [3]

III

It was somewhat fortunate, in view of Cleveland's family responsibilities, that he had the income of the sheriff's office, for the sudden death of two of his brothers in 1872 left him the unassisted mainstay of his mother. Since their discharge from the army, Richard C. Cleveland and Lewis F. Cleveland, known as Cecil and Fred, had passed

[1] Wm. Dorsheimer, *Grover Cleveland*, 35.
[2] Mrs. E. L. Yeomans, Memorandum. Cleveland Papers.
[3] Dorsheimer, *Cleveland*, 34, 35.

through varied experiences. Fred, the younger, was the more successful. Going into the hotel business, he became owner of the Fairfield House at Fairfield, Conn., a summer resort. For winter occupation he acquired a lease of the Royal Victoria Hotel at Nassau in the Bahamas, a government property still widely known for its size and comfort. It was his energy and shrewdness which first made it popular with Americans. Cecil was associated with him in its management. On October 17, 1872, they sailed from New York to open the hotel; their steamer, the *Missouri,* burned at sea twenty-five miles off one of the Bahamas, the Great Abaco, on the 22nd; and they and some eighty other passengers were lost. On seeing the first telegrams Cleveland hastened to Holland Patent to comfort his mother and remained there with five of the other children while confirmation was being obtained. The *Courier* remarked that he would have "the heartiest sympathy of thousands who know him hereabouts." A simple stone erected to the two sons in the Holland Patent graveyard bears the felicitous inscription: "Loving and pleasant in their lives, and in their deaths they were not divided."

The management of the substantial estate which Lewis F. Cleveland, though only thirty-one, was able to bequeath, fell to Grover. He and William W. Stephens, a New York attorney, were executors under the will, and he assumed the principal burden. Most of the property passed to a favorite sister, Louise, who had accepted the burden of staying with and caring for the mother; Fred bequeathing her the Holland Patent house, which he had bought for his mother's use, with the stipulation that it must not be sold during Mrs. Cleveland's lifetime.[1] A bequest of $500 was made for a school library in Holland Patent. Under the will, the Royal Victoria might be carried on by the executors for a time, and when the lease and furniture were sold, $10,000 was to be paid to Cecil (now dead) and the rest to the mother. Cleveland chose to continue the operation of the Royal Victoria, and according to family tradition, made a journey to Nassau—his only trip, save those across the Niagara, and two late in life to Cuba and Bermuda, outside the country. The panic of 1873 had depressed all property values, and he had to act slowly. After several years he sold the Fairfield House and its furniture for $5,266, most of this going to Louise. Meanwhile he advanced considerable sums to meet claims on the estate, and carried on an active correspondence with the colonial

---

[1] L. F. Cleveland's Will and other legal MSS. Cleveland Papers.

authorities in making the best use of the Royal Victoria lease. This correspondence shows his familiarity with every detail of the management—the best dates for opening and closing, the danger from yellow fever, the jealousy of Florida hotels, and so on.

Completing the term as sheriff at the end of 1873, Cleveland joined Lyman K. Bass and Wilson S. Bissell in establishing a new firm, with offices in the Weed Block. His shrievalty had been, on the whole, an unfortunate deviation from his career as lawyer. There were some compensations: his friends variously estimated his three years' savings at from $20,000, which is too little, to $60,000, which is far too much.[1] Whatever the sum, he for the first time had a small competence at hand, a fact which increased his sense of independence. Dorsheimer states that he really had found time for the extra legal study which he acknowledged that he needed. The training in administration was not without value, and there were men in Buffalo who would remember that he had proved a firm incumbent of a trying office. Nevertheless, the cheap political associations of the position, the rough men it brought around him, and the unsavory nature of its tasks, rendered it an office that he should have avoided.

In the next half dozen years Cleveland was to make his principal mark as an attorney. His partners were men after his own heart: Bass had been one of his closest friends for years, while Bissell was to be his most intimate confidant long after he entered the presidency. He had served his professional apprenticeship, and was held in solid esteem by everyone at the bar. For the first time he was free from financial worries. Still in his middle thirties, he presented a figure of abounding health and virility. His fondness for beer and lack of regular exercise had rendered him excessively fat, yet the primary impression which he made upon observers was of strength. His shoulders were broad, his legs large and muscular, his arms large, his head large. His movements were not clumsy, but possessed a slow ease. In vigor and energy, he seemed ready for any task that his profession would bring.[2]

---

[1] Parker, *Saturday Evening Post,* Aug. 28, 1920, gives the larger figure; George C. Level in Armitage, *Cleveland as Buffalo Knew Him,* 58, the smaller.

[2] Timothy Mahoney, H. M. Gerrans, and others to author, June 4–11, 1929.

THE ruling principle of all the Clevelands, from the time of the first English settlers in Massachusetts, was to do right, work hard, and be useful. None of them had shown any taste for adventure as such. They were thrifty, but none had made an energetic effort to grow rich. While proud of their good name, they had never manifested any desire for fame, even the two Aaron Clevelands regarding their reputation as merely incidental to their work for the church and for good causes. But they had always displayed a strong sense of duty and a disposition to labor at the task which lay directly ahead. Cleveland simply followed his forefathers when he gave wholehearted devotion to the work of his profession, never sparing himself and never thinking of unusual rewards. Following his term as sheriff, he cherished the hope that some day he would be appointed to the bench. Meanwhile he applied himself to the legal business of his three successive firms—Bass, Cleveland, and Bissell; Cleveland and Bissell; and Cleveland, Bissell, and Sicard.

In the square, whitish, five-story brick building at the corner of Main and Swan called the Weed Block, an ugly boxlike structure with stores below, offices above, and a heavy jutting roof at the top, Cleveland spent most of his time. The stores, with plate-glass windows behind which flared the gaslights of the period, took up the entire Main Street front. The Swan Street side presented simply a flat wall of bricks, against which a steep flight of stairs led up to an entry-way on the second floor by which callers reached the attorneys and business men upstairs. It was an ingenious device to avoid placing a large hallway on the ground floor, where space was valuable, and the fact that it added to the hideousness of the building gave citizens of Buffalo no concern. The offices of Cleveland's firm, on the second floor, were plain and unprepossessing. A photograph of the main room shows booklined walls, a great central table, a barrel-stove at one end, its four feet resting on a zinc plate, and a gas fixture bearing two large white globes. On the third floor of a brick addition at the rear of the Weed Block Cleveland took a small apartment, with southerly windows opening on Swan Street, while he ate his meals at Gerot's French restaurant a block east of his office, in some saloon, or later, at the City Club.   ·

Since Buffalo prided itself on being a city of beautiful homes, it was unusual for even bachelors to live in a business block; but Cleveland cared little for appearances and wished to be near his work. On the same floor was the apartment of Powers Fillmore, the eccentric only son of the ex-President and a frequent companion of Cleveland, while others lived from time to time in the building. Cleveland's rooms were furnished with great comfort. A young nephew who sometimes came and spent brief vacations with "Uncle Jumbo," as the family began to call him when in the seventies he became corpulent, felt that he possessed everything that heart could desire. There were deep easy chairs, polished tables, books, cigars in boxes and humidors, and fishing and hunting trophies. There was even an icebox. When the nephew inquired what was kept in it, Cleveland's eyes twinkled as he replied, "Watermelons!" [1] One of the young law clerks, Harlow C. Curtiss, occasionally brought Cleveland's laundry over from the office to the apartment, and noted that his personal library was fine as to quality though not large. "That he had read it was proved by what he wrote and what he said; it was his English and his writing that made me his sincere friend and admirer long before he achieved fame." [2] Living so near his work, he could pore over his cases as late as he liked and be in the office again before the clerks arrived in the morning.

From the beginning he was the real though not nominal head of the firm. Lyman K. Bass, whose name preceded his on the door, was a member of the Forty-third and Forty-fourth Congresses (1873–77), and as such was absent in Washington for from three to eight months in each of these four years. Moreover, Bass was fond of society and movement, knew many political and financial leaders, and travelled much. Touched by tuberculosis, in 1877 he removed to Colorado Springs, there becoming counsel for the Denver & Rio Grande, though continuing to visit Buffalo. After 1877 the firm was practically Cleveland and Bissell, though it did not take that name until 1880. It may be mentioned in passing that by Cleveland's second Presidential term, Bass's widow had become conspicuous in Washington society as the

[1] Cleveland Bacon to the author, Nov. 8, 1931.
[2] H. C. Curtiss to author, Feb. 14, 1931.

wife of the witty and unfortunate Colorado Senator Edward O. Wolcott, who was a close friend of Roosevelt, Hay, and Henry Adams. George Sicard, the last partner, was a graduate of Hamilton College and a cultivated man of scholarly tastes.

II

By dogged industry and reliability rather than any striking talents, Cleveland lifted his firm to the front rank among Buffalo law offices. Business men liked him because he was instinctively conservative and gave safe advice, and because he devoted untiring attention to their cases, never letting a brief enter the courtroom till it had been made as nearly impregnable as possible.[1] When he erred, it was on the side of caution. He continued to show no desire to join the ranks of the money-making lawyers, and in later life once told William L. Wilson that he could never bring himself to ask large fees. He continued also to leave most court-room appearances to his partners—to Bass, a polished speaker, or Bissell, a quick-witted, jovial young man, whose sympathetic temperament made him a good pleader. The firm did an active business of a miscellaneous nature, principally for corporations, and Cleveland found that it required all his time. He never took a continuous vacation of more than a fortnight, though when the wild ducks flew or the bass bit he could be found tramping along the waters near Buffalo. When he had a free week-end he frequently ran over to Holland Patent to see his mother and sister, walk with his young nephew, and talk with the villagers, whose views he enjoyed.

By the middle seventies his abilities were universally acknowledged. His apprehension was slow but sure; he had a genius for application, and a resolute purpose to master every question which came before him. He never relaxed over a case until he had searched every precedent and thought every argument through to its conclusion, no matter how varied its ramifications. "His power of concentration was only limited by physical demands," writes a fellow-attorney, Edward W. Hatch,[2] "and he worked for twenty-four hours at a stretch without feeling the need for rest—indeed, I think he was insensible to his physical requirements. When his task was ended, his physical reaction was like that of a suddenly released spring." He was not infallible;

[1] Bissell, quoted in Parker, *Grover Cleveland*, 40, 41.
[2] Hatch's Memorandum, July 29, 1920. Cleveland Papers.

sometimes the judges, through their fault or his, disagreed sharply
with his process of reasoning. But once he had reached a conviction
upon any question, no matter how much the opposing lawyers or the
bench might assail it, nothing ever shook his views. "This," says Judge
Hatch, "made him at all times an exceedingly dangerous antagonist."
His exceptionally retentive memory, enabling him to deliver long arguments without notes, added to this formidability.

His deliberation, industry, and stubbornness were no more remarkable than his honesty. One of the most distinguished attorneys Buffalo
has ever produced, John G. Milburn, at whose house President
McKinley died in 1901, began his career as a clerk in Cleveland's
office. Cleveland, he has written, was "a very distinct personality at
the bar, forceful, deliberate, rather slow-moving, impressive, genial; a
very earnest advocate, confining himself to the main points in question without any of the arts of the rhetorician." [1] In his last days
Milburn recalled as Cleveland's principal trait in the courtroom the
quintessential integrity that he radiated; "everybody felt it." When in
1879 William B. Hornblower went to Buffalo in behalf of some New
York clients he had occasion to choose a referee to look after some
important litigation against a prominent Buffalo citizen. He asked
various Buffalo attorneys as to the selection. They agreed unanimously
in recommending Cleveland as a sound lawyer and a man of unequalled
courage and impartiality, who would decide without fear or favor,
however influential or locally powerful the defendant might be.[2]

His partner Bissell has stated that two facts were of cardinal importance in Cleveland's legal career: [3]

One, that in all his varied relations with clients, lawyers, and courts his
every act was characterized by the highest sense of honor and by the most
delicate appreciation of and compliance with all the rules of professional ethics;
and the other, that every professional engagement, great or small, received
the best judgment, thought, and energy of which he was capable. Nothing he
undertook was slighted; therefore all his work was done well.

Judge Hatch bears testimony to the same effect:

He was a good jury lawyer, and frequently became eloquent before juries.
He practised no subterfuge. This was impossible for him. His great strength

1 Scribner's Magazine, Vol. 81, p. 345 (April, 1927)

was his candor, his thorough integrity. These elements, coupled always with an intense conviction, were an exceedingly strong factor before a jury, while before the courts they gave him a standing and insured him a respectful hearing at all times.

His thorough nature was averse to impromptu effort, and he knew that if he relied on inspiration he would probably fail. Before a trial, according to Bissell, he was "always timid and self-distrustful," and hence prepared himself to the utmost. He would devote the noon hour, when his partners were lunching, to study, and when pressed would stay at his desk till two or three in the morning. "Once pushed or dragged into court by his client," adds Bissell, "he was not only part and parcel of the case, but bold and self-reliant; and through much practise he acquired great skill and sagacity in marshalling his facts before a jury."

Ambition for distinction or wealth was emphatically not a motive in his hard work. His Buffalo friends, noting how constantly he labored, sometimes wondered that he should be so utterly devoid of a desire for either professional or political eminence. More than once it was said in print that he was among the first, if not the first, of the Buffalo lawyers of his own age. Yet he showed no desire for a conspicuous list of clients, or the honor of representing diverse and important interests. He did not wish a place among the corporation lawyers who were frequently called to New York and Washington. Bissell has pointed with pride to the fact that he undertook one of the most important lawsuits in western New York in the seventies—the case of Alberger and Williams vs. C. J. Hamlin and the American Grape Sugar Company. Williams had invented a grape-sugar formula, on which a thriving industry was built up. He was unfortunate in his associates, found that he was being robbed of control of the plant by unlawful manipulation of the stock, and with his partner John L. Alberger brought a suit for damages. Cleveland was counsel for the plaintiffs, and secured an award of $247,000, the largest in the history of the region. But such cases were few. Mr. Milburn, puzzling over his apparent inertia, believed that he found the explanation:

My only explanation to myself was that in his scheme of life professional eminence as such was not a controlling factor: but rather such a degree and amount of employment as would produce a sufficient income for all his purposes and leave him free to control fundamentally his time and efforts to his own liking. One illustration of this attitude was that he was always inclined to be impatient if the argument or trial of a case took him out of town to Rochester or Syracuse or Albany, though these are the opportunities of extending a lawyer's contact and acquaintance outside of his own bar and courts. I remember the difficulty I had in persuading him in 1881 to lead me, in the absence of my senior partner, in the trial of an important case in an adjacent county that would occupy four or five days, simply because he would have to be away from home and his usual round of life for the time.

His ideal was a substantial business of limited proportions, to which he could give personal attention in every detail. It was not a bad ideal. America, as a young country, has always been full of men doing brilliantly superficial work, hurrying from one half-finished task to another; but Cleveland had rather the spirit of a conscientious craftsman, intent upon thoroughness and completeness. In this he differed from Folsom. While Cleveland liked to study Folsom hated it. Once while they were partners Folsom asked Cleveland for a point of law. "Go look it up," said Cleveland, "and then you'll remember what you learn." Folsom, as Cleveland loved to tell the tale, turned away with a fine disdain. "I want you to know," he said, "that I practise law by ear, not by note."

In his profession he took great pride, and was willing to spend time and money for its advancement. He became prominent at meetings of the bar in Buffalo, and was made president of the local Bar Association just before he became mayor. At professional gatherings he was recognized as invaluable whenever some recently dead attorney was to be eulogized, for his sensible words would cut in a refreshing way across the stream of platitudes. Once an attorney from outside was present when a dead judge was being honored. The speakers dilated tiresomely upon their personal relations with the judge, until a heavy man with blue eyes and brown hair and moustache arose and dealt forcibly with the character of the judge himself. The stranger was struck, inquired his name, and was told that it was Grover Cleveland.[1] Different hearers have testified that in these speeches he manifested much real acquaintance with the English classics. Frequently, according to Henry Ware Sprague, a junior at the bar, "he used poetic quotations to convey and embellish his thought. For the wide range of

[1] Robert L. O'Brien to the author, June 4, 1929.

reading and retentive memory he then displayed he has received general credit only for the latter."

He was liberal in advice to younger members of the bar, helping them deal with complicated cases and assisting them in trials where he knew that his pay would be small or nothing at all. In the courts he gained such a reputation for fairness and principle that the bench often made use of his services. It was then a frequent practice of judges, whenever an issue was complex and difficult, to call in open court on some impartial attorney for an opinion. Whenever Cleveland was present he was almost sure to be the man thus recognized. He was generous in other ways. Though a Buffalo friend once remarked that "he was a great Sunday worker and a very thrifty man with money," he gave in his own fashion. Bissell recalled that his first act, when he returned to the bar in 1874, was to lend a large sum to a client in distress. Professional service was always at the command of the worthy poor. "He tried many a case without fee or the expectation of it, and often intervened to prevent the doing of injustice because of his hatred of injustice." A Buffalo attorney has left an illustrative anecdote:

I remember one time a country milliner came to Buffalo in great distress to seek a lawyer. She saw Cleveland's sign over his window—a proof of the efficacy of signboards—and went upstairs to find him. She told him afterward with fine frankness that she had never heard of him before, but that her uncle lived in Cleveland and she liked the name, and being a stranger dropped in. Her business was a foreclosure suit. Somebody had a mortgage on her house. She had let the payments and the interest run behind, and she wanted a lawyer to get her out of the scrape without money. There wasn't much time to do it, but he told the lady to call again, and meanwhile he'd think it over. He did so. The result of the thinking was the sending of Mort Robbins to the country town she hailed from with instructions to settle the suit with $1200 he gave him and take an assignment of the mortgage. This done, of course proceedings dropped. He had won her suit for her by paying her debt. I believe she paid him years afterward, delaying restitution because she said she "had a boy to bring up." Cleveland used to tell that as a joke. He would say: "I've got a right of action in a foreclosure against a woman—a client of mine—but she's got a perfect defence—she's got a boy to bring up." [1]

III

Socially, Cleveland remained a man's man. So rare were his appearances at evening parties that they were long remembered. Buffalo was

[1] Warren F. Miller in Buffalo *Courier,* April 11, 1885.

the first American city to borrow from England the admirable plan of the Charity Organization Society, an English clergyman named S. H. Gurteen establishing such a body in 1877. From the outset it was supported in part by an annual charity ball. When Cleveland became mayor it was his duty, *ex officio,* to attend, and there was amusement when, supported by George J. Sicard, he actually appeared on the floor. An unnamed Buffalo woman thought the event worth com-memorating in verse:

> "Let's dance the step-over," said genial Grover.
> "Who'll be your pard?" said George J. Sicard.

He cared little for dining out, and if he ever escorted a young woman anywhere the fact was not recorded; indeed, he noticeably kept his distance from the belles of the city. His sisters once asked him whether he had ever thought of getting married, to which he replied: "A good many times; and the more I think of it the more I think I'll not do it." A few years later they again interrogated him, and this time he an-swered with more truth than he supposed: "I'm only waiting for my wife to grow up." [1]

It was partly because he worked so intensely that he still liked a robust kind of relaxation. He was fond of amusement, but not the amusement of the parlor or theatre. He was happiest in a hotel lounge; in a friend's room full of tobacco smoke, glasses, and cards; in one of the cheerful saloons—particularly a back room; off on the duck-marshes with a gun, or on the Niagara River with a rod; or at a clam-bake near the lake, with a dozen good fellows scattered about. He kept a fine bird-dog and was an expert on shotguns. He enjoyed Race Week, which brought such men as General Sheridan to Buffalo. Sometimes when the strain of the law had been severe, he relaxed in proportionate degree. He used later in life to acknowledge, with a chuckle, that he had not been a saint. [2] In his gayer moods he liked an intimate friend at hand, and Oscar Folsom was long a boon companion. Bright, frank, and broadly-educated, Folsom moved in much wider circles than Cleve-land, while he had some sporting tastes that Cleveland did not share—for example, he loved fast trotters, and his mare White Cloud was locally famous; but they were much together. When Folsom's little

---

[1] Mrs. Yeomans' Memorandum. Cleveland Papers.
[2] Hatch's Memorandum. Cleveland Papers.

girl was born and named Frances, Cleveland and Bass went together to see the baby.[1] Later he fell back more and more upon Bissell for companionship, and found in him sterling qualities. Bissell, who had been brought up in Buffalo and graduated from Yale, had entered the Laning, Cleveland, and Folsom firm as a clerk in 1869, and soon formed a special esteem for Cleveland as the "working member" of the organization. To the end of his life, though not without petulant fits, he was Cleveland's devoted admirer.

Buffalo had a number of Alsatians who prided themselves upon the excellence of their food and drink. Considering his bulk, Cleveland all his life was a sparing eater, but he appreciated a well-cooked dinner of the German type, served with wine or beer. Spirits he drank occasionally, but beer constantly. When he was running for district attorney against Lyman K. Bass, they agreed that during the campaign they would take only four glasses of lager daily. It was hot summer weather. Meeting in the evening at some saloon to talk the contest over, they found the allowance inadequate. At Bass's suggestion, they began to "anticipate" their future supply. It was not long before Bass announced, as they finished quenching their thirst one night: "Grover, do you know we have anticipated the whole campaign?" The next evening he brought forth two huge tankards, by courtesy called glasses, and there was no more trouble with the rule.[2] Cleveland soon became attorney for the Brewers' Association, and even owned some stock in a brewery.

Buffalo of the seventies was a democratic community, and no man could be sheriff in such a city without knowing many different kinds of people. In saloons like Louis Goetz's or Gillick's Cleveland chatted with everybody and anybody. He liked to play pinochle, poker, and a card-game called "sixty-six." Another saloon where he might be found was "the Shades," at Main and Swan near his office, where the patrons drew their own liquor from barrels and kegs picturesquely ranged about the wall, for there was no bar, and made their own change from a peck of loose silver on the table. Still another was Bass's. In general it was food, not drink, that drew Cleveland to a saloon, as it drew other professional and business men. Sunday evenings would often find him at Schenkelberger's restaurant, famed for its sausages and sauerkraut.

---

[1] Frances M. Wolcott, *Heritage of Years*, 41.
[2] Parker, *Saturday Evening Post*, Aug. 28, 1920.

But as the years passed his dignity increased. He was seen less frequently in saloons, and more often at the better hotels and restaurants. In 1877 he helped found the City Club, which took up pleasant quarters in a remodelled house at 351 Washington Street; in fact, he was one of the original board of directors. It had an excellent dining room, while the 350 resident members included many good friends. A few years later, as mayor, he became an honorary member of the older and smaller Buffalo Club. At the City Club he made the acquaintance of a very capable mulatto named Sinclair, the steward, whose son William he later took to Albany and then to Washington. During the seventies the principal hostelry of Buffalo was the Tifft House, which was not supplanted by the Genesee Hotel until shortly before Cleveland left; and here for a long time Cleveland had a corner table with friends. Once the "seven bachelors," a group to which he and Bass belonged, commandeered the house and gave an entertainment that was long remembered.[1] All the accounts of his personal appearance in the later seventies emphasize the severe correctness of his dress. He usually appeared in black broadcloth, immaculate linen, and a top hat, and it was said that he was even seen fishing at the Beaver Island clubhouse in this attire.[2]

Three events of the seventies did much to make Cleveland a more sober and thoughtful man and curb his occasional laxities. One was the drowning of his two brothers, already recorded. Of another, the Halpin affair, we shall speak later. The third was the tragic death of Oscar Folsom, who while driving with Warren F. Miller on July 23, 1875, was thrown from his buggy and almost instantly killed. At the time Cleveland was working in his room with another friend, George S. Wardwell. As he said afterward, he could hardly believe the news; it was almost impossible to think of anyone so full of irrepressible spirits and the joy of life lying cold in death. The blow was one of the heaviest he had ever felt, and he could not easily recover from it.[3] Folsom had died without a will. The court appointed Cleveland administrator of the estate, and thereafter he felt a special duty toward Mrs. Folsom and her little girl Frances.

Thus the quietest decade in Cleveland's life—the decade between

[1] Frances M. Wolcott, *Heritage of Years*, 39.
[2] Deshler Welch, *Grover Cleveland*, 31, 32.
[3] Buffalo *Courier*, July 24, 1875; August 11, 1884.

his early struggles to gain a footing in the world and his political activities—rolled by. He labored hard at what came to his hand, and avoided other fields of possible effort. After leaving the sheriff's office he was too busy to engage in politics. He continued a good Democrat, faithful at ward meetings and city conventions, serving on party committees, and giving advice on tickets, but he made no effort to take a hand in State affairs. "He did not seek or maintain relations with prominent Democrats throughout the State for political purposes," writes Milburn, "and, I should say, was acquainted with very few of them." He never but once went to a State convention. He was simply a spectator as Tilden, whom he never liked, won and lost the presidency; in 1874 he wished to see a western New York man, George Magee, nominated for governor instead of Tilden, and in 1876 he favored the nomination of Thomas F. Bayard for President. At the same time he was a loyal party man, and in 1880 scolded Milburn for complaining that the Democrats were running Hancock for a great civil office on his military record.

Nor did he take time from the law for participation in the public affairs of Buffalo. A careful search of the press reveals a conspicuous absence of his name from the roll of speakers at public meetings, the subscription lists of various "causes," and the trustees of institutions.[1] He was not a member of the Buffalo Historical Society, of which Henry W. Rogers became president in 1868. He was not interested in the Buffalo Hospital, or in raising money for the sufferers from the Chicago fire. Buffalo was now an alert little city, reaching out hungrily for culture and self-improvement. It had an Oratorio Society and occasionally an operatic troupe; some of the best stock companies offered theatrical performances in which Adelaide Neilson played Juliet, Charlotte Cushman Meg Merrilies, and Sothern Lord Dundreary; Wilkie Collins gave readings, and in 1882 Oscar Wilde lectured. The only Buffalo organizations in which Cleveland was active were the Bar Association, the City Club, and, at the close of the seventies, the Beaver Island Club. This was a sports club which purchased an island in the Niagara River, erected a clubhouse, and used the place in summer for fishing, boating, and swimming, and in spring for duck-shooting. Cleveland had helped clear the grounds, and as one member said, "was no slouch with an axe." At night the members were

[1] The author has been assisted in studying Buffalo files by Mr. Robert L. O'Brien.

carried back to their homes in a little steam launch. The organization was exceptionally congenial, for some of Cleveland's best friends, including Bissell and Milburn, belonged to it. As a bachelor he was felt to have time for club business, and came to be regarded almost as manager of the club. Years later men recalled seeing him in its grounds, leading the chubby little girl, "Frankie" Folsom, by the hand.

We have evidence that he continued to read general literature. When he was in the White House in the second Administration he was entertained at dinner by Secretary Morton, who showed him a silver punch-ladle sent by Ambassador Bayard, and read him Bayard's letter quoting the lines:

> So fares it since the years began,
> Till they be gathered up;
> The wit that flies the flowing can,
> Will haunt the vacant cup.

Cleveland instantly declared that the word "wit" should be truth; and when his statement was questioned, he turned in Tennyson to "Will Waterproof's Lyrical Monologue," and proved that he was right.[1] He still had one interest of a purely business character, the active oversight of the Royal Victoria Hotel at Nassau. It was sublet to various experienced men, chief among them James M. Morton, manager of the Morton House on Union Square in New York. When in 1880 the lease from the colonial government had to be renewed, Cleveland bargained carefully, insisting that his manager must not be compelled to open the hotel before the first week in December or keep it in operation after the first week in April. A six-year lease having been signed, he and his fellow-executor soon sold it, together with the furniture and fixtures, for almost $10,000—evidently a shrewd stroke of business.

IV

Late in the seventies Cleveland formally assumed the headship of his firm. After his partner Bass left Buffalo he and Bissell carried on the firm alone until late in 1881 Sicard was brought in as a partner. The business grew steadily, but Cleveland insisted on keeping his clientage local, and retained all his old professional conservatism.

[1] Cleveland Papers for 1895. Undated clippings quoting Secretary Morton.

Among his clients were the Standard Oil Company, the Merchants' and Traders' Bank, the Buffalo, Rochester, & Pittsburgh Railroad, and the Lehigh Valley Railroad. His friends began to say that he would eventually take his seat on the Supreme Court of the State.

One incident near the close of this period illustrates the esteem in which he was held at the bar, his unwillingness to enter new fields, and his independence. When his former partner Laning died in September, 1881, the New York Central, for which Laning had been general counsel in western New York, looked about for a successor of equal ability. The railroad was temporarily served by two lawyers who proposed a merger with Cleveland and Bissell, Cleveland to be the head of the reorganized firm. Most attorneys would have seized the opportunity without hesitation. Bissell was eager in urging the step, and many of Cleveland's friends, including Milburn, advised it. To become chief counsel for the Central in western New York would bring him into association with leading attorneys of the East and place him at one stride in the front rank of the State bar. Chauncey Depew, now vice president of the road, besought him to take the place, saying that it would add $15,000 a year to his income. He was strongly tempted and tried a number of Central cases. Yet after prolonged deliberation, he refused. He knew that Laning had been compelled to rush for trains, stay in bad hotels, and prepare cases under pressure for hurried presentation. He told his friends that having saved about $75,000, he did not need the money, and that acceptance would restrict his personal freedom in the choice of his work and the control of his time more than he could endure.[1] Milburn and others misinterpreted this, thinking he was intent upon his own comfort, when actually he was intent upon his freedom. For mere comfort he cared little. This was shown in his long hours of labor, his refusal to shirk drudgery, and his indifference to a house or personal possessions. But he had no intention of becoming the slave of a great corporation, compelled to try its designated cases on its fixed terms; he preferred to maintain his identity and pull his own boat. It was a fateful decision that he made, for if he had accepted he would never have consented to run for mayor— and would never have been President.

Thus at the beginning of the eighties Cleveland seemed to have found his permanent place in the life of Buffalo. A substantial, highly-

---

[1] C. M. Depew, *My Memories of Eighty Years*, 124, 125; Hatch's Memorandum.

regarded lawyer, who worked hard and kept to his well-worn round; a good Democrat who performed routine labors but showed no ambition for party leadership; a bachelor who meant to stay single—in short, a useful, earnest, and very limited man. No one could see him without being impressed with a sense of character. His powerful figure, his massive head set on broad shoulders, his air of bluntness and determination, gave those who observed him closely a feeling of rugged strength and integrity. Already there was something monumental about the man. He had his evident defects; he was slow, unimaginative, and narrow, and there seemed nothing about him that could be touched into incandescence. But these were after all the defects of his qualities. It is hard to find rocklike strength without a certain admixture of rocklike inertia.

Probably no man in the country, on March 4, 1881, had less thought than this limited, simple, sturdy attorney of Buffalo that four years later he would be standing in Washington and taking the oath as President of the United States.

CLEVELAND's life, thus far a slow and placid stream running through narrow banks, was now to rush suddenly into a channel which broadened with startling rapidity. As the seventies closed, there was general and rising discontent in Buffalo with the city government. It was this wave of discontent which lifted Cleveland, unexpectedly to himself or his friends, out of his quiet law office and into politics. Once this was done, the transformation of an unknown attorney into a successful party leader and a President proceeded with amazing rapidity.

The dissatisfaction of the Buffalo electorate rose from the fact that the city government had fallen into the hands of an aldermanic "ring," which conformed precisely to Samuel J. Tilden's definition of that term as a combination of corrupt politicians of both parties. Since Republicans predominated in the ring, their party was held chiefly responsible. But the mayor, who was elected every two years, might be a Republican or Democrat—it did not matter; the ring always remained in control. In 1878–79 the position fell to a Bavarian-born brewer of wealth, jollity, and general popularity named Solomon Scheu, a Democrat, personally honest but not at all inclined to interfere with the politicians. Cleveland knew Scheu and helped to elect him. During 1880–81 the mayor was a rich brick-manufacturer named Alexander Brush, a conservative Republican whose personal integrity was never questioned but who had not the slightest inclination for reform. Taxes had risen heavily. Early in 1880 the local Republican machine had obtained the passage at Albany of two bills reconstructing the Buffalo police and fire departments in a way to assure ring control for years to come. Under Mayor Brush, the cost of the fire department increased by almost $60,000 a year, and that of the police by almost $25,000, while graft was suspected in many city contracts. A feeling seized the citizens that it was time to stop electing easy-going brewers and brickmakers, choose an aggressively honest mayor, and support him in clearing out the ring.

This feeling crystallized when it became evident that the Republican leaders expected to elect as Brush's successor a highly dubious machine man. Their city convention on October 19, 1881, nominated for mayor the president of the common council, Milton C. Beebe, a crafty politician whose membership in the G. A. R. and position as Grand Master of the Ancient Order of United Workmen in the State were valuable assets.[1] For controller the convention selected a German-American of equally low reputation. At once many reputable Republicans rose in open rebellion. The party regulars called them "Ishmaelites," "scratchers," "mutineers," and "croakers," but as they persisted in their revolt it became evident that the Democrats had only to name a reform candidate to win their support.[2] A committee of five under Chairman Peter C. Doyle of the Democratic County Committee began a search for a nominee.

Cleveland was not the first man approached, for others were proposed and refused to consider the place; but when his name was suggested, it seemed an inspiration.[3] His work as sheriff was well remembered. Being what was called "ugly-honest"—pugnaciously honest—he would command instant and general confidence. When asked to take the nomination, he showed reluctance but indicated that he might possibly accept if the rest of the ticket suited him and in particular if John C. Sheehan was denied a renomination for the controllership. This stipulation simply expressed the resentment which many Buffalo Democrats had felt against the man ever since his despicable treachery to the party two years earlier. Sheehan, leader of the First Ward, a rough Irish constituency, had long been reputedly corrupt and prone in close contests to sell out to the Republicans. In 1880 he had run for controller on the same ticket with Solomon Scheu, then seeking re-election, and by adroit vote-trading had won while Scheu was defeated. Cleveland did not intend to expose himself to a similar knifing. It is evidence of the value placed on Cleveland's name that the slate-makers, with Doyle and Charles W. McCune, editor of the *Courier*, at their head, promptly agreed to the conditions. Sheehan was told that he must retire, and the *Courier*, the principal Democratic organ, announced that he had dropped out.

Cleveland's formal nomination occurred at a city convention of ward delegates in Tivoli Hall on Tuesday afternoon, October 25. Despite all the preparations, this body met in great uncertainty. As part

---

[1] Buffalo *Courier*, October 20, 1881.
[2] *Ibid.*, October 29, 1881.
[3] Armitage, *Cleveland as Buffalo Knew Him*, 80.

of the bargain with Cleveland, a resolution was first passed to defer the nominations for mayor until the remainder of the ticket was completed. There was evident fear that the First Ward men would kick over the traces. After some trouble with Sheehan's followers, suitable candidates were chosen for controller, city attorney, and city treasurer, and a committee was then appointed to wait upon Cleveland and urge his acceptance of the nomination for mayor. John G. Milburn and others had meanwhile been laboring to overcome Cleveland's reluctance. For a long time, writes Milburn, "he stood fast to the position that there were others who would do the job just as well or better than he; that his tastes did not run in that direction; that the claims of his clients were urgent and paramount; and that it was too radical a dislocation of his life. There was to him no lure in the prospect of political honors. We gave him no peace, but it was only at the last moment that he surrendered." [1] The committee found Cleveland in the Supreme Court, arguing a case before Justice Albert Haight, who has described what followed: [2]

The committee came into court and attracted the attention of Cleveland, who stepped aside and held a brief, whispered conference. Then he came up to my desk, leaning his elbows on it, and talking across in low tones.

"This," he said, indicating the committee with a nod, "is a committee from the Democratic city convention, and they want to nominate me for mayor. They've come over to see if I'll accept. What shall I do about it?"

"I think you had better accept," was Judge Haight's reply. "The Republicans have gotten into a tangle. A good many are dissatisfied with the candidate nominated. Your chances may be pretty good."

"But I'm practising law and don't want it interfered with," objected Cleveland.

"The mayoralty is an honorable position," urged Judge Haight. "We are all interested in having a good city government. You're an old bachelor. You haven't any family to take care of. I'd advise you to accept."

Had Cleveland refused, the deputation was under instructions to ask Alderman Patridge to take the nomination. The convention had adjourned to a saloon under Tivoli Hall. At half-past four a committeeman elbowed his way inside and proclaimed: "He's accepted, boys, He's accepted! Let's have a drink!" [3] They trooped upstairs, Daniel

[1] *Scribner's Magazine*, vol. 81, p. 346.
[2] Armitage, *Cleveland as Buffalo Knew Him*, 86, 87.
[3] Buffalo *Commercial Advertiser*, Oct. 26, 1881.

N. Lockwood made a nominating speech, and Cleveland received a unanimous vote. Amid cheering, he appeared in the hall for a brief address, saying: [1]

I hoped that your choice might fall upon some other and worthier member of the city Democracy, for personal and private considerations have made the question of acceptance on my part a difficult one. But because I am a Democrat, and because I think no one has a right, at this time of all others, to consult his own inclinations as against the call of his party and fellow-citizens, and hoping that I may be of use to you in your effort to inaugurate a better rule in municipal affairs, I accept the nomination tendered to me. I believe much can be done to relieve our citizens from our present load of taxation, and that a more rigid scrutiny of all public expenditures will result in a great saving to the community. I also believe that some extravagance in our city government may be corrected without injury to the public service. There is, or there should be, no reason why the affairs of our city should not be managed with the same care and the same economy as private interests. And when we consider that public officials are the trustees of the people, and hold their places and exercise their powers for the benefit of the people, there should be no higher inducement to a faithful and honest discharge of a public duty.

In his letter of acceptance he put the same idea more crisply— "Public officials are the trustees of the people;" and an able journalist, William C. Hudson, later induced the public to credit Cleveland with the slogan, "Public office is a public trust." The phrase had actually been invented long before, and Dorman B. Eaton, the reformer, had given it wide publicity in an official report made early in 1881 on the civil service system.

Cleveland's election, in view of the Republican revolt, was never in doubt. In the two weeks following his nomination he was incessantly busy making speeches, and their character throws light upon the man. They were not eloquent or witty; they presented no constructive programme for city affairs. Their unvarying burden was simply that the government must be honest and efficient. "A Democratic thief is as bad as a Republican thief," he said. "Why," he demanded, "should not public interests be conducted in the same excellent manner as private interests?" He attacked the Republican county government, and especially the system by which the county treasurer was allowed to pocket the interest on public moneys of which he was the custodian.

[1] Buffalo *Courier,* Oct. 26, 1881.

He promised the city laborers that he would pay them weekly instead of monthly, and thus end the operations of the professional money-lenders. "It is a good thing," he told a rally at Schwabl's Hall, "for the people now and then to rise up and let the officeholders know that they are responsible to the masses." He said elsewhere that "We believe in the principle of economy of the people's money, and that when a man in office lays out a dollar in extravagance, he acts immorally by the people."

It is interesting to note that the opposition press and speakers were at a loss for material in attacking Cleveland. One former quartermaster came forward with an affidavit that he had badgered Cleveland a few weeks earlier for a contribution to help take a deputation of veterans to the centenary celebration at Yorktown, and that Cleveland had refused, saying: "I am sick and tired of this old-soldier business. You fellows have been well taken care of, and I am opposed to it on principle." This attack fell flat, for many were sick and tired of the old-soldier business. The principal Republican newspaper admitted that he was "a wealthy old bachelor who is pretty well thought of," and found nothing worse to allege than that "he carries his head so high, as a rule, that he cannot see ordinary persons." [1] Cleveland declined to spend a cent in treating voters in the saloons, or to do any personal soliciting for votes. Repeatedly importuned to call on men who were believed to control electors, and to make a tour of close districts where a sight of his pocketbook was wanted, his refusal resulted in fresh charges that he was a "kid-gloved" and "white-vested" aristocrat; [2] but it probably won him votes. The *Courier* printed an editorial estimate which emphasized his honesty, inflexibility, and contempt for meanness.

The election showed Cleveland far ahead of his ticket. He polled 15,120 votes against 11,528 for Beebe, a majority of 3,592. The Democratic candidate for city attorney had a majority of 1,896, that for controller 1,707, and that for city treasurer scraped through with a margin of only 313 votes. At the same time, the Republican State ticket carried Buffalo by a decisive lead. All the circumstances of the election gave Cleveland a position of unusual authority.

[1] Buffalo *Commercial Advertiser*, Oct. 26–Nov. 7, 1881.
[2] Editorial in Buffalo *Courier*, Nov. 10, 1881.

II

On January 1, 1882, at the age of forty-four, he took the oath of office. For the time being he did not give up his place in the law firm. During 1882 his name was still carried on the door of Cleveland, Bissell, and Sicard at 284 Main Street, and he assisted the partners with advice. The office of mayor paid only $2500, and it was not expected that its holder should sever all professional connections. Cleveland still lived in Room F of the Weed Block, and still took his meals chiefly at the Tifft House or City Club. He applied himself as unsparingly to his work at the City Hall as he had to his law cases, and since he knew little about deputing labor to others, his burden was heavy. However, in certain details he did rely much upon his secretary, Harmon S. Cutting, an attorney versed in municipal law and an efficient aide.

He was expected to be a fighting mayor, and he became one. It was not a fight to carry through constructive new plans; it was simply a fight to stop the constant perpetration of jobs. As such it suited his temperament precisely. He was yet far from being a leader, but he could stand immovably against what he knew to be wrong. In his inaugural message he revealed the temper that would actuate his administration. One section of this document arraigned the street department for "shameful neglect of duty" and the "wasting (to use no stronger term) of the people's money," while another passage, designed to stop unnecessary gifts to favored party newspapers, demanded that the council should thereafter let the contract for the publication of its proceedings (a contract not subject to the mayor's veto) to the lowest bidder. A third section pointed to palpable evidence of extravagance in the bills for the repair and refurnishing of the schools. A fourth insisted that the city auditor should no longer be content with merely testing the arithmetical correctness of the accounts laid before him— a work that "might well be done by a lad but slightly acquainted with figures"—but should make an expert inquiry into the *merits* of the claims presented to him. Finally, Cleveland gave notice that the closing of city offices at four o'clock must stop, and that the employees must perform a full day's work.

In the single year that Cleveland served as mayor he distinguished himself principally by two great exploits: by his successful contest against an unblushing attempt to rob the city of approximately $200,-000 on a street-cleaning contract, and his equally successful struggle to obtain expert and efficient treatment of the sewage problem in Buffalo. If he had never been elected to higher office he would long have been remembered in western New York for these achievements. At the same time, he was vetoing a multitude of petty bits of graft which the alderman, or rather a corrupt combination of fifteen aldermen and certain contractors, with singular pertinacity were trying to thrust past him.

The street-cleaning veto was the most spectacular single event of the administration. On June 19, 1882, the council passed a resolution awarding a contract for cleaning the paved streets and alleys of the city during the next five years to George Talbot at $422,500. The circumstances indicated that a large part of this sum would be divided among the politicians as graft. Five other bids were much lower. One, by Michael Shannon & Company, was for $315,000; another, by Thomas Maytham, was for $313,500—$109,000 less than Talbot's. Most suspicious of all was the fact that Talbot had actually first put in a bid for $372,500, and had then raised it, indicating that at least $50,000 would find its way to the pockets of aldermen or the men who controlled them. Of course the aldermen had various excuses. Several alleged that the low bid offered by Maytham would land the city in trouble, for he had no financial standing and could not carry out his contract, while others declared that the wicked John C. Sheehan was behind Michael Shannon & Company. Cleveland's veto cut through these excuses like a knife through wet paper. He wrote:

This is a time for plain speech, and my objection to the action of your honorable body, now under consideration, shall be plainly stated. I withhold my assent from the same, because I regard it as the culmination of a most barefaced, impudent, and shameless scheme to betray the interests of the people, and to worse than squander the public money. . . .

When cool judgment rules the hour the people will, I hope and believe, have no reason to complain of the action of your honorable body. But clumsy appeals to prejudice or passion, insinuations, with a kind of low, cheap cunning, as to the motives and purposes of others, and the mock heroism of brazen effrontery which openly declares that a wholesale public sentiment is to be set at naught, sometimes deceives and leads honest men to aid in the consummation of schemes which, if exposed, they would look upon with abhorrence.

"Rarely," said the *Courier*, "have we heard such a universal and unanimous round of public applause as that which everywhere yesterday greeted Mayor Cleveland's message." The aldermen had accepted the bid by a vote of 15 to 11; when they received Cleveland's veto message, they rescinded their action by a vote of 23 to 2. One alderman confessed that "I have made the greatest mistake of my whole life." The contract went to Maytham, who cleaned the streets to general satisfaction.

III

The question of sewers for Buffalo was more complicated and difficult altogether. Nearly all American municipalities, at this period, were dilatory and unenlightened in providing for public sanitation. New York had not built a trunkline sewer to carry her wastes out into the bay until after the Civil War; Philadelphia then and for years later cast a mass of sewage into the Schuylkill above the unprotected water-mains; and Chicago filled the area about her cribs in Lake Michigan with filth, and then directed her citizens to boil their water. Though Buffalo was by no means exceptional in letting the problem go unsolved year after year, by the beginning of the eighties it had become urgent.

Placed on ground that sloped to the lake, the city could easily have drained its sewage away had it not been that a part of the Erie Canal, called the Main and Hamburg Street Canal, intercepted the natural line of flow. As a result, the sewage of a large section of the city passed directly into the canal, where it baked in the sun. The canal became a great brewing vat for disease. As population thickened, it constantly grew more offensive and dangerous. The citizens debated the subject at endless length. Plans were proposed for conducting Buffalo Creek through the canal to cleanse it; for filling the canal up; and for placing a great water-wheel at the Lake Erie end to create a current inland. As the discussion went on, the conviction grew that the only permanent remedy would be a large intercepting sewer to cut off the sewage from the canal, and carry it northward to be emptied into the Niagara River. But save for the erection of a small water-wheel, which simply propelled the sewage farther up the canal, arousing heated protests from the population along its banks, nothing had been done when Cleveland took office.

In his inaugural message Cleveland devoted several paragraphs to the situation. The number of deaths in the previous calendar year, he pointed out, approximated 4,000, of which 1,378, or more than a third, were from epidemic diseases, typhoid being the most prominent. He declared that the abatement of the Hamburg Canal nuisance could no longer be postponed; and assuming that the intercepting sewer would be built, stated that it would be money well spent to employ "the best available engineering skill" to plan and perhaps superintend its execution.

Cleveland returned to the subject on February 20 in a more forcible message, insisting upon a prompt decision and again proposing that the best engineering skill be employed. But to this he added an important new recommendation. For general administration of the enterprise, he suggested that the city ask the legislature to create a commission of citizens, to have full control of the construction until it was completed. He explained that the work would be the most extensive, complex, and costly in the history of Buffalo; that both the council and the city engineer were too busy with routine affairs to give it the necessary attention; and that "it does no harm to bring the non-office-holding portion of the community into more intimate relations with public affairs." He argued that since three years was the least estimate of the time required for completing the sewer, and during that period the terms of all the city officers would expire, it was desirable to have the work commenced and completed under the same continuing authority.

At once the politicians rose in revolt. The aldermen wished to keep their hands on these huge new appropriations. Already they had advertised for proposals and had received a number of bids, the lowest being $1,568,000. The city engineer, his official pride sorely wounded, declared that he was quite capable of supervising the construction. In March the aldermen joined him in concerted steps to defy the mayor, and the number of assistants in the engineer's office was increased to enable him to do the work. By this time Cleveland was thoroughly aroused, and on March 27 he descended upon the council with a crushing message. The engineer had made the blunder of saying that the task would be easy. At this Cleveland avowed himself surprised. For eleven years the sewer had been regarded as a work of urgent importance; the city years ago had been actually indicted for maintaining a nuisance; and yet nothing had been accomplished except the mistaken installation of a wheel which was forcing part of the sewage up to Tonawanda and Lockport, where the irate citizens were threatening legal proceedings. Moreover, the mayor pointed out, a number of years earlier the council had directed the city engineer to perfect plans for the elimination of the Hamburg Canal nuisance. What had he done with this "easy" task? Skilled advice had been employed, much money had been spent—and not an inch of progress had ever been made.

For a short time the aldermen continued trying to defy the mayor. When State Senator Titus introduced a bill in the legislature for the creation of such a commission as Cleveland wished, the aldermen passed a resolution condemning it and requesting Titus to withdraw it. But the press—the *Courier, Commercial, Express, News,* and *Telegraph*—rallied with unanimity behind Cleveland, and public sentiment was manifestly on his side. Indignation meetings were held in some wards. Before the end of April the aldermen gave signs of weakening, and adopted a substitute bill for a sewer commission, which they forwarded to the Buffalo assemblymen in Albany for introduction in the legislature. The commission which it proposed to set up would possess no real powers, and the members would, as Cleveland said, be nothing more "than dignified inspectors of the work," and "next to useless." Cleveland condemned the bill in another message—and the aldermen finally gave way. On June 8, 1882, the legislature passed an act creating just such a board of sewer commissioners as Cleveland had been demanding. The main battle had been won.

Yet two little skirmishes still had to be fought out to make Cleveland's victory complete. During May, with their accustomed stupidity, the aldermen carried a resolution asking the legislature to allow payment for the new sewer in twenty-to-fifty year bonds. It was obvious that the debt could easily be discharged in ten years, and Cleveland vetoed the resolution. A little later Cleveland sent in his list of five appointees to the sewer commission. The aldermen, 14 to 12, showed their teeth by rejecting all five names. Cleveland brought out the whip in another stinging message, sending back the same five names, and saying that he felt sure that their previous rejection "was the result of haste and confusion." With a tail-between-legs air the aldermen thereupon confirmed all five by a vote of 17 to 8. This commission, it may be added, conferred with the best sanitary engineers of the country, and on their advice adopted a plan that met all requirements at an estimated cost of only $764,370.[1]

IV

It was a stirring battle, this running contest of the spring of 1882 with the venal and stupid council; it resounded not only in western New York, but in Albany. June, the month the sewer bill passed, was the month also of the street-cleaning veto. That month Norman E. Mack's Buffalo *Sunday Times* published an editorial proposing Cleveland for the governorship. He was ceasing to be merely a local figure.

His two main achievements attracted the greater attention because he had kept up a constant fire of minor veto messages. Had the corrupt aldermen tried deliberately to play into his hands, they could not have succeeded better. He vetoed a silly grab by which $800 was to be paid each of the three local German newspapers for publishing a synopsis of the aldermanic proceedings. The chief of these newspapers, the *Demokrat*, heartily approved his action. He vetoed a series of pettier grabs by which officers of the street department tried to charge the city for personal livery hire. He vetoed a gift of $500 for the Firemen's Benevolent Association. He vetoed bills for unnecessary sidewalks, for the printing of unnecessary notices of tax sales, and for a donation to the Fourth of July fund of the G. A. R.—he himself making a handsome personal gift. He refused to be good-natured about small matters. He would not wink at little devices for getting public work done without competitive bids, and he had a blunt way of calling attention to all sorts of abuses. For example, the city government had been in the habit of accepting gifts of land for streets in new sections, and permitting these new streets to be laid out in any length and width the previous owners desired, thus consulting the private interests of realty speculators, and not the future needs of the city. Cleveland stopped the practise. Meanwhile City Auditor English was checking over all the contractors' bills and challenging many of them.

Cleveland showed a disposition, also, to work with the progressive

[1] See the review of this episode in the Buffalo *Courier*, July 12, 1884.

elements in city life. Now and then his message sounded a distinctly humane note, as when in June, 1882, he supported a request by the Society for the Prevention of Cruelty to Children for a protective ordinance:

It seems to me that no pretext should be permitted to excuse allowing young girls to be upon the streets at improper hours, since its result must almost necessarily be their destruction.

The disposition of the boy (child though he be) to aid in his own support, or that of others, in an honest, decent way, ought not to be discouraged. But it does not call for his being in the street at late hours, to his infinite damage morally, mentally and physically, and to the danger of society.

Again, he stood by the board of health in its fight to remove filthy dairies in which the cows were being fed on distillery wastes, and to close up some of the worst of the open wells about the city that were furnishing bad water. A description of the attack on the unsanitary cow-barns may be found in P. L. Ford's *The Honorable Peter Stirling*. As for the wells, a test case was afforded by an especially foul one at William and Watson Streets. In May, 1882, a chemist submitted a report to the board of health on this and twelve other wells, certifying that their water was "vile, and disgustingly contaminated with filth." Of the thirteen, this one stood third in the extent of its contamination. The council on June 5 declared it a public nuisance and ordered the street commissioner to fill it. Many local residents at once took steps to connect their houses with the city mains, but others made vigorous protests. As a result, on August 28 the aldermen rescinded their action and directed the street commissioner to replace the pump. In vetoing this order, Cleveland waxed sarcastic. He did not accept the theory that a good deal of nastiness in water was all right, he said, nor the theory that if people wanted to violate all sanitary regulations they should be allowed to do so:

. . . If there is in the mind of anyone the idea that it is not necessary to supply the poor and laboring people in the vicinity of this well with water as pure and healthful as that furnished to their richer and more pretentious fellow-citizens, I desire to say that I have no sympathy with such a notion. On the contrary, I believe that the poor who toil should of all others have access to what nature intended for their refreshment—pure and wholesome water. . . . There is no place in this enlightened age for the proposition that the authorities of a city may maintain an unwholesome public well, known to be such, even though the people are willing to take the risk to life and health in the use of the water.

Cleveland would not have claimed any credit for either special insight or courage in the series of acts which won him a wide reputation as the "veto mayor" of Buffalo. He could justly have claimed credit for unusual vigilance and steadfastness. Now and then he made an error, and when he did, confessed it with refreshing frankness. Thus he approved a resolution with regard to the public printing under the careless impression that only a small sum would be involved. When he learned that the costs would approach $4,000, he revoked his assent, adding: "Though there may be a slight excuse for my approval of this resolution in the first instance, I desire to acknowledge that my action in the matter was hasty and inconsiderate. A little examination and reflection would have prevented it."

A minor event of 1882 unquestionably had its effect in awakening Cleveland's ambition for larger political opportunities. The previous year one Martin Flanagan, a scooper in a Buffalo grain-elevator, had killed his foreman John Kairns. He was tried, convicted of murder in the first degree, and sentenced to be executed on January 20, 1882. Appeals to the higher courts having failed, Flanagan's counsel petitioned Governor Cornell for commutation of sentence, and Cornell refused. The execution was imminent when some prominent citizens of Buffalo, headed by John Allen, a director of the New York Central, appealed to Mayor Cleveland for aid. They believed that Flanagan should have been convicted of second degree murder or manslaughter. Pointing out to Cleveland that one of Flanagan's counsel had been drunk at the trial, that the murder had been committed with a short-bladed Barlow knife, which no one would have supposed capable of inflicting a mortal wound, and that Flanagan was a confirmed dipsomaniac, who did not know the quality of his act, they enlisted Cleveland's sympathies. The mayor undertook a painstaking inquiry, interviewing Judge Beckwith, who had presided at the trial, and going to the jail for several long talks with Flanagan. On January 19, at his request, Governor Cornell consented to a three weeks' postponement of the execution and a public hearing on the question of commuting the sentence to life imprisonment. Cleveland, convinced that lenity was demanded, resolved to appear in person.

It was well known that Cornell would be difficult to move. He was a man of firm will and cold temperament, deliberate and stern in all his acts, and notoriously disinclined to use the pardoning power. On the day preceding that set for the hearing, February 2, Allen provided a special car to carry a large deputation to Albany. It included jurymen and witnesses, the district attorney, Edward W. Hatch, prominent lawyers and other citizens, among them Millard Fillmore's son, and the mayor. Franklin D. Locke joined the group in Albany. These men were ushered into the Governor's chamber. His set jaw warned them that their task would be difficult. Mayor Cleveland opened the hearing with a review of all the facts and the laws involved, urging with great power that Flanagan had no motive for the murder, since the man was his friend, that the act could not have been premeditated, and that it was not even rightly understood. The jury, he said, had not realized that they could take the fact of intoxication into account. After this the affidavits and recommendations of the jury were heard. Cornell asked for the district attorney, who made a rather hostile statement. Then a Buffalo attorney, Henry W. Box, attempted to speak. Two hours had now been consumed, Governor Cornell was growing tired and irritated, and he harshly bade Mr. Box to sit down. Judge Hatch has described what followed: [1]

His attitude and expression succeeded in squelching Mr. Box, but they aroused Mr. Cleveland. The governor sat in a swivel chair in front of his desk. Mr. Cleveland sat a little to the right of the desk, but when he rose to address the governor he stood behind it directly facing the man in authority. The governor, in order to squelch Mr. Box, had partially risen from his chair, with his arm extended toward Mr. Box, when Mr. Cleveland sprang to his feet and in a determined manner, evidently under great excitement, faced the governor, and in a ringing, impressive tone he said: "We come to you as the king, pleading for mercy. It is your duty to hear us and hear us to the end."

Here were two men, both very large physically, both determined in character and in habit; both had been used to the exercise of command in the spheres in which they had moved; both were powerful in will. The governor was angered and roused, possessed the power and knew it. Mr. Cleveland was roused and presented a majestic appearance in the conviction that his cause was just and that the rights of a citizen were being infringed by the governor. The attitude of the two, the tension of the occasion, the commanding force of both men, it is impossible to describe. The whole chamber was hushed. Gradually the governor let his hand fall, resumed his seat in the chair, and Mr. Cleveland

[1] Quoted in Parker, *Saturday Evening Post,* Aug. 28, 1920.

proceeded to address him for fifteen minutes with tremendous impressiveness, and the governor listened without any attempt to interrupt. He realized that for once he had met his master.[1]

Cleveland was deeply stirred. Going into the anteroom, and asking the pardon clerk when they would be likely to hear the result of the application, he received what he thought was an insolent answer; and he blazed up angrily. But he won his object. The governor, who later spoke to others of the impression that Cleveland's earnestness had made upon him, granted the commutation. In later years more than one Buffalo observer attributed to the Flanagan incident a share in the change in Cleveland's outlook. In his first venture into a sphere of action outside of western New York he had won a victory, and he took pride in it.

[1] The Buffalo *Courier* had a reporter present, who gave a slightly different account of the affair. He wrote: "Governor Cornell interrupted, 'It is a waste of your time and mine to discuss this matter further, Mr. Box,' but Mr. Box continued for a few sentences. The Governor stated that there were no less than twenty-one murderers in New York City alone charged with homicide, and that a large portion of these were the result of strong drink. He should regard it as a very serious question to put this forward as a basis for the plea that a man was too drunk to deliberate. This brought Mr. Cleveland to his feet, and with an exhibition of warmth he quoted, with a thrilling effect that was felt by all present, the words of Blackstone: 'The king himself condemns no man but leaves that rugged task to his courts.' Cleveland followed this with a repetition of previous arguments and pointed out that the punishment which they were asking for was the extreme penalty in some States. This closed the hearing." The *Courier* gave four columns to the hearing in its issue of February 3, 1882.

THERE were doubtless a hundred mayors in the United States in the year 1882 who served ably and incorruptibly, and there were doubtless a number who showed the same kind of courage that Cleveland manifested. It is seldom that even the most notable of American mayors has climbed high on the political ladder. In this very decade Brooklyn elected an executive of shining qualities, Seth Low, and New York city one of still greater gifts, Abram S. Hewitt, but neither was ever strongly thrust forward for the governorship—much less the presidency. Why was it that the mayor of Buffalo fared so much better? The answer is simply that circumstances favored him. All his common sense, his superb courage, his physical and mental strength, his cautious sagacity, would have availed him little but that the stars were with him.

Ordinarily in the history of New York the governorship has gone to men previously identified with either State or national affairs. Those whose names everyone recalls, from Martin Van Buren and Silas Wright to Alfred E. Smith, were usually well known at Albany or in Washington before they entered the executive mansion. If they had not held office in these capitals they had made themselves, like Charles E. Hughes, conspicuous in connection with issues of State-wide or nation-wide importance. Between Grover Cleveland and immediate promotion there seemed to rise insuperable barriers; yet a few touches of fortune's wand, and they had been cleared magically from his path.

One important fact was that he had made himself conspicuous as a reform mayor at the happiest possible time. The months in which he fought his dramatic series of engagements with the Buffalo ring were those which just preceded the election, at this time triennial, of a governor. It cannot be said that his name was known east of Utica. But various of his acts, and particularly his veto of the street-cleaning contract, had stirred passing attention in newspapers all over the State, while west of the Finger Lakes his stubborn honesty was appreciated at its full value. As early as May the editor of the *Courier*, Charles W. McCune, a quick, keen Irishman, had told a meeting of the Democratic State Committee, of which he was a member, that Cleveland was the best man available, and some committeemen remembered this when they read the news from Buffalo during June and July. The man stood ready; he lifted himself from obscurity at the critical moment; and then, like cogs in some neat mechanism of fate, one circumstance after another snapped into the requisite pattern.

II

Into the minutiae of New York politics at the moment it is unnecessary to inquire too closely. The salient elements in the Democratic situation in the summer of 1882 may be briefly delineated. There were two principal aspirants for the nomination for governor, Roswell P. Flower of Watertown and Gen. Henry W. Slocum of Brooklyn. The former was a debonair young leader, who, while he had made a dashing record as a financier in Watertown and New York city, and had served capably in Congress, was principally qualified in the eyes of the politicians by his wealth, which promised large and careless campaign disbursements. Later he was to become a governor of the standard machine type, but his hour had not yet struck. Slocum was an older, stodgier, and more commonplace man, whose principal asset was his record as the leader of one wing of Sherman's army in the march to the sea, and who would be forgotten today but that he gave his name to an excursion steamboat which figured in one of the most horrible of American disasters. Each man hated his rival, and was prepared to fight him to the last.

In the background stood the organization leaders who were the real arbiters of party destiny. The immense influence of the Tilden organization, now wielded by the shrewd and imperious Daniel Manning of Albany, was thrown behind Slocum. It was hostile to Flower because he had opposed Manning in various State affairs and because he had made overtures for the support of Tammany Hall. No matter how much men might praise Flower's ability and generosity, Manning would have none of him. He exerted his power as chairman of the State committee against him, and assailed him through his Albany *Argus*, still a great political organ. Tammany meanwhile was playing a cautious hand. The boss, John Kelly, was determined to support a winner, and ready to divide his votes till the winner really emerged;

Flower would receive some, Slocum some, and some would be scattered. The Brooklyn Democrats under Boss McLaughlin were of course aligned behind Slocum. A fourth power in the party was the new reform organization in New York city, the County Democracy, which fortunately for Cleveland refused to join the Tilden organization in supporting Slocum. They attacked him on the ground that he was secretly friendly to Tammany; they declared that he had been implicated in gross frauds in the erection of Brooklyn Bridge; and they insisted that he was of mediocre ability.

Although divided into all these and other groups, the Democratic party tended always to coalesce about two hostile poles, Tammany and Anti-Tammany. Ten years previously the wigwam had been laid prostrate by the destruction of the Tweed Ring, but a new Tammany had quickly arisen on its ruins. The leader, John Kelly, was far more adroit than Tweed and less audacious—or, to put it differently, more smoothly hypocritical. But he was too short-sighted and too much addicted to private animosities to make a great leader, while he exerted little effort to prevent his subordinates from pursuing graft in the good old fashion.

What Kelly's Tammany lacked in rapacity and impudence it made up in cunning. It never went to the corrupt lengths of the Tammany of Croker, much less of Tweed, but it was distinguished by a vengeful meanness. Falling out with Tilden, it had fought him tooth and nail in the Democratic convention of 1876. Three years later it betrayed the Democratic governor, Lucius Robinson, a friend of Tilden, in his campaign for reëlection, and helped to make Alonzo Cornell governor instead. In 1880 its delegates had gone to the Democratic convention in Cincinnati as party outlaws, detested by everybody. When they were contemptuously denied seats, they took up headquarters in a neighboring hotel and filled its lobbies with threats of what they would do if Tilden were renominated. Tilden withdrew, Hancock was named, and the Tammany men pledged him enthusiastic support. Nevertheless, late in the campaign Kelly recklessly sacrificed even Hancock to his greed for local power. Against a storm of protests, he insisted on the nomination for mayor of an Irish-Catholic candidate, William R. Grace, who alienated the German voters and raised the issue of free public schools, and New York was lost to Garfield by 21,000 votes.

Stung to exasperation by this final example of Kelly's perfidy, the better Democrats of New York city determined to teach him a lesson. They turned to the County Democracy. This organization was founded in April, 1881, with Abram S. Hewitt, Hubert O. Thompson, and William C. Whitney as its most conspicuous leaders. Hewitt, the wealthy ironmaster and son-in-law of Peter Cooper, was a man of the true Roman stamp, who held the complete confidence of all good citizens; he had long sat in Congress, had managed Tilden's campaign in 1876 with consummate ability, and was a recognized leader in all civic undertakings. Whitney was a brilliant young lawyer, handsome and magnetic, who had become corporation counsel. He was wealthy, irresistibly attractive, and a bit ruthless in business and private life. Thompson was a promising, likable, and weak young man with a fatal ambition for a machine of his own. This triumvirate, of which Hewitt was much the most important member, gave the County Democracy certain arresting features. Chief among these was a huge managing committee of 678 members, designed to impart to all nominations a popular character. In October, 1881, Hewitt triumphantly announced that the County Democracy had 26,500 enrolled members, and the following month, against a union of Tammany and Irving Hall, it swept the local elections—choosing four of the seven State senators, twelve of the twenty-four assemblymen, and twelve of the twenty-two aldermen. When the time came for organizing the State Convention of 1882, the State leaders recognized the County Democracy as the principal regular party organization in the city, and allotted it thirty-eight votes as against twenty-four to Tammany and ten to Irving Hall.

Ordinarily men would have expected the Tilden-Manning forces and the County Democracy to unite on the same candidate; but the unsatisfactory character of either Slocum or Flower prevented that. Manning had fairly made up his mind. Kelly had not. The County Democracy had not. Many up-State Democrats had not. The situation invited a search for a strong new man, standing apart from the old factional antagonisms and jealousies.

By midsummer a number of Democratic leaders were wondering if Cleveland were not just the man required. The most important of these leaders was Edgar K. Apgar of Albany, a spirited orator and organizer who played a meteoric part in the political history of these years. All

admirers of Cleveland have reason to remember his name with gratitude and to wish that his activities might have been prolonged. Frail,
boyish-looking, gifted with restless energy and an inexhaustible vein of
idealism, he seems a precursor of that still more attractive spirit of
Cleveland's second Administration, William E. Russell. His career may
be briefly summarized. A native of Ithaca; a Yale student who threw
aside his books to join the Union army; a young lawyer who entered
State service, becoming deputy secretary of state and deputy treasurer;
a party worker who soon burned his candle to the socket, dying in 1885
—such is the story. An eminent scholar of the day, Moses Coit Tyler,
has celebrated his talents in a little book that glows with feeling.[1] No
one in the country studied political management more closely, kept
better informed on every current and intrigue, or thought more intensely upon party problems. Back of this interest lay a fervent concern for the elevation of public life. A man of intense feeling, he was
kindled to enthusiasm by any instance of remarkable courage in civic
affairs, and plunged into dejection by any political baseness. He shed
tears of anger when in the State convention of 1876 someone suggested
that Tilden should conciliate certain Brooklyn malcontents by making
a disreputable Brooklyn man the head of the State delegation to the
national convention. His sincerity and fervor rendered him a singularly
inspiring orator.

It was Apgar's habit, as part of his tireless political labors, to read
newspapers from all over the State. During the spring of 1882 he was
unhappy over the prospect that the party might nominate Flower
simply for his money. An Albany friend has described the sequel in an
anecdote that illustrates Cleveland's special appeal at the moment: [2]

Mr. Apgar did not believe in such a policy. He came to my office almost
daily, and we looked about and discussed men and ways to bring about a
different state of things. One evening he came in with a rapid step and il-
luminated countenance, which at once indicated to me that he had something
new and important to communicate. He asked me if I knew Grover Cleveland
of Buffalo. I answered that I did not. He said that he had just been reading in
a Buffalo paper at the reading-rooms a message which Mayor Cleveland had
transmitted to the Buffalo common council, vetoing a street-cleaning job, and
which contained sentiments which could only come from an ugly-honest man
of good purposes and undaunted courage, and that to his mind this man

[1] Moses Coit Tyler, *In Memoriam E. K. Apgar.*
[2] Quoted in Tyler, 32 ff.

Cleveland would make a good candidate for governor. That was the beginning. Cleveland was studied and watched, and the young men of the party organization rallied about Apgar. . . .

One other leader, of equal astuteness but very different character, early marked Cleveland as a possible candidate. The name falls on the page like a sinister shadow. David B. Hill, a follower of Tilden and former Speaker of the Assembly, now at thirty-nine mayor of Elmira, cherished an ambition to be nominated for lieutenant-governor, and early in the summer wrote begging for Daniel Lamont's influence with Manning.[1] Visiting a fellow-attorney, Major H. R. Rockwell, he chatted of the party prospects. "Who do you figure will be our candidate for governor?" inquired Rockwell. "I've been looking the ground over," said Hill, "and it looks to me as if it would be this man Cleveland." "Cleveland?" echoed Rockwell; "who in hell is Cleveland?"[2]

III

Cleveland had instantly realized that the nomination for governor was a far greater prize than the seat on the bench of the Supreme Court which had previously been his ambition. Early in July he was called to the deathbed of his mother in Holland Patent. She lingered until July 19, and he remained for the funeral. All seven of the surviving children were present—even the oldest daughter, Mrs. Hastings, happened to be back from Ceylon. From a room of the parsonage Cleveland quietly transacted business and answered letters and telegrams.[3] To none of the family did he breathe a hint that he might be a candidate for governor. But plans were being steadily laid, and on July 18 the *Courier* fired the opening gun.

Within a few weeks the Cleveland "boom" was well under way in western New York. On August 23 Apgar wrote the mayor offering his services and suggesting that Cleveland pay a visit to Chairman Manning as head of the old Seymour-Tilden wing of the party. To this Cleveland returned a decided negative. Since his strength lay in the fact that he was a free candidate, he must not enable his opponents to charge him with entangling alliances: [4]

[1] Sept. 2, 1882. Lamont Papers.
[2] Armitage, *Grover Cleveland as Buffalo Knew Him,* 157, 158.
[3] Memorandum of Mrs. Yeomans.
[4] August 29, 1882. Cleveland Papers.

I am entirely certain that if there is anything of my candidacy, it rests upon the fact that my location, and an entire freedom from the influence of all and every kind of factional disturbance, might make an available candidate. If my name is presented to the Convention, I should think it would be presented upon that theory. And I am sure, if I were nominated, and could be the instrument of bringing about the united action of the party at the polls, I should feel that I had been of great value to the people and to the party.

When an interview with Mr. Manning was first suggested some time ago, my impulse was at once to find my way to him by way of showing my regard for his position in the party, and the regard I have learned to entertain for him as a gentleman.

Upon reflection, however, it has occurred to me that if we meet by appointment, it will of course be known that we have been together, and it will not the less surely be falsely alleged, that an understanding has been arrived at between us, and pledges made which make me his man.

Would not this lying interpretation be used in answer to the claim that I am free from any alliance?

It would have been folly to make any other answer, for the central question was that of Cleveland's position as a candidate able to reconcile quarrelling factions. A visit to Manning would make Tammany his enemy and would arouse the suspicion of all Slocum's supporters. Further evidence that he was giving careful thought to his strategy appeared when he requested the city controller, Timothy Mahoney, to work for him among the members of the Catholic Mutual Benefit Association, a fraternal order of importance. Mahoney, who had been in correspondence with members of the Association, made a tour of upper New York, visiting Syracuse, Canandaigua, Wellsville, and other towns, and obtaining assistance of great value. Western New York, in fact, was easily enlisted for Cleveland. That part of the State had reason to feel slighted politically, for no United States Senator had ever been elected from beyond the Genesee, and only one governor.

In addition, Cleveland prevailed upon his friends to carry out an important tactical measure touching the nomination for lieutenant-governor. If he were placed at the head of the ticket, it would not do to assign the second place to any man from near Buffalo. Albany or even Elmira might be admissible territory, but anyone from Rochester must be discouraged. George Raines of that city—not the man who later wrote New York's unhappiest temperance law—was a candidate, and there was danger that he would trade votes with the Flower or Slocum forces. Cleveland's friends, including Bissell and Goodyear, made desperate efforts to induce Raines to retire; the task had its difficulties, but they were aided by David B. Hill, and ultimately he withdrew.

IV

The Democratic State Convention met in Syracuse on Thursday, September 21. It was known by the beginning of that week that Slocum and Flower would be fairly tied. Out of 385 delegates both were sure of approximately 100. So energetically had Cleveland's friends labored that he had risen to third place, with more than sixty delegates. No one yet knew where the County Democracy would turn if their candidate, Allan Campbell of New York, failed to develop strength. Cleveland's supporters were keyed to the highest pitch, ready to seize every opening. Then on Thursday the 21st, as politicians trooped in by every train, a bombshell was exploded. News came that the Republican Convention the previous day in Saratoga had proved completely subservient to the dictates of Chester A. Arthur, Roscoe Conkling, and Jay Gould, who had used purse and patronage to coerce it; that Governor Cornell had been denied the renomination he had richly earned; that Charles J. Folger, Secretary of the Treasury, had been named instead; and that already independent voters were loud in their wrath.

During Friday the popular indignation grew. As within two days everything connected with machine politics thus became hateful, the Democratic delegates who had expected to compromise on some machine candidate grasped the demand for an independent man, and prepared to put Slocum and Flower aside.[1]

Even before this bombshell burst Cleveland had been infected by the high spirits of his associates, and was making every exertion to grasp the prize. Bissell had already gone to Syracuse, where he was to be joined by two of Cleveland's aides, Daniel N. Lockwood and ex-Mayor Scheu. Cleveland sent them instructions. They were not to allow themselves to be bought off by any minor nomination. He wrote: [2]

John B. Manning has been in to see me tonight and has much to say about treachery etc. I listened to all.

He talks Congressman at large.

I still listened.

[1] Cf. editorial review in Albany *Evening Journal,* April 13, 1883.
[2] To Bissell, Sept. 19, 1882. Cleveland Papers.

Now do just as I tell you without asking any questions.

When Dan and Scheu get there, have them go the first thing to Daniel Manning and urge with the utmost vehemence my nomination.

Never mind what he says—pound away.

I am quite sure he thinks these two good friends are cool and jealous and don't want to see me nominated. And I am sure he has in his head the idea of Congressman-at-large and I think it is based upon what he thinks as to the real feelings of some of my friends—or that we think are friends.

Of course I know how it is, but I want Manning to be convinced that he is wrong in his premises.

I heard the some old song—if I had come to see him nomination would have been assured but Flower has much money, etc.

I think if Dan and Scheu would go separately to see D. M. they would soon convince him he was reckoning without his hosts. You may be sure the thought is that I will not get Governor but the Western part of the State will be placated by Congressman at large.

This letter reached Bissell and Lockwood on the 20th. Finding in their talks with arriving politicians many who wished to see Cleveland, they telegraphed him that day, and on the 21st he took a train to Syracuse, arriving at dusk.[1] It was the evening on which the full effect of the Republican nominations were just being felt. Cleveland held an informal levee, coatless, in the lobby of his hotel. Perspiring delegates were introduced to him; he went to call on Manning, mistakenly thinking that he controlled his fortunes; and it was not until two o'clock in the morning that he took a train back to Buffalo. Years later he told George F. Parker that he rather enjoyed the ordeal. "It was a novel experience, but after the training I had had, did not impress me, after all, as having in it so many difficulties as I had anticipated."[2] It is interesting to note the impression he made upon reporters. The *Times* correspondent wrote that Cleveland

is a little above the medium height, with a portly and well-proportioned figure. His head, which is set squarely upon a pair of broad shoulders, is well shaped, and is surmounted by a thin layer of dark hair tinged with gray. His features are regular and full of intelligent expression. His eyes are dark and penetrating in their glance. He wears no beard, but a heavy dark mustache completely covers his mouth, and underneath is a square, firm chin. In his movements Mr. Cleveland is deliberate, dignified, and graceful.

When next day the roll-call was about to begin he was placed in

[1] Buffalo *Courier*, Sept. 21, 1882.
[2] Parker, *Cleveland*, 52.

nomination by Lockwood, who made a short, forcible, and inaccurate speech reviewing his previous career. Slocum and Flower had already been nominated. Usually the seconding speeches at such gatherings amounted to nothing, but this time the convention was roused to eager attention by the ablest address that any such body had heard in years. The slight figure of E. K. Apgar was seen advancing to the rostrum. He was lifted to a level of emotion unusual even for him. Beginning with forced calmness, he pointed out the danger of selecting a candidate from either of the great hostile factions of the State Democracy. Then, naming Cleveland, he launched into a eulogy of his qualities as disclosed in his record as mayor. He pointed to his strength as a reformer and independent, and showed that it would be greatest in those western counties where the Republican split seemed the deepest. His eloquence produced an obvious impression, and the friends of Flower at the front of the hall, noting this with alarm, tried to drown his voice by shouts and tramping. When the chairman intervened, Apgar resumed his speech, and received long-continued applause at the close.[1] He had achieved that rare result in a political convention—he had changed votes.

The first ballot showed that Slocum had 98 votes, Flower 97, and Cleveland 66, with five other aspirants trailing behind them. John Kelly, determined that he would somehow be on the bandwagon, had given Flower seven of Tammany's votes, Slocum six, Cleveland six, and Corning five. The County Democracy voted for Campbell. As for Manning, he threw his entire strength, as was anticipated, behind Slocum. On the second ballot the deadlock remained unbroken. Slocum and Flower were tied with 123 votes apiece, while Cleveland had obtained a total of 71. The third roll-call began. The danger now was of a sudden break to Slocum, for Manning's influence was tremendous, and if the County Democracy turned to the Brooklyn general, he would be within reach of a majority. But at this juncture the County Democracy, directed by Hewitt's iron will and Whitney's foresight, swung in a body to Cleveland. A cheer rolled through the hall. John Kelly, never quick-witted, failed for the moment to realize the opportunity of making the victory partly his own, and the Tammany delegation split its vote much as before. But Albany, Rensselaer, and other counties fell into line behind Cleveland, the Flower delegates going over almost in

[1] Buffalo *Commercial Advertiser*, Sept. 23, 1882.

a body. Cleveland's nomination was as good as won when Kelly, beating his chair and bellowing in a stentorian voice, changed Tammany's vote. The final count gave Cleveland 211 ballots, Slocum 156, and Flower 15.[1]

Thus Cleveland won his nomination without incurring any political debts of importance. He was bound neither to Manning nor to Tammany; his sole obligation was to his friends in western New York and to the County Democracy. Buffalo celebrated his nomination with cannon and bunting. The leading Republican newspaper there congratulated the Democracy on placing its standard in the hands of "a man of Grover Cleveland's personal ability, personal integrity, and party loyalty." Meanwhile, Cleveland was writing the nominee for lieutenant-governor, Hill: "Accept my hearty congratulations on your nomination. Now let us go to work and show the people of the State what two bachelor mayors can do."

V

Already his election was assured; for the Republican split had forged the final link in the chain of circumstances which was to make him governor by an unequalled majority. For years the Republicans had sown the wind, and now they were reaping the whirlwind. They had permitted the party to be torn by a protracted feud between the Stalwarts, or followers of Grant and Conkling, and the Half-Breeds, or followers of Blaine and Garfield, and the inevitable disaster had followed. Cornell's firm and honest administration had been one of the best in the history of the State, but Roscoe Conkling and President Arthur had marked him for a cruel humiliation. When Senators Conkling and Platt had resigned their places in 1881 because of a quarrel with President Garfield over patronage, and had appealed to the New York legislature for reëlection, Cornell had failed to bestir himself on behalf of the resigning men, and both Conkling and Arthur resented the fact. The legislature had refused to reëlect the Senators, and Conkling had passed from public life in humiliation. He shortly became attorney for Jay Gould's predatory interests, and as such was further angered by Cornell's veto of legislation favorable to the Gould corporations. He was determined to end Cornell's career, and ruthlessly did so.

[1] N. Y. *Times, World, Tribune,* Sept. 23–25, 1882.

In the revolt which followed the nomination of Folger in place of Cornell, many men later prominent as Mugwumps took a vigorous part. "When Cornell went out," said Henry Ward Beecher, "Avarice and Revenge kissed each other." Folger's nomination, declared George W. Curtis in *Harper's Weekly*, "was procured by the combined power of fraud and patronage, and to support it would be to acquiesce in them as legitimate forces in a convention." Many of Folger's friends urged him to withdraw. He had been a decidedly receptive candidate, and he refused. His letter of acceptance admitted that fraudulent practices had vitiated the acts of the convention, though he truthfully denied that he had taken any part therein; but no excuses could placate the angry element in the Republican party. Had Cleveland been a weak instead of a strong candidate, the result would still have been decisive.

There was little smoke or fury in the brief six weeks' campaign. Cleveland, who had an opportunity to see how skilfully Manning could organize a canvass, entrusted his personal interests largely to Bissell. The State Committee asked him for a contribution of five or ten thousand dollars, and he and his immediate friends raised the larger amount.[1] It was unnecessary to take the stump, which he would have refused to do in any event. The Republicans struggled vainly against forces far too strong for them. Folger went about the State raising the alarmist cry that a Democratic victory would unsettle industry and cause a shrinkage of stock values. "Do the business interests of the country dread a return of the Democratic party to power?" he demanded. "Will the election of Cleveland increase this dread? These are questions for hesitating Republicans to ponder." But the Republican candidate was doomed; in a vote of 915,539, Cleveland received 535,318, and Folger 342,464, Cleveland's plurality thus being 192,854.

The Buffalo reporters on election day were impressed by his calm. He cast his vote in the first district of the Ninth Ward as in years past, transacted some business in the mayor's office, and returned to his law office.[2] At six o'clock a Mutual Union wire was run into his office and an operator began rattling off returns. Bissell, Sicard, and "Charley" McCune were at hand, and others came and went; among them Sherman S. Rogers, who had been active in his behalf as an independent Republican. The mayor read the returns as they came in, making

[1] Bissell to Lamont, Oct. 23, 1882. Lamont Papers.
[2] Buffalo *Commercial Advertiser*, Nov. 8, 1882.

comments with characteristic composure. At midnight it was plain that he had been chosen by a landslide vote, and after general handshaking he went to the rooms of the Democratic Club, where he was presented with a "handsome" chair, its arms and backs made of the horns of Texas steers, and the evening ended in a celebration.

As the historian of New York politics says, the victory of the Democrats was so astounding that they did not claim it as a purely party victory. It could not be denied that Cleveland had helped to swell the majority. His record as a "veto mayor" had been made known to the whole State. Campaign orators had expatiated upon his diligence and courage. His professional career, unlike Tilden's, disclosed no dubious spots. But the result was primarily a rebuke to presidential bossism and to unblushing fraud in politics. The one tragic feature of the election was the humiliation of Folger, a man of fine qualities thus suddenly hurled from the Secretaryship of the Treasury to obscurity. Cleveland felt this keenly, and later remarked: [1]

To me, it seems the very irony of fate that a man of this type, with a career distinguished by conspicuous and honorable service, and of such unusual capabilities, well known to the public, should have been defeated by me, then wholly unknown outside my own small community. I must confess that, even now, a quarter century after the event, I am unable to understand it. . . .

I have no doubt, either, that coming suddenly into the higher public life in this way, I was warned of one of the worst pitfalls to be found there. Even if it had been possible for me to use the power of a great office for purely partisan or political purposes, the effects of such a policy stood out before me so prominently on the very threshold that I could only have heeded the warning. I encountered a great deal of abuse when President for my refusal to take part in local politics in my own and other States; to help my friends, as it was called. If I had ever been tempted to do so, I should only have had to think of the gubernatorial campaign of 1882, and the rebuke then administered to such a policy.

[1] Quoted in Parker, *Cleveland,* 244, 245.

To BE governor of New York in the eighties was to occupy a position which might be distinguished or unimportant, according to the man who held it. Most of the executives of the State in the period after the Civil War are today totally forgotten. Who now recalls Hoffman or Robinson, Flower or Black? Even Alonzo B. Cornell, able as he was, is little more than a name. Yet a man of preëminent abilities, especially if favored by fortune, might make a great reputation in the office. Horatio Seymour, as war governor, had done so, and everyone in the country was familiar with Samuel J. Tilden's irresistible attack upon the bipartisan Canal Ring, and his feat in almost halving the taxes of the State. For these two leaders the office had been the stepping-stone to a Presidential nomination, and men knew that a governor who equalled their record would again find the national party convention laying the prize at his feet. Cleveland was facing a supreme test of his abilities. Within one year, or at most, two, he would either be an exploded hope, a disappointment tossed to one side, or the most promising leader in his party, a champion striding from State to national position.

A sense of this fact weighed upon him during his six last busy weeks in Buffalo. His work as mayor had to be wound up; his message to the legislature had to be written; his mail had swollen into an avalanche of letters. He resigned his office at the first opportunity, and turned over his law partnership to Bissell and Sicard. An appeal to State Chairman Manning brought to Buffalo Daniel S. Lamont, one of the most brilliant young politicians in the party, who spent three weeks helping him with his message and advising him as to men and policies. Cleveland formed an instant liking for this energetic, boyish-looking journalist, who as clerk to the Assembly, secretary of the Democratic State Committee, and a member of the Albany *Argus* staff had become a past master of party affairs in New York. There were meetings to be addressed, and early in December Cleveland attended a glittering reception offered him by the Manhattan Club in New York.

Naturally at first, as he took up the work of preparation, he felt a certain self-distrust. On election day he had laid his deepest feelings bare in a letter [1] to his brother William. He realized, he wrote, the magnitude of his new responsibilities. "The thought that has troubled me is, Can I well perform my duties, and in such a manner as to do some good to the people of the State? I know there is room for it, and I know that I am honest and sincere in the desire to do well, but the question is whether I know enough to accomplish what I desire." He spoke also of his anxiety over the social life which seemed to await him. "I have a notion that I can regulate that very much as I desire, and if I can, I shall spend very little in the purely ornamental part of the office. In point of fact, I will tell you, first of all others, the policy I intend to adopt, and that is to make the matter a business engagement between the people of the State and myself. . . . I shall have no idea of reëlection or any higher political preferment in my head, but be very thankful and happy if I can serve one term as the people's governor." In closing, he struck the religious note that was to vibrate so often in his letters. "Do you know that if mother were alive I should feel so much safer? I have always thought her prayers had much to do with my success. I shall expect you to help me in that way."

The second morning after his election a Buffalo friend had found him alone in his office. Cleveland showed the caller some letters from his sisters, and remarked; "I have only one thing to do, and that is to do right, and that is easy." He added: "Let me rise or fall, I am going to work for the interests of the people of the State, regardless of party or anything else." [2] At the Manhattan Club reception he spoke in the same spirit. The fine parlors of the clubhouse at 96 Fifth Avenue were crowded with Democrats. General Hancock, the titular head of the party, was there; Mayor Grace and Mayor-elect Edson; John Kelly, Abram S. Hewitt, S. S. Cox, and many of only less note—eight hundred in all. "God knows how fully I appreciate the responsibilities of the high office to which I have been called," Cleveland told this assemblage, "and how much I sometimes fear I shall not bear the burden well." He added, in effect, that the size of his majority and the fact that many Republicans had voted for him would only increase his conscientiousness in office.

There was no evidence of a lack of self-confidence as he entered

[1] Nov. 7, 1882. Cleveland Papers.
[2] Buffalo *Courier*, Aug. 10, 1884.

office on January 1, 1883. The previous afternoon he had arrived in Albany with Bissell, walking through the quiet streets to the executive mansion without being recognized. The ceremonies were simple. It was a clear cold day, the sun shining brightly on the snow. Shortly before noon Cleveland met Governor Cornell in the senate chamber, and the powerful forms of the two men, their massive heads and broad shoulders so much alike, were seen ascending the rostrum. Reading from manuscript, Cornell extended his wishes for a successful administration. As usual, Cleveland used no notes. In a ringing voice he thanked Cornell, and expressed the hope that he could look back from the end of his own term upon an official career equally honorable. In the audience was a man later his close friend, Dr. Joseph D. Bryant, who has recorded the impression which Cleveland's self-possession made upon him. As he took the oath of office, he seemed fairly to radiate physical energy. Eastman Johnson, in the fine portrait of Cleveland as governor which hangs in the capitol, has caught the abounding vigor which in these years marked his robust figure and ruddy face.

II

His first act was symbolic. Cleveland at once threw the doors of his office open to all comers, transacting his business virtually in public. At times the big executive chamber took on the appearance of a town meeting, and Lieutenant-Governor Hill suggested that the governor might as well place his desk on the grass in front of the capitol; he would be no harder to approach, and he would have the advantage of the fresh air.[1] He handled politicians with the brusqueness of a man who knew his own mind. Men who came in to ask for office were greeted politely; but when they demanded, "Don't I deserve it for my party work?" they would see Cleveland's eyes narrowing and hear him frigidly remarking: "I don't know that I understand you." Those who tried to whisper to him were disconcerted by a reply audible to everyone in the room. In dealing with party men the governor found the tact and experience of Lamont, whom he at once appointed military secretary and soon induced to become his private secretary, absolutely indispensable. "Lamont is a wonderful man," Cleveland told a friend.

---

[1] W. C. Hudson, *Random Recollections of an Old Political Reporter*, 138.

"I never saw his like. He has no friends to gratify or reward and no enemies to punish." For his part, Lamont soon learned that the governor was best handled with indirection, and that to combat him often meant to confirm him in his course.

While not a distinguished document, the governor's initial message showed competence and grasp. It recommended civil service legislation and a reform in the tax system, two crying needs of the day. More space was given to the Erie Canal, a sempiternal source of expense and controversy for the State which it had helped to make great. Most important of all, practical suggestions were made for reforming the militia forces, the immigration department, the banking and insurance departments, and the harbor-masters' system in New York city. On the need for local home rule Cleveland, remembering some of his experiences as mayor, came down with hearty emphasis.

But Cleveland was not destined to be either a great constructive or a great reform governor. There were no Augean stables to be cleansed in Tilden's fashion, while the governor did not have before him any such contest for progressive measures as Alfred E. Smith brilliantly waged a generation later in carrying through his social legislation and the reconstruction of the State government. Cleveland was to make his mark in another fashion—by giving battle to the baser wing of his own party. The tidal wave of election day had brought with it the inevitable danger of Democratic factionalism and arrogance. It was by his determination in insisting that the victory belonged to the reform element, and that the spoils elements could claim none of its fruits, that Cleveland showed his true stature.

The political arena in which this battle was to be waged was somewhat confused. To say that the legislature was composed of Democrats and Republicans would be to simplify the situation beyond all recognition. There were Tammany Democrats and County Democrats, who hated each other like Montagues and Capulets. There were the Democrats of Boss McLaughlin's Brooklyn fiefdom, and the haystack-and-cheesepress Democrats of the up-State counties. The organization Republicans ruled by Platt and the minor bosses of New York city, such as "Barney" Biglin and John J. O'Brien, glowered at the little knot of independent Republicans headed by young Theodore Roosevelt, whose ability had quickly made him the minority leader in the Assembly. Both branches of the legislature this year were decisively Democratic, the Senate standing 18 to 14, the Assembly 84 to 42. But for years a bipartisan alliance had existed in the Senate between the Tammany Democrats and the machine Republicans, and Cleveland was aware that at any moment the upper chamber might be ruthlessly swung against him.

The Governor knew, like everyone else who mingled with politicians and read the newspapers, that New York politics were both corrupt and merciless. The forms of corruption had changed since Tweed's day. No longer did two or three great municipal bosses and railway magnates manipulate the legislators like puppets. The forces of graft were more numerous, protean, and expert. Most of the corruption was arranged for directly with the members and on the spot, for fully a third of the legislature had its price, and the price was known.[1] At the height of the bitterest contests, as when two street-railway corporations were arrayed against each other, lobbyists would sometimes invade the floor of the Assembly and draw venal men into the halls with no concealment of their purpose.

Half the legislation that was introduced concealed some job or steal, and intelligent members like Roosevelt spent much of their time in trying to ascertain the hidden wickedness in measures that looked innocent. The new mayor of New York, Franklin Edson, set up a committee to perform the same work on city bills—with the result that it condemned forty out of the first forty-four that were examined. Dishonest tactics on the part of big business by no means constituted the principal menace. For every bill corruptly introduced in behalf of corporations, ten "strike" bills were introduced in an effort to blackmail them. They would progress to a certain point, and then payment would be made to stop them. But the machine leaders kept in close partnership with predatory business interests, and both were quick and relentless in punishing men who dared vote against their interests. Roosevelt in his autobiography tells the story of Peter Kelly, a fine young attorney, who was ruined in both politics and law because he opposed the Brooklyn bosses; and Kelly was but one among dozens. Upright men were shadowed by detectives trying to pin some scandal on them, and woe betide the legislator who, in that wide-open city, was caught— as Platt himself had once been—in doing something he should not have done. Roosevelt tells how one honest man, thus trapped, was thence-

[1] Theodore Roosevelt, *An Autobiography*, 71 ff.

forth the terror-stricken tool of political gangsters.

Cleveland also knew that the principal enemy to be faced by any decent governor was Tammany, and that Tammany in all essentials meant John Kelly. The determined Irish leader had dared to throw down the gage of battle before Tilden himself, and for all the need of party harmony in 1884, he was not likely to hesitate to attack Cleveland. Nearing the end of his long career, the sixty-one-year-old boss was now almost as powerful as ever.[1] By a long series of services, he had endeared himself to the Irish voters of New York. Of Tyrone stock, he had been born in Hester Street on the lower East Side and had grown up when the old sixth ward was famous for its wakes, picnics, and street-battles. He had gained his education partly in the parochial school attached to the old St. Patrick's cathedral in Mott Street, and partly in the *Herald* office under James Gordon Bennett. When the Native American movement reared its head in New York, he distinguished himself as its opponent, won the warm friendship of Archbishop Hughes, and was rewarded by the Irish and Germans with a seat in Congress, which he held for two terms in the stormy years just before the Civil War. From that hour his influence grew steadily. When the Tweed Ring became insolent with power, he had the good fortune to be of the discontented Tammany faction which charged that it had usurped control of the Hall. Though his honesty was not above suspicion, and he had become a rich man no one quite knew how, after Tweed fell he persuaded Tilden and Charles O'Conor to confirm him as the leader of a "new" and better Tammany. For a time the fiction of a regenerated organization was maintained, but it was soon found that neither the tiger's spots nor his greed ever changed. Meanwhile, Kelly had confirmed his hold upon the Irish Catholics by his marriage in 1876 to a niece of Cardinal McCloskey, the American head of the church, had travelled, and had set up pretensions to culture, even delivering an historical lecture occasionally for charitable objects.

Kelly could threaten Cleveland with one hand, and offer him rewards with the other. Men were already talking of the Presidential nomination; but of the three "tidal wave" governors whom the Democrats had just elected, Pattison of Pennsylvania was below the constitutional age limit, Ben Butler of Massachusetts was detested by the South, and Cleveland alone had a chance against such elder Democrats

[1] The only biography is J. Fairfax McLaughlin, *Life and Times of John Kelly.*

as Thomas F. Bayard. Could he afford to throw away the support of Tammany Hall? Kelly had turned against Governor Robinson when the latter had removed one of his best friends as clerk of New York County for taking swollen and illegal fees. In his thirst for revenge the boss himself had run for governor in 1879, had stumped the State, assailing Tilden as "the old humbug of Cipher Alley," and Robinson as "sore-eyed," and by polling a vote of 77,566 had caused Robinson's defeat. He could be equally vindictive toward Cleveland.

Though it was taken for granted that Cleveland would cultivate friendly relations with the two Nestors of the party, Seymour and Tilden, whose political strength he had inherited, only the latter really counted. The querulous Seymour was now well past seventy, rounding out his last years in Utica. For a time it was gossipped that he was one of Cleveland's advisers, but he shortly dispelled these reports by an interview, saying that he had never given Cleveland any counsel by word or letter, nor had he seen him since his inauguration; he had sent him many communications, but they were all at the request of office seekers.[1] He might have added that Cleveland had paid scant attention to them. Tilden also, now sixty-nine, was in retirement at Greystone, and almost a recluse; but the Tilden organization remained one of the great political forces of the country.

From the outset Cleveland was naturally surrounded by the leaders of this organization. Manning and he were much together. They had a good deal in common, for Manning, a self-made banker and newspaper owner, was a man of burly physique, unresting energy, great conservatism, and a simple common-sense outlook upon life. Lamont, who retained some connections with the *Argus* even after becoming Cleveland's secretary, was a link between the two. So was St. Clair McKelway, the young editor of the *Argus*, who developed a strong admiration for Cleveland. As for Tilden himself, Cleveland shared the general willingness of Democrats the country over to defer to the great leader who had been cheated of the presidency. He disliked the unsavory episodes of Tilden's career at the bar and his disreputable political allies in Erie County. But he admired his acute intellect, his transcendent legal abilities, and the courage and address he had shown as governor. Most of all he respected Tilden's views on finance. Then and later, he believed that if Tilden had been inaugurated President in

[1] Albany *Evening Journal*, March 1, 1883.

1877, the silver movement which gained its first victory in the Bland-Allison Act of the following year might have been crushed in infancy, that Tilden's expository vigor would have diffused sound ideas on the subject throughout the Democratic party, and the fiat money idea might gradually have withered away.[1]

But at no time could Cleveland be called a member of the Tilden-Manning group. He went his own way, and while at first Manning's influence may have been as perceptible as the footprints of a fox after a light fall of snow, the astute State chairman never felt really sure of the governor. Cleveland was in control, and Cleveland alone.

III

The initial test of Cleveland's quality lay in his appointments. One office after another, in the first two months, was filled with a man selected for merit alone. Sometimes Manning or Lamont suggested him, and sometimes Francis Lynde Stetson, the New York attorney whom Cleveland had first met at the Manhattan Club reception; sometimes Cleveland chose him unaided. The first important nominations were to a board of railroad commissioners which the legislature had established the previous year. The famous Hepburn investigation in 1879 had aroused general indignation over railway rate abuses, while a series of accidents had increased the feeling against the roads; and the new commissioners were expected to keep a close watch upon capitalization, rates, management, and safety. Cleveland rejected the demand of leading Democrats that he appoint an able editor, Purcell of the Rochester *Union,* and selected W. E. Rogers and J. D. Kernan, who had never been in politics and were known only for their technical qualifications. Rogers was a West Point engineer. A still heavier blow to the politicians followed. The superintendency of public works had to be filled, and there was a general demand from Democratic legislators for the appointment of a former assemblyman, James O'Brien. He had Manning's support. But on January 12 Cleveland named James Shanahan, a professional engineer, who possessed no political connections whatever. He had helped in building the first bridge across the Hudson at Albany, the Cohoes Dam, and several important viaducts, while he had served as assistant secretary of public works.

[1] Parker, *Cleveland,* 288.

The superintendency of insurance, one of the juiciest plums, was eagerly coveted by a politician named George M. Beebe, who travelled from Montauk to Dunkirk stirring up support, had one of the principal Tammany legislators circulate a petition in the Assembly for him, and even induced prominent Democrats in other States to write Cleveland. The Republican press pointed out that Deputy Superintendent John A. McCall was a better man, but that he had refused to remove qualified Republicans from office, and that there would be "an explosion of wrath" if he were promoted. Cleveland promptly appointed him. At a later date McCall rose to be head of the New York Life Insurance Company, and not precisely an ornament to American finance, but Cleveland could not foresee his future. The governor acted in the same way in selecting the commissioner charged with that architectural hodge-podge which now adorns Albany, the "new Capitol." He appointed Isaac G. Perry of Binghamton, an esteemed architect who had not sought the place, and who, though a Democrat, was so little a party man that Republicans were among his chief sponsors. Perry added to the consternation of Democrats when he announced that the enterprise was to be devoid of patronage.

Good as were Cleveland's appointments, his vetoes were better. The most famous and the one which aroused the most ill-will, particularly among Tammany men, was the veto of the Five Cent Fare bill. The earliest elevated railroad in New York city had been partially completed in 1870 in Ninth Avenue, and had quickly been followed by one on Sixth Avenue. At first regarded as risky undertakings, they had proved highly successful, and had developed the northern part of the island with magical rapidity. By 1883 Jay Gould was in control of the roads, and their capital had been watered to twice the sum actually invested. Even on this swollen capital the railways earned five per cent. It had been distinctly understood that they were to furnish not only quick but cheap transportation; and a demand arose that the fare, which was a nickel at rush hours and ten cents at other times, should be reduced to a general level of five cents. It was a popular cry, the more so because everyone detested Jay Gould, and the fare bill passed both houses almost by acclamation. In the senate the fight was led by the dissolute Thomas Grady, Boss Kelly's personal representative, and after hearing Grady describe the bill as "a measure of justice," the senators passed it 24 to 5.

Various accounts of this episode have treated Cleveland's veto as the act of a single strong man standing out against universal selfishness and delusion. Actually the bill was opposed by numerous public-spirited citizens, and its justice and constitutionality alike were sharply challenged before Cleveland had expressed himself. Immediately after its passage Mayor Edson wrote the governor that it was neither judicious nor just, and was an act of "bad faith toward these chartered companies." Comptroller Campbell vigorously attacked it, as did the New York *Tribune*. Nevertheless, the weight of even intelligent opinion was at first strongly in favor of the measure. Many argued that Gould's Manhattan Company, formed to consolidate two originally competing lines into a monopoly, possessed no legal right to succeed to their charter privileges, and that by its illegal practices it had forfeited all moral claim to consideration. No one could deny that it had employed trickery to conceal its profits and evade its due share of the taxes. It was asserted that it had also violated an implied contract by its faulty service, for it had irritated people by discontinuing all late night trains, Gould unctuously declaring that New Yorkers were so dissipated that pressure had to be applied to make them go home at a respectable hour. The *Times, Sun, Herald*, and *Star* all approved the bill. Cleveland could easily have signed it, accepted hearty public applause, and left the courts to decide upon its constitutionality.

On the night that he sent his veto message to the legislature, Cleveland remarked to himself as he was throwing off his clothes for bed: "By tomorrow at this time I shall be the most unpopular man in the State of New York." The next morning, as he told a friend years later, he went down to the Capitol feeling very blue, but putting the best face that he could on the situation: [1]

"I didn't look at the morning papers; I didn't think that they had anything to say that I cared to see. I went through my morning mail with my secretary, Dan Lamont, pretending all the time that I didn't care about the papers, but thinking of them all the time, just the same. When we had finished I said as indifferently as I could, "Seen the morning papers, Dan?" He said, "Yes." "What have they got to say about me, anything?" "Why, yes, they are all praising you." "They are? Well, here, let me see them." I tell you, I grabbed them pretty quickly, and felt a good deal better.

[1] Joseph Bucklin Bishop, *Memories of Many Years*, 185.

Indeed, the governor's argument against the bill was irresistible. The measure was palpably unconstitutional. The franchise legislation constituted a clear contract, protected by the first article of the Federal Constitution. Even if this objection were waived, and it was agreed that the State had power under its general railway law to reduce the fare, it had promised in the railway law not to do so except under certain circumstances, and after a certain examination; these circumstances did not exist, and the examination had not been made. And quite apart from the constitutional and legal arguments, there were important moral objections. For many years rapid transit had been a crying need of New York city; capital was timid; the government had gladly offered investors the inducement of liberal fares and other concessions, and now forgetting these facts, it was repudiating the promises which had persuaded business men to enter a field full of risk and danger. Cleveland closed his message with the appeal to high ethical considerations which so often touched his words to eloquence: [1]

But we have especially in our keeping the honor and good faith of a great State, and we should see to it that no suspicion attaches, through any act of ours, to the fair fame of the commonwealth. The State should not only be strictly just, but scrupulously fair, and in its relations to the citizens every legal and moral consideration should be recognized. This can only be done by legislating without vindictiveness or prejudice, and with a firm determination to deal justly and fairly with those from whom we exact obedience.

Yet the veto message seemed to fall upon the Assembly, and particularly upon Tammany, like a clap of thunder from a clear sky. It was received on March 1. The clerk had not read three paragraphs before the Tammany members were huddling together. If possible, the supporters of the bill would at once have carried it over Cleveland's veto, but it was evident that many members had changed sides. Theodore Roosevelt, who had been conspicuous in advocacy of the measure, gained the floor to make a confession of error. "Mr. Roosevelt said," according to the Albany *Evening Journal*,[2] "that when he voted for the bill he believed he was wrong. He never voted before against his conscience. He voted for the bill in weakness, in a revengeful spirit toward the infernal thieves of the elevated railway. They had bought the legis-

[1] Charles Z. Lincoln, ed., *Messages From the Governors*, VII, 850 ff.
[2] March 2, 1883.

lature, corrupted the judiciary, and hired newspapers. Jay Gould and his friends should be sent to jail, but the bill breaks the plighted faith of the State. . . . It is not a question of feeling toward them. It is a question of justice to ourselves. Mr. Roosevelt said he would rather go out of politics than go wrong." That night the Tammany legislators went down the river in a body to obtain instructions. The press was now against them. The *Times* and *Sun* agreed that the veto was legally sound, though they regretted Cleveland's failure, in discussing the ethics of the situation, to give full weight to the crimes of the corporation; and the *Tribune, World,* and *Mail and Express* warmly commended him. The backers of the bill surrendered, and on March 7 the veto was sustained by a decisive vote.

IV

More important, though less spectacular, was a veto of the following month which wiped out a bill for reorganizing the fire department of Buffalo, and indirectly destroyed Tammany's half-hatched scheme for revising the New York city charter. The fire department bill was an attempt to break up an efficient city department in order to create patronage and plunder. Harold Frederic, the young Republican editor of the Albany *Evening Journal,* hailed the veto as a tremendous stroke for sound government. The whole Democratic organization in Buffalo, including the *Courier,* the local officials, and the State senator and assemblymen, had been behind the measure. Cleveland might have quietly induced them to recall it, as was often done; he might have held it under advisement for a time, to soften the blow; instead, he struck it down with scorching language. "The amazement and wrath," wrote Frederic, "with which these politicians learned last night that they had counted without their host, defy the power of statement. The Democracy of Erie is one white-hot, hissing globule of rage. . . . If the Bourbon Democracy made a mistake last November, the people didn't. Grover Cleveland has shown himself what we took him on tryst to be last fall—bigger and better than his party." [1]

It was an act which meant more than superficial observers supposed. Tammany members had been quietly preparing in the Assembly committee on cities a new charter for the metropolis, the distinctive feature

[1] Albany *Evening Journal,* April 10, 1883.

of which was that it concentrated authority in the board of aldermen. It was opposed by the Republicans. Cleveland's veto of the fire department bill was taken as evidence of what he would do to a bad charter, and Tammany forthwith gave up hope for it.[1] A Democratic senator from Brooklyn had been pushing a bill to legislate certain Brooklyn excise commissioners out of office. Now he suddenly announced, as if he had seen a great light, that the bill violated home rule, and would be withdrawn. "Perhaps," sarcastically remarked the *Tribune*, "a little talk which Mr. Kiernan had with Mr. Cleveland about this bill the other day accounts for its badness. It is said that the Senator left the Governor's presence looking sadder and wiser." [2] Another veto, amply justified on legal and constitutional grounds, defeated an effort to appropriate State money for a Catholic protectory or orphanage in New York city.[3]

The Tammany leaders were not of the stoic mould. A momentary outburst had occurred early in February, when Cleveland sent the Senate an unexpected nomination for superintendent of the State's salt works. Enraged by the appointment, Senator Grady bristled, demanded that the nomination be referred to a committee, and was with difficulty pacified. He was a weak man, notorious for his open patronage of the worst saloons and bawdy-houses of the capital, and like most weak men he was vindictive. By the end of April the emotions of Tammany had reached the boiling point. The inevitable explosion came when Cleveland treated two branches of the State service particularly important to New York city, the immigration department and the harbor-masters, with his customary attention to efficiency and total indifference to politics.

Both branches needed reform, and both had offered fat pickings for Tammany. The immigration commissioners were an unpaid group of four officers supposed to protect newly-landed immigrants, care for the sick and helpless, and help others to find homes and employment. As a Republican body on working terms with Tammany, they had lately proved incompetent and dishonest, and the $200,000 appropriated for them in 1882 had been largely wasted. Robbery and exploitation of the immigrants by sharpers and ward-heelers continued un-

---

[1] New York *Tribune*, April 10, 1883.
[2] New York *Tribune*, April 14, 1883.
[3] Lincoln, ed., *Messages From the Governors*, VII, 914–916.

checked. The harbor-masters were a set of minor functionaries in New York city who assigned ships to piers and docks, performed a few other duties, and collected fees for the service; they were almost totally useless, and were chosen for their ability to swing districts, not vessels, into their proper channels. The Federal Supreme Court had decided in 1876 that their fees were a tax on commerce and hence unconstitutional, but they still levied them by a kind of blackmail. Cleveland wished the immigration department thoroughly reorganized, while he asked that the harbor-masters be abolished, if possible, and if retained, be placed on a salary basis.

To a certain extent Tammany was willing to coöperate with Cleveland in this; it was ready to pass the necessary legislation, but insisted that part of the new patronage which thus fell to the disposal of the governor should be reserved for it. Late in April a measure was carried placing the immigration department under a single commissioner, to be appointed by Cleveland at a salary of $8,000, and to have two ex-officio associates, the presidents of the German Society and the Irish Emigrant Society. The legislature also passed an act giving the harbor-masters, of whom a fresh set were to be named by the governor, salaries of $2,500 each, and reorganizing the port-warden service. Cleveland had other nominations to make late in April—a banking superintendent, and the members of a newly-created State board of claims. Tammany eyed the whole list hungrily. The city department of public works was in the hands of the hostile County Democracy, and Kelly's anxiety for a hearty helping from the State platter, now that many city jobs were lost, was unconcealed.

In this situation Cleveland acted with his usual bluntness. He and Manning regarded Kelly's organization as only partially readmitted to the party fold, as remaining there on probation, and as entitled to no courtesies. In especial he had no intention of placing the immigration department, where a drastic housecleaning was imperative, under Tammany control. On April 27 he nominated ex-Senator William H. Murtha, of Brooklyn, for immigration commissioner. It was not a strong nomination, for Murtha was a second-rate political aide of Boss McLaughlin in Brooklyn; but Francis Lynde Stetson had recommended him, he was noted for his charitable work, and the Governor had been impressed by an interview with him. Tammany instantly showed its teeth. On orders from Kelly, Senators Grady, Trainor, and

Browning joined forces with the fourteen Republican Senators, and referred the nomination to a committee.

This was in effect an ultimatum to Cleveland. The harbor-masters and port wardens remained to be appointed. Moreover, Tammany wished to know what disposition Murtha, if confirmed, would make of the two hundred subordinate offices at his command. If the governor included some Tammany men in his new appointments and if Murtha showed a conciliatory temper, harmony would be restored. If they did not, the Tammany tomahawk was ready. Murtha would be defeated, control of the immigration department would remain with the O'Brien-Biglin Republicans, and the Governor would find Tammany fighting his nomination in 1884. As Cleveland said later, "there began an astonishing pressure to secure a promise that the patronage of the office should be duly apportioned between the different political factions in the Senate, and that this promise should be a precedent to confirmation." [1]

In such a situation there could be no doubt of Cleveland's stand. With rising anger he waited to see if the Tammany-Republican coalition would act upon Murtha's name. On May 4, the final day of the session, the deadlock remained unbroken. That morning he sent the Senate the last of his appointments—and not one place was offered to Tammany. The nominees included quarantine commissioners, port-wardens, and harbor-masters. Senator Grady, just before Cleveland acted, had grovelled on his knees for a few crumbs. He had sent Cleveland a note begging him "as a special favor" to name Bryan Reilly, a former alderman, as a harbor-master. "I hope that you will kindly make the appointment for me," he pleaded, "as it will place me in a most humiliating position with my people here if, with eleven appointments to be made, I should fail in securing one of them for so good a man as Mr. Reilly." [2] Tammany men could hardly believe their eyes when they saw how total was their rebuff. "Out of all the three hundred places that would have come into Democratic hands through these nominations," growled one brave, "Tammany was not guaranteed so much as a night watchman at Castle Garden." Grady, Browning, and Trainor at once joined the Republicans in holding up the entire list of nominations, and word was carried to the Governor that

[1] Interview with Ballard Smith, N. Y. *World*, Sept. 7, 1887.
[2] Grady to Cleveland, May 4, 1883. Cleveland Papers.

they would all be stifled.

The result was just such an ebullition of Cleveland's wrath as produced his veto of the street-cleaning contract in Buffalo. "Give me a sheet of paper," he ejaculated to Lamont; "I'll tell the people what a set of d—d rascals they have upstairs."[1] He sat down and wrote a message to the Senate which was brief and sharp as a Roman sword. He pointed out the importance of carrying into effect the new law reorganizing the immigration department. He recalled the extravagance, the corruption, the disgraceful dissensions, and the swindling that had marked the work of the existing officers. Murtha, he declared, was a man of acknowledged honesty and experience, whose benevolence would insure a kindly administration; yet the Senate, rather than confirm him, would continue the familiar scandals and abuses. It did so at a time when various officers of the old department were in the Capitol conducting an impudent lobby for the retention of their places. "The refusal to confirm the appointee," he concluded, "is not based upon any allegation of unfitness, nor has such a thing been suggested. It concededly and openly, as I understand the situation, has its rise in an overweening greed for patronage which may attach to the place, and which will not be promised in advance, and in questionable partisanship."

In effect, the message was an appeal over the heads of the Tammany Senators to the people of the State. A crowded Senate chamber listened to it. When the clerk finished, Grady, flushed with anger, made the insulting motion that it be referred to the committee on grievances. Senator Jacobs defended Cleveland, asserting that Boss McLaughlin did not know that Murtha's name had been suggested until after the Governor decided on the nomination. Amid confusion the legislature adjourned *sine die*. Next day Harold Frederic wrote its epitaph in the Albany *Evening Journal*. "The senate of 1881–83 came to the capitol a body without a political majority," he declared. "Without a political majority it departed. During the two brief hours that preceded the close of its session the Democracy, reunited at Syracuse, broke into its component parts over the patronage of Castle Garden."

In Cleveland's opinion it had broken in parts over a question of principle—the same principle that Garfield had defended against Conkling and Platt, the principle that the appointive power of the

[1] Henry Murlin to author, April 11, 1928.

executive is not, under the rules for legislative confirmation, to be prostituted to the political greed of this or that group of senators. For a time he hesitated over the question of calling an extra session. He was perfectly content to let the harbor-masters pass out of existence. "Let the merchants and shippers of New York see if they cannot get along without these men," he remarked. As everyone expected, the city department of docks competently took over their duties. But he regretted the lapse of the immigration department into its old position, and consulted Manning, Stetson, and others on the question of recalling the legislature. They were emphatically against it, and he dropped the idea.[1]

V

In reviewing the session, Cleveland could well feel a certain satisfaction. He had been an inexperienced governor, he had possessed few constructive ideas, and he had not urged them with much aggressiveness. Yet he had been able to lend his shoulder to important new advances. The most striking was a civil service law which, in answer to the demand of public opinion, passed the reluctant legislature on the last day with only a few dissenting votes. Theodore Roosevelt had introduced it and fought hard for it. The public expected to see men of outstanding rank appointed as commissioners to administer it. Cleveland named Andrew D. White, Harry Richmond, and Augustus Schoonmaker, and when White pleaded his presidential duties at Cornell University as a reason for not accepting, he chose another conspicuous reformer, John Jay, in his place. Other enactments included a reapportionment of the State into Congressional districts, a measure looking toward the abolition of contract labor in State prisons, another creating a State board of claims, the abolition of some useless State offices, and a new military code dealing with the organization of the State militia. All of these subjects had been treated in his first message.

He had stood firm against Tammany and the spoilsmen; he had also stood firm against two flagrant abuses of the day—special legislation for private claimants, and bills which infringed the principle of local home rule. All over the State, villages and towns which wished to spend money for special purposes, such as fire equipment, libraries,

---

[1] Stetson to Cleveland, May 16, 1883. Cleveland Papers.

or paving, had been coming hat in hand to the legislature for permission. The State laws plainly gave local authorities, such as the county boards of supervisors, the duty to act in most such matters. Cleveland stopped the practice by a few sharp vetoes, one of which killed a bill authorizing his old village of Fayetteville to buy a fire-engine. He gave equally short shrift to a long list of bills appropriating money to various persons injured in State employ, each appropriation being labelled a "gratuity in full for all claims;" for as he said, the new court of claims should deal with these cases.

If the people were pleased with him, he had an increasing confidence in the people. Soon after arriving in Albany he had written Bissell,[1] apropos of some appointments, that "I sometimes think the people of this State act like 'a passel of boys.'" But this mood passed. At the close of the session he replied to a letter of congratulation: [2]

I must not fail to give expression to the satisfaction I feel, upon the approval of such friends as you have always been, of my course thus far.

I sometimes feel that the fight for the good against the bad is a discouraging contest with odds on the wrong side; this is when it seems to me that the people and the press are omitting to give me aid and encouragement. But I straightway grow ashamed of my unbelief, when I win a word of encouragement from men whom I *know* are right.

I look for better things. I am where I *must* and *have* and *shall* feel the strain and wrenching of the change.

I hope I shall hold fast. I believe I shall.

It is exceedingly unfortunate that those who in public places battle with the jobbery and treachery fronting them, must constantly feel that malice, uncharitableness, and misrepresentation are treacherously fighting them in the rear.

I don't know but this is a foolish letter; but it is written.

The plodding, restricted Buffalo lawyer found in these first five months of 1883 a valuable bit of schooling. Within three years he, as President, would have to meet a Senate intent upon abusing its powers of confirmation; would have to fight back hungry spoilsmen in thousands; would have to resist special legislation in its most difficult forms, with the Grand Army of the Republic supporting it. He was becoming acquainted in Albany with some of the political dragons whose scaly coils and fiery breath he would have to face in Washington.

[1] Jan. 6, 1883. Cleveland Papers.
[2] To Sherman S. Rogers, May 20, 1883. Cleveland Papers.

CLEVELAND'S first six months in the governorship had effected two conflicting results. It had given him excellent lessons for the Presidency, and it had produced a quarrel with Tammany which, if not healed, would make his election to the Presidency highly improbable. No Democrat could be President without carrying New York State; no Democrat, barring a truly extraordinary conjunction of circumstances, could carry New York against the full enmity of Tammany. The sufficient proof of this statement is the fact that without at least four accidental factors, which we shall presently review, he would almost certainly have been defeated in New York in 1884; that is, Tammany's hostility would have cost him the Presidency.

Yet he never thought for a moment of composing the quarrel. His downright unhesitancy in breaking with John Kelly becomes explicable only when we take account of several facts. One is that, to a degree almost incredible, he kept the Presidency out of his mind; it would be fatuous to say that he did not think of it, but he really thought very little of it. His lack of imagination about himself helped him centre his attention entirely upon his governorship. A contributing circumstance was that he had inherited the Seymour-Tilden attitude toward Tammany—an attitude of instinctive and uncompromising hostility. When up-State Democrats thought of Tammany they thought of the draft riots, the Tweed Ring, the political gangsterism of an ignorant, venal Irish element that was deeply repugnant to their own Anglo-Saxon traditions. Since they neither understood Tammany nor wanted to understand it, they had no tolerance for it. At a later date Roosevelt, who possessed the advantage of being born in New York city, showed a certain respect for the boss-system, for he realized that it was a symptom of definite social conditions, and that even Tammany performed some useful functions; but to Cleveland it was a pernicious growth. Finally, his Palmerstonian quality, his "you-be-damnedness," as a friend once called it, came into play. Tammany was interfering with his honest work and was threatening him, and he brusquely thrust Tammany aside.

From a broad national standpoint, he builded better than he knew. His breach with Tammany caught the public imagination as nothing else could. The groping moral forces that were slowly gathering strength below the surface, and were ready to break forth in a powerful movement, demanded a moral hero; and the spectacle of the stolid, stubborn Cleveland smiting Tammany without thought of the consequences appealed to it. The episode of the port-wardens was inadequate to bring him before the country in this rôle of moral knight, and to impress the nation with his strength of character. More was required. But Cleveland quickly supplied that more. Whereas on May 4th Tammany was the aggressor, and Cleveland merely parried its blows, within a few months he carried the warfare into the enemy's country. And after he had done this, Tammany by opposing his nomination tooth and nail dramatized his public fearlessness of the whole country. While weakening his political strength in New York, and reducing his fate there to a question of chance, he strengthened himself everywhere else and took the first long steps in creating the Cleveland Tradition.

II

Cleveland's friends became aware at this period that interesting changes of personality were going on in the man. The dry and narrow attorney, interested only in his lawbooks and fishing-rod, solicitous of his personal routine, was becoming broader in his outlook, fresher in his sympathies, more sternly self-sacrificing. In his limited Buffalo environment he had been in danger of stiffness if not of mental petrifaction. Yet he had responded to the new demands with surprising suppleness, and showed reserves of power which his intimates had hardly suspected.

Socially, he found it easy, as a bachelor of simple tastes, to adjust himself to his Albany position. He had taken up his residence in the executive mansion which a decade earlier the State had acquired on the brow of a hill a mile south of the Capitol, and of which he was the fourth occupant, Tilden having been the first. The State provided the residence and furniture, but all other expenses had to be met out of his annual salary of $10,000. It was a modest yellow brown house of double turrets, half-covered with Virginia creeper, facing a beautiful stretch of lawn. There was an arched porte-cochère in front, of which he made little use, for he kept no horses. Beyond installing a billiard-table, he made few alterations in the interior. Visitors found the same parlors, dining-room, and big library, all panelled in the black walnut of the period, filled with the same heavy, old-fashioned furniture, and adorned with the same steel engraving of St. Peter's and the same large bronzes. His only important change was to convert the wide upper hallway, breezy in summer, into an extempore office for Sunday work. The mansion had a fine greenhouse, and for the first time he learned to appreciate cut flowers. Tilden and Cornell had numerous servants in Albany and entertained lavishly, but Cleveland lived simply. One of his sisters, usually Mrs. Hoyt, acted as housekeeper, and he brought William Sinclair from his Buffalo club to look after details.

Most of the governor's time, indeed, was spent in his office. He rose at seven, breakfasted at eight, and walked to the Capitol before nine. At half-past twelve he walked back for lunch, returning in an hour, at five dropped his pen, and after chatting for an hour with friends, walked home for dinner. Tilden, with his French chef borrowed from Delmonico's, had made dining an art, but Cleveland's table was plain. Once we find him complaining that, after a reception, the tyrannical William was compelling him to eat up all the left-over food: "I've worked like the devil, and am told that my redemption is near." [1] In the evening he usually returned to his office to labor again with Lamont from half-past eight to well after eleven, finally pushing away his papers with his stock witticism: "Well, I guess we'll quit and call it half a day." Sometimes, his labor finished, he would linger to write a letter to Bissell or Goodyear. Usually he would go straight home, accompanied by Lamont or the eagerly talkative Apgar; and after a few hours' sleep, the round would begin again.

His long hours disturbed his associates. Early in his first year one newspaper correspondent complained that he was overtaxing himself. "The visitors who go into the executive chamber are met affably by the large-headed man, and he listens patiently to what they have to say. Still there is only a slight glimmer of ideas in response. The words are few and they are listlessly said. The eyes of the large man look glassy, his skin hangs on his cheeks in thick, unhealthy-looking folds, the coat buttoned about his large chest and abdomen looks ready to burst with

[1] To Bissell, Feb. 11, 1884. Cleveland Papers.

the confined fat. Plainly he is a man who is not taking enough exercise; he remains within doors constantly, eats and works, eats and works, and works and eats. . . . There was not a night last week that he departed from the new Capitol before one A. M. Such work is killing work." [1] The governor valued hard labor not only in itself but as an example to his associates. As at Washington later, he wished a working administration. In his second annual message he rebuked the legislature for its accustomed weekly adjournment from Friday to Monday. But late in the session even he admitted to Bissell that he was overtaxed: [2]

I will tell you as the deadest secret in the world, that for the last few days I have felt the effects of long hours, steady work, and worse than all, incessant pressure about office. I honestly think I can't stand it more than two weeks longer. My head a good deal of the time doesn't feel right, and when a man begins to talk about office I begin to feel irritable and my head begins to ache.
Lamont acts and looks as if he needed rest too.

His habits of Sunday work did not escape notice. He took a pew in the Fourth Presbyterian Church, whose pastor, the Rev. Charles Wood, was a former Buffalonian and had officiated at Folsom's funeral. Once Wood sent word that he was sorry not to see him oftener at services. "Tell him," Cleveland grinned, "that an ass fell into a pit." Sometimes on Sunday evening he attended the Catholic Cathedral, hard by the executive mansion.

Yet when opportunity offered he fell back upon the amusements of his Buffalo days. He frequently relaxed on Sunday afternoons over a game of draw-poker with a twenty-five cent limit, remarking: "My father used to say that it was wicked to go fishing on Sunday, but he never said anything about draw-poker!" [3] Occasionally he attended a large dinner. In January, 1883, he went down to New York to dine at ex-Governor Cornell's Fifth Avenue mansion with a long list of distinguished guests—Hamilton Fish, William M. Evarts, General Hancock, John Jacob Astor, Leland Stanford, Joseph H. Choate, William C. Whitney, and J. Pierpont Morgan. Later Whitelaw Reid asked him to a Union League dinner to meet Lord Rosebery, but he refused. He was seen in some of the best Albany homes, and more than

---

[1] Albany *Evening Journal*, March 21, 1883.
[2] April 22, 1883. Cleveland Papers.
[3] Simon Rosendale of Albany to author, April 15, 1928.

one belle set her cap for him. Naturally he had little time for general reading. Yet the *Argus*, in commenting on his remarkable memory, stated that "he can repeat pages of poetry or of prose, after a single reading. . . . He remembers prose substantially and poetry literally. The music and rhythm of the latter chain and charm his mind. Long after he has forgotten who the author of some noble and diverting verses is . . . he can repeat them with correctness and admirable feeling if only some event or some incident in conversation makes them apposite. Those nearest to him find that his mind is stored with these gems of the muses." [1] He read snatches of history and biography, and mastered Hammond's dull *Political History of New York*.

At the proper seasons he still found the fishing grounds irresistible. His assistant secretary, Col. William Gorham Rice, used to watch him and Manning set off for an island down the Hudson with a dinner of planked shad in prospect. Their nickelled tackle gleamed in the spring sun. The future President and Secretary of the Treasury both wore large Panama hats; their shoulders were broad, and they had the same generous waist measure. "There was indeed a pervasive atmosphere of rotund jollity about them both which it is a pleasure to remember." [2]

But the Hudson flats, as Cleveland soon learned, compare badly with the lakes and forests of the Adirondacks. He became friendly with an Albany physician, Dr. S. B. Ward, later a boon companion, who expatiated upon the delights of the northern woods. In August, 1883, after visiting his sister Rose at Holland Patent and his brother William at Forestport, he set out on his first Adirondacks trip. Accompanied by the Rev. A. H. Corliss, Dr. Claude Wilson, and J. K. Brown, he drove to Studor's Hotel at White Lake Corners, then crossed to Camp Corliss on the Woodhull Reservoir, where Bissell joined him, and after a week went on to the Fulton Chain of lakes, a route which combined good fishing with easy communications to Albany. The letters he sent back to Lamont were full of high spirits. Late in August he enclosed to his secretary a note which accused the party of stealing bait. "I think," ran his comment, "that this is pretty mean treatment to begin with, and I suspect that this is a pretty tough country. At this rate I am liable to be accused of rape before I get back." He added that "I went to church three times yesterday, and had big audiences on all occa-

[1] *Argus*, July 17, 1883.
[2] Wm. Gorham Rice, *State Service Magazine*, April, 1918.

sions." A few days later he was writing: "I am in disgrace, with my-self at least, just at present. I had a beautiful shot at a deer Saturday and missed him. We are now preparing to start again for my last chance." [1]

III

Such vacations, however, were short. Cleveland gave himself to routine duties with a thoroughness that was almost unexampled. He was the first governor, for example, who ever attended *ex officio* a meeting of the trustees of Cornell University. He pried into the opera-tion of every department and State institution, and gave such con-scientious study to all recommendations for pardons that he was ac-cused of softheartedness. While he was at work in midsummer a rumor that he was enjoying the delights of Newport obtained currency, and he showed his indignation to a reporter for the Brooklyn *Eagle*: [2]

"I hope, Governor," said the reporter, "you enjoyed your visit in New-port?"

"Newport?" returned his excellency, laying down his pen and swinging around in his chair. "I have not been to Newport."

"Why," said I in some surprise, "the papers of New York City announced you as spending some days there with Dorsheimer, Belmont, and some others."

"Yes," replied the Governor, "I know they did. I received an invitation to go to Newport, but I declined it, for the reason that I had so much business here to do. But that fact did not prevent certain of the newspapers of New York from stating it as if it were really so. How is it that they get these things in the newspapers out of nothing? Alongside of the very columns announcing my presence in Newport were statements of doings here in this chamber show-ing that I was here at work. Yet, notwithstanding that, the New York *Times* read me a lecture on its editorial page nearly a column long about my 'junket-ing' and roaming about for pleasure. 'Junketing' would have been far pleas-anter than working at this desk hard all day. When an officer junkets and is blamed by the press for it I suppose he has the consolation and compensation of having had a very good time. When he doesn't junket and yet is criticized he has the consolation of duties performed. The *Sun* about the same time said I was away pleasuring, and that the lieutenant-governor was the governor. These papers keep well informed."

While the vials of his indignation were thus uncorked, he answered

[1] C. to Lamont, Aug. 20–Sept. 3, 1883. Cleveland Papers.
[2] Quoted in *Argus*, Aug. 2, 1883.

the critics who accused him of excessive lenity in pardoning criminals. Sending a clerk for the official records, he burst out:

"I have been listening to many applications, and I shall pardon when I see fit. I shall be governor until the end of my term, notwithstanding all the would-be governors there are in the State. I am going to do just as I have a mind to about this pardoning business, whether the newspapers like it or not. I am going to be governor one term, and then if these editors want to be, and the people will let them, they can be. One of these days I'll grant a pardon just because, in my judgment, it ought to be granted, and I shall say that that is my reason, and shall not give any other. Justice, mercy, and humanity are the things alone to be considered in the application for a pardon. And if I find a poor fellow has been unjustly imprisoned, or there is any good reason why he should be pardoned, I'll pardon, and will not regard the record at all. That's all there is about that business. There are a whole lot of people who want to be governor. All of these people will have to wait till I have got done, and the people have turned me out."

At that moment the clerk arrived with the official record, showing that up to July 15th, 1883, Cleveland had pardoned twenty men and commuted six sentences, while in a similar period Cornell had issued thirty pardons and fifteen commutations. "Well," replied Cleveland, "I don't care what the records of previous governors were. The idea that an executive should refuse a pardon when it is justified in order to make a record for himself is very dreadful to me."

He never hesitated, in fact, to temper justice with kindness. He released one defaulting county treasurer from the penitentiary on condition that he abstain from intoxicants for five years. In the summer of 1883, pardoning a forger whose term was half completed, he included with his legal reasons a frank additional statement. "My sympathy was moved by the distress of the convict's mother," he wrote, "his only parent, who was then represented to be in very poor health. But notwithstanding all this, upon a full examination of the case I was so fully convinced that the prisoner had, at the time of his arrest, entered upon a career of crime, and that his own good and the protection of society would not be subserved by his release, that on the 11th day of June, 1883, I denied the application for his pardon. I was asked on the 20th day of June, 1883, to reconsider my action. The convict's mother died the day before, and his uncle and aunt, whom I was satisfied were respectable and worthy people, promised to give him a home and employment. I could not refuse, in view of the additional and saddening circumstances presented, to allow the prisoner to look upon the face of his dead mother and to avail himself of the opportunity offered to gain a respectable place in society. I hastened to place the pardon in the hands of his aunt, who personally applied for it."

During his first year the governor made general friendships which signally helped to broaden his outlook. The ablest man in the capital, whose influence on Cleveland has never been rightly appreciated, was Manning. From him Cleveland derived a substantial stock of information, and still more a fixed set of convictions, upon various subjects which interested Manning intensely—notably the currency and the tariff. As owner of the *Argus* Manning kept its editorial page filled with sound money doctrine, writing many editorials himself. He never ceased to inveigh against the "silver swindle." He continually insisted that the poorest money reached the poorest people, because the rich, dealing in large sums, could choose what currency they would use.[1] Arguing against the Bland-Allison Act, he declared that if any crisis or disaster forced the United States to a silver basis, prices would instantly go up the fifteen or twenty per cent difference between the nominal and the real value of the metal in the silver dollar, and wages would be reduced by a proportionate amount. "It is folly and knavery to base money on any other than a gold standard," he declared. Though Manning's views simply confirmed Cleveland's previous opinions, they were of the utmost importance. Meanwhile, from Lamont the governor was learning a few lessons upon practical politics and the way to handle politicians.

One of his most interesting friendships lay outside of office or party. Harold Frederic, a talented young man of twenty-seven, born in the rural New York environment to which he later gave its finest literary depiction, had just become editor of the Albany *Evening Journal*. He imparted a fresh distinction to the fine old paper which Thurlow Weed had so long conducted. Reared in a Republican family, calling himself a Republican, and directing an influential Republican organ, he was actually an independent. While a mere stripling he had been attracted by Tilden's reform ideas and had enlisted under the new banner. In a few years he had risen on the Utica *Journal* from proofreader to editor. The repudiation of Tilden at the Cincinnati convention

[1] "The Truth About Trade Dollars," *Argus*, July 5, 1883.

William C. Whitney   Daniel Manning   Daniel S. Lamont

THREE NEW YORK ASSOCIATES

in 1880 had snapped the last ties binding him to Democracy, and he felt able to accept the conduct of the *Evening Journal*. Yet he remained a liberal, advocating tariff reduction, civil service reform, and other progressive changes. Frederic often dropped into the governor's office and gradually developed an enthusiastic admiration for Cleveland. It repeatedly cropped out in the supposedly Republican editorials of the *Evening Journal* like veins of gold in a cold quartz ledge. When Cleveland broke with Tammany over the city appointments Frederic applauded his stand, and when the governor decided not to call a special session he declared that this wise determination crowned his work during the session. "The commerce of New York is getting along very well—and so is the governor." [1]

Frederic's wit and cultivation appealed to Cleveland as a welcome change from the shoals of politicians. He occupied the place which Richard Watson Gilder was later to fill more completely. Versatile, light-hearted, full of ideas, his talk diverted the governor, while his editorials were among the few which Cleveland read. For Cleveland had his own sprightly and cultivated side. Going to the Albany high school one day, he made a little address on education which was a model of felicity.[2]

IV

As the summer of 1883 passed Cleveland thought much and said little about politics. Cautious men in both the Tammany and the Tilden-Manning factions hoped to patch up a peace between him and Kelly, for a legislature and a secretary of state were to be elected that fall. Cleveland's letters show that his own ideas were very different. He cared nothing for harmony except on terms that safeguarded the cause of reform. He wrote Lamont on September 3 that "I am not anxious to be beaten and cuffed about too much, and yet I want to subordinate all things except honor and consistency to the good of the party." Meanwhile, he was taking a hand in Buffalo politics, for through his friends he labored to have reform delegates sent to the State convention from Erie County, and was pleased when this was done. He talked of writing McCune "a little United States language,"

---

[1] Albany *Evening Journal*, May 24, 1883.
[2] In Albany *Argus*, June 14, 1833.

and his letter to Bissell on September 12 took an uncompromising stand: [1]

The most important of all things is that the delegates at my home act together and in the manner which aids my administration, and the cause of good government. I have never seen a more earnest desire evinced to accomplish anything, in a sincere unselfish way, than is now apparent on the part of my friends, looking to a supplement of last year's results by another step in the same direction, thus giving the party a firmer place in the confidence of the people. The lines will be sharply drawn, though there will probably be a great effort to conceal them. All the spoilsmen, little and big, all the disappointed seekers after personal interest, all those hoping to gain personal ends, and all those who desire a return to the old, corrupt, and repudiated order of things in party management, will, under one specious guise or another, be ranged on one side. . . . On the other side will be found the true and earnest men. . . .

On October 18 Cleveland attended the centennial exercises at Washington's headquarters at Newburgh. It was an occasion of great pomp and display, with a military parade, brass bands, bunting, and enthusiasm. Addresses were made by Senator Bayard and William M. Evarts, while the guests included Secretary Chandler, Chauncey Depew, Senator Hawley, ex-Governor Curtin, Gen. Horace Porter, and General Schofield. One incident greatly tickled Cleveland. He, Lamont, and Rice led this distinguished gathering up the hill to the headquarters, the military men furnishing a glitter of uniforms. As they reached the top the caretaker, recognizing Cleveland and his secretaries, opened the gate to them and then shut it with a bang. "The band goes up the other way," he announced, pointing Evarts, Depew, the Senators and the generals to a dusty by-road. Thanks to this episode, Cleveland always remembered the day joyously. Yet at the beautiful headquarters above the blue Hudson he was meditating a dramatic stroke. The rumor had reached him that John Kelly planned to renominate the treacherous Grady for the Senate. Two days afterward, on October 20th, he sat down in the executive chamber and addressed Kelly in these terms: [2]

It is not without hesitation that I write this. I have determined to do so, however, because I see no reason why I should not be entirely frank with you.

[1] Cleveland Papers.
[2] At this time the governor held office for three years, the Senators for two, and the Assemblymen for one. There were thirty-two Senators.

I am anxious that Mr. Grady should not be returned to the next Senate. I do not wish to conceal the fact that my personal comfort and satisfaction are involved in the matter. But I know that good legislation, based upon a pure desire to promote the interests of the people and the improvement of legislative methods, are also deeply involved.

I forbear to write in detail of the other considerations having relation to the welfare of the party and the approval to be secured by a change for the better in the character of its representatives. These things will occur to you without suggestion from me.

Having finished this letter, he showed it to Lamont. The secretary disapproved. "Well," ejaculated Cleveland determinedly, "I'm going to send it!"

This letter marked the beginning of Cleveland's marvelous career as a national leader. Other governors, like Robinson, had waited for Kelly to strike, but Cleveland boldly carried the war into an aggressive phase. Widening circles in New York had noted Cleveland's political courage; now the whole nation could note it. Many Democrats, when they later learned of the letter, were astounded by it. Nearly a month earlier their State convention had nominated a Manning slate for the principal offices, and Kelly had acquiesced in it. Yet now, three weeks before election day Cleveland had deliberately struck out at Kelly and Grady, had broken open the slowly healing wound in the party, and had apparently ensured the defeat of the Democratic ticket.

For more than a fortnight Kelly carried the letter, which Cleveland regarded as confidential, in his pocket. He did not reply to it, and Cleveland said nothing publicly. But secretly Kelly and his friends were busy. It immediately appeared that he meant to disregard the letter and obtain Grady's nomination; but the leaders of the Sixth District told him that Grady could not be elected in his home constituency. The Democratic nomination there went to former Justice Timothy J. Campbell. Kelly then made a weak effort to have Grady nominated in the Fifth District, where Colonel M. C. Murphy had already been named in pursuance of an understanding between all the party groups—Tammany, Irving Hall, and the County Democracy. When this failed, Grady withdrew from the canvass entirely. At this point the chagrined Kelly, who from the outset had been openly seeking the defeat of four Democratic Senators outside New York city, published Cleveland's letter in the New York *World*, omitting the name of the recipient. With characteristic sensationalism the *World* played it up, and with less than its usual astuteness attacked Cleveland for trying to interfere with the people in choosing their own representatives. The governor was dictating nominations! A little later Kelly printed a facsimile of the letter in the Tammany organ, the *Star*, heading it "How Harmony Fell Through in New York." At the same time Kelly made a bitter statement, accusing Cleveland of being the fount and origin of all the Democratic disaffection which existed in New York County, and of being actuated in his attitude toward the inoffensive Senator Grady by a mean spirit of personal revenge. He declared that Grady's reply to Cleveland's message just before the adjournment of the last session "was dignified, and his grounds for the statements uttered at the time were, to my mind, well taken."

The letter perhaps contributed to a partial Democratic defeat, which did not greatly matter. The Republicans carried both houses of the legislature and elected the secretary of state. The really important result was that the letter produced a complete and irreparable Democratic schism. From that moment Tammany hated Cleveland with a sleepless vindictiveness. A few days after the election Grady assailed the governor in an acrid and mendacious speech in Tammany Hall. He was soon busy spreading the story, which he gave open currency in the campaign of 1884, that Cleveland had been bribed to veto the Five Cent Fare bill—that a large sum had been placed where Bissell and Sicard could transfer it to him. Bourke Cockran and other Tammany orators lent their assistance in an unremitting campaign of abuse. Naturally, Cleveland had known that, in Daniel Webster's phrase, there were blows to be taken as well as given. To the New York *Herald* he gave an interview in which he expressed himself vigorously and summarized his position in a few pregnant if heavy sentences: [1]

The Governor was alone. He looks vigorous and buoyant. The Hancock standard of 250 pounds has evidently been long since reached.

"That letter of yours to Mr. Kelly," said the correspondent, "has caused a good deal of talk."

The heavy armchair was rolled a little nearer the interviewer and the Governor's lips were compressed.

"Indeed? Well, I suppose so," he replied. "Why?"

"That is for you to say."

"I hold that it was the proper thing, under the circumstances, to send that letter."

[1] N. Y. *Herald*, Nov. 23, 1883.

"You think Grady was not a proper representative to send back to the Senate?"

"I do, most assuredly. His action in the Senate has been against the interests of the people and of good government, and his ready tongue gave him power to be of great aid to bad men. I believe that the Democratic party could not afford to indorse such a course, and that his rejection would be a great benefit to the party and to the people. What's the use of striving for the Senate, country Democrats argued, and have Grady holding the balance of power to sell us out to the Republicans?"

"But about that letter, governor?"

The big armchair rolled closer still. "I sat down without the knowledge of any person and wrote to Kelly—this man who has been assuring me of his anxiety to give me aid in my work." (The Governor here raised his hand and forcibly slapped the desk in front of him.) "I suggested, not for my personal comfort, which I did not deny would be subserved, but for the good of the public service, that he who had the power to say 'Go' or 'Come' should not force the nomination of Grady upon the Democrats of the State. No man ever acted with a more positive desire to serve the State than I did when I wrote that letter to a man claiming to be my friend."

When the reporter pressed his questions, mentioning the newspaper attacks on Cleveland for "interference," the governor banged the desk again. The letter, he said, had shown New Yorkers the true facts of Democratic politics:

"Its reception proved to me that the man who has been assuring me of his friendship was my enemy, and that of the cause which I had espoused. It gave an opportunity for this enemy to openly and coarsely insult me as Governor of the State. To say that this letter should not have been written from one gentleman to another—the one anxious to better the public service, and the other having it in his power to do it—is nonsense. To say that a man should go three hundred miles to say what he should not put on paper is the rankest kind of hypocrisy. This criticism can only be based on the assumption that a man might say in conversation with another what he might afterward in policy find it convenient to deny when there was no corroborating evidence to be brought forward as to the facts."

On Evacuation Day Cleveland visited New York city to address the powerful Chamber of Commerce of the State of New York. When, speaking of business, he demanded whether enough care was taken to send champions of this all-important interest to the Legislature, the responsible men of the metropolis caught the significance of the reference and rose in vigorous applause. From other sections of the State

Cleveland obtained assurances of support. Christmas was pleasant that year. "O Boy!" he wrote Bissell, "what a nice dressing-gown I found here. It fits like paper on the wall." And a few days later he wrote again: "Like Blind Tom, I congratulate myself upon the close of my first year of gubernatorial life—and a close, I'll say to you and myself, which brings no disgrace or regret." [1]

V

On January 1, 1884, Cleveland faced his second legislative session with the advantages of a year of experience, a rising tide of public confidence, and the fact that the legislature was now controlled by the Republicans, who would be responsible for its misdeeds. His experience showed in his annual message, much longer and more expert than the first. "My idea," he confided to a friend, "has been to deal lately with the practical things relating to State affairs and in which my people are interested. The fact is I am growing to be a kind of crank on all that pertains to the commonwealth and the citizens of New York. I haven't the material, I think, to do more for the people, the party, nor myself than I can do in that role." [2] His authorized biographer gives the impression that the message dealt largely with the question of monopolies. Actually Cleveland steered wide of national issues, upon which any pronouncement would have been interpreted as a bid for the Presidency.

He called attention to the inequity of the tax laws, and especially to the provisions under which the debts of the city man might be deducted from his personal property assessments, while the farmer's mortgage could not be deducted from his realty assessment. He pointed to the urgent need for a compulsory State examination of all banks at least once a year. He furnished some sensible suggestions on prison management, and devoting seven pages to the abuses in charitable institutions, called for remedial legislation. Noting that the new Railroad Commission was requiring all railways to file a quarterly report on their financial position, he declared that it would be a healthy reform if all corporations were compelled to lay similar financial statements, in great detail, before some vigilant State department. Reckless financing might thus be exposed, investors given better protection, and the use

[1] C. to Bissell, Dec. 27, Dec. 31, 1883. Cleveland Papers.
[2] C. to A. C. Chapin, Dec. 18, 1883. Cleveland Papers.

of money in lobbying checked. It was an interesting suggestion—in principle anticipating Roosevelt's plan for a Federal Bureau of Corporations—but it came to nothing. He strongly recommended legislation to buy lands surrounding Niagara Falls and create a State reservation there. At one point only did his vision falter—in the section in which he opposed the State purchase of private lands in the Adirondacks for the preservation of the forests and the water-courses; for he mistakenly believed that the object might be secured without purchase.

If the outstanding feature of the first legislative session had been Cleveland's clash with Tammany, that of the second was his working partnership with Theodore Roosevelt. It was a happy conjunction of stars which brought together the two greatest men New York had produced since Jay and Hamilton. In 1882, then twenty-three and fresh from Harvard, Roosevelt had entered the Assembly from the Twenty-first district in New York. Observers saw a bullet head, close-cropped sandy hair, steely eyes, a strong jaw partly hidden for the time by burnsides, and a general air of youth and self-assertion. His frail physique, dudish dress, and boyishness excited derision. One newspaper-man, as he first saw him wipe his eyeglasses and learned that he was called Theodore—a name then classified with Algernon and Percy—muttered to himself: "What on earth will New York send us next?" [1] Roosevelt had much to learn, but he learned rapidly. The "black horse cavalry" or professional politicians had soon found that the aggressive and terribly earnest young man was not to be taken lightly.

In 1882 he and others got hold of the correspondence of Judge Westbrook of Newbury with Jay Gould, and found that it showed a shocking readiness to use the judicial office in any way that Gould might dictate. Westbrook had written that "I am ready to go to the very verge of judicial discretion to serve your vast interests." Roosevelt demanded his ejection and brought about a committee investigation, in the course of which Francis Lynde Stetson made a powerful argument for impeachment; but the legislature refused to act. Reëlected in the year in which Cleveland swept the State, Roosevelt again made an energetic record. He unsuccessfully urged action to vacate the charter of Gould's Manhattan Railway Company, pressed a civil service reform bill, and received the Republican nomination for Speaker. Reëlected again, he entered the legislature of 1884 an influential figure, and at the open-

[1] Edgar L. Murlin to author, April 15, 1928.

ing of the session achieved a key position. The Republican Speaker, Titus Sheard, appointed him chairman of the Committee on Cities, with authority to bring in measures for their better government; and with characteristic zeal Roosevelt began drafting a broad set of reforms.

He and his associates prepared the way for their bills by having committees appointed in both houses to investigate the various departments of both the city and county of New York. Democratic and Republican politicians in previous years had always united to choke off such investigations as soon as they became really dangerous. But this time Roosevelt was made chairman of the Assembly committee, and refused to be diverted from his goal. Hearings were held, witnesses grilled, and revelations shortly made which startled the State and arrested the attention of the whole country.

It was shown that under the fee system the county clerk's term of office had yielded him a total of $250,000, a large part of which he had paid to the political leaders who gave him his position. The register of deeds and mortgages, also a beneficiary of the fee system, could not tell what his income was, and had forgotten whether he had paid more or less than $50,000 for his place; while the surrogate's office was found to be "largely run by his subordinates simply for the purposes of blackmail." Hubert O. Thompson, the commissioner of public works and a pillar of the County Democracy, was discovered to have administered his office with reckless extravagance if not downright corruption. He was not only condemned by the legislative committees, but was indicted by a grand jury, and the *Times* compared his record with that of Tweed, who had held the same office twenty years earlier. Sheriff Davidson, head of the Irving Hall Democracy, had received $85,000 in fees in one year, for most of which he had no legal authority; his office was described by the committee as "a great nursery of corruption and peculation," and he also was indicted.

Having thus shown the necessity for reform, Roosevelt and his associates brought in three closely-linked bills to strike at the heart of the abuses. One substituted salaries for the fee system in various county offices, thus stopping the levy of blackmail and saving $200,000 a year. Another gave the mayor power to appoint the heads of city departments, commissioners, marshals, and police justices, and to remove them for cause with the approval of the governor. The third and most important took away from the aldermen their power of confirming the mayor's appointments to city offices. The aldermen were the creatures of Boss Kelly and his Republican allies like Barney Biglin and John O'Brien, and so long as they held the power of confirmation Kelly was almost sure to control the mayor by corrupt bargains over offices. Taken together, the three bills concentrated the principal authority of the city government in the mayor, and purged the county government of its worst defects.

Inevitably, heavy Democratic pressure was brought upon Cleveland to veto these bills, and in especial the vital measure destroying the aldermanic right of confirmation. The scope of the opposition went far beyond Tammany. Many respected members of the party, many County Democrats and members of the Tilden-Manning wing, argued in favor of a balance of powers, and against the subversive tendency of a concentration of municipal authority in one man. But Cleveland never hesitated. Not only did he sign the measure, but he sent the legislature a memorandum indicating that he was willing to go much further on this same path. His action enabled Harold Frederic, now about to be forced out of his editorship, to fire a last salute: [1]

The Democratic game of bluff and bulldozing did not succeed with Governor Cleveland, as we predicted from the moment the Roosevelt bill went to the executive chamber that it would not. The timid Democratic papers which contented themselves with announcements that the Governor would veto the bill because he was so good a Democrat, and the bold Democratic papers which threatened him with political annihilation if he dared to sign it, were alike astray in their estimation of the man. There has probably never been any doubt in his mind from the beginning about signing the bill; but if there had been, the tactics of his party papers were of precisely the sort best calculated to destroy the doubt. The governor's action is another wedge driven into the split in the Democracy of New York State—and one which goes much further toward completing a complete and obvious rupture than any which have been driven before. The old chronic antagonism within the party, which dates back to the days when the label "Half Puritan, half Hibernian" was first affixed to it, is deeper and fiercer today than ever before.

Cleveland also signed the two other principal bills. *Harper's Weekly* published a cartoon showing him and Roosevelt, arm in arm, surveying the dejected form of the Tammany tiger as, in a state of utter collapse, its teeth and claws scattered about, it slunk out of the arena

[1] Albany *Evening Journal*, March 18, 1884.

where the young legislator and the governor had deprived it of all its weapons.

VI

Yet Cleveland at one point disagreed with Roosevelt and as a result was later warmly attacked by him. In a widely-printed speech of 1884, Roosevelt showed indignation because Cleveland refused to sign the so-called Tenure of Office bill authorizing the next mayor to appoint a new register of deeds and commissioner of public works. This was specifically intended to effect the removal of Commissioner Hubert O. Thompson, who richly deserved to be ousted. As a leader of the County Democracy, Thompson had done much to nominate Cleveland. The governor vetoed the bill. To the New York *Tribune*, Roosevelt, and Republicans in general, this proved that Cleveland was not strong enough to punish an unfit officer who happened to be a powerful member of the Tilden-Manning organization. "George W. Curtis knows now," said one pessimist, "that his idol has clay feet." Roosevelt expressed himself still more stingingly. "Now, we had several bills that bore upon Tammany Hall. The Governor signed those most unflinchingly—with reckless heroism. Then we had several that affected the County Democracy and the leader of the County Democracy—my esteemed fellow-citizen, Mr. Hubert O. Thompson—and these measures came to an untimely end."

This accusation deserves a moment's examination. Cleveland's real reason for vetoing the bill was simply that the legislature, after repeated warnings from him not to pass measures imperfect in form, had let this one go through in a shape almost incredibly "defective and shabby." The governor was able to point out a long list of confusions, absurdities, and contradictions, some of which would absolutely defeat its purpose.[1] It was so slipshod in language that Mayor Edson could easily take steps to keep Mr. Thompson in office; it would throw the appointments of the next mayor into a hopeless tangle; in one section it applied to certain men and in others totally failed to apply to them; and in a single sentence it provided two terms for the same officers—one to run four years from May 1, 1885, and one to run one year and eleven months from February 1, 1885! Of all the careless leg-

---

[1] Charles Z. Lincoln, ed., *Messages From the Governors*, VII, 1072 ff.

islation ever sent him, declared Cleveland, this was the worst. And his judgment was corroborated by the author of the bill. Assemblyman Scott wrote the New York *Times* that "As the draughtsman of the original Tenure of Office Act and one of its most ardent supporters, I am constrained to agree with Governor Cleveland that in the shape in which it reached him it was a very shabby piece of legislation, quite unfit to find a place in the statute book." [1] The main defects had been introduced in an amendment written by one of John O'Brien's assemblymen.

Before the session of 1884 closed, several other measures of value, for which Cleveland deserves partial credit, had been enacted. He secured a law for the compulsory examination of all banks and trust companies, and had the satisfaction of seeing the first steps taken for the business reorganization of all State charitable institutions. He approved an aqueduct bill for New York city which was severely criticized, but which had more merits than defects. With the natural pride of a western New Yorker, he signed an appropriation of almost a million and a half for a reservation at Niagara Falls. Many eminent men had been interested in the movement—Emerson and Longfellow, Carlyle and Ruskin. His predecessor, Cornell, had been chilly toward the plans; when a bill was brought before him, he listened with frigid attention while the arguments were being presented, and then demanded: "But, gentlemen, **why** should we spend the people's money when just as much water will run over the Falls without a park as with it?" But to Cleveland it meant the preservation of one of the imperishable glories of the State. Years later, in 1891, he described the innocent political art he had helped to give the undertaking: [2]

There was a suggestion made while I was in Albany that an effort should be made to have a reservation at Niagara Falls for the purpose of preserving the great natural beauty of the place. I must confess that the project seemed to me a rather discouraging one to attempt. I was full of sympathy, but not full of hope. Its warmest supporters hardly dared to predict that their hopes would be realized, yet they were realized and I will tell you how.

If we had then gone to the legislature for a bill asking so much money to buy so much land around the falls, we certainly would have failed. We might have gone there and pleaded that we only wanted $1,500,000 until we were black in the face, and we would have been answered every time that the

[1] N. Y. *Times*, June 18, 1884.
[2] Speech at Adirondack Park meeting, Jan. 24, 1891.

$1,500,000 we asked for was only an entering wedge. Our opponents would have pointed to the Capitol building at Albany and shaken their heads.

What did we do? We got the legislature to pass a law authorizing an appraisal of the lands we wanted to preserve. As good luck would have it, the appraisal amounted to just about the amount we said the lands would cost. We had continued to win supporters for our project. We then asked the State to buy the lands, and to her credit be it said, she did so.

I used to say to people that Niagara Falls was the great natural wonder by which we were known throughout the world.

The legislature sat late that year—till May 16th. Declining a dinner invitation on the 13th, Cleveland wrote that he was in a whirl of work and perplexity. "I had my lunch brought to me and have directed my dinner to be also brought, and with this economy of time I am afraid the night will not be long enough to do all I have on hand. Need I say any more—except to assure you that 'It's fun to be governor?' " [1] He had thirty days in which to sign or veto bills, and it was the middle of June before he could rise from his desk with a sense of relief. By that date one national convention had come and gone. The Republicans had gathered in Chicago on June 3 and nominated James G. Blaine. The Democratic national convention was to meet in Chicago on July 8, and already one name was on everybody's lips—Grover Cleveland.

[1] To Mrs. Pruyn. C. S. Hamlin Papers.

FOR several reasons the campaign of 1884 will long be counted among the most memorable in American history. It is the only campaign in which the head of a great party has gone down to defeat because of charges impugning his integrity. Only once or twice in our political history has victory or defeat hung on so delicate a hair, for the change of six hundred votes in a single State would have reversed the verdict. Seldom have the fortunes of a political contest been affected by such spectacular incidents as Burchard's Rum, Romanism, and Rebellion speech or the "Belshazzar's Feast" at Delmonico's. We may add that never but once since the Civil War—in 1896—has popular excitement in a campaign risen higher, and that never at any time has so much scandal entered into such a struggle.

When 1884 opened, the nomination of James G. Blaine by the Republicans was almost a certainty. He had now been a candidate before the party for eight years. In 1876 he had been the strongest aspirant until on the eve of the convention the publication of the so-called Mulligan letters dealing with his dubious railroad operations,[1] followed by his unexpected physical collapse, had shattered his chances. Four years later Appomattox and its apple-tree—Grant's stubborn candidacy—barred the way until Garfield was chosen. Now the death of Garfield, the weakness of Arthur, and the complete eclipse of Conkling had opened the road to his ambition. There was still a rumble of warning from many Republicans that they could not overlook the Mulligan letters and that Blaine's nomination would be the signal for a revolt. But the politicians paid little attention. On the first ballot Blaine had nearly four times as many votes as the reform candidate, George F. Edmunds, and on the fourth he was nominated. The enthusiasm of the organization leaders was unfeigned.

Yet the nomination was the signal for a revolt which took the most

---

[1] The gravamen of the charges against Blaine is that when Speaker in 1869 he made a decision that saved a land grant for the Little Rock & Fort Smith Railroad; and after calling the attention of the railroad officials to this favor, he received the privilege of selling the road's bonds on a secret and highly generous commission. J. F. Rhodes, *History of the United States*, VII, 194 ff. James Mulligan of Boston had kept some books for Warren Fisher, Jr., of the Little Rock line, and held many of Blaine's letters.

experienced observers by surprise, for in volume and intensity it surpassed the hopes of the Democrats and the fears of the Republicans.
Cleveland had felt the ground-swell before the shock actually came,
remarking just before the Republican convention: "O, neither Blaine
nor Arthur will be nominated. I have observed that in time of crisis
the moral sense of the Republican party comes uppermost. The crisis
is here. The Republican situation demands the nomination of Edmunds,
and Edmunds will be nominated." [1] To thousands of Republicans the
selection of Blaine, with his dubious railroad transactions, his liking for
the bloody shirt, and his belief in the spoils system, was an affront
which made them turn anxiously toward the Democratic party.

II

On the Democratic side one figure had loomed at the outset above all
others—Samuel J. Tilden. In the eyes of his party he was a martyr
still awaiting vindication, while its admiration for him as a reformer,
a thinker, and a man who had sacrificed ambition to national peace was
as deep as ever. The friendship between Manning and Cleveland was
steadily gaining warmth, and there is no reason to believe the story
that Manning had resented Cleveland's signing of a bill which abolished the use of the *Argus* as a State paper; Manning was too big a
man for that. Nevertheless, as State Chairman, Manning felt that his
first duty was still to Tilden. So did Samuel J. Randall, leader of the
Pennsylvania Democrats, and many Southerners.

The insuperable impediment was Tilden's frail health. Seventy years
old in February, 1884, he had suffered a paralytic stroke which left
him unable to speak above a whisper or walk except with tottering gait.
His mind was as keen as ever, but he knew that the strain of a campaign might be fatal. When Clark Howell of the Atlanta *Constitution*
called at the Gramercy Park mansion he was shocked to see Tilden
totter into the room on a cane, one arm useless, one eyelid drooping,
and his voice hardly audible. To the young man's remark that he
hoped he would be nominated, Tilden, smiling gently, responded: "My
boy, don't you see it is impossible?" [2] His good eye twinkled as he told
other newspapermen that Thomas A. Hendricks wanted the old ticket

[1] J. B. Bishop, *Presidential Elections*, 64.
[2] Clark Howell to author, June 14, 1930.

of Tilden and Hendricks—"and I do not wonder, considering my weakness!" On June 10 he published a decisive letter asserting that "I ought not to assume a task which I have not the physical strength to carry through."

The field was thus left open to three national figures, Thomas A. Bayard, Allen G. Thurman, and Grover Cleveland, and to the usual galaxy of favorite sons—Hendricks, Randall, McDonald of Indiana, Morrison of Illinois, and Carlisle of Kentucky. Of the national figures, Cleveland held the advantage. Eminent as Senator Bayard was, he came from the minor state of Delaware; he seemed an aristocrat, and he had made an unfortunate speech in 1861 defending the right of secession. Allen G. Thurman of Ohio, "the old Roman," was growing infirm, while his views on money were distrusted. In addition to these men, one interloper, Ben Butler, hoped to fish in the troubled Democratic waters. This impudent adventurer in law, war, and politics, having slipped into the Democratic ranks by way of the Greenback party, had failed of reëlection as governor of Massachusetts, but still made use of every opportunity to keep himself conspicuous. Receiving in May at Indianapolis the nomination of the two little Anti-Monopoly and Greenback parties for President, he made overtures to Tammany Hall, and prepared to move on to the Chicago Convention with as much swagger as in Civil War days he had moved on Bermuda Hundred.

In New York the withdrawal of Tilden resulted in an immediate mobilization of the Tilden-Manning machine in behalf of Cleveland. To be sure, so many Tilden men were now warmer admirers of Cleveland than of the Sage himself, that it is impossible to speak of a hard-and-fast Tilden organization. Manning was in a measure right in denying that any machine was conducting the Cleveland canvass, and in declaring the movement "spontaneous." During May and June encouraging news came from every part of the State. In New York city the County Democracy under Abram S. Hewitt and William C. Whitney were active, and had the support of Sheriff Davidson and Irving Hall. In the southern tier Lieutenant-Governor Hill, anxious to get Cleveland out of the governorship, was indefatigable. State Treasurer Maxwell lent assistance in the western counties to the Buffalo organization and to such friends of Cleveland as Bissell and Lockwood. Alton B. Parker and Deputy-Comptroller Benedict were behind the scenes when the Ulster County Democrats declared for Cleveland, while in St. Lawrence

County Daniel Magone was hard at work, and in Clinton and Essex no effort was spared by Smith M. Weed. Meanwhile, Apgar, brilliant and resourceful as ever, toured the whole State.[1]

Thus while Cleveland's opponents were declaring that his own State was hesitant, he was fast being made irresistible there. Henry Watterson of the Louisville *Courier-Journal,* a supporter of Carlisle, called Cleveland impossible on the ground that he was inexperienced, that his position on national affairs was unknown, and that he was opposed by Tammany, the trade unions, and the Catholic hierarchy. Dana of the *Sun* attacked him with equal vigor. He had taken a violent dislike to Cleveland because the latter had refused to nominate a friend, Col. Franklin Bartlett of the State militia, to his staff. To Dana the request had seemed simple and legitimate, and its rejection an insult, while to Cleveland it had seemed an attempt to interfere with his freedom in making appointments. The episode made Dana a lifelong enemy, and he now whetted his sarcasm upon Cleveland's "plodding mind, limited knowledge, and narrow capacities." The Tammany men and the friends of Bayard and Thurman were eager to block Cleveland in any way possible.

The Democratic State Convention met at Saratoga on June 18 with the heavy port and imperious voice of Manning, like some Jupiter of politics, constantly in evidence. Having taken counsel beforehand with Tilden, he dictated all its principal acts. The authors of the platform aimed their shots directly at Blaine. Nothing was more important, they declared, "than the election of a President whose character and public reputation shall give to the whole people assurance of an honest, impartial, and efficient administration of the laws, without suspicion of personal ends or private interests." A crust was tossed to Tammany, which was given half the national delegates for New York County, and a crumb to the futile little Flower-for-President group, which was allotted a delegate-at-large. But, while making these concessions, the Manning-Cleveland forces were adamant in requiring the convention to declare for an ironclad unit rule at Chicago. Of the seventy-two State delegates, twenty-two would be opposed to Cleveland, and at least nine were counted uncertain; but the others were all for him and the unit rule would give him the total of seventy-two votes.

Only a few hours before the State Convention had thus done its

[1] Albany *Evening Journal,* June 5, 1884.

utmost for the governor, a distinguished committee of Republican bolters met in New York city and adopted resolutions condemning Blaine and calling on the Democrats to make a nomination which they could support. A conference of Independents in Boston a few days earlier, on June 13, had taken the same step. No name was mentioned at either gathering, but George W. Curtis in *Harper's Weekly* on July 5 came out flatly for Cleveland.

Immediately after the Saratoga meeting, Manning sent William C. Hudson to Chicago to open the Cleveland headquarters at the Palmer House and talk with the arriving delegations. Hudson was provided with a list of the New York delegates, divided into three groups: those certain to support Cleveland, those certain to oppose him, and the six or eight who were doubtful. Manning impressed upon him that it was essential to get at the doubtful men immediately they arrived, and to employ the utmost pressure, "political, commercial, and moral." [1] Tammany had already taken similar action. When Hudson arrived he found Thomas F. Grady on the scene, laboring energetically to influence the local press against Cleveland, and filling the saloons and lobbies with his whispering campaign. While he accused Cleveland of being anti-Catholic and anti-Irish, up-State allies of Tammany spread broadcast reports that Cleveland was a dissolute drunkard. Grady's main goal at the outset was to induce the convention to free the New York delegation from its unit-rule instructions, while he and Kelly hoped to hold more than one-third of the 840 convention members against Cleveland. In all these developments Cleveland naturally showed a deep interest. He feared nothing so much as that at the last minute his chances might be bartered away for the Vice Presidency, and on June 30 wrote an emphatic letter on the subject to Manning. After some general remarks he declared: [2]

No one has a better appreciation of the greatness of the office of President of the United States, and of the supreme honor that attaches to the citizen holding the same. . . . And yet I have not a particle of ambition to be President of the United States. Every consideration which presents itself to me tends to the personal wish on my part that the wisdom of the Democratic party in the coming convention may lead to a result not involving my nomination for the Presidency. If, however, it should be otherwise and I should be selected as

[1] Hudson, *Recollections*, 160 ff.
[2] Cleveland to Manning, Albany, June 30, 1884. Cleveland Papers.

the nominee, my sense of duty to the people and my party would dictate my submission to the will of the Convention.

But there is another subject which has frequently been a topic of conversation between us, upon which I desire here to particularly express myself.

I should not, in any condition of affairs, or under any imaginable pressure, deem it my duty to relinquish the trust which I hold from the people of my State, in order to assume the duties of the Vice Presidency; and the nomination for that office, I could not accept upon any consideration whatever.

III

On July 4 the delegates began to gather in Chicago in force. Cleveland that day was in Buffalo with Gen. Stewart L. Woodford, reviewing a patriotic parade. Driving along the line in an open barouche, his staff in uniform clattering behind, he received something like an ovation. In Chicago there was a new feeling in the air. For the first time since the war the gathering Democratic hosts showed a genuine confidence of victory. Everyone recognized that it was Cleveland against the field, and the immediate question was whether he would command an impressive backing from his own State, or whether Tammany would succeed in making him seem a weak candidate. At dawn on Sunday the County Democracy arrived with three brass bands, their Cleveland banners gleaming silver and gold under the first rays of sunlight. Later in the day came two long trains, twenty-five cars in each, bearing Kelly, Croker, and. seven hundred Tammany braves, all wearing tall white hats. Kelly had been interviewed on the rear platform as his train passed through Syracuse, and in answer to a question about Cleveland had shrugged his shoulders, remarking: "Butler is a good man." [1] Another long special train drew in with the Democrats of Irving Hall and Hill's followers of the southern tier. Manning was early on the ground, taking charge of the Palmer House headquarters—three immense parlors, with a life-size portrait of Cleveland over the entrance. With him came Smith M. Weed, Abram S. Hewitt, ex-mayor Edward Cooper, Apgar, Whitney, and others, who ranged the hotel corridors posting pickets and carrying on a systematic propaganda.

It was only for a single day that there was any uncertainty as to the size of Cleveland's New York vote. On Monday the Brooklyn delegation announced that it stood by him, making a total of at least forty-

[1] New York *Sun*, July 6, 1884.

five delegates. Bissell, Lockwood, and Goodyear were observed joyously celebrating in the bar. "Fire and smoke burst from the nostrils of Tammany," reported the New York *Sun*. "Spinola, Grady, Bourke Cockran, and other faithful henchmen paced the lobbies raging like lions." In their chagrin the Tammany men indulged in lurid utterances. Kelly declared that the Knights of Labor controlled 700,000 votes—all hostile to Cleveland. His up-State ally John C. Sheehan talked in the most scandalous terms of Cleveland. But as the Southerners arrived, "Fighting Joe" Wheeler heading the Alabama delegation and Wade Hampton the South Carolinians, the Cleveland sentiment increased.

By the opening day, Tuesday, July 8, it was clear that the convention was to be nothing more than a savage fight of two party marplots, Butler and Kelly, against Cleveland. The result could hardly be in doubt. All the States except those with favorite sons and the Pacific Coast preferred Cleveland because of his character and because they believed he could win. Nor were the favorite sons in a position, by vote-trading, to defeat him. Samuel J. Randall was weak in the West because of his protectionist opinions; John G. Carlisle and Morrison were weak in the East because of their low-tariff views. As for Butler, who seized an early opportunity to deliver a tub-thumping speech from a window of the Palmer House, the South would have none of him. "We may be willing to eat crow," ejaculated one Georgia delegate, his eye bent in disgust on Butler's stocky figure, "but we'll be d—d if we'll eat turkey buzzard." Meanwhile, a second letter from Tilden, repeating that he was not a candidate, was interpreted as a declaration in Cleveland's favor.[1] The one momentary burst of enthusiasm for anyone else occurred when Thurman, his tall figure conspicuous in spats, white tile hat, and a gray suit, entered the hall at the head of the Ohio delegation. The delegates rose and cheered, while hundreds of red bandannas waved at the end of the canes. An exuberant Westerner shouted: "The California delegation, after traveling twenty-five hundred miles, catches its first glimpse of paradise in the person of Allen G. Thurman."

On this first day the fight raged about the unit rule, Cleveland's opponents fighting in the last ditch. Butler, Voorhees, John M. Palmer, and Morrison all held earnest conferences with Kelly. Bourke Cockran told the convention that Cleveland was "one of the men who in two years have reduced the 200,000 Democratic majority in New York to

[1] N. Y. *Times, Tribune,* July 8, 1884.

17,000." Kelly himself stepped into the aisle, broad-shouldered and square-jawed, and made a brief speech pointing out that only ten of the sixty-two New York counties were Democratic, and that Tammany's county outweighed all the others. It was in vain, for the unit rule was upheld by a vote of 463 to 322. Manning, as chairman of the New York delegation, was empowered to cast the entire 72 votes.

On Wednesday the ninth came the nominating speeches. The bands played selections from the new operas *Patience* and *Iolanthe;* Northerners cheered *Dixie,* and Southerners *Yankee Doodle.* The galleries were so friendly to Cleveland and so hostile to Tammany that Mayor Carter H. Harrison felt it necessary to issue a formal denial of the report that his police had packed the hall with Cleveland men. Most Westerners detested Tammany. The bulk of the Cleveland delegates had front seats. Here Manning was repeatedly in conference with Hill and the distinguished-looking Smith M. Weed, later to become a constant correspondent of Cleveland and in 1892 a leader of the "anti-snappers." Apgar, who had been sick in his hotel room, came in late to take his place with the suave and handsome Whitney, occasionally polishing his eye-glasses, and Hubert O. Thompson. The Tammany men waited sullenly to make the most of any opening, and two temporary allies, August Belmont and William Travers, whispered with them. As the speechmaking proceeded, the indifference to the favorite sons became oppressive, and it was only when Lockwood arose to nominate Cleveland that the convention awoke to a sense of excitement. Lockwood's remarks were carefully shaped to avoid offending the older leaders, for he did not praise Cleveland as the ablest man before the convention, but as the man most available; and he closed with the prediction that Cleveland would give the party New York's electoral vote.

This statement ushered in the only dramatic hours of the convention. While seconding speeches were made Grady was clamoring for recognition. At their close he was instantly on his feet, proclaiming: "Cleveland cannot carry the State of New York." After being temporarily silenced on a point of order, he declared amid a hostile uproar that the labor interests of the State and all other enemies of corporate greed would refuse to support Cleveland. Bourke Cockran, gaining the floor to second Thurman's nomination, attacked the governor in scathing language. "We have been told that the mantle of Tilden has fallen upon Cleveland," he said. "The mantle of a giant upon the shoulders of a dwarf!" The battle was protracted throughout the afternoon of the ninth and the morning of the tenth. Apgar spoke with effect, recalling that Kelly had gone astray eight years earlier in predicting Tilden's defeat in New York, and asserting that a hundred thousand New York Republicans would turn to Cleveland if he were nominated. But it was the speech of Gen. Edward S. Bragg, of Wisconsin, which best expressed the feelings of the majority. The fact was that the convention was sick of Tammany; sick of its greed, its jealous spirit, its squabbles, its predictions of defeat. It was always kicking and bolting; it had opposed Tilden and stabbed Hancock in the back; it was responsible for nothing but mischief.

Bragg turned upon Tammany with unfeigned anger. He spoke, he said, for the young men of Wisconsin. "They love Cleveland for his character, but they love him also for the enemies he has made." Those who saw Grady's face at that moment, only a few feet in front of Bragg, recall that it was contorted with rage as he uttered a yell of defiance.[1] Kelly replied, "In behalf of his enemies, I accept your statement." The galleries shouted, "A little more grape, Captain Bragg," and Bragg, levelling his finger at the Tammany delegation, delivered another shot: "Riddleberger of Virginia, whose treachery caused a Democratic defeat in that State, would not be permitted to speak here. Gentlemen, behold the Riddlebergers of New York!" Some observers said later that if the galleries had at that moment been turned loose on Kelly and his associates, their lives would have been in danger.

The platform, reported by Morrison of Illinois, was rapidly read and adopted, though not without a minority report just after midnight from the irrepressible Butler. Then, in the early morning of July 11, the first vote was taken. It was disastrous to Cleveland's opponents, for it showed him far in the lead: he had 392 votes, Bayard 168, Thurman 88, and Randall 78. The convention, with the Cleveland forces vainly calling for a second ballot, thereupon adjourned at 1:30 A. M. That night Hill, Whitney, Weed and others, fearing an anti-Cleveland combination, got only snatches of sleep. But the last-minute attempts at a hostile coalition proved futile. Indeed, the one bargain made that night was to Cleveland's advantage. Manning, at an early-morning hour, met Samuel J. Randall in the hotel room of the Philadelphia editor

[1] Edgar L. Murlin to author, April 15, 1928.

A. K. McClure, and on the understanding that Randall should control the patronage of his State, received a promise of the Pennsylvania delegates.

On the second ballot on July 11th there was an effort to stampede the delegates for Hendricks. Illinois suddenly transferred one vote to him, and at the same instant the bland Indianian was seen entering a door directly facing the delegates. Kelly and Grady leaped to their seats, shouting hoarsely; Indiana sent Voorhees to the platform to withdraw McDonald in favor of Hendricks; the usual band-playing and parading began. Hendricks sat pale and quiet. But the movement was instantly checked. Another Illinois delegate announced that the State increased its vote for Cleveland from 28 to 38, and Missouri raised her Cleveland vote from 6 to 21. As the end of the ballot came in sight it was evident that Cleveland had almost 500 votes, while Bayard had lost ground. Immediately State after State, led by North Carolina, which had been voting for Bayard, changed its vote; and the official count gave Cleveland 683 votes, Bayard 81½, and Hendricks 45½. The Democratic old guard was consoled by Hendricks' nomination for the Vice-Presidency—a shrewd move, for his strength proved the decisive factor that fall in carrying Indiana.

While the final ballot was being taken, Cleveland was at his work in his private office in Albany, where he and Adjutant-General Farnsworth were disposing of business connected with the State militia camp. A number of friends had dropped in. Every few minutes a messenger brought a bulletin from the Assembly telegraph-office. At about 1:45 P. M. Farnsworth heard against the westerly wind what he thought was a cannon shot. A second later there was an unmistakable roar from a brass piece which the Young Men's Democratic Club had placed at the foot of State Street. Farnsworth leaped to his feet, remarking, "They are firing a salute, governor, for your nomination." "That's what it is," said Lamont. "Do you think so?" said Cleveland. "Well, anyhow we'll finish up this work," and at it they went again.[1]

If any doubt remained, it was soon dispelled by a telephone call which conveyed the news of the second ballot. Cleveland, not at all excited, smiled as Lamont took the message. There was general hand-shaking. Then the governor said suddenly: "Lamont, I wish you would telephone that to the mansion. Sisters will want to hear it."

[1] Albany *Evening Journal*, July 11, 1884; N. Y. *Sun*, July 12.

Cleveland had always been a favorite of the newspapermen, who liked his blunt, downright ways. A number of them telegraphed hasty sketches of his personality and ways to their journals, and perhaps that which appeared in the Boston *Advertiser* said in a few sentences as much as any: [1]

Cleveland is stout, has a well-fed look, is indeed a good liver, has the air of a man who has made up his mind just how he ought to behave in any position where he may find himself. He is getting bald; he is getting gray—though his white hair does not show conspicuously, as his complexion is sandy. He dresses well, carries himself well, talks well upon any subject with which he is familiar, and upon subjects with which he is not familiar he does not venture to talk at all. He has the happy faculty of being able to refuse a request without giving offence. It has been my fortune to see him several times during the past winter upon business in connection with some of the State institutions. He has impressed me always as one heartily desirous of getting at the bottom of any matter he may have in hand, and of acting wisely in it.

[1] Boston *Advertiser*, July 12, 1884.

THE campaign had already taken on the quality of a great moral crusade. The uprising of the independent voters to vindicate the principle that the presidency must forever be barred to any man of doubtful integrity had gained tremendous momentum, arousing a fervor such as tens of thousands had not felt since the Civil War. In 1872 there had been a momentary burst of the same spirit of patriotic idealism, but it had quickly been damped by Greeley's nomination. Now the crisis seemed to have met its leader, and a host of voters leaped their party frontier at a bound to enlist under a new banner. The Independents or Mugwumps, so called by a name first taken out of Eliot's Indian Bible in 1872, and now revived by Dana's *Sun,* became virtually a new party—from 1884 to 1897 a Cleveland party. They were able to decide at least one national election, and their faith was to be a leavening force in politics for a long generation.

The hour was ripe for precisely such a movement. The health of a nation requires, from time to time, a far-reaching moral movement to awaken men from old lethargies and fix their eyes upon some new city in the heavens. Ever since Appomattox the government had in great part been subject to the selfish materialism of the worst wing of the Republican party. The Congressional oligarchy which had humiliated Andrew Johnson and crushed the South; the placemen and corruptionists who had moulded Grant to their desires; the favored groups which had obtained land-grants, subsidies, pensions, and tariffs; the quarrelsome gangs of Stalwarts and Half-Breeds who had kept the Hayes and the Garfield-Arthur Administrations in turmoil—all these had aroused an increasing irritation. Men were in revolt against the entire system of government by special favor of which Blaine was simply the emblem. They knew that he would not take bribes in the White House. But they also knew that by virtue of his record, his associates, and his coarseness of fibre, his election would give new encouragement to the crew of lobbyists, spoilsmen, and seekers after privilege. They wanted an honest man who stood in hostility to the whole discreditable and dangerous tradition.

At the Republican Convention the rebels had mustered but a corporal's guard. Before the week was over, it was a brigade; before June ended, an army. The New York *Times* on June 8 printed three columns of letters from bolting Republicans, selected from a mass of such communications. Carl Schurz bolted; Henry Ward Beecher bolted; ex-Secretary Bristow bolted; George Haven Putnam wrote that the Republican nominations were "a farce and an absurdity, not to say an anachronism." On the afternoon of June 7 the Massachusetts Reform Club brought together at the Parker House a large part of the brains and character of the Bay State, and feeling ran high. A letter was read from Charles Francis Adams, Jr. "I presume there is no question as to the attitude of the members of the club toward the nominations," he wrote. "We will at once organize to defeat them." The committee which was appointed to mobilize the voters seemed a list of the best names of Massachusetts. It included Adams, Edward Atkinson, Moorfield Storey, Leverett Saltonstall, William Everett, James Freeman Clarke, John C. Dodge, Richard H. Dana, Josiah Quincy, Winslow Warren, T. W. Higginson, and Frederick J. Stimson. Higginson announced, after talking with a "multitude" of people, that the sentiment against Blaine in Boston was powerful, "and in Cambridge, where I live, almost universal." Lowell was bolting; so was Charles Eliot Norton; so were President Eliot and most of the Harvard faculty. Another meeting on the 13th brought new names—Theodore Lyman, Francis W. Bird, and George Fred Williams.[1] Several of the Hoars joined, though Senator Hoar stood by his party.

Still more ominously for the Republicans, newspapers all over the East halted, veered uncertainly, and then swung to the Democratic party. In New York city new colors were hoisted by the *Times, Herald,* and *Evening Post,* and by *Harper's Weekly,* the *Nation,* and *Puck.* A squadron of influential journals elsewhere in the State joined them. In New England there was an equally impressive list, including the Springfield *Republican,* the Boston *Transcript* and the Boston *Herald.* All these journals began printing long lists of former Republicans who refused to tolerate Blaine's nomination.

When Cleveland was nominated, the Mugwumps rose to the reform governor with an enthusiasm that owed something to his record and something to the fact that he was a new man. They would have been

[1] Boston *Daily Advertiser,* June 14, 1884.

chilly to Bayard and hostile to Thurman or Randall; but so far as *Harper's Weekly* and the *Nation* knew anything of Cleveland, they admired him. In Boston and New York strong organizations, amply financed, were formed. The influential Boston Committee of One Hundred, in which George Fred Williams, Moorfield Storey, William H. Forbes, and Charles R. Codman were conspicuous, was soon sowing all New England with its publications. In New York the leaders included Schurz, Everett P. Wheeler, R. R. Bowker, George Haven Putnam, Beecher, Godkin, and Curtis. Oscar S. Straus was instrumental in forming the Cleveland and Hendricks Business Men's Association, 40,000 strong. The Middle West mustered such men as Louis Howland and Lucius B. Swift of Indianapolis, and Franklin Mac-Veagh of Chicago. Not least important, young men everywhere rallied to Cleveland. He was a young man himself, and his dramatically rapid rise appealed to them. David F. Houston later spoke for many who were first voters at the time when he said that "There was nothing . . . in the ideals, practices, or leaders of either party which commanded my admiration or aroused my enthusiasms till the nomination of Grover Cleveland by the Democrats, in 1884." [1] The generous spirit which fired thousands of such political novices, the bright outlook which they saw for a rejuvenated republic, were reflected in an eloquent letter which Harold Frederic shortly wrote from London to Cleveland: [2]

Truly, my friend, I think I realize now for the first time that stalwart pride, as of the ancient Roman citizenship, which the Clays and Bentons and Jacksons of a past generation felt in their birthright of a whole continent, and which we of a punier growth, smarting under foreign criticism, aping foreign customs, seeking in the race for dishonored wealth to win class distinction and the idleness of the aristocrat in older countries, had almost completely lost. I have felt that the public tendency since the war, in business, in politics, in social life, has rotted and infected almost every condition of our existence. Moral sensibility has been blunted, the keen edge of honor turned, the standards of justice clogged, the ardor of patriotism chilled, the confiding ignorance of the half-educated tampered with, the ambitions of good men perverted. So long had I seen and hated these modern tendencies in our people; so trivial and selfish and unworthy had seemed to me the aims and ends for which Americans worked, the gods before which they did fetish worship, and the political harangues by which they justified themselves, that I may be said to have grown up with more indignation at than pride in my country and my countrymen. In

[1] *Eight Years With Wilson's Cabinet*, I, 1, 2.
[2] London, Nov. 8, 1884. William Gorham Rice Papers.

my little way I tried to do what I could to set things right—and you know how I was broken on the wheel for it.

But, as in a burst of sunlight, the pride of country, of race, yes, of state, comes to me now, and I am almost intoxicated by its radiance and power. It is true, after all, that nobody who through the years behind us has worked for the right has wrought in vain. It is true that in the end corruption wins not more than honesty, that there *is* a public conscience—that all the greed and scoundrelism and prejudice and folly of our political, race, and business sides, massed into one grand desperate effort for control, are not able to stand before the simple weight of an honest man and an upright cause.

It was impossible to conduct such a campaign except upon an emotional plane. Men who were intent upon a change in the very spirit of government could not be bound down to prosaic issues like the tariff and currency. Seldom has so little account been taken of platform or pledges, for as George W. Curtis truly said, "the platforms of the two parties are practically the same." Both sides made ostentatious affirmations regarding civil service reform. There was some truth in Godkin's statement that Blaine, while Secretary of State, had wallowed in spoils like a rhinoceros in an African pool; but now he declared himself in favor of placing even consuls and secretaries of legation in the classified service. On the tariff the parties were almost equally close together. Both declared in favor of revision to reduce the burden upon the taxpayer, but both promised to move with caution and to protect business and the workingman. Thus the Democrats asserted that they would bring to revision "a spirit of fairness," and take precautions against "depriving American labor of the ability to compete successfully with foreign labor." A few low-tariff men like Morrison tried hard to interpret the Democratic plank as a promise of a tariff for revenue only, but Henry Watterson more accurately called it a straddle.

II

Though the Blaine forces dreaded the task of fighting on the defensive, at first the rôle seemed unescapable. In vain did Blaine direct Whitelaw Reid to "agonize more and more on the tariff issue." To make the party position more difficult, the manager selected for the campaign was Stephen B. Elkins of West Virginia, a typical business man in politics. He had first come into prominence in New Mexico as a Federal district attorney under Johnson and Grant, and later as a territorial delegate in Congress for two terms. During this period he became interested in mining ventures, which were usually connected with special Congressional grants, territorial court decisions, or other political complications which made his influence valuable in promoting them. One of the most interesting of the enterprises that he took up was the Maxwell land grant, a claim with a Mexican title and a Congressional bill back of it; Elkins was largely instrumental in having this bill passed, and the grant was later sold to a Dutch syndicate for several million dollars. Prolonged litigation followed, and was accompanied by ugly charges of irregularity on the part of the men pushing the claim. While still a delegate in Congress Elkins became a close friend of Blaine, then Speaker. "Some of Mr. Blaine's most profitable investments," a veteran newspaperman has written,[1] "were made on Mr. Elkins's advice." One episode of their relations was a little later the subject of heavy criticism. Elkins became attorney for an American adventurer who had a fifty-million-dollar claim against the Brazilian government for alleged guano discoveries; he asked Blaine as Secretary of State in 1881 to take it up, though Secretary Evarts had already rejected it; and Blaine very improperly did so. Thus the choice of Elkins as executive chairman further estranged the Mugwumps.

The Democratic managers were determined to force the fighting— and seldom has their unlucky party had managers of equal ability. It is true that the national chairman, ex-Senator Barnum of Connecticut, was a political hack of low reputation. But the real leader was Arthur Pue Gorman of Maryland, head of the executive committee, and his principal lieutenants were Manning and Whitney—three of the ablest political organizers of their generation. They played their cards with the utmost skill, and they wisely determined to maintain a persistent attack upon Blaine's official record and upon departmental inefficiency in Washington.

In this they received invaluable aid from the Mugwumps, who soon struck the heaviest single blow of the campaign. The New York Independents had a tiny office, little money, and so few workers that they welcomed a young volunteer just out of college, Frederic Bancroft, with enthusiasm. But Schurz, Bowker, Curtis and others had brains. They saw that the original Mulligan letters which Blaine had tried to suppress in 1876 must be reinforced, and they sent an able Brooklyn

[1] O. O. Stealey, *Forty Years in the Press Gallery*, 271.

attorney, Horace Deming, to Boston to search for more.[1] He found Mulligan and ascertained that he possessed additional letters from Blaine to Warren G. Fisher, fitting in with the missives which eight years earlier had almost ruined Blaine's career. Some leading Boston Mugwumps were apprised, and Mulligan came to Moorfield Storey's office for advice as to the best disposition of the papers. Storey urged him to release them unconditionally. Mulligan finally said that he would consult Dr. James Freeman Clarke and abide by his decision. When Clarke told him that he should make the letters public property, Mulligan brought them to a little meeting of Independents, where they were examined and discussed till two o'clock in the morning.[2] He wished to publish them with a long prefatory statement written by himself, but Storey dissented, pointing out that if this were done, Blaine would attack the preface and throw a cloud of dust in the eyes of the public. In the middle of September they appeared, without comment, in the Boston *Journal*. Simultaneously it was announced that the originals were in the custody of one of the best-known legal firms of Boston, where they might be inspected by any accredited person.

These new Mulligan letters were an amazing series. Blaine himself, when interviewed by the *Kennebec Journal,* declared that they left him unscathed: "There is not a word in the letters which is not entirely consistent with the most scrupulous integrity and honor. I hope that every Republican paper in the United States will republish them in full." But many Republican newspapers suppressed part of them, or gave misleading summaries. When read with Blaine's defence in 1876, they convicted him of "taking 44,000,000 of his countrymen into his confidence" and feeding them perversions of the truth. One letter in particular had a stunning effect—an epistle which Blaine had sent from Washington to his old business associate Fisher in Boston on April 16, 1876, when under threat of the House investigation of his railroad transactions. For greater secrecy he had mailed it to the Parker House, though he knew Fisher was at the Commonwealth Hotel, and had then telegraphed Fisher to call for it. He enclosed a draft letter exonerating himself. "I want you to send me a letter such as this enclosed draft," he wrote. "Regard this letter as strictly confidential. Do not show it to anyone." And he endorsed on the back, "Burn this letter." Taken with

[1] Statement of R. R. Bowker to author, July 11, 1931.
[2] Moorfield Storey Papers.

Blaine's solemn statement of April 24, 1876, that "My whole connection with the road has been open as the day. If there had been anything to conceal about it, I should never have touched it," this disclosure was damaging in the extreme.

The reformers fell upon the letters with exultation. Carl Schurz, in a series of address as unrelenting as his brilliant German mind could make them, drove home the full meaning of Blaine's apparent use of the Speakership to advance his railroad interests. His speech in Brooklyn on August 5 was a masterpiece of logic and sarcasm, and it stung Blaine into a libel suit which was never pushed. While the *Nation* hammered its condemnation into the intellectuals, and *Harper's Weekly* into its large popular following, the English-born cartoonist Gillam in *Puck,* with a ferocity which even Nast had scarcely equalled, depicted the Republican candidate as "the tattooed man." Various editors did not fail to stamp Blaine's misstatements in plain language. He had said, for example, that following his purchase of bonds of the Little Rock & Fort Smith Railroad, only a single act of Congress had been passed applying to the line and it merely rectified a previous error in legislation; whereas the bill had actually repealed the proviso that the railroad's land grant should not be sold for more than $2.50 an acre, thus making the property more valuable. Week after week Godkin reprinted a series of Blaine's contradictory utterances in damning parallel columns, and the Independents circulated the list in hundreds of thousands of pamphlets. The whole assault was, apart from Gillam's cartoons, kept at a dignified level, and the speeches and editorials dealt in legitimate arguments—that is, in undeniable facts affected with a public interest. Yet the attacks were perhaps pressed too far. At any rate, a later generation has been more lenient with Blaine. We are probably safe in saying that this fascinating and adroit leader was not deliberately dishonest—he was simply a man of lax principle who was found out and who now paid a terrific penalty.

III

It was inevitable that many Republicans should regard this line of attack as slanderous and seek to retaliate by some personal assault upon Cleveland. As early as July 21 the great bombshell of the campaign was exploded. A despised Buffalo rag, the *Evening Telegraph,* spread broad upon its pages what it called "A Terrible Tale," showing that Cleveland had once maintained a connection with a Buffalo woman named Halpin whose illegitimate son was later placed in an orphan asylum. The story was garnished with unctuous detail, and concluded with a quotation of the history of Mordred and Margaret from Lowell's *Legend of Brittany*. Instantly it was telegraphed all over the United States. The Republican press took it up with cackling glee, while the most powerful of church organs, the *Independent*, encouraged the pulpit to interpret it as requiring Cleveland's defeat. After reciting the initial charges, the *Telegraph* gradually added a series of allegations venomous in their falsity. As mayor, Cleveland had offended the worst elements of the Buffalo population, and from saloons and dives there poured forth a flood of scandalous inventions. Two Buffalo ministers, feeling the moment auspicious to strike a blow for morals and notoriety, thrust themselves into the limelight. One, the Rev. C. W. Winchester of the Plymouth Methodist Episcopal Church, drew a crowd to a salacious sermon on "Absalom the Fast Young Man." His Absalom was crudely identifiable as Cleveland. The other, the Rev. George H. Ball, D.D., of the Hudson Street Baptist Church, a former editor of the *Baptist Union*, made himself a national nuisance by Chadband letters to the Boston *Journal* and other papers. Posing as Buffalo's exponent of decency, he actually gave currency to indecent falsehoods.

To his friend Goodyear, who wrote asking what the party should do, Cleveland replied with the historic phrase: "Tell the truth." It was a common-sense decision which penetrated the heart of the situation. From the truth he had little to fear. Part of the original story was true; admit the facts, and the falsehoods would disappear like noxious fumes before a fresh gale. Within a few days, indeed, the hounds of truth were on the heels of the worst fabrications. Not only were investigations made in Buffalo by agents of the New York Mugwumps, but a thorough inquiry was conducted for the *Independent* by the Rev. Dr. Kinsley Twining, whose vindication of Cleveland's general character was emphatic. The Boston Committee of One Hundred sent to Buffalo an efficient lawyer named Hodges, who on invitation from Dr. Ball investigated his "proofs" of general dissipation and found them worthless. The Buffalo *Courier* forced Ball to write a letter in which he lamely admitted the falsity of certain of his statements. Meanwhile, an interesting event had occurred in Albany. Dr. James Freeman Clarke suddenly appeared there—the great Unitarian minister of Boston, the friend of Emerson, Margaret Fuller, and Sumner, the champion of liberty in every form. Half the people of America were familiar with portraits of his fine old face framed in silvery hair and beard, his shrewd, kindly eyes peering through spectacles. He had an hour's conversation with Cleveland. The governor told him everything, and Clarke emerged his firm champion.

Henry Ward Beecher took the same course. On October 22 he appeared before a great Brooklyn meeting, read a manly letter which Cleveland had written to Mrs. Beecher repudiating all the principal charges, and declared that he would fight harder for the Democratic candidate than ever. In all the history of politics, he said, he did not believe that "lies so cruel, so base, so atrocious as those concerning Mr. Cleveland" had ever been set in motion. Several of the best Buffalo clergymen defended Cleveland. The conclusion of fair-minded investigators was summed up by the report of sixteen well-known Republicans of Buffalo, including Ansley Willcox, Henry W. Sprague, and the historian J. N. Larned, who declared:

Our examination of the general charges which have been made against Governor Cleveland's private character shows that they are wholly untrue. In every instance in which the reports and insinuations have been tangible enough to furnish us a clue to guide us in our investigations they have been positively proved to be false. The attack upon Governor Cleveland's character is thoroughly discredited when we consider the sources from which it comes.

The simple truth, which reveals a transient weakness on Cleveland's part but also throws light upon his latent strength, requires a brief statement.[1] Maria Halpin was a young widow of Pennsylvania family who, leaving two children behind her, came to Buffalo from Jersey City about 1871, and found employment first as a collar-maker and then in the drygoods store of Flint & Kent, where she was soon placed at the head of the cloak department. She was tall, pretty, pleasing in manner, and spoke French. She attended the fashionable St. John's Episcopal Church and made numerous friends. For a time she accepted the attentions of several men, including Cleveland, who was a year

[1] These pages are based on a careful study of the Buffalo press for 1876 and 1884; on Cleveland's letters, including many yet unpublished; on the Democratic campaign pamphlet which contains the record of the investigation by a committee of Buffalo citizens; and on the files of the hostile N. Y. *Tribune* and *Sun.*

her elder—she was thirty-six in 1874. When a son was born to her on September 14 of that year, whom she named Oscar Folsom Cleveland, she charged Cleveland with its paternity. Although, as he wrote a Boston friend when President, he did not know whether he was really responsible,[1] he consented to make provision for the child. Those closest to him believed that Mrs. Halpin was uncertain who was the father; that she fixed upon him because she hoped to make him marry her; and that he did not question her charge because the other men in the scrape were married.[2] As the Rev. Kinsley Twining declared, "After the preliminary offence . . . his conduct was singularly honorable, showing no attempt to evade responsibility, and doing all that he could to meet the duties involved, of which marriage was certainly not one." His subsequent indifference to the child was due to his doubts about his fatherhood.

Through a series of trying events his course continued to be straightforward. While nursing the child, the mother, then living at 11 East Genesee Street, began drinking heavily and neglecting it. In these circumstances Cleveland turned to a much older friend who had been county judge while he was sheriff, Roswell L. Burrows, and placed the entire matter in his hands. Burrows, after investigation, and without Cleveland's immediate knowledge, had the woman taken to the Providence Asylum, an institution for mentally deranged persons managed by the Sisters of Charity. Mrs. Halpin was persuaded to remain here for a short time, while legal steps were taken through the Overseer of the Poor to commit the boy to the Protestant Orphan Asylum on Main Street (March 9, 1876), at the usual board rate of $5 a week, which Cleveland was to pay through Judge Burrows. At the same time, Cleveland gave Mrs. Halpin the means of establishing a business of her own in Niagara Falls. But growing lonely for the child and finding that by surrendering him she had lost her claim on the supposed father, she immediately returned to Buffalo and employed Milo A. Whitney as her attorney in efforts to recover her son. When these failed she took the desperate step, on April 28, 1876, of kidnapping him. Judge Burrows intervened again, and in July there was a final commitment of the boy to the orphanage, from which later he was adopted by one of the best families in western New York, in time becoming a distinguished pro-

---

[1] Cleveland Papers.
[2] Cleveland Bacon to author, Dec. 15, 1931.

fessional man. He thus disappeared from Cleveland's life.

Mrs. Halpin, who had admitted to her lawyer that Cleveland had never made any promise of marriage, also disappeared. We hear of her only once more. Twenty years later, in 1895, when she had remarried and was living in New Rochelle, N. Y., she sent President Cleveland two letters, one of which is still preserved, asking for money,[1] and threatening to publish facts in her possession.

All these events of 1874–76 were kept out of the press, and but for partisan malice need never have been lifted from the sphere of Cleveland's private concerns, where they belonged. Those who knew all the facts were never inclined to judge him harshly. A weaker or more callous man in his place would have tried, with some prospect of success, to deny responsibility for the child; but Cleveland saw the matter through in the most courageous way. He might have said, in the words that Alexander Hamilton used after the Mrs. Reynolds affair, that "I have paid pretty dearly for the folly;" but at any rate, like Hamilton, he had acted a man's part.

Had this scandal been brought out during the Chicago convention, it would doubtless have prevented Cleveland's nomination; had it been brought out in the last fortnight of the campaign, it would doubtless have defeated his election. But appearing when it did, it soon fell into its proper proportions. It was evident that the real issue was the public integrity and capacity of the two candidates, and that old questions of private conduct were essentially irrelevant. This view was neatly expressed by one of the Mugwumps. A great national meeting of some eight hundred Independents was held in the University Club Theatre in New York on July 22 to endorse Cleveland. Much enthusiasm appeared.[2] As the members trooped forth they were handed copies of the lurid attack by the Buffalo *Telegraph,* and were thrown into consternation. That evening a select few of the Mugwumps met at the University Club for dinner. Carl Schurz, who sat at the head of the table, was depressed, and when later George W. Curtis and others came in, Curtis also was laboring under a profound shock. As he expressed his discouragement a Chicago gentleman broke in to ask if they would like his opinion. "We are told," he said,[3] "that Mr. Blaine

---

[1] Sept. 9, 1895. Cleveland Papers.
[2] Solomon B. Griffin, *People and Politics,* 92 ff.
[3] Cf. M. A. De Wolfe Howe, *Moorfield Storey: The Portrait of an Independent.*

has been delinquent in office but blameless in private life, while Mr. Cleveland has been a model of official integrity, but culpable in his personal relations. We should therefore elect Mr. Cleveland to the public office which he is so well qualified to fill, and remand Mr. Blaine to the private station which he is admirably fitted to adorn." Godkin phrased the issue with equal pith. Which was better for the Presidency, he asked, a man who, like Cromwell, Franklin, Hamilton, and Webster, had been unchaste, or a man who had sold his official influence for money, and had broken his word in order to destroy documentary evidence of his corruption?

The precise origin of this scandalous attack remains unknown. Before the convention Cleveland had spoken frankly of his "woman scrape" to ex-Speaker Chapin and others,[1] and Tammany had spread hints of it in Chicago. At a later date one of the principal Democratic newspapers of the country formally charged that the national Republican leaders were responsible: [2]

Mr. Cleveland was nominated for the presidency on July 11. Some intimations of this scandal had attended the discussions at Chicago. On July 12 there arrived at Augusta by the first train Col. Zimro A. Smith, editor of the Boston *Journal*, about the only prominent newspaper in New England which was supporting Mr. Blaine's candidacy. He had been secretary of the Maine Republican State Committee, was one of Mr. Blaine's most confidential workers, and owed his position in Boston largely to Mr. Blaine's money and influence. He was in secret consultation with Mr. Blaine for several hours during the morning of July 12. He took the afternoon train for Boston, arriving there late that night. On the following morning a reporter of the Boston *Journal* was sent to Buffalo with the sole object, as was afterwards explicitly stated in the *Journal*, of inquiring into the circumstances of the scandal concerning Mr. Cleveland.

The reporter was in Buffalo until the morning of July 21. On the afternoon of July 21 the publication was made in the poverty-stricken Buffalo newspaper of ill repute before referred to. The scandal fell flat. Not one respectable newspaper in the East referred to it, and only one newspaper of extended circulation in the West. If it was the purpose of the Republican managers to make use of it as a campaign force they must give it a more influential parentage. On July 22 the Boston *Journal* printed all its scandalous story on its first page, with glaring headlines, editorial reference, and all the devices which a newspaper may employ to secure attention to one of its articles.

[1] A. C. Chapin to author, July 20, 1931.
[2] N. Y. *World*, May 19, 1885.

It would be painful to believe that Blaine had any connection with the matter, and there is no evidence for doing so. But the Republican leaders never rebuked the attacks, and as the *Nation* pointed out in the last week of the campaign, a systematic organization somewhere kept the scandal alive to the very end.

And what of Cleveland? His letters show that, while outwardly little perturbed by the attacks, at heart he was filled with anguish. That his old friends in Buffalo, who had celebrated his nomination with a hundred guns, with fireworks and parading bands, should listen to these slanders; that a venerable minister like Dr. Ball should stab at him with such malice! Never again was he able to feel at home in Buffalo. Manning, Whitney, and Gorman paid no attention to the scandal, which was dealt with by his Buffalo friends, Bissell, Goodyear, and John G. Milburn. He never flinched, and there is a revelation of character in the angry letter to Lockwood at the end of July: [1]

I don't know but I am all "out," but I am going to be frank enough to say to you that it does not seem to me that things are getting into just the right shape in Buffalo. What is the matter with Rohr?

I learned last night that McCune had started the story and told it to newspaper men (one at least) that I had nothing to do really with the subject of the *Telegraph* story—that is, that I am innocent—and that my silence was to shield my friend Oscar Folsom. Now is this man crazy or does he wish to ruin somebody? Is he fool enough to suppose for a moment that if such was the truth (which it is not, so far as the motive for silence is concerned) that I would permit my dead friend's memory to suffer for my sake? And Mrs. Folsom and her daughter at my house at this very time!! I am afraid that I shall have occasion to pray to be delivered from my friends.

How often I wish that I was free and that some good friend of mine was running instead of myself. I wish I knew what, if anything, is the matter. Can't you tell me frankly some things I want to hear? This story of McCune's of course must be stopped. I have prevented its publication in one paper at least.

McCune's story was eight years later popularized by Paul Leicester Ford in his sentimental novel *The Honorable Peter Stirling*. Cleveland was enormously relieved when the whole subject gradually died away. He wrote Bissell on September 11 that "I hope now that the scandal business is about wound up that you have a little freedom from the annoyance and trouble which it necessarily brought in its train. I think

[1] July 31, 1884. Cleveland Papers.

the matter was arranged in the best possible way, and that the policy
of not cringing was not only necessary but the only possible way. King's
intrusion made me trouble. And now Cochrane has published something just as bad in a Chicago paper. I don't see what possessed him
to do it."

It is amusing to mention, in conclusion, that one of his allies got into
trouble. Godkin, with his Irish love of battle, published in the *Evening
Post* an editorial on Dr. Ball in which he asserted that he had had a
disreputable early career in Indiana, and had left a city there in haste
for insulting a lady. Unfortunately for Godkin, there were two Rev.
Dr. Balls. The unprincipled minister who was run out of Owensville,
Ind., was another—and a libel suit resulted.[1] Godkin had to fight it
out in the courts with the angry Buffalo cleric, but thanks to a skilful
defense by John G. Milburn, who undertook the case, finally escaped
without paying damages. Cleveland, with his usual sense of duty, paid
most of Milburn's bill. It should also be mentioned that Cleveland
forbade any use of his opponents' tactics. A nasty and mendacious
story sprang up regarding Blaine's marriage. Once a packet of alleged
"evidence" upon Blaine's private life was brought to Cleveland. It was
for sale, and he paid for it. "Are all the papers here?" he demanded.
Then, without looking at the packet, and adding to it some similar
documents which had reached him, he drew up a waste-basket, slowly
tore the sheets to bits, called a porter, and stood over him as he burned
the material in the open fireplace. "The other side," he remarked, "can
have a monopoly of all the dirt in this campaign." [2]

IV

The principal factors in the campaign, apart from the dominant issue
of Blaine's integrity, were five: the Democratic schism in New York,
where Tammany was in revolt; the old-soldier vote, vigorously appealed to by the Republicans through Pensions Bureau officials; the
Prohibitionist vote, cutting into Blaine's strength; the lingering distrust of the South, and the business depression of 1884, engendering a
certain discontent with Republican policies. In addition, there were the
accidental but unforgettable occurrences of Blaine's last fatal week

[1] Denis T. Lynch, *Grover Cleveland*, p. 231, makes the curious error of accepting
Godkin's libelous editorial as true.
[2] Bishop, *Presidential Nominations and Elections*, 66–68, quoting Lamont.

in New York city.

Tammany was important for the votes it controlled in New York and for its influence upon the Irish-Americans throughout the country. This total Irish vote was estimated by careful judges to approach a half-million, and the Republicans made assiduous efforts to win it.[1] Blaine's mother had been an Irish Catholic, and his sister was the mother-superior of a Catholic convent. He had been outspoken in his sympathy for the Irish cause, and particularly for the Irish Land League which, under Parnell and Davitt, was striving to abolish absentee landlordism in the island; and when Secretary of State he had shown a distinct animosity toward the British Government. His nomination was the signal for the *Irish World,* a weekly edited by Patrick Ford and the greatest agency in marshaling Irish sentiment in the United States, to swing to his side. John Devoy's *Irish Nation* followed suit. On July 28th a great Blaine rally was held at Chickering Hall in New York by the Irish-American Independents, with prominent Tammany men on the platform. Judge John Brennan of Iowa hurled a gibe at Beecher and Curtis: "If ever I go to heaven and meet them there, I hope God will let me camp on the outside!" Many Catholic priests believed that Cleveland's veto of the Catholic Protectory Bill, though fully explained, indicated a latent hostility. However, some of the clergy, including the Bishop of Albany, resented the effort to drag the church into politics, and declared for Cleveland. In New York city the influential Dr. Edward McGlynn, Henry George's friend, praised the Democratic nominee warmly and rebuked the display of clerical antagonism. The governor wrote Bissell on October 5 that "The Catholic question is being treated, and so well treated in so many different ways that I should not be at all surprised if what has been done by the enemy should turn to our advantage." [2] Gorman paid special attention to the subject.[3]

For week after week John Kelly hesitated, while most Tammany leaders remained hostile toward the national ticket. The veteran boss actually hoped for a time that Cleveland might be forced to retire as

[1] The Irish-born in the U. S. in 1880 numbered 1,855,000, of whom 499,455 were in New York State. Tenth Census.
[2] Cleveland Papers.
[3] See M. P. Curran, *Life of Patrick A. Collins,* 86–89, for a letter from a Catholic bishop denouncing Cleveland as a "cowardly bigot," and threatening use of the church against such supporters as Collins. Collins called on the governor, was convinced of the falsity of the charges against him, and delivered a speech of which a million copies were printed.

a candidate, and was encouraged in this by Dana of the *Sun*, who in his shrill abuse of the governor repeatedly demanded that he resign the nomination. In 1887 some interesting letters of Kelly's came to light in the New York *World*.[1] Under date of August 27th, he informed Gunther K. Ackerman, the secretary of Tammany, that he had talked with many politicians who disliked Cleveland and wished he might be thrust aside. "I have no hope or expectation that that can be accomplished. The Governor is surrounded only by those who give him encouragement and persuade him that his success is beyond peradventure. This is always the case. Candidates very rarely see or speak to their enemies. I am strongly of the opinion even now, that if he were to withdraw and Allen G. Thurman were to be nominated in his place, that the Labor, Anti-Monopoly, and Greenback agitation would subside. And I am also of the opinion that Butler would leave the field to Thurman and support him enthusiastically." Active efforts were being made by Tammany elements and other anti-Cleveland Democrats to nourish Butler's Greenback candidacy in the hope that it would cost Cleveland New York State, and these efforts were abetted by the Republicans.[2]

But in the end Kelly was forced into line, and carried most of his Tammany subordinates with him in a sullen and tepid adherence to Cleveland. His correspondence with Ackerman and others, as later revealed in the *World*, showed that he was carefully weighing the arguments pro and con.[3] Much as he hated Cleveland, he hated the Republican party more, and he saw that it could do nothing for Tammany. Early in September he called the district leaders into a caucus. Though some were truculent, he lectured them angrily, declaring that Tammany Hall always had been Democratic and always would be, and that it must now swallow the Cleveland pill. His decree was formally ratified at a meeting of the Tammany General Committee on September 12, at which Thomas F. Gilroy read a humble-pie address, and which voted 810 to 87 to endorse the national ticket. Nevertheless, Grady delivered a fiery denunciation of Cleveland, and was presently making stump speeches for Butler and the Greenbackers. Dana also, at almost ruinous cost to the *Sun*, which in a few months lost half its circulation, lifted the Butler banner.

[1] See long *World* article, April 17, 1887.
[2] Cf. N. Y. *Sun*, Aug. 10, 1884.
[3] Cf. Kelly's letter of Aug. 4 in *World*, April 17, 1887.

For reaching the Union veterans the Republicans had a perfect agency in the Pensions Bureau, which was all but avowedly a political machine, and they showed singularly little scruple in employing it. In September the head of the Bureau, Col. W. W. Dudley, handed in his resignation to take effect not immediately but on November 10, and set out for Ohio. For two months, while drawing pay from the government at $5,000 a year, he devoted all his time to mobilizing the soldier vote for his party. The arguments were obvious—Democratic stoppage of pensions, Democratic hostility to all veterans, increased Republican generosity in the event of victory, and so on. The *Nation* later characterized his operations as "disgraceful, being nothing less than the use of the Pension Bureau, with all its power and influence, as a bribe for votes." [1] When his Democratic successor, Chauncey F. Black, wrote his first annual report, he was equally severe, declaring that the Republicans had utilized the Bureau to pour "a tide of men and money" into the doubtful areas. [2] Though the phrase was exaggerated, highly improper work had gone on during the fall of 1884. The official figures show that the sums paid for the field expenses—not the salaries—of special pensions examiners in the first four months of 1884 had averaged $28,250 monthly. But in September and October the field force was increased by fifty per cent, and the expenditures rose to an average of nearly $46,000 monthly. In the Indiana district the amount paid in April for examiners' expenses was not quite $1,500, and in October $2,885; in the Ohio district the sum paid in June was $3,950, and in October $7,550. Unquestionably thousands of veterans who might have voted for Cleveland were persuaded that the continuance of the pension system depended upon Republican success.

But this was merely part of a larger effort. Strenuous exertions were made by the Republicans to prove that Democratic rule would be a dangerous experiment, for low tariffs would bring the business structure down in ruins, while the disloyalty of Southern politicians would sap the foundations of the Union. As John G. Carlisle put it later: [3]

It was said that the election of a Democratic President would be immediately followed by the prostration of our manufacturing industries, the derangement of our finances, the debasement of our currency, and the destruction of the

---

[1] Feb. 26, 1885.
[2] Report, Commissioner of Pensions, 1885.
[3] Speech of June 29, 1888; N. Y. *Times, World*, June 30.

public credit; and that even the civil and political rights of the people would not be secure. According to these partisan prophets, the Supreme Court of the United States was to be reorganized and the Constitutional amendments annulled; the soldiers and sailors of the Union were to be deprived of the pensions and bounties heretofore granted to them, and all the terms and agreements of the adjustment which succeeded the late civil war were to be entirely disregarded.

This, remarked the *Nation*, was "a simple and strictly accurate description of the view taken by a large proportion of the Republican party." [1] It is difficult today to believe that such statements could find credence. Yet from a hundred platforms it was declared that fearful perils would flow from Democratic success, and tens of thousands believed that the hard-won victory of Lincoln and Grant might yet be undone. The negro would not only lose his ballot, but be virtually re-enslaved.

The business depression of 1884, which began to lift in the autumn, assisted the Democratic campaign far less than Gorman had hoped. The British Minister reported to his government that from the very beginning of the year the tariff agitation and the steady coinage of silver had disturbed industry.[2] Before the campaign opened, the shocking failure of Grant & Ward, sinking the aged general into utter poverty, had created a national sensation. This occurred in May, and ruined many trusting investors. Other disastrous failures of the year included the Northern Pacific Railroad and the North River Construction Company. Stocks sank to a low level, there were many defaults, and unemployment increased. Inevitably this bred discontent with the party in power, especially in New York.

Some business interests, on the other hand, feared the unsettling effects of a change, while the Republicans made adroit use of Butler's candidacy to draw workingmen's votes away from Cleveland. The old Labor-Greenback movement had been powerful in the East in 1878, and there seemed a possibility of its revival. The Democrats, in their fear of the Greenback ticket, early sent Samuel J. Randall to Butler in an effort to get him to withdraw, but in vain, for he had already obtained a direct subsidy from Elkins. It later leaked out that during July Secretary Chandler and other Republican leaders had met Butler

[1] July 5, 1888.
[2] Foreign Office 5, No. 1903. Sackville-West Papers.

aboard a warship in Portsmouth harbor, N. H., promised him funds for his Eastern canvass, and secured his acceptance. Gossip of the time had it that Jay Gould supplied the funds. At any rate, all the expenses of his special train in New York and Massachusetts were paid from Republican sources. At the outset, but not later, Butler had the support of John Kelly.[1]

Of all the special factors in the campaign, that which most clearly and emphatically assisted Cleveland was the prohibitionist movement under John P. St. John of Kansas, whose hopeless fight was one of the dramatic features of the struggle. A remarkable story lay back of it. St. John was a Republican governor of Kansas, a convert to Prohibition, who in 1882 had stood for a third term. A popular Democrat named Glick, with the aid of the anti-prohibitionist elements in the Republican ranks, had defeated him. Nevertheless, having the churches and temperance organizations enthusiastically back of him, St. John remained powerful, and as the Republican national convention approached in 1884, he headed a strong Western movement in favor of some declaration favorable to the prohibitionist cause. In this he was abetted by Senator Preston B. Plumb of Kansas, who wished him sent to the Chicago convention as a regular Republican delegate.[2] But the anti-prohibitionists of the State proved able to block his ambitions. When the convention opened, St. John was there—but only as an unwelcome observer.

At Chicago the Republicans painfully humiliated the temperance forces. Miss Frances E. Willard, head of the W. C. T. U., had obtained through that organization some 20,000 names to a petition asking the convention to support the temperance cause, and she presented it in person to the platform committee. She was politely bowed out, and a delegation of distillers and brewers was shortly bowed in. Some of the politicians derisively showed them the temperance petition, and asked what should be done with it. "Kick it under the table," was the reply. When the convention adjourned this massive document, with its host of names, was found on the floor, covered with dust and stained with tobacco-juice; the platform was silent on temperance; and Miss Willard's indignation was extreme. When her followers urged St. John to

---

[1] M. P. Curran, *Life of Patrick A. Collins;* B. F. Butler, *Butler's Book,* 983; Lynch, *Cleveland,* 263.
[2] W. E. Connelley, *Preston B. Plumb,* 274 ff.

accept the nomination of the Prohibition party, he did so, shortly setting up remarkably efficient headquarters under the attic of the Fifth Avenue Hotel in New York. The Republicans were to rue their indifference to him.

v

Cleveland remained hard at work in Albany throughout most of the campaign, the managers frequently running up from New York to consult him. The first of his few public appearances was at the official notification meeting in Albany on July 29, a curious affair. Col. W. F. Vilas of Wisconsin and the notification committee arrived at the executive mansion in a drizzle, with a band playing the doxology! There was a small gathering—Manning, Perry Belmont, Lamont, Erastus Corning, some of the governor's staff, two of his sisters, two nieces, and Mrs. Oscar Folsom and her daughter Frances. The speeches were short and undistinguished. Later the occasion was remembered for an inspired remark by Colonel William Gorham Rice. Encouraging the young aides to be gallant, he said, "If one of you young fellows doesn't take an interest in that pretty Miss Folsom, the governor is likely to walk off with her himself!" [1]

Early in August Cleveland went to the Adirondacks with Dr. S. B. Ward and others, meanwhile struggling to finish his letter of acceptance. "I am having a good time and find this place very quiet and nice," he wrote Lamont from Derby's Prospect House on the Upper Saranac.[2] "None the less I worked on the letter until two o'clock this morning, and was up at half past six. I don't know whether I just like it or not, but such as it is, I regard it as nearly completed." He spoke of Tammany and the Greenback party. "Now this is for you personally. I want to tell you just how I feel. I had rather be beaten in this race than to truckle to Butler or Kelly. I don't want any pledge made for me that will violate my professions or betray and deceive the good people that believe in us. Of course I appreciate my relations to the party and the earnest desire on the part of many good men to win at almost any price. But I cannot forget that a stiff upper lip may be the best means of bringing about a united action, and that if such a thing is not accomplished the chance to win without the element that threatens trouble is

1 Wm. Gorham Rice to author, June 11, 1930.
2 Aug. 11, 1884. Cleveland Papers.

only a forlorn one." Three days later he mailed the letter of acceptance, completed at midnight, to Lamont with an expression of deference to Tilden: [1]

The subjects I have treated of I have tried to put in on the theory that they are very closely connected with the very framework of the government and that their treatment does not constitute a commentary on the platform. . . .

I wish both Mr. Tilden and Mr. Hendricks could be consulted about it and that it could be read to them. Can't Mr. Manning see them both Saturday?

I want the thing to suit those who are wiser than I, but I have given it a good deal of thought, and seriously hope that it will not be deemed necessary to change it. If, however, it is thought necessary to change the form of expression it may be done, but if the substance must be changed of course it must be submitted to me.

The letter, like Blaine's, was not a document of great importance. Blaine had devoted half his space to the tariff, and the rest to what the *Nation* called "a collection of platitudes drawn out to the utmost limits of verbosity." Cleveland gave his general approval to the Democratic platform, endorsed the principles of civil service reform, called for laws promoting the welfare of the workingmen, declared his opposition to prohibition, and announced that he favored a constitutional amendment limiting the President to a single term. That announcement was destined in 1888 to cause him some embarrassment. But the document lacked the boldness and definiteness that were to characterize his best state papers.

Partly because of his official duties and partly from innate reserve, Cleveland refused to be drawn into active campaigning and followed the example of Tilden, Hayes, and Garfield in keeping aloof from the hurly-burly. When the Republicans made an attempt to exploit his failure to enlist in the Civil War, he wrote a frank letter on the subject. The attempt did not get far, for it was obvious that the plumed knight had kept equally distant from the firing line; eight years earlier Hayes's friend, Gen. E. F. Noyes, had bracketed Blaine, Conkling, and Cameron as men "invincible in peace and invisible in war." Cleveland also wrote a short letter to Curtis on civil service reform,[2] and was at pains to answer misleading statements regarding his official attitude toward labor. He constantly gave advice to the campaign managers,

[1] August 14, 1884. Cleveland Papers.
[2] Oct. 24, 1884. Cleveland Papers.

and furnished some helpful information. But as the campaign grew in excitement he remained calm. Great torchlight parades, with bands and transparencies, roared through the cities. The Democratic hosts clamored in unison:

> Blaine, Blaine, James G. Blaine,
> The continental liar from the State of Maine,
> *Burn this letter!*

and the Republican cohorts chorused back:

> Ma! Ma! Where's my pa?
> Gone to the White House,
> *Ha! Ha! Ha!*

At Albany the governor quietly kept on with his tasks while troops of speakers took the field. Blaine set forth on a six weeks' campaign trip to the West, speaking to four hundred audiences, and was seconded by John Sherman, Hoar, Allison, Logan, and Depew. Young Roosevelt and Henry Cabot Lodge were expected to bolt, but they declined. Early in October Roosevelt came back from his Dakota ranch, and New York reporters found him at his house, very sunburnt, walking up and down around a pile of red apples and purple grapes, and sipping sherry. He mentioned that he had shot three grizzlies—"three terrors;" one had weighed 1200 pounds. He was out for Blaine. Asked about Cleveland, he declared: "I think he is not a man who should be put in that office, and there is no lack of reasons for it. His public career, in the first place, and then private reasons as well." He was soon giving New York and Massachusetts audiences a history of Albany affairs in which his own rôle was not minimized. On the Democratic side Randall, Thurman, Carlisle, Bayard, and Morrison were all busy, while particular importance attached to the efforts of Hendricks in Indiana. This urbane leader, who had been both governor and Senator, proved a tower of strength. At one moment he was exposing the defalcations under Secretary Chandler; at another crawling unscathed from a train wreck in Illinois; at a third addressing 30,000 people at a Shelbyville, Ind., barbecue. In New York his influence was far from negligible, for he was a friend of Kelly and Tammany, and did much to prevent the threatened bolt.[1] On election day in Massachusetts 45 per cent of the

[1] Cf. J. W. Holcombe and T. W. Skinner, *Life of Thomas A. Hendricks.*

voting population remained at home; in Illinois 21 per cent; but in Indiana, only 7 per cent.

In the list of Republican speakers there were two conspicuous absentees. Roscoe Conkling despised the "man-milliner" Curtis and his Mugwump associates, but he detested Blaine far more. After delivering his classic retort to the question why he did not speak for Blaine—"I do not engage in criminal practise"—he began secretly enlisting his Utica friends against the plumed knight. A dramatic moment in the campaign occurred when Blaine reached that city on his electioneering tour. The *Press,* a Republican paper, declared that not more than 1500 people came to greet him, half of them curious Cleveland men. "The sky was softly clear and the atmosphere warm, but Blaine thought it a cold day. There were a few cheers and some hisses. And when the train began to move again, someone cried out, 'All aboard for Little Rock!' " [1] In Vermont Senator Edmunds, who had long been convinced that Blaine was a political menace, was equally recalcitrant. Indeed, he had once said that "Whenever Thurman and I have joined hands against Jay Gould and fellows of that sort in the Senate, James G. Blaine has invariably started up from behind Gould's breastworks, musket in hand." [2] After much urging, this grim Puritan now made one speech which was notable chiefly for its frigid avoidance of Blaine's name. Two years after the election Edmunds published a letter explaining his silence, in which he said that he had not felt able to tell untruths about the candidate even to retain his party in power. [3] When Blaine met him at the funeral of Chester A. Arthur in 1886, and Edmunds offered his hand, Blaine refused it.

Cleveland was prevailed upon to make only two set speeches. With his usual moral courage, he declined to attend a Tammany rally, but late in October he visited Newark, N. J., and Bridgeport, Conn., speaking to large audiences on civil service reform, tax reduction, and the needs of labor. His most interesting and picturesque trip, however, was that earlier in the month to Buffalo. A tremendous demonstration had been arranged as a testimonial of the city's affection, and its enthusiasm, color, and childish display typified the picturesque side of the campaign.

[1] See C. E. Russell, *Blaine of Maine,* 403, for the evidence that Conkling contributed to the N. Y. *World* the scathing attacks on Blaine signed "A Stalwart Republican."
[2] N. Y. *Sun,* Sept. 7, 1884.
[3] *Nation,* Nov. 25, 1886.

Cleveland was welcomed on the evening of October 2 by railway yards aflare with bonfires and the whistling of scores of locomotives. The units of a parade of 20,000 men already filled the side streets, their torches and lanterns seeming to observers from upper windows to present a sheet of flame. At nine o'clock Cleveland took his place in the line, band after band broke forth, and the march began. There were ward clubs, the Buffalo Democratic Legion, the Batavia Guards, the Lockport Cleveland Club, and organizations from Rochester, Elmira, Syracuse, Erie, and other cities. Nothing like it, men boasted, had ever been seen outside New York City. The costumes were ingeniously varied: a corps garbed in gray trousers, white flannel shirts, and white helmets, performing military evolutions; a dignified block of men in black silk hats, frock coats, and white gloves; a mediaeval-looking crew in chain-armor bearing battle-axes; a platoon in army blue, and so on. The Niagara Falls Cleveland Club carried a black sphere painted, "The Rev. Dr. Ball To Go Over The Falls." Everywhere waved transparencies with the shibboleths of the day: "No Star Route Frauds; No Sanborn Contracts; No Whiskey Ring"—"Soap Won't Wash Out the Record"—"Grady Can't Scare Us"—"Sumptuary Laws Destroy Personal Liberty"—"No Jay Gould Lobbyist For Us." Most pleasing of all to Cleveland were the decorations of the city, for the business buildings were covered with bunting and colored mottoes, while the residential districts showed festoons of Chinese lanterns or his portrait brightly illumined. On his return to Albany he wrote Bissell with simple-hearted gratification: [1]

We arrived here safely yesterday morning and I did a good day's work. All our party agreed that the trip had been a pleasant one, and that the ovation was much beyond anticipations and in point of fact the largest they have ever seen. I was very much pleased that Corning thought so well of it. He said: "O Hell! Of course the procession could be gotten up with money, but a man don't decorate and illuminate his house unless he wants to!" The people here seem to be as much pleased at the success of the demonstration as I am, and express themselves freely on the subject. I attended a very nice dinner party this evening, and I was handsomely congratulated by some of the best people here.

Such parades were nowhere more spectacular than in New York, where the Mugwump fervor burned brightest. "I well remember,"

[1] Oct. 5, 1884. Cleveland Papers.

writes William B. Hornblower, "the anti-Blaine parade of 1884 in which I participated. It was a typically bleak fall day, but the enthusiasm of the occasion kept us warm. The Lawyers' Division formed on Pine and Cedar Streets about noon. . . . It was past five and quite dark when we marched past the reviewing stand at Madison Square and disbanded. It was certainly a wonderful object-lesson to the Blaine Republicans. In our ranks were hundreds of lawyers, among them some of the best-known men at the bar. Veteran Democrats marched side by side with gray-headed men who had participated in the formation of the Republican party. Of the active men at the bar between the ages of twenty and forty, it seemed as if all but a handful were with us. As we marched up Broadway and Fifth Avenue with ranks reaching from curb to curb and with inspiring strains of martial music, we could see ahead of us as far as the eye could reach the divisions which had preceded us, with their banners waving, and we could hear constantly repeated the war-cries of 'Blaine, Blaine, James G. Blaine, The monumental liar from the State of Maine,' 'Burn this letter,' and 'Kind regards to Mrs. Fisher.' " [1]

Yet in the final weeks it became evident that the result would be decided by a small margin. The State election of September in Maine showed a greater Republican majority than in 1880, but that in Vermont, where Edmunds' chilliness had spread to the voters, gave the party a lessened vote. The October elections in Ohio were eagerly awaited. While Blaine spent two weeks there, and he, McKinley, and John Sherman all laid emphasis on the tariff, Schurz made powerful speeches for the Democrats. The result was equivocal. Though the Republican ticket—merely a State ticket, of course—triumphed by majorities averaging about thirteen thousand, and their showing was better than in 1883, it was not so good as in 1880. Efforts were redoubled in all the critical States. In Ohio the Federal marshal appointed a host of deputies for election day, 2500 in Cincinnati alone thus being placed temporarily on the Federal payroll. Meanwhile, the Democrats were unfortunately hampered by lack of funds. A typewritten memorandum in the Cleveland papers lists the chief donors, showing that William H. Barnum gave $27,500, Cooper & Hewitt and Abram S. Hewitt $25,300, William L. Scott $24,000, and Oswald Ottendorfer $18,000, while others who gave between $10,000 and $16,000 included Whitney, Man-

---

[1] Memorandum. Cleveland Papers.

ning, Roswell P. Flower, and Gorman. Cleveland himself contributed $10,000, half of it through Bissell. But the listed total came to less than $460,000, a meagre sum.

As November opened, both sides made confident predictions of success. It was clear that the election would turn on New York, Connecticut, New Jersey, and Indiana, and each party claimed all four States. As a matter of fact, the Republican boasts were the better grounded. As the Democratic leaders received confidential reports from local managers throughout New York, they saw little chance of carrying the State. For forty years the Irish Catholic vote of New York city and the up-State municipalities had been the very backbone of Democratic strength.[1] Now, despite Kelly's reluctant professions, it remained largely indifferent or hostile. There seemed little chance that the Irish and Greenback defections would be offset by the desertions of the Mugwumps and Prohibitionists from Blaine. But at the final moment fate intervened.

VI

Cleveland in the very last days of the campaign dropped everything else. Meanwhile Blaine, returning from the West, was met at Jamestown, N. Y., the home of ex-Senator Fenton, by Andrew Sloan Draper, the Republican State chairman. Draper implored him not to go to New York city. He said: "Go up the line of the New York Central to Syracuse; stump the northern counties—they need it; and then go home to Portland." Blaine was tired. He stood at the window watching the falling rain, hesitated, and then stepped into his carriage for the New York train.[2] By that act, he lost the election.

At the end of Blaine's ride were crowds, receptions, plaudits, and the fateful events of October 29th. These events need not again be described in detail. In a sense the Burchard affair and "Belshazzar's feast" were accidents; in a truer sense they fitted logically into the pattern of the unprincipled campaign which the party was conducting, and their penalty was deserved. For the morning of October 29th New York clergymen had been called, by an advertisement in flagrant bad taste, to meet Blaine at the Fifth Avenue Hotel. To many the invitation

[1] Cf. *Nation*, Jan. 1, 1885, for charges of Tammany treachery.
[2] Edgar L. Murlin to author, May 30, 1930.

seemed an echo of the Ball affair. No minister of high reputation in New York city responded, but a crowd of obscure clergymen were there. The Rev. S. D. Burchard, pastor since 1879 of the Murray Hill Presbyterian Church, acted as spokesman, and addressing Blaine, referred to the Democrats as the party of "Rum, Romanism, and Rebellion." If the phrase was new, the idea was old. James A. Garfield in 1876, when he thought Tilden elected, had written in a private letter of the Republicans as worsted by "the combined power of rebellion, Catholicism, and whiskey." [1] As it happened, Blaine was too fatigued to catch Burchard's remark. To their eternal discredit, the newspaper men present also missed it.[2] But the ever-alert managers of the Democratic headquarters had taken the precaution of shadowing Blaine with a shorthand reporter. He returned forthwith to headquarters, and began reading Burchard's speech.

Oscar S. Straus, who was present, saw Gorman's eyes flash as he caught the fateful phrase [3] and heard him exclaim: "Write that out!" Within a few hours the principal cities were being placarded with the insulting alliteration. When Blaine passed through New Haven the next day he was greeted with a shower of Rum-Romanism-Rebellion handbills. The effect was profound. Blaine's managers were relying heavily upon his strength with the Irish Catholics, and a hurricane had burst upon the fields white for the harvest. When he finally repudiated the utterance it was too late. Chauncey M. Depew quotes a high Catholic dignitary as saying that "We had to resent an insult like that, and I estimate that the remark has changed fifty thousand votes." This was an exaggeration—but it did change many.

The "prosperity dinner" at Delmonico's occurred on the evening of the 29th. As if ashamed of it, the managers excluded all reporters but an Associated Press representative, and when the speeches were over and the guests retired to the parlors, even he was dismissed. This secrecy naturally bred suspicion. One motive for the dinner lay in the hope for last-minute campaign contributions from the millionaires invited, and another in the desire to impress business men all over the country. Elkins, far too shrewd to approve of it, did all that he could to prevent Blaine from going, and refused to attend himself. The principal re-

[1] R. G. Caldwell, *James A. Garfield, Party Chieftain*, 251.
[2] H. L. Stoddard, *As I Knew Them*, 132.
[3] Oscar S. Straus, *Under Four Administrations*, 39.

The Rev. Samuel D. Burchard

John Kelly

TWO FIGURES OF THE 1884 CAMPAIGN

sponsibility for it rested with Cyrus W. Field, and for many weeks afterward he and Elkins were not upon speaking terms.[1]

At seven o'clock long lines of carriages were leaving their occupants at the doors. At half-past seven Blaine, amid handclapping, entered the ballroom where the covers had been laid. He was escorted to the post of honor by William M. Evarts and Cyrus W. Field, and took his seat as the room resounded with three cheers proposed by A. R. Whitney. The decorations were elaborate—smilax, roses, and costly orchids, expensive confectioneries, and in front of the principal guest a magnificent bed of hothouse flowers lettered J. G. B. Among the guests were Jay Gould, the best-hated man in America; Russell Sage, famous for his griping hand; John Roach, a wealthy government contractor; Henry Clews, Levi P. Morton, D. O. Mills, Charles L. Tiffany, Cornelius N. Bliss, Whitelaw Reid, and Lloyd M. Aspinwall. Evarts presided and made a harmless speech. In his response Blaine seemed to talk of nothing but money. The next day the New York *World* filled half its front page with Walt McDougall's cartoon of "The Royal Feast of Belshazzar Blaine and the Money Kings," and the comments of many newspapers were scathing. At a time when the press was filled with news of factories closing down, when three-fifths of the iron furnaces were banked, and when business of all kinds was at a low ebb, with multitudes out of work, Blaine had appeared at a banquet offered by wealth and privilege, and had made a speech which was one long glorification of plutocracy. At a stroke he had lost the votes of thousands of workingmen.

Cleveland watched the close of the campaign in a deeply thoughtful mood. He travelled to New York on the Saturday before election to review the great Democratic business men's parade, and he read the eloquent speeches with which Schurz and Beecher closed the canvass, and the editorials in which Godkin and Curtis touched the highest notes of idealism. But there was no complacency in his attitude. Instead, his feeling was of humility, tinged with the simple religious emotion which had flowed down to him from so many Puritan generations. Something of all this he expressed in a note to Harold Frederic in London: [2]

You do not know how all this political work and talk appear to me. I sometimes feel that I do not fully appreciate the solemn responsibilities of my posi-

---

[1] See Elkins' statement in the Chicago *Tribune,* June 18, 19, 1888.
[2] Frederic published this letter in the *Pall Mall Gazette,* Nov. 8, 1884.

tion, and, again, that I do not fret enough and am not anxious enough. At times the whole question is presented to my mind in such a way that in the midst of wonderment I say to myself, "There is a God!"

Imagine a man standing in my place, with positively no ambitions for a higher position than I now hold, and in constant apprehension that he may be called upon to assume burdens and duties the greatest and highest that a human being can take upon himself. I can not look upon the prospect of success in this campaign with any joy, but only with a very serious kind of awe. Is this right?

I have in this written more of my inner feelings than I have said or penned since my nomination. I shall say no more on the subject. This would not have been written except that your letter brought the mood on me, and that it was to go "beyond the seas."

Election day dawned with squalls of chilly rain in up-State New York. Cleveland voted in Buffalo, and returned to the executive mansion in Albany. After dinner he retired with Lamont, Apgar, Judge Peckham, General Farnsworth, John Boyd Thacher, and a few other intimates to the front room of the second floor. There was no telegraph wire at the mansion, and early in the evening the telephone went out of commission in a rainstorm that as the hours passed became almost a deluge. Congratulatory telegrams shortly began to pour in by messenger, with friendly newspaper dispatches claiming New York State, but few detailed figures were obtainable. In this uncertainty William Gorham Rice went to the *Argus* office and by means of the press wire began to compile exact though fragmentary returns. The first news from New York city had been remarkably encouraging. When word came that Cleveland had polled a tremendous vote in such normally Republican sections as Murray Hill and Brooklyn Heights, many observers leaped at the conclusion that he carried the State by a large majority. But Blaine men who knew the situation discounted these early reports. "Wait till you hear from the slums," they said—the slums filled with Tammany's Irish voters. They were right. In the more prosperous areas the Mugwumps had turned out in force, and Murray Hill (the 21st Assembly district) gave Cleveland a plurality of 561 where Hancock had been defeated by 1,109. But in the First Ward, filled with Irish-Americans, Blaine received 2,275 votes where Garfield four years earlier had been given only 1,885; the Fourth Ward gave Blaine 2,390 votes where it had given Garfield 1,543; and the Second Ward gave

Blaine 2,130 votes as against 1,146 to Garfield.[1]

As the figures piled up, and Colonel Rice made close calculations based upon percentages of comparative gain or loss over previous years, it became plain that the roseate messages arriving at the executive mansion were misleading. There was a perceptible drift toward Cleveland, but it was so slight that Rice became satisfied that the governor's majority would not be more than 2,000. Lamont, studying the dispatches by Cleveland's side, arrived at the same conclusion. Cleveland was especially interested in comparing the returns with those of 1882, but made few comments. When some discouraging totals from Jefferson County were read he remarked, "That hurts." [2] A supper was served, William having decorated the table in the gayest fashion. Then about midnight Cleveland announced that he was going to bed, and advised everyone to do the same. "If you stay up much longer," he said, "you will be counting me out."

In the minds of all Cleveland's friends was the fear of a repetition of the events of 1876. Shortly after midnight Lamont, Apgar, and Rice, taking counsel together, began to dispatch telegrams to two or more prominent Democrats in every county, instructing them to act: [3]

The only hope of our opponents is in a fraudulent count in the country districts. Call to your assistance today vigilant and courageous friends, and see that every vote cast is honestly counted. Telegraph me your estimate, and let me hear from you from time to time until actual figures are known.

To this telegram they signed Manning's name. Early the following morning they sent additional messages to leading Democrats all over the State, asking them to go at once to the nearest county clerk's office, remain there till the returns were filed, obtain a certified copy, and send it at once to Albany by special messenger.

VII

For three days the election remained in doubt. On Wednesday, November 5, a few counties in New York State still remained to be heard from. Impartial estimates showed a majority of several thousand for

[1] See *Tribune Almanac*, 1885; *Nation*, Feb. 2, 1888.
[2] Wm. Gorham Rice, *State Service Magazine*, April, 1918.
[3] Wm. Gorham Rice Papers.

Cleveland, but the vote was dangerously close, and the Associated Press, which was receiving returns from election districts instead of counties, made extravagant claims for Blaine. As reports gained currency that Jay Gould's Western Union lines were delaying and falsifying the returns, fifty eminent lawyers in New York city, including Whitney, Francis Lynde Stetson, James C. Carter, Carl Schurz, and Roscoe Conkling, devoted themselves to scrutinizing the count. Meanwhile in all the great cities crowds predominantly Democratic manifested a temper which justified Blaine's later statement that he feared that a contested election would result in civil war. In New York city on Wednesday the multitudes in front of the bulletin boards cheered madly for Cleveland. As night fell the concourse swelled to immense proportions, and a mass of men and boys marched down Broadway to the Western Union building on Dey Street, threatening violence, while another crowd moved up Fifth Avenue toward Gould's house, singing "We'll Hang Jay Gould to a sour apple tree." In Indianapolis a great Democratic crowd headed by Congressman English gathered downtown. In Boston there were wild scenes before the newspaper offices in Washington Street, and when the *Journal* posted a bulletin of Blaine's election there seemed danger that the building would be gutted. Everywhere these crowds cheered Cleveland's telegram of November 6 to Edward Murphy of Troy:

> I believe I have been elected President, and nothing but grossest fraud can keep me out of it, and that we will not permit.

The charge was shortly made by many Republicans, and has been repeated by Senator Hoar in his *Autobiography*,[1] that Blaine had an actual plurality in New York, but was deprived of it by fraud—particularly by tellers in Long Island City who counted Ben Butler's Greenback votes for Cleveland. These statements have been subjected to a searching and destructive review.[2] Few elections in New York have been more carefully watched and supervised than that of 1884. In the metropolis as well as up-State the election machinery was much more nearly under Republican than Democratic control, for while every election district possessed two Democratic and two Republican inspectors,

[1] I, 408; cf. Edward Stanwood, *James G. Blaine*, 291.
[2] W. G. Rice and F. L. Stetson, "Was New York's Vote Stolen?" *North American Review*, Jan., 1914.

the Democrats were in many instances Tammany men, hostile to Cleveland. The chief of the Bureau of Elections was the Republican leader, John J. O'Brien, who was later accused of accepting, two days before the election, checks of $50,000 each from Jay Gould and the Union League Club to be used in buying blocks of Democratic votes.[1] As for Long Island City, the careful bipartisan scrutiny of the votes rendered fraud impossible, but even if all of Cleveland's plurality over Blaine there, amounting to 727 votes, had been rejected, he would still have carried the State!

The whole cry of fraud, like the charges of mismanagement shortly brought against Chairmen Elkins and Jones, was essentially an effort to obscure the real cause of Blaine's failure. The vote cast in Republican districts for St. John; the rain that kept rural Republicans at home; the loss of more than 2,000 Republican votes in Conkling's home, Oneida County; the Burchard alliteration—these all counted. But the great central explanation of the defeat was simply that Blaine was morally suspect.

As late as Friday the *Tribune* still claimed New York for Blaine. But that day the *Sun* and the Albany *Journal* conceded Cleveland's election, and at 1:30 A. M. on Saturday the Associated Press announced it as certain. Within a few hours Blaine admitted defeat. "I am glad of it," Cleveland told his friends. "I am glad they yield peaceably. If they had not, I should have felt it my duty to take my seat anyhow." [2]

His margin in New York was of less than 1200 votes, but it was decisive. He had carried every Southern State, together with Indiana, New Jersey, and Connecticut, and though his popular majority over Blaine was less than 25,000 in a total vote of more than ten millions, he had 219 electoral votes to Blaine's 182. Butler had polled some 175,000 votes, running best in Michigan, fairly well in Massachusetts, and very badly in New York, where he received only 16,994 votes. The damage he did to Cleveland in that State was not nearly so heavy as the damage done to Blaine by St. John, who polled 25,016 votes in New York, and

---

[1] For this extremely interesting charge see the interviews of an active Republican worker, Col. George Bliss, in the N. Y. *Herald,* June 8–14, 1885, and editorial comment in the N. Y. *Evening Post,* June 15, 1885. Bliss said that Gould's money "was paid under some assurance that it was to be used upon Democrats with the concurrence of Mr. Kelly." But the money was not thus used—it was pocketed. Blaine was in consultation with Gould on Nov. 2 in the house of Elkins on 58th Street, and on Nov. 3 the *Tribune* published an editorial article headed, "Trust This City," and promising up-State New York that the results in the metropolis "certainly will not displease you."

[2] McElroy, *Grover Cleveland,* I, 97.

more than 150,000 in the nation as a whole. Even in New Jersey the vote for St. John was nearly twice that for Butler. After all, the Eastern workmen had not been hoodwinked.[1]

When it became certain that the Democratic party was restored to power, the rejoicings of its members all over the country, but especially in the South, were impressive. In city after city guns thundered salutes, and fireworks lit up the evening skies. Surging crowds in Richmond and New Orleans sang hymns of joy. In Atlanta the legislative session was interrupted by a concourse of five thousand citizens who invaded the capitol. Henry W. Grady bore down the aisle of the House shouting, "Mr. Speaker, a message from the American people," the band struck up, and the legislators rose cheering. Proportionately great was the gloom among the Republicans. At the North a few men ostentatiously sold their securities, while many expressed fears that the Democratic leaders would pursue disloyal policies. Numbers of Southern negroes leaped to the conclusion that slavery would be restored; and the distressed butler of Dr. J. L. M. Curry appeared before him pleading that, as he must now belong to someone, Dr. Curry would claim him.[2]

Most striking of all was the rejoicing of the Independents. As their moral enthusiasm during the campaign had been greater than that of any other element, so now their exultation was unrestrained. Schurz, Moorfield Storey, Bristow, Eliot, Seelye, all expressed a sense that the republic had been rescued from a grave danger. The *Nation* and *Harper's Weekly* declared that a great principle had been vindicated. A few friends touched a personal note. On the day of assured victory Harold Frederic in London, his eyes misty, was writing Cleveland: [3]

"How proud I am to have known you, to be privileged to call you my friend!"

[1] Edward Stanwood, *History of the Presidency*, I, 448.
[2] M. L. Avary, *Dixie After the War*, 286.
[3] Nov. 8, 1884. Wm. Gorham Rice Papers.

THE winds had whistled and the waves had swept high in this turbulent campaign of 1884, but the fountains of the great deep had not been broken up. It seemed, after all, but a superficial change which had capsized the Republican party. Following the overturns of 1800, 1828, and 1860, the national life had set into strong new currents. Would 1884 take its place with these three dates? A foreign observer, arriving just after the election, and seeing how exultant were the Democrats and how gloomy were the forebodings of the Republicans, might have inferred that some far-reaching transformation was at hand. An Englishman would have thought at once of the Liberal triumph in 1868, and the far-reaching social and political reforms which Gladstone's Ministry had then initiated. But shrewd Americans knew that the Eastern leadership of the Democratic party was conservative; they perceived in the Democratic platform an assurance that no radical innovations were planned, and they realized that Cleveland's temper was caution itself. The nation, moreover, was not facing any crisis which obviously demanded a bold leap forward. Reconstruction was safely in the past; the agrarian problem, the labor problem, and the trust problem were only slowly coming to national attention, and belonged to the future. Beneath the surface powerful forces were at work, and grim spectres would soon loom out of the smoke of the Haymarket Riot, but outwardly all was still calm.

A change not so much in policies as in spirit—this it was that the new Administration represented. The last great Democrat in office, Andrew Jackson, had given the country a hard-riding, hard-hitting government. But his pioneer age was gone, and a prosperous, settled democracy is always cautious in dealing with policies, though often violent in its enthusiasm for a new spirit. Men expected Cleveland to display not an excursive boldness, but simply a greater honesty and earnestness than his predecessors, and he understood this perfectly. His campaign speeches, reticent upon policy, had been emphatic in hammering upon the need for a new moral attitude toward the business of government.

It would have been better, it would have been a great national benefit, if Cleveland had entered office in 1885 as Roosevelt did in 1901 and
Wilson in 1913, with a progressive programme which caught the beam
of the future like a mirror flashing back the sunrise. He might have anticipated problems that were to become menacing as the years gave
them size. It would also have been better had he been more fully
trained. Yet the issue made by Blaine's nomination had been simply
that of honor in government, and unquestionably one of principal
needs of the hour—perhaps the principal—was for corrective as distinguished from constructive action. Twenty years had passed since
Lincoln had died. In only four of those years had liberal men felt that
the government in Washington pursued high aims with high-minded
means, and during those four years Hayes had been crippled by party
jealousy and the blot on his title. Looking backward, men recalled the
cruel military government of the South, the impeachment, the Crédit
Mobilier, the Whiskey Ring, the railway land-grant scandals, the
third-term movement, the disputed election, the Star Route exposure,
and all the rest of the disreputable story. In a youthful democracy the
objects which a government seeks to obtain are of less importance than
the methods by which it gains them, for if it takes care of its own character, growth and wealth will take care of themselves. This was a truth
which Washington had done his utmost to impress upon the country;
since Lincoln's day it had been ignored, and Cleveland's first task was
to burnish the letters of the precept into brightness.

II

Cleveland's emotions were always simple and powerful. He emerged
from the canvass swayed by two natural feelings: resentment for the
villification which he had endured, and a sense of dedication to the
office before him. Both sentiments found expression in an early letter
to his best friend, Bissell: [1]

I suppose I may now address you as the President-elect. We have just heard
that eleven of the twenty-four districts in New York have been canvassed with
no reduction in our majority. They include that part of the city in which
informalities and mistakes, our friends think, would be found if anywhere. So
I should think the count might be concluded tomorrow or Monday at the

[1] Nov. 13, 1884. Cleveland Papers.

furthest.

As I look over the field I see some people lying dead whose demise will not harm the country, some whose wounds will perhaps serve to teach them that honesty and truth are worth preserving, and some whose fidelity and staunch devotion are rewarded with victory, and who have grappled themselves to me with "hooks of steel." In this last array stand my two Buffalo friends. You don't, I am sure, want me to be invidious, but you must trust me to fully appreciate all that you have done. I am busy all day long receiving congratulations of friends in person while through the mail and by telegram they are counted by thousands. It's quite amusing to see how profuse are the expressions of some who stood aloof when most needed. I intend to cultivate the Christian duty of charity toward all men except the dirty class that defiled themselves with filthy scandal and Ballism. I don't believe God will ever forgive them and I am determined not to do so.

I look upon the next four years to come as a cheerful self-inflicted penance for the good of my country. I can see no pleasure in it and no satisfaction, only a hope that I can be of service to my people. . . .

This is not much of a letter, but I want to hear from you, and perhaps it will do to accomplish that object. Give my love to Charley [Goodyear], Frank [Locke], and G. J. [Sicard], and all the good friends.

A man of less sensitiveness, in that triumphant moment, would quickly have forgotten the hurt, but Cleveland's heart was still sore when he wrote Bissell again: [1]

Yours just arrived. I shall not come to Buffalo—just yet, at all events. As I feel at this moment, I would never go there again if I could avoid it. Elected President of the United States, I feel that I have no home at my home. . . .

I wish to make some financial arrangements. Perhaps it would be safe for me to arrive there some morning and leave at night.

Bayard is coming here tomorrow night and will spend Sunday with me.

I am so overwhelmed with all kinds of things and perplexed more than I can tell you; but nothing is so annoying to me as my thoughts concerning Buffalo.

In this mood Cleveland concluded his work as governor. Characteristically, he retained his office till January 6, 1885, for though David B. Hill thirsted for its emoluments and powers, he chose to subject himself to a double pressure in order to round out his second year and prepare his third annual message. He worked stubbornly every night till after midnight, and when Christmas came spent the whole day, with a brief interruption for William's festive dinner-table, over letters and

[1] Dec. 5, 1884. Cleveland Papers.

public documents. His last message contained a number of important recommendations flowing from his full experience. For his final two months in Albany he removed to a curiously-built house called "The Towers," where Mrs. Hoyt continued to act as housekeeper. While his furniture was being settled there he made a brief business trip to Buffalo, terminating his partnership with Bissell and Sicard, and attending the Charity Ball. As he went, he once more uttered a few growls to Bissell about the "dirty and contemptible part of the Buffalo population," and expressed a special hope that the "scum" of the town would keep out of his path.[1] In Albany the winter was marked by more social appearances than he had usually made. In December he was the principal guest at the brilliant wedding of Manning, who took as his second wife a handsome and socially ambitious woman much his junior. Cleveland's final reception in the executive mansion was attended by a large group of Buffalo friends and he was enormously pleased by the favorable impression which his old comrades made. They were gentlemen; they were men of education, affairs, and character, and after what had been said of his Buffalo associates, he was delighted to have Albany see them in a true light.

But as the pressure upon him grew, he chafed because he had so little time for the study of public questions. To a little group of New York Mugwumps he declared that he wished he might drop everything, go off to the North Woods, and spend a month in studying the issues before the country.[2] As the old year ended amid the importunities of office-seekers, he wrote Bissell that everyone seemed to have an axe to grind:[3]

The plot thickens. I am sick at heart and perplexed in brain during most of my working hours. I almost think that the profession of most of my pretended friends are but the means they employ to accomplish personal and selfish ends. It's so hard to discover their springs of action and its seems so distressing to feel that in the question as to who shall be trusted, I should be so much at sea. I wonder if I must for the third time face the difficulties of a new official almost *alone?*

Hundreds of voices, eminent and obscure, clamored in Cleveland's mail, urging him to adopt this policy or that. Almost every congratu-

[1] Dec. 31, 1884. Cleveland Papers.
[2] R. R. Bowker to author, June 10, 1930.
[3] Dec. 25, 1884. Cleveland Papers.

latory note contained some attempt to influence the first Democratic President in a generation. James Freeman Clarke wrote how happy he was to believe that Cleveland would support civil service reform, tariff reform, and friendship between North and South. Horace White, declaring that he had never rejoiced so profoundly over any election since Lincoln's in 1860, expressed the hope that Cleveland would press for immediate repeal of the silver purchase law. George Ticknor Curtis sent a long letter of advice upon the enforcement of the Fourteenth and Fifteenth Amendments; Abram S. Hewitt proposed that Cleveland utter some reassuring words to the Southern negroes; and Carl Schurz, always prodigal of counsel, wrote that the principal test of the Administration would not lie in the tariff, "for that, I am confident, will settle itself more easily than many now suppose," but in the civil service policy. He urged Cleveland to be a St. George against the spoils dragon. By extending the merit system, rebuffing the greedy politicians, and lifting party aims to a purer plane, "you can thus bring about a state of things in which public questions can once more be discussed on their own merits." Samuel J. Randall asked him to weigh carefully the arguments of protectionist Democrats. Tilden, happily, made no effort to press his views upon Cleveland, but in a pathetic note to Manning simply volunteered to give his best advice if any were needed, adding that this would probably be the last service that he could hope to offer his country.[1]

III

The formation of any Cabinet is a delicate piece of mosaic work, and in dealing with it the greatest Presidents have committed costly blunders, as Washington did in making Edmund Randolph Secretary of State, and Lincoln in appointing Simon Cameron Secretary of War. When Cleveland set to work he confronted special difficulties. The only Democrats of political experience, save a few governors, were in Congress, and it would be dangerous to weaken the party there by removing too many leaders. The Northwest, New England, and the South all had to be satisfied. Moreover, all the seasoned politicians, led by Manning and Gorman, were apprehensive lest Cleveland neglect the party machine, and Gorman placed before him a list of men who should be called to Albany for interviews;[2] the Southerners alone including L. Q. C.

---

[1] Various letters, Dec., 1884–Jan., 1885; Tilden's is dated Nov. 12, 1884. Cleveland Papers.
[2] Gorham to Manning, Jan. 5, 1885. Cleveland Papers.

Lamar, M. W. Ransom, Joseph E. Brown, Wade Hampton, Isham G. Harris, and George Vest—representatives of the whole area from Carolina to Missouri. Meanwhile little booms, like dust-tornadoes on a windy day, were whirling frantically in every direction. There was one in Illinois for William M. Springer as Secretary of the Interior; one in New Jersey for George B. McClellan as Secretary of War; one in Georgia for John B. Gordon; [1] and one in Ohio for George M. Hoadly.[2]

The basis of the Cabinet was quickly laid, for Cleveland knew from the outset that he wanted three men, Bayard, Manning, and Whitney. The first was an almost inevitable choice as Secretary of State. He stood second only to Cleveland as a party leader. He represented one of the great American families, for his great-grandfather, grandfather, father, and uncle had all been Senators; and it was a family peculiarly influential in the South. For sixteen years he himself had sat in the Senate, where he had gained a high reputation for soundness and conservatism on all financial and legal questions. Cleveland could implicitly trust his views on the currency, the tariff, and international affairs, and his experience of Washington ways would be invaluable. Moreover, he was a man of high culture, with a grave, stately courtesy and a polished if heavy eloquence that would make him an excellent spokesman for the Administration. Tilden would have preferred to see his close friend John Bigelow, who had been minister to France, in the State Department, but he was never even considered. Bayard took his elevation to the first place in the Cabinet with reluctance, for he modestly said that he knew little of foreign affairs, and he feared the expense of his social duties; but his choice greatly pleased the party.

Cleveland desired Manning as Secretary of the Treasury for a variety of reasons. He was a trusted and admired friend, and his loyal work in the campaign deserved a reward. He stood at the head of the powerful Tilden wing of the party, and possessed a devoted following. Above all, he was a man of burly, elemental strength and of immense driving capacity, demonstrated in his rise from a ragged newsboy and printer's devil to wealth and authority; and he had a firm grasp of financial principles. Whitney was widely distrusted. But he had made a brilliant record ever since he had helped fight the Tweed Ring, and as corporation counsel he had saved New York city many millions by

[1] Senator Colquitt to C., Nov. 18, 1884. Cleveland Papers.
[2] S. J. Tilden, *Letters and Literary Memorials*, II, 649 ff.

contesting plausible but fraudulent claims. Cleveland knew that in the right post his energy, brains, and influence with moneyed men would be valuable; and that post was found for him in the Navy Department.

Inevitably these selections met with criticism. Randall and the protectionists never concealed their dislike of Bayard. The fact that Manning was an experienced banker and business man, and the very soul of conservatism on financial questions, escaped many shortsighted critics. Godkin wrote the President-elect [1] that one prominent Mugwump had called Manning "the machine incarnate," and warned him that the appointment would send many independents back to the Republican party; while Abram S. Hewitt believed that he lacked proper training, and that McDonald of Indiana would make a much abler Secretary.[2] To offset these criticisms, Randall urged his appointment and it was obviously pleasing to Tilden.

But it was upon Whitney that the storm burst most fiercely, for already he was recognized as a representative of corporation finance in politics. Angry mutters came from the West when it was hinted that he might go into the Treasury, while Eastern reformers wished him left out altogether. He disavowed any claim upon Cleveland. "Governor," he wrote in his impetuous scrawl,[3] "pay no attention to newspaper or other advocacy of me. You owe me nothing and I would feel really hurt if I thought you would have any feeling of obligation to me. What I have done was from a sense of duty to our party and country. It was right (the result has proved it) and that's enough. I want you to succeed and you will. If for reasons personal and sound you should desire me, that's one thing, but I hope you will believe this of me—that if you shouldn't it wouldn't make the slightest difference in our relation nor in my feeling nor in what I would do for you. I must free my mind by saying this." Cleveland never had the slightest reason to regret the choice of any of the three. They were the backbone of the Cabinet, its ablest men, and from beginning to end his most trusted advisers.

The lesser Cabinet positions were not so easily filled, and on February 4 Cleveland came to New York to hold a series of conferences on this and other subjects. His richly furnished suite on the second floor

[1] Godkin to Cleveland, Feb. 26, 1885. Cleveland Papers.
[2] Hewitt to C. Feb. 17, 1885. Cleveland Papers.
[3] Whitney to C., no date, 1885. Cleveland Papers. Later Whitney, in accepting the appointment on March 1, wrote that "on the whole I think it was a necessity in view of the exigencies of the party that are upon you at the outset."

of the Hotel Victoria, decorated with a half-dozen pictures which the
artist Bierstadt hastily sent over, was soon thronged. Barnum, Gorman,
Don M. Dickinson, and other national committeemen arrived, and with
them Senators Pugh, Camden, Lamar, and Kenna. The President-elect
told reporters that "I came for information—the idea of this trip is
to widen my information on public needs." [1] His final selections soon
followed. By the end of the month he had chosen a Wisconsin attorney,
William F. Vilas, to be Postmaster-General; a scholarly Senator, Lucius
Quintus Cincinnatus Lamar of Mississippi, to be Secretary of the Interior; a Massachusetts jurist, William C. Endicott, to be Secretary of
War; and a Senator from Arkansas, Augustus H. Garland, to be
Attorney-General. In ability the whole group had not been surpassed
since Lincoln's day, though it had certainly been equalled by Hayes's
Cabinet.

One member, Endicott, distinctly represented the reform Democrats.
In early life he had belonged to the Whig party, but in 1856 had followed Rufus Choate and other conservatives in joining the Democratic
organization. Later a Republican governor had placed him on the
supreme bench of his State. A clear-headed and learned lawyer of
Salem, wealthy, widely-travelled, and of aristocratic manners, he was
selected over the protests of the practical politicians. For a time Cleveland had hesitated between him and John Quincy Adams, Jr., and Francis Lynde Stetson had made the choice.[2] Vilas also was a reform Democrat. He was a man of striking personal attractions—tall, with chiselled
features, lustrous eyes, and curling hair, looking like a darker Roscoe
Conkling; and he was the recognized leader of the Wisconsin Bar, with
a rank unsurpassed among Northwestern attorneys. Graduating from
the University of Wisconsin in 1859, he had flung down his lawbooks
to enter the Civil War, had made a gallant record at the siege of Vicksburg, and had become one of Grant's best friends. A few years later he
had gained one of the largest practises in the West, and had become
an orator of note—his speech of welcome when Grant returned to Chicago from his tour of the world was long famous. As yet he had held
only minor offices. But as chairman of the national convention in
Chicago his skill and courage had attracted Cleveland's attention, while
he had made an instant impression as head of the notification party. For

[1] N. Y. *Times*, Feb. 5, N. Y. *Evening Post*, Feb. 11, 1885.
[2] Griffin, *People and Politics*, 279–282.

no other member of the first Cabinet, not even Bayard, did Cleveland develop so warm an affection.

The most pleasing appointment, to lovers of fine American types, was that of L. Q. C. Lamar. This old-school Southerner, a member of the Huguenot family which gave the republic of Texas its first president, had drafted Mississippi's ordinance of secession and served for two years in the Confederate army, becoming a colonel. After the war he had distinguished himself as a champion of sectional reconciliation. During four years of studious poverty he had preached reunion from a chair in the University of Mississippi. Elected to Congress, he had delivered a eulogy of Charles Sumner so eloquent and yet so loyal to Southern principles that it was long afterward recalled with praise by Blaine; while in the disputed election of 1876 no one was more prominent in counselling peace.[1] Simple-hearted, childlike, and in many ways impractical, he always leaned heavily on his first assistant secretary, and when his desk became intolerably cluttered with papers, would go away for several days while others cleared it up. But Chief Justice Fuller declared years later that he had the most suggestive intellect he had ever met, and Senator Hoar paid tribute to the "profound and farsighted wisdom" which lay beneath his chivalry. President Barnard of Columbia had written Cleveland that he had never known a man whose character was more admirable. "He is true, noble-hearted, honorable, and generous; no persuasion could induce him and no power could drive him to deviate by a hair's breadth from what he may believe to be the path of duty." The chief quality needed in the Interior Department was courage, and Lamar, for all his pensive look, slow gait, and habit of stroking his beard and quoting Horace, had plenty of it.

The other Southerner in the Cabinet, Garland, who had opposed secession but had sat in both houses of the Confederate Congress, was the one weak appointment. Cleveland did well, despite some protests, to choose two representatives of the South for his official family; for to slight that section would have been to subscribe to the theory that there were two grades of citizenship, Northern and Southern, and that eleven States did not yet fully belong to the Union. But he could have found a better Attorney-General. It is true that Garland possessed much capacity.[2] As governor of Arkansas he had lifted that State out

[1] J. G. Blaine, *Twenty Years of Congress.*
[2] See the three-column article on Garland, "A Well-Equipped Lawyer," N. Y. *Herald,* Jan. 8, 1885.

of the mire of carpetbag corruption, and when men of both parties had united to reward him with a seat in the Senate, his legal knowledge and clear logic had shortly impressed his fellow-members of the Judiciary Committee. He had successfully argued the noted case of *ex parte Garland* in the Supreme Court, upholding his right to practise before that tribunal without taking the test-oath prescribed by Congress. Tall, broad-shouldered, smooth-faced, with a humorous, genial look, ready to boast that he had never owned a dress-suit, he possessed a host of friends. His broad-constructionist view of the Constitution was to his credit. But he had two great defects. He lacked judgment, giving Cleveland bad advice and soon becoming involved in a distressing financial scandal; and as the one Cabinet member from west of the Mississippi, he felt too much sympathy with the interests which were exploiting the national domain.

Nothing was more important for Cleveland's efficiency and comfort than the fact that the shrewd Lamont went with him to Washington as private secretary. He was the first presidential secretary to give that position the importance it has ever since held. When he demurred, Cleveland had said, "Well, Dan, if you won't go, I won't, that's all." He completed an executive group that young Roosevelt sneeringly called the Apotheosis of the Unknown. In reality its members were as well known as those of most Cabinets; three of them possessed long experience in Washington; it was well distributed geographically; and its character silenced the partisans who had expected Cleveland to surround himself with low politicians. There were nowhere in the country two finer patricians, in the American sense of that word, than Bayard and Endicott.

IV

Even before his Cabinet was completed Cleveland had to make a statement on the civil service question. A horde of hungry office-seekers looked up to him to be fed; day by day their voracity was increasing, and if it were not checked at once it threatened to become uncontrollable. At the same time, thousands of reformers demanded some proof that their confidence had not been misplaced. They believed that the civil service was the burning question of the hour. It did indeed possess an importance which later generations can but faintly realize;

Vilas   Whitney   Endicott   Garland

Bayard   Cleveland   Manning   Lamar

CLEVELAND'S FIRST CABINET

for the disease having long ago been cured, its pain and fever are now difficult to describe.

Cleveland realized the seriousness of the situation. Out of approximately 126,000 Federal employees, some 110,000, a veritable army, were political appointees, chosen by the President or his immediate subordinates, and only 16,000 were as yet in the classified service. This was a tremendous evil in itself, but there were aggravating circumstances. It had long been customary to multiply temporary employees for political purposes. In recent years the situation in the Treasury and Postoffice Departments had been especially deplorable. At one time, out of 3400 persons employed in the former, almost 1800 filled no permanent positions, but were put on and off the rolls at the pleasure of the Secretary, who paid them out of funds that had not been appropriated for that purpose. Superfluous employees abounded. Not long before Cleveland took office an investigation showed that of 958 minor workers in the bureau of printing and engraving, 539 were unnecessary. The demand for spoils was so eager that when $1600 and $1800 positions became vacant, the salaries were often allowed to accumulate, and then divided among political placemen. Instead of one $1800 clerk, three would be employed at $600 each "on the lapse." In one instance thirty-five persons had been put on the lapsed funds of the Treasury for eight days at the close of a fiscal year to sop up some money that was in danger of being returned to the government.[1]

Every large postoffice, custom-house, internal revenue collector's office, and navy yard, moreover, had been a centre for the systematic distribution of spoils. To make them go as far as possible a system of rotation had been introduced. One collector of the port of New York had removed, on the average, one employee every three days, while a more efficient successor had removed 830 of his 900 subordinates at the rate of three in every four days. Still worse was the unblushing use of "assessments" for party purposes; for officeholders were systematically blackmailed by party heads into paying a fixed percentage of their salaries—usually two per cent—into the campaign treasury. Year after year the National Committee and Congressional Committee had sent out letters requesting every employee to furnish a definite sum. It was a request—but the penalty for refusal was certain. In 1880 and 1882

[1] See the first two reports of the Civil Service Commission, 1884–1885, for conditions just before Cleveland entered office.

Jay A. Hubbell, chairman of the Republican Congressional Campaign Committee, had thus shaken the patronage tree, while such party associates as Allison, Aldrich, and McKinley clubbed its branches. The scandal created by his work and by Garfield's letter of 1880 encouraging him had done much to force the passage of the Pendleton act in 1883. Throughout the country enlightened citizens supported this civil service law, but there were Herods eager to slay the infant reform. As Senator Hoar had remarked a few years earlier, many men grown gray in high station preached "that the true way in which power should be gained in this republic is to bribe the people with offices created for their service. . . ."

Would Cleveland stand up to fight these men? The clumsy and indifferent Grant, surrounded by bad advisers, had permitted civil service reform to be trampled underfoot, and the Independents were nervous lest it suffer again. Schurz, Godkin, Curtis, John Jay, and Moorfield Storey wrote urgent letters, and R. R. Bowker went to Albany to press the subject. Godkin told Stetson that he earnestly hoped that Cleveland would make an early pronouncement. "The sooner it comes the more effective it will be. The hopes and delusions of the officehunters are rising every day, and so are the doubts of Grover Cleveland's well-wishers as to whether he will have the courage and strength to meet them. The time to check these tendencies is now." [1]
But Cleveland never hesitated. It was arranged in December that he should receive a letter from the National Civil Service Reform League, and issue a public reply. In this letter the reformers—Curtis, Schurz, Silas W. Burt, Everett P. Wheeler, and others—pointed out that the great party overturn offered a searching test of the new reform. [2] Cleveland replied that he believed in the new civil service law of 1883, and had repeatedly promised to enforce it: [3]

I am not unmindful of the fact to which you refer, that many of our citizens fear that the recent party change in the National Executive may demonstrate that the abuses which have grown up in the civil service are ineradicable. I know that they are deeply rooted, and that the spoils system has been supposed to be intimately related to success in the maintenance of party organization; and I am not sure that all those who profess to be the friends of this reform will stand firmly among its advocates when they find it obstructing their way to

[1] Godkin to Stetson, Dec. 16, 1884. Cleveland Papers.
[2] Dec. 20, 1884. Cleveland Papers.
[3] Dec. 25, 1884. Cleveland Papers.

patronage and place.

But fully appreciating the trust committed to my charge, no such consideration shall cause a relaxation on my part of an earnest effort to enforce this law.

Cleveland went on to lay down two additional principles. One was
that he would not merely enforce the terms of the law, but observe its
spirit in dealing with the huge class of employees "which are not within
the letter of the Civil Service statute, but which are so disconnected
with the policy of an Administration" that they should not be removed
during their terms on merely partisan grounds. These persons he
divided sharply into two classes: efficient employees, who would be
kept for their full terms, and inefficient employees, offensive partisans,
and unscrupulous manipulators of local politics, who would be removed. The third principle was in effect a warning to the hungry Democrats. He told them frankly that faithful party work could not always
be rewarded by office, and that appointments would be based upon
careful inquiry as to fitness. It was a cautious letter, and required subsequent development, but the reformers found it satisfactory.[1]

V

Immediately afterward, a month before the inauguration, the silver
question had to be faced, and here Cleveland took a much bolder stand.
Only a genuine national exigency would have justified him in thus taking up so controversial a question. East and West were already divided
on the expediency of continuing the silver coinage, feeling was rising,
and leaders in both parties preferred to avoid the issue. Suddenly,
menacingly, "brief as the lightning in the collied night," the emergency
did appear. It was appropriate that Cleveland was thus compelled to
take an immediate position on the currency problem, for it and the
tariff were the two binding threads which ran through his eight years
in the White House, and his greatest single service to the nation was to
be his stubborn defence, against terrific assaults, of a sound financial
system.

The unemotional Abram S. Hewitt, chairman of the House Ways and
Means Committee, wrote Cleveland in great alarm on February 2: [2]

[1] Carl Schurz, *Speeches, Correspondence, and Political Papers*, IV, 414.
[2] Hewitt Papers.

I am satisfied that we are in the presence of a great peril. When in New York yesterday I ascertained that the receipts of the Custom House are now mainly in silver certificates. The stock of gold in the Treasury is being exhausted, and cannot be replenished, except through practical purchase, which will soon put gold to a premium—already the banks and trust companies are hoarding gold, or investing in sterling exchange. The Secretary of the Treasury is striving to maintain gold payments until the 4th of March, so that the inevitable suspension shall take place under a Democratic Administration. He has had a conference with the Republican presidents of the United States banks who are being appealed to and have agreed to take silver certificates at the New York Clearing House, so far as may be necessary to keep up the balance of gold in the Treasury to the point needed to avoid suspension.

This alarm was well founded. Under the Bland-Allison act of 1878, which required the coinage of from two to four million dollars' worth of silver bullion monthly, the government had now minted nearly 200,-000,000 dollars. It had exerted every effort to force this vast amount of silver into circulation. Much of it had actually gone into the channels of trade. But during and after the business depression of 1884 it began to come back again; [1] and obligations due the government were now being steadily paid in these dollars, while gold was being drawn from the treasury by the use of both silver and greenbacks. In other words, the government was compelled to accept silver from all its debtors, while it had to pay out gold to all its creditors—for any other course would have ruined its credit. It must keep its silver money and gold money at a parity. At the same time it was expected by all financial authorities to maintain a reserve of at least $100,000,000 in gold to protect the redemption of the greenbacks, and early in 1885, as Hewitt's letter indicates, this reserve was gravely threatened.

Hewitt and other sound money men, fearing that if the gold reserve once dropped below a hundred millions specie payments would have to be suspended, believed that legislation to stop the coinage of silver would arrest the danger. A law to halt all silver coinage would certainly have had a reassuring effect, and Randall and Hewitt hastily drafted a suitable amendment to the pending civil appropriations bill. They also laid siege to Cleveland, demanding that he come out boldly in its behalf. Tilden heartily favored such action, and Manton Marble, the former editor of the *World*, urged the President-elect to act.

[1] The tariff of 1883 also reduced revenues; A. Barton Hepburn, *History of Currency in the United States*, 293.

Meanwhile the silver men had also risen in arms, and were bringing equal pressure to bear upon Cleveland. By scores the representatives from the West and South rushed to the fray. Excited conferences were held, and on February 11 ninety-five Democratic Congressmen, including such leaders as S. S. Cox, W. S. Rosecrans, John H. Reagan, and William L. Wilson, sent Cleveland a letter expressing the hope that he would not yield to the men who were calling for the suspension of silver coinage. In 1873, they argued, a Republican Congress had demonetized silver, and in 1878 the Democrats, aided by part of the Republicans, had given force to the national will by providing for its limited coinage. They had done so against the arrogant opposition of the bankers, bondholders, and all those having fixed incomes, and since that date the classes which would profit by an appreciation in the value of money had sleeplessly endeavored to demonetize silver again. It was a plot of the rich to injure the poor, and the great masses of the plain people expected the new President to help them frustrate it. Two-thirds of the Democrats in Congress, continued the letter, had for six years been a united phalanx in defence of silver coinage, and would continue to be. Representative Lowndes H. Davis of Missouri warned Cleveland in a separate letter that he was rushing against a stone wall: [1]

There is great apprehension among Democratic Representatives from the West and the South that your Administration will favor the stoppage of the coinage of silver, and fail to recommend a remedy for the contraction of our currency, which is going on at the rate of three or four millions a month. This House will not aid in stopping its coinage, the next House will not do it, and there must be a wonderful change in the South and West before such action can be expected from the Fiftieth Congress.

The question, then, is what necessity there can be for a Democratic Administration to press a measure with no hope of its success, with at least three fourths of the Democratic Party opposed to it, and which will inevitably result, if not in the party's disruption, at least in losing Missouri, Texas, and Indiana, and every foot we have gained in Illinois, Iowa, Wisconsin, and Michigan, and of course with this loss, *the loss of every hope of reform in the Government.*

These may seem wild statements, but ask somebody else.

Imbued by Manning's and Tilden's financial ideas, Cleveland welcomed an early opportunity to demand, as Hayes and Arthur had done before him, an end of silver coinage. Though the crisis had been as

[1] Feb. 15, 1885. Cleveland Papers.

alarming as Hewitt pictured it, for various reasons it was transitory. By February 24 Randall had become convinced that there was no immediate need for interference, but Cleveland had already determined to act. "I have some delicacy in saying a word that may be construed by anybody as interfering with the legislation of the present Congress," he had written Randall. "But so grave do I deem the present emergency, that I am willing as a private citizen to say that I think some legislation of the character suggested is eminently desirable." [1] Believing that the subject required an expert hand, he allowed Manton Marble to draft the emphatic letter addressed to Representative A. J. Warner and others which he signed and published on February 24. [2] A flat defiance of the silver men, it pointed out that the Bland-Allison act had heaped the vaults of the Treasury with 85-cent dollars, which, with the silver certificates representing them, were receivable for all public dues:

Being thus receivable, while also constantly increasing in quantity at the rate of $28,000,000 a year, it has followed of necessity that the flow of gold into the Treasury has steadily diminished. Silver and silver certificates have displaced and are now displacing the gold in the Federal treasury now available for the gold obligations of the United States notes called "greenbacks." If not already encroached upon, it is perilously near such encroachment. . . .

These being the facts of our present condition, our danger, and the duty to avert that danger, would seem to be plain. I hope that you concur with me, and with the great majority of our fellow-citizens, in deeming it most desirable at the present juncture to maintain and continue in use the mass of our gold coin, as well as the mass of silver already coined. This is possible by a present suspension of the purchase and coinage of silver. I am not aware that by any other method it is possible.

The result was a sharp rebuff by Congress. Two days after Cleveland's letter the House defeated the amendment for suspending silver coinage by a decisive majority, 118 Democrats and 52 Republicans against 54 Democrats and 64 Republicans. The first Democratic President in a quarter century had been slapped in the face by his own party before he took his seat. Nevertheless, the letter was a statesmanlike piece of initiative. It served notice that Cleveland, following in the footsteps of Seymour and Tilden, would turn a face of granite against all inflationist schemes. By its very vigor it put heart into frightened bankers and restored confidence. His only regret, as he said later, was

[1] Feb. 9, 1885. Cleveland Papers.
[2] Full text in McElroy, *Grover Cleveland*, I, 107–109.

that the letter was composed by Marble instead of himself [1]—though its ideas were certainly common property, and most Presidents have accepted help on important papers. In the East, where a catastrophe had been feared, the letter was universally applauded. Tilden wrote Cleveland that it was the only silver thing he knew that transmuted itself into gold. At a time when it had been determined on but not published Horace White met on Broadway George S. Coe, president of the American Exchange Bank, who had supported Blaine. "Mr. White," said Coe, "I am glad that the *amiable man* was not elected. This is the time for a President who has a big hand and a heavy foot."

VI

In the field of foreign relations the activities of the Arthur Administration had rendered another immediate decision unescapable. For many years the eyes of the State Department had been fixed upon a possible canal across Nicaragua. Garfield's Secretary of State, Blaine, had made an attempt to abrogate the Clayton-Bulwer treaty, which gave Great Britain the same measure of control over any isthmian canal which we ourselves should enjoy. When Arthur came in the controversy with the British Foreign Office was continued by Blaine's successor, Frederick T. Frelinghuysen, but with no success. Finally Frelinghuysen determined to defy the old compact, and in 1884 negotiated with Nicaragua the so-called Frelinghuysen-Zavala treaty, which provided that the United States should build a canal in Nicaragua, to be owned by it and Nicaragua jointly, that there should be a perpetual alliance between the United States and Nicaragua, and that the United States should guarantee the territorial integrity of the little republic. This was a deliberate violation of the Clayton-Bulwer treaty, a direct challenge to Great Britain, and an attempt to establish a virtual protectorate in Central America. It threatened a grave quarrel with England and serious complications in the Caribbean. Bayard was one of the foremost opponents of the treaty in the Senate. His appointment as Secretary of State was therefore a virtual notice that Cleveland would reject the Blaine-Frelinghuysen policy. The treaty was at once accepted as dead, and no one was surprised when Cleveland, on taking office, immediately withdrew it from the Senate and never again submitted it.

[1] McElroy, *Grover Cleveland*, I, 110.

VII

When Cleveland left Albany for Washington in a special train on the evening of March 2, he had thus blocked out the main lines of his policy on civil service reform, silver, the tariff (for his Cabinet were all low-tariff men), and isthmian relations. He was accompanied by Lamont, Manning, and several members of his family. He had refused the railway's offer to furnish his train free, and he also refused Arthur's invitation to come to the White House. Hewitt had suggested that the colored people would appreciate it if he went to Wormeley's, which was managed by a Negro, but he spent March 3 quietly at the Arlington Hotel.

When he took the oath of office the next day it was upon a little Bible, his cherished possession, which bore in faded ink on its flyleaf: "My son, Stephen Grover Cleveland, from his loving Mother." Later the Bible was carefully bestowed in the upper lefthand drawer of the great desk which Queen Victoria had given the White House in token of British appreciation of American efforts to rescue Sir John Franklin.[1] The initial impression which Cleveland made upon Washington observers was not altogether happy. Robert M. La Follette, watching him and Arthur enter the Senate and seat themselves, felt a momentary shock. "The contrast with Arthur, who was a fine handsome figure, was very striking. Cleveland's coarse face, his heavy inert body, his great shapeless hands, confirmed in my mind the attacks made upon him during the campaign." La Follette adds, however, that he came later to entertain a deep respect for Cleveland and "to admire the courage and conscientiousness of his character."[2] The inaugural address, delivered in vibrant tones, struck most hearers as fine, while everyone was impressed by Cleveland's bold refusal to use a manuscript. "God, what a magnificent gambler!" exclaimed Ingalls.

The address dealt less with specific questions of the hour, though several were mentioned, than with the great general considerations raised by the change in party authority.[3] The government was still for all the people, Cleveland said, and should be the object of their affectionate solicitude; and now that the campaign was over, all the animosi-

[1] McElroy, *Grover Cleveland*, I, 110.
[2] Robert M. La Follette, *Autobiography*, 52.
[3] Richardson, *Messages and Papers*, VIII, 299 ff.

ties of partisan strife should give way to a sober concern for the general weal. He spoke of the evils of sectional rancor, and of the need, in a nation so large and variegated, for a spirit of mutual concession in Congress. He promised economy, a policy of independence and isolation in foreign affairs, and a cautious observance of the due sphere of the executive branch. That is, he expressed a distinctly limited conception of the President's functions. The keynote of the address was struck in an emphatic sentence near its close: "The people demand reform in the administration of the government, and the application of business principles to public affairs."

That evening, while Sousa's Marine Band played for the inaugural ball, the doors of the White House closed upon a President who felt hardly the respite of an hour from the demands of the office-seekers. Every friend had his pleas. Alton B. Parker asked for a good consulship. Abram S. Hewitt requested positions for three well known Democrats, one being George W. Julian, the political diarist, now old and poor. Apgar, after writing Cleveland that he had destroyed more than a bushel of petitions for his influence, asked a postmastership for an acquaintance. St. Clair McKelway petitioned that the chief clerk at the custom house be given the important office of collector of the port in New York. Even Harold Frederic wrote from England requesting that a former member of the *Argus* staff, now in distress, be sent to London as deputy consul-general. Secretary Bayard announced that more than one hundred applications for the post of consul-general in Paris had been received; one of them was from Cleveland's old friend Tifft, the Buffalo hotelkeeper! The President's former partner Bissell was hurt that he was not taken into the Cabinet. All the Democratic governors had names to suggest. There were some thirty well-supported applicants for the position of minister to Belgium—and so the flood rose.[1]

The whole country, thanks to the Washington correspondents, soon knew what was going on. George W. Curtis telegraphed Cleveland on March 15: "I beg the President to remember Charles Sumner's advice to Stanton—Stick!"[2] Cleveland astonished one delegation, which urged the appointment of a Democrat to an office filled by an efficient Republican, with the cutting remark: "Why, I was not aware that there was a vacancy in that position." He bluntly told another deputation

[1] Cleveland Papers, Feb.–March, 1885.
[2] Cleveland Papers.

that there was a tenure of office act. He informed a third that the commissions of gentlemen they sought to remove had some time to run, and nothing was known against them. "And," said one crestfallen man, "if you see him once and look at that face and jaw, you will believe he means what he says." Senator Butler, of South Carolina had to bow to the rule that Cleveland would grant no interviews to job-seekers and that the papers of applicants must be left at the departments. He appeared at the Interior Department with endorsements for a political favorite, saying pathetically, "I have ascertained that this is the place to file them." [1] Two Minnesota Democratic leaders, Patrick Kelly and Michael Doran, who came to Washington with a slate of proposed appointments, secured just one party office, and as a result they were burned in effigy at home. One resigned his place on the Democratic National Committee, and the other departed for Europe.[2]

Cleveland planned to dispose of the appointments in a rough order: first, the diplomatic service; second, the territories; third, the District of Columbia; fourth, the postoffices; fifth, the marshalships; and sixth, the collectorships.[3] The principal diplomatic nominations attracted nearly as much attention as the Cabinet. James Russell Lowell was just quitting London. The legation there, with the Irish and the Northeastern fisheries questions pending, required an able lawyer. To the surprise of everybody, including Bayard, Cleveland appointed E. J. Phelps, a conservative Vermont attorney who had recently been president of the American Bar Association. Though little known, he was admirably fitted for the position, possessing cultivation, broad experience, and a decided will of his own. He was soon desirous of pressing England more vigorously on certain questions than Bayard would permit. Senator Edmunds declared that he had the best legal mind in the North, but the public identified him more quickly as an essayist and the author of some excellent humorous verse.

George Pendleton of Ohio—"Gentleman George," whose devotion to civil service reform had just cost him his Senate seat—was sent to Berlin. Having studied at Heidelberg long before the war, he spoke German fluently. The French mission went to Robert M. McLane of Maryland, a well-equipped diplomatist. He could recall when his father

---

[1] N. Y. *Evening Post*, March 9, 10, 1885.
[2] *Ibid.*, May 23, 1885.
[3] Cleveland Papers; cf. N. Y. *Evening Post*, April 20, 1885.

had been minister to England and Secretary of the Treasury under President Jackson; he himself had received a part of his education in Paris, had travelled widely, had served as commissioner to China, and had been our minister in Mexico City just before the Civil War. Two better appointments could hardly have been made.[1] Cleveland sent the witty S. S. Cox as minister to Turkey. He offered Abram S. Hewitt, who deserved a better place, the ministership to Russia, Austria, or Spain, but with his usual instinct for duty Hewitt declared that his proper post was in the House, and that having given ten years to the cause of tariff reform there, he did not wish now to drop it.[2] The President pleased the Mugwumps by appointing one of them, a Scandinavian-American professor at the University of Wisconsin, as minister to Denmark.

The one bad error in the diplomatic field lay in the selection of Anthony M. Keiley as minister first to Italy and then to Austria. Keiley was a Virginia Catholic with an unfortunate record. Attending a public meeting in Richmond in 1871 to protest against the destruction of the Pope's temporal authority, he had made a speech denouncing the Italian government as a usurper. Now his harsh utterances regarding Victor Emmanuel and Italian unity were dug up and given wide publicity. It is strange that Keiley himself had not realized that they would debar him. The Quirinal naturally refused to receive him and the appointment, to the chagrin of Archbishop Gibbons, who had urged it upon Cleveland, had to be revoked.

This would have been a trifle had not Cleveland immediately made the mistake of appointing Keiley as minister to Austria. Had he given the matter careful consideration, or received proper advice from Bayard, he would not have done this. Austria had to reject Keiley not because she was in close relations with Italy, but because her relations were exceedingly strained. On both sides of the Italo-Austrian border Irredentism persisted and despite all repressive measures was continually breaking out. There was constant danger that some "incident" would bring the two nations close to war. Under these circumstances Austria could not afford to accept as minister a man whose insulting references to Italy had just been given the widest publicity in Europe.

---

[1] See *Nation*, March 26, 1885, for commendation of these appointments.
[2] Hewitt's letter, dated March 29, indicates that he thought Cleveland insufficiently concerned with the problem of leadership in the House. Cleveland Papers.

To do so would have been regarded by even sober Italians as a needless affront. When Count Kalnóky came to reject Mr. Keiley, he felt that the dignity of the Dual Empire would not permit him to disclose this real reason, and hence took refuge in allegations touching the social ineligibility of Mrs. Keiley; she was a Jewess, and he declared that she would not be acceptable in the diplomatic circle of Vienna. The State Department rejoined with asperity that the American Government could tolerate no religious tests in such a matter, but Keiley never reached Vienna. The whole episode was unfortunate. No experienced European government would have made the error of choosing for the foreign service a man with Keiley's record.[1]

During March an excited interest was taken by reformers in New York city in the question whether the Republican postmaster, Henry G. Pearson, who had been appointed by Garfield four years earlier, would be removed. He had Republican as well as Democratic enemies, for he had been of the Half-Breed faction. Preposterous charges were levelled against his honesty. Actually he was a public servant of unusual merit, and the reformers felt that his fate would supply a test of Cleveland's sincerity. Schurz sent Cleveland one of his irritating letters, warning him [2] that if he yielded he would not only make enemies of all the Mugwumps, but fire the patronage-brokers to still more insistent demands. Hewitt was equally emphatic but more tactful.[3] "The office is not a political machine," he wrote Cleveland, "and you cannot afford to make it so. The Independent will be justified if he be reappointed, and you will be free to act in other cases as you may choose." Many business men of both parties requested that Pearson be kept in office. On the other hand, the spoils politicians, especially in the Tammany camp, made energetic efforts to influence the President, one of them writing Lamont that the appointment would cost the Democrats not less than ten thousand votes. John Kelly visited Washington late in March and obtained an interview with Cleveland, from which he emerged patently dissatisfied. Cleveland waited only to make a brief investigation of the charges against Pearson, and as soon as possible (March 31), reappointed him, writing an anonymous statement for

---

[1] Upon the Keiley affair, see *Foreign Relations*, 1885, 549 ff; the well-informed European correspondence of the *Nation*, Jan. 21, 1886; N. Y. *Evening Post*, April 16, 1885, Jan. 2, 1886.
[2] March 22, 1885. Cleveland Papers.
[3] March 29, 1885. Cleveland Papers.

the press with his own hand. "The Democratic party," he declared, "is neither hypocritical, unpatriotic, or ungrateful—they will understand the whole matter, and be satisfied." [1]

Cleveland's own feelings in these crowded weeks were no secret to his few intimate friends. He was pleased by his initial reception and by his success in giving the lie to the Republican sneers at him as "a conundrum in the flesh," a tool of the "New York gang," and "a man without ideas." But he found the pressure at times almost intolerable. He wrote that "this dreadful, damnable office seeking" had become a "nightmare." [2] In its intervals he was trying hard to put the executive machine to work and inspire the Cabinet with his own zeal for administrative efficiency. The sense of duty which had attended so many of his Puritan ancestors was heavy on his shoulders. A few days before his inauguration he had written Bissell a letter containing one of his frequent bits of self-revelation. He might be taking life seriously, he declared, "but a man in my position learns how serious a thing it is to live. I think so often of the legend over the head of my bed at home." [3] He was recalling the Biblical motto in his little Buffalo room, the verse upon a man's days and his strength. His own days he was filling with honest endeavor, and trusting that his strength would endure.

[1] McElroy, *Grover Cleveland*, I, 130, 131.
[2] N. Y. *Tribune*, Jan. 9, Feb. 13, 1885.
[3] Feb. 19, 1885. Cleveland Papers.

Chapter XIII   *A Summer of Practical Reform*

TILL his midsummer vacation in the Adirondacks in 1885, Cleveland found that one exigent task crowded on the heels of another. He settled at once into a fairly comfortable routine of life in the White House. As compared with Arthur, who had entertained lavishly, he made it a simple ménage. Miss Rose Cleveland was the first chatelaine, assisted sometimes or even relieved by her sister, Mrs. Hoyt. The President's mulatto servant, William Sinclair, had come with him from Albany, receiving the title of White House steward and a salary of $1800 a year. There was a French chef, M. Fortin, who had acted during the Arthur régime and was expert in his duties, but Cleveland never cared for his cuisine. "I must go to dinner," he once wrote Bissell. "I wish it was to eat a pickled herring, Swiss cheese and a chop at Louis' instead of the French stuff I shall find." [1] So great was his desire for a plain cook that he begged Governor Hill to let him have one, Eliza by name, from the executive mansion in Albany. "I do not know whether she desires or is willing to leave," wrote Hill, "but I shall say to her that she can do as she pleases about it." [2] There were few other servants, for while Arthur, a wealthy and fastidious man, had kept butlers and a valet, Cleveland wanted no personal attendants.

He found that the White House, where Arthur and his sister, Mrs. McElroy, had insisted on a general renovation, had been greatly improved. The furniture in 1881 had been worn and soiled, the china chipped, and the storerooms filled with a miscellany left by former Presidents. Arthur, declaring that he would not live in a house looking as this one did, had cleared out twenty-four wagonloads of goods of all descriptions and, to the great delight of souvenir-hunters, sold them at auction. A silk hat and a pair of trousers once belonging to Lincoln, an ancient portmanteau of Abigail Adams', and the sideboard which Lucy Hayes had disdainfully banished, were among these wares—a local saloon taking the sideboard. [3] Arthur had a huge stained-glass screen installed by Tiffany in the entrance hall to give more privacy to the

[1] Dec. 14, 1885. Cleveland Papers.
[2] April 10, 1885. Cleveland Papers.
[3] Edna M. Colman, *White House Gossip*, 170 ff.

inmates. Upstairs, during his term, the main corridor was decorated with a number of florid western pictures lent by Bierstadt, which remained during Cleveland's first years.

The social side of the Presidency gave Cleveland little concern. His sister Rose, a woman of large stature, not unattractive in features, but with a masculine manner and an air of decision, made a distinctive and indeed an impressive hostess. Like her brother, she was obviously a person with clearcut purposes and stern will. Her tastes were literary and historical, and she was one of the most cultivated women who ever reigned over the White House. A graduate of Houghton Seminary, she had taught in that school and later in a "collegiate institute" at Lafayette, Indiana, and had lectured widely. Visitors to the White House found that she was an excellent conversationalist, and that though she preferred educated people to mere politicians, she had enough of her brother's natural democracy to unbend to the plainest visitors. Now and then she seemed a little grim, but she met her social duties well. The first reception, when on March 21 the diplomatic corps and members of Congress were invited to meet members of the Cabinet, was a distinct success, and some press reports called Miss Cleveland charming. Among the guests were James G. Blaine and his son Walker, who came early, shook hands with Cleveland, and left almost immediately.

Though Cleveland has been described in these first months as almost "alone in the White House," guests were constantly present. Early in the spring John G. Milburn came from Buffalo, and just after him Bissell. The President's sister had a Miss Van Vechten, of an exclusive Albany family—a handsome young woman of aristocratic manners, who had once been reported engaged to General Sheridan and by some was believed to be setting her cap for Cleveland—at the White House for a month; while in April Mrs. Oscar Folsom and her daughter Frances were guests for a fortnight. The daughter was to be graduated from Wells College in June, and the *World's* Washington correspondent reported that "during her short sojourn here she made many friends." Cleveland worked almost without intermission, but he could at least see these friends at table. He particularly liked having the Lamonts at the mansion, and often in the morning walked down to the fountain in the south grounds with their two little girls to feed the goldfish. At the end of April he asked them to come live with him for a time, writing that "I am sure we can arrange matters in quite a nice way and I should certainly be much pleased if such a scheme could be consummated." [1]

So far as public affairs would permit, the President quickly settled into a routine not unlike that which he had maintained in Albany.[2] He and Lamont dropped a number of superfluous clerks in the executive offices and set an example of industry to all the others. Rising early and eating breakfast at eight o'clock or earlier, Cleveland was at his desk in the executive office on the second floor before nine. For more than an hour he and Lamont attended to correspondence and other business. Then at ten he began to receive business visitors, devoting two or three hours to their affairs. Those whose calls were of a personal or social nature were requested by public notice [3] to come only at 1:30 on Mondays, Wednesdays, and Fridays, when he shook hands in the East Room with long lines who wished to pay their respects. The luncheon hour was about two o'clock. Twice a week, on Tuesday and Thursday afternoon, Cabinet meetings were held in the Cabinet room adjoining his office. In the evenings he and Lamont worked in the library, their lamps often burning till two o'clock in the morning. Cleveland had learned the need for outdoor air, and in fair weather usually fitted a late afternoon drive into his program, while early in the morning he walked in the park and down to the Washington monument. "I have taken him every drive around Washington," said his coachman, "but when he goes outside the city he gets out of the carriage and walks, keeping it up with him so that he can see what time he is making." [4] Arthur had used the little naval vessel *Dispatch* for cruises on the Potomac, but Cleveland dispensed with it. He probably worked for longer hours, day after day, than any other President since James K. Polk, who had worked himself to death.

II

The first great task which Cleveland wished to undertake was the reform of the executive departments, for he correctly believed that a generation of uninterrupted Republican administration had resulted in rust and decay. Men like Schurz thought the repulse of the spoilsmen

[1] Cleveland to Lamont, April 25, 1885. Cleveland Papers.
[2] See *Harper's Weekly,* Jan. 23, 1886.
[3] For example, N. Y. *Herald,* June 15, 1886.
[4] Washington *Post,* Sept. 16, 1885.

the immediate test of the Administration, but Cleveland expressed a wiser view. "To me," he said later, "the importance of general administrative reform has appeared to be superior to the incidental matter of civil service reform. Good government is the main thing to be aimed at. Civil service reform is but a means to that end." This emphasis upon reform must constantly be kept in mind in measuring the achievements of his first administration. In the half century following the Civil War a clear distinction can be drawn between the reformer and the progressive. While the one was intent upon purifying the existing processes of government and effecting more completely its traditional aims, the other was fired rather with the ambition to bring in wholly new processes of government and achieve novel aims. Both types, upon the plane of true statesmanship, were rare. Cleveland, like Tilden before him and Charles E. Hughes after him, was instinctively a reformer; Theodore Roosevelt and Woodrow Wilson, beginning as reformers, developed into progressives. In the middle eighties, a prosperous and conservative period, the hour of progressivism had not yet struck, but the need for more efficiency and earnestness in government was great.

Expert observers agreed with Cleveland as to the opportunity. "Mr. Manning and Mr. Whitney," exclaimed the *Nation* the week after inauguration, "have a chance of honest fame which does not come to men once in fifty years." Secretary Lamar, it might have added, had an equal opening. The first Cabinet meeting was devoted exclusively to departmental reform, and the next half dozen dealt almost entirely with it. Late in the summer the *World* was able to declare, with a little exaggeration, that the Administration "has already in a little more than five months destroyed nests of corruption in the Navy Department, the Treasury, the Indian Bureau, the Land Office, the Coast Survey, and the War Department." [1] Better than that, it had instituted new departmental policies of a far-reaching kind.

Reform may be a celestial votaress, but she is a rather dull one; and it was fortunate for Cleveland that not only his Cabinet but many of the assistant secretaries and bureau heads were fired with zeal in her behalf. There was a notable body of these men, who must be credited with much of the success of the Administration. The most conspicuous and effective was the Assistant Secretary of the Treasury, Charles S. Fairchild, a favorite of Manning and destined to be his successor. Be-

[1] Aug. 13, 1885.

fore entering office Manning had called Fairchild up the Hudson from New York city to insist that "now we are in the scrape, you must help." [1] The two belonged to the same political and financial school. The son of a loyal up-State Democrat, Fairchild had helped Tilden prosecute the canal ring, had served as attorney-general of the State, and had practised law with incidental attention to banking. He used to say later [2] that he had learned Democracy first at the knees of Seymour and later at the side of Tilden, while the warmest friendship of his manhood was with Manning. He soon became intimate with Cleveland, who frequently had him for a companion on his late afternoon drives. Only less active in Treasury affairs was Conrad N. Jordan, who was called from the Third National Bank in New York to become Treasurer of the United States, and of whom much was to be heard in the second Administration.

In the Interior Department Lamar leaned heavily upon his First Assistant Secretary, Henry L. Muldrow, a fellow-Mississippian who had been in Congress since 1877, and who by committee work had learned much about Interior affairs; he was as brisk as Lamar was slow and philosophical. More important still was the new Land Commissioner, William Andrew Jackson Sparks, an explosive Illinois Democrat who had also served for eight years in Congress. He was a born crusader, chosen by Cleveland because of his known belligerence and independence, the two qualities most needed in his office. [3] He sometimes disregarded strict legal rules in his work of protecting the public domain in the West, and finally quarrelled with the more cautious Lamar, but before his resignation he made a striking record. In more ways than one he was a worthy predecessor of Gifford Pinchot. The Commissioner of Agriculture in the same department was not so happy a choice. Norman Colman of St. Louis, named despite the opposition of Chairman W. H. Hatch of the House Agricultural Committee, was editor of *Colman's Rural World* and had been prominent in many rural organizations, but he was a prosy, old-fashioned, quiescent individual. [4] The chief of the Indian bureau, however, could not have been bettered. Cleveland appointed John DeWitt Clinton Atkins

[1] Fairchild's speech to Brooklyn Democratic Club, May 19, 1888; MSS in Manton Marble Collection, University of London.
[2] Speech of Feb. 11, 1892.
[3] Cf. E. S. Osgood, *The Day of the Cattleman*, 203 ff.
[4] L. S. Ivins and A. E. Winship, *Fifty Famous Farmers*, 359 ff.

of Tennessee, who had been in Congress half a dozen terms, was greatly interested in the Indians, and was as fearless as Sparks. It did not sweeten reform to some Northern tastes that, counting Lamar, Muldrow, and Atkins, three former Confederate colonels were prominent in the Interior Department.

III

In the Navy Department subordinates did not count for so much, for Whitney's impetuous energy was equal to a dozen men; and this was the department which received the greatest blaze of publicity. The precise nature of Whitney's work has sometimes been questioned, and some critics have insisted that the rebirth of the American navy dates from Arthur's and not Cleveland's administration. Yet the facts are simple. Legislation had been carried through under Arthur, but the work authorized had been bungled, and it was now necessary to turn back and start anew.

Cleveland and Whitney found that the navy in 1885 had just entered upon what was of necessity a rapid and violent transition from old equipment and methods to new. The ocean defences of the country, which were still those of Matthew Perry's and Farragut's day, had to give way at once to the fleets of Dewey and Sampson. Wooden ships were to be abandoned for steel, smoothbore cast-iron batteries for steel rifles and torpedo tubes, old designs for blue-prints requiring swifter hulls, watertight compartments, and powerful engines. Compared not merely with European but with some South American warships our navy was hopelessly antiquated. With the exception of two vessels of the so-called *Alert* class, iron sloops with three masts, we possessed nothing but wooden hulls, and apart from a few Palliser converted rifles of eight-inch calibre, our armament consisted of old-fashioned guns which had been hardly respectable in 1865. The government had first awakened to the situation in the autumn of 1881, when a naval advisory board had made an alarming report on our weakness and had called for the rapid building of steel cruisers. Congress responded on March 2, 1883, by authorizing the construction of three cruisers, later called the *Atlanta, Boston,* and *Chicago,* and a dispatch-boat, the *Dolphin.* Two years later, as Arthur was packing his bags in the White House, it authorized four additional vessels, which were left for Whitney to build.[1]

Fumbling and blunders were impossible to avoid. Up to the time of the building of the first cruisers, no steel for ship-plates had ever been rolled in the United States; no vessel of any kind had been built entirely of steel of domestic manufacture.[2] The country had no yards which compared in skill with the British yards, no steel-mills which had ever proved their ability to make armor, and no foundries which could be relied upon to make modern steel guns. Yet if in Arthur's administration a really able Secretary of the Navy had pooled his brains with those of the nation's best industrialists, the new navy might have been well launched. Instead, the Secretary was a hack politician, William E. Chandler, and the shipbuilder he chose was a single illiterate, elderly, infirm ironmaster named John Roach. In his own day Roach was a picturesque and not unimpressive figure.[3] An Irish orphan, he had come to the United States at the age of sixteen, had shown indomitable pluck and energy, and after using his savings of $100 in buying, with three other mechanics, the bankrupt Aetna Iron Works in New Jersey, had gradually built up a fortune. The iron industry flourished during and after the Civil War. In the flush years preceding the panic of 1873, Roach purchased plant after plant—the Morgan Iron Works in 1867, the Neptune Works in 1868, the Allaire Works in 1870, and a shipyard at Chester, Pa., in 1871. Seized with an ambition to restore the American merchant marine to its pristine vigor, he constructed so many iron ships at Chester that in the seventies and early eighties most of those under the American flag came from his yard. He and Chandler were close friends, for he contributed money to Chandler's political campaigns and made him personal gifts of as much as $1,000.[4] When Congress authorized the first new vessels, Chandler saw that he was awarded the contracts for all four. Other bidders were offended, and the Cramps angrily declared they would never again offer a contract on work for the Navy Department. Whatever Roach's qualifications—and in Grant's time he had undertaken the six iron monitors then ordered, so that he possessed some experience—the look of favoritism was deplorable.

---

[1] Annual Reports, Secretary of the Navy, 1884–1885.
[2] Cf. Rear-Admiral Edward Simpson, "The United States Navy in Transition." *Harper's Magazine*, June, 1886.
[3] See articles on Roach in *Appleton's Annual Cyclopedia*, 1887; N. Y. *Herald*, Jan. 11, 1887.
[4] E. P. Oberholtzer, *History of the U. S.*, IV, 343.

Immediately after Cleveland took office Whitney was informed that the dispatch-boat *Dolphin,* the first of Roach's four new ships, had been completed and its acceptance recommended by the naval advisory board. Both Cleveland and the Secretary were suspicious. The latter demanded a new trial, and appointed a board of expert examiners which included Commander Robley D. Evans. Early in June, after four trips, this body made a scathing report.[1] It declared that the single effective gun was so placed that it could not be fired directly ahead; that the ship could not consistently make the required sea speed of fifteen knots; that the engines and other machinery were of such bad design as to require a disproportionate engine-room and fire-room force; that the bow of the ship was not strong enough to resist heavy seas; that the steel shafting had broken on the first trial; that the armory was wet; and that there were minor structural defects. The question of rejecting the vessel was then laid before the Attorney-General. Garland reported that as neither the law nor the terms of the contract had been properly complied with, the government was not bound to accept the ship; and that the contract was illegal anyway.

The implications of this decision were far-reaching. Roach's contracts for the *Chicago, Atlanta,* and *Boston* were of equally questionable validity. He was already financially embarrassed, had received money advances from Chandler, and was worried to illness by the possibility of an exposure of his dubious relations with him. Now he made a hasty assignment of his property to friends, and the Navy Department had to meet the emergency by taking over the uncompleted vessels and using his plant and working force to complete them.

Meanwhile other aspects of Chandler's management of the navy were coming under scrutiny. Due in part to carelessness, and in part to politics, spoils abuses, and bad precedents that stretched back to Robeson's long and corrupt régime under Grant, the establishment had been a scene of hopeless waste.[2] Chandler in his annual reports had pointed out some of the extravagance, but without applying any remedy. Between 1868 and 1885 the government had expended more than $75,-000,000 upon the construction, repair, equipment, and upkeep of a heterogeneous array of wooden vessels, and had almost nothing to show for it. Secretary Whitney instanced the *Omaha* as an illustration of

---

[1] See text of report in N. Y. *Evening Post,* June 19, 1885.
[2] *Annual Report,* Secretary of the Navy, 1885.

the futile dissipation of government funds. This antique craft, good only for scrapping, had lately been rebuilt at a cost of $572,000, a sum which would have paid for a small steel ship of modern efficiency. The *Mohican*, a little tub of 910 tons, had cost $908,000 for repairs in twelve years, while the contract price of the new steel cruiser *Atlanta* was only $675,000. Whitney ordered an inventory of stores, which showed an appalling accumulation of junk; more than twenty million dollars' worth of supplies had been brought together, of which four million dollars' worth was already obsolete. At the eight navy yards, for example, there were almost 50,000 augurs and bits, of which about half had been lying for years in closed yards where no work was done. The track of the politicians was evident everywhere. Repairs had been farmed out to Republican contractors, who gave lavishly to campaign funds. At the principal yards work was slackly managed during most of the year, but just before election they were scenes of busy activity. Hundreds of laborers, hastily hired, were marched to the polls in Kittery for Tom Reed, in Charlestown for Henry Cabot Lodge, in Philadelphia for Boss Leeds, and in Brooklyn for Platt's local favorite.

It was found also that the "new navy" was being carelessly and inexpertly planned. American naval designers were a generation behind their times, and men like Roach, indifferent to fine technical skill, could not fabricate fast or powerful vessels. When the *Boston, Atlanta,* and *Chicago* were completed they compared very unfavorably with British work. Since the government itself had finished them, it had to accept them. But the armament was weak, the machinery poor, and the speed so slow that they could neither overtake the best modern merchantmen nor escape the speediest armored ships of Europe. They would be of limited usefulness as commerce destroyers, and hopelessly at a disadvantage in any fleet encounter. Whitney said in his report for 1886 that "the experience of the department in its first attempt at the creation of modern vessels of war has been such as to excite the greatest concern and disappointment." While the blame fell partly upon Chandler's selfish management of contracts and the carelessness of the Arthur Administration, a good deal of it was assignable merely to the dead weight of years of departmental inefficiency and to sheer ignorance and inexperience.

Manifestly the first requisite was a reconstruction of the department, and upon this Cleveland and Whitney agreed. "Our Navy Department as at present constituted is Chaos," French E. Chadwick had written Robley D. Evans early in 1885.[1] "A worse organization for the purpose intended could scarcely be devised." Although the basis of administration in any such organization should always be a careful division of duties and continuity of method, the department consisted of eight uncoördinated bureaus, each of which arrogated to itself as much independent authority as possible and issued orders to the service which had the force of orders from the Secretary himself. Every bureau head seemed to act as if his were the paramount branch of the administration, and adopted a *noli me tangere* attitude toward his associates. Each bureau had its own secretariat. The result was confusion, duplication, and worst of all, spasmodic instead of continuous effort. There was no Assistant Secretary, and when the Secretary went out to lunch, the department was headless. The organization of the British Admiralty was far superior.

After repeated consultations with Cleveland, Whitney urged a reconstitution of the department into three principal branches: one to deal with naval personnel, one with construction and materials, and one with finance, accounts, contracts, and purchasing.[2] This was a sensible plan, and without waiting for Congressional action Whitney put as much of it into effect as the statutes would permit. Borrowing some features from the British organization, he made sure that the work of the bureaus was coördinated, that policies fixed by himself were carried out by his subordinates, and that responsibility was rigidly established. At the same time he plugged many leaks. He ordered the Mare Island authorities to halt their repair work on the *Mohican*, curtailed other wasteful activities, and gave rigid orders for the extirpation of politics from the department.

In his first message Cleveland supported the demand for an effective navy, and as public sentiment favored it, fresh appropriations were made. During the summer of 1886 Congress added a new cruiser, two armored warships, and a torpedo boat to the list. Within a short time Whitney had let contracts, this time carefully executed and supervised, for five protected cruisers averaging about 4,000 tons in displacement —the *Charleston, Baltimore, Newark, Philadelphia,* and *San Francisco.* The work was distributed among different shipbuilders; Cramps re-

---

[1] Jan. 23, 1885. Cleveland Papers.
[2] *Annual Report,* 1885; cf. review of Whitney's work in *Public Opinion,* April 29, 1893.

ceived their share, and by a special decision of Cleveland's, one cruiser was awarded to the Union Iron Works of San Francisco. In addition, Whitney placed under construction in the Brooklyn and Norfolk navy-yards the second-class battleship *Texas* and the battleship (at first called an armored cruiser) *Maine*, both destined to become famous in the Spanish War.[1] He had meanwhile taken over the *Dolphin* from the builders, his naval experts having assured him that the blame for its defects rested rather upon the government's designers than upon Roach.[2] The utmost business vigilance attended the construction of all the new ships.

Looming behind the new keels was the formidable problem of making the United States independent of Europe, and especially Great Britain, in the manufacture of armor and rifled guns. The subject was investigated in 1884–86 by two naval boards and two committees of Congress, and evoked vehement discussion on the part of steel manufacturers. It was impossible to begin fabricating the new armor and ordnance without heavy initial expenditures, and the steelmakers demanded contracts of proportionate value. As a result, Whitney in the summer of 1886 consolidated in one advertisement all the navy's requirements for armor and gun-steel on the warships then authorized, giving the bidders an average of two and a half years to furnish it. He stimulated offers by correspondence with the leading steel manufacturers and induced Congress to appropriate a lump sum of $4,000,000 to foot the bill. On March 22, 1887, he reported to Cleveland that he had opened bids from five different companies, the Bethlehem Company making the lowest offer on the armor-plate contract, and the Cambria Iron Company that on the gun forgings.[3] The Bethlehem interests set about erecting a special mill which Whitney predicted would furnish armor and gun-steel "second to none in the world." [4]

Cleveland was never interested in a large navy equipped for offensive operations. He did believe that a wealthy country with a long coastline and rapidly growing commercial investments should cease to be an impotent leviathan and build up an efficient naval protection. It always gave him pleasure to think that the false start made by the Arthur

[1] *Annual Reports,* Secretary of the Navy, 1886, 1887, 1888; N. Y. *Herald,* Aug. 16, 1887, describes some of the contracts in detail.
[2] Roach, broken by the worry and humiliation of the naval scandals, died on Jan. 10, 1887.
[3] See N. Y. *Herald,* March 23, 1887, for description of bids.
[4] *Annual Report,* 1887.

Administration had been retrieved, and an unassailable beginning made by his own. Whitney has been generally credited with giving the United States a new navy, but he and Cleveland did more—despite the refusal of Congress to pass the legislation that Whitney asked, they gave it a new navy department. By the close of the first Administration the United States was taking pride in its fleet. The White Squadron was still so weak that a few British battleships would have brushed it aside. But the press published pictures of the cruisers rushing through foam-torn waters, their funnels belching smoke, their guns spitting fire, which made them look like floating Gibraltars. A growing propaganda nourished the desire for maritime power. Mahan, who in these years (1886–89) was head of the naval war college at Newport, was writing his first notable book, the *Influence of Sea-Power Upon History, 1660–1783*. Back of the ships were plants capable of building better vessels, yards that for the first time since Gideon Welles were economical, and a department which worked with precision.

IV

By far the greatest administrative responsibility of the government was in the West. Here it was still the possessor of a vast domain of approximately a million square miles, or more than six hundred million acres, of public land—glebe, timber, mineral, and desert. Here it still held suzerainty over eight great territories, several of them now populous—Dakota alone had more than four hundred thousand people. It was protector, landlord, inspector, creditor, and policeman to a motley array of Indians, cattlemen, miners, railwaymen, and officials. Here it applied laws, rules, and traditions dating back to 1787; sought to adjust the conflict between rancher and farmer, Indian and white; and tried to reconcile the Eastern demand for conservation of government resources with the Western demand for their rapid utilization.

In the lavish years following the Civil War the public domain had been administered as if it were illimitable. The West had been thrown wide open to settlers by the Morrill Act of 1862, while in the fifties and sixties munificent grants were also made to railroad promoters and agricultural colleges. The donations to railroads were indignantly halted by Congress in 1871; within a dozen years, however, the government had given more than 160,000,000 acres to railroad corporations. As homesteading increased and smoke rose from thousands of sod houses in the trans-Missouri country, the area of good farm land declined so rapidly that both the census of 1880 and the report of the General Land Office for that year warned the government of its imminent exhaustion. Nevertheless, in Dakota in the year Cleveland took office the area of land homesteaded or purchased was equivalent to Connecticut and Rhode Island combined.[1]

One evil to be attacked was the stubborn retention by various railways of land-grants which they had never earned. Most of these grants had contained forfeiture provisions providing for a reversion to the government if certain conditions were not met. When Cleveland took office the area subject to forfeiture was equal to New York, New Jersey, Pennsylvania, Delaware, Maryland, and Virginia; but under Republican Administrations the railroads had tended to treat forfeiture clauses as a dead letter. Another evil lay in the abuse of the so-called indemnity lands. When the railroads were endowed with strips along their proposed routes, it was realized that these areas contained bits of land already in private hands. As indemnity, the railroads were permitted to select generous additional tracts within certain fixed limits beyond their grants. It sometimes happened that homesteaders, in ignorance of the risks they ran, would settle within these indemnity areas. The agents of some railroads, with greedy eagerness, took every opportunity of claiming the lands thus improved by innocent settlers. Moreover, compliant officers of the Interior Department, under pressure from the corporations, had withdrawn excessive tracts of indemnity land and were keeping them locked up from the would-be homesteaders. The railroads would eventually select the cream of these areas. In great sections of the West the antagonism between the settlers and railroads had, for these and other reasons, risen to fighting pitch.

Another source of constant loss lay in fraudulent surveys of government land. It had become customary for Washington to allow the surveyor-generals of the various States and Territories to let contracts for public-land surveys to their deputies. Under this system laxity and dishonesty flourished. Syndicates were formed to control all surveying contracts and the government was cheated out of valuable land rights. Moreover, lumber and cattle corporations had learned to manipulate the system for their own benefit. A still greater evil lay in the practise

[1] *Annual Report,* Secretary of Interior, 1886, p. 68.

of land-grabbing by false entries. Systematically planned, and practised from the Canadian line to the Rio Grande by an array of predatory interests, it overspread the West with a dark cloud of fraud. When superintendents of lumber companies or ranchers hired their loggers or cowboys, they often stipulated that each should file homestead papers upon the best timber or grazing lands available. Experienced prospectors then sought out the lands for them. Expert attorneys prepared a brazen "proof" of settlement, and witnesses were hired to support it. When all was finished, the lands thus fraudulently obtained were sold or given away to the corporations. The true homesteader arrived to find that the best areas had thus fallen to interests which clung to them with the grip of a tiger.[1] In 1887 the Land Commissioner reported that "bold, reckless, and gigantic schemes to rob the government of its lands" had been exposed in every State and Territory; that over 5000 cases of perjury or subornation of perjury had been discovered; and that everywhere State and Territorial officers had connived at the frauds.[2]

No early problem of his Administration worried Cleveland so much as this wholesale spoliation of the West. He saw one of the richest treasures of the government slipping like sand through its indifferent fingers. Railroads, cattle-barons, lumber companies, slippery surveyors, Western politicians, all had a share of the spoils. When the land could not be seized its products were often stolen. A well-financed corporation behind which the Northern Pacific was supposed to lurk, the Montana Improvement Company, organized in 1883 with a capital of four millions to exploit the forests of Montana and Idaho, ruthlessly despoiled government lands, and by buying up witnesses, laughed at threats of prosecution.[3] Elsewhere in the West valuable woodlands along rivers and creeks were impudently sheared to the ground. The rulings of most previous Secretaries of the Interior, Schurz being an honorable exception, had proved an assistance rather than an impediment to these nefarious enterprises. Arthur's Secretary, Henry M. Teller, was personally honest but had leaned in a deplorable way to the Western demand for rapid exploitation of our natural wealth.

It seemed difficult to find a point at which to attack the accumulated evils. Cleveland later wrote that "The history of the department, and

[1] *Annual Reports*, Department of Interior, 1885, 1886.
[2] *Ibid.*, 1887, 136 ff.
[3] *Ibid.*, 1886; *Democratic Campaign Book*, 1886, 108–112.

especially that of the General Land Office, as it has been communicated to the President, has been that of a contest waged on the one hand by wealth, represented by the most capable and accomplished lawyers, overflowing with precedents and arguments, and an overcrowded office almost buried under accumulated work and ill-supplied with men to bring the delayed cases to conclusion." [1] Commissioner Sparks of the Land Office declared with equal resentment: [2]

The tract books of this office show that available public lands are already largely covered up by entries, selections, and claims of various kinds. My general information leads to the conclusion that no large amount of public land remains in the Western States and Territories east of the cattle belt which an actual settler can take up without first buying off a speculative claim, or avoiding some invalid entry by contest proceedings, while within the cattle region it is notorious that actual settlements are generally prevented and made practically impossible outside the proximity of towns, through the unlawful control of the country maintained by cattle corporations. The demand for free land for the homes of American citizens, which is daily increasing in intensity, can no longer be met, unless unpatented lands now unlawfully held or claimed can be recovered to the public domain, and future illegal and fraudulent appropriations decisively stopped.

Within sixty days after taking office Cleveland, Lamar, and Sparks had put a decidedly new face on the situation. Years before, Congress had made a large land grant to the New Orleans, Baton Rouge & Vicksburg Railroad Company, attaching a time limit which expired while the road was still unconstructed. The grantee sold its claim to the New Orleans Pacific Railroad Company and this organization during Arthur's Administration filed selections of more than one million acres between New Orleans and Shreveport. Despite protests by residents of this area, on the Friday preceding Cleveland's inauguration Secretary Teller ordered an additional force of clerks to prepare the necessary patents. They were kept hard at work all day Sunday, and on March 3 patents were actually issued for 680,000 acres—this sudden assiduity causing much talk in Washington. Secretary Lamar on March 10 issued an order suspending the further issuance of patents, while the Senate shortly debated the subject. Van Wyck of Nebraska, a radical Republican, hotly attacked Teller, who had just taken his seat in the

[1] Interview with Cleveland, N. Y. *Times*, Feb. 23, 1889.
[2] *Annual Report*, 1885.

Senate from Colorado, declared that Jay Gould and Collis P. Huntington were at the bottom of the whole scheme, and asserted that the whole
recent history of the Interior Department had been a record of subserviency to corporations.[1]

Meanwhile, Sparks early in April issued a sweeping order which
suspended action in the General Land Office upon all entries in most of
the trans-Mississippi West except private cash entries and certain land-
scrip locations. This was to permit an investigation of the mass of
fraudulent claims. A clamor arose against the Administration for this
sudden stoppage of the greater part of the public-land machinery, but
it was absolutely necessary until further precautions could be taken.
Forty-two special agents were kept busy in the West, during the next
fiscal year, reporting upon more than 3,000 cases of suspected fraud,
and their findings were sensational. One such agent, after examining
a part of the Duluth and St. Cloud land district, wrote that in this
single tract 4,300 homestead claims had been proved up and certified
for patents where fewer than a hundred persons were living by cultivation of the soil.[2] Nor was this the worst of the situation. The agents
reported numerous instances in which settlers on the plains had been
driven from their land by fraudulent entries alongside them, corporations placing their cowboys or other workers on homesteads in such a
way as to cut the newcomers off from water, markets, or the society
they had expected to grow up about them.[3]

In August, 1885, Cleveland struck at the ranchers who were fencing
in government lands and water courses; he issued a proclamation denouncing unlawful enclosures and calling upon Federal officers to de-
molish them. There had been a mania for unlawful enclosures since
1878, and the government had recently learned of fenced-in areas of
public land reaching 30,000 acres. One rancher took down 34 miles of
fence after Cleveland's order.[4] Sparks meanwhile took steps to purge
the surveying system. Men who had destroyed monuments to make
resurveying necessary were punished, and the surveying "rings" were
broken up. He suppressed the pseudo-homesteading by cowboys and
lumberjacks, while timber-thieving was checked by a vigorous patrol.

[1] Edward Mayes, *Life of Lamar*, 476; *Cong. Rec.*, March 9, 1885; vol. 17, p. 9 ff.
[2] See N. Y. *Evening Post*, Jan. 5, 1886, for Eaton's activities.
[3] *Annual Report*, Secretary of Interior, 1885, 1886.
[4] *Ibid.*, 1886, 30 ff.

Sparks' predecessor had gathered evidence during 1884 of thievery which aggregated more than $7,000,000,[1] and by suits both criminal and civil the guilty corporations—the Sierra Lumber Company in California offered a conspicuous example—were brought to book; during 1885 alone the actions for recovery prepared in the Interior Department totalled $3,000,000.

v

Of a similar nature was the immediate work done by Cleveland and Lamar in protection of the Indians. The immemorial feeling among pioneers that the savages had no rights worth respecting was heightened by the fact that their Western reservations were actually much larger than they required. When Cleveland took office a raid was under way which required emergency action on his part. On February 27, 1885, only five days before the inauguration, a great part of the Old Winnebago and Crow Creek Reservations on the east bank of the Missouri River in Dakota Territory were restored by Arthur to the public domain and thrown open to settlement beginning May 1. Arthur's order is difficult to explain, for it was a palpable violation of a solemn treaty; and certain circumstances point strongly to collusion between officers of the Interior Department and land speculators. A tract of 494,778 acres, worth not less than a million and a half of dollars, was wrenched from the Indians and coolly handed over to expectant Westerners. The date May 1 meant nothing to many of these men. When the order was issued the plains around the reservations were already dotted with the camps of hungry settlers, and the ink was hardly dry on the document before they thronged over the boundary. Within a few days two thousand persons had staked off their homesteads, and houses were going up by the hundred. Thousands of more law-abiding settlers had gathered in convenient Western cities and were ready to enter at midnight on April 30.[2]

Friends of the Indian appealed to Cleveland, who at his first Cabinet meeting directed Lamar to make an investigation. As the Secretary pressed his inquiry, he became convinced that Arthur's order was an imposition upon an ignorant, confiding people which would cause much

---

[1] *Ibid.*, 1884, 15 ff.
[2] *Annual Report*, Secretary of Interior, 1885, I, 30 ff.

distress and retard the progress of the northern tribes toward civiliza-tion. Cleveland also consulted Garland, who held that the order was illegal. On April 17 the President issued a proclamation declaring it "inoperative and of no effect," and warning all persons who had entered the reservations that they would be summarily ejected.[1] Again Western teeth were gnashed, but justice was manifestly served.

In the Southwest the cattlemen, as the range grew crowded, had for some time been pressing upon both the Indian lands and public lands in the so-called Indian Territory, a fertile area of almost forty-five million acres. One of the resulting problems had to be met by Cleve-land forthwith. Various Presidents had issued proclamations warning the ranchmen to keep away from the Indian Territory, and declaring that military force would be used if necessary, and Cleveland in March followed their example. Unfortunately, this by no means ended the trouble. It was shown that parts of the Cheyenne and Arapahoe reserva-tions were occupied by white cattlemen who claimed the right to graze stock thereon by virtue of agreements with the Indian owners. These leases had been obtained in 1883 over the protests of many of the Indians affected; they were manifestly illegal, though Federal agents had acquiesced in them; and Cleveland determined that the govern-ment would not recognize them. The situation presented a constant menace of warfare. Many of the savages were accusing the ranchers of robbery and fraud; many of the ranchers, on the other hand, were pointing to their heavy investments and the scarcity of land, denying that the lazy Indians needed such large areas, and accusing "bad" Indians of killing cattle and threatening the lives of cowboys. There was danger of a collision. While Endicott prepared to concentrate troops in the region, Cleveland sent General Sheridan westward with orders to ascertain the facts, and especially to invite the tribes to lay their complaints before him.[2] The President's sympathies were obviously with the Indians.

There was something to be said for the cattlemen; their speculative business had been feverishly expanded, herds had been crowded to-gether till every square mile was in use, and new pastures were des-perately needed. But Sheridan discovered that the grass-leases were a

---

[1] Richardson, *Messages and Papers,* VIII, 305.
[2] Cleveland directed Sheridan to call for Indian statements "as to any real or fancied injury or injustice towards them." Cleveland Papers, April (no day), 1885.

clear injustice to the two tribes. The use of about four million acres of grazing land had been obtained at a yearly rental of one or two cents an acre; and under the leases the Indians were liable for the loss of cattle by depredations, these damages being deducted from the rent. Hundreds of thousands of cattle were thus being fattened by ranchers who got the use of the land for almost nothing and paid no taxes. Sheridan proposed drastic action—the expulsion of the cattlemen forthwith, with only forty days to drive the stock out of the territory. In accordance with his views, Cleveland on July 23, 1885, proclaimed the forty days' notice.[1] More than 200,000 head had to be driven out upon the already overcrowded ranges. There was vigorous protest from Eastern investors and Western ranchers that the notice was inadequate and that thousands of cattle would perish from the hardship of enforced drives. The herds reached the overgrazed ranges as the Southwest was about to undergo one of the bitterest winters in its history, and the following spring the cattlemen found more than four-fifths of their stock dead in the ravines or piled up along the range fences.[2]

It was an instance in which Cleveland had done right, but had done right too recklessly and harshly. One of the investors who had requested a longer notice was Abram S. Hewitt, for whom Cleveland had the deepest respect. His losses under the edict approached a quarter of a million dollars, and he found it difficult to forgive Cleveland.[3] There is evidence that in 1886 Cleveland regretted his peremptory action. Yet Sheridan had informed him that immediate action was necessary to avert an outbreak of hostilities, and the local Indian Agent, Dyer, had agreed.[4] Bissell had a little joke on the subject which amused Cleveland. He wrote that the order should have been given in Latin— "Hinc illae lachrimae"—"Hence! these steers!"[5]

VI

In all this hardworking Administration there was no one who labored more grimly than Manning. He had come to Washington with reluctance, for he was growing old, loved his friendly little circle in

[1] Richardson, *Messages and Papers*, VIII, 307.
[2] Osgood, *The Day of the Cattleman*, 217, 218.
[3] Hewitt to Cleveland, Oct. 20, 1885. Hewitt Papers.
[4] See article on the subject in *Harper's Weekly*, Aug. 29, 1885.
[5] N. Y. *World*, July 24, 1885.

Albany, and knew that his health was precarious. One factor in inducing him to accept the Secretaryship of the Treasury was his loyalty to Cleveland. All the ill-natured gossip which John Bigelow presents in his life of Tilden as evidence that Manning's relations with the President were unhappy may be dismissed as unfounded. David B. Hill, for reasons of his own, enlarged upon this gossip, even going so far as to declare later in print that friction between Manning and Cleveland was constant and that it had "killed Manning." [1] The fact is that the two men trusted and admired each other in rare degree, and no one can examine their papers without realizing that they were completely in harmony. A second reason for Manning's acceptance was the desire of his bride, a vivacious and charming woman, to share in Washington society. She insisted upon taking a large house and entertained brilliantly. But once Manning had passed between the tall pillars of the Treasury he threw himself into his tasks with exhausting ardor. It is mild praise to say that he was one of the ablest of those Secretaries of the Treasury who fall into secondary rank. He was not a Hamilton or Gallatin, not even a Chase or McAdoo, but among the others he holds an eminent place. Night after night his carriage waited for him till midnight. He told a friend that his office was at once so exacting and fascinating that he could not leave it. It was impossible for him to make concessions to expediency. The silver-coinage act he called a dangerous fraud; the tariff he characterized as robbery; the greenbacks he termed a delusion. His blunt frankness and courage, precisely matching Cleveland's own traits, dulled the edge of the opposition to him. He offered "a splendid example," wrote Godkin, "of the superiority of candor over cunning as a political force." [2]

Though Manning was a dogmatic believer in low tariffs, he signalized his advent in Washington by an attack upon the systematic undervaluation of imports at the custom houses. This practise had been going on for years, enriching foreign manufacturers and dishonest importers at the expense of honest American merchants. In New York city in particular a group of importers had allied themselves with slippery members of the Appraiser's staff. When the custom-house valuations did not suit them they had the Appraiser recall the invoices for "corrections." Man-

---

[1] See Hill's long, characteristic, and amusing review of Bigelow's *Tilden* in N. Y. *Times*, May 5, 1895.
[2] N. Y. *Evening Post*, Sept. 23, 1886.

ning found that in 1884 the Appraiser, a Mr. Ketchum, had thus altered no fewer than 1709 invoices, a proceeding both arbitrary and illegal. Though Ketchum protested that most of the corrections had been made by subordinates and were merely incidental in character, there was a mass of sworn testimony to show that he had issued nearly all the orders himself, and that they had almost invariably resulted in material reductions.[1] Manning saw to it that the laws which had been disobeyed for fifteen years were now met to the letter; in other words, he came to the rescue, as a matter of duty, of the protective system whose principle he detested. An impressive list of the most respected drygoods merchants of the country signed a memorial applauding the new regulations and declaring that they constituted the first attempt by the Treasury in years to protect honest importers.[2]

A long series of departmental reforms was also introduced at the Treasury. Within three weeks after entering office Manning appointed a commission under Fairchild to overhaul the whole machinery and recommend means of placing it on a business basis. There was general agreement that at least 500 of the 2300 clerks could be spared; while upon the recommendation of Conrad N. Jordan valuable changes were introduced in the method of Treasury bookkeeping and in the monthly balance sheet.[3] The running expenses of the custom-houses were drastically diminished. The so-called "fraud roll," which had cost the government $90,000 the previous year, was reduced to $15,000; this being a salary-roll of party hacks who were supposed to be detecting customs frauds, but who had generally attended to politics.

Everywhere the new Administration was taking hold with a firm grasp. Even Endicott, who looked after one of the tiniest armies in the world, found something to accomplish. He abolished the system by which officers who possessed political or social influence had been allowed an indefinite tenure in Washington or other desirable places; this order bearing harshly upon ballroom ornaments, but welcomed by unfavored officers in bleak Western posts. It is true that no serious scandals were uncovered. The loud campaign promises of the Democrats were not redeemed by the exposure of any new Crédit Mobilier

---

[1] *Nation,* June 18, 1885.
[2] Cf. Manning's special report on customs collections, December, 1885.
[3] N. Y. *Evening Post,* March 21, April 2, 1885.

or Star Route frauds.[1] But the reforms of Whitney, Manning, and Lamar nevertheless showed insight and courage, and proved that Cleveland had selected his aides well. One of the opposition cries had been that the Democrats were too inexperienced to be useful. Yet these "inexperienced" men were going into the departments, and within a few weeks stopping old scandals and substituting vigilance for laxity.

"I knew," Cleveland said in 1888, "that abuses and extravagance had crept into the management of public affairs; but I did not know their enormous power, nor the tenacity of their grip."

[1] Yet the N. Y. *Evening Post* of June 13, 1885, estimated the loss to the Treasury from the custom-house frauds in 1884 at $65,000,000.

WHILE thus engaged in invigorating the government services, Cleveland was waging a continuous struggle with the spoilsmen. The phrase civil service reform, it must be confessed, does not possess either a mellifluous or an exciting sound. The very dustiest shelf, in political libraries, is that occupied by books on the subject. Yet it needs only to be lifted from the category of dull abstractions and placed against its true background of human appetite and passion to become interesting. Its various friends—the tall, spidery Carl Schurz, the somewhat unctuous G. W. Curtis, the disdainful Godkin—spilled too much ink upon it and made it a bit tiresome. Yet actually there played about it, in the seventies and eighties, some of the fiercest struggles of American politics. We shall do well to think not alone of reports, editorials, and associations, but of Grant's cronies filling him with fierce suspicion of Bristow and other reformers; of Conkling in the New York State Convention hurling his gibes at Curtis and proclaiming that when Dr. Johnson said that patriotism was the last refuge of a scoundrel, he ignored the enormous possibilities of the word reform; of Garfield caught between contending camps of Stalwarts and Half-Breeds and shot by a fanatic who proclaimed that "I am a Stalwart, and now Arthur is President!"; of Ingalls telling a responsive Senate that purity in politics is an iridescent dream. Not least dramatic, in this succession of pictures, is the spectacle of Grover Cleveland sitting in the White House library while surges of hungry politicians swept up the stairs to his door.

About Cleveland's treatment of civil service reform and the spoilsmen history has less to say than to unsay. In his own day there were two diametrically opposed views of his course: that of admirers who praised extravagantly his steadfast courage, and that of critics who were sure that his professions were largely pretence. There has since gained ground a compromise opinion—that he tried hard, that he resisted the pressure better than anyone else would have done, but that he yielded a good deal. Yet this is too simple a dismissal of a difficult problem. It should be recalled that Cleveland, a strong believer in government by party, never made any really sweeping promises to the reformers. If we scrutinize his attitude toward appointments, we shall

234

see that he laid down certain definite principles and tried to apply them to definite problems; that at first he did extremely well, though from inexperience and reliance on poor advisers he made some bad appointments; and that his record was best where the reform spirit was strongest, as in New York and Massachusetts, and worst where it was weak, as in Indiana and Maryland. We shall also see that the result of his efforts was a dismaying revolt in his own party within a year, and that he then hastily took steps to maintain party unity. He realized that if a division developed within the Democracy he might be fatally crippled in all his policies; he did what he could for reform up to the limit where a disastrous schism really threatened, but no further.

II

The amount of pressure upon Cleveland from office seekers in 1885 has been exaggerated. Experienced observers declared it less than Garfield had faced four years earlier. Yet it was bad enough. Godkin's trenchant pen pictured in it an editorial on "The President as Sheikh"; a hundred years hence, he wrote, the country would find it hard to believe that Cleveland, Bayard, and Manning had spent their first months like Arab chieftains, sitting under a big tree outside the city gate, hearing individual demands for rewards and punishments, and distributing bounty. Cleveland in June, dashing off a grateful note to Apgar, who had taken steps to discourage some hundreds of place-hunters, closed with the words; [1] "The clock has just struck ten, and the doors must be opened to the waiting throng. The question with me is, When (if ever) will this thing stop?" A little later he confessed to a reporter:

I go to bed after a long day with the feeling that I must be the meanest man in the world, for I seem to say only "no" where I would be only too glad to say "yes." But this office-seeking is a disease—I am entirely satisfied of that. It is even catching. Men get it, and they lose the proper balance of their minds. I've known men to come here to Washington on other business, with no thought of office, but when they had been here a couple of weeks they had caught it. They seem suddenly to get a mania.

The principles which Cleveland quickly laid down can be extricated from a half dozen separate pronouncements. He had determined that in

[1] Cleveland Papers.

the offices filled by Presidential appointment for four-year terms inoffensive and efficient Republicans should not be removed "during the terms for which they were appointed." [1] The minor officeholders were all appointed for unfixed terms, but Cleveland decided, as a second rule, that they should stand on precisely the same footing as their superiors. "My idea has been," he wrote, "that those officials who have held their places for four years should as a rule give way to good men of our party"—but if they were good public servants, not till the end of the four years.[2] A third principle was that "those who have been guilty of offences against our political code" (that is, who had shown what Cleveland elsewhere called "pernicious partisanship") "should go without regard to the time they have served." [3] A fourth principle was that he would appoint no Democrat for mere political service, without being assured of his competency, honesty, and readiness to devote himself to his office. And as a fifth rule, he was resolved to give no offices to personal friends merely because they were friends.

A President in Cleveland's position was certain to find it impossible to please either of the opposing groups of extremists. The spoilsmen were full of angry objections. They did not wish to wait till the expiration of a four-year term before seizing an office; they did not wish the task of proving that a Republican officeholder was an offensive partisan before ejecting him; and they did wish to place their political henchmen in office without a cautious inquiry as to their fitness. The reformers also regarded the rules at two points with much uneasiness. They objected to the principle of a rotation in office after four years. Cleveland should be content, Schurz and the National Civil Service Reform Association said again and again, when approximately half the offices were filled by Democrats. That is, both parties should be willing to strike and maintain a balance, and this could be done only by leaving the fittest Republicans in office for more than four years. Again, who should decide just what constituted "offensive partisanship"? The reformers feared that the term would cloak unjust removals.

We have said that at the outset Cleveland made an exemplary record, though one marred by a few bad errors. In New York city he delighted

[1] Letter of Dec. 25, 1885, to National Civil Service Reform League. Cleveland Papers.
[2] Letter to Manning, June 20, 1885. Manning Papers.
[3] *Ibid.*

the independents by restoring Silas W. Burt to the post of Naval Officer: a Republican with fifteen years of service in the custom house to his credit, and a staunch believer in civil service reform, who had been ejected by Arthur for political reasons. The Naval Officer, as the auditing authority in the custom house, holds a highly responsible position. He nominated Malcolm Hay, a public-spirited attorney of Pittsburgh, who had no interest whatever in spoils, to be First Assistant Postmaster-General; that is, the officer in charge of all fourth-class appointments. During Hay's short tenure the politicians detested him. The leaders of the Democratic machine in Massachusetts had united upon Peter Butler for the collectorship of the port, but Cleveland passed him by to name a Mugwump, Leverett Saltonstall, one of the ablest of the "solid men of Boston." Reformers again expressed gratification when Secretary Manning appointed E. O. Graves, who had worked his way up from a clerkship and had been Assistant Treasurer under a Republican President, as chief of the bureau of engraving and printing, which with its 1200 employees offered a rich field for the spoilsman.

Secretary Manning, with Cleveland's approval, announced that bureau heads in the Treasury Department would not be removed except for cause, and the same rule was enforced in the War and Navy Departments. In Indiana the organization headed by Vice President Hendricks received so few plums that its dissatisfaction was unbounded, and Hendricks filled his last days with covert attacks on Cleveland.[1] In Ohio the disreputable faction led by Senator Henry B. Payne was studiously ignored. When a political delegation from Chicago, numerous and arrogant, reached Washington with a slate which included representatives of the professional Irish, professional Germans, and the ruling Mike McDonald organization, it also was given a cold shoulder. Seven Democratic Congressmen had endorsed the machine selection for Federal marshal, but Cleveland appointed an Ogle County man who was quite unknown to politics.[2] The Massachusetts regulars, headed by John Quincy Adams, Jr., and Patrick Collins, protested to Cleveland that he was unjustly slighting them. An impression rapidly spread over the country that the President was impervious to political influences of the baser sort.

[1] N. Y. *Evening Post*, March 23, 1885.
[2] *Ibid.*, June 10, 1885.

III

Cleveland showed more resolution than his predecessors, including Lincoln, in stubbornly refusing to appoint personal friends to office, and felt genuine anguish when this offended some of his old associates. He was hurt because so many Buffalo men expected him to offer them gifts in the careless fashion of President Grant. Bissell wished a seat in the Cabinet—but there were two New Yorkers there already. He then asked to be made consul-general in London, the fees of $40,000 a year rendering this the most lucrative of all government offices. He was tired and needed a change, he wrote, the money would be useful, and his family would enjoy London society! For good reasons, Cleveland again refused. Although he offered Bissell several other positions, including the Comptrollership of the Currency and the office of Treasurer, his old partner felt slighted. He grumbled to his friends of his rebuff, even shedding tears,[1] and in his frequent letters to Cleveland hinted at ingratitude. All this stung Cleveland to the quick. Writing Bissell late in June, he declared with asperity that "I cannot rid myself of the idea that I owe so much to the country, that all other obligations shrink almost to nothingness before it":[2]

And if, in carrying my present burden, I must feel that my friends are calling me selfish and doubting my attachment to them and criticizing the fact that in my administration of my great trust I am not aiding them, I shall certainly be very unhappy, but shall nevertheless struggle on. The end will come; and if on that day I can retire with a sure consciousness that I have done my whole duty according to my lights and my ability, there will be some corner for me where I can rest.

You must not think I am always blue and always unhappy. In the midst of all I have to do, daily and hourly come the assurances from the people in all parts, that they are satisfied and pleased. If I could only, by giving up all I have or expect, liquidate the debts and obligations to my friends, a terrible load would fall from my shoulders. You say that there were very few and could be counted on the fingers of one hand. I am sure that five thousand have claimed that they were spent in my behalf to an extent that can never be compensated. What a nice thing it would be if my *close* friends could see a compensation in my successful Administration.

As Bissell continued his complaints and they were echoed by other Buffalo men, Cleveland a few weeks later delivered himself of a sharper

---

[1] Simon Rosendale to the author, Albany, June 18, 1930.
[2] McElroy, *Grover Cleveland*, I, 134.

letter, addressed to Goodyear but intended for Bissell's eye. Declaring that he could never give the lie to his pretensions that merit and not favoritism would count in the public service, he burst out indignantly: [1]

I have been here five months now, and have met many people who had no friendship for me, and were intent on selfishly grabbing all they could get, without any regard to the country, the party, or to me; but I have managed to get along with them as well as with my Buffalo friends. And now I am done. I feel sick at heart. I don't want to let these friends go; but I am tired of this beating about the bush and all this talk about "second-handed invitation" and "holes in a plank" and that sort of thing. If people lie in wait for me to discover things that may be construed into slights and offences, they will find plenty of them. I am not much on my guard with friends.

I have no complaints to make. Of course I thought it strange that with the hundreds of invitations to visit hundreds of places during my vacation, my friends in Buffalo did not seem to care to see me; but I am not going to say that I can get along without Buffalo or Buffalo friends. I care much—very much—for the latter. But by God! I have something here that cannot be interfered with; and if my Buffalo friends or any other friends cannot appreciate that, I can't help it. . . .

For God's sake, Charley, don't think that I am any way out of sorts with you.

No predecessor of Cleveland had ever given such close personal scrutiny to applications for appointments. He spent endless hours, far into the night, going over bundles of recommendations. While other Presidents had bothered only with the first, second, and third-class post-offices (that is, those having an income of more than $2,000 a year), Cleveland frequently had Vilas bring him material bearing upon the fourth-class appointments. As in Albany, Lamont was indispensable as a political adviser. The sandy-haired secretary, with the genial smile lighting up his Scotch sharpness, tipped back his chair and received the Congressmen and State committeemen tactfully. He carried on so voluminous a correspondence that his papers, as now preserved in Washington, constitute a virtual directory of Democratic leaders from Kittery to San Diego. Some of his best-trusted advisers wrote him continually—Francis Lynde Stetson and Abram S. Hewitt in New York; D-Cady Herrick in Albany; George Fred Williams in Boston; William M. Singerly of the *Record* and A. K. McClure of the *Times* in Phila-

[1] *Ibid.,* 137.

delphia; W. L. Scott in Erie; Melville W. Fuller in Chicago; and Don M. Dickinson in Detroit. The President would have done well to trust more to Lamont and Vilas on petty appointments, devoting himself to broad policies, but that was not his way.

When he committed errors, and the reformers made them the subject of noisy criticism, he tried honestly to correct them. If the uproar which was raised over some bad appointments now seems excessive, we must remember that the civil service law of 1883, applying to all the minor employees of eleven custom houses and twenty-three great post-offices, raised these places conspicuously in the public eye. One of Cleveland's mistakes was the appointment of Aquilla Jones as postmaster in Indianapolis—a politician who was shortly accused of discharging all Republicans within reach, of invading even the classified service, and of permitting Democratic candidates to cheat in the civil service examination. Lucius B. Swift took up the matter with Cleveland, assuring him that in any fight with the spoils politicians the people would stand by him. "That has nothing to do with it," said Cleveland, irritated. "We must find out what is right and do it regardless of the result." There was an investigation, which sufficiently exonerated Jones to permit of his retention under strict promises of good behavior. Another bad appointment was that of J. Parker Veazey as postmaster of Baltimore. Soon coming under fire, he resigned, to Cleveland's relief, in May, 1886. Still another was the selection by Manning of a member of Gorman's Maryland machine, Eugene Higgins, to be chief of appointments in the Treasury Department. But much the worst blunder was the choice of E. L. Hedden as Collector of the Port of New York— a blunder which caused Cleveland great anxiety before he could repair it.

Hedden, a well-recommended business man and a friend of Hubert O. Thompson, gave a signal exhibition of weakness in managing the Custom House, the very citadel of machine politics in New York. In June and July, 1886, the New York *Times* published articles exposing his incompetence, showing that the spirit of civil service reform had been habitually outraged, and indicating that Thompson was the real villain behind the arras. Cleveland, after writing several patient admonitions to Hedden, had already made up his mind to get rid of him, and brushed aside Manning's expostulations. "The chief is determined to make a change," Manning wrote Thompson. "He cannot be talked out of this determination. There is much mischief abroad. Many good men are victims of this mischief and many more will perish of it." Thompson, now fast drinking himself to death, his brief career closing in discredit, burst forth in a letter to Manning which indicates the fury that the cheaper politicians were developing against Cleveland: [1]

Mr. Cleveland, who you, Mr. Tilden, and myself made President, and you recollect all the circumstances, wrote Francis Lynde Stetson a letter asking him to get Mr. Hedden's resignation, simply, solely, and entirely because the New York *Times* and the *Evening Post* had abused Mr. Hedden for not being a strong civil service man. In spite of all my feeling against Mr. Cleveland, I have held my peace. I have done everything in his interest and in the interest of all our friends in Washington; I have been loyal and true, in spite of the gross indignities which I was subjected to, but which we need not refer to any further now, as I am perfectly satisfied on that subject; but to think that the President should dream of asking Mr. Hedden to resign, is the greatest mortification that has ever been experienced by myself in my life. My dear Manning, pardon me for intruding on your illness, but this is such an important thing. It means my political destruction; it means the destruction of many men who supported Mr. Cleveland in New York; it means absolutely ruin all around. I must appeal to you, I must ask you to intercede. This thing must not be done.

You know that I do not want to threaten. I do not want to do what is unwise or thoughtless, but if Mr. Cleveland does this dirty, dastardly act, I think I will be justified in going to any extremity that I see fit. He is so afraid of the papers that I will be compelled to publish him in the papers to show what a cowardly knave and fraud he is. I have facts which you know of yourself; I have facts which I have received from Mr. Bissell; I have facts which I have got from a dozen other sources, which could show him in a shape that would ruin him. . . . This thing has driven me fairly to desperation. To think of such a dastardly act as this man asking my friend to resign, and through that awful sneak Frank Stetson.

In place of Hedden, who resigned August 7, Cleveland appointed Daniel Magone, a lifelong resident of Ogdensburg, one of the best lawyers of northern New York, and a man long active in the Tilden organization. He was an ideal officer. Near the end of the Administration Silas Burt wrote Cleveland a confidential letter on Magone's qualities, praising his "lightning-like quickness of perception as to facts and their relations," his judgment, his untiring industry, which had extinguished all the arrears of business, and his skill in improving business methods.

[1] Cleveland Papers.

IV

But while the *Nation* was publishing a laudation of Cleveland's record in his first six months, while the National Civil Service Reform League in its convention of August, 1885, was praising his courage "amid immense perplexities and difficulties," a party storm was rising. There was much to be said for the rebellious politicians. For better or worse, the United States had always been governed by party and parties had always been nourished by patronage. Tilden had once bitterly declared that the opposition party in America would have to be supported by two-thirds of the voters to be sure of success, for otherwise the leverage which the Administration could exert by its control of offices and appropriations would be irresistible. Was Cleveland now to throw away the advantage which the Democrats, after twenty-four years, at last held in controlling more than a hundred thousand Federal offices? Men began to talk of dry-rot and discouragement in the party; they asserted that if Cleveland persisted, the workers who had borne the heat and burden of the day would desert him.

The first angry voice was lifted from the South. In Louisiana political power had long been concentrated in an odious ring, of which Senator Eustis was the most prominent leader and the New Orleans *Times-Democrat* the principal newspaper supporter. Cleveland, learning of the ring's character, broke its hold on the State by the appointment of honest and businesslike men to the New Orleans custom house, post-office, and other Federal positions. Naturally Eustis burned for revenge. On August 4, 1885, he declared that Cleveland was "a conspicuous and humiliating failure," charged him with "treacherous conduct toward the party he claims to represent," and threatened that if the Administration were not made Democratic "in the full significance of the term, Mr. Cleveland and his Cabinet shall fall and be buried in the ruins they have made."[1]

Foremost among Cleveland's journalistic critics were Henry Watterson of the Louisville *Courier-Journal* and Joseph Pulitzer of the St. Louis *Post-Dispatch* and the New York *World*. Both were brilliant, hotheaded, and irresponsible. Pulitzer in particular, intensely earnest, cocksure, and belligerent, and gifted with a remarkable flair for making his newspapers interesting and aggressive, set out to discipline the

[1] N. Y. *World*, Aug. 5, 1885.

President. He saw everything in vividly contrasting blacks and whites, and to him the Democrats were white and the Republicans black. Battling like a Roland in 1884, he had made the *World* a veritable horn of Roncesvalles, which Cleveland later declared was one of the decisive factors in carrying New York. As thick-and-thin party men, he and Watterson regarded the Mugwumps with contempt and demanded that the fight against the Republicans be pressed without a truce. In their systematic campaign to force Cleveland to drop the Independents and pay more attention to the Democratic regulars they were supported by the Omaha *World-Herald*, Atlanta *Constitution*, Cincinnati *Enquirer*, Chicago *Times*, Boston *Globe*, and other newspapers.

"Cleveland must remember," said the *World*, "the obligations which an Administration elected by a great historical party owes to that party." [1] Pulitzer reprinted Jefferson's famous letter of 1801 to the citizens of New Haven who objected to the displacement of a customs collector, in which Jefferson explained that he had to make removals, for the public service was wholly in Federalist hands and "few die and none resign." Reporters were sent out to interview Democratic leaders, a long list of whom expressed approbation of Pulitzer's opinions. The Washington correspondent wrote that even Manning and Whitney, while refusing to say anything for publication, had told their friends that they heartily approved of the *World's* editorials. Adlai E. Stevenson, who had just become first assistant postmaster-general, was bold enough to give out a statement commending the newspaper. "Although it is daily asserted that hundreds of postmasters are being appointed," he declared, "yet the six months which have elapsed since Cleveland's accession finds only between ten and twelve per cent of the offices occupied by Democrats." [2] Meanwhile, direct pressure upon the President and his advisers was becoming steadily heavier. One Congressman warned Bayard that "the men who do the voting and give their time and their money to secure party success will say that, if Republicans only are fit to fill places, they will quit work."

In the midst of this uproar Cleveland carried the patronage problem off with him on his summer vacation. The season was unusually hot in Washington. He had thought for a time of imitating Lincoln and taking a cottage near the Soldiers' Home, but decided that the White

[1] N. Y. *World*, Sept. 10, 1885.
[2] N. Y. *World*, Sept. 12, 1885.

House was cool enough. Already he had found the best spots on the Potomac for brief fishing trips, on which several Cabinet members occasionally accompanied him, but it was evident that he should get away from Washington for at least a fortnight. The death of General Grant, who painfully breathed his last at Mount McGregor on July 23, made it necessary to go to New York for the imposing funeral; and seizing the opportunity, he went on to the Adirondacks for a short vacation.

This first Presidential excursion, taken in company with Dr. S. B. Ward of Albany and a few other friends, was planned with a simplicity that would now be impossible. No secret service men, clerks, secretaries, or servants accompanied Cleveland. He simply set off for the wilderness as any jaded business man might do. His party had engaged four of the best guides of the North Woods: Gard Maloney, a skilful navigator of the northern lakes, Charley Brown, an expert hunter, Wesley Wood, who acted as cook, and most important of all Dave Cronk, a tall, powerful man who gave special attention to Cleveland. The President grew fond of Cronk, though as he later wrote, "I have never been able fully to understand why he should charge me half a dollar a day more than anyone else." [1] The party moved from point to point in the southern Adirondacks and was soon lost to civilization.

Some rumors that Cleveland was ill gave the *World* an excuse for sending a reporter into the woods to hunt up the "lost" President. After an exhausting tramp the correspondent finally overtook the party, introduced himself, and was received with more affability than Cleveland usually showed to newspapermen. He was assured that the President was in superb health, and observed the rough and primitive style in which he camped: [2]

The President asked me to join them at breakfast and told the cook to "place one more plate." The meal consisted of broiled venison, baked potatoes, hot biscuits, and tea with condensed milk. It was served on a rough board supported on stakes. Large logs were used as chairs. Everything was primitive in the extreme. There was not the slightest thought of form or formality. While we sat at table, I had an excellent opportunity to observe the President's appearance. He seemed even to have gained considerable flesh since he entered the mountains, and his manner betokened some fatigue and lassitude. I was told by one of his guides that the arduous journey through the forest had exhausted him so much that for two days after reaching camp he had

[1] Cleveland to S. B. Ward, June 14, 1886. Cleveland Papers.
[2] N. Y. *World*.

been unable to move freely about. Small wonder, speaking from my own experience! The life he is leading in his retreat in the wilderness is evidently too much for him. It is totally unadapted for any but the hardiest woodsman.

Cleveland found his principal delight in fishing, and left the more strenuous sport of deer-hunting chiefly to Dr. Ward. Like his successor Mr. Coolidge, he seldom fished with flies, finding that he could catch more trout with bait. At night in fine weather the whole camp sometimes indulged in the unsportsmanlike practice of jack-hunting or torch-hunting for deer. If it rained or drizzled, they played euchre till the small hours. The result, as a guide told the reporter, was that they obtained only four or five hours' sleep in the twenty-four, a fact which accounted for Cleveland's jaded appearance. Their sleeping quarters were a low-roofed cabin, twenty-seven feet long and ten wide, half of which was used for the stores and guides and the other half by Cleveland and his companions. When ready for bed they simply threw off their outer clothing, wrapped themselves in blankets, and hunted for the softest spots on the balsam boughs with which the ground had been covered. Several deerhounds were kept and were used at times in coursing game. A college student who passed several of the President's camp sites just after he had gone was struck by the number of empty bottles tossed into piles near by; some of them were water-bottles— and some were not.[1]

While on this vacation, and while the resentment of party men and editors was waxing hottest, Cleveland wrote a long letter on appointments to a prominent Northwestern politician. It is noteworthy that the letter stated with extreme stiffness his determination to adhere to a reform policy; it is still more noteworthy that the letter was never mailed. From the sylvan quiet of Saranac Lake, Cleveland recalled to his correspondent that he had explicitly promised that minor office-holders would not be removed during the continuance of their terms merely to make way for Democrats. Declaring that public sentiment was now strongly hostile to a wholesale change in governmental officers, he added that he shared this feeling and intended to remain steadfast in his policy. Wherever officeholders were found to be using the influence of their positions for partisan ends, they would be dismissed; "but the enjoyment, in a decent manner, of their political privileges and

[1] W. H. Hooper to author, March 17, 1930.

rights, should not be made a pretext for removal for the purpose of putting in their place our political friends." [1] The letter went to Lamar and other Cabinet members for their advice, and it was deemed inexpedient to send it.

V

The fact is that late in 1885, under the full impact of party demands, Cleveland began to modify his position on appointments. Some recession was inevitable. The vital question was not one of formal rules, but of interpreting the rules, and the thrust for a more liberal interpretation was irresistible. Party government, as organized in the eighties, simply could not exist on the austere basis demanded by Schurz. That Cleveland was faced by the threat of a formidable party revolt is shown by the expressions of even the best Democrats. There was no finer young Congressman than William L. Wilson, recently president of the University of West Virginia. To reform in all its aspects he was a friend, yet he wrote in his diary for August 31, 1885: [2]

Since my return [to Washington] I have been at work upon the Post-offices and have had quite a number of changes made. On the 10th July Mr. Malcolm Hay, the First Assistant Postmaster-General, was obliged to resign on account of his ill-health, and Hon. A. E. Stevenson of Illinois succeeded him. This has been a great relief to the members. The First Assistant Postmaster-General makes appointments of all fourth-class postmasters, and the long absence of Mr. Hay after his qualification, his ill-health, and his reluctance to make removals except upon strong and compelling evidence, made our work very slow and burdensome. In Mr. Stevenson we have found a man whose service in Congress taught him how to understand our position. He is naturally prompt, energetic, and accommodating. There are in my district six Presidential postoffices, and over 330 minor (fourth-class) postoffices.

When Cleveland emerged from the Adirondacks he found that the opposition in New York to his reform policy had consolidated itself about David B. Hill, whose character represented nearly everything that Cleveland did not. Already Hill was in evil odor with the independent press and voters, for his record as governor was discreditable. He had given executive support to the costly fee system in Brooklyn offices, had opposed the Niagara reservation, had shown hostility to prison

---

[1] Mayes, *Life of L. Q. C. Lamar*, 486, 487.
[2] Wm. L. Wilson, MS. Diary.

labor, and had proved a thorough spoilsman. Compared with the great Democratic executives since Silas Wright he was a small and tricky man, yet he now possessed a powerful following, and his nomination for governor at Saratoga in September, 1885, was a dramatic occurrence. All the heterogeneous elements which hated Cleveland—Tammany men, liquor dealers, Buffalo machine men, office jobbers—were on the scene. The County Democracy and the Mugwumps, which were aligned in opposition, were swept aside like straws.[1] As the delegates assembled, Cleveland published a letter to Dorman B. Eaton, who was just resigning as chairman of the Federal Civil Service Commission, which Hill's supporters construed as a blow aimed at the governor. "I hope," Cleveland wrote Eaton, "the time is at hand when all our people will see the advantage of a reliance . . . upon merit and fitness, instead of a dependence upon the caprice or selfish interest of those who impudently stand between the people and the machinery of their government." The President's enemies had a direct answer. Bourke Cockran placed before the convention a resolution assailing civil service reform, dictated by Hill himself, and it was received with a rousing demonstration.[2]

The Gradys, Cockrans, and Spinolas of New York City, with a phalanx of up-State politicians, exerted every nerve to give Hill a staggering majority over the Republican candidate, Ira Davenport; but they were not thinking of Davenport alone. They were striking past him at Cleveland. Hill's election in November by a plurality of 12,000 was a signal for wild rejoicing, and it accentuated the chorus of reproach levelled at the President. Men pointed out that the governor's lead in the State was ten times as great as Cleveland's in 1884. "It means, above all," trumpeted the *World*, "that the fact that Governor Hill was the representative of real Democracy and not of sham Mugwump Democracy secured his election by a majority probably fifteen or twenty times greater than the State gave Mr. Cleveland last year. This is the lesson of the election." Hendricks, "Vice President of the spoilsmen," remarked that the result in New York was "a straightout Democratic victory, *with all that that implies.*" No taint of reform about it! Nast published in *Harper's Weekly* a cartoon drawn with all

---

[1] For the Mugwump attitude toward Hill, see *Harper's Weekly*, Oct. 17, 1885.
[2] Don C. Seitz, MS. Life of Bourke Cockran. Cf. D. S. Alexander, *Four Famous New Yorkers*, 66 ff.

his old verve.[1] The spoilsmen had raised Hill high on a dais overlooking a Roman arena; the Tammany tiger below was about to leap upon the defenceless figure of liberty; and politicians looked gloatingly on beneath banners which read, "We are the Rulers, We are Hungry, Now we will Raise Hill to the White House." The simultaneous election in Maryland, where Gorman's machine swept the State, was regarded as another stinging rebuke to Cleveland's policy.[2]

One by one the barriers were partly lowered. "I haven't finished my message by a good deal and am almost crazy over it," Cleveland wrote Bissell on November 25. "I am afraid it will be a bad one; the d—d everlasting clatter for office continues to some extent, and makes me feel like resigning, and Hell is to pay generally." There was no haste and no surrender of vital principle. But party leaders were permitted to state their cases to Stevenson and Lamont, and a steady flow of suspensions and removals followed. In January, 1886, Hale of Maine rose in the Senate to complain that out of 984 fourth-class postmasterships in his State, about 100 changes had been made, nearly all on the recommendation of the Democratic State Chairman. In other States the record was much the same. Cleveland himself showed more generosity with the Presidential appointments. It became evident, also, that the four-year rule would ultimately result in a replacement of most Republican officeholders. Vilas in April had issued a confidential letter (which was soon published) to several Congressmen, urging them to go over the list of postmasters, pick out offensive Republican partisans to the number of a sixth or a quarter of all, and propose good Democrats in their places. It would be sufficient proof of partisanship, he declared, for a Senator or Representative to affirm that the postmaster had been a partisan editor, stump speaker, or political committeeman, that his office had been a political headquarters, or that his clerk had been assigned political duties.[3] This general rule by Vilas was now put into effect. By midsummer of 1886 most Democratic politicians felt distinctly better, and the party revolt was subsiding.

Early in the summer Senator Hoar, whose literary gifts and polished demeanor could never conceal his intense partisanship, assailed Cleveland in the Senate for his retreat upon the patronage. He charged him

---

[1] *Harper's Weekly*, Nov. 14, 1885.
[2] See interview with Gorham in N. Y. *Herald,* reviewing this campaign. Oct. 10, 1887.
[3] For hostile comment see N. Y. *Evening Post, Times,* May 11–14, 1886; special report National Civil Service Reform League, March, 1887.

with trying to serve God and the Democratic party at the same time. Holding direct control of about 3,500 positions, he had nominated more than 2,000 Democrats to office, and, Hoar asserted, had frequently dismissed worthy men for mere party reasons. The Independent press rallied to Cleveland's side and showed that some Republican Presidents had made many more changes than he. Indeed, dismissals upon purely factional and personal grounds had been continuous under Grant, Garfield, and Arthur. Nevertheless, there was much force in what Hoar said. That autumn the *Civil Service Record* published statistics which showed how heavy a sweep had been made in the Interior Department alone.[1] Up to the beginning of October, more than 70 per cent of the offices at the disposal of the President there had been refilled.

The impression of an uneven and somewhat fumbling record which Cleveland thus made upon reformers was accentuated by the curious Benton and Stone affair late in 1886, in which he showed himself well-meaning but signally maladroit. Under pressure from various reformers, and in anticipation of the coming Congressional campaign, Cleveland on July 14, 1886, had issued a letter of warning to officeholders against the use of their positions "in attempts to control political movements in their localities." [2] He had told them to keep out of the manipulations of primaries and conventions, to avoid the active conduct of any campaign, and to abstain from "pernicious activity" in general. Hayes had issued a similar order, but it had not been well enforced. During the autumn two men, District Attorneys M. E. Benton of western Missouri and W. A. Stone of Pittsburgh, made a number of campaign speeches, were reported to the President, and in October were suspended from duty for their alleged violations of his order. Benton was a Democrat and a favorite of Senator Vest; Stone was a Republican, who had shown such extreme partisanship for Blaine in the campaign of 1884 that when Cleveland first entered office his removal had been seriously considered, and he was kept in office only on what Cleveland believed was a clear promise to refrain from offensive conduct.

Neither man had now made speeches of a violently partisan nature, and both had so ordered their political engagements as not to interfere with their official duties. Cleveland had specifically written a Texas officeholder that he did not regard a temperate and decent political

<hr>

[1] Oct., Nov., 1886.
[2] Richardson, *Messages and Papers*, VIII, 494, 495.

speech made by an official to his neighbors as objectionable.[1] It seems clear that neither should have been removed, though both deserved a caution or reprimand; and certainly it was highly unwise to treat the Republican more harshly than the Democrat. Yet this was precisely what Cleveland did. Shortly after the November elections he accepted Benton's defence and reinstated him, but at the same time dismissed Stone, declaring that he did so not because his speeches were a graver infraction of the rule than Benton's, but because to make Republican speeches at all was an act of treachery: [2]

Mr. Stone when permitted to remain in office became a part of the business organization of the present Administration, bound by every obligation of honor to assist within his sphere in its successful operation. The obligation involved not only the proper performance of official duty, but a certain good faith and fidelity, which while not exacting the least sacrifice of political principle, forbade active participation on his part in purely partisan demonstrations of a pronounced type . . . conducted upon the avowed theory that the administration of the government was not entitled to the confidence and respect of the people.

It was a graver count against Cleveland's management of the civil service that by 1887 his Civil Service Commission had proved signally weak. The voluntary retirement of Dorman B. Eaton had been followed in the fall of 1885 by Cleveland's demand for the resignation of the two other commissioners, John M. Gregory and Leroy D. Thoman.[3] He meant to reorganize the body completely, and for a time he searched hard for able men. He asked Leverett Saltonstall of Boston to serve as chairman, but he refused. Melville W. Fuller of Chicago was appealed to, but felt unable to give up his practice of $30,000 a year.[4] The President would gladly have given Bissell a place on the commission, but his old law-partner also declined to make the sacrifice. In the end the reorganization proved a complete failure. As chairman Cleveland named, at the solicitation of Chief Justice Waite, an old-style Indiana politician named A. P. Edgerton, seventy years of age, who in 1888 shocked the reformers by describing the merit system as "a hollow and extravagant fraud." As the junior Democrat he appointed a former superintendent

[1] Oct. 29, 1886. Cleveland Papers.
[2] Cleveland to Garland, Nov. 23, 1886. Cleveland Papers.
[3] Oct. 12, 1885. Cleveland Papers.
[4] Oct. 15, 29, 1885. Cleveland Papers.

of Indian education, John H. Oberly, who was little better. By all odds
the strongest commissioner was the Republican, Charles Lyman. Cleveland missed an opportunity by not obtaining a man of national reputation and influence, as Harrison did later when he appointed Roosevelt.

Yet in other directions Cleveland tried his best to make fresh gains
for the reform principle, and the general impression which he diffused
was favorable. It was easy for Senator Hale in 1888 to fling a formidable
set of statistics at Cleveland's head. He cited official figures to show
that up to June 11, 1887, out of 52,609 fourth-class postmasterships,
the Administration had refilled about 40,000; out of 2,359 presidential
postmasterships, Cleveland had refilled about 2000; and that he had
replaced 138 out of 219 consuls, 100 out of 111 customs collectors, 84
out of 85 internal revenue collectors, 64 out of 70 marshals, and 22 out
of 30 territorial judges. But the apparent force of these statistics is
largely broken by the fact that the mere expiration of four-year terms
would account for a general overturn by 1888. Cleveland consciously
broke none of his promises, and he did not permit a clean sweep or
anything like it. He kept and promoted numerous deserving Republicans; for example, he and Bayard in 1886 advanced the brilliant Alvey
A. Adee, a Republican, from the Third to the Second Assistant Secretaryship of State, against indignant Democratic protests. He insisted
upon a reorganization and extension of the civil service rules which
made the merit system more efficient; and he made repeated additions
to the classified list, so that when he left office it included about 27,000
places instead of 14,000. A single order placed more than five thousand
employees of the railway mail service under the new system. He claimed
also, and with justice, that he had wrought a substantial alteration in
the attitude of his party toward office. Ballard Smith of the *World*
talked with Cleveland late one night in 1887 as he finished his work on
the second floor of the White House. Said the President: [1]

This has been the room which has witnessed very many trials and perplexities, but I feel that it has been, too, the scene in which a great improvement has been made in civil service ideas. In the first year and a half of
my Administration the same battle was fought day after day. Men came here
by the hundred—by the thousand—each company filling the room and
there was always the same formula: "I have come, Mr. President, to
ask that Blank be removed." "The reason?" I would say. "Why, he is a

[1] N. Y. *World*, Sept. 7, 1887.

Republican," would be the uniform answer. I had always, I could have, but the same response: "You must bring me a proof of his unfitness as a public servant." I understood very well their inability to comprehend this. But now the formula has altogether changed. I have not heard that expression for many months past. It is now, at the outset of every application for a change, "This man is unfit, a faithless public servant, and these are the reasons." Is not this a great deal to have accomplished? Is not this a sufficient answer, for the time that has intervened, to those who complain that no more has been accomplished?

In even a summary view of the first Cleveland Administration, its four successive years stand out in clear distinction from one another. The year 1885 was a time of beginnings, with a green and nervous President struggling against the spoilsmen, insisting at Cabinet meetings on a higher standard of departmental zeal, and learning enough about national affairs to write his first annual message. The year 1886 was a year of hurried grappling with a half dozen difficulties: the tenure of office law, silver, the Morrison tariff, labor, and the fisheries question. The year 1887 witnessed Cleveland's first strong assertion of leadership in an effort to solve the combined problems of the surplus and the tariff; and the year 1888 brought a desperate fight, both in Congress and the Presidential campaign, to make that leadership successful.

Of these four years the most crowded and animated was the second, 1886—as eventful a year as the dull, flat decade of the eighties offered. All over the world, if we consider Gladstone's first home rule bill, the gold rush in South Africa, the emergence of Boulanger as war minister in France, and conflict and upheaval in the Balkans, it was an interesting twelvemonth. Congress had no sooner met than Cleveland was locked in a close-matched wrestle with the Republican Senate on the question of appointments. Thereafter national problems developed so rapidly that he was soon struggling with a bewildering variety at once— with the questions raised by the Gould strikes in the Southwest, the attacks of the silverites upon the Treasury, the hornetlike buzzings of veterans outraged by his battleflag order, the party schism over the tariff, official appointments, and the Congressional elections. His marriage took place in the midst of the hurly-burly, and he snatched his five-day honeymoon from a clutter of tasks. Not one of the subjects with which he dealt was of first-rate importance, but several had dramatic aspects and tested his qualities severely.

The Republican majority in the Senate had assembled in December, 1885, in a hostile mood. As Republicans they nursed a smouldering resentment over their defeat in 1884, they had been stung by the exposure of lax methods in the departments, and they were irritated by the sharp reversal of their Nicaraguan policy. They felt that they needed some bold stroke to restore their party prestige and reduce the President's growing popularity. As Senators, they particularly welcomed any opportunity to humiliate the executive. It was natural that their first onslaught should be aimed at Cleveland's nominations, for constitutionally the Senate shares with the President the control of the more important appointments, and in this joint control it has repeatedly found the Achilles heel of the Chief Magistrate. Such a concerted attack had occurred once before in our history. When Jackson took office the jealous Senate had adopted a proscriptive policy toward the men he appointed. Against the vain protests of Daniel Webster himself it had cut off head after head; had debarred from office one large group, the Jacksonian editors, by a general rule; and had outraged more than a few Democratic States by its acts.[1] Jackson had fought back hard and successfully, but the Senate now had an additional weapon in the Tenure of Office Act.

It was impossible for Senators in 1886 to adopt so ruthless a policy as in 1829. There had been no such spoilsman's sweep as in Jackson's day, Cleveland having made relatively few suspensions from office— only 643 when the Senate met; and public sentiment would not tolerate excessive interference with the President. But with the additional law at hand, the Republicans prepared to be as truculent and unyielding as the situation allowed. They held nightly caucuses to lay plans, and gusty laughter echoed down the Senate corridors as their meetings broke up. They would make Cleveland beg for mercy, not by boisterous or aggressive acts, but with neat Italian—or Yankee—adroitness. Senators Edmunds, Hale, Ingalls, Sherman, and Harrison all bared their cold steel.

The Republican motives in this appeal to the old Tenure of Office Act were mixed. Beyond the desire to humiliate Cleveland lay their wish to placate many of the ousted Republican officeholders. The President had declared emphatically that he would remove major officials only when they had completed their four-year terms, had proved inefficient or dishonest, or had shown an offensive partisanship. Among the 643 men suspended were many who protested that they did not fall into any of these categories; and yet their neighbors might suppose that some secret charge had been proved against them. They besieged their

[1] Bowers, *Party Battles of the Jacksonian Era,* 87.

Senators for a "vindication," more than five hundred pleas soon being received,[1] and the Senators were only too glad to demand it. The Republican leaders loudly affirmed that they were not trying to estop the Administration from replacing Republicans with Democrats, but were merely insisting that Cleveland should admit that he was doing it, in the main, for partisan reasons. If he would make a frank confession, they would confirm his appointees without further ado. Nevertheless, some Senators secretly hoped to check the stream of suspensions.

The result was as pretty a fiasco as party conspirators ever experienced, but the reasons for its failure have perhaps never been properly analyzed. The Republican Senators were basing their scheme upon an Act of 1867, originally used to restrict the powers of Andrew Johnson, which had been modified when in 1869 Grant protested against having such a dangerous weapon left about. The original enactment had provided that no civil officer appointed with the consent of the Senate could be removed except with Senatorial acquiescence. During a recess of the Senate the President might suspend an officer for misconduct or crime, but within twenty days after the Senate met again he must report the fact with the "evidence and reasons," and obtain its concurrence, or the officer would legally return to his post. Senator Edmunds had been one of the principal authors of this Act, and in 1869 he was one of the men who prevented its complete repeal. The modification of that year changed and weakened it in three important particulars. It provided that the President might suspend an officer in his discretion, instead of merely for misconduct or crime. It dropped the clause which had required the President to send the Senate his evidence and reasons for the suspension. Finally, it deprived the suspended officer of the right to return to his old place if the Senate refused to concur in his removal; instead, the President might keep on making nominations until the Senate approved of one.[2] In other words, under the original law a hostile Senate could compel the retention of a man whom the President disliked; under the modified law, it could not.

It was obvious to impartial observers that the President, being responsible for the execution of the laws, ought to be unhampered in his power of dismissal. If an officer was dishonest, inefficient, unfriendly to

[1] N. Y. *Herald,* Feb. 3, 1886.
[2] For a careful outline of the legislation of 1867–69 see Senator George's speech, *Cong. Rec.,* 49th Cong., vol. 17, 2656 ff.

Administration policy, or merely uncongenial, it should be possible to get rid of him at once and completely. Grant, Hayes, and Garfield in turn had assailed the Act in strong terms. Cleveland had not been President a month before he felt the outrageous disadvantages of the law. The Republican postmaster at Rome, N. Y., a drunken scamp, had failed to make the required monthly reports to the Postmaster-General. Investigators were sent to his office and unearthed evidence of what Cleveland called "the most disgraceful confusion" in all that pertained to its finances, with heavy deficiencies. Here was a thievish and incompetent man—and yet Cleveland could not dismiss him. He had presented the case to the Senate in March of 1885, asking it to confirm a new appointee, but it had adjourned without acting. Cleveland, suspending the man, wrote an angry note to Vilas upon the case: [1]

> To me it clearly seems my duty to exercise all the powers which the present condition of the law has left in my hands, so far as it may be done independently of the Senate, to protect the interests of the government, to vindicate the laws which have been enacted for the regulation of the postal service, and to impress upon Federal officeholders that no indulgence will be granted by the Executive to those who violate the law or neglect public duty.

II

From the outset Cleveland carried the brunt of the battle without much effective aid from the Democratic Senators. Without exception they rallied to his side, and a number of them, notably Pugh, Isham G. Harris, Kenna, and Vest, made well-meant speeches. But it was left for the President to force the fighting, to bring the issue squarely before the country, and to make the most forcible statement of his own case.[2] He put all the heart into the battle. At the beginning most of the Democrats in Congress believed his cause to be tactically weak, and feared ultimate defeat. So did the Democratic press, the *Herald* remarking of the Administration [3] that "They are in the wrong and fatally in the wrong; they are in a pitiful case." On the Republican side Edmunds and Sherman maintained a grim discipline by caucus meetings and personal labors, while their speeches on the controversy were among the most ambitious of their careers. Yet as the fight dragged on

[1] April 4, 1885. Cleveland Papers.
[2] Cleveland describes his steps in *Presidential Problems*.
[3] N. Y. *Herald*, Feb. 9, 1886.

their followers broke ranks, and it was with increasing difficulty that they marshalled a united front. One weakness of their campaign was that Edmunds wished to go much further than Sherman in asserting a Senatorial control over dismissals and nominations, and even Sherman went further than many other Senators. But their principal weakness was that they miscalculated their power, under the law, of coercing the President.

The Republicans determined at the outset that they would approve of all Cleveland's nominations to office in which the previous dismissal seemed to them justified; but that in doubtful instances they would demand that the President send them information upon his suspensions and upon the new appointees. This information they would use to show the public that he was in the wrong. As the nominations came to the Senate, they were forwarded to the appropriate committees for reports. The majorities in these committees, after some study of the various names, began to call upon the Cabinet members for information upon both the causes of the removals, and the qualifications of the new nominees. A number of resolutions for such information passed the Senate. Thus it shortly sent a demand to Postmaster-General Vilas for an explanation of certain dismissals and appointments in Maine postoffices. The President reached the conclusion, as he said later, that the authors of these resolutions had but one real intent.[1] "They assume the right of the Senate to sit in judgment upon the exercise of my exclusive discretion and Executive function, for which I am solely responsible to the people from whom I have so lately received the sacred trust of office."

A weak President would have tried to compromise; instead, Cleveland ordered the department heads to refuse flatly the Senate's demands for information upon suspensions, and to send only the official papers dealing with appointments. This distinction between information upon suspensions, and information upon nominations, cannot be too strongly emphasized. Cleveland and his Cabinet advisers knew that the Constitution gave the Senate no authority whatever in the matter of dismissals; they knew also that in the modified legislation of 1869 the Senate had expressly surrendered the right to demand "reasons and evidence" upon suspensions. Appointments were a different matter. In dealing with them the Senate, under the Constitution, obviously held an equal partnership with the President. But even in furnishing informa-

[1] Richardson, *Messages and Papers*, VIII, 381.

tion regarding his appointees, Cleveland drew another vital distinction. He was willing to send the Senate all formal papers, and all open endorsements of the men he had selected for office, but he insisted that confidential letters and memoranda relating to them must be withheld. And, he declared in effect, it was he alone who should judge which documents were official or open, and which were confidential.

At Cleveland's direction, the departmental heads began following a set form of reply to the Senate requests or resolutions. Naturally an open clash was not long in coming. Edmunds and his allies made haste to select a test case. As chairman of the judiciary committee, Edmunds on December 26 had asked Attorney-General Garland to send him all the papers dealing with the suspension in the previous summer of George M. Duskin, Federal Attorney for the southern district of Alabama, and the appointment of John D. Burnett in his stead. As it happened, special circumstances made this a weaker test case than Edmunds supposed, but this did not affect Cleveland's handling of it. A fortnight later Garland transmitted the formal documents describing Burnett's qualifications, but refused to send those which touched upon the suspension of Duskin. Edmunds thereupon turned to the Senate majority. He prepared a resolution which the Senate forthwith passed,[1] ordering the Attorney-General to transmit copies of all documents filed in the Department of Justice during the previous year in relation to the conduct of the office of the district attorney in question. When the Senate gave orders, it expected to be obeyed! But in this instance it was not. Three days after the passage of the Senate resolution, Attorney-General Garland, obviously acting for Cleveland, declined in courteous but decisive terms to furnish the required documents.

Thus at the beginning of February in 1886 the President and Senate majority were confronting each other in open battle with the whole country looking on. The Senate demanded information upon suspensions which the President would not give; the Senate demanded confidential papers upon appointments which the President also refused. Which side would force the other to retreat? On February 17 the Republican caucus adopted a set of resolutions, drawn up by Edmunds, which embodied a distinct threat against the executive. One feature of these resolutions was a formal censure of the Attorney-General for refusing to yield the information asked of him. Another was a complaint

[1] *Cong. Rec.*, Jan. 25, 1886, vol. 17, p. 2212.

regarding the removal of Union veterans. But the vital section was a threat—a declaration that the Senate could not and would not confirm persons nominated to succeed suspended officers unless the reasons for the suspension were furnished. That is, the Republicans would block the whole appointive machinery unless Cleveland surrendered. An elaborate report by the Judiciary Committee, again from Edmunds' pen, furnished an adroit argument for the resolution; the essential question, it contended, being simply "whether it is within the constitutional competence of either House of Congress to have access to the official papers and documents in the various public offices of the United States, created by laws enacted by themselves."

There can be no doubt that when Edmunds lifted his angular form from the table on which this report was written, it was with a triumphant feeling that both abstract right and concrete power were on his side. He believed that the Senate majority held the whip hand. The Constitution certainly gave the Senate coördinate authority with the President over appointments, which might be made only with its advice and consent. From the very beginning of the government Congress had demanded from the departments official documents relating to their work, and had received them. Surely his legal position, and Edmunds prided himself on his mastery of constitutional law, was impregnable. On the surface it appeared that the practical position of the Republican Senators was equally strong. If they refused confirmation of one appointment after another, what could the President do? Would he not have to capitulate in the end? Finally, Edmunds, Sherman, and their associates must have congratulated themselves that they could appeal to public opinion with every hope of rallying it to their side. They could tell the American people that Cleveland was trying to conceal official information regarding his appointments, and that he was doing so because many nominations had an indefensible political basis. The President would be left in a sorry light if he maintained the concealment, and in a still sorrier if he told the full truth—or so they reasoned.

Yet as a matter of fact, on all three points Edmunds was mistaken. Abstract right lay with the President. He did not deny that the Senate had a constitutional and statutory claim, bulwarked by precedent, to all the official information upon appointments which lay in the departmental files. The Cabinet officers had consistently furnished such information. But he did deny that the Senate had any right to information upon his dismissals or suspensions. It possessed no constitutional authority over them, and it had surrendered its very dubious statutory authority in 1869. He denied also that the Senate possessed any right to confidential information upon appointments. The justification for this denial was a matter of mere common sense.[1] The President could not know personally one man in ten whom he appointed. He must rely on statements by others, and these statements would often be worthless unless confidential, for men would not tell the truth except under a pledge of secrecy. If confidential papers were sent to the Senate, the Republicans there would publish or expose all papers that would injure the President or his advisers, and would pigeonhole the others. As a consequence men would stop giving frank advice to the President. There was not an unprejudiced man of affairs in the United States who did not recognize this point.

More important was the fact that, as the chagrined Republicans shortly found, practical power in the matter also lay with the President. Suppose the Senate did refuse to confirm—still all the cards would be in his hands. To begin with, the law declared that when a nominee was rejected, the President must nominate some other person "as soon as practicable." He might interpret this as meaning weeks or months. In the second place, Cleveland, after making one or more unsuccessful nominations, might simply wait until the end of the session. He could then consider the office vacant, recommission his first appointee, and keep him in his place till the Senate sat again, continuing to play this game, if necessary, to the end of his administration. It is an historical fact that several American Presidents have, by a succession of recess appointments, kept an office occupied, despite the non-concurrence of the Senate, for several years.[2] Senator Kenna was shortly pointing out to the Republicans [3] that Cleveland had this clear power of reappointment, and Senator Ingalls, of the judiciary committee, was shortly admitting it.[4] The Senate's power of defeating nominations was a broken sword.

Finally, and most important of all, Cleveland occupied a ground on which he could call for public support with far greater chance of suc-

---

[1] See the shrewd statement on this by E. P. Wheeler, N. Y. *Herald,* Feb. 24, 1886.
[2] W. B. Munro, *The Government of the United States,* 203.
[3] *Cong. Rec.,* March 12, 1886, vol. 17, p. 2332 ff.
[4] See statement of Ingalls, N. Y. *Herald,* Feb. 22, 1886. "The public service will not suffer, nor will the removed Republican get back his place."

cess than could the hostile Senators. At first many Americans refused to take the affair seriously, regarding it as a characteristic piece of manoeuvring by rival political leaders—a sham battle which would end without casualties. But when men realized that Cleveland was aroused in defence of what he regarded as the fundamental rights of the Presidency, they took his side. In any such collision the instinct of most Americans is to align themselves with the executive. Andrew Jackson, in his famous message of April 15, 1834, protesting against the resolution of censure passed by the Senate, had declared the latter a body "not directly amenable" to the public, whereas "the President is the direct representative of the American people." There was truth in the statement then, and still more truth in Cleveland's day. Men distrusted the Senate for its big-business character. Moreover, the very phrase Tenure of Office, with its memories of Andrew Johnson's period, recalled an aspect of previous Senatorial tyranny which men were beginning to appreciate in its true light.

III

On March 1 the President made his formal appeal to the country, and the Republicans were able to read the handwriting upon the wall. The Democratic members of the judiciary committee had written a verbose reply to Edmunds, which had produced little impression; but now Cleveland's own statement was distinctly the report of a piece of heavy artillery. He gave it to the public in the form of a message to the Senate which defined the true nature of the contest. While perhaps not ranking high among American state papers, this document is one of the most dignified, concise, and logical of all his writings. Senator Edmunds a few days before had rather absurdly spoken of the contest between Parliament and the tyrant Charles I. Cleveland for his part was willing to furnish a tacit reminder of the tyranny of the Long Parliament which Cromwell had so decisively and beneficially ended.

The President based his reply upon the three theses which have already been indicated. In the first place, he declared, the Constitution gives the chief executive the sole power of suspension or removal, and he is responsible for the use of this power to the people alone. He believed that Congress had never possessed a constitutional right to enact the first Tenure of Office law—a contention which has since been sustained by the Supreme Court. In the second place, even granting that it possessed this right, the sections of the Act directing the President to report his reasons for any suspension had been repealed. As Senator Kenna had said a few days before, the Senate was now trying to re-enact them by its unsupported resolution! In the third place, the papers which the Senate had demanded as being official papers of a department created by Congress were often not official at all. He had always been willing to send any really official document upon appointments. But some of these papers were private and privileged, and some were negligible and open to misconstruction if published:

They consist of letters of representation addressed to the executive or intended for his inspection; they are voluntarily written and presented by private citizens who are not in the least instigated thereto by any official invitation or at all subject to official control. While some of them are entitled to executive consideration, many of them are so irrelevant or in the light of other facts so worthless, that they have not been given the least weight in determining the question to which they are supposed to relate. . . . I consider them in no proper sense as upon the files of the department but as deposited there for my convenience, remaining still completely under my control. I suppose if I desired to take them into my custody I might do so with entire propriety, and if I saw fit to destroy them no one could complain.

In this message there were some unusual bits of sarcasm. Cleveland remarked that while the executive departments might have been created *by* Congress, they were not created *for* the Senate, and it had no peculiar authority over them. He mentioned with contempt the Senatorial belief that papers became official simply because temporarily kept in official files. "There is no mysterious power of transmutation in departmental custody, nor is there magic in the undefined and sacred solemnity of Department files. If the presence of these papers in the public offices is a stumbling block in the way of performance of Senatorial duty it can easily be removed." In attacking the Tenure of Office Act he recalled Grant's protests against the law. "After an existence of almost twenty years of nearly innocuous desuetude," he wrote, "these laws are brought forth—apparently the repealed as well as the unrepealed . . ." But the part of the message which carried the most weight was the final ringing series of paragraphs. Here he declared that he took his stand upon his oath to support and defend the Constitution, upon his responsibility to a people who had chosen him to exercise the powers of office and not to relinquish them, and upon his duty to the Chief Magistracy itself, which he must preserve in all its vigor:

Neither the discontent of party friends, nor the allurements constantly offered of confirmations of appointees conditioned upon the avowal that suspensions have been made on party grounds alone, nor the threat proposed in the resolutions now before the Senate that no confirmations will be made unless the demands of that body are complied with, are sufficient to discourage or deter me from following in the way which I am convinced leads to better government for the people.

After this blow from the shoulder the disintegration of the Republican ranks proceeded rapidly. Already John Sherman had made a speech in which he surrendered much of the ground upon which Edmunds had originally drawn his lines.[1] He utterly repudiated the idea that he had any right to call upon the President for his motives in making an appointment. The Senate, he said, had no more authority to demand of Cleveland, "For what reason did you do this thing?" than Cleveland had to demand of the Senate, "Why did you pass this law?" It could ask only that the President give it the same sources of information that he himself possessed. Other Senators admitted that whatever they might request as to appointments, they had no just claim to meddle with dismissals. Several Republican members, notably Ingalls of Kansas, Mitchell of Oregon, and Logan of Illinois, made little secret of the fact that they thought Cleveland right and Edmunds wrong. Logan took the view that only when the Senate gave up secret or executive sessions upon appointments—as he wished to do—could it castigate the President for secrecy. Because of special motives some other Senators were unwilling to wage a determined contest against the President. It was common knowledge that a number of them had gone to Cleveland and asked him to remove Republican officeholders who happened to be obnoxious to them, and had furnished him with facts to justify the dismissal of men of their own party![2] They had good reason to fear that if the battle continued, Cleveland would make their requests public. Indeed, he included a quiet hint to that effect in his message.

By the middle of March it was evident that the Republicans were

[1] *Cong. Rec.*, Feb. 8, 1886, vol. 17, p. 1204.
[2] *Cong. Rec.*, March 26, 1886, vol. 17, p. 2810. On April 2 the Republican caucus, without taking a vote, made it clear that a majority believed Edmunds' course unwise and untenable; N. Y. *Herald*, *Tribune*, April 3, 1886.

beaten. The full token of their defeat came on March 12 in the temporary confirmation of a Democrat as surveyor-general of Utah. It was a vulnerable appointment, the man being ill-qualified; the previous Republican holder of the office had been highly efficient; and yet because the nominee was a friend of Logan's, and "Senatorial courtesy" was invoked in his behalf, seven Republicans joined with the Democrats in voting him into office. When the result was announced, Edmunds' face was a study in chagrin. He knew that the President would have little trouble thereafter in getting his appointments confirmed by Republican votes. Late in the month Edmunds' resolution of censure, as adopted by the caucus, came up for passage. The Senate voted, by a strict party majority, 32 to 25, its condemnation of Garland's refusal to transmit the papers requested of him. But the accompanying resolution which declared it to be the Senate's duty to refuse its confirmation in all such cases was adopted by a margin of but one vote. Three Republicans stood with the Democrats, and one of them, Senator Mitchell, vigorously attacked the programme of Edmunds.[1]

On March 29 the Washington and New York newspapers announced, on the authority of several Republican Senators, that there would be few if any further calls for information on appointments. It was all over! Yet bitter as this defeat was for Edmunds, worse was to come. The debates in both the House and Senate, for Democratic Representatives had angrily discussed the question, had revealed the fact that many capable lawyers within the Republican party believed the Tenure of Office Act to be both unconstitutional and pernicious. The whole drift of the times was toward a greater concentration of power in the hands of the executive. As the spring wore on, the efforts to interfere with the President's powers of removal and appointment were practically given up, and it was everywhere admitted that his interpretation of the law had become fixed and irrefragable. This being so, why not repeal the legislation altogether? In June, 1886, Senator Hoar mustered the courage to bring in a bill for the purpose; towards the end of July it was favorably reported by the Judiciary Committee, with Edmunds alone dissenting; and that winter it passed.

Cleveland had thus triumphed over the Republicans of the Senate in a spectacular contest. Matched in a duel against the veteran Edmunds, with weapons which Edmunds himself had chosen, he had

[1] *Cong. Rec.*, March 24, 1886, vol. 17, p. 2703 ff.

OLIVER CROMWELL (CLEVELAND) AND CHARLES I (EDMUNDS)
(A cartoon by Thomas Nast in *Harper's Weekly*, May 1, 1886.)

struck the sword out of his antagonist's hand. For the Vermonter the defeat was a personal tragedy of lasting import. Never again could he assume his old position as arbiter of the Senate on constitutional questions. For years he had been one of the most irritating as well as ablest members of the upper house. No one save Ingalls equalled him as a master of cutting sarcasm and waspish retort. When his victims cried out in their agony, he would show his delight by characteristic gestures —by scratching his elbow, or with his forefinger stroking the side of his nose. Partisan, unrelenting, and sometimes malignant, he had loved to goad the Southern Senators into unwise exhibitions of anger. Now he had met more than his equal.

INTERESTING as the tenure-of-office contest was, it was essentially an episode detached from the central current of events in the eighties. The main conflict was always joined about the three issues of the currency, the tariff, and civil service reform. Long before the last shots had been fired in the Senate upon the President's powers of appointment, stubborn battles had broken forth upon the silver question and the reduction of duties. Of these the former was particularly striking in that it involved Cleveland in a direct collision with the majority of his own party in the House. The tenure-of-office controversy had revealed again Cleveland's redoubtable qualities of resistance; the new battles were to expose his still decided limitations as a leader of attack.

Both the emphasis on financial topics in Cleveland's first message and Washington gossip had created a general expectation that he would press aggressively for repeal of the silver purchase law. A portentous conflict of sections and classes was dimly taking shape. Cleveland and Manning, as representatives of Eastern banking, investing, and commercial circles and of the Seymour-Tilden tradition, saw arrayed against them a heavy Congressional bloc representing the silver miners, the small farmers of the West, and the debtor groups generally. The views of the two forces were quite irreconcilable. While the Administration desired to blot the Bland-Allison Act from the statute books, the Westerners were eager to obtain the free and unlimited coinage of silver. Cleveland and Manning foresaw disaster if the gold standard were even shaken; Bland of Missouri, Morrison of Illinois, and A. J. Warner of the Marietta district in Ohio believed that its total destruction would be a great national blessing. The silverites, unfortunately, were the better prepared for offensive battle.

Cleveland in his annual message of December, 1885, made the calm assumption that abandonment of the gold standard would disrupt business, impair all confidence, and reduce the income of the farmer and workingman while cancelling at one blow a large part of the savings of thrifty people. On this assumption, which was never for a moment questioned by most business and professional men, the necessity for stopping the coinage of silver seemed plain. Ever since the Bland-Allison Act took effect in 1878, he recalled, the government had been buying silver bullion and coining it at the rate of more than two million dollars a month. The mints had thus far stamped more than 215,750,000 silver dollars, a total far greater than the country needed or could absorb; for despite every effort by three Administrations only about $50,000,000 had gone into circulation. The Treasury did not know what to do with the $165,000,000 clogging the government vaults; yet "every month two millions of gold in the public Treasury are paid out for two millions or more of silver dollars, to be added to the idle mass already accumulated." He pointed to the inevitable result if this went on. Years later, in the dark days of 1894–96, the truth of his prophecy might have been recalled:

If continued long enough, this operation will result in the substitution of silver for all the gold the government owns applicable to its general purposes. It will not do to rely upon the customs receipts of the government to make good this drain of gold, because the silver thus coined having been made legal tender for all debts, and dues, public or private, at times during the last six months 58 per cent of the receipts for duties has been in silver or silver certificates, while the average within that period has been twenty per cent. The proportion of silver and its certificates received by the government will probably increase as time goes on, for the reason that the nearer the period approaches when it will be obliged to offer silver in payment of its obligations the greater inducement there will be to hoard gold against depreciation in the value of silver or for the purpose of speculation.

This hoarding of gold has already begun.

When the time comes that gold has been withdrawn from circulation, then will be apparent the difference between the real value of the silver dollar and a dollar in gold, and the two coins will part company.

The message exasperated the silverites, who were already irritated by the events of the preceding summer. At the time of the threat to the gold reserve in March, 1885, Cleveland and Manning had adopted rigorous measures to protect it. They had discontinued Arthur's policy of bond redemptions, allowing the Federal revenues to accumulate in the vaults; and they had used greenbacks wherever possible for disbursements instead of gold coin or silver certificates. They also made an arrangement with the New York Clearing House to keep the existing stock of gold in the Treasury intact and if possible augment it. The result surpassed Cleveland's brightest expectations. In the first year his Administration, aided by a favorable turn in business, actually built up the gold reserve from $125,000,000 to $151,000,000. [1]

Because the peril was so quickly averted, the public soon forgot that it had ever existed, and history has passed it over with little comment. But as Abram S. Hewitt later pointed out in Congress, the country had really stood close in those March days to disaster. The gold reserve had fallen to the smallest sum since the resumption of specie payments; public faith in its adequacy was ebbing. The hoarding of gold had begun, not by the people, but by the masters of finance. To his personal knowledge, three great New York banks had secretly accumulated more than $25,000,000 in gold for the apparently imminent change. "Did the change come?" sarcastically asked Mr. Brown. "It did not," answered Hewitt, "thanks to Grover Cleveland and that superb management of the Secretary of the Treasury which has made the name of Daniel Manning famous throughout the financial world." [2]

The very success of the new Treasury policy angered the free-coinage men, for they would have liked nothing better than to see the nation forced to a silver standard. Congress had no sooner met than there ensued a series of attacks on the President. The leader of the assault in the Senate was the picturesque Scotchman James B. Beck of Kentucky, who, emigrating from Dumfriesshire in his youth, had been graduated from Transylvania University in Mexican War days, when that Blue-Grass institution was one of the best in the country. He was a fighter who frequently showed more zeal than discretion. No native-born Southerner was readier to resent a Yankee taunt. His combativeness made him a strong debater, and he was an indefatigable worker, laboring so strenuously in the Committee on Appropriations that he and Allison almost monopolized its functions. He frequently said he would rather be Senator than President, and he had resented the resignations of Bayard, Lamar, and Garland to enter the Cabinet. The whole conservative tenor of the Administration disgusted him, and he particularly denounced Cleveland's policy of "locking up so much money in the Treasury," saying that if a cyclone came and scattered all the

[1] *Annual Report,* Secretary of Treasury, 1885, pp. xxxi–xxxii.
[2] *Cong. Rec.,* July 14, 1886, vol. 17, p. 6923. The N. Y. *Evening Post,* Feb. 28, 1885, described the threatened withdrawals of gold by large bank depositors, and the means adopted by leading bank officials "to assure them that the crisis was not yet at hand."

government funds to the four winds of heaven, and the people ran pell-mell to gather up the currency, that would be better than the Administration's course. Senator Eustis of Louisiana was equally bitter.[1]

In the House Bland, Warner, and Weaver of Iowa led a motley array of Democrats and Western Republicans who accused Cleveland and Manning of open subserviency to Wall and Lombard Streets. Taunts were hurled which anticipated those of the great silver struggle of 1895–96. It was charged that Cleveland had practised a gross deception. He had predicted a dire calamity, a financial crisis, and none had come; it had all been a "transparent cheat" in the interests of the money-changers and the creditor classes.[2]

In this situation the Administration should have forced the fighting. Cleveland closed the discussion of finance in his annual message with the sharp challenge to Congress: "I recommend the suspension of the compulsory coinage of silver dollars, directed by the law passed in February, 1878." But it quickly became evident that firm leadership was lacking. When Speaker Carlisle appointed the House Committee on Coinage, Weights, and Measures, its membership of thirteen was almost equally divided between advocates of continued coinage and of suspension. The chairman was Bland, a strong silverite, and he had four Democrats and two Republicans with him; five members were anti-silverite, and one was counted uncertain. Worst of all, Cleveland at this juncture committed what must be called a blunder of the first magnitude. If he had put all his driving power, in Jacksonian fashion, behind a programme of financial and tariff legislation, he had a hopeful prospect for accomplishing much. But by a needless and most unfortunate public statement, he abdicated his proper position of influence and temporarily ruined in both fields what chances he possessed.

In a New Year's dispatch the Washington correspondent of the New York *Herald* predicted that Cleveland would take a strong line with Congress. The Administration, he wrote, would use both pressure and patronage to give effect to its recommendations. Cleveland's eye fell on the dispatch. Already he had been resisting party associates who were urging him to take just this course. "It doesn't look as though Congress was very well prepared to do anything, but maybe it will get into shape," he had written Bissell in December. "If a botch is made at the

---

[1] *Cong. Rec.,* Jan. 18, 1886, vol. 17, p. 708 ff.
[2] *Cong. Rec.,* April 3, 1886, vol. 17, p. 3101. Cf. *Nation,* Feb. 18, 1886.

other end of the Avenue, I don't mean to be a party to it." And again a few days later, "I think some men are pretty busy digging their political graves. I tell them I shall keep right on doing executive work. I did not come here to legislate." [1] Now he felt that he was being publicly misrepresented, and he made the error of speaking out.

To the press correspondents on January 4 he declared that the *Herald* was quite mistaken. "I believe," he said, "the most important benefit that I can confer on the country by my presidency is to insist upon the entire independence of the executive and legislative branches of the government, and compel the members of the legislative branch to see that they have responsibilities of their own, grave and well-defined, which their official oaths bind them sacredly to perform." The Constitution, he went on, directed him from time to time to make recommendations to Congress and gave him the power to veto bills, and he meant to be a strictly constitutional President. "I believe that this is an executive office, and I deem it important that the country should be reminded of it. I have certain executive duties to perform; when that is done my responsibility ends. The office is one of the coördinate branches of the government. The Senators and members have their duties and responsibilities. They put their hands upon the Bible and take the same oath of obligation upon assuming office as does the President." Asked whether he thought Congress would carry out his recommendations regarding the tariff and silver, he said he had no means of knowing. It was a subject which had now passed beyond his control. He had no desire to influence Congress in any way beyond the methods he had employed in directing their attention to the topics.[2]

It was unmistakably an error. Washington echoed with discussion of Cleveland's "go-as-you-please policy," and the *Herald* summarized the prevalent feeling under its headlines: "Belief That The President's Non-Interference Will Disorganize Parties—Democrats Without a Leader." All who had been hostile to his message, and especially the silverites and high tariff men, were delighted, while Administration men were in dejection. To both sides the statement had been a complete surprise; the tone of the message, the positive language which Cleveland had sometimes used to Congressmen, and his reputation as a man of immovable convictions, had led many Democrats to believe they

[1] Dec. 24, Dec. 27, 1885. Cleveland Papers.
[2] N. Y. *Herald, World*, Louisville *Courier-Journal*, Jan. 5, 6, 1886.

would find in him another Jackson, or at least another determined program-maker like Polk. He was an experienced cardplayer, and yet here he had needlessly given up the best part of his hand.

"If only Mr. Cleveland had been content to say nothing," remarked one of the shrewdest men in Congress,[1] "he had the game in his own hands. The opposition to his policy was melting away like snow in a thaw. He need not have done anything, if only he had said nothing. We should presently have had a united party, confident and happy, with the President as our natural and proper leader. It makes me sad—for what he so needlessly said is a direct invitation to confusion and discord." For a time Cleveland clung to his conviction that a President should interfere with Congress only under stress of an emergency. "You know, I think," he wrote Randall as late as July, 1886,[2] "that I am not at all inclined to meddle with proposed legislation while it is pending in Congress." Little by little he had to alter his opinion; within a few weeks he was using all his influence with Democratic Senators on the Tenure of Office question, and within a few months was urging Representatives to vote right on the Morrison tariff. But meanwhile the opening for the silverites was irresistible, and it was they who at once assumed the offensive.

II

The first of their three separate waves of attack was a demand upon Secretary Manning for an explanation of his arrangement with the New York Clearing House. In September the New York financier George S. Coe had described to the American Bankers' Association the methods used by the Treasury to prevent the submergence of the gold standard. Bland seized upon this speech as if it were some revelation of treason. He pushed through the coinage committee a resolution calling upon the Treasury for a history of its agreement with the bankers, a statement of its authority in law for making it, an account of its use of silver in paying the public debt, and a definition of its future policy. After Hewitt had been defeated, 168 to 58, in an effort to modify this demand, it passed by a viva voce vote.

The Administration reply was an 18-page report which Manning sent

[1] Quoted in N. Y. *Herald*, Jan. 6, 1886.
[2] July 14, 1886. Cleveland Papers.

the House early in March, 1886, cool, dignified, and vigorous in tone.[1] He was emphatic in asserting that there had been a real peril to the national finances. The gold in the Treasury had fallen on June 3, 1885, to the alarming level of $114,650,000, and to meet this crisis he had agreed with the bankers to exchange subsidiary silver and silver certificates for gold, greenbacks, and other lawful forms of money—"a transaction wherein the New York banks showed again, as during the war, their perception of an enlightened self-interest in the dictates of a sterling patriotism." He had no difficulty in demonstrating that this arrangement was fully warranted by law. After some elementary explanations about the impossibility of forcing more silver into current use than the public wished to take, he went on to present his argument for calling a halt to the Bland-Allison purchases. True bimetallism, he declared, could never be attained except by international action, and "international concert we can never have, except by stopping our present coinage and stopping it unconditionally." By this he meant that Europe would never coöperate with the United States to establish bimetallism while the Bland-Allison Act stood, partly because she inclined to a ratio of 15½ to 1 instead of 16 to 1, and partly because she hoped that we would soon go off the gold standard altogether, so that she could pour her silver into this country in enormous quantities.

Already, it should be noted, the Administration had made a gesture toward an international agreement. The British Government, supported by Germany, had blocked all plans for a world arrangement at the international bimetallic conferences of 1878 and 1881. Early in May, 1885, Cleveland had sent Manton Marble to Europe as a special commissioner to inquire into the subject. This astute former editor of the *World*, who had lost his place when Pulitzer bought the paper, and who held Tilden's views on the currency, talked with high officials in London, Paris, and Berlin.[2] The months just following his arrival witnessed several encouraging events. The Indian Government had for some time been badgering London to take steps favorable to silver. Lord Randolph Churchill, as secretary of state for India, took up the subject energetically, and in September, 1886, the British Government actually went so far as to create a Royal Gold and Silver Commission to make an exhaustive report on the world's currency. For a time there was

---

[1] House Exec. Docs., 49th Cong., 1st session, no. 100.
[2] On Marble's mission, see Annual Report, Secretary of the Treasury, 1885, p. xxi.

some reason to think that the faraway dream of international bimetallism might actually be taking on tangibility. Then in 1888 the British Commission made its report, and the iridescent bubble vanished again. [1]

The silver men were realists. They had no intention of giving up a silver coinage of two millions or more each month in order to catch at a bird in the European bush; moreover, the extremists wanted free coinage without waiting for other nations. "The great question is," declared Senator Bowen of Colorado, "shall this government issue a declaration of financial independence—a declaration not only against Europe, but against the organized enemies at home?" [2]

It was with such statements that the second wave of attack was launched against Cleveland's policy. This was Bland's bill for the free and unlimited coinage of silver, introduced soon after Congress met. The committee on coinage unexpectedly gave it an unfavorable report, the doubtful member, John Hemphill of South Carolina, taking the Administration side completely. Most of the debate, which opened on March 20, was stale and dull. Easily the best address was that of Hemphill, who dealt with the subject from the standpoint of the Southern farmer and trader, showing how much they would be injured by a fluctuating currency. When the bill came to a vote early in April there was no excitement, for its defeat was a foregone conclusion. Bland was beaten 163 to 126. But at the same time Congress showed much more decisively that there was no hope of stopping the limited coinage against which Cleveland had inveighed. Another South Carolinian, Mr. Dibble, had introduced an amendment declaring that unless silver were remonetized by international action before July 1, 1889, the silver purchase clause of the Bland-Allison Act should then lapse. The vote against this was 201 to 84. And Eastern Democrats who analyzed the vote on the Bland bill found the result discouraging, for of the 163 noes, only 70 were Democratic, while of the 126 yeas, 97 came from that party.

But the Western and Southern members had still a third and more formidable measure to bring against the Administration: the Morrison surplus resolution. For some years the revenues had produced an embarrassing surplus. Since Cleveland and Manning had stopped using it for buying bonds, it had grown more troublesome than ever. It occurred

[1] H. B. Russell, *International Monetary Conferences;* Manton Marble Papers.
[2] *Cong. Rec.,* March 8, 1886, vol. 17, p. 2182.

to the silver leaders that Cleveland might now be ordered to use it to cancel bonds, on the ground that this would both increase the monetary circulation and cut down the government's interest bill. Chairman Morrison of the Ways and Means Committee lent himself to this step; a strange manoeuvre, for though he was a mild silver man, he had a tariff bill before the House and there were a hundred reasons why he should not alienate the Administration. Late in February his committee brought in a spiteful report declaring that the government held almost $180,000,000 in excess of all other liabilities than the greenbacks, and that this was far too much. The money should be used to pay the public debt, "and not unnecessarily held to lure the agents and representatives of the people on to improvident expenditures." With the report went a joint resolution, requiring the Treasury to employ all its money, over and above the sacred $100,000,000, in sums of not less than $10,000,-000 a month to buy and destroy government bonds.[1]

In the East this resolution was greeted with dismay. Manning had already sent Morrison's committee a statement of the reasons which constrained him to display caution in lowering his gold reserve. Now Hewitt, in acting for the committee minority, presented a still more powerful argument. He showed that the Treasury, like any bank or store, needed a reasonable working balance, and that $100,000,000 was far from enough. Careful business firms usually kept on hand a sum equal to one month's disbursements. Measured by this rule, the working balance in the Treasury should be approximately $30,000,000 above the redemption fund maintained for the greenbacks; and as he put the proper redemption fund at $138,000,000, the total balance in the Treasury should be approximately $168,000,000. If the reserve were paid too low, there would be constant danger of upsetting the gold standard. Speculators could accumulate a large body of demand notes, present them for payment in a mass, bring the reserve below the safety line, and profit by the ensuing panic.

For four months the country vigorously discussed the Morrison resolution. The Knights of Labor, who this year were at the height of their power, threw their influence behind it; [2] indeed, they later claimed credit for disinterring it from the Ways and Means files and forcing Morrison to take it up. The extreme silverites really felt no great inter-

[1] *Cong. Rec.*, Feb. 23, 1886, vol. 17, p. 1704.
[2] Report, Legislative Committee, Knights of Labor, 1886.

est in the purchase of bonds *per se*. They wanted to do just what Hewitt was warning them they would—bring the gold standard to a point where it could be overthrown. Senator Beck declared resentfully that the financial policy of the Administration had carried the 4 per cent bonds up 28 points, and made it clear that he would have liked to see them selling at 75 instead of 128. If the Western Congressmen could carry the resolution, they would reduce the national finances to a level where any extraordinary shift in foreign exchange, unfavorable to America, would bring a financial crisis. To cloak their design some pretended that a crisis was impossible. Senator Vest remarked that "when there is a run on the United States Treasury, there will be a run on the Maker of the Universe," adding that he said this "with reverence." Godkin caustically retorted that Vest was much better acquainted with the laws governing the distribution of post traderships in the Indian Territory than the laws of finance.[1]

III

Early in this phase of the great "silver blizzard" of 1886 occurred one of the unfortunate events of the Administration, the sudden breakdown of Manning. Long hours, overwork, and worry produced their natural result upon a man who was far older in body than his fifty-five years would indicate. Throughout the winter he had been looking worn and exhausted, and had complained of indigestion. As we have said, the talk of friction with Cleveland was quite baseless. On March 23 Manning attended the regular Cabinet meeting. As he walked up the Treasury stairs on his return, he was seized with vertigo and fell heavily. Helped to his carriage and taken home, he was found by physicians to have burst a blood vessel at the base of the brain. Though he repeatedly offered to resign, Cleveland in appreciative language refused to permit it,[2] telling him that he had so ably organized his department that he should simply leave it to Fairchild and go away for a rest until October 1.

For a few days the worst was feared, one official writing Tilden that death might occur at any moment. Then it was seen that he might recover. Tilden offered to place his steam yacht, the *Viking*, at Manning's

---

[1] N. Y. *Evening Post*, Aug. 19, 1886.
[2] Cleveland to Manning, June 1, 1886. Cleveland Papers.

service, but he could not accept.[1] When Cleveland was married in June the Secretary, a mere ghost of the robust man of 280 pounds who had come to Washington fifteen months earlier, was helped from his carriage to witness the ceremony. He went to Hot Springs to recuperate, Cleveland meanwhile writing him the kindliest letters upon public affairs and the work of the Cabinet. When he came back in July Cleveland was on the platform to greet him, and arm in arm the two walked to the street. Then Manning, whose shyness made travel in America uncomfortable, settled down temporarily in Bournemouth, England. Fairchild made an admirable substitute. But C. N. Jordan was correct in saying that in one sense Manning was irreplaceable—"there isn't a member of the Cabinet who has made the impression he has, either on Congress or the people with whom he has been brought in contact"[2]—and his loss was felt severely in the latter part of the silver struggle.

The Democratic House was determined to misbehave, and on July 14, by a vote of 207 to 67, passed the Morrison resolution. A pitiful corporal's guard of 14 Democrats were opposed, while 143 of the President's party voted aye! Conservatives were shocked, but the vote was not taken seriously, for there was little expectation that the Senate would concur, and it was certain that Cleveland would veto it if it ever reached his desk. A few hours before the vote, Cleveland had despatched a letter to Randall in an effort to rally all the friends of the Administration in the House to his side. It is curious because it was written so tardily, and was so cautious and tentative in character. He said:[3]

My object in sending this is to express in writing, to avoid all misunderstanding, my regret that many of our friends in the House should deem it necessary to aid in such action as is contemplated by the resolution now pending. I am unable to see why the Treasury Department should not be trusted as previously it has been in other Administrations.

I do not speak of these things as presenting any reason why this legislation should not be passed.

It is because I deem it dangerous that I am sorry to see the determined effort made . . . to do in Congress what I think can better be left to the Treasury Department.

---

[1] S. J. Tilden, *Letters and Literary Memorials*, II, 713 ff.
[2] Samuel J. Tilden, *Letters and Memorials*, II, 719; "the only Democrat in the Cabinet," Jordan called him.
[3] July 14, 1886, Cleveland Papers.

With full appreciation of the irony of the situation, the Republican Senate came to Cleveland's rescue. Its Finance Committee amended the Morrison resolution to remove its sting. A maximum of $130,000,-000 and a minimum of $110,000,000 were fixed for the Treasury reserve, and the Secretary was authorized to suspend the operation of the enactment whenever he feared an emergency. In this shape, the resolution simply expressed a pious opinion on the part of Congress that the surplus should ordinarily not exceed $130,000,000 or drop below $110,000,000; and there was no objection to that. The objection had been to the mandatory and inflexible terms of the House resolution. The silverites in the Senate were indignant. They managed to screw the permissible treasury balance down to $120,000,000, but the executive was still given authority to suspend the bond purchases at will, with an explanation to Congress. In this form the Senate passed the resolution by a vote of 42 to 20. Cleveland was still distinctly irritated by it, and gave it a pocket veto. In his papers is an unpublished memorandum on the subject. "This resolution," he wrote, "implies so much and is of such serious import that I do not deem it best to discuss it at this time. It is not approved because I believe it to be unnecessary and because I am by no means convinced that its mere passage and approval at this time may not endanger and embarrass the successful and useful operations of the Treasury Department and impair the confidence which the people should have in the management of the finances of the government." [1]

Manning, hovering on the Rhode Island coast before going to Europe, wrote the President: [2]

I have been anxiously watching the doings of Congress. It seems to me that the Senate has relieved you of many embarrassments that the House sought to plant in your way. The planting was done clumsily and the weeds sown by the leaders are likely to choke them out of the field. Certainly the leaders have not been able to do anything to hurt your record.

IV

When Congress adjourned in the August heat, a deadlock had been reached on the silver issue. Cleveland had proved totally unable to

[1] Cleveland Papers. Undated.
[2] From Watch Hill, R. I., Aug. 1, 1886. Cleveland Papers.

obtain a repeal of the silver-coinage clause, pregnant as it was with danger to the gold standard. The Western silver men had been totally unable to obtain free and unlimited coinage. In the two and a half years which remained of the Administration, the deadlock was never broken. In a sense, this stalemate represented a victory for the silver men. Every year not less than $24,000,000 was added to the silver flood. The Administration, helpless as yet to dam the stream, had to devote itself to precautions for minimizing its evil effects.

Persistent efforts were made by the Treasury to thrust more silver into circulation. It accomplished this in various ways, but principally by making silver coin or silver certificates the only money available in small denominations. Secretary Manning had discretionary power to suppress the one and two dollar greenbacks, and he used it. The one and two dollar banknotes had previously been suppressed by law. As the greenbacks came into the Treasury in ordinary business transactions they were cancelled, and larger notes were substituted in order to keep the whole amount of greenbacks up to the sum fixed by statute. Silver dollars and silver certificates became conspicuously more common, and during the years 1887–89 inclusive more than $36,000,000 in one-dollar silver certificates alone were issued. [1]

Nevertheless, the future was to be faced with nervousness. What course would the party take on this dangerous question? All of the weather signals to the west and south were set to the signal "storm." It was disheartening to note how one Democratic leader after another filled the air with demagogic cries. Senator Beck had talked of the common man embattled against "the most powerful body of capitalists" in the country. Senator Vance had declared that the republic must awaken to "one of the grandest conspiracies against the rights of the people ever inaugurated by human greed." [2] From Vest, Brown, Maxey, Pugh, Eustis, Voorhees, and others poured forth vitriolic allusions to "Wall Street gamblers," "plutocratic rule," "heartless creditors," and "Eastern Shylocks."

Another circumstance certain to create foreboding was the continuous growth of the Treasury surplus, with the shadow which it cast across all governmental policy. The Treasury, which during the crisis

[1] *Annual Reports*, Treasurer of the U. S., 1886, 1887. For comment, *Nation*, May 27, 1886.
[2] *Cong. Rec.*, Jan. 12, 1886, vol. 17, p. 605, 606.

of 1885 had refused to buy bonds, shortly began to redeem those which had reached maturity. But by the close of 1886, nearly all the bonds which might be taken up at the pleasure of the government had been called in. In using the surplus to buy non-callable bonds the government had to compete in the open market with other purchasers, and this was a costly policy. Higher and higher premiums had to be paid. This meant that large sums which by means of the tariff and internal revenue taxes had been collected from the consuming population, and above all from the masses of poor wage-earners and farmers, were used to pour into the pockets of the investing classes, especially in the East, a heavy unearned increment. The injustice was too obvious to escape notice.

UNTIL the spring of 1886 Cleveland had not been keenly interested in the tariff question. He shared the general Democratic predilection, a fixed party position ever since the passage of the Walker tariff under Polk, for low duties; but, preoccupied with administrative reform, at first he paid little attention to the controversy. It received less space than the silver issue in his first annual message, and less than the surplus in his second. In other words, Cleveland had not enlisted under the banner of aggressive tariff reform which political independents then carried forward in close alliance with the civil service movement. Carl Schurz has told a somewhat dubious story of how, interviewing Cleveland shortly after his election, he urged him to take up the tariff. "I shall never forget what then happened. The man bent forward and buried his face in his hands on the table before him. After two or three minutes he straightened up and, with the same directness, said to me: 'I am ashamed to say it, but the truth is I know nothing about the tariff. . . . Will you tell me now how to go about it to learn?' " Cleveland might well have expressed his comparative ignorance, but it is unlikely that he did it with this sentimental gesture.

From the moment of his election the tariff reformers had exerted every possible ounce of pressure upon Cleveland, talking with him, writing him letters, and sending him books. Just before his inauguration he received a long petition signed by a group of eminent Mugwumps in New York—Henry Ward Beecher, David A. Wells, George Foster Peabody, R. R. Bowker, and others. Pointing to the "shameful" accumulation of surplus revenue, they declared that it was continued "for no other reason than that the maintenance of many of these taxes involved the levying of a much larger tribute by a few thousand capitalists, and that their influence over Congress has been too powerful to allow the public burdens to be lessened, for fear that the incidental profits of a few, at the expense of the many, should be lowered." Quite apart from the question of the surplus, they made a frontal attack upon the entire protective principle. With their arguments and those he had often heard from Manning, Cleveland was unquestionably impressed; and Schurz's testimony that early in his Administration he read many books on the tariff question is borne out by his papers.

Cleveland was peculiarly receptive to the pleas of the tariff reformers, for they included many of the men who gave continuous vigor to the struggle against spoils politics. For years they had been organizing a movement against the high post-war tariffs, which by 1885 had become a broad crusade. Although they did not neglect political activity, the movement was primarily propagandist in nature—a movement of economists, educators, editors, and other intellectuals. David A. Wells, a Connecticut Republican who had been special commissioner of revenue just after the war, deserves as much as anyone the honor of being considered the pioneer leader. Wells had distinct limitations as an economic thinker, but in his official annual reports of 1866–67 his analysis of the effect of the war tariff in raising prices, yielding outrageous profits, and fostering monopoly was unanswerable. He was quickly joined by two disinterested groups, economists of the Manchester school, and publicists who were irritated by the tariff abuses; and they in turn received support from two interested bodies, the Eastern importers and the Western farmers. Among the economists were William Graham Sumner, A. L. Perry, and General Francis A. Walker; among the publicists were Godkin, George W. Curtis, Watterson, and James Russell Lowell. Such political liberals as Schurz, Jacob D. Cox, Hugh McCulloch, Montgomery Blair and Lyman Trumbull gave enthusiastic aid to the cause. It was unlike most radical movements in keeping its feet on the ground and avoiding any lunatic fringe, and it made steady progress.

By 1880 there were flourishing Free Trade Clubs in New York and Boston—the name being an unhappy misnomer, for even the radicals believed in free trade only as the English Fabians believed in Socialism, as a far-off goal. The older generation of New England reformers, represented by William Lloyd Garrison and Charles Francis Adams, had helped establish the Boston club. The young publisher George Haven Putnam, with E. P. Wheeler, Hewitt, Beecher, and that meteoric House humorist, S. S. Cox, were prominent in the New York organization. In the campaign of 1880 the tariff reductionists supported special Congressional candidates in certain districts of Massachusetts, Kansas, and Minnesota. The movement was beginning to show formidable energy.[1] Hancock might have won the Presidency that year had he possessed the courage to lead an aggressive attack upon the existing schedules, which even Republicans admitted were too high. Instead, he accepted the advice of Democratic protectionists to evade the question. His remark that the tariff was a local issue struck the country as ridiculous and tariff reformers as timid, and possibly cost him the election. Though in the campaign of 1884 the tariff issue was kept almost out of sight, everyone realized that the Mugwumps were overwhelmingly in favor of a reduction, and that they assailed Blaine with all the more zeal because of his protectionist opinions.

Encouraged by Cleveland's election, the enthusiastic agitators held a convention in Chicago in November, 1885, and established a National Tariff Reform League, of which David A. Wells was chosen president.[2] Beecher, using some of the hottest pulpit phrases he could muster—"protectionism is the jugglery of the devil," "a paternal government is an infernal government"—made an address which received national attention. The reformers resolved that at the next election they would elect as many low-tariff Congressmen as possible, and with R. R. Bowker as their untiring secretary, strengthened their organization and treasury for this purpose. They formed an alliance with the importing interests, represented by such men as Isidor and Oscar Straus, later two of Cleveland's best friends; they offered every labor union a "workingman's economic library"; and they began to scatter pamphlets broadcast.

II

But while Cleveland sympathized with the tariff reformers, two facts made him approach the subject cautiously—the fear of injuring established American industries, and the grave danger of a party schism. As he said in his first message, justice dictated that in any tariff revision "the industries and interests which have been encouraged by such laws, and in which our citizens have large investments, should not be ruthlessly injured or destroyed." These interests had their representatives among the Democrats, for from the days of Jackson there had been a determined protectionist school in the party. Vice President

[1] Cf. H. E. Starr, *William Graham Sumner*, 233 ff.
[2] E. P. Wheeler, *Sixty Years of American Life*, 150 ff.

Dallas, a wealthy Philadelphian, had warned Polk that the Walker tariff would cost the party Pennsylvania, and it did. Now his political heir, the great surviving Pennsylvania leader in the party, Samuel J. Randall, headed a compact group of some forty Democratic protectionists in the House. We shall see that its gradual contraction was one of the most significant political facts of Cleveland's first Administration.

Randall had lost no time in issuing a warning to the new President. Two weeks before the inauguration he had sent Cleveland a letter almost menacing in tone. "From what I deem authentic newspaper correspondence and from reliable and mutual personal friends who have recently seen you," he wrote,[1] "I am led to write and guard you against a serious error, as I think, on your part. The gentlemen as far as indicated as likely to compose your Cabinet are all of the same disposition on the tariff, with tendencies toward the free trade line of thought. This I can stand and it will make no difference in my steady support of your Administration, for we all have to stand on and execute the tariff utterance of the Chicago Democratic platform—but the people in general will consider that your selections, in case of such appointments, point only to one part of our party and you will cool the friendship of many of those who differed at the last session with the majority of the Ways and Means Committee on the tariff and such feeling will find expression among the people of our party who approved the action at last session referred to." Cleveland selected no protectionist for his Cabinet. But it was impossible to disregard such a warning, reënforced as it was from various quarters.

In histories of the period, especially those written from Cleveland's point of view, Randall usually appears as a sinister figure; yet he was not a small man, nor did he act from merely selfish or unenlightened motives. A man who lived and died poor and who had so little money that in his last illness his friends had to make up a purse to send him to the country, he did not represent, like Aldrich, a few wealthy manufacturing interests, but what he regarded as the broad welfare of his State. Pennsylvania, with her mines, her oil-refineries, her steel foundries, her laboring population awakened every morning by the scream of multitudinous mill-whistles, all dependent on a vigorous American market, was constantly before his eye. He was one of the ablest members of the House. His commanding presence, unfaltering

[1] Cleveland Papers.

courage, and the mental resourcefulness which animated his quick speech and snapping black eyes, made him a formidable antagonist. Beginning life a Whig, he had been active in Democratic affairs ever since his attendance at the Cincinnati convention which nominated Buchanan in 1856. In the Civil War he had temporarily left politics to fight, commanding a company at Gettysburg; but after 1862 his service in Congress was never interrupted. The district which he represented for almost thirty years was a Philadelphia constituency lying along the Schuylkill and filled with the plainest people—stevedores, petty shopkeepers, and workers in the navy yard.[1] From time to time Republicans proposed that it be gerrymandered in order to defeat Randall, but the party chiefs always vetoed the idea. They knew that he was far more valuable to protection than any Republican could be.

Randall knew it too, and he always preferred to work from inside a half-hostile party, though his principles would have made it easy for him to exchange camps. From 1867, when he protested against the tariff-reduction bill for which David A. Wells was responsible, his defence of protection never faltered. In 1871 he was responsible for a step which proved decisive in fixing the character of our subsequent tariff system: on March 13 he introduced the momentous bill—for momentous is not too emphatic a term—repealing the duties on tea and coffee. The essential issue then before the nation was whether a reduction of the revenues should be effected by lowering the protective duties, and the removal of the tea and coffee levies forestalled at one stroke any extensive disturbance of the protective schedules.[2] In 1872 Michael Kerr of Indiana attacked the tariff as extortionate. Randall replied that in Philadelphia there were 8,300 manufacturing establishments large and small, and that at the last census their annual production had been valued at $334,000,000. "And yet gentlemen who stand here would strike down such interests as that," said Randall, "I am glad that I have the nerve and courage sufficient to resist them, whether they are inside or outside my party." Repugnant though his doctrines were to the Democratic tradition, in 1880 he had been seriously considered for the Presidential nomination. Everyone respected him. "From crown to toe," later said his fiercest opponent, Roger Q. Mills, "he was an honest man."

[1] S. I. Pomerantz, *Samuel Jackson Randall: Protectionist Democrat*, 113.
[2] F. W. Taussig, *Tariff History of the United States*, 171 ff.

Beside Randall in the House in 1885 stood Andrew G. Curtin of Pennsylvania, who had been war governor, and three other Democrats of that State; William McAdoo and two other Jersey Democrats; ten New Yorkers; four spokesmen of the Louisiana sugar interests; three representatives of the Ohio wool-growers; members from iron districts in Maryland and Alabama; and protectionists from other industrial constituencies scattered as far west as California. The Democrats seemed irreparably divided by the question. It was also obvious that even if tariff reform were victorious in the House it would be defeated in the Republican Senate. There was as yet little evidence of a great national impulse toward downward revision of the tariff. What popular demand existed came principally from the Southern and Western areas which were vociferous for unlimited silver coinage, and whose Congressmen showed little desire to act in harmony with the President. Altogether, it is not strange that Cleveland hesitated.

III

This hesitation was patent in Cleveland's message of December, 1885. Though he called for tariff legislation, it was in cautious terms. Established industries must not be ruthlessly injured, and the interests of labor must be conserved, but "within these limitations a certain reduction should be made in our customs revenue." There was a striking contrast between his utterance and that of Secretary Manning, whose annual report treated the tariff question at length and with aggressive energy. Unquestionably Cleveland had read this report before its publication and approved it, but it went far beyond his own words. Manning's own investigation of the customs service had proved that the tariff laws were "a chaos rather than a system." He pointed out that like the laws on currency and banking, the tariff acts were a legacy of the war. Through a long era of falling prices the war duties had been maintained and even increased, though Arthur's Tariff Commission had demonstrated that many rates were actually injurious to the interests supposed to be benefited, and that a reduction would conduce to prosperity. He struck a note of angry protest:

They have been retained at an average ad valorem rate for the last year of over 46 per cent, which is but 2½ per cent less than the highest rate of the war period, and is nearly 4 per cent more than the rate before the latest revision. The highest endurable rates of duty, which were adopted in 1862–64 to offset internal taxes upon almost every taxable article, have in most cases been retained now from fourteen to twenty years after every such internal tax has been removed. They have been retained while purely revenue duties upon articles not competing with anything produced in the thirty-eight States have been discarded. They have been retained upon articles used as materials upon our own manufactures (in 1884 adding $38,000,000 to their cost), which, if exported, compete in other countries against similar manufacturers from untaxed materials. Some rates have been retained after effecting a higher price for a domestic product at home than it was sold abroad for.

It was well known that the House Ways and Means Committee would immediately bring forward another tariff revision bill. The head of this committee, William R. Morrison of Illinois, had offered an ill-planned and abortive measure for a horizontal reduction of rates in the previous Congress. As a leader Morrison unfortunately left much to be desired. His career, to be sure, had been richly picturesque. An Illinois farm boy, a graduate of McKendree College, a private at Buena Vista, a forty-niner who had actually found gold in California, a colonel at the capture of Fort Donelson—he was one of the representative Americans of his time. But while a man of ability, he was tongue-tied and had never made a successful speech. Moreover, with his impracticable temper and strange tactlessness he was ill-equipped for parliamentary management either on the floor or in the caucus. At the beginning of the session he antagonized Randall by a proposal for revision of the House rules, taking away from Randall's Appropriations Committee a large part of the powers with which it was vested; while as if deliberately to offend Cleveland, he shortly declared that the President "is surrounded and influenced by people and interests not such as would lead him to what I believe correct conclusions on tariff reform." The statement was as false as it was ill-timed. No one believed that Speaker Carlisle would supply much of the leadership which Morrison was incapable of furnishing, for Carlisle's conception of his official functions was excessively mild and conciliatory.

Yet however unfavorable the circumstances, something had to be done. The fact was that the tariff constituted an irrepressible challenge to the party, both in itself and in its connection with the growing problem of the Treasury surplus. The Republicans themselves, finding it barely escapable in Grant's Administrations and quite unescapable in Arthur's, had made a desperate effort in 1882–83 to get rid of it by creating a temporary tariff commission, but had failed. Hewitt, one of the leading American industrialists, correctly said in 1886 that the existing schedules were a blight upon large sections of industry, that both parties had acknowledged the fact in their platforms, and yet that neither had taken an effective step toward reform. Any prolonged evasion by the Democratic leaders was impossible, for as Hewitt remarked, Cleveland's party was the responsible party in Washington, and if it did not keep its promises, it deserved to be turned out.

The new bill, drawn by the Ways and Means Committee with a special eye to Western farming interests, was almost completed by the end of March, 1886. Meanwhile, at Morrison's instigation Mills, McMillin, and other members were trying desperately to placate Randall, and finally Morrison himself sought out his old enemy—without result. On April 8 the bill was reported to the House. Many articles, including lumber, salt, wool, hemp, and flax, were put on the free list; the specific duties on woolen textiles were replaced by lower ad valorem duties; and the rates were reduced on cottons, sugar, pig iron, steel rails, and window glass—the three products last-named being close to Randall's heart.[1] Although the public hearings on the bill had been attended by a clamorous crowd of lobbyists, it was a moderate and fair measure. During May it was thrust to one side by the silver debate. Meanwhile Morrison, Mills, Carlisle, and others labored to gain converts—and Cleveland, despite his resentment of Morrison's surplus resolution, took a hand.

Early in June the President was interviewing doubtful Congressmen. "He has summoned a number of men to his presence," wrote the Washington correspondent of the *Herald*,[2] "and told them that in his opinion the good of the party demands action on the tariff. . . . So far as is known Mr. Cleveland has not made a single convert. But all who have listened to him admit that he has been very much in earnest." No Democratic caucus could be held, for as one Congressman said, if the doors were locked the chairman would have to call in a squad of police to keep the peace. The grand object was simply to cut down the dissident vote to such a point that the bill might actually be debated.

At 1:30 on the afternoon of June 17 the test came. Morrison, his

---

[1] F. W. Taussig, *Tariff History of the United States.*
[2] N. Y. *Herald*, June 17, 1886. "This kind of missionary effort does not seem to be in his line," added the correspondent.

heavy beard hiding an unemotional face, moved that the House go into Committee of the Whole to consider his bill, and called for the yeas and nays. The roll proceeded slowly, a forty-minute process. Once the House stopped to cheer the entry of W. S. Holman, who had hastened back from Indiana. Five Republicans, one from New York and four from Minnesota, voted for consideration, while thirty-six Randallite Democrats voted against it. The total stood 157 to 140 against consideration. It was crushing defeat for Morrison, and as the *Herald's* correspondent said, a rebuff for Cleveland as well. The correspondent quoted a Congressman: [1]

It is a black eye for the President, and I for my part am not sorry for him. If he had not declared in January that he took no interest in the silver suspension question he could have carried that. He chose to go back on his policy in that matter, and he ought to have kept out of this tariff business. He fancied he had some influence, and he brought pressure to bear on some of us to vote for the Morrison bill, and got snubbed, as he deserved. A President of the United States ought to have great influence with his party, but Mr. Cleveland deliberately threw his away, and he can't now pick it up again. That so many New York men should go against him is undoubtedly a mortification for him, but he has himself to blame for it.

"Do you call yourself a Democrat?" demanded Cleveland harshly of a New Yorker who had voted against consideration. He felt the result keenly and made others realize that they were on his blacklist. Randall followed his victory by introducing a tariff bill which lowered some rates and raised others, to show how the protectionist Democrats would grapple with the problem. It was a mere gesture, and was buried in committee, but he insisted that it constituted a true interpretation of the Democratic platform.

IV

With the adjournment of Congress, the tariff issue went over into the Congressional campaign of 1886—the one issue of real importance. Studiously ignored in parts of the country, in other areas it burst to the surface with irrepressible force. The reformers had to make an effort to force the fighting, for inertia was defeat. At the outset national interest seemed slight. When the Philadelphia *Press* in August published several

[1] N. Y. *Herald,* June 18, 1886.

columns of interviews on the political issues of the day, Benjamin Harrison stated that "the question of primary importance in Indiana will be the gerrymandering of the State." Senator Allison and David B. Henderson of Iowa agreed that railroad regulation was the most burning topic; Senator Manderson of Nebraska mentioned prohibition; and Frank Hiscock of New York declared the financial policy of the Democratic party the most important question. Patrick Collins bluntly said, "There are no issues." But late in August the American Free Trade League held a meeting in New York under David A. Wells, and demanded "aggressive and uncompromising political action."

In Massachusetts, encouraged by the Independents, two men began to stress the tariff question—John E. Russell, Democratic candidate in the Worcester district, and Gen. Hazard Stevens, a Boston Independent. Sixty-nine prominent Mugwumps issued an appeal to the voters to support Democratic candidates, presenting various arguments, including Cleveland's excellent record, but giving most emphasis to the point that the Democrats had sought in good faith to redeem their tariff pledges, while the Republicans had balked them.[1] Charles W. Eliot announced that he would vote the Democratic ticket on the tariff issue, and a great Independent rally for Stevens, with David A. Wells as principal speaker, was shortly held in Tremont Temple. In Connecticut a similar movement seemed to be declaring itself. A State association had been set up in New Haven, with one of the largest Connecticut manufacturers, J. B. Sargent, as its president. It enlisted many Democratic leaders, including the State chairman, and prepared to support low-tariff candidates.

In Pennsylvania the standard of revolt against Randall was unfurled with surprising boldness. Here the leader was W. L. Scott of Erie, one of Cleveland's best political friends: an iron manufacturer, banker, railroad builder, holder of so much coal land that he was sometimes called "the coal king," landowner, cattle-breeder, and twice mayor of Erie. He was one of the important men of northwest Pennsylvania, and in the old Buffalo days Cleveland had heard much of him. He had extended the Rock Island Railroad to the Missouri River during the Civil War, and had later done more than anyone else to build the New York, Philadelphia & Norfolk road. Such a man might be expected to be on the protectionist side. But somewhere in his versatile career Scott had

[1] N. Y. *Evening Post*, Oct. 14, Oct. 20, 1886.

become imbued with liberal doctrines on the subject. Perhaps it was
when he was being educated in Virginia at what is now Hampden-
Sydney College; perhaps when he was a page in the House in the days
of Polk. He had supported the Morrison bill in the Forty-ninth Congress. Now he hesitated to run for reëlection, but changed his mind
when nearly 1500 Republicans in his district petitioned him to be a
candidate.[1] Representative C. E. Boyle of Uniontown, in the Connells-
ville coke region, was refused a renomination because of his vote against
the Morrison bill.[2]

Naturally, however, it was in New York that the most ardor was exhibited. A host of Democrats there recalled with a sense of outrage
that ten Representatives had opposed the Morrison bill.[3] The Democratic press of the metropolis—the *Herald, Times,* and above all, the
World and *Evening Post*—were low-tariff sheets. Manning's followers
were active, and the Free Trade Club early set to work. Even more
important were the activities of the Young Men's Democratic Club in
New York city, which in July appointed a committee under E. P.
Wheeler to carry the contest into the Congressional districts. This body
demanded that all candidates for nomination declare themselves; it led
a victorious effort for the election of S. S. Cox, who had resigned his
Turkish post, as successor to Joseph Pulitzer; and it found a low-tariff
successor to Hewitt, who was now engaged in a spectacular campaign
for mayor of New York. It particularly advocated free raw materials,
and all the Democratic candidates were committed to tariff-revision on
that principle. One convert was even made among the Republicans—
Ashbel P. Fitch, who ran on a tariff-reform plank against a Randallite
Democrat, Egbert L. Viele, and with Independent help was elected.[4]
There could be no question that the party in Cleveland's own State was
overwhelmingly for lower duties on raw materials.

In the Northwest it proved equally impossible to suppress the tariff
issue. No sooner did the Republican conventions begin to meet than it
became evident that a party revolt was threatened. The farmers were
tired of being taxed for the benefit of Eastern industrialists. "We believe," ran the platform of the Iowa Republicans, "the tariff should be

[1] N. Y. *Evening Post,* Oct. 4, 1886.
[2] *Ibid.,* Oct. 2, 1886.
[3] E. P. Wheeler, *Sixty Years of American Life,* 175 ff.
[4] The N. Y. *Evening Post* of Sept. 23, 1886, contains a long statement by Wheeler on
the tariff reformers' work in the campaign.

revised and reduced." Thus early had the Iowa idea, later to be made famous by Cummins, appeared. The Republican platform in Nebraska demanded that "a revision of the tariff shall be made at the earliest practicable day." The Indiana plank called for reduction, while the Minnesota Republicans drew up a platform worthy of the finest traditions of that progressive State. They endorsed Cleveland's reforms in the civil service; indicated their willingness to repeal the Bland-Allison Act if legislation to promote the free international coinage of silver were carried into effect; and demanded such tariff revision as would simplify the duties and bring them below the level of Civil War times. In addition, they commended the four Republicans who, led by Knute Nelson, had voted for consideration of the Morrison bill.[1]

The Republicans and the harried little Randallite wing of the Democratic party were ready to return blow for blow. It did not form part of the Republican strategy in 1886 to try to carry the House; the party leaders were content to maintain control of the Senate, and leave the responsibility for the unruly lower chamber with the Democrats. No special Congressional campaign fund was raised, and the subscriptions received were insufficient to pay for the printing.[2] Yet with an eye upon 1888, the Republican leaders resolved to exploit the tariff issue wherever profitable, and lost no time in enlisting rich manufacturers.

Blaine, who had just completed his *Twenty Years of Congress*, showed special alacrity in bringing the tariff issue before the country again. Emerging from his new mansion at Bar Harbor, he prepared to take the platform in August. An unfortunate occurrence marred his entrance. Senator Frye preceded him by a speech delivered at Houlton, Me., on August 21st, which cost Blaine a heavy pang. Explaining the defeat of 1884, Frye remarked: "You take a magnificent bridal dress, with its ribbons and splendid laces, and put it on exhibition with a little inkspot on its skirt, and you will find plenty of men and women who will see nothing but that spot. Now the people of this country, with an exquisite fidelity to the best interests of the nation, saw the little bit of a smirch on the skirt of Mr. Blaine's coat . . ." This indiscreet admission kept Frye busy explaining for days. Blaine's first speech, at Sebago Lake on August 24, lacked his usual pyrotechnic quality, but one-third of it was devoted to the tariff. At that date

---

[1] See review of these platforms in N. Y. *Herald*, May 3, 1888.
[2] N. Y. *Evening Post*, Nov. 4, 1886.

America rejoiced in a little instrument called the chestnut-bell. Attached to the waistcoat, it was rung whenever anyone made a peculiarly stale remark. All over the green that afternoon these little signals tinkled numerously, punctuating Blaine's discourse on the beauties of protection.[1] Other speeches in Maine were followed by a tour, in which he gained fire and vigor, through New Jersey and Pennsylvania, talking everywhere of the tariff.

In Ohio a special drive was made by the protectionists to defeat Frank Hurd, a brilliant Toledo attorney who, though a hard-money man and civil service reformer, was above everything else a tariff-reductionist.[2] In Illinois the eyes of the country were shortly fastened upon the Belleville district, where Morrison was engaged in a death-grapple with his foes. Money was poured into it by the Republicans. In October John Jarrett, secretary of the American Tin-Plate Association, arrived with ample funds, which he declared came from a "working-man's tariff club" of Pittsburgh, but which were probably from the American Iron and Steel Association. He employed a small army of men at $3 a day and "legitimate expenses"; travelled all over the district making speeches; and obtained the assistance of the Knights of Labor. Jarrett admitted that when Morrison had defeated in Congress a proposed increase in the duty on tin flakes he had threatened to follow him into his district. By strenuous efforts and skilful use of money the operatives in the glass factories, rolling mills, and other protected industries of Alton, Belleville, and East St. Louis were not only marshalled against Morrison, but induced to threaten a boycott of all merchants who did not join them. Saloonkeepers were also dragooned into opposing him.[3]

The one State in which the protectionists gained full control of the Democratic as well as the Republican organization was Connecticut. Just before the delegates to the State convention were chosen, a quasi-secret order went out from ex-Senator William H. Barnum, whose authority was absolute, that the tariff reformers were to be suppressed. All his life Barnum, a rough boss whose code of political ethics had landed him in more than one scandal, had been interested in iron manufacture. At his instigation nearly all the Democratic candidates for the

[1] N. Y. *World*, Aug. 21–29, 1886.
[2] Stealey, *Twenty Years*, 323 ff.
[3] Chicago *Daily News*, Nov. 4, 1886, describes Jarrett's activities in detail.

State convention who were hostile to protection were now defeated, and the convention rejected a resolution commending the two Democratic Representatives for their support of the Morrison bill. A week later a harsher stroke fell. Edward Seymour, one of the ablest Democrats in Congress, was refused a renomination simply because of his low-tariff votes. Soon afterward the Congressional convention in the Hartford district, which had adopted resolutions favoring a tariff for revenue only, was reconvened and made to pass protectionist resolutions instead.[1]

No one who watched the campaign could doubt that industrial organizations, and especially the iron and steel interests, were using money lavishly. In a speech at Erie William L. Scott disclosed some of the motives at play. Eighteen months previously he had had occasion to buy 10,000 tons of steel rails, and going to a rolling-mill, secured them for $25.50 a ton. About six months later the seven or eight steel-rail mills of the country combined, agreed to divide the home market, and gradually forced the price up to $33 a ton. This represented a gross increase of $7.50, which Scott estimated gave the manufacturers a totally unfair profit of $5 a ton. Their production being about 1,500,000 tons of steel rails a year, the seven or eight mills were dividing $7,500,-000 annually.[2] Naturally they wished to bulwark themselves against British competition, and were willing to pay handsomely to save the protectionist cause. Godkin, writing more loosely, estimated the unjustified profits of all the iron and steel mills of the country under the existing tariff at $25,000,000 a year.

v

A number of unpleasant complications entered the campaign. In New York a storm was fast gathering about the enigmatic and unsavory personality of David B. Hill; in Ohio much indignation had been excited by the scandal of Henry B. Payne's purchased seat in the Senate, a subject on which we shall touch later. Most embarrassing of all to the Administration was the criticism to which Attorney-General Garland, by deplorable indiscretions, had subjected himself, and which came to a head this summer.

[1] See N. Y. *Evening Post*, Oct. 30, 1886, for matter on Barnum's activities. Barnum was national chairman 1876–1889.
[2] Erie *Herald*, Nov. 1, 1886.

Garland three years before, when Senator, had been presented with shares to a nominal value of $500,000 in a new corporation called the Pan-Electric Company, and had been made its attorney. The company possessed no capital or credit, and its sole property was the so-called Rogers telephone patent, which was worthless unless the Bell patent was declared invalid. But if Bell's claims to priority could be broken down, the company would become rich. As attorney, Garland had furnished the company an opinion that its rights did not in any way infringe upon those of the Bell Company. When he became Attorney-General he did not surrender his stock, although he must have known that it would become an embarrassment. The Pan-Electric promoters had meanwhile been offering gifts of shares to various Congressmen, which astute men like Cox and Hewitt refused. In 1885, Attorney-General Garland was asked by the company to institute a government suit to test the validity of the Bell patent. He declined, very properly feeling disabled by his ownership of the stock. But a few weeks later he left Washington for a vacation at his estate, Hominy Hall, near Little Rock; and it was shortly announced that the Solicitor-General had decided to commence the suit.[1]

There immediately ensued a popular outcry, and Garland's relations with the Pan-Electric were described in unpleasant detail in the press. It was shown that he actually held one-tenth of the whole stock of the company. Cleveland called upon him for an explanation, and it was given in a long communication dated October 8. Garland admitted his close connection with the promoters, and asserted that the Solicitor-General's permission had been granted without his knowledge or consent; but he did not say that he had warned the Solicitor-General against acting! Of course he should have given such a warning. Cleveland had already issued peremptory orders to the Solicitor-General to revoke the steps taken to begin the suit, and to refer the whole question to Secretary Lamar of the Interior Department. Early in 1886 Lamar, to the general surprise, decided that the suit ought to be pressed, and this revived the national chorus of criticism. It was pointed out that the Department of Justice would have entire charge of the case, and that if it succeeded Garland would forthwith become a very rich man. "His continuance in office under the present conditions," wrote Godkin

[1] See *Harper's Weekly*, Feb. 27, 1886, for a review of the Garland case.

in February, "is doing the Administration irreparable injury." [1] An investigating committee, hurriedly appointed by Congress, began to hold public hearings. On April 19 Garland testified frankly and fully, making a good impression. He denied that the stock was a gift—he had helped organize the company, and had paid an assessment for that purpose, the stock being his remuneration. He asserted that he had never had any idea of using his official influence in its behalf; and that when he had gone to Arkansas he had ordered that no departmental mail whatever was to be forwarded to him.[2] The majority of the Congressional committee brought in a report completely exonerating him, though the minority censured him sharply.

Cleveland was convinced that Garland had done no actual wrong, and never for a moment thought of dismissing the man. This was correct, but Garland's failure to resign was improper and unfortunate. At the best his conduct had constituted a refusal to avoid the appearance of evil, and it showed a lack of proper delicacy of feeling. He by no means escaped without a penalty. He had been a popular officer, and the country had regarded with favor his well-known ambition for a seat on the bench of the Supreme Court; but now he was largely discredited. Despite the Congressional whitewashing, echoes of the attacks upon him reverberated throughout the summer and fall, coming to a climax when in November the circuit court at Cincinnati quashed the case against the Bell Company on the ground that it lacked jurisdiction. It would manifestly have relieved the President and his party had Garland given up his place. *Harper's Weekly* joined the *Sun* and *World* in calling upon him to do so; and Nast published a cartoon which showed Garland plaintively declaring "Nobody will take the stock off my hands," and Columbia responding: "Can't I get somebody to take you off my hands?" [3]

VI

The result of the elections in 1886 was indecisive. Cleveland awaited the returns with much concern, for they offered the first test of public sentiment upon his Administration, but he had no reason to feel dis-

[1] *Nation*, Feb. 4, 1886.
[2] N. Y. *Herald*, April 20, 1886.
[3] *Harper's Weekly*, Feb. 27, 1886.

turbed by them. There was more popular interest in the mayoralty contest in New York than in anything else, and Hewitt's decisive victory over Henry George, Theodore Roosevelt running a bad third, caused nation-wide rejoicing among conservatives of both parties. Cleveland was among those who congratulated the mayor-elect. He and Hewitt had not recently been on cordial terms, but each respected the iron integrity and self-reliance of the other. The result in the Congressional elections seemed to prove anything or nothing, according to the mood of the observer. The Democratic majority in the House was cut down from 184 to 160, giving the party a scant majority of 8 over the Republicans; but in the Senate the prospective Republican margin was reduced from 8 to 2.[1]

On the surface, it at first appeared that the tariff reform forces had suffered a severe setback. Their outstanding champion, Morrison, was defeated by a sharp overturn, the normal Democratic majority of 2600 in his district changing to a Republican majority of 750. Frank Hurd in the Toledo district went down; even Carlisle barely escaped defeat in Kentucky. With Hewitt gone from the House, who would lead the next tariff battle? Yet the losses were not all on one side, and a calmer view showed no ground for uneasiness. In Minnesota the Democrats carried three of the five Congressional districts. In Massachusetts the tariff reformers elected John E. Russell. William L. Scott was returned in Pennsylvania, and in New Hampshire one of the two Congressional districts was gained by a Democrat for the first time in years. All the New York Democrats chosen to Congress, and one Republican as well, were now pledged to vote for tariff reduction. If the Democrats had suffered in Indiana, Kentucky, and Illinois, the Republicans had suffered in Connecticut, New Jersey, Colorado, and California. There was little evidence of popular distrust of the President, and still less of a reaction against tariff reform.

Fortunately, Cleveland regarded the elections as a challenge to increased vigor in stating the low-tariff position, and his annual message the next month demonstrated the fact. Watterson also regarded it as a challenge. The Democracy had two great enemies, he wrote—the Republican party, "unscrupulous, corrupt, and insatiable in its thirst for power," and the tariff party, "an army of mercenaries and monop-

olists, with a treasury filled by millions of dollars, wrung remorselessly
year by year from an overburdened, overtaxed people." He went on: [1]

The defeat of Hurd and Morrison and the narrow escape of Carlisle should
awaken the Democracy from its slumbers and destroy its false sense of
security. In the result of today we hear a trumpet call to battle. There are
traitors in the camp, there are spies everywhere, there are dangers that
threaten us that can only be conquered by relentlessness, by unremitting, un-
wavering warfare. The House is saved to us, but if lost it should only impress
on us the necessity of putting on the whole armor of Democracy. The gigantic
power of concentrated and ill-gotten wealth of the North is arrayed against
us.

In the final session of the Forty-ninth Congress, just before Christmas of 1886, a last effort was made to give life to the Morrison bill.
The House leaders decided to put all their energy behind the measure.
Cleveland, now fully aroused, sent word that if the session declined to
heed his recommendations on the silver and tariff issues, he might call
an extra session of the Fiftieth Congress. For a time there was talk of
a caucus in which Cleveland's appeal could be forcibly presented.
Morrison and other members of the Ways and Means Committee
favored one, but the Randallites threatened to bolt to the Republicans
if it were called.[2] They still turned a defiant ear to Cleveland's message, in which he had said that the popular demand for lower duties
"should be recognized and obeyed," and that "a cheerful concession
sometimes averts abrupt and heedless action." [3] When the vote was
taken just before the holiday recess, consideration of the bill was again
defeated. But this time the margin was significantly narrower, 154 to
149, and the protests of the regular Democrats were ominously angrier.
The Chicago *Tribune,* voicing a general Western sentiment, was declaring that reduction was "imperative." Morrison's wife telegraphed him,
with feminine defiance, to "Call it up again—keep them uncomfortable." [4]

"I happened to see the President the afternoon the tariff was rejected," said S. S. Cox a few days later; "he expressed himself very

[1] Louisville *Courier-Journal,* Nov. 4, 1886.
[2] The N. Y. *Evening Post,* Dec. 10, 11, 12, 1886, describes Cleveland's activities.
[3] Richardson, *Messages and Papers,* Vol. VIII, p. 510.
[4] *Public Opinion,* Dec. 25, 1886.

intensely as to his disappointment." [1] Yet Cleveland was not discouraged. Some Congressmen told him that with a little more strenuous effort, and two or three conciliatory changes, the attempt at consideration would have succeeded. He looked forward hopefully to the next Congress.

To the tariff reformers the year 1886 had been pregnant with important events. The Democratic party had been brought to a searching test, and notice had been served that the protectionist members must alter their views or be cast into outer darkness. In New York, Massachusetts, and the Middle West Democratic candidates for Congress had been compelled to pledge themselves to tariff reduction. Tariff-reform clubs and leagues the country over had been awakened to new activity. And above all, Cleveland had been converted to the necessity of lending active assistance. The President who in January declared that he would not use his executive influence for any legislation had in June called Representatives to the White House and argued with them and in December had threatened an extra session. It was a momentous change.

[1] Interview in N. Y. *Herald,* Jan. 3, 1887.

Chapter XVIII   *Marriage: The President and the Public*

WASHINGTON had watched with critical eyes as Cleveland took up his quarters in the White House, and as Democratic Cabinet officers prepared to play their part in the society of the capital. Beyond Washington, a curious nation had also watched. The slanders of the campaign had imbued multitudes with a certain distrust of the new President. Did he possess the dignity, poise, and decorum that were expected of a Chief Magistrate, or would the nation have to blush for him as it had sometimes blushed over Lincoln's stories and over Grant's fast trotters and vulgar companions? During his first year in the Presidency Cleveland was constantly aware of being under an unfriendly scrutiny. He knew that hostile journalists and politicians were ready to seize every opportunity to perpetuate the legend that he was a rough, uneducated man of coarse instincts, lifted to a position far above his due level.

Socially, Washington expected little from the Administration—and correctly. Unlike Arthur, Cleveland cared nothing for dinners or receptions, accepted few invitations, and until his marriage did little entertaining except that which was *de rigueur*. Several Cabinet members were equally indifferent to social life. Attorney-General Garland refused nearly all invitations. Secretary Lamar dined out more frequently, but in 1885–86 lived in modest bachelor quarters. Vilas had a small house and entertained in restricted fashion. Endicott took the handsome mansion of George Pendleton in Sixteenth Street, but his tastes were those of an austere New Englander, while Bayard also lived with the utmost quietness. The social burden of the Administration fell at the outset upon Manning and Whitney. To please his bride the former leased a large house and gave numerous dinners and receptions. Whitney, after renovating the fine Frelinghuysen house on I Street, used his wealth in a decidedly glittering hospitality, his weekly receptions and balls, with superb catering, being attended by the smartest people of both Washington and New York. It was said that at a single party two hundred gallons of terrapin soup and eighty cases of champagne disappeared! Dinners and cotillions were numerous. Mrs.

Whitney's Wednesdays at home attracted large numbers, and she paid special attention to readings and musicales, with authors and musicians of note as guests of honor. Indeed, some critics complained that Whitney's use of his fortune was vulgar and unrepublican.

It was important for Cleveland to accomplish two objects: to show the country that the White House would be managed with the utmost decorum, and at the same time to prove that with all his ruggedness of character he could be genially human. In the former undertaking he was capably aided by his sister Rose. She was a model of propriety. Some people, indeed, found her strong personality, energy, and purposeful movements rather terrifying. There could be no question that she governed all White House affairs strictly as Lucy Hayes had done. Though really democratic and on occasion a charming conversationalist, her learning made her seem a good deal of a bluestocking to simple Congressional wives. It was soon reported that she had confessed to relieving the monotony of an hour of handshaking by conjugating Greek verbs behind her formal smile. Somewhat to the President's annoyance, she made a public statement in praise of Mrs. Hayes' cold-water rule in the executive mansion and frowned upon wine at dinner—though wine continued to be served. He was also annoyed by her worriment lest he should appoint too many Catholics to office, and her efforts to awaken him to the Romanist peril. Cleveland rather preferred Mrs. Hoyt to his severe maiden sister, but the latter's appeal to religious folk and temperance people—she was an active member of the W. C. T. U.—was invaluable to him.

Within a few months after she came to Washington Rose was receiving columns of news-space as the author of *George Eliot's Poetry and Other Studies,* which appeared in June, 1885. "The book is not of a kind to suit the masses," she admitted, "but it will, I hope, be read by students, for whom every line of it was originally written. Those who have appreciated my life work thus far think that it should seek expression in this form, and such kindly suasion and the sincerity which I know underlies it have led me to publish it at this time. I hope it will fill some good purpose." It certainly filled one excellent purpose, for running through twelve editions in a year, it was said to have brought Miss Cleveland more than $25,000.[1]

A President can humanize himself only by letting the public know of

[1] Peck, *Twenty Years of the Republic,* 61.

a hundred incidents which show him in his informal and workaday moods. Little by little the American people realized Cleveland's true qualities. They learned how he called his secretary "Dan" and how Lamont called him "Governor," and how the two labored together, as in the old Albany days, till one or two in the morning. They heard stories of his fineness of feeling. In January, 1886, Secretary Bayard lost in rapid succession his daughter Kate and his wife, the latter an invalid for years. The newspapers gave a touching picture of his grief at the second funeral as, with bent shoulders and tottering steps in sharp contrast with his usually robust stride and erect head, he followed the coffin to the picturesque yard of the Old Swedes' Church in Wilmington. Cleveland's cheeks were wet as he drove with him from the Bayard residence to the Washington station. The President pleased old Washingtonians by a call upon that venerable survivor of the antebellum era, the banker-philanthropist W. W. Corcoran. Seventy-seven years old, Corcoran might be seen daily, a carnation in his buttonhole, pushing his vigorous way to his office in the Riggs Bank. And Cleveland took equal pains to show courtesy to a more distinguished octogenarian, the historian George Bancroft.[1] In his house on H Street, within a square of Corcoran's, where he kept his private library of 12,000 books and manuscripts, Bancroft was now completing the final revision of his history of the United States. He also was a spare, erect, vigorous man, who loved to work in his rose-garden. A graceful horseman, he was often seen riding with his friend Spofford, the librarian of Congress, his blue eyes sparkling with enjoyment and his white beard fanning his ruddy cheek. Cleveland took pains to ask him to the White House and accepted invitations in return.

The President regularly attended the First Presbyterian Church, where the Rev. Byron Sunderland preached. He shook hands at 1:30 with long lines of callers. Sometimes he cracked a joke with one of them. Once a Chicago minister, the Rev. Hugh J. Field, remarked that "I was against you, Mr. President. I labored diligently among my flock and prayed that you might be overthrown, but now—" "I like that," vigorously interjected Cleveland; "I like the *but now* especially. Go on." [2] He would occasionally lean over and whisper in the ear of an

---

[1] See W. M. Sloane, "George Bancroft in Society, in Politics, in Letters," *Century Magazine*, Jan. 1886.

[2] N. Y. *Herald*, March 3, 1886.

old lady, who smiled as she passed on. Now and then a witticism got into the press. "Whenever I see a Bland dollar," he once remarked, "I am reminded of the aphorism about the cloud with the silver lining. It is 80 per cent silver and 20 per cent mist." At his inaugural he had been surrounded with men in derby hats. The photographer Jarvis took a view from the Capitol pediment, which Cleveland later scrutinized. "I wonder," he commented, "if Oliver Cromwell ever had so many Roundheads about him as I did when this picture was made!" [1]

II

But the event which did most to dispel the prejudices that first clustered about Cleveland was his marriage in the White House on the evening of June 2, 1886. So much has been written of it that there is no need to relate the story again in full. The secret of his engagement to Frances Folsom had been well kept. Rose Cleveland said later that she had known for two years that the marriage was probable, and for one year that it was agreed upon, but the two families told almost no outsiders. Cleveland, who since 1875 had regarded himself as a virtual guardian of Frances Folsom, had seen something of her when she attended the Central High School in Buffalo. Once or twice he had brought her legal papers to fill out. Soon after he was elected governor he had written her mother regarding the sword Oscar Folsom had carried in the Civil War, which had passed into Cleveland's possession; and he had then asked permission to correspond with Frances. He wrote to her assiduously while she was in Wells College, and sometimes sent flowers. Once during the week of the Music Festival in Buffalo, when he was attending with members of his staff, he had come to call; she had just returned home through a drenching rain and had gone to bed, and she kept the governor waiting while she struggled into a frock. "Five minutes more that time," he used to say later, "and we should never have been married!" Mrs. Folsom and she had visited him in the governor's mansion in Albany, and she had taken an intense interest in his election to the presidency. In April following his inauguration she and her mother used the spring vacation at Wells College to visit Miss Cleveland in the White House, and were guests there for perhaps ten days. From her babyhood there had been the warmest affection between her and

[1] N. Y. *Herald*, March 23, 1886.

Cleveland, and it now ripened into a more romantic feeling.

To a friend Cleveland later remarked: "I often say to my wife, 'Poor girl, you never had any courting like other girls,' " and added: "It is true I did say some things to her one night, when we were walking together in the East Room, when she was here visiting my sister." He tried to get her to prolong her visit, but she insisted upon her college duties. With his usual delicacy of feeling, he did not wish to propose till she had graduated at Wells. But in August he wrote her in Scranton offering marriage, and the engagement at once followed.[1] At the time she was twenty-two years old; tall, graceful, very pretty, with dark eyes that could be called beautiful, and with charmingly unaffected manners.

The management of the wedding could not have been in better taste. While the country justly felt entitled to some knowledge of the event, vulgar curiosity was held at arm's length. Miss Folsom and her mother had been travelling in Europe, and did not return till late in May. So well had the secret been guarded that it was not until April 19th that the New York *Herald*, preëminent for society news, mentioned the topic. Then it blazed out with the skeptical headlines: "Washington Gossip—Society Incredulous About the President's Marriage—What if it Prove True?—Official Precedence and Other Matters to be Affected." The Washington correspondent believed that the report was a canard circulated by certain interested social groups in Buffalo. When on May 27 Miss Folsom and her mother arrived in New York, Lamont met them down the bay, whisked them aboard a waiting vessel, and conducted them to the Gilsey House. Immediately afterward, at ten o'clock on the evening of May 28th, the engagement was officially announced at the White House. Cleveland visited New York city on Memorial Day to review parades there and in Brooklyn, Governor Hill having refused to share the burden with him. The press chronicled every movement. His evening visit at the Gilsey House when he first reached the city; his early morning departure from Secretary Whitney's home to witness the Brooklyn parade; his return to the reviewing stand in Madison Square, where with Endicott, Whitney, Vilas, Sheridan, and Schofield he watched the blue-coated veterans file past; the moment when, catching the flutter of Miss Folsom's handkerchief from the balcony of the Gilsey House two blocks down Fifth Avenue, he lifted his

[1] Mrs. Thomas J. Preston to author.

silk hat to her; the cheers of the crowd as P. S. Gilmore's Twenty-second Regiment band broke into Mendelssohn's Wedding March, and other bands played "He's Going to Marry Yum-Yum" or "Come Where My Love Lies Dreaming";—all this was told in columns of fine print. In the cries of "Long Live President Cleveland and his bride!" there was a warmth he had never before felt.

Miss Folsom had intended to be married at the home of her grandfather, John Folsom of Folsomdale, near Buffalo. But his death just before she reached America made that impossible. Cleveland refused to be married in a hotel; he belonged to no church, and so objected to a church wedding. After much debate, it was finally decided that under the circumstances there was but one fitting place.[1]

The ceremony took place on Wednesday, June 2, in the White House. It was the second time in our history that a President had been married during his term of office, and the first time that one had been married in the Executive Mansion. The arrangements were simple. Early on the wedding day Miss Folsom, with her mother and cousin, arrived in Washington, were met at the station by Miss Cleveland, and went to the White House. Cleveland worked that day as usual. During the afternoon Secretary Vilas sent a messenger to inquire if he would sign two or three postmasters' commissions.[2] With a comical expression the President lifted his face above his pile of paper and exclaimed: "Yes, I will sign—but tell him to get the documents here as quick as the good Lord will let him."

An army of florists had transformed the Blue Room into a bower of roses and pansies, over which tapers in the two five-foot candelabra given to the White House by President Jackson threw a mellow illumination. At half-past six a few near relatives and friends had gathered, including Bissell and all the Cabinet members save Garland, with their ladies—twenty-eight in all. A few minutes before seven Sousa lifted his baton and the scarlet-and-gold Marine Band began the wedding march. As it closed, Miss Folsom and the President descended the great staircase unattended to where Dr. Sunderland awaited them. The service had been specially written for the occasion and revised and condensed by Cleveland, the bride promising to "love, honor, and . . . keep." As the Rev. William N. Cleveland closed the ceremony with a blessing, a

---

[1] Mrs. Thomas J. Preston to author. See also Appendix I.
[2] W. H. Crook, *Memories of the White House,* 176 ff.

MR. AND MRS. CLEVELAND IN 1886

salute of twenty-one guns boomed from the navy yard, and all the church bells of the city rang a merry chime. There followed an informal reception and supper in the state dining room, during which messages of congratulation, including one from Queen Victoria, arrived. Among the table decorations, the great mirror brought by Dolly Madison and used by every President since made a realistic sea for the full-rigged ship *Hymen,* built of pansies and pink roses, with the national colors at the mainmast and tiny flags embroidered C-F on the other masts.

Unfortunately, the wedding was followed by an anti-climax. In any civilized country the honeymoon of a ruler would have been respected, but the America of 1886 was not fully civilized. Cleveland erred in not selecting some large estate whose gates could be closed upon himself and his wife. They left soon after nine o'clock in the evening on a special train of two cars for Deer Park in western Maryland, which they reached at sunrise the next morning in a drizzling rain. Here Cleveland had rented for a few days a cheerful little cottage, embowered by trees and commanding a view of the Blue Ridge Mountains. The place had many advantages.[1] There were well-stocked trout streams, the President having remarked that "if I am going to keep my reputation as a fisherman I must go where there are plenty of trout." There were lovely drives with long views across the misty Blue Ridge. There were historical associations, for near Deer Park ran the old road over which George Washington had led part of Braddock's army, and near by John Brown had prepared for his raid at Harper's Ferry. Nor was the spot a solitude. Henry Gassaway Davis, who had begun life as a poor brakeman on a railroad not far from Deer Park and was now a multi-millionaire, had developed much of the land as a summer resort, and was residing there. At one of the cottages, occupied by Senator Elkins, many of the leaders of the Republican party—Grant, Sherman, Garfield, Blaine—had been entertained.

The serpents in this Eden were the newspapermen, some of whom gave an exhibition of Paul Pry journalism, or as it was then called, Jenkinsism, which shocked the decent public. A carload of reporters followed the President on an express train, arrived at daybreak, roused an operator to take their messages and took up their post in a pavilion several hundreds yards from Cleveland's cottage. The irate owner of the house stationed pickets about it, but in vain. On the first day long

[1] N. Y. *Herald,* June 5–11, describes Deer Park and its attractions fully.

dispatches were sent to the Eastern newspapers describing the appearance of the couple on the piazza at ten o'clock, Mr. Cleveland's black frock coat and Mrs. Cleveland's blue tulle, their breakfast, their afternoon drive, their seven-course dinner, and their evening stroll. Some reporters lifted the covers of the dishes sent from the hotel to inspect their contents; others counted the President's letters. The idea that the metropolitan papers should hire a pack of writers to infest the shrubbery at Deer Park and use spyglasses to watch every movement of the bridal pair struck most Americans as detestable. The remarks of the New York *Evening Post* and other self-respecting newspapers upon "keyhole journalism" were scorching.[1]

Cleveland's first instinct was to take the national interest in his marriage good-naturedly. In humorous vein he had himself written Secretary Endicott to express the hope that "in this grave crisis" he might have the "support" of his Cabinet. The solemn Tyler on his marriage with Miss Gardiner had unbent sufficiently to crack a joke about an annexation without the advice or consent of the Senate. Cleveland smiled when Representative Bland said he hoped the two would live to celebrate their silver wedding, and when Representative Springer expressed uneasiness because "I promised on the stump that I'd try to have Mr. Cleveland married to one of my constituents." A telegram came from the Michigan Press Association: "In the little government today established may there be no conflicting policies, no unexpected vetoes, no offensive partisanship, and may the affection and esteem that prompt this union never pass into innocuous desuetude." Cleveland laughed heartily at his, and corrected a correspondent who remarked that the phrase "innocuous desuetude" had been attributed to Lamont. "Oh, no," replied the President. "It was my idea. I used those words and thought they would please the Western taxpayers, who are fond of such things." [2]

Nor did he object to the innocent jocosity of professional funmakers. Eugene Field, for example, was entertaining Chicago with humorous comments which had more ebullience than brilliance, but were not unkind. In a high-spirited series of "White House Ballads" he celebrated various incidents of the marriage. As a satire upon Cleveland's bachelor awkwardness he sang "The Tying of the Tie":

---

[1] For comment, see *Public Opinion*, June, 1886.
[2] N. Y. *Herald*, June 9, 1886.

Now was Sir Grover passing wroth—
"A murrain seize the man," he quoth,
"Who first invented ties!
Egad, they are a grievous bore,
And tying of them vexeth sore,
A person of my size."
Lo, at his feet upon the floor
Were sprent the neckties by the score,
And collars all awreck . . .

The President was rescued by Sir Daniel, who mounted a chair to help him with the look of one saying, "Odds bobs, I vow, there's nothing like the knowing how." Subsequent ballads described a Deer Park fishing expedition and similar occurrences.[1]

III

But Cleveland, with his combined shyness and deep innate dignity, felt that the more intrusive spying of reporters, the sniggering desire to make copy out of a sacred personal experience, was unforgivable. He wrote Lamont with heat regarding the "newspaper nuisances," the "animals"; "I can see a group of them sitting on a bridge, which marks one of the limits, waiting for some movement to be made which will furnish an incident." The smouldering resentment which he had felt against sensational newspapers ever since 1884 was fanned into flame. He was shortly penning for the New York *Evening Post* a vitriolic condemnation of the correspondents:

They have used the enormous power of the modern newspaper to perpetuate and disseminate a colossal impertinence, and have done it, not as professional gossips and tattlers, but as the guides and instructors of the public in conduct and morals. And they have done it, not to a private citizen, but the President of the United States, thereby lifting their offence into the gaze of the whole world, and doing their utmost to make American journalism contemptible in the estimation of people of good breeding everywhere.

Fear of the press haunted him while he made plans for his summer trip to the Adirondacks. "You don't know how I sometimes am perplexed when thinking of my vacation," he wrote Dr. Ward.[2] "Occasion-

---

[1] Slason Thompson, *Life of Eugene Field*, 228 ff.
[2] Washington, June 21, 1886. Cleveland Papers.

ally I almost feel like giving the thing up and remaining here where I know what I must meet rather than fly to ills I know not of. . . . You have no idea how I fairly *yearn* to be where I shall be *let alone*. I'll fly from any spot where the poor privilege of being no trouble to any human being is denied me." He and Mrs. Cleveland started for the Adirondacks on August 16. A week earlier he wrote his crony Dr. Ward [1] that as his destination would be well known, "I begin to fear that the pestilence of newspaper correspondence will find its way to our retreat. And Mrs. Cleveland's presence will, I presume, increase this probability." He thought of selecting a single correspondent to give the Associated Press all the news that could properly interest any citizen, and announcing that other reports would be spurious. "One thing is certain," he burst out. "If the newspaper men get there *I shall leave*. I will not have my vacation spoiled by being continually watched and lied about, and I won't subject my wife to that treatment."

During the summer his irritation with the press increased. Mrs. Cleveland, in her movements from Washington to New York and Buffalo, was beset with reporters. When she was admitted to membership in Dr. Sunderland's church in Washington, an offensive description of her first communion service was printed, lurid stories that Cleveland had quarreled with Secretary Manning were continually appearing, and there were equally well-garnished accounts of the President's supposed tiffs with his quite devoted sister Rose. In September his uncle, Joseph Neal, died in Baltimore. Two days later the *World* printed a dispatch under the headlines: "President Cleveland's Uncle; His Death at Baltimore; Neglected by his Nephew and Niece." The story beneath charged the President with gross discourtesy to his relatives.[2] The *World's* subsequent account of the funeral accused Cleveland of disrespect in not attending it, and played up expressions of censure by Neal's friends. The truth was that Cleveland, who had always treated his uncle with affection, had absented himself by the express desire of the Neal family, who realized that his presence would draw a crowd of curious people. Worst of all were various references to Cleveland's marital relations. Rumors that Mrs. Cleveland was abused and unhappy presently began to appear in print, and filled him with silent fury.

In the autumn of 1886 Harvard College, celebrating its 250th birth-

---

[1] August 8, 1886. Cleveland Papers.
[2] N. Y. *World*, Sept. 29, Oct. 1, 1886; cf. N. Y. *Herald*, Nov. 11, 1886.

day, invited the President to attend with Mrs. Cleveland and receive an honorary degree. He accepted the invitation but refused the degree. Bayard, who had been made LL.D. by Harvard in 1877, and Lamar, who was to receive the same honor this year, urged him to consent; while Endicott pointed out that he would simply follow the unvarying practise of former Presidents when they had visited Cambridge—even Andrew Jackson, much to J. Q. Adams' disgust, had manifested no hesitation in the matter. But Cleveland modestly declared that he was not a suitable candidate, for his education was scanty and he could not figure as a man of letters or even a distinguished lawyer. "My disinclination to receive the degree," he wrote Endicott,[1] "is based upon a feeling which I cannot stifle and which I hope may be humored without any suspicion of lack of appreciation or churlishness."

Cleveland's visit was marked by two incidents which showed how deeply he was suffering under the current scurrility of the press. Arriving the day before the celebration, he spent the night at President Eliot's house. Mrs. Cleveland was to arrive in the morning. Eliot, rising early, found the President already walking restlessly about the hall and parlor, which commanded a view of the avenue. "As we stood together in the hall, a station hack drove up, out of which came quickly Mrs. Cleveland. Her husband walked rapidly toward her with both hands outstretched, and they met on the threshold. She seized both his hands and they kissed each other tenderly. By a natural impulse as host I had followed him, only a step or two behind; but I wished I had not done so when I saw the tears running down his cheeks." James Russell Lowell, as orator of the day, delivered an eloquent address, closing with a tribute to the President who held the helm of state: "So long as it is entrusted to his hands we are sure that, should the storm come, he will say with Seneca's Pilot, 'O Neptune! you may save me if you will; you may sink me if you will; but whatever happens I shall keep my rudder true.'" Cleveland was manifestly affected.

That afternoon there was a dinner in Memorial Hall for alumni and guests, at which Cleveland spoke. He began with an expression of thanks for his reception. "Then," continues Eliot, "he chanced to look up to the ladies' gallery at the end of the great hall, and caught sight of Mrs. Cleveland sitting beside Mrs. Eliot. At once his voice and posture changed; he turned pale and exclaimed, 'O, those ghouls of

[1] Nov. 5, 1886. Cleveland Papers.

the press.' There were two long rows of reporters sitting at a table immediately in front of him and within a few feet. He uttered several denunciatory sentences on the conduct of the press towards himself as a man and towards the President of the United States; and again tears rolled down his cheeks, but they were tears of wrath and indignation. He recovered himself quickly, and spoke briefly in his ordinary quiet and rather heavy way on the obligations of the country to its universities." [1]

By these denunciatory sentences on the unscrupulous journals Cleveland produced a sensation. The occasion for the outburst was ill-chosen; at this academic celebration the President was expected to choose a larger topic, and his attack on the newspapers seemed malapropos and petulant. But the provocation was great and the rebuke was heeded. He had no desire, he said, to check the utmost freedom of criticism of all his official acts, but as President he should not be put beyond the protection which fair play should accord every American citizen. If the people realized the extent and tendency of this evil, they would stamp out "the silly, mean, and cowardly lies that every day are found in the columns of certain newspapers which violate every instinct of American manliness, and in ghoulish glee desecrate every sacred relation of private life." This was a shoulder blow at Dana's *Sun,* Pulitzer's *World,* and Murat Halstead's *Commercial Gazette.*

IV

After Cleveland's marriage both he and the White House underwent a striking change. His friends observed that he was happier, brighter, and more companionable. There were some curious contrasts between him and his bride. He was ponderous, a little lethargic, and indifferent to most plays and to concerts; she was eager, full of spirits, fond of social life, and ready in her girlish way to see everything. After his marriage he seemed to have been rejuvenated; he worked better, went out oftener, and spent more time in amusements congenial to them both.

There survives a pretty story of the first reception held by Mrs. Cleveland. Mrs. Folsom came to the library where the President was at work, begging him to step in a moment to make sure that all was

[1] Charles W. Eliot to William Gorham Rice. Rice Papers.

well. They were presently unobserved in a corner, watching the First Lady greet the admiring stream. The President touched his mother-in-law on the arm and proudly observed: "She'll do! She'll do!" [1] Another anecdote, told by Cleveland himself, related to an afternoon when they were to go driving together. The President was busy. At the appointed time he put on his overcoat, and stood waiting. Minute after minute passed; finally, concluding that he would teach her a lesson in punctuality, he threw off his coat and gloves, resolved that he would not go driving that day. Presently he heard her voice at the foot of the stairs. "Come along," she cried, "I am ready now." "And what do you suppose I did?" asked the President. "Why, I got up, put on my coat and gloves again, and went driving." [2]

The country rapidly became aware that the new mistress of the White House was the most charming woman seen in that mansion since Dolly Madison, though unlike "Queen Dolly" she made no effort to be a belle. One of Cleveland's political enemies expressed his hatred, when other superlatives failed, by saying: "I detest him so much that I don't even think his wife is beautiful." Col. W. H. Crook, a veteran of the White House, wrote that "I am an old man now and I have seen many women of various types through all the long years of my service in the White House, but neither there nor elsewhere have I seen anyone possessing the same kind of downright *loveliness* which was as much a part of Mrs. Cleveland as her voice, or her marvelous eyes, or her warm smile of welcome." Numerous observers have recorded the impression she made. General Sherman, dining with the Clevelands at his brother's home, thought her a fine sample of a beautiful young woman, with not the least particle of affectation. In conversation she "made things lively." [3] Cecil Spring-Rice describes her at the Whitneys', "a tall, very pretty and direct person," and very amusing; telling of the President's tour of the North, where people were discontented because she, who went along for her looks, had a bandaged eyelid, while Cleveland, who was there for his talking, had a sore throat; telling also how her husband had recently gone on the loose and bought himself an orange-tawny suit, which she used every artifice in her power to prevent his

---

[1] Edna Colman, *White House Gossip*, 170 ff.

[2] Chicago *Tribune*, Dec. 7, 1887.

[3] *Home Letters of General Sherman*, 394 ff.

wearing. She had finally told him that he would certainly lose the Irish vote if he wore it, and this argument prevailed! [1]

Few young women fresh from college would have met the exacting demands of her position, which gave her hardly a free hour, without complaint. She carried her zest for life and her unselfish interest in people into the routine of dinners and calls. Holding two receptions weekly, she assigned one to Saturday afternoons so that women and girls in Washington offices might attend. She once espied in line a woman holding a baby, and obviously hot and tired; and instantly sent one of the Secretaries' wives to conduct her to a parlor for rest and refreshment. She settled the matter of wines by merely turning down her own glass, without trying to impose her views upon others. Before her coming the White House had been a mannish place. She filled the private rooms with flowers, and showed a fondness for canaries and other birds. Once Cleveland, trying late at night to fix his mind upon business, called a servant to carry a noisy mocking-bird to a dark room. Later he felt uneasy lest his wife's pet should take a chill, and lumbered stealthily down the corridor to put it out of the draft.

Early in 1886 Cleveland had purchased a country house just outside Washington. His new property comprised about twenty-seven acres and a house on the Tenallytown road, nearly two miles north of Georgetown and more than three miles from the White House.[2] The move had become exigent, for the White House had grown monotonous, it was hot in midsummer, and it offered insufficient quiet for continuous work. Secretary Whitney had just purchased a thirty-acre farm on the Georgetown Pike, with a house nearly a hundred years old, and his example impressed the President. For $21,500 Cleveland obtained a property which a few years later he sold for far more. The little stone dwelling was an ugly affair, square, gray, and flat-roofed, and the grounds were unkempt. But an architect added an extra story, a stone addition was built for the kitchen and servants' rooms, and the interior was remodelled, while the grounds were landscaped. Before long the Clevelands had a home which, while far from beautiful, was smart and comfortable. The glory of the place was its view. Placed on Georgetown Heights, it offered a fine sweep of the Virginia hills, the Potomac, and the capital. From the gallery of the two-story piazza thrown about the

---

[1] *Letters and Friendships of Sir Cecil Spring-Rice*, I, 72, 73.
[2] See description in *Harper's Weekly*, June 12, 1886. The road is now Wisconsin Avenue.

southern and western part of the building was visible the whole city, the great dome of the Capitol lying in the centre. On moonlight nights in summer the prospect was superb. A slight mist rose to veil the lights and structures of the sleeping city; the silver sweep of the Potomac lay like a great crescent to the southeast; the moon poured its radiance upon the figure of Liberty above the halls of Congress and upon the ghostly shaft of the Monument.[1] Every summer week-end in 1886, and if possible oftener, the Clevelands sought refuge in this enchanted spot.

During the first summer Cleveland had the roof painted red, and despite his wife's wish to call the house Oak View, the newspapermen's name of Red Top stuck. It was by no means a solitary place. Near by was Woodley, formerly the property of Philip Barton Key, and not far away was Grasslands, the home of Secretary Whitney. Within sight stood the house once occupied by Madame Iturbide, daughter-in-law of the unfortunate Mexican Emperor. Here, little by little, the Clevelands accumulated the belongings of a complete farm. George W. Childs presented them with a cow named Grace, which presently bore a calf named after his friend Randall. Other animals appeared; a coachhouse was built; and a large kitchen garden was made. In the early summer of 1887 we find Cleveland writing Bissell that his wife had gone to Red Top to stay, and that he meant to drive out and in every morning and evening. For that purpose he had bought a light roadwagon. The weather was delightful, "and I honestly think I have one of the handsomest places in the United States." [2]

Social life in Washington was materially brightened by the advent of Mrs. Cleveland, for she delighted in receptions and dinners. The pre-Lenten season in 1887 was the liveliest the city had seen for years, and the Washington *Post* actually thought there was too much society. "Every day in the week is given up to receptions, balls, teas, luncheons, and theatre parties. On the face of things it looks foolish to see the streets of a large capital thronged with private carriages whose occupants are on pleasure bent." Washington, though its population was still only about 150,000, was gradually ceasing to be a provincial place. It did not take on the air of one of the world's great capitals till the first ambassadors arrived in 1893; but Whitney's rich New York friends, the wealth of various Senators, and the intellectual sparkle of

---

[1] See description by Ballard Smith, N. Y. *World,* Sept. 7, 1887.
[2] June 30, 1887. Cleveland MSS.

the "five of hearts"—the Henry Adamses, the John Hays, and Clarence
King—had wrought a change. In 1885–86 Adams and Hay had built
fine adjoining houses, designed by H. H. Richardson, on Lafayette
Square, and had expected to gather a brilliant group about themselves,
the Lodges, and the Don Camerons. The tragic death of Mrs. Adams
in December, 1885, had defeated this prospect, and Adams in 1886
went to the Orient with John La Farge. But early in 1887 Roosevelt
and his bride took a modest house for the season. Mrs. Leiter, with her
marriageable daughters, one soon to marry George Curzon, and the
novelist Frances Hodgson Burnett, were beginning to cut figures in
society.

Most of these people entertained very quietly. John Hay was busy
bringing his life of Lincoln to the point of publication. "After fifteen
years of work," he told a reporter, "one approaches the sixteenth without many qualms." Secretary Bayard liked to prepare the terrapin for
his guests in his own chafing-dish. Roosevelt would ask his friends to
drop in for a simple beefsteak and a glass of claret. But a note of greater
ostentation was struck by such residents as Senator and Mrs. Leland
Stanford, who had taken a house on K Street. Mrs. Stanford wore dia-
monds, as the press put it, "like a coat of mail," and at one reception
bore $250,000 in gems on her ample throat and bosom. It need not be
said that the Clevelands, and all the Cabinet save Whitney, avoided
show. There was much less splendor at the White House than at the
British legation, where the three daughters of Sackville-West made
brilliant hostesses. It was a high honor to be asked to one of the Minister's balls, beginning at eleven, and ending at three A. M. with a Sir
Roger de Coverley and "God Save the Queen," and the catering and
decorations far surpassed in elegance anything attempted by the President.

Cleveland's principal friends in the Cabinet were Bayard, Vilas, and
Fairchild, with Lamar following at a long remove. He could not help
respecting the first. The tall Secretary of State was intellectual and cultivated, he had a charming manner, and he united dignity with geniality.
He excelled in courtly speeches. "Grace *after* meat," ran a characteristic note following one of Cleveland's shooting excursions.[1] "The ducks
came and the ducks have gone—and I render many thanks to the sender
of the ducks." But Bayard did not make friends easily, for as Spring-

---

[1] Nov. 8, 1888. Cleveland Papers.

Rice wrote, the politicians and business men in the Senate hated him. "They don't like to call him their superior and so say he is a pompous ass." He showed also an emotional strain, sometimes going beyond sentiment to sentimentality, which somewhat repelled the rugged, practical Cleveland. Fairchild, who with his wife was socially popular, fully took Manning's place. But it was in Vilas that Cleveland found a man after his own heart. He was often at the White House, drove frequently with the President, and was a constant adviser. When he went back to Madison in 1886 he stopped in Buffalo, and Cleveland wrote Bissell a letter about him. "You know," he stated,[1] "I think he is one of the most complete men, mentally, morally, and politically, I ever met." Vilas' *bonhomie* appears in the letter he sent back to Cleveland, describing how he visited the Buffalo city hall, "where the veto business took on its early development," and in Bissell's pleasant home "exchanged the Carolinian compliments." [2]

Cleveland sometimes had out-of-town guests at the White House. In December, 1886, he even wrote Governor Hill inviting him for several days of "a comfortable visiting sort of time," an offer which Hill accepted. "Please let me hear from you as early as you can determine the question," Cleveland added. "A fellow who has his message off his hands ought seriously to wish the other fellow who has his in the pains of parturition 'a safe deliverance,' and I do this most sincerely." [3] In the summer of 1887 Richard Watson Gilder first appeared. He delivered the commencement address at Wells College in June, met the White House bride there, and escorted her back to Washington. A little later he stayed for several days at Oak View, delighting in its umbrageous grove and finding Cleveland extremely interesting, confidential and kind—ready to talk over his forthcoming public utterances in detail.

V

A score of States had their first sight of Cleveland in the long journey which he took in 1887 to the West and South. This was prefaced early in the summer by a brief but enjoyable visit to Clinton, Holland Patent, and other towns of central New York. On July 13, Clinton celebrated its centennial. Cleveland arrived early that day in the pretty com-

[1] Aug. 14, 1886. Cleveland Papers.
[2] *Ibid.*, Sept. 8, 1886.
[3] *Ibid.*, Dec. 19, 1886.

munity, nestling under its elms in the Oriskany Valley. He reviewed a picturesque procession of militia, civic societies, the G.A.R., and a band of Oneida Indians, shook hands with hundreds of citizens, and made a brief address. Genuinely moved, he imparted an unusual felicity to this speech, and its reminiscences of his early life contained some touching passages. Clinton Scollard, who had been born in the town some years after Cleveland left it, read a poem, and at an evening banquet Elihu Root responded to the toast, "Clinton, A Good Place to Come From." After visiting his brother William at Forestport, on the edge of the Adirondacks, and the Fairchilds at Cazenovia (travelling from Utica to Oneida behind the same engine which had brought Lincoln through the State in 1861), Cleveland found himself on July 19 at Fayetteville. The grocery store where he had clerked was draped in bunting. Here he made another happy speech, recalling his old friends and many former scenes and incidents. No one can read these informal talks without feeling that if he had given himself free rein a little oftener, dropping his ponderous verbal dignity, he might have made all his addresses far better. He spoke at Fayetteville [1] of "old Green Lake and the fish I tried to catch and never could; the traditional panther on its shores which used to shorten my excursions thitherward. I have heard so much roaring in the past two years that I think I should not be frightened by the panther now. If some of the old householders were here I could tell who it was that used to take off their front gates. I mention this because I have been accused of so many worse crimes since I have been in Washington that I begin to consider taking off gates a virtue."

It was evident that Cleveland delighted in being among the quiet up-State folk with whom he had been reared. On arriving at Holland Patent he gazed hungrily about the depot, pointed out the familiar objects to his wife, and then tucking a bundle under his arm, set out afoot for his sister's house, "The Weeds." At Forestport he fraternized with the postmaster, and went for a long walk with a reporter. On arriving at Fayetteville he greeted Mrs. Hoyt with a noisy kiss, and bestowed a boyish greeting upon all his old schoolmates. The press described his informal manner: [2]

After breakfast Mr. Cleveland sat out on the verandah, the picture of contentment. He had not been there long when Dr. Crane drove by with his

[1] N. Y. *Herald, World,* July 20, 1887.
[2] N. Y. *World,* July 13, 1887.

chaise and sorrel mare. He was on his way to visit a patient and had his little medicine chest with him.

"Hullo, doctor," shouted the President. "Glad to see you, sir."

"The same to you," shouted the doctor, reining in his steed. Mr. Cleveland came down to the gate and the two conversed for a few minutes. Then the doctor asked the President if he wouldn't like to take a ride.

"Wait till I get my hat," was the reply, and Mr. Cleveland entered the house and returned with his high white tile. The doctor took him over to the neighboring town of Steuben, chatting sociably by the way, and occasionally pointing out familiar places. The President entered the house of the patient and conversed with the lady of the house, and it was not till he was leaving that the doctor introduced him as the President of the United States. The good woman with whom he had been talking so freely was so surprised that she nearly fainted.

A public reception was tendered to Mr. and Mrs. Cleveland at "The Weeds" from two to four o'clock in the afternoon. The villagers arrayed themselves in their Sunday clothes and turned out *en masse*. Farmers drove in from Remsen, Prospect, Trenton, and villages for ten miles around. The street leading up to the house was full of gay dress, gaudy parasols, and flying ribbons all the afternoon. Mr. and Mrs. Cleveland stood in the back parlor and the callers were introduced by Miss Cleveland. The President and his wife had a pleasant word for everyone. Mr. Cleveland entered into the spirit of the occasion. Among those received . . . was a former sweetheart of Mr. Cleveland, Miss Mary Burlingame, daughter of a cheesemaker. Mr. Cleveland once presented her with a pony, and for a long time they were reported to be engaged.

VI

Cleveland's Western and Southern tour, beginning September 30, and taking him as far west as St. Paul and Omaha, was both pleasant and successful. The President wished it to be divested of all political aspects, and to be merely "a social trip and every-day-kind-of-visit to the people." He insisted that Lamont and Bissell go along, and that on the train they regard themselves as "a family party with every freedom from restraint which that implies." [1] The first stop was for four hours at Indianapolis, where the party lunched with the widow of Vice-President Hendricks. Everywhere Cleveland and his wife were received with interest and in some places with enthusiasm. In a large number of short speeches he said nothing brilliant, but unlike Andrew Johnson, Winfield Scott, and other swingers round the circle, he also said nothing

[1] Sept. 2, 1887, Cleveland to Bissell. Cleveland Papers.

regrettable.

The sole criticism made of the speeches, which abounded in facts of local interest, was that he had consulted an encyclopaedia and followed the text rather closely. But as his admirers asked, What is an encyclopaedia for? In Indianapolis, for example, he showed that he knew when the city was founded, what its population was, the number of its railroads, and the fact that the State House was one of the few large public buildings in the country erected within the original estimates. The *World* pointed out that "this style of touching upon local history and statistics was introduced in this country by Louis Kossuth in his famous tour of 1851." Whoever introduced it, it was not happy. Cleveland would have done well to avoid these pedestrian discourses, and to intersperse several carefully-written speeches upon national policy with a number of informal talks. But if the discourses did not arouse enthusiasm, Mrs. Cleveland did. The *Ohio State Journal* remarked acidly at the end of the first week that Cleveland had now seen at least ten thousand men who were as well fitted to be President as he, but it admitted that almost nobody was so well fitted to be a President's wife as Mrs. Cleveland.

In Chicago, which was reached October 5, the President received an ovation. A holiday had been declared all over the region, and people from four States poured into the city on excursion trains. The presidential party alighted at Twenty-third Street, two miles from the heart of the city, and proceeded downtown in a procession so long that Mrs. Cleveland, worn out, left it when she had covered three fourths of the line of march. There was a monster reception at the Palmer House, where Cleveland shook hands with 6,000 persons—"forty-seven handshakes a minute!" He expressed a desire to see the site of the Haymarket Riot, which Mayor Roche showed him. There ensued some pleasant days with Vilas at Madison, where he dined with President Chamberlain of the University of Wisconsin, and caught bass in Lake Mendota. At St. Paul he made a reference to Mrs. Cleveland's schooldays there, thanking the people that "they had neither married nor spoiled my wife," and adding that they were "related to that in my life better than all earthly honors and distinctions." Everywhere he showed the keenest interest in Western sights—in Lake Michigan gleaming with white sails; in the goldenrod and purple asters lining the edges of the northern woods, red with autumn; in the Corn Palace at

Sioux City, with its wax maiden in cornhusk satin, on a throne of golden ears; in the Veiled Prophets' parade passing in St. Louis amid a blaze of torches; in the gilded saloon-deck of the Mississippi steamboat on which he rode. His physical endurance impressed the reporters. Repeatedly kept up till two o'clock in the morning, he would smoke till three with Bissell before going to bed.[1]

The climax of the trip was his visit to the South. At Nashville he called on the widow of President Polk, and Mrs. Cleveland and Mrs. Polk compared notes on White House life. Near that city he spent Sunday at one of the most famous of Southern plantations, Belle Mead, owned by Judge Howell E. Jackson, a former Senator. Great crowds at every station cheered him as he passed southward by way of Chattanooga to Atlanta, where he was to visit the Piedmont Exposition. While he dined at General Gordon's, and attended an evening reception at the Capitol City Club, the city was filling with throngs of visitors from all over the South, who slept in freight cars and on billiard tables, and next day cheered him at every turn. The "new South" was dinned into his ears everywhere, and Grady was at his elbow to explain the significance of the phrase. Cleveland had feared lest some untoward incident mar his journey. "The paper last night," he had written Lamar just before his tour began,[2] "contained a dispatch from Atlanta stating that a movement was on foot to have Jeff Davis there with us. I cut it out and sent it to Grady, commending it to his consideration. If any such business as that is indulged in, the people of Atlanta will find that one of their expected guests will not listen to their talk." But all went smoothly.

The one incident that was remembered later by certain people of Atlanta occurred when Cleveland returned from Exposition Park through a sea of mud, and in a driving rain. He was to be entertained that evening at the home of Senator Colquitt, who had been a Methodist minister and was one of the pioneer prohibitionists of the South. Cleveland was cold and wet when he arrived. His first words after shaking hands with his host were, "Senator, I must have a drink right away." The astounded Colquitt was for a moment nonplussed. As he said later, "There hadn't been a drop of liquor in the house since I lived in it." But the difficulty was easily solved; a neighbor across the street sup-

[1] See *Harper's Weekly*, Oct. 8, Oct. 15, for many details.
[2] August 28, 1887. Cleveland Papers.

plied some Bourbon, and in a moment the President had the only drink that Colquitt ever served in his life.[1]

In Montgomery, Senators Pugh and Morgan welcomed Cleveland to the old Confederate capital. Then, with stops at Tecumseh and Asheville, the special train, laden with mementos, lumbered northward, reaching Washington on October 22. The journey had done something to erase the ill-feeling caused by the events of recent months, and Cleveland recalled with special pleasure a sign he had seen at Chattanooga: "Our Grover: he has filled the bloody chasm." [2]

This long tour through two curious sections did much to make the American public better acquainted with Cleveland; and so also did the publication, year by year, of interviews and letters which struck a personal note. The country which in 1885 had thought of him as an honest but coarse man had learned four years later that this was an inadequate view. His integrity went beyond the plain everyday honesty of the good business man or officeholder. It was the integrity of a man of unbending principle and sleepless conscientiousness, founded upon a deep if simple religious conviction of which the outside world occasionally caught a glimpse. Coarse he might be in some physical tastes, but it began to be understood that he possessed a remarkable delicacy about certain human relationships. He never learned to be tactful. He lost his temper frequently and sometimes unjustly; he could swear violently. Shouldering his way through difficulties like an elephant lumbering through a jungle, he thrust annoyers away with a rough gesture. But the country thought none the less of him for his brusqueness to dishonest men. A letter to a machine politician just before the campaign of 1888, preserved among his papers, exemplifies the blunt you-be-damnedness which people found refreshing: [3]

Dear Sir: I must ask you to excuse me from my engagement with you this morning. When I made it I did not know who you were nor the object of your regard. I have learned both from your letter and I am satisfied that I can improve my time much more profitably at this extremely busy period than by talking politics with you. Yours truly, Grover Cleveland.

A hundred examples of his punctiliousness, his tenderness beneath a gruff exterior, and his responsiveness to certain emotional appeals,

[1] Clark Howell to author, May 29, 1931.
[2] Lynch, *Cleveland*, 348.
[3] Undated. Cleveland Papers.

gradually reached the public. Sometimes they became known as an answer to slanderous assaults. The story that he had refused to assist a former partner in his hour of need, and had allowed him to be buried in a potter's field, was met by a circumstantial denial from a man who knew the facts. He related how a visitor to a certain cemetery found this partner's grave beautifully cared for and marked by a handsome stone; and that when he inquired who had paid for it, he was told that it was Grover Cleveland. Cleveland's intimates knew how devoted he was to even the Buffalo men who charged him with ingratitude. They knew how searching was his sense of responsibility to family, public service, and, despite his dislike of dogma, to God. Richard Watson Gilder testified publicly in 1888: [1] "The thing to me most attractive about the President is the moral atmosphere of the man, his lofty and devoted views and aims. Circumstances have made me well acquainted with not a few other public men since the war, but without intending derogation of them, I must say that the President strikes me as remarkable and well-nigh unique for a certain moral fervor in his views of public affairs. The fact is that the 'preacher blood' of the President has told in him more and more as his public and private responsibilities have increased."

[1] Letter in N. Y. *Times*, Dec. 12, 1888.

AMONG all the cares of the crowded year 1886, the issues presented by pensions legislation and the political activities of the G.A.R. gave Cleveland a peculiar anxiety; for they bore directly upon the painful antagonism between North and South. No Democratic President could hope to escape a multitude of difficulties growing out of the resentments left by the Civil War. These sectional antipathies, still so real and grim, overshadowed our national life to a degree now difficult to realize. Only twenty years before Cleveland's inauguration millions of Americans had been straining every nerve to kill, cripple, and abase other millions; blood had been poured out in streams deep enough to keep the Mississippi and Potomac tinged red; hatred had been fanned to an intensity like that which Sparta and Athens had once felt for each other. Great griefs and passions are dimmed in the minds of individuals only by long years, and in the minds of nations still more slowly. Many Southerners in 1886 yet mourned the "lost cause" with a proud defiance, and many Northerners taunted the "rebels" with a suspicious disdain.

Cleveland's election and the prosperous beginning of his Administration were expected to do much to exorcise the evil spectre of Northern distrust of the Southerners. In his inaugural address he expressed a hope that the people would "cheerfully and honestly abandon all sectional prejudice and distrust, and determine, with manly confidence in one another, to work out harmoniously the achievements of our national destiny." The *Nation*, in an Independence Day editorial entitled "Twenty-one Years," shortly declared that at last the North was free from the haunting fear "that irreparable harm might yet be done the country by the section which attempted secession." [1] Former Confederates were proving themselves among the most patriotic of national officers. Their work strengthened a sane Northern sentiment which Howells had put into his *Rise of Silas Lapham* several years earlier. "What are they doing now?" young Corey had asked Lapham as the latter showed irritation over his morning paper. "O, stirring up the Confederate brigadiers in Congress," growled Lapham. "I don't like it.

[1] July 8, 1886.

Seems to me if our party hain't got any stock in trade, we'd better shut up shop altogether."

In making appointments Cleveland deliberately shaped his policy to remind the South that it was a part of the nation and could claim its share in the government as an indefeasible right.[1] Charles Dudley Warner, after a tour to the Gulf, wrote of the success of this policy and of the new progressiveness evident in the Southern spirit. "Immense satisfaction was felt at the election of Mr. Cleveland, and elation of triumph in the belief that now the party which had been largely a non-participant in Federal affairs would have a large share and weight in the Administration. With this went, however, a new feeling of responsibility, of a stake in the country, that manifested itself at once in attachment to the Union as a common possession of all sections." [2] The North Carolina correspondent of the New York *Evening Post* similarly declared that the President's appointments in that section had greatly lessened the sensitive irritability of Southerners. Some manifestations of this changed attitude were touching. In New Orleans, when on Confederate Memorial Day the grizzled veterans of the Armies of Virginia and Tennessee had marched out to the Confederate Monument, they disbanded without any speeches. A lady explained to Warner that oratory had been given up. "So many imprudent things were said that we thought it best to discontinue it." Advised by Lamar and Garland, Cleveland distributed patronage in the South in such a fashion as to discourage the Bourbon or unreconstructed element, and bring forward younger men; and the *Evening Post* was soon able to print a series of articles entitled "Southern Bourbons to the Rear." [3]

The most powerful forces making for national unity were, however, not political but economic and sectional. A new South, interested primarily in business, was being born. As Watterson put it, "The South, having had its bellyful of blood, has gotten a taste of money, and is too busy trying to make more to quarrel with anybody." [4] Smoke from a dozen steelmills was swirling over the roofs of Birmingham. At Atlanta, with its factories and busy distributing trade, Henry W. Grady was preaching a hardheaded attention to the real problems of Southern

[1] See A. G. Bradley, "Southern View of the Election of Cleveland," *MacMillan's Magazine*, March, 1885.

[2] "Impressions of the South," *Harper's Magazine*, Sept., 1885.

[3] For example, Aug. 16, Sept. 28, 1886.

[4] N. Y. *Herald*, July 19, 1887.

development. Warner concluded that the South was more interested in getting rich than in settling the negro question or anything else. A valuable new industry had just arisen in the utilization of cottonseed, of which 600,000 tons were crushed for oil in 1885. Careful writers estimated that in the five years 1882–6 the wealth of the South had increased by more than 40 per cent, while the population had risen by only 16 per cent.[1] Northern visitors were becoming more and more numerous—Cleveland's friend A. K. McClure was one who wrote a friendly book; Northerners were giving money to such Southern institutions as Vanderbilt University; and migration between the two sections was growing. Anyone who looked at the counters of a bookstore was aware that Cable, Page, Joel Chandler Harris, and Charles Egbert Craddock were winning literary laurels as gleaming as those of any Northern author.

Left to themselves, such healthy forces would soon have triumphed. But two powerful groups possessed a selfish interest in keeping sectional rancors alive; the politicians, North and South, for whom they spelled votes, and the newspaper owners to whom they yielded revenue and influence. Moreover, a pernicious sentimentalism had crystallized about all symbols of the struggle, and to many it seemed actually unpatriotic to undermine the old resentments. If men stopped hating the section against which Grant or Lee had fought, they would stop admiring these heroes! Charles Sumner in 1872, with a noble gesture, had tried to induce the Republican majority in the Senate to vote for erasing the names of Civil War battles from the Army Register and from the regimental colors of the United States. He was at once assailed as a man lost to patriotism, and the Massachusetts legislature passed unqualified resolutions of censure; his supporters, including Schurz, were howled down, and his bill was ingloriously defeated.[2]

In the spring of 1886 evidences of the old feeling cropped out in warning fashion. Jefferson Davis, now almost eighty, emerged from his Mississippi home "Belvoir" to lay the cornerstone of a Confederate monument in Montgomery, and two days later unveiled a statue of B. H. Hill in Atlanta. The speeches of the poor old Confederate Polonius awakened fierce echoes of the war. Longstreet appeared at Atlanta in his

[1] W. F. Tillett, "The White Man of the New South," *Century Magazine*, March, 1887.
[2] Moorfield Storey, *Charles Sumner*, 419 ff.

Confederate uniform, Grady shouted that "this Easter week is the most glorious since the resurrection," and Southerners everywhere applauded Davis' reference to the past struggle as "a holy war of defence." [1] In Albany an indignation meeting sang "We'll hang Jeff Davis to a sour apple tree." The New York *Tribune* excoriated "this unrepentant old villain and Union-hater who should have been hanged twenty-one years ago," [2] and the Kansas City *Journal* writhed to think that the South was biding its time "to strike for lost empire and revenge." Davis, who was well known to be unreconstructed, was a fair target for criticism. But it was deplorable that so few Northerners appreciated the reverence of the South for the valor of its soldiers, or realized that the memory of their devotion was a precious national possession.

In dealing with this feeling, Cleveland's peculiar virtues were as effective as any. He had little imagination, little tact, and no diplomacy. A President with Roosevelt's boldness might have executed some dramatic stroke, but he might also have spoiled everything by another incident like the invitation of Booker Washington to lunch; Lincoln's composing touch might have been valuable, but it might also have struck radical Northerners as weak. Cleveland's directness and courage, his blunt way of ignoring sectional lines, were worth more than subtle methods. As always, he satisfied his own conscience without much regard to queasy criticism. When he wanted to go fishing on Memorial Day in 1887, he went fishing. Though Melville W. Fuller sent him a special plea to visit Lincoln's tomb at Springfield on his western tour, he refused to disarrange his schedule for the purpose. When he visited Gettysburg, feeling that Lincoln had said for all time what needed to be said there, he stubbornly declined to make a speech. For all this he was attacked. He knew he would be assailed when he wrote a letter on the unveiling of a monument to Albert Sidney Johnston, saying that every American might take pride in the Confederate general's nobility of character; but he wrote it. [3] There was no nonsense about him in dealing with prejudices that he regarded with contempt. And in the end, his blunt honesty exposed much of the selfishness and silliness of the sectional clamor.

---

[1] Atlanta *Constitution*, May 1, 2; Charlestown *News and Courier*, April 30, May 1, 1886.
[2] April 30, 1886.
[3] Cleveland to W. H. Rogers, April 1, 1887. Cleveland Papers.

II

At this period there was always one uncertain item, one elastic figure, in the annual budget of the government—the pensions list, which in 1884 demanded more than sixty millions. Except for the interest charge on the public debt it presented the largest single channel of Treasury disbursement, and it was the only channel of no known bounds. It showed that a democracy which raised great popular armies for war was subject to peculiar after-dangers; that the armies, after disbanding peaceably, might re-form for an attack on the Treasury. A formidable host had arisen to support ever bolder demands on the national purse. It comprised the veterans, armed with their own and their relatives' votes; many Republican politicians who sought these votes; a swarm of claim agents and pension attorneys; and the local shopkeepers who knew that the pension money would ultimately reach their tills.

The general evil was tolerated by that immense good nature which is rather an American vice than a virtue. It was agreed in Washington before Cleveland took office that probably one-fourth of the existing pensions list was fraudulent. By the basic enactment of 1862, the government had instituted a far-reaching system of disability pensions; every soldier or sailor who could trace some bodily ailment directly to his wartime service was compensated, while provision was made for widows, orphans, and other dependents. The total number of pensioners, after rising to 238,411 in 1873, began a slow decline; but this was checked in 1879 by a law placing the whole pension system on a new basis—the famous arrears of pensions act. This arrears legislation was intended to do justice to those veterans who, having incurred some wound, disease, or other cause of future disability during the war, had neglected to apply for a pension until many years after discharge. As the law was signed by President Hayes, himself a veteran and a G.A.R. man, it provided that all pensions which had been or should be granted should commence from the date of the discharge of the veteran in question—that every claimant, in other words, might recover the full amount which he would have received had the pension begun when he was mustered out.

The most significant feature was that these arrears should be paid on all claims *thereafter to be granted*. This offered a golden incentive to the presentation of new claims, and encouraged claim agents to drum the country for veterans who might press a fairly plausible demand. With the aid of such veterans' publications as the unscrupulous *National Tribune,* they reaped a munificent harvest. By 1885 there were 325,000 Civil War pensioners on the roll, and the list was steadily lengthening.[1] It was notorious when Cleveland appointed Col. John C. Black of Illinois as Commissioner of Pensions that the administration of the laws needed overhauling. Harvey W. Scott of the Portland *Oregonian* said that to his knowledge about every shirk and worthless veteran of his brigade had been a successful applicant under the arrears act. There were thousands of "invalid" pensioners who were robust and able-bodied. There were other thousands pensioned for diseases really incurred in civilian life. There were "dependent relatives" who were quite independent, and "widows" who had long ago remarried. There were still more glaring cases of successful fraud by swindlers who impersonated dead pensioners and continued to receive their checks. The system had been at fault in three principal ways. The evidence upon which pensions was granted was all *ex parte,* being furnished by comrades and neighbors; the examining surgeons were local physicians, often glad to help a friend and bring more money into the community; and the gauge of a pensioner's disability was his unfitness to do manual labor, without regard to his mental capacity or private income.[2]

It was Cleveland's object to call sharp attention to the carelessness of the system; and in a special veto message of May 8, 1886, he unlimbered his artillery against the most careless feature of all—the host of special pension bills which Congress had fallen into the habit of passing without real consideration. He complained that Congress had recently sent him in one day 240 special bills, of which 198 covered claims already rejected by the Pensions Bureau. Any veteran whose claim was too silly or impudent to get past the pension authorities was at liberty to take it to his Representative or Senator. The resulting bills became as thick as autumn leaves in Vallombrosa. The House had set aside Friday evenings for enacting them with a jubilant whoop, while the Senate in a single field-day (April 21, 1886) voted some four hundred of them. As Cleveland said, many of them were the result of nominal sessions held for their express consideration and attended by a small mi-

---

[1] W. H. Glasson, *Federal Military Pensions in the United States,* 123 ff.
[2] See E. V. Smalley, "The United States Pension Office," *Century Magazine,* July, 1884.

nority of the members of the respective houses.[1]

The principle involved was simple: The nation had in its Pensions Bureau a virtual pensions court, hearing cases fairly and interpreting the laws in a liberal spirit. Congress was setting itself up as a rival pensions court, and reversing hundreds of decisions made by the proper tribunal. It is not too much to say that three out of four of the special bills were flagrantly bad. The President's method of dealing with them was to send back measure after measure with brief and sarcastic messages of exposure. He approved many—several times as many as he rejected; but by the middle of August, 1886, he had penned more than a hundred vetoes. He thus fixed the eyes of the country upon a gross perversion of Congressional energy, which combined robbery of the Treasury with a vicious time-wasting habit of attention to special and local bills. As he pointed out, Congress should either rely upon the Pensions Bureau, or reorganize it to make it reliable. If it really constituted itself a supreme court to deal with claims, in justice to the veterans it would have to attend to *all* that were offered. Indeed, the number of private bills was increasing by leaps and bounds; Representative Warner showed that in about six months 4,127 pension bills had been introduced in the House, and a larger number in the Senate—enough, if given ten minutes apiece, to consume four months of Congressional time.[2] No earlier President had ever vetoed one of these bills! Cleveland signed far more than he vetoed, and far more than any previous President had ever signed; but he took a stand against the enactment of an indiscriminate and unconsidered mass of legislation.

His brief, pointed veto messages were so good that it was a pity he weakened their effect by occasional gibes or ridicule. It was easy to find objects for his humor. One claimant explained that he had been registered "at home" and had set out on horseback *intending* to complete his enlistment, that on the way his horse had fallen on his left ankle, and that he was thus entitled to a cripple's pension.[3] A widow whose husband had been killed by a fall from a ladder in 1881 traced this to a slight flesh-wound in the calf in 1865! A Louisville policeman demanded a pension for the death of his son ten months after desertion from the army. A similar claim was made by the family of a Pennsyl-

[1] Richardson, *Messages and Papers*, VIII, 437.
[2] *Cong. Rec.*, July 30, 1886, vol. 17, p. 7765.
[3] Richardson, *Messages and Papers*, VIII, 422 ff.

vanian who, after deserting, had been drowned in a canal six miles from home. An Illinois soldier who had been captured and released on parole had been injured at his home in 1863 by the explosion of a Fourth of July cannon, and now in 1886 asked for a special pension. The widow of a captain who had died in 1883 from cerebral apoplexy swore that it was the result of a hernia contracted in 1863. One gallant private claimed that a disease of the eyes had resulted from army diarrhea. So the stories went; a plain recital of facts, without comment, would have been quite sufficient to expose their absurdity.

The defence of Congress offered by its members was lamentably weak. John A. Logan's reply, in a Chicago speech, was to demand a pension bill for all Union soldiers on the ground that every one had come out of the war weaker than when he entered it! A large part of the Republican press simply showed a surly resentment. The New York *Tribune* accused Cleveland of "sending the destitute, aged mothers of soldiers to the poorhouse, in order that the Democratic party may gain a reputation for economy," and the St. Louis *Globe-Democrat* found that his messages recalled "the way the Copperheads used to talk about soldiers whose bodies were brought home for burial after some great battles." Even ex-President Hayes referred to his policy as penny-pinching. But the great body of independent opinion took a different view. Scores of newspapers, Republican as well as Independent, heartily approved of Cleveland's course. In reality, he was battling for a principle infinitely more important than the petty appropriations involved, and far from being unfriendly to the soldier, he was quite sincere in writing that the pension list should be kept "a roll of honor": [1]

I have not been insensible to the suggestions which should influence every citizen, in private station or official place, to exhibit not only a just but a generous appreciaton of the services of our country's defenders. In reviewing the pension legislation presented to me many bills have been approved upon the theory that every doubt should be resolved in favor of the proposed beneficiary. I have not, however, been able to entirely divest myself of the idea that the public money appropriated for pensions is the soldiers' fund. . . . This reflection lends to the bestowal of pensions a kind of sacredness which invites the adoption of such principles and regulations as will exclude perversion as well as insure a liberal and generous application of grateful and benevolent designs.

[1] *Ibid.*, VII, 554.

It was at once urged against Cleveland's pension vetoes that they represented a waste of the President's time; that he showed a lack of proportion in laboring till nearly dawn over trivial legislation when large policies called vainly for his time. But the labor which so forcibly illustrated one or two great principles of sound government was not wasted. It has also been urged that he hardly checked the evil, for special pension bills were revived in great numbers again under Harrison. But anyone who scrutinizes this legislation will observe that flagrant impostures became far rarer after Cleveland had appealed to public opinion and to the consciences of those Congressmen who happened to possess them. Moreover, his minor vetoes paved the way for stopping completely if temporarily a dangerous piece of general pension legislation—the long-pending Blair bill of 1887.

By this measure it was proposed to take the costly stride from pensions granted for wartime disabilities only to pensions granted for any disabilities whatever, including those of mere old age. The bill offered a government stipend to every disabled veteran of at least three months' honorable service who was dependent upon his own exertions for support, and also pensioned the dependent parents of soldiers who had died in the service. The G.A.R. posts labored sleeplessly in its behalf, raising a tremendous clatter of arguments and excuses, and dolefully announcing that they had discovered 7,000 veterans in poorhouses. Their officers declared, without a trace of humor, that the ten thousand G.A.R. posts throughout the country would guard against the pensioning of unworthy veterans! All the myriad financial and political parasites who battened upon the veterans joined forces behind the bill. Its author, Senator Henry W. Blair, of New Hampshire, himself a veteran, lightly estimated that it would cost anywhere from thirty-five to fifty millions a year. Logan, who thirsted for the Republican nomination in 1888, and did something every few days to show the party the wisdom of nominating somebody else, actually wished the measure to cost more, and offered an amendment raising the minimum pension rate. The bill passed the House on January 17, 1887, and the Senate ten days later, with almost a unanimous Republican vote in each.

From the nation in general there came such an uproar of protest as Congress had seldom heard.[1] It was obvious that the measure would make the ninety-day soldier who, long after the war, fell ill of chronic

[1] Summary in *Public Opinion*, Feb. 12, 19, 1887.

alcoholism, the legal equal of the man who gallantly sacrificed a limb at Gettysburg or Cold Harbor. The Chicago *Tribune* remarked that it would "put a serpent of temptation at the ear of every veteran" to cheat the Treasury; the Washington *Post* called it one of the most reckless specimens of legislation ever presented in Congress; the *World* pointed out that the pensions expenditures of the United States, now $76,000,-000 a year, represented the interest on a debt of two billions. General Bragg of Wisconsin declared that it should be termed "a bill to pension the rubbish of the United States, and to revive the business of claim agent in Washington." All this sentiment, so largely the creation of Cleveland's recent minor vetoes, sustained him in the formidable veto message that went to the House on February 11. He could not believe, he wrote, that the host of Union veterans who took pride in the pension system wished it extended to include an indiscriminate body of charity-seekers; and referring to the widespread disregard for truth already fostered by careless pension legislation, he recalled that the estimates of the future cost of such laws always fell far below the actual sum required. Hardly even a feeble effort was made to carry the Dependent Pensions Bill again while Cleveland was President.

That his veto of the Blair bill was an act of principle, without a trace of partisanship, was shown by another veto of the time which rested upon the same basic theory. Early in 1887 both houses of Congress passed a bill—the so-called Texas Seed bill—which sharply challenged Cleveland's views. Certain Texas counties had suffered from a drought and were in urgent need of seed-grain. Congress generously appropriated $10,000 to enable the Commissioner of Agriculture to distribute seed. The amount was trifling; but Cleveland, who had just vetoed the Dependent Pensions bill, saw that the same underlying delusion—the delusion that the government ought to give alms to anybody in distress—was involved. The Texas legislature could easily meet the need, or popular subscriptions could be circulated. On February 19 he disallowed the measure, sending the House a remonstrance that has more than once been quoted by his successors. As late as 1930, in objecting to demands for direct Federal assistance to the needy, President Hoover thus appealed to it. Cleveland believed it wrong, as he wrote, "to indulge a benevolent and charitable sentiment through the appropriation of public funds" for this purpose. "I can find no warrant for such an appropriation in the Constitution, and I do not believe that the power and duty of the General Government ought to be expended to the relief of individual suffering which is in no manner properly related to the public service or benefit." Once more he struck out one of his few memorable phrases:

A prevalent tendency to disregard the limited mission of this (the Government's) power and duty should, I think, be steadfastly resisted, to the end that the lesson should constantly be enforced that *though the people support the Government the Government should not support the people.*

III

It was unfortunate that immediately after this salutary veto Cleveland unnecessarily placed a weapon in the hands of the claim agents, the G.A.R. officials, and all the others who, stung by his exposure of pensions greed, were berating him as a mere tool of the South. They were eager to exploit the sectional spirit as a means of undermining his influence, and in his famous order of June, 1887, for the return of captured Confederate battle-flags to the South, he gave them a perfect opportunity.

Though this battle-flag order was not impulsively given, it was issued as a mere piece of executive routine and without careful reflection. In April, 1887, it occurred to Adjutant General Richard C. Drum that the Union and Confederate flags stored in the basement and attic of the War Department, and rapidly falling into dust, were a nuisance. Survivors of Union regiments had sometimes applied for the return of their colors and had always gotten them. Drum, a Republican and a member of the G.A.R., suggested to Secretary Endicott that it would be a graceful act to anticipate such requests by transmitting all the flags, both Union and Confederate, to the various States. The President verbally assented, and on May 26 Endicott returned the adjutant-general's memorandum with the endorsement, "The within recommendation approved by the President." Both Cleveland and Endicott thought the step felicitous and certain to advance sectional amity.

The actual response, once the order was published, was a stunning surprise. It is important to discriminate between a great body of sincere protests, intended merely to induce Cleveland to retrace his step, and a body of purely malicious and partisan protests intended to discredit the President. The sincere utterances merit some respect. Governors

Rusk of Wisconsin and Thayer of Nebraska telegraphed vigorous protests, while Governor Martin of Kansas wired the President that the act was "an insult to the heroic dead and an outrage on their surviving comrades." Senator Manderson of Nebraska sent Cleveland a long letter citing Vattel, Halleck's *International Law,* and other authorities in opposition to a return of captured flags. Senator Hawley of Connecticut wrote the President that he was "deeply saddened," and that the flags taken from "our misguided brothers and wicked conspirators" should be burned, for if sent south they would be cherished as more than mere "mementoes of misapplied valor." All these men spoke from the heart. Rusk had been a lieutenant-colonel of Wisconsin volunteers, Thayer a brigadier-general of Nebraska troops; Manderson had led an Ohio regiment at Shiloh, and Hawley had fought gallantly as a brigadier before Richmond. Pensions Commissioner Black, who was at Norwalk, O., when the President's order appeared, at once telegraphed Lamont:[1]

> The report of alleged order returning captured flags has provoked deep feeling. If order not authentic should it not be disavowed at earliest practical moment? Mischievous men are taking extreme advantage of the situation. The public mind seems unprepared for the sentiment of such a course. I earnestly advise of the feeling as I find it.

But the sincere objectors were respectful, whereas a host of insincere demagogues rushed forward merely to traduce the President. The keynote for this attack was sounded by the national commander of the G.A.R., Lucius Fairchild of Wisconsin, who had commanded a regiment of the "Iron Brigade" at Gettysburg. At a Grand Army meeting in Harlem he declaimed: "May God palsy the hand that wrote that order. May God palsy the brain that conceived it, and may God palsy the tongue that dictated it." Thereafter to half the press of the country he was "Fairchild of the three palsies." The New York *Tribune* blazed out with such headlines as "The old slave whip cracking again;" "Now pay the rebel debt;" and "Slapping the veterans in the face."[2] But worst of all was the conduct of Gov. J. B. Foraker of Ohio. Not content with telegraphing Cleveland that "the patriotic people of this State are shocked and indignant beyond anything I can express,"[3] he wrote

[1] Cleveland Papers, June 16, 1887.
[2] June 16, 17, 1887.
[3] Cleveland Papers, June 15, 1887.

an inflammatory letter declaring that "No rebel flags will be surrendered while I am governor," which he circulated broadcast; and when Cleveland revoked the order, he spoke of the President as having "sneaked like a whipped spaniel." For on June 15 Cleveland, finding that he had exceeded his legal authority, did revoke it.[1]

It was obvious that Foraker was thinking of politics. He was running for reëlection this year, and cherished a hope that in 1888 he might obtain Ohio's support over John Sherman for the Presidential nomination. It was obvious also that Fairchild was thinking of pensions legislation. Later in 1887 there was a centenary celebration in Philadelphia of the drafting of the Constitution. Mrs. Cleveland, in the crush of the principal meeting, failed to greet Governor Foraker and his brilliant wife, and many assumed that it was because of his gross discourtesy to the head of the nation. This was not so; Cleveland took pains soon afterward to give publicity to a statement that Mrs. Cleveland had simply been carried in another direction by the irresistible crowd. But his letters show that his contempt for Foraker was scathing.

Though it was bad enough to have a President abused in terms worse than any used since Andrew Johnson's time, it was worse to hear section taunting section again. The North listened to excited talk about rebels and slave-drivers, and the South to angry denunciation of tyrants and robbers. While the *Tribune* spoke of the battleflags as "mementoes of as foul a crime as any in human history,"[2] the New Orleans *State* said that it looked forward to the day when some foreign war "will compel the cowardly rapscallions of the Republican party to recognize that the South will do far more than they to protect the flag about which they are always croaking."[3] Nevertheless, some men had risen nobly to the level of Cleveland's aim. It was compensation for the ignoble features of the incident to hear the generous statement of Robert E. Lee's nephew, Governor Fitzhugh Lee of Virginia:[4]

The proposition to return the Southern battleflags did not originate with Southern soldiers. While they would have accepted again their banners bathed

---

[1] Cleveland, looking into the matter more carefully than at first, found that the flags were national property which was not subject to executive order and could be given up only by act of Congress. In a public letter to Endicott he acknowledged the fact, and requested that no further steps be taken except to inventory the flags and adopt measures for their preservation. McElroy, *Grover Cleveland*, I, 207. For Foraker's role see his *Notes of a Busy Life*, I, *passim*.

[2] June 19, 1887.   [3] June 17, 1887.

[4] Petersburg, Va., *Index-Appeal*, June 20, 1887.

in the blood of brave comrades, they recognized that flags captured in battle are the property of the victors, and were content to let them remain in their charge. Flags captured from Northern troops by Southern soldiers have been returned in some cases with ceremonies. The country should not again be agitated by pieces of bunting that mean nothing now. The South is part and parcel of the Union today, and means to do her part toward increasing the prosperity and maintaining the peace of the republic, whether the flags rot in Washington or are restored to their former custodians. If any man hauls down the American flag shoot him on the spot, but don't let us get into trouble because another flag changed its resting place. It will not get into the hands of a standard-bearer.

In the spirit of this statement the Second Alabama Regiment, through Cleveland, shortly restored to the Sixteenth Connecticut their colors, captured in battle. In the same spirit occurred a reunion at Gettysburg, on the following Fourth, of Pickett's division and the Philadelphia brigade. The heroine of the occasion was Mrs. George Pickett, before whom the Virginians and Pennsylvanians, after clasping hands at the stone wall where they had last met in blood and smoke, passed in review. Those who saw the handsome Virginia woman—she had been but fifteen when she married Pickett in 1863—with her classic features and challenging eyes, could not but feel a thrill in recalling the history she had witnessed. Pickett had written her a letter while his troops lay in line at Gettysburg, waiting for the signal to charge, the thunder of Lee's cannonade passing over their heads. Her husband had been appointed to West Point by an Illinois Congressman named Abraham Lincoln, and in April, 1865, just after Appomattox, Lincoln had called at her door in Richmond and asked affectionately for George. In the sad years of Reconstruction she had shown the same gallant spirit as other Southern women, teaching school and translating articles to eke out the family income. Cleveland sent this gathering of Northern and Southern veterans at Gettysburg a letter hailing their honest desire for peace and reconciliation: [1]

The friendly assault there to be made will be resistless because inspired by American chivalry; and its result will be glorious, because conquered hearts will be its trophies of success. Thereafter this battlefield will be consecrated by a victory which shall presage the end of the bitterness of strife, the exposure of the insincerity which conceals hatred by professions of kindness, the condemnation of frenzied appeals to passion for unworthy purposes,

[1] Cleveland Papers.

and the beating down of all that stands in the way of the destiny of our united country.

While those who fought and who have so much to forgive lead in the pleasant ways of peace, how wicked appear the traffic in sectional hate, and the betrayal of patriotic sentiment. It surely cannot be wrong to desire the settled quiet which lights for our entire country the path to prosperity and greatness; nor need the lessons of the war be forgotten and its results jeopardized, in the wish for that genuine fraternity which insures national pride and glory.

This was the year in which the talented W. A. Rogers first fully replaced Thomas Nast as the principal cartoonist of *Harper's Weekly*, and in midsummer a spirited drawing of his caught the public fancy.[1] It showed the pathetic figure of Grant, seated in the armchair of his last illness, and above it his fine words: "I have witnessed since my sickness just what I have wished to see ever since the war—harmony and good feeling between the sections." Below, in contrast, was the squat figure of Foraker, attempting to paste over Grant's sentiment the malignant accusation with which he had attacked Cleveland:—"And, on such a basis, to establish a *sentimental fraternity* of feeling for the present, to be followed with payment for Cotton, Slaves, and Confederate Bonds by and by." Between these views the enlightened public was easily able to make its choice.

IV

Then came the episode of Cleveland's cancellation of his proposed visit to the G.A.R. Encampment to be held in St. Louis in September, 1887. He wished to see the West; moreover, this was the first time that a national convention of the G.A.R. had been held in any Southern or border city, and it seemed fitting that a Democratic President should attend. Early in the spring of 1887 the St. Louis *Post-Dispatch* proposed a mammoth popular invitation; beautifully lithographed sheets were signed by 200,000 citizens; and Mayor David R. Francis, at the head of a committee, went to Washington to urge Cleveland to come.[2] At the same time, the executive committee of the G.A.R. requested

---

[1] *Harper's Weekly*, Aug. 6, 1887.
[2] Walter B. Stevens, "When Cleveland Came to St. Louis," *Missouri Historical Review*, XXI, 145 ff.

Cleveland's presence, and local posts throughout the country passed cordial resolutions. He accepted. But suddenly the battle-flag order, evoking denunciatory resolutions by numerous bodies of veterans, changed the atmosphere. It was evident that if Cleveland went to the St. Louis encampment, he would risk encountering some public outrage. As a matter of fact, when the Army of West Virginia held a reunion late in August at Wheeling, with Foraker present, many veterans offered a studied insult to the Chief Executive. One of the banners hung over the line of march bore the words, "God Bless our President, Commander-in-Chief of our Army and Navy." Most of the posts, on reaching this, halted. Then, declining to pass beneath it, they folded their flags and marched around it in the gutter, some even trailing their colors.[1]

Under such circumstances Cleveland was not a man to hesitate. Mayor Francis, at the time of the battle-flag order, was in the East. Cleveland, hastily calling him to Washington, sent him back to St. Louis to sound popular sentiment. The mayor's report was clear:[2]

The resident members of the G. A. R. whom I have met disclaim any feeling of antipathy to you and profess a desire to have you attend the encampment. They express at the same time, however, a fear lest your presence will deter many posts from coming.

I find a growing sentiment among the local G. A. R. to have you decline the invitation to the encampment, and to enable you to do so gracefully they are asking me to originate a movement inviting you to attend our annual Fair and Veiled Prophet pageant to be held the week after the encampment.

A few days later, after much mental turmoil, Cleveland recalled his acceptance of the Grand Army's invitation. Secretary Whitney was violently opposed to this step, thinking that Cleveland should wait till an aroused public opinion demanded the cancellation. The President's worry over the subject led him to write out not one but several rough drafts of his withdrawal. He felt no concern regarding the feelings of the G.A.R., a thoroughly partisan organization, which had never elected a Democratic head and had often supported Republican national tickets. But he wished the country to understand perfectly his position. In a letter to Mayor Francis,[3] he referred to the intimations that he might

[1] *Nation,* Sept. 1, 1887.
[2] St. Louis, June 22, 1887. Cleveland Papers.
[3] N. Y. *Herald, World,* July 7, 8, 1888.

be unwelcome and said that he refused to believe that the G.A.R. wished to intimidate the President of the United States. His real reason for declining he gave in blunt terms:

Rather than abandon my trip to the West and disappoint your citizens, I might, if I alone were concerned, submit to the insult to which it is quite openly asserted I would be helplessly subjected if present at the encampment; but I should bear with me there the people's highest office, the dignity of which I must protect . . .

This letter threw the G.A.R. upon the defensive. Its officers had never repudiated the outrageous utterances of such members as Fairchild, and were left in an unhappy position. Scores of editorials denounced them. When Cleveland attended the Clinton centennial in July he devoted his brief evening speech before his old neighbors to the subject of the dignity of the Presidential office. Moreover, he showed unusual adroitness in heightening the popular impression that the G.A.R. was in the wrong. When the letter to Mayor Francis was published, 150 veterans of Lynn, Mass., had just arrived in Washington from a tour of the Virginia battlefields. A newspaper quoted one of them as saying that they would not call upon the President— "We can see enough rebels South." The indignant post thereupon obtained permission to wait upon Cleveland, marched into the East Room, and cheered him vigorously. "I want you to understand," said Cleveland, "that I have lost no confidence in the G.A.R. as an organization. . . . It is incomprehensible to me that men who have risked their lives to save the government should return home to abate one jot or tittle of the respect and support which every good citizen owes to the constituted authorities." He shook them all by the hand, and forming anew in front of the White House, they gave him and Mrs. Cleveland the marching salute as he went for his afternoon drive.[1] Cleveland presently drove home his attack on the intolerant element among the veterans by a letter to a Pennsylvania post which had asked for a donation—and got it: [2]

No one can deny that the Grand Army of the Republic has been played upon by demagogues for partisan purposes, and has yielded to insidious blandishments to such an extent that it is regarded by many . . . as an organization which has wandered a long way from its original design. . . . Such a sentiment not only exists, but will grow and spread unless *within* that

[1] N. Y. *Herald*, July 8.
[2] Cleveland to E. W. Fosnot, Oct. 24, 1887. Cleveland Papers.

organization something is done to prove that its objects are not partisan, unjust, and selfish.

Cleveland's nomination of Lamar to the Supreme Court at the close of 1887 brought forth a new spasm of the old rebel-baiting. The fine old Mississippi sage was so admirably suited for the place that it was difficult to find fault with him. Yet Ingalls, a waspish New Englander transplanted to Kansas, declared that he represented all that was bad in the past, dangerous in the present, and menacing in the future of the country! Others, including Sherman and Edmunds, announced that they would do everything in their power to prevent confirmation. The Judiciary Committee delayed action until the party vote could be worked up to the point of rejection, and then made an adverse report. Fortunately, several Western Republicans refused to stand with the Northeast on the issue, and with the aid of Stewart of Nevada and Leland Stanford of California, Lamar was confirmed by the narrow margin of 32 to 28. Stewart wrote a courageous letter to a constituent, declaring that rejection would be taken as a permanent bar against all Confederate veterans, and that he would not support so unreasonable an act. The vote was thus a notable victory for sectional tolerance; and now that one of its old soldiers was on the Supreme Bench, the South had further reason to think of the national government as its own.

As the campaign of 1888 approached, the disappointed Ingalls made one final effort to wave the bloody shirt in the agonizing manner of Blaine and Ben Butler. He gained the floor on May 1, delivered a long and vituperative speech, and declared that "the success of the Democratic party means the triumph of the Confederacy, which is today as much an organized, active, aggressive force in our politics as it was in 1860." But the oratorical bomb, for such he had expected it to prove, fizzled and died like an empty firecracker. And during the campaign, for the first time since Appomattox, the Confederacy was virtually forgotten.

Sectionalism was subsiding. The reason for this subsidence lay chiefly, of course, in the workings of time and of irresistible economic and social forces. But a not unimportant contribution was made to it by Cleveland's calm scorn for sectional outbursts, and his calm exposure of the pensions grabs and other selfish schemes lurking behind the carefully-manufactured attacks on the South.

Chapter XX   Varied Problems of National Growth: 1886–87

ALWAYS men came back, in the late seventies and the eighties, to three great subjects—currency, the tariff, and administrative reform. Politics was like a weary waltz in some huge triangular ballroom; the airs and the partners changed, but the circling dancers still pivoted upon the three identical corners. After 1884 the orchestra was new and was ringing out livelier music; a fresh set of dancers, more alert and interesting, was on the floor; but the three corners remained and the evolutions followed the same general lines. When would someone break down a partition and lead the rout in new directions?

The time was arriving, though few perceived it, for striking departures in public policy. A few men, in general obscure rather than prominent, had caught the glint of light on peaks ahead. One was a tall, lean, sunburnt Texan, John H. Reagan, once postmaster-general of the Confederacy, who was insisting that the government should deal vigorously with the railroads. Three members of Congress, Breckinridge of Kentucky, Bacon of New York, and Edmunds of Vermont, had been struck by the menace of the trusts and were attempting to devise remedies. A third herald of the future was a squat, large-browed Jew of Anglo-Dutch origin, Samuel Gompers of New York, who held the secret of the effective organization of labor, and who during Cleveland's governorship had appeared in Albany to demand the first important laws against the exploitation of workers.[1] A fiery young Representative from Wisconsin, Robert M. La Follette, was observing with growing indignation the evils of lobbying, log-rolling, and secret combinations in Washington. Congress, he found, represented less the people than the special interests intent upon defrauding the people—tariff interests, railroad interests, timber interests, mining interests, and pork-barrel interests.[2]

Looking back from our vantage-point upon the eighties—the decade of the first electric power station, the first horseless trolleys, the first trusts, the first ten-cent magazines, the first American battleships—we can see that politics was coming under the impact of several great eco-

[1] Samuel Gompers, *Seventy Years of Life and Labor*, I, 207 ff.
[2] La Follette, *Autobiography*, 54 ff.

340

nomic facts. The industrial revolution which had been halted and chastened by the depression of 1873–78 had resumed its stride and was reaching some of its principal objectives. Great business organizations, the most ruthless in the world, were deriving enormous profits from a monopoly of production or of marketing. At the same time, the frontier was rapidly being closed. Though homesteading continued, the best land was fast being exhausted, the discontented workman or shopkeeper of the East could no longer find open portals in the West, and the fluidity of the American population was being lost. It was as if a sun had gone down, a source of roseate optimism had been extinguished. The empty West had been the principal wellspring of America's sense of freedom, and hence of her optimism and comparative lack of social friction. Moreover, worldwide conditions were rapidly throwing a sombre shadow over the prairies. The wheatgrower and cattlegrower were facing the enlarged competition of the Canadian and Australian plains, the Argentine pampas, the Russian steppes, and the Indian fields suddenly brought close to Europe by the Suez Canal. Gold production was slackening and prices were falling. The Western farmer was ceasing to be the hopeful worker of James Hall's chronicles of pioneer life and becoming the drudge of Hamlin Garland's mordant tales.

In the grip of these economic forces, the government was like a ship on a sea dominated by powerful submarine currents. The pilots looked to wind, wave, and tide, and made sail by surface indications; and all the while their craft was being hurried on by forces they could neither understand nor calculate. It is easy, long after the event, to say that the captain and mates should have seen these currents and used them. Where was the statesmanship which, in these formative years, might have faced the trusts and pools and brought them under partial Federal control? Where was the statesmanship that might have turned to the farmer and lessened his growing discontent by a bold system of land-banks and by aids to marketing? Where was the statesmanship which might have done for labor, in the national sphere, what Massachusetts through her Labor Bureau had been doing for it since 1869 in the State field? [1] These questions, ignoring the fact that in a democracy problems must ripen slowly toward a solution, and that public opinion must be educated to any decisive action, are partly unfair—but not wholly so.

[1] There was a Federal Bureau of Labor, organized in 1885 under Carroll D. Wright, but it was weak.

Cleveland, as Woodrow Wilson pointed out a few years later,[1] showed little power of vigorous leadership till past the middle of his term. His tariff message of December, 1887, was his first bold stroke. Administrative reform, appointments, and the terrific pressure of routine consumed all his time in the first two years. His original conception of his office did not involve any display of parliamentary leadership. On the contrary, in his inaugural address he promised a strictly constitutional interpretation of the presidency. Twenty years later he, like others, thought that Roosevelt's aggressive leadership in Congressional action was contrary to the whole spirit of the Constitution. Finally, his temperament must be kept in mind. He was always markedly deficient in imagination. His power of doing was a power *ad hoc*—he saw the task directly before him, and attacked it with superb courage and directness, but he never peered far ahead. He was hampered by the lack of range in his education, his failure to read widely, and the fact that he had paid almost no attention to governmental problems till three and a half years before his inauguration. His faculty of leadership had to grow.

II

One impediment to leadership lay in Congress, which at the time of Cleveland's inauguration as President was singularly ill-adapted for important or progressive legislation. The House was Democratic and the Senate Republican, placing them at cross-purposes. The Senate suffered from the presence of a large and powerful group of men representing corporate interests, while the House suffered from overgrowth and from perhaps the worst set of rules cursing any important legislative body in the world.

By the middle eighties public opinion was becoming outspoken upon the Senate. *Harper's Weekly* remarked that the people were convinced "that it is becoming a club of rich men, and that Senators are not sensitive to the charge of voting upon questions in which they have a pecuniary interest." Similar terms were used by the Washington correspondent of the Springfield *Republican:* "It is growing more and more aristocratic, more and more regardless of public opinion, more and more separate from the House, and some people say more and more corrupt." It seemed to stand less for an American democracy than an American

[1] *Atlantic Monthly,* March, 1897.

plutocracy. When Senator Van Wyck in the spring of 1887 proposed a constitutional amendment for the direct election of Senators, he based his argument upon the ease with which money controlled the choice by the legislatures. The House contained a long list of men, such as Carlisle, Morrison, Hewitt, Mills, Reagan, and the two Breckinridges, who were passionately devoted to the interests of the common man; but in the Senate the passionate interest was turned in a different direction.

Wealth was conspicuous in half of the Senate seats. The richest Senator was James G. Fair of Nevada, who had wrested some $30,000,000 from the mines of Virginia City and was now intimately associated with the heads of the Southern Pacific. Leland Stanford, part-builder of the Central Pacific, did not represent the voters of California half as energetically as the western railroads. Joseph N. Dolph, an Oregon attorney, had grown rich from the clientage of the Northern Pacific, and was vice-president of that line when chosen to the Senate in 1882. John P. Jones of Nevada was a millionaire and during his thirty years in the Senate an unwearied champion of the powerful silver mining interests. Brown of Georgia, noted for his stubborn opposition to railway rate regulation, was one of the richest holders of Southern railroad stocks. Allison of Iowa, Don Cameron of Pennsylvania, a State at this time largely ruled by the Pennsylvania Railroad and the Standard Oil, and Aldrich of Rhode Island, were all closely connected with great corporation interests. Indeed, the last-named had developed a political philosophy by which his allegiance to these moneyed influences—his biographer dignifies them by the term "economic constituencies" [1]—was converted into a semi-patriotic duty. We need give only passing mention to Camden of West Virginia, a man wealthy in railways, coal, iron, and petroleum; Gorman of Maryland, closely associated with the Chesapeake & Ohio Canal and the Central Maryland Railroad; and William J. Sewell, whom all-powerful railroad and manufacturing interests had just sent to the Senate from New Jersey.[2]

A picturesque place in the list was occupied by Spooner and Sawyer of Wisconsin, so vividly described by La Follette in his autobiography; two wealthy, self-made, and assertive leaders who regarded corruption as inevitable if not proper, and who were interested in government chiefly as a means of enriching the lumber and railway interests of Wis-

[1] Nathaniel Stephenson, *Nelson W. Aldrich,* 60, 61.
[2] See N. Y. *World,* Jan. 8, 1887, for a caustic description of the Senate.

consin. It was Sawyer who made the error of trying to bribe young La Follette himself.[1] A more scandalous prominence attached to Henry B. Payne of Ohio, an elderly Democratic politician who had married the daughter of Nathan Perry and still occupied the fine Perry mansion in Cleveland. Possessing family, education, and wealth, and connected with the Standard Oil by his son Oliver H. Payne, its treasurer, he stood for all that was most aristocratic in the Western Reserve. Yet when he took his seat in 1885 his title was tainted with impudent corruption. Officers of the Standard Oil had supplied his managers with huge sums to bribe the legislature and wrest the senatorship from Pendleton. The backroom headquarters of these managers in Columbus was described as looking like a bank, littered with canvas bags of coin and cases stuffed with greenbacks; and one of them admitted to a friend that he had carried $65,000 to the Capitol "next his skin." [2] There were of course numerous Senators who were patriotic, high-minded, and liberal, and several even of the richest members, such as McPherson of New Jersey, showed a marked hostility to predatory corporations. But the general trend revealed a dangerous subservience to railroads, banks, and powerful manufacturing interests.

As for the House, in these years it might well have been symbolized by the central figure in some new conception of the Laocoön. During the previous decade every session had demonstrated a more urgent need for the drastic reformation of the rules which was finally carried out in 1890 by Speaker Reed. The situation when Cleveland took office had grown almost intolerable. Henry Watterson aptly called the House the great lumbering Gulliver-snail of politics. Debate could be protracted interminably, and an active minority, by dilatory motions and filibustering, could create preposterous delays. But worst of all were the difficulties which arose from the lack of any machinery to give due precedence to important measures. As they were reported from committees they all went on the calendar helter-skelter, and one could be reached out of due order only by suspending the rules, which required a two-thirds vote. A special priority had naturally been given to appropriation bills, to which, under the "Holman rule," general legislation might be attached, but this availed little for efficiency. Reed did not

---

[1] La Follette, *Autobiography*, 59.
[2] On Payne see Senate Report 1490, 49th Cong., 1st Sess., 1886; H. D. Lloyd, *Wealth Against Commonwealth*, ch. 27.

exaggerate when he declared in December, 1885, that "for the last three Congresses the representatives of the people of the United States have been in irons. They have been allowed to transact no public business except at the dictation and by the permission of a small coterie of gentlemen"—that is, the majority group in the Appropriations Committee. Morrison's change in the rules struck down the tyranny of this committee, but in doing so left the House more rudderless than ever. An iron-willed Speaker might have done much even with the old rules, but Carlisle consistently regarded himself as a mere moderating officer and declined to exercise real leadership.

It was therefore always with a feeling of surprise that the country found that important legislation had actually been passed. The Forty-ninth Congress was compelled by the death of Vice-President Hendricks to take up the question of the Presidential succession, and Hoar offered a well-devised bill in the Senate. Though it met with some slight opposition from the Republicans, it passed the House on January 15, 1886, and was signed by Cleveland four days later. By providing a long line of succession—Vice-President, Secretary of State, Secretary of the Treasury, and so on—it forever removed the contingency that the country might be left without a chief executive. Within little more than a year it was followed by an act regulating the counting of the electoral votes, approved February 3, 1887—an act which rendered impossible a repetition of the dispute of 1876. Neither law owed anything whatever, in its inception or progress, to Cleveland, but he gladly signed them both.

III

Not because times were bad but because they were slowly growing better, the year 1886 was one of great labor restiveness; in militant temper, workingmen the country over were demanding better wages and working conditions. The year opened with riots among the coke workers of western Pennsylvania. In March, Bradstreet's reported that 51,000 men were out on strike in the bituminous mines of Pennsylvania, Maryland, and Ohio, in the textile, shoe, and metal industries of New England, and in nail factories west of the Alleghenies. Few parts of the country, as the months passed, were left untouched by walkouts and lockouts. There were twice as many strikes as in any previous twelvemonth in all American history. This also was the year in which the Knights of Labor, stimulated by their victory on the Wabash Railroad the preceding autumn, reached their greatest vigor, and in which Henry George, running on a labor ticket, made his gallant fight against Hewitt and Roosevelt for the mayoralty of New York. Never before in our history had the press, the pulpit, and other agencies of discussion paid so much attention to the labor question—a question still too new to be sympathetically understood.

The struggle this spring on the Gould railway system in the Southwest—the Missouri Pacific, Texas & Pacific, and other lines—raised a question of immediate import to the government. The Knights of Labor, whose ill-organized, amorphous strength is difficult to estimate, but which may have had 800,000 members, had recently established strong and troublesome lodges in this system and had forced Jay Gould's managers to recognize them.[1] When the Texas and Pacific, becoming bankrupt, passed under the control of the Federal courts, the Knights grew uneasy over their status and presented the receiver with a set of demands designed to safeguard themselves against harsh measures of economy. These were rejected, and soon afterward the receiver discharged a mechanic at Fort Worth who had been a prominent knight. When he refused to reinstate the man, on March 1 the shopmen struck.[2] Within a week they were joined by employees on the Missouri Pacific; and the strike quickly spread through Texas, Missouri, Arkansas, Kansas, and Illinois, affecting some 6,000 miles of railroad, and paralyzing many communities. At its height not less than 10,000 men had thrown down their tools. The blockade of freight west of the Mississippi was felt from one side of the continent to the other, and the loss to the railroads and the public was tremendous. Many farming communities suffered severely, and St. Louis was for a time in almost as much distress as if besieged by a hostile army. Perishable goods rotted on the tracks, provisions soared, coal reached $40.00 a ton, and many factories and all the flourmills closed down.[3] So great was the resentment created by the strike that there sprang into existence throughout parts of the Southwest a so-called Law and Order League, whose object was to combat the Knights. The sympathy of most people, however, was naturally

[1] Norman J. Ware, *The Labor Movement in the United States*, 1860–95, 139–145.
[2] F. W. Taussig, "The Southwestern Strike of 1886," *Quarterly Journal of Economics*, I, 184–222.
[3] N. Y. *Times*, April 18–29, 1883; three-column letter in the *Nation*, April 15, 1886.

against Jay Gould.

Most alarming of all was the violence which ensued. Negotiations between Gould and Terence V. Powderly, the head of the Knights, having come to nothing, on March 26 the governors of Missouri, Kansas, Arkansas and Texas issued proclamations calling on the managers to send out their trains as usual, and on all officers of the law to afford them protection. But at many points the strikers disabled the engines, uncoupled the cars, and otherwise deranged traffic. Early in April there was an affray between deputies and strikers at Fort Worth, with several killed, and a week later another battle at East St. Louis resulted in more casualties. Answering a public demand, the House appointed a committee of seven to investigate the "existing labor troubles," [1] and in April passed a bill for the voluntary arbitration of railway disputes, the government to pay the expenses up to $1,000 in each case. Before the end of that month it was evident that the strike was breaking down and would end in surrender. On May 4 it was formally terminated, not more than one-fifth of the strikers being taken back on the Missouri Pacific.

At this juncture the country was startled by the famous Haymarket riot, which grew in part out of a lockout of 1400 employees at Cyrus McCormick's reaper works in Chicago, and in part out of a prolonged and radical agitation in that city. During the spring of 1886 Chicago was the scene of constant unrest, marked by various labor disturbances, much brutal clubbing of workmen by the police under Captain John Bonfield, and a wildly vocal anarchist movement led by August Spies, Albert R. Parsons, and Sam Fielden. On May 1 occurred an impressive demonstration by trade unions in favor of the eight-hour day, between 40,000 and 60,000 men dropping their tools.[2] Two days later a collision between the police and some 7,000 workmen and roughs at the McCormick plant resulted in the death of one man and the serious injury of half a dozen others. The excitable Spies, losing his head, published at the press of his radical paper, the *Arbeiter-Zeitung,* a circular headed "Revenge! Workingmen! To Arms!" "Your masters sent out their bloodhounds—the police—they killed six of your brothers at McCormick's this afternoon," the circular inaccurately stated. "To arms, we call you, to arms!" Another circular convoked a general meeting for the night of May 4 in Haymarket Square to denounce "the

[1] House Reports, 49th Cong., 2nd session, No. 4174.
[2] *Centennial History of Illinois,* IV, 169, gives the larger figure.

latest atrocious act of the police, the shooting of our fellow-working-men," and in a few copies an inflammatory sentence exhorted the workers to prepare to fight.

On the night named a small crowd of perhaps 1300 gathered in the Haymarket, and in orderly fashion listened to speeches which were shot through with resentment and class-feeling, but by no means incendiary. Shortly after ten o'clock rain began to fall, the crowd commenced to break up, and the mayor, who was watching, departed. As Fielden, mounted on a wagon, was closing the speaking, a platoon of police needlessly marched on the remnants of the gathering to break it up. Fielden had just shouted "We are peaceable," when a bomb from some unknown hand exploded in the platoon, cutting down more than fifty police and killing or fatally wounding seven. The remainder drew their pistols and fired volley after volley into the crowd, which instantly broke for shelter.

As a result of the riot, Chicago fell under a spell of passion and fear. A frenzy seemed to seize the leading newspapers and most business and professional groups. Alarmed capitalists set on foot a movement for the establishment of a large army post near the city, and quickly raised $500,000 to buy the site of what became Fort Sheridan. All anarchists and Socialists, and particularly all Germans and Poles of radical tendencies, were ferociously denounced. The wave of excitement spread over the country: a lurid double-page drawing of the riot, published by the artist T. de Thulstrup in *Harper's Weekly,* symbolized the exaggerated view taken of it. There was rioting and bloodshed in Milwaukee, an anarchist editor was jailed in New York, and arrests were made elsewhere.

Ten alleged anarchists were promptly indicted in Chicago, of whom two were released for lack of evidence. Parsons at first eluded capture, but on the day the case was called, July 21, 1886, he walked into the courtroom and voluntarily surrendered. The atmosphere of the community was implacably hostile to justice. When the jury was impanelled, men were admitted to it who confessed that they had read all about the affair and had formed distinct prejudices regarding it. The presiding judge, Joseph E. Gary, showed a highly discreditable bias in his conduct of the case and his charge to the jury. It proved impossible to identify the bomb-thrower, whose name has remained a mystery to this day. It was of course impossible to prove that the unidentified man had been influenced by the speeches or writings of the defendants. But the judge held that since they had "generally by speech and print advised large classes to commit murder," and murder had resulted, they were guilty. Four, Spies, Engel, Fischer, and Parsons, were hanged; one exploded a bomb in his mouth and killed himself; and two whose death sentences were commuted were years later, with fine courage, pardoned by Governor Altgeld.[1]

Cleveland, intensely interested in all this, had already taken notice of the labor problem. In consequence primarily of the Southwestern strike, on April 22 he issued the first message to Congress upon the subject of labor in our history.[2] It was not only an innovation which riveted public attention, but a notably liberal pronouncement. After clumsily referring to "the problems which recent events and a present condition have thrust upon us," he laid down several broad and sympathetic principles. The relations of the day between labor and capital, he declared, were highly unsatisfactory. Workingmen felt that there existed a "discrimination in favor of capital as an object of governmental attention," and that they were suffering from "the grasping and heedless exactions of employers." He believed that the workers had a right to a full share of the benefits of legislation; and as a beginning, he proposed that the government try to improve affairs by setting up a permanent board for voluntary arbitration in labor disputes. The tone of his message elicited applause from the labor papers, and criticism from such organs of the propertied class as the *Nation*.

His suggestion regarding arbitration came to much less than he expected. Cleveland of course knew that compulsory arbitration was an impossibility, even on the railways—citizens cannot be made to labor against their will. His scheme differed sharply from the O'Neill bill passed by the House, which provided that each railroad dispute might be settled by its own special board representing employees and employer. The President proposed that instead of relying on "arbitrators chosen in the heat of conflicting claims," the government should create a permanent labor commission of three men to whom disputants might appeal. Moreover, he believed that this board, which should be engrafted upon the Bureau of Labor, should be empowered to offer its

---

[1] For this affair, see the printed *Brief and Argument for the Plaintiffs in Error*, 18–86; Spies, *Autobiography;* Altgeld, *Reasons for Pardoning Fielden, Neebe, and Schwab;* and the press of the day. Neebe had been sentenced to fifteen years.

[2] *Messages and Papers*, VIII, 394 ff.

services in any dispute whatever, not merely those on interstate railroads; and that it should investigate the causes of all labor troubles. Its decisions would obviously have no legal weight, but he hoped that their moral authority would in most instances prove decisive. For a few weeks the press eagerly discussed the whole subject. Many newspapers of both parties approved of Cleveland's proposal; many others clung to the view that labor difficulties were quite beyond the reach of easy legislation. Some result immediately useful might have been attained but for a shameless display of partisan manoeuvring by the two houses.

Both House and Senate were eager to win labor votes for their respective parties. The Senate therefore let the O'Neill bill and Cleveland's proposals languish while it passed various measures of its own. One was a bill legalizing the incorporation of national trade unions, which the House accepted and Cleveland signed. Another was a bill giving letter-carriers an eight-hour day. The House, making its own record, passed a long-pending bill prohibiting the importation of contract labor, which met opposition in the Senate but after some delay became law. Finally, at the close of the session the Senate took up the O'Neill bill and passed it. Although it conflicted with his ideas Cleveland signed it.[1] But near the end of his term he won a partial victory. By an Act of October 1, 1888, provision was made for the voluntary arbitration of railway disputes, and the President was also authorized to appoint a commission to investigate any labor quarrel whatever, acting at the same time as a board of conciliation. It was too late for him to give vitality to the law. Within a few months Harrison was President. But we shall later see what use he made of this authority after the great Pullman strike of 1894.

IV

To some of Cleveland's critics in 1886, including the *World*, the railroad problem seemed the most important and urgent of all the riddles facing the Administration. At the moment it presented a Janus face; on the one side were the mismanaged Pacific railroads, in which the government held a mortgage interest, and on the other was the general regulation of interstate commerce, with Congress still wrangling over the best method to be adopted.

[1] *Cong. Rec.*, March 1, 1887, vol. 18, p. 2460.

The Union Pacific indeed offered a painful issue. The day in 1869 upon which it and the connecting Central Pacific in California had been completed as our first transcontinental railway had been hailed as a bright moment in the nation's history. The government had given both roads lavish support, making not only enormous land grants, but generous loans; and the Union Pacific thus received a little more than $33,500,000 in government bonds, the debt being made a second mortgage on the property. Yet at first Congress felt sure of repayment, for in the exuberant days after the war the obligation did not seem heavy.[1] Indeed, if the Union Pacific had not been robbed by the outrageous construction costs of the Crédit Mobilier and by subsequent financial manipulations, it could have met its obligations without difficulty. But instead of being efficiently managed it became a booty to be plundered unmercifully, and as late as 1880 Jay Gould made more than ten millions at its expense by unloading on it the Kansas Pacific and Denver Pacific at exorbitant prices.[2] In 1885, when brought under the able presidency of Charles Francis Adams, Jr., it was in bad repute, with a demoralized service, and already on the verge of bankruptcy. The government in 1878 had tried to safeguard itself by the Thurman Act, which required both the roads to pay into the Treasury 25 per cent of their net earnings, up to a yearly limit of $1,500,000 apiece. But this attempt to extinguish the mortgages by creating a sinking fund did not prove satisfactory.

When Cleveland entered office he encountered a noisy demand for drastic action. Part of this outcry was a natural public response to the misdeeds of previous managements; part of it represented an effort by stock speculators to depress Union Pacific values for their own profit.[3] The Chicago *Tribune*, which as a mouthpiece of agrarian sentiment bitterly denounced the two roads, demanded that the government foreclose its mortgage and either lease them or operate them as a check upon other greedy railroads. In 1886 it began taunting Cleveland with a betrayal of the people. "Soon after his inauguration," wrote the editor, "it was given out that he would take up the Pacific Railroad problem in a special message to Congress and urge the appointment of a receiver to secure the many millions due the government from the de-

[1] *Public Opinion*, Jan. 28, 1888, has a good review of the whole question.
[2] R. I. Warshow, *Jay Gould*, 140.
[3] Nelson Trottman, *History of the Union Pacific*, 222.

faulting railroad. Two regular messages have now been sent to Congress and only the most perfunctory mention was made of the Pacific Railroad swindle." [1] The *World* was equally vehement. Cleveland, it proclaimed, should have compelled the Pacific Railroad ring to open its books, stop diverting business from the subsidiary roads into its own pockets, and cease its lobbying and corruption; instead, he had waited for the press to force Congress to act.[2] It was evident that Congress was eager to seize the tomahawk. In the winter session of 1885–86 nine bills were offered dealing with the indebtedness of the two lines, eight bills dealing with their lands, five resolutions for an investigation, and one resolution to prosecute the heads of the Union Pacific.[3]

Cleveland had no intention of taking hasty steps. Either foreclosure or the surrender of the unpaid claims of the government was out of the question, the former being impracticable and the latter unjust to the taxpayers. The one really feasible plan was to revise the Thurman Act and refund the debt at a lower rate of interest, incidentally improving the government's security by including the branch lines in the mortgage. Early in 1886 Cleveland threw his influence behind this general settlement of the question. A bill had already been drafted by a former Railroad Commissioner, and now it was reported to the Senate by the Judiciary Committee. It provided for a series of fixed annual payments, sufficient to wipe out the debt in eighty years, enlarged the security, and made the whole debt due immediately if the roads defaulted. The bill was endorsed by the Interior Department, while the *Nation* remarked that "it must be acquiesced in by every thoughtful and disinterested person." [4] But there at once arose the expected protest from farmers, labor leaders, and the whole anti-corporation press, and it failed. The President tried to revive interest in it at the beginning of the second session of the Forty-ninth Congress, but in vain.[5]

Cleveland had made a serious error. If he had coupled with this bill a plan for a thorough investigation of the two railroads, which would have satisfied the insistent public demand for a full exposure of the undoubted thefts and abuses, he might have carried its passage. Pitiless publicity for the errors of the past, a sober, constructive scheme for

[1] Chicago *Tribune,* Dec. 30, 1886.
[2] N. Y. *World,* April 6, 1887.
[3] Trottman, *Union Pacific,* 222.
[4] *Nation,* May 20, 1886.
[5] *Messages and Papers,* VIII, 526.

the future—both were needed. When Cleveland failed, the *World* stepped forward. Waiting till Congress met, it published a startling mass of facts showing that Collis P. Huntington and Leland Stanford, as heads of the Central Pacific, had during the years 1869–80 used more than two million dollars of railroad money, without an accounting, in Washington.[1] The obvious inference was that their agents in the capital had practised bribery on a colossal scale. An inquiry now became imperative, and Congress promptly provided for a commission to conduct it. Cleveland, after signing the act on March 3, 1887, appointed three men who were able but who unfortunately lacked national prominence: ex-Governor Robert E. Pattison of Pennsylvania, E. Ellery Anderson, of New York, a railroad lawyer, and D. L. Littler of Illinois.

The investigation was exhaustive in character. Jay Gould, Russell Sage, Sidney Dillon, and many officers and directors of the companies were haled to the stand and reluctantly gave sensational testimony. A corps of expert accountants went through the books and records with a fine comb. Not a single fact of importance—and some of the facts were staggering—was allowed to escape.[2] Though most of the evidence referred to water that had long since flowed under the mill, it was followed with almost bated breath by the public. Huntington admitted, under oath, that his company had expended more than $6,000,000 between 1874 and 1885 (with one year missing) for "legal" and "miscellaneous and general purposes." He admitted that his Washington agent, Franchot, was paid $20,000 a year for "explaining things" to Congressmen, and had received as much as $30,000 or $40,000 a year additional, for which no vouchers were asked. Huntington maintained other representatives in Washington to "see that the position of the company received no damage," and granted them equally large sums without asking an accounting. The robbery of the Union Pacific by Gould was exposed in all its sordid grandiosity. There was a mass of testimony upon rebates, pooling, and the evil manipulation of the branch lines.

The majority report, signed by Anderson and Littler, was an able document. After a review of the wholesale looting of the railroads and the dissipation of the government subsidies, it went on to propose se-

[1] *World*, Jan. 15–19, 1887.
[2] See the nine large volumes of the *Pacific Railroad Report;* Sen. Ex. Docs., No. 51, 50th Cong. 1st session.

vere but not impossible terms for the future. Facts were cited to show that the roads would have to be given a long term for the payment of their debt in instalments. The report proposed that the Union Pacific debt be fixed at $50,757,000, and the Central Pacific debt at $49,331,-000, and that the annual charge for interest and sinking fund should rise in each instance from approximately $1,750,000 in the first decade to approximately $2,000,000 afterward. Such payments were really beyond the capacity of the roads at this moment. Simultaneously Commissioner Pattison brought in a minority report which met the widespread clamor for vengeance. He concluded a bitter arraignment of the past misdeeds of the lines by demanding prosecutions, fines, and jail sentences; while he also reported against any refunding of the debts, though he failed to offer an alternative plan.[1]

It was evident that the majority report was the sounder document. Pattison's policy of vengeance would have led to protracted lawsuits and criminal trials, to the postponement for weary years of a settlement already overdue, and to the impairment of property values on which the government held a mortgage. It required courage to take the side of the unpopular conservatives. Cleveland supplied it. "I suppose," he wrote in his message to Congress accompanying the reports,[2] "we are hardly justified in indulging the irritation and indignation naturally arising from a contemplation of malfeasance to such an extent as to lead to the useless destruction of these roads or the loss of the advances made by the government. I believe that our efforts should be in a more practical direction, and should tend, with no condonation of wrongdoing, to the collection by the government, on behalf of the people, of the public money now in jeopardy." He thought that the majority plan gave at least partial promise of the results sought. In short, he wished the government to take the role not of an avenging angel but of a practical, hardheaded business creditor.

But the sands were running out. When he penned this message his campaign for reëlection was about to begin. With greater time he might have brought Congress to a more reasonable view of the situation; he would certainly have tried. Harrison accomplished nothing, Congress still wavered, Jay Gould in 1890 again took control of the Union Pacific, and three years later the road was in receivership.

[1] *Pacific Railroad Report*, I, 1–217.
[2] *Messages and Papers*, VIII, 596 ff.

The year of the Pacific Railroad investigation was that in which the insistent demand for Federal regulation of interstate commerce bore its first fruit. With the passage of the Cullom bill Cleveland had little to do, though Senator Cullom tells us that he was "keenly interested" in the subject.[1] The long struggle for the enactment was approaching its final stages when he became President, and much as he believed in regulation, it was unnecessary for him to exert himself in its behalf. He knew, at the time he took office, that there were two opposed views on railroad legislation. Reagan and most of his Democratic associates in the House, with their State Rights background, disliked executive commissions and centralized authority. They proposed to pass a law clearly prohibiting various abuses and enjoining certain duties, and then to let the Federal attorneys and courts do the rest. Cullom and his friends, impressed by British practice, preferred a radically different plan. They wished to prohibit exorbitant rates, discriminations, and other evils, and to set up a permanent administrative commission to hear complaints, bring witnesses before its bar, and enforce the law. Cleveland agreed with this latter view, and his influence doubtless had something to do with its victory. In 1886 the Senate passed the Cullom bill by a huge majority, the House the Reagan bill by a small margin, and the familiar deadlock ensued. Cleveland soon afterward called attention to the decision of the Supreme Court in the Wabash case, specifically denying the States power to regulate interstate traffic, and asked Congress to act. Early in 1887 the two bills were sent to a conference committee, Reagan's supporters gave way, and the Cullom measure, in strengthened form, was passed. Cleveland's friends announced that he had long believed in the necessity for such legislation,[2] and waving aside all talk of its unconstitutionality, he signed it.

To no appointments of his first term, the Cabinet excepted, did Cleveland give such painstaking attention as to those for the Interstate Commerce Commission. The subject filled his mind for weeks early in 1887, for he realized that the effectiveness of the law depended upon two factors—the kind of men he chose, and the attitude of the courts. The corporation baiters were apprehensive lest he name a limp commission, and talked of the danger that savage and powerful rail-

[1] Shelby M. Cullom, *Fifty Years of Public Service*, 227.
[2] N. Y. *Herald*, Jan. 30, 1887.

road lawyers would toss the members like a set of mad bulls. Meanwhile, a pitiful whimpering came from the railway capitalists. Many were hysterical in their predictions of ruin. Chauncey Depew, president of the New York Central, declared that the law would depreciate Western farm-lands by one half, both Leland Stanford of the Southern Pacific and Clarke of the Illinois Central predicted a panic, and H. V. Poor asserted that it would ruin much of the nation's foreign and domestic commerce.

Cleveland's first decision was to name Thomas M. Cooley of Michigan, whose work as a jurist he knew well, as chairman of the Commission. Cooley until 1885 had sat on the supreme bench of his State, and until 1884 had been dean of the law school of the University of Michigan. More recently he had been receiver of the Wabash lines east of the Mississippi, in which position he had shown marked administrative capacity. Cleveland sent Don M. Dickinson to Ann Arbor to sound him, and the result being satisfactory, made a formal tender of the position on March 8.[1] The appointment, which Cullom had endorsed in advance —Cooley being a Republican—received universal applause. Indeed, Cooley's experience, energy, and shrewdness were chiefly responsible for the early success of the Commission. Immediately thereafter the President encountered difficulties. Bissell, Andrew D. White, ex-Senator Thurman, and George D. Robinson of Springfield, Mass., all refused nominations.[2] Yet before the end of March the slate had been made up. Besides Cooley, it included William R. Morrison; Augustus Schoonmaker, a Kingston lawyer and former attorney-general of New York State; Aldace T. Walker, who as a member of the Vermont legislature had given special attention to railroad questions; and Walter L. Bragg of Alabama, who while president of the railway commission of his State had made a reputation for compelling corporations to toe the line. He had insisted, for example, that they give first-class accommodations to colored people who paid first-class fares. The list deserved and received wide approval. "Better selections," Thurman wrote Cleveland, "I do not believe could have been made," adding that he had done well not to name "practical railroad men." [3]

In the two years before Cleveland went out of office a thoroughly

[1] Dickinson to Cleveland, Detroit, Feb. 13, 1887. Cleveland Papers.
[2] Cleveland Papers, Feb.–March, 1887. Secretary Bayard urged the appointment of Arthur Twining Hadley of Yale. Feb. 11, 1887. Cleveland Papers.
[3] March 25, 1887. Cleveland Papers.

hopeful beginning was made in railroad regulation, but a beginning that was to be blighted in the bud. The railways for a time endeavored to obey the law in both letter and spirit. In 1888 the Commission was able to report that the lines had "conformed promptly" to its orders. Many desirable alterations were effected in railway practice. Tariffs were changed all over the country to meet the long-and-short haul clause, and Westerners and Southerners found that local rates had been cut in every direction. Many pools passed out of existence, while others were remodelled to make them inoffensive. Accounting practices were widely reformed. This honeymoon of the new Commission and the railroads lasted for three years, or until after Cleveland had given way to Harrison; but then the corporations suddenly began to show recalcitrance, and beginning in 1890, secret rate-making and defiant appeals to the courts became common.[1]

V

By this time the Indian, to well-informed Americans, was ceasing to be the bright creation of Cooper's romances and Longfellow's *Hiawatha*, and had become a "problem." According to the point of view, he was either a whiskey-drinking nuisance or a much-cheated and neglected brother; and fortunately Cleveland held to the latter conception. It was high time that he was placed in a new relationship to the government and the land-hungry settlers. In 1887 there were about 264,000 Indians, owning 137,765,000 acres of land (nearly all in reservations, and worth not less than $160,000,000), and possessing trust funds to the amount of some $18,000,000.[2] There was much force in the Western complaint that they occupied a grossly excessive amount of the tillable land beyond the Mississippi. If every Indian family were given a quarter section, they would need a total of only 10,400,000 acres, or one-thirteenth of what they actually held. Friends of the Indians were equally dissatisfied because under the reservation system, supplemented by government distributions of money, blankets, and beef, they received little training for self-support or self-improvement. The evils incident to the tribes' position were nowhere better illustrated than in the Indian Territory, where some 97,000 Indians occupied al-

---

[1] *Report*, Interstate Commerce Commission, 1898.
[2] Proceedings of Lake Mohonk Conferences, *Annual Reports Board of Indian Commissioners*, 1883-1885.

most 45,000,000 acres, comprising twenty-five separate reservations. A number had attained a high degree of civilization, and Chief William P. Ross of the Cherokees boasted of the houses, farms, and stock which his people held. But most of them were in barbarism, without schools, without churches, without profitable farms, without a made road, and without any way of securing contact with white culture.[1]

Cleveland and Lamar, discussing the situation, were soon able to devise one definite recommendation. In his first two annual reports Lamar, with Cleveland's support, urged Congress to appoint a commission to visit every reservation, suggest needed reforms in agency affairs, and survey the requirements of the Indians in general.[2] Such a commission, they thought, could do something to allay the Western discontent, to inform the public upon the merits of the strong movement for opening the Indian Territory to white settlement and erecting a territorial government there, and to suggest means of civilizing the Indians. The Administration also continued its measures to protect the Indian reservations against the greedy cattle companies. Though Congress at first failed to do anything, public opinion shortly became aroused. A part was played in this by the bloody and needless Apache revolt under Geronimo in 1886, and another by the publication in 1885 of Helen Hunt Jackson's scathing book, *A Century of Dishonor*. Mrs. Jackson sent her volume to Cleveland through his old law-partner, Bass, with the request that he take up the problem in earnest. Meanwhile, a group which since 1883 had been holding an annual conference at Lake Mohonk on Indian affairs had given prominence to proposed legislation under which the Indian tribes could gradually be dissolved, their members be admitted to full citizenship, and their lands be distributed to them in severalty or individual ownership.

To this demand Cleveland lent his shoulder. The Mohonk Conference was shortly able to boast that "we have reiterated our faith in this policy from year to year, and now the President, the Secretary of the Interior, the Commissioner of Indian Affairs, the Lieutenant-General of the Army, and the common sentiment of the people East and West alike are substantially united in its favor." Senator Henry L. Dawes of Massachusetts pushed forward an appropriate bill, empowering the President, whenever he believed that any tribe had

---

[1] See the excellent articles on Indian affairs in N. Y. *Herald,* Feb., March, and April, 1886.
[2] Cf. Richardson, *Messages and Papers,* VIII, 520.

reached the proper stage of development, to divide its reservation and allot every man, woman, and child a farm of from 40 to 160 acres; each Indian to be then invested with all the privileges of citizenship except the right, for twenty-five years, of selling or encumbering his land. All surplus land was to revert to the public domain after a fair payment to the tribes. Early in 1887 the Dawes bill passed and Cleveland signed it. He could reflect that he had done something to make the Indian a man instead of a mere helpless ward, and, though the disposition of the district later called Oklahoma Territory was left quite unsettled, to satisfy the complaints of white settlers that great areas were being held as idle wastes.

Immediately afterwards Cleveland performed a memorable service for the homesteader. Within two months (April 28, 1887) he issued his famous order to Secretary Lamar regarding Guilford Miller's farm, an act which did more than anything else to warm the heart of Western settlers toward him.[1] Miller was a poor homesteader in Washington Territory who had settled upon a piece of land in 1878 and had belatedly filed claim to it under the Homestead Act at the close of 1884. Immediately afterward the Northern Pacific had swooped down upon his little holding, claiming the farm as part of its indemnity grant—that is, of the lands assigned it as compensation if part of its original land-grant proved unavailable. The railroad officials asserted that they had selected the tract in 1883, more than a year before Miller filed his claim. Cleveland and his Cabinet inquired into the matter. They found that the railroad had indeed been granted a large indemnity area in 1872. "In 1880," as Cleveland later wrote, "upon the filing of a map of definite location of the road, the land in controversy, and much more which had been so withdrawn, was found to lie outside of the limits which included the granted land, but its withdrawal and reservation from settlement and entry under our land laws was continued upon the theory that it was within the limits of indemnity lands which might be selected by the company as provided in the law making the grant." The question was whether this continued withdrawal had been legal.

Attorney-General Garland, with his unfailing instinct for the wrong side of questions, declared that the withdrawal and reservation were at all times effectual, and operated to prevent Miller from acquiring any right to the land. Lamar leaned to the same view. But Cleveland, in

[1] A full history of this is given in the *Democratic Campaign Textbook*, 1888, 215 ff.

his sternly vigorous letter, ordered Lamar to take the position that all such lands belonged to the government and that the railroads must surrender them. He called for justice to this unprotected settler and wrote in condemnatory terms of Garland's view: [1]

With this interpretation of the law and the former orders and actions of the Interior Department it will be seen that their effect has been the withdrawal and reservation since 1872 of hundreds of thousands if not millions of acres of these lands from the operation of the land laws of the United States, thus placing them beyond the reach of our citizens desiring under such laws to settle and make homes upon the same, and that this has been done for the benefit of a railroad company having no fixed, certain, or definite interest in such lands. . . .

There seems to be no evidence showing how much, if any, of this vast tract is necessary for the fulfillment of the grant to the railroad company, nor does there appear to be any limitation of the time within which this fact should be made known and the corporation obliged to make its selection. After a lapse of seventeen years this large body of the public domain is still held in reserve to the exclusion of settlers, for the convenience of a corporate beneficiary of the government.

Such a condition of the public land should no longer continue. So far as it is the result of executive rules and methods these should be abandoned, and so far as it is a consequence of improvident laws these should be repealed or amended.

This letter, which contained many additional admonitions upon the necessity for a careful guardianship of the national domain, was regarded as a rebuke to Garland and in lesser degree to Lamar. It had the effect of an executive order, and not only safeguarded thousands of poor settlers whose position had been precarious, but laid the foundation for action which took great areas of indemnity land away from the railroads and restored them to settlement. Nothing in the first Administration was more creditable than Cleveland's jealous regard for Federal property and settlers' rights in the West. The landgrant railroads, the cattle kings, the land syndicates, and the lumbermen completely controlled the action of the Senate; they had shrewd advocates in the House; and Garland inclined toward them in the Cabinet. They possessed a well-armed lobby and could employ the sharpest lawyers of the country. Yet the Administration again and again dealt them staggering blows. Lamar was so slow and cautious that Commissioner

[1] Cleveland Papers.

Sparks quarreled with him on a point of law in 1887 and resigned, but his aims were sound. Cleveland at the close of his term confessed to "special gratification" that since he had entered office, the railroad and wagon-road corporations had been compelled to disgorge 81,000,000 acres granted them under stipulations which they had not met, and that all this land had become subject to homesteading. He had reason to hope that another 65,000,000 acres would, as the Interior Department had recommended, soon also be forfeited. This was not precisely conservation in the modern sense, but it was a good substitute.

Lamar was succeeded at the Interior Department in 1887 by Vilas —the Postmaster-Generalship falling to Don M. Dickinson of Michigan, whom Cleveland once called "the most unselfish friend I ever had"; and thereafter more vigilance than ever was shown in dealing with the public domain.

VI

But the nearer West received no such benefits at Cleveland's hands. For the discontented agrarian interest between the Wabash and the Platte, the grain-growing farmers who intermittently hummed like a hive of angry bees, the Administration did little. Probably at this stage in our political and economic development little could have been accomplished by even the most alert statesmen, but it is to be wished that Cleveland and his Cabinet had devoted more thought to the problems involved. One reason why they did not lay in the temporary subsidence of rural agitation in the middle eighties. During the seventies the granger movement had risen to its height; the overtaxed, overmortgaged, overworked, and ill-paid farmers had captured many Western legislatures and enforced their demands for a squarer deal. The first victories in the long battle for the governmental control of corporate greed were registered in statutes written by agrarian blocs in the Middle West.[1] But in the decade from 1877 to 1887 the farmers held a position of comparative security, and the discontent ebbed. It never really died out and in some localities remained fierce and angry, but its militant edge was dulled. The grange declined in numbers and vigor, and following the heavy vote by the Greenback-Labor party in 1878, nearly all the farmers gradually returned to the old parties. The sum-

[1] Cf. Nevins, *Emergence of Modern America*, 154 ff.

mer of 1887 was the first of the series of terrible drought years which gradually made western Kansas and Nebraska a land of desolation,[1] and it marked the beginning of a new and stronger agitation. This year, for the first time, the Farmers' Alliances and the Agricultural Wheel attained national strength.[2]

One urgent and definite demand of the farmers was answered in 1886 —that for a Federal tax upon oleomargarine. Within a decade a gigantic traffic in artificial butter had grown up. It was said that oleomargarine could be made for seven or eight cents a pound; that the average value of the fifteen million cows in the United States had declined from $40 to $30; that more than four million Americans engaged in the cattle or dairy business had been injured by this unfair competition; and that State legislatures had been unable to cope with the evil. A bill passed both Houses to tax oleomargarine two cents a pound, and to regulate its manufacture and sale. Cleveland hesitated over it as an improper interference with private enterprise, and signed it with reluctance— but he signed it.[3]

Meanwhile, the movement for a national Department of Agriculture forced itself upon his attention. Since 1862 there had been a so-called department, but it was essentially a bureau, headed only by a commissioner and restricted in its activities. Representative Hatch of Missouri had for some time been pressing a bill to create a department of Cabinet rank, and pointing in justification to the vast extent and complexity of the farming interests. The measure found its most stubborn opponents among conservative Republicans. Senator O. H. Platt of Connecticut, for example, argued against it as a piece of dangerous class legislation, asking why the farmer should be given this special position, and not the manufacturer, the merchant, or the laborer. Chandler of New Hampshire opposed it on constitutional grounds. The older departments, he pointed out, all represented interests connected with the political affairs of the nation, but agriculture was an economic interest; once open the door in this way, and there was no telling how wide it might swing.[4]

In this discussion Cleveland during 1886 took a keen interest. Early

[1] J. D. Hicks, *Populist Revolt*, 30 ff.
[2] Solon J. Buck, *Agrarian Crusade*, 116 ff.
[3] August 2, 1886, *Messages and Papers*, VIII, 407 ff.
[4] H. B. Learned, *The President's Cabinet*, 335 ff.

the next year he asked for Cabinet advice, and several members presented written memoranda, both Garland and Whitney believing that the Hatch bill ought to be vetoed. They took a narrowly legalistic view of the subject. "There is no express authority in the Constitution for the creation of the office or the department," wrote Garland, "and it is impossible to find any such authority by a just and proper inference or implication from any language used in, or any power conferred by, the Constitution." Besides, he argued, there was no need for such a department. What work could it do? "The Cabinet is in session, and after the usual call upon the officials for anything they wish to submit, the President says: 'Mr. Colman, have you anything to submit?' Mr. Colman: 'Yes, sir, I have quite a number of letters discussing the question whether it is best to plant potatoes in the dark or the light of the moon, and many inquiries as to whether the black land is better for cotton than the red sandy soil, and whether the Southdown sheep is adapted down South or up North, etc.' These now are about fair samples of the matters that would come before the Cabinet from that department. Now, what on earth has the government to do with these?" [1]

Fortunately, Cleveland took a different view. In his annual message for 1888 he devoted fully five hundred words to the admirable work of the old department, and commended the movement to develop it.[2] When the Hatch bill reached him in February, 1889, he immediately signed it and nominated Colman as the first Secretary of Agriculture.

But Cleveland failed, as indeed nearly everyone else did, to seek for an answer to the very problems that meant life and death to the farmer. The most important of these problems, the disposal of surplus production, has never yet been solved. But one great difficulty of the day, the lack of farm credit on easy terms, might at least have been approached and studied by the government. The crushing burden of mortgage debt at ten or even fifteen per cent then borne by Southern and Western agriculture, with high renewal-charges, was nothing less than a national outrage. In Europe there existed various credit institutions, such as the Landschaften of Germany, the Raiffeisen banks of that country, with their counterparts in Scandinavia and elsewhere, and the Lands Improvement Company of England, which might have given Americans

[1] Garland to Cleveland, March (no day), 1887. Cleveland Papers.
[2] Richardson, *Messages and Papers,* VIII, 798, 799.

some useful ideas. One of the principal Populist demands of the next few years was for some plan by which the Federal Treasury might loan money on land or crops at low interest rates. C. W. Macune of Texas originated a plan for loans on warehouse receipts which, much ridiculed in his own day, was in essence not greatly different from the Warehouse law enacted in 1916 by Congress.[1] It would have been a happy stroke if Cleveland had at least proposed an investigation of this subject by a Congressional committee or an executive commission.

The subject was the more important because it already involved a serious resentment on the part of the debtor West toward the creditor interests of the East. There was not a single State of the Middle West or South which was not to some extent under mortgage to New England and the Middle Atlantic States. In Kansas it was estimated in 1888 that half the entire wealth of the State was tied up in debts to the industrial centres of the seaboard. Even the older States of the Mississippi Valley, such as Ohio, Illinois, Minnesota, Michigan, and Indiana, found that from one-half to three-fourths of their railroad properties were owned by Eastern investors. The insurance companies of Hartford were said to hold $70,000,000 in Western farm mortgages, the loan companies of Boston $76,000,000, and even the investors of the little State of New Hampshire some $35,000,000. Senator Saulsbury of Delaware, in a speech on the subject, quoted a declaration that "if the whole debt claim of the industrial States on the farms and railroads of the agricultural States could be ascertained, it would probably be not less than three billions, bearing an annual interest of $180,000,000." This burden was felt the more keenly because both the financial and tariff policy of the government had been so shaped as to favor the East.

Moreover, the West suffered with special severity from the current credit stringency and the shrinkage in national banknotes; for the amount of such banknotes in circulation fell from $344,500,000 in 1880 to $318,600,000 in 1885, and to $186,000,000 in 1890. The national banking law required so high a capitalization for banks that rural communities were poorly served. Yet even the soberest economists of those days heaped a shortsighted derision upon all suggestions for a Federal system of farm credits. Western resentments might have been mollified by a little attention to the subject.

[1] J. D. Hicks, *Populist Revolt*, 188 ff.

VII

One token of the changing times was the steady passage of the older generation of leaders—the Civil War and post-war generation—from the national stage. Late in 1886 occurred the deaths of Charles Francis Adams and Chester A. Arthur, both evoking a tribute of nation-wide respect. The homage paid the former was not surprising, for everyone remembered how in the bitterest days of the war, as minister in London, he had shown the unfriendly British leaders a temper more dogged, independent, and dauntless than their own, and inch by inch had forced them to recede. But Arthur was a man of different type. This machine leader, this Prince Hal of politics, so long regarded with contempt, had filled the great office to which he was unexpectedly called with a surprising discretion. Men now remembered how quickly he had demonstrated his gentle breeding and how firmly he had wielded his authority. The most caustic of American editors wrote that his Administration was "certainly above the average that the country has known since that of Lincoln, and not inferior to any." In the spring of 1887 it was a preacher-statesman who died. Cleveland on March 8 was telegraphing Mrs. Beecher: [1] "Accept my heartfelt sympathy in this hour of your bereavement, with the hope that comfort may be vouchsafed from the heavenly source you know so well." He had a special interest in this dramatic life, so entangled with American history, so closely associated with great currents of opinion and emotion, its dark chapter of scandal still a subject for debate, but its balance for good so unquestionable. He could not forget how manfully Beecher had campaigned for him in 1884, "not because I am a Democrat, but because I am a Republican."

But the most striking of these events was the long-expected death of Samuel J. Tilden. His funeral in August, 1886, was everywhere regarded as marking the end of an era in the history of the Democratic Party, and it left Cleveland more nearly isolated than ever as a leader. The President went to Greystone for the ceremony. In the spacious "blue room" on the first floor Tilden's body lay on a catafalque in full dress, with a white pink in the buttonhole, the fine features only slightly emaciated. A large and distinguished gathering, including Dana,

[1] N. Y. *Herald*, March 9, 1887.

Randall, Bigelow, Hewitt, and Hill, gazed with emotion on the only really great Democratic leader between Jackson and their own day. Cleveland, lingering in the reception room to talk of Tilden's career, was one of the last to leave the house.

The President was left for the moment in lonely eminence in his party. Tilden was dead, Thurman was retired by age, Randall ill, Manning stricken, younger men like George Gray, who had succeeded to Bayard's seat in the Senate, were still unproved, and Hill was shadowed and pursued by his sinister reputation. Cleveland was the undisputed leader. The leadership he furnished was as yet neither dynamic nor far-sighted; but it was sound, and it fitted that rather curious decade, the eighties.

Interposed between the hungry seventies and the stormy nineties, two periods which witnessed terrible panics and ensuing depressions, the eighties were by comparison a quiet, unambitious, and almost complacent decade. Any national Administration was bound to partake of their temper. Cleveland's conception of his duties also fitted the constitutional ideas then held by a majority of men in both parties—cautious ideas which were well described at precisely this time by James Bryce. Richard Olney years later declared that the President's concepts of government had been clear and simple; that he had believed that Congress, the Judiciary, and the Executive should stick to the written definitions of their powers; that "the comparatively modern doctrine that the Constitution is an organic growth, naturally and inevitably evolving not merely constitutional provisions but vital changes in the provisions themselves, he would have felt unable to understand;" and that the proposition that the national government needs greatly increased power, which must be got through executive action as well as by legislation, "would have struck him as treachery to the people." Certainly he had not believed in aggressive presidential policies. His conceptions, finally, were suited to the peculiar position of the Democratic party at this time. Recalled to power after twenty-five years, it was regarded nervously by large economic and social groups, and a policy of experiment and innovation would have increased these apprehensions. Nevertheless, in his slow way Cleveland was groping toward a firmer exercise of his initiative in legislation and his influence over public opinion. The year 1887 was to bring a bold display of leadership.

As THE year 1887 arrived, both parties turned their attention to the presidential contest near at hand. The Republican politicians were frankly pessimistic. They knew that by virtue of his record Cleveland deserved reëlection, and they were not sure of their own leader. Blaine had gone to Europe, and reports drifted back that his health was bad. Moreover, the party had no issue upon which to fight. The Southern question was barren; the country was prosperous; the currency issue was too dangerous to touch. The Democrats, on the other hand, were confident, though a singular amount of ill-temper was mingled with their complacency. Most of the party leaders disliked the President because he was unmanageable, stubborn, and plainspoken, and because he continued to withhold patronage from the politicians who wanted it most. But they knew that they could win with him and with nobody else. Moreover, they could not help taking pride in the grudging admission by Republicans and the frank boasting by Independents that he was making an excellent President. On May 11, 1887, the Federal Club in New York gave a banquet at Delmonico's to Roosevelt, the speakers including Lodge, Depew, and Choate. When Roosevelt in the course of his address said: "I come now to Mr. Cleveland's Administration. I give him the credit for all the good he has done," there was an unexpected burst of applause. George W. Curtis repeatedly said in *Harper's Weekly* that he was both better than his party and stronger than his party.

The Republicans tried to make the most of Cleveland's few errors in dealing with Federal appointments, but they knew that this was futile. They attacked him on the score of inconsistency—for vetoing a petty seed bill while signing a rivers and harbors bill full of jobbery; they accused him of wasting his time on petty details. Efforts were made to prove that Cleveland was indifferent to the West, and that he never really tried to acquaint himself with its people, resources, or views. Yet all this produced little impression. It was clear that if the Democrats walked carefully and avoided offending important sectional or economic interests, their victory was assured. They needed only to continue Cleveland's work of departmental reform and play safe. But party safety was never uppermost in the President's mind. Before 1887 ended, despite the imploring appeal of half the party leaders, he had precipitated the most contentious of issues and offended the most powerful of American economic interests.

II

Congress adjourned on March 3, 1887, with much done, but with its most important responsibility completely untouched—the problem of the national surplus. The steadily increasing income of the government, far in excess of its needs, was becoming a grim menace to national health. Enormous sums were being withdrawn from general circulation and locked up in the Treasury in a way certain to disturb business, while simultaneously offering a constant temptation to extravagance on the part of Congress. To avoid direct contraction the government had increased its purchases of outstanding bonds. In the fiscal year 1886 it had bought $50,000,000 worth; in 1887 $125,000,000 worth. But this was a temporary expedient.

In his annual message at the close of 1886 Cleveland had called emphatic attention to the predicament.[1] With receipts of $336,000,000, and expenditures of $242,000,000, the surplus for the fiscal year just closed was very nearly $94,000,000. The application of the government's growing accumulation of gold to the purchase of such bonds as might be called at par would retire that class of Federal indebtedness within a year. What then? The nation must either consent to allow a large part of the circulating medium of the people to be "hoarded in the Treasury when it should be in their hands," or it would be drawn into lavish expenditures, "with all the corrupting national demoralization which follows in its train." The tariff had furnished the principal part of the revenues, and it must continue to do so; but a careful revision of the tariff downward was needed immediately. So Cleveland had written, calling attention to the fact that duties were still on the average but little lower than during the war, and on some articles were far higher. Early in 1887 he had talked with party leaders on the advisability of a special message on the tariff and the revenues, and several, including Henry Gassaway Davis, had urged him to write one.[2]

---

[1] Richardson, *Messages and Papers*, VIII, 507.
[2] Charles M. Pepper, *Henry Gassaway Davis*, 142.

Secretary Manning had simultaneously called attention to the surplus in still sharper terms and with more radical recommendations. His last annual report—for he finally resigned in February, 1887—was written with the same fire that had characterized all his previous productions and the same unflinching positiveness of opinion. He stated the plain facts about the surplus revenue. There were two ways, he declared, of dealing with it. Congress might and should attack the tariff, which he characterized as an "incompetent and brutal scheme of revenue;" but if it would not do this, he offered an alternative. Let Congress employ the surplus in retiring the whole volume of greenbacks, amounting to $346,681,000. No such proposal had been made by a head of the Treasury since Secretary McCulloch had brought it forward just after the war and Congress after a brief trial had rejected it. The primary reason for its rejection at that time was that it involved a contraction of the currency. But Secretary Manning's plan contemplated no such reduction. For every greenback dollar cancelled, he proposed to pay out a new gold or silver dollar, keeping the volume of the currency exactly what it had been. At the rate of a hundred million a year, it would take three and a half years to dispose of the greenbacks by means of the surplus.

This was not only a bold but a feasible and sagacious plan, the one valid objection being that its adoption would lessen the demand for tariff reduction. But the greenbacks were more than money: to millions ever since Peter Cooper's day they had been a great symbol. The West in particular regarded them as the money of the people, "the best currency ever devised," and the proposal to give them up met with indignant derision. Abram S. Hewitt suggested another safety valve for the overflowing Treasury. He introduced a bill permitting the Secretary of the Treasury to anticipate as much of the interest on the bonds of the United States as might be in excess of three per cent annually; that is, to make advance payments to the holders of the four and four and a half per cent bonds.[1] William L. Scott had still another bill, which the New York *Herald* called "a cry of despair"—it simply authorized the President to loan the surplus to the banks.[2] All these proposals met a stony hostility from the short session of Congress. As they failed, the gravity of the approaching crisis grew plainer. When the remaining

[1] N. Y. *Evening Post,* Dec. 14, 1886.
[2] N. Y. *Herald,* Jan. 1, 1887.

callable bonds, the three per cents, were all bought in, there would en-
sue an interval of three and a half years before the four and a half per
cents became callable. The surplus meanwhile could not be allowed to
pile up in a golden heap. Business needed it. To be sure, bonds might
be bought in the open market. But this meant paying a high premium;
meant, in other words, transferring the dollars taken by unjust tariffs
from the farmer and workman to the coffers of the investing classes.

III

The inevitable result of the discussion, all over the country, was to give
edge to the demand for lowering the tariff. Even after the second failure
of the Morrison bill a constant agitation for tariff reform ran through
Congress. As summer came on party conventions began to be held. On
May 4 the Kentucky Democrats at Louisville denounced the tariff as
"a masterpiece of injustice, inequality, and false pretense." They spoke
not only for Watterson and Carlisle, but for the plain Kentuckians.
On July 21 the Ohio Democratic Convention declared for a tariff which
should produce "a revenue sufficient only to meet the expenses of an
economical administration of the government, and the payment of liberal pensions to Union soldiers and sailors, and the payment of the
interest and principle of the public debt." Other Western States took
similar action,[1] and on the prairies the Republicans stood side by side
with the Democrats. By the middle of July the Republican convention
in Minnesota had called for "a simplification and reduction of the customs revenues;" that in Iowa had asserted that "the tariff should be
revised and reduced;" and that in Nebraska had stated that "the business of the country now demands a revision of the tariff."[2] The Iowa
Democrats used particularly vigorous language in condemning the al-
ternatives: [3]

We call upon Congress for the immediate revision of our tariff laws to a
revenue basis to the end that every industry and every section may enjoy
perfect equality under the law, and we favor the retention of the internal
revenue tax on intoxicating liquors and tobacco, and protest against its proposed reduction for the purpose of continuing the present high tariff on the
necessaries of life.

[1] See N. Y. *Herald*, July 21, 1887, for summary.
[2] *Harper's Weekly*, July 14, 1888.
[3] N. Y. *Herald*, Sept. 21, 1887.

The mounting agitation against the tariff had at last reached even Pennsylvania. Here the Democratic State convention had been called in Allentown for the closing days of August. In every part of the country eyes were fastened upon it, and the New York press published long stories of the preliminary manoeuvrings. Would it endorse Cleveland's policy, or would it pass the customary protectionist resolution for abolition of the internal revenue taxes? Randall embattled all his forces, including delegates drawn from among the employees at the mint, the internal revenue office, and the Philadelphia custom house; for in 1885 a great deal of Federal patronage had been placed at his disposal. But feeling ran high against him not only on account of the Morrison bill, but because he had attacked Cleveland's civil service policy and had voted to override the veto of the Dependent Pensions bill. On Cleveland's side Representative Scott and William M. Singerly had made every effort to obtain delegates. With the President's approval, Singerly had sown broadcast a circular quoting Cleveland's recommendation that the tariff be reduced on necessaries and on raw materials needed in manufacturing, and at the same time had filled his newspaper, the Philadelphia *Record*, with arguments. Cleveland himself took a hand by sending a letter to the superintendent of the mint ordering that no employees should participate in political affairs.[1]

The convention ended in a compromise, but a compromise which came close to defeat for Randall. The redoubtable ex-Speaker appeared at noon on the 30th with his own platform; that evening Scott and a group of reformers arrived with another platform. On the 31st Randall was forced to agree to sweeping concessions. The plank as adopted declared for immediate extinction of the surplus by "a wise and prudent reduction of internal taxation *and of duties on imports.*" This last demand, said the New York *Times*, was one "which has not been made in any Pennsylvania platform since Randall became a power." The convention gave a strong endorsement to the Administration.[2]

IV

By the end of July, Cleveland had made up his mind that a bold blow must be struck for tariff reduction, and before the close of August he was in correspondence with his friends on the subject. His first im-

[1] N. Y. *Times*, Sept. 13, 1887 (editorial).
[2] N. Y. *Herald, Times*, Aug. 30–Sept. 2, 1887.

portant step was to call a meeting of leaders at Oak View—the famous "Oak View Conferences." Speaker Carlisle and his wife were the President's guests for four days. While they remained, on September 5 Fairchild, who was summoned to Washington by telegraph, Mills, and William L. Scott all came out. Carlisle and Cleveland had already discussed the question whether the emergency demanded a special session, and as Carlisle opposed it, had decided in the negative. On this very day Cleveland told a *World* correspondent that he wished for public opinion to ripen: [1]

I gave the subject the most careful study and consideration. There was much to be said on both sides, but after considering the matter carefully in all its bearings, I decided that an extra session was not imperatively demanded. The convening of Congress in extra term has often failed to realize the anticipations of good to proceed from it. But in this particular exigency I should have called the extra session if at any time the needs of the country seemed to demand it. The expedient we adopted of disposing of that part of the surplus, the retention of which from the channels of trade might have proven too great a strain upon the country, by calling the bonds, ought to subserve what is imperatively required. It appeared more to the public interest that the members of the new Congress should spend the usual recess among their constituents, and learn there by as long and intimate communion as possible just what the people required of them.

On September 6 and 7 Cleveland, Carlisle, Fairchild, Scott and Mills continued their discussions at Oak View. Randall had come to Washington, ostensibly to put his boy in school, but Cleveland coldly ignored him. His visit gave rise to insistent press rumors that a tariff compromise was being mooted—rumors which produced an explosion of wrath in Watterson's *Courier-Journal*, the Charleston *News and Courier*, and other papers.[2] Such reports were wide of the mark; Cleveland was ready to present Randall not with concessions, but with an ultimatum. The Oak View conferrees decided that tariff reductions were imperative, that all the loyal party leaders should be so informed, and that Carlisle and Mills should begin work on a bill, Fairchild advising them as to its financial effects.[3] A circular describing the emergency was prepared for Democratic Congressmen, and Carlisle began mailing copies to trustworthy men. Cleveland remained intensely anxious. He feared

[1] N. Y. *World*, Sept. 7, 1887. Interview with Ballard Smith.
[2] See Washington dispatches, N. Y. *Times*, Sept. 8, 9, 10; N. Y. *Tribune*, Sept. 10, 1887.
[3] Cleveland Papers, September, October, 1887.

that in view of the heavy autumn demands for money to assist crop movements, the locking up of the surplus might produce a disastrous squeeze and a panic. After Carlisle left he wrote him again about a special session, asking how many days members of Congress would require, in an emergency, to reach Washington. Carlisle replied that ten or fifteen should suffice, but that he still believed a special session inadvisable. "By the time of your return from your Western tour, the results of the Treasury policy will be so fully developed that the question of calling Congress together will be more easily solved than it is now."[1]

The Oak View conferences not only attracted national attention; they sent a thrill of expectation throughout the party. At last a vigorous Presidential leadership was emerging. From sources close to Carlisle came the statement that Cleveland and he had agreed upon stern measures to compel a unified front in Congress. The New York *Herald* published an editorial entitled, "Will Mr. Cleveland Take His Place at the Head of His Party?" Referring to his unfortunate decision of January, 1886, it remarked that his restricted idea of the functions of the Executive—the idea that he was not to be the head of his party or give leadership to Congress—had "engendered a painful lukewarmness where only enthusiastic cooperation should exist," but that Cleveland was now showing his statesmanship:

> The conference which he has invited marks an era in his Administration. It will create a better feeling everywhere, and prepare the party for an attack upon some important problems during the next session of Congress. If he is successful in his present plan the Democrats will have a thoroughly live issue to go to the country with next year, and one which will compare so favorably with the petty sectional hatred and the wretched and disgusting three-palsy business of the Republicans that they will present an invincible front. What the people want is big ideas . . . and the party which sees the whole continent and fits its policy to the magnificence of the opportunity is the only party worthy of the times in which we now live.

While Cleveland was absent on his Western trip, the tariff was being warmly discussed in several State campaigns, most notably in New York. The Democrats carried the State by pluralities of from 13,000 to 17,000, and interpreted their success as a low tariff victory. On his return the President found that Secretary Fairchild's measures had ren-

---

[1] Carlisle to Cleveland, Wichita, Sept. 30, 1887. Cleveland Papers.

.

dered an emergency session of Congress unnecessary. He also found that the debate on the surplus continued to hold public attention. A hundred leaders offered as many different views. Carlisle was telling reporters that the tariff must be carefully reduced, wool and other raw materials placed on the free list, and the taxes on tobacco be repealed. Randall proposed to abolish almost the whole internal revenue system. At a bankers' convention in Pittsburgh John Jay Knox, long comptroller of the currency, explained a plan for refunding all the outstanding bonds into new securities paying two and a half per cent interest, the holders to be compensated by a cash premium. Senator Evarts asserted that the surplus taxation was only a flea-bite, not felt by the prosperous American people; that the existing tariffs and internal taxes ought to be maintained, and the excess revenue spent on pensions, coast defence, internal improvements, and public buildings.[1] John Sherman, who had outlined his remedy for the swollen treasury in a Lincoln Day statement,[2] was repeating his prescription. He believed that the tariff required some use of the knife; the duties on sugar should be cut down, while all rates on tropical products and exotic luxuries might be reduced or abolished. But above all, the government should enter upon a course of free spending. It should establish a system of coast defences; strengthen the navy, subsidize the mercantile marine; assist in the construction of an Isthmian canal; and "give assistance and encouragement to all American republics founded upon our example"—whatever that meant. Senator Voorhees gave general approval to this program.[3]

But Cleveland had already made up his mind that the one statesmanlike policy to be followed lay in a frontal attack upon the tariff, and the tariff alone. He intended it to be an attack of the most determined and uncompromising character. Before he left for the West, he had taken shrewd steps to find out just what course Randall meant to follow. Appealing to Representative Scott, he asked him to sound out the stubborn Philadelphian, and the two men met at the Fifth Avenue Hotel in New York. Scott's report, after an hour's talk, showed that Randall would consent to nothing:[4]

So far as his professions for the Administration go, no one could speak more favorably of it. He is, however, thoroughly impressed with the idea

[1] See a summary of proposals in N. Y. *Herald,* Oct. 18, 1887.
[2] Published in N. Y. papers, Feb. 13, 1887.
[3] Interview in N. Y. *Herald,* Nov. 11, 1887.
[4] Scott to Cleveland, Erie, Pa., Sept. 16, 1887. Cleveland Papers.

that he is the master of the situation; that he can carry through the House his ideas of revenue reform, and he stated to me that he knew that he could accomplish this, for he had Virginia, North Carolina, Kentucky, and Tennessee with him. I did not dispute this fact with him, but when we came to discuss the policy of the future with him and I urged upon him harmony and united action of the party as an absolute necessity and endeavored to arrive at what his views were, I soon discovered that his plans were by no means matured. When I put it up to him that the question was one of the reduction of the surplus revenues and not of protection or free trade, and asked him if he proposed to take the internal tax off of whiskey and beer and leave the duties on the necessities of life, he immediately replied that more revenue could be obtained on whiskey at 40 or 50 cents than at the present tax of 90 cents, evidently proving to my mind that he had abandoned the idea of abolishing internal revenue, and that his scheme will be to take off all the tax on tobacco and reduce the tax on whiskey and beer and thereby accomplish a reduction of about sixty millions in revenue, hoping thereby to catch not merely the tobacco men of the South, but the moonshiners of North Carolina and eastern Tennessee, and by such a policy to escape the hue and cry that would be raised against him should he favor free whiskey. When I spoke to him about sugar and wool and salt, he virtually said he was opposed to any reduction of the present duties on imports. . . . The impression created on my mind, growing out of this interview, is that today Mr. Randall feels very confident of his position and believes in his ability to defeat any programme which our party may bring forward in connection with revenue reform. I have no doubt that he has had assurances from Virginia and North Carolina that make him more confident than he would otherwise be.

Scott suggested a flank attack upon Randall's border-State supporters, using men like Vance of North Carolina and John S. Barbour of Virginia to convert them. But flank attacks made no appeal to Cleveland's blunt mind. Secretary Fairchild had furnished him with facts that were too menacing for evasion. All the three per cent bonds had now been cancelled. The sinking-fund requirements for the current fiscal year had already been met. By December 1, 1887, the Treasury would have a surplus of more than $55,000,000. By the end of the fiscal year this surplus would reach $140,000,000. Under these circumstances, Cleveland resolved to devote his entire annual message to a demand for tariff revision.

As he spent November in writing this message he must have smiled grimly at the last-minute efforts of both protectionists and tariff reformers to exert pressure upon him. From both camps came volleys of letters. Carlisle, Hewitt, and Mills all knew that some sort of onslaught was coming from him, and encouraged his intention. So did Henry Watterson and Frank Hurd. Others were vehement in protest. George Hoadly, formerly Governor of Ohio and now a New York attorney, was invited by Cleveland to come and confer with him upon the message. He declined, but sent a cautionary letter. His advice was "that in the matter of the revision of the tariff, you 'go slow.' Not to be understood, I mean that I think it is a perfectly safe position to stand on before the country, that you seek to reduce the duties on raw materials and to impose duties on luxuries. The danger of alienating large bodies of workingmen, who are thoroughly organized, whose ignorance is crass, and whose employers are extremely jealous of any danger of loss of profits, is to my mind the danger of the situation. You have both the manufacturer and the Knights of Labor to be afraid of." He thought that "you have now the opportunity to make a very great success, but that if the counsels of Henry Watterson and Frank Hurd are fully followed, the success would be converted into a defeat." [1]

Col. A. K. McClure gave similar advice. Cleveland invited him to Washington and he spent the evening of November 23 at the White House, Carlisle also being present. The President gave him a hint of his tariff message, and McClure earnestly appealed to him to change it. It was all true; it stated what the country ought to know; but it would certainly defeat him the next year for reëlection. "I shall never forget the quiet firmness with which he declared that it was a duty he should perform for the nation, and that it must be performed regardless of personal consequences to himself." [2] At the same time the New York *Herald* suddenly veered to the safe side. It published a letter signed "A Democratic Tariff Reformer," who declared that the President should move cautiously and not frighten people; for "if you lose the election next year you will put back tariff reform a dozen years." Watterson, seeing this, replied hotly. The *Herald* thereupon spoke editorially against provoking an immediate tariff battle: [3]

The *Herald* has urged tariff reform as earnestly as the *Courier-Journal*, but this reform has been so long bungled and so often lost by Mr. Watterson's friends in Congress that we would rather have it delayed another year or two than, by an untimely attempt now, to risk next year's election. Will Mr. Watterson answer the following plain questions?

[1] Cleveland Papers.
[2] McClure, *Recollections of Half a Century*, 128; N. Y. *Herald*, Nov. 24, 1887.
[3] N. Y. *Herald*, Nov. 18, 1887.

First—Does he believe it necessary for the country's best welfare that the Democratic party shall stay in power another four years?

Second—Is he certain that the passage or attempt to pass a general tariff reform bill at the coming session will help the party to carry the election next year?

Third—If so, New York and New Jersey being, as we believe, protectionist States, and therefore likely to be lost by attempted tariff legislation at this session, will he name the States formerly Republican which can be carried by the Democrats next year to replace New York and New Jersey?

Fourth—Have the Democratic leaders ever attempted to instruct the people thoroughly in all the States on tariff reform?

Fifth—If not, would it not be wise to do this before proceeding to action, and especially on the eve of a Presidential election, if the Democrats lose which tariff reform and all other reforms will undoubtedly receive a discouraging blow?

But Cleveland—unlike Clay, who flinched in a like juncture in 1844— proved that he would rather be right than be President. He looked one timid adviser in the eye and said: [1] "Do you remember my letter of acceptance? Do you remember that I opposed a second term on the ground that, human nature being what it is, the President would work for his reëlection instead of for the country's good? . . . The fact of my being a candidate does not alter the necessity for the message— rather emphasizes it; and since I would stultify myself by withholding it, the message will certainly be sent in." He told another: "What is the use of being elected or reëlected, unless you stand for something?" [2] It was a thoroughly courageous step. It was not the less courageous because in some tired and discouraged moments he felt that he did not care whether he were reëlected or not. On December 1 he wrote to Bissell: [3]

My message is done. I think it is pretty good but you will be surprised when you see it.

Things are improving here and I think we can get some pretty good legislation.

I want more and more to get out of this thing. When Doyle and Wiley said that Sheehan was about the county trying to get delegates for Hill, I did not feel so bad as they thought I did.

[1] A. B. Farquhar in *Harper's Weekly*, Aug. 1, 1908.
[2] McElroy, I, 271.
[3] Cleveland Papers.

Few of Cleveland's acts have been so famous as this tariff message, and few acts by any President have been so much acclaimed, yet it may be doubted if the precise character of the courage exhibited has been generally understood. This courage did not lie in calling forcible attention to the dangers of the surplus; for no President could have failed in that duty. It did not lie in demanding tariff reduction, or even in devoting the whole message to the need for revision. Where it did lie was in the unflinching attack upon one kind of duties—the duties upon necessities. A less courageous President might well have called attention in equally forcible terms to the emergency; he might well have said with Cleveland that "it is a condition, not a theory, that confronts us;" he might well have devoted his whole message to the problem. But a less courageous President would have compromised at one or both of two points where Cleveland refused to yield an inch.

What were these two points? Cleveland knew that in raising $336,-110,284 by taxation in the fiscal year 1886–87, the government raised roughly $113,000,000 more than it needed. Of the whole government income, the internal revenue taxation furnished $118,823,000; the customs taxes furnished $217,286,893. Here lay the first opportunity for a compromise. Men like Randall said, "Place part of the tax reduction on the internal revenue page of the ledger. Cut down the taxes on whiskey and tobacco." This doctrine was popular with all the whiskey-and-tobacco states from Missouri to Maryland and Virginia. It would have been easy for an amiable President to accept the compromise. Cleveland refused, and demanded that the entire reduction fall upon the tariff.

But in attacking the tariff there was room for another general compromise. Men like Hoadly declared: "Cut down the luxury taxes— raise less money by tariffs on silks, wines, tropical products, and the like; leave the other duties, protecting our factories, where they are." The rates on sugar and molasses alone yielded a revenue of about fifty millions a year, or approximately half of the troublesome surplus. But here again Cleveland's message returned a defiant answer. "The taxation of luxuries presents no features of hardship," [1] he wrote, and he declined to recommend the reduction of a penny upon them. It was the tariff on necessities which he attacked.

[1] Richardson, *Messages and Papers*, VIII, 589.

V

The date on which the message went to Congress was December 6. The next day every important newspaper in the country published it in full, and it was read as no Presidential messages since Lincoln's had been. Cleveland began by a brief exposition of the financial emergency. The surplus had become an acute danger to business health. He explained the impracticability or unwisdom of various expedients proposed to abolish it. The scheme for depositing the surplus in banks throughout the country for general use he pronounced extremely objectionable, as establishing too close a relationship between the Treasury and private business, and fostering an unnatural reliance of the latter upon public funds. He then launched into the heart of his doctrine.

Filling a dozen octavo pages of close print, the message was a sweeping arraignment of a tariff system by which protection had been raised to a ridiculous extreme, continued upon many articles long after it was needed, and used as an excuse for viciously unjust burdens upon the poor. The tariff, as Cleveland pointed out, was precisely the system of taxation under which the ill-paid workingman and hard-pressed farmer bore the heaviest burden. A tariff on necessities, on sugar, coffee, carpets, and clothing, cost them almost as much as it cost the millionaire. He waxed sarcastic in treating the "infant industries." Americans were in the midst of a series of centennial celebrations; they were boasting of their skill, their ingenuity, their rich natural resources; and yet when the tariff was discussed, "it suits the purposes of advocacy to call our manufacturers infant industries still needing the highest and greatest degree of favor and fostering care that can be wrung from Federal legislation." In a slashing passage, he pointed to the tariff as a prolific mother of trusts:

The fact is not overlooked that competition among our domestic producers sometimes has the effect of keeping the price of their products below the highest limit allowed by such duty. But it is notorious that this competition is too often strangled by combinations quite prevalent at this time, and frequently called trusts, which have for their object the regulation of the supply and price of commodities made and sold by members of the combination. The people can hardly hope for any consideration in the operation of these selfish schemes.

The message, marked by a practical tone throughout, was prepared as an argument for the farmer by his fireside and the shopkeeper by his barrel-stove. Cleveland told R. R. Bowker that "they made me leave out a good deal that I had written." [1] He did not use two arguments which Manning had forcibly employed. One was that the United States ought to cast away the swaddling clothes of needless protection in order to enter the world market. Protection, Manning had written, implied that we were children while the European Powers were adults; but everywhere abroad it was believed that when we released ourselves from bad laws and entered competition unmanacled—that is, with free raw materials—we would outdistance all rivals. This was the argument for lower tariffs which McKinley used in the Buffalo speech which closed his career. A still more striking assertion by Manning was that high wages and efficient production go hand in hand: the very argument of a host of economists in Ford's day a generation later. Manning applied it simply and logically to the tariff question, declaring that since high pay meant high production, we need not fear Europe's pauper-labor. [2] But Cleveland, intent upon a simple, forcible message, rightly excluded such ideas.

In one sense the message was not radical, for Cleveland never believed in stringent low-tariff views and hung back from the extreme doctrines of Godkin and Watterson. He again made room for some reassuring words to the workingmen, declaring that the interests of American labor should be carefully considered. But the message was radical in the slashing vigor of its attack upon "our present tariff laws, the vicious, inequitable, and illogical source of unnecessary taxation." It was radical in its denunciation of a type of protection "which, without regard to the public welfare or a national exigency, must always insure the realization of immense profits instead of moderately profitable returns." Above all, it was radical in its complete disregard of anything except the tariff, and of anything but the necessaries of life within the tariff.

In confining his annual message to this one subject, and thus departing from immemorial usage, Cleveland displayed again the hard practical sense which served him so much better than brilliancy or profundity. If he had made his tariff doctrine merely one section of a varie-

[1] R. R. Bowker to author, June 29, 1931.
[2] *Annual Report*, 1886, li, lii.

gated paper, it would quickly have been forgotten. By presenting it without entanglements, he made it seem the only important topic of national concern. Everyone was talking of it. It cleared the atmosphere. Even those who assailed the President's views confessed admiration for his method. "A thousand thanks to President Cleveland for the bold, manly, and unequivocal avowal of his extreme free trade purposes!" exclaimed the Philadelphia *Press*. "We do not approve the President's recommendations," said the Boston *Journal*, "but we may frankly say that we like the tone of his message." The New York *Commercial Advertiser* remarked that the "concise, able, and manfully candid message will have a decisive weight in the future of parties and of legislation."

The reformers everywhere were jubilant. All the low-tariff organs applauded enthusiastically. Carl Schurz forcibly expressed his delight. Melville W. Fuller telegraphed from Chicago, "My gratification is intense." R. R. Bowker wrote that "It clears the air like a thunderstorm on a sultry day." [1] That fine-spirited Southern liberal, Dr. J. L. M. Curry, asserted: "It has the ring of the good old Democratic days of the republic; it reminds me of the utterances of Polk, Wright, and Woodbury. I should like to make one hundred speeches in the Presidential campaign with that message as the platform." [2] The readiness of the Independents to rally again to Cleveland's side was at once made clear. James Russell Lowell shortly seized upon a meeting of the New York Reform Club to declare himself on the President's side. The country, he said, was face to face with the question whether it wished to endure the swollen war tariff forever, or would adopt a revenue system harmonizing with the new era which had dawned. The simple and powerful way in which the issue had been brought before the nation illustrated the old truth "that it is a duty of statesmen to study tendencies and probable consequences rather than figures, which can as easily be induced to fight on both sides as the condottieri of four centuries ago." [3]

The praise was deserved, and the verdict of history must be that Cleveland was at fault in only one respect. His message should have come earlier. It was belated by six months or a year. George Hoadly

---

[1] Dec. 6, 7, 1887. Cleveland Papers.
[2] Dec. 19, 1887. Cleveland Papers.
[3] N. Y. *Times*, April 14, 1888.

was right when, in pledging his support to Cleveland, he wrote him that the whole subject should have been dealt with before.[1] "It takes time for our countrymen to recover from a blow and the danger is that thousands of them will be swept off their intellectual bearings for a period long enough to endanger the results of the next Presidential election." The ground should have been prepared in 1886, and the blow struck at the end of that year or the beginning of 1887. But apart from this, the message was a magnificent act of statesmanship, magnificently executed.

[1] Dec. 8. Cleveland Papers.

THE two parties, like armies, had been manoeuvring for position—scouting, deploying, and bringing up their column in confusion. Cleveland's message of December, 1887, was like the sudden echoing boom of a great cannon signalling the commencement of a decisive battle on unexpected ground. The lines stiffened, took fixed position, and fell into fighting array. A fire of musketry ran down the opposing ranks, and the contest had begun.

The most prominent and impetuous of the Republican leaders at once caught up the President's challenge, and discharged the first salvo in answer. James G. Blaine was in Paris; a *Tribune* correspondent quickly saw him; and on December 8 an interview was telegraphed throughout the nation. It was accepted everywhere as a proclamation that Blaine considered himself the brevet champion of protection, and as such would enter the Presidential lists. Sherman and Evarts were momentarily silent, but the plumed knight did not need to hesitate for arguments. His statement had characteristic adroitness, and all his peculiar intellectual qualities appeared in its first lines:

I have been reading an abstract of the President's message and have been especially interested in the comments of the English papers. These papers all assume to declare that the message is a free trade manifesto, and evidently are anticipating an enlarged market for English fabrics in the United States as a consequence of the President's recommendations. Perhaps that fact stamped the character of the message more clearly than any words of mine can.

Blaine went on to explain that he would keep the tariff high; that he would repeal the internal revenue tax on tobacco at once, before Christmas, thus giving millions of Americans their cigars and plugs at lower cost while foreigners continued to contribute to our revenue; and that he would use the whiskey taxes, which he would maintain, to fortify the Atlantic cities as Samuel J. Tilden had proposed in his letter to the Democrats in 1885. In twenty lines he managed to appeal to high protectionists, lovers of cheap tobacco, haters of England, temperance advocates, coast-defence enthusiasts, and those who thought that Cleveland was a poor Democrat compared with Tilden. His interview was a masterpiece and the protectionist press made the most of every point. A new hopefulness and energy instantly diffused itself throughout most of the Republican party.

Yet it immediately became evident that a grave division of opinion on the tariff ran through both parties, and that each would have to whip stubborn minorities into line. On the Republican side, while monitory growls came from Knute Nelson and other Minnesota Congressmen, the Northwestern press rose in opposition to Blaine. Many newspapers praised Cleveland's message and attacked the Paris interview. The Chicago *Tribune* declared emphatically that the Western farmers paid dearly for the tariff; that Blaine was unwilling to give the poor man cheaper clothing, cheaper lumber for his house, or cheaper tableware, but would allow him a cheaper "chaw" of tobacco. The stand of this powerful journal worried Blaine's friends, and Joseph Manley threatened that if it really bolted from Blaine there would be an opposition paper in Chicago within sixty days. "Bring on your bears, Joe," answered the editor, "but don't bluff on a pair of deuces," and added: "The last national Republican platform pledged the party 'to correct the inequalities of the tariff and to reduce the surplus,' and that pledge cannot be violated without disloyalty to Republicanism. The monopoly trusts and rings which have combined to capture the Republican party have undertaken a bigger contract than they can reasonably hope to carry out." [1] Newspapers like the New York *Commercial Advertiser* and men like Don Cameron warned the party that an extreme protectionist stand would be unstatesmanlike and untenable.[2]

In the Democratic ranks the unchastened Randall lifted a banner, not of revolt, but of dissent. He had carried to Washington, at the time he was so conspicuously not invited to the Oak View conference, a belief that there might be a party compromise on the tariff; and now he indicated that he meant to fight for one. Questioned on December 6 by the Washington correspondent of the *Herald*, he predicted that the new session would reduce the revenues by $60,000,000 or more, but not just as Cleveland had proposed.[3] "A large part of the reduction will be in the repeal of internal taxes, which the President does not seem to favor—

[1] Chicago *Tribune*, Dec. 11, 12, 1887.
[2] Philadelphia *Times*, Dec. 27, 1887.
[3] N. Y. *Herald*, Dec. 7, 1887.

and a large reduction will also be made in the rate of duty on imports." He believed that the House would cut off the taxes on tobacco, on fruit distillates, and on licenses. Admitting that the free list would be enlarged and duties lowered, he thought it would be done conservatively, "without the least injury to any of our established and useful industries, and without lowering in the least the remuneration now awarded to labor." One of his sentences embodied a threat—"A conservative course of action will secure the desired legislation; a radical course will not." Randall was close to George W. Childs and Anthony J. Drexel, owners of the *Public Ledger,* which had supported Cleveland in 1884. Already this newspaper had declared that Cleveland's message was a shortsighted lecture based on defective information, reproducing hackneyed arguments, couched in overwrought phrases, and vehemently partisan.[1]

Not only did various Democratic journals in Ohio, Pennsylvania, and New England take Randall's side, but even in the South a number of voices spoke up in his behalf. He had repeatedly invaded that section; in 1886 he had been greeted at Birmingham by banners reading "Peace, Pig-Iron, and Prosperity," while in the fall of 1887, formally opening the Piedmont Exposition in Atlanta, he had received an ovation. Several Georgia newspapers, notably the Atlanta *Constitution,* the Macon *Telegraph,* and the Augusta *Chronicle,* had recently, on the basis of the growing industrialization of the South, been expounding protectionist ideas.[2] Senator Brown of Georgia, who boasted that he had purchased the first hundred tons of Bessemer steel produced in the Birmingham district, declared that tariff revision downward would prove more disastrous to the South, to the extent that it had manufacturing establishments, than to New England—for the South had little skilled labor.[3]

II

Yet in times of crisis and danger no party brooks a division. A hundred forces of loyalty and discipline acted to unite all the Democrats behind tariff reform, and all the Republicans behind tariff preservation. The great protectionist organizations, galvanized into action by Cleveland's message, had already joined with the Republican leaders to un-

[1] Philadelphia *Public Ledger,* Dec. 7, 1887.
[2] The Atlanta *Journal,* May 20, 1892, ably reviews the situation just before and after Cleveland's message.
[3] *Cong. Rec.,* March 14, 1888, vol. 19, 2048.

loose a deluge of high-tariff propaganda. On the Democratic side, with Cleveland thoroughly aroused, the day had passed when Randallism would be tolerated. Immediately after the message word went out from Washington that no follower of Randall's need expect any patronage or other benefits. Two important organizations, the Randall Club of Pittsburgh and the Eleventh Ward Democratic Association in Philadelphia, hastened to repudiate their old leader and endorse Cleveland's message. On January 18,1888, the Democratic State Committee met in Harrisburg to elect a chairman and adopt resolutions. Randall was on the ground, but he was overthrown in dramatic fashion. His nominee for chairman lost to W. L. Scott's low-tariff candidate by the decisive vote of 42 to 35, and the committee voted its hearty endorsement, in language prepared by Scott, of Cleveland's proposals for tariff revision. It was generally agreed that Scott must be recognized as the new Democratic leader of the State.[1] Aged, infirm, bereft of his old fire, Randall had been humiliated and deprived of most of his power to combat the President's policies. The Southern protectionist newspapers were also quickly crowded into line.

Meanwhile, the all-important question was what the business men, laborers, and farmers would think of Cleveland's proposals. A thousand voices came from that murky cave of the winds called public opinion. The principal Eastern dailies sent out reporters to interview industrialists, merchants, and financiers, and they learned in the main just what their editors instructed them to learn. Yet a few indisputable facts emerged from the long columns of talk.[2]

Many business men, then as now, were essentially timid and greedy, and their instinct was to demand caution and support the *status quo*. That fact alone would have made most of the responses to Cleveland's message unfriendly. An overwhelming majority of the manufacturers who depended upon home materials were instantly in arms. The *Herald* found that the makers of cotton goods in Philadelphia and New York were unanimously opposed to any change. John J. Glazier, a leading Pennsylvania mill-owner, declared bitterly: "I have always voted the Democratic ticket, but I am a protectionist on principle as well as from personal interest." Edward Risborough, another Philadelphia manu-

---

[1] *Nation,* Jan. 26, 1888; Philadelphia *Press,* Jan. 19, 22.
[2] The N. Y. *Herald* had four columns of interviews on Dec. 9, and more up to and including Dec. 16; the N. Y. *World* had many interviews Dec. 8 and 9; the N. Y. *Tribune* Dec. 8–12.

facturer, remarked: "This thing will kill Cleveland. Tariff for revenue killed Hancock. I have never voted anything but the Democratic ticket, but I never voted for free trade and never will." In Troy the shirt and collar manufacturers showed a united front against tariff revision. Thirty thousand people, said William S. Earl of Earl & Wilson, would be thrown out of work if rates were lowered. The inland steel and iron manufacturers, both of Pennsylvania and upper New York, took the same attitude. The vice-president of the Troy & Albany Steel & Iron Company grumbled that Congress ought not to meet but once in four years: "This constant agitation of the tariff question stagnates business. I want the tariff left just where it is." Similar declarations came from Cleveland, Bethlehem, Fall River, Lawrence, Lowell, and other manufacturing centres.

Importing interests naturally favored the message, but they were weak. The principal bank presidents of New York divided almost evenly. Most significant was the appearance on Cleveland's side of a large body of manufacturers who wished cheap raw materials and knew that foreign competition would help to provide them. Iron manufacturers on the seaboard, such as the managers of the Manhattan Iron Works and Phoenix Iron Company in New York city, declared that they would be glad to see raw materials enter free. Most makers of machinery all over the East took the same attitude. The great arms manufacturers of Bridgeport, led by the Union Metallic Cartridge Company, desired a lower tariff on copper, of which they used thousands of tons annually.[1] The Wheeler & Wilson Sewing-Machine Company, through Mr. Wheeler, declared for reduced rates on metals, while Warner Brothers and other corset manufacturers complained of the high tariff on sisal grass and other materials. Even typewriter manufacturers advocated a reduction of duties. But most emphatic of all on this subject were the makers of woolen textiles, including carpets.[2] The Keystone Mills of Philadelphia asserted that raw wools and yarns were better protected than the finished product, which meant that a premium was placed on foreign labor. Beach & Company, of Hartford, declared that after making woolens for fifty years, "We have learned that a high tariff is not of necessity protection, either to laborers or employers. On the contrary, it is usually a snare and a delusion. The labor of our country would be

---

[1] See N. Y. *Herald*, Sept. 25, 1888, for a long article on Bridgeport manufacturers.
[2] N. Y. *Herald*, Dec. 15, 1887.

better protected and manufacturers be upon a much sounder basis with free raw materials and a moderate duty upon manufactured products."

Compared with business sentiment, the opinion of the farmers and workingmen seemed inchoate and inarticulate. In Minnesota there was an aggressive hostility to the tariff, yet just across the line in Wisconsin Senator Sawyer could call Cleveland's message "a weak, flabby document—free trade rot of the worst description." Unquestionably much agrarian opposition to protection needed only to be awakened by proper appeals. Labor sat in Delphic silence. One leader alone, Henry George, flashed out a phrase as winter fell: "They don't promise the poor protection from the cold; it is protection from coal." [1] While so much of the public mind remained unfathomable and cross-currents churned the waters of public discussion, both sides appealed to propaganda.

III

Cleveland had of course determined that his message must be followed immediately by a bill translating it into new tariff schedules. Morrison was gone. Upon the President and Speaker Carlisle fell the task of choosing a successor. Some distrust was expressed when the latter named Roger Q. Mills as chairman of the Ways and Means Committee. It seemed unfortunate to turn the bill over to the Texan head of an overwhelmingly Southern group, for the Democratic majority of the committee comprised McMillin of Tennessee, Breckinridge of Arkansas, Turner of Georgia, Wilson of West Virginia, Scott of Pennsylvania, and Bynum of Indiana; moreover, Mills was comparatively obscure. But no mistake had been made.[2] Mills was a tall agile man of fifty-five, a former Confederate colonel who had been wounded at Missionary Ridge, and who had been in Congress since 1873. A persistent interrupter in debate, he had impressed his fellow-members with his quick and irascible disposition. But he was also an intense and enthusiastic worker, who passed his life between the Capitol and his boarding house, and who had long concentrated his energies upon one question, the tariff. Year after year he had studied it, literally burning the midnight oil, and now he rose admirably to the occasion. Those who looked at the loose figure, the long mustaches, the quiet blue eyes, the typical old-school dress—frock coat,

[1] N. Y. *World*, Dec. 21, 1887.
[2] See article on Mills in *Harper's Weekly*, May 19, 1888.

soft black hat, dangling watch-chain—might underrate Mills' capacities. But when he spoke, they realized that he possessed dignity, sense, and a profound knowledge of the subject.

During December Mills had completed a tentative tariff bill. It was too radical for Cleveland and for Mills' seven colleagues, and the latter revised it completely. On March 1 the general provisions of the act were made known, and five days later the internal revenue features were published. Judged in the light of our subsequent enactments, this Mills bill made but moderate changes in rates. The average reduction in duties was to be about seven per cent, the principal cuts falling on raw materials. Hemp, flax, lumber, salt, copper ore, tin plate, jute, and most important of all, wool, were to enter free, while the compensating duties on woolen goods were to be abolished.[1] Heavy diminutions were made on finished iron and steel, ranging for the most part from $4 to $6 a ton; but iron ore and pig iron were treated with great caution. Sugar duties were cut down much less than had been expected, by not quite one fifth. On the whole, it effectively embodied most of Cleveland's ideas. The principal criticism was that it appeared excessively sectional in character. It was obvious that the heavy reductions on finished metal products, glass, wood, and crockery, would be severely felt at the North. On the other hand, the light cuts on sugar favored Louisiana, and on iron ore the Alabama and Tennessee foundries. Duties on starch, a Northern product, were sharply reduced, while those on South Carolina's rice were left untouched. The low-grade cotton goods made in the South suffered little in the revision while the woolen textiles of the North lost much of their protection. This was not true tariff reform, declared the critics—it was tariff reform marred by selfish local interests.[2] But Mills had simply done for his own section what a long line of Pennsylvania, New York, and Maine tariff-makers had done for theirs.

On a day of bright spring sunshine, April 17, there began what some members of Congress later called "the great tariff debate of 1888." At one o'clock Mills rose, looked anxiously about him, and moved that the House go into committee of the whole to deal with the tariff bill. The Republicans had promised not to oppose the motion, and as Tom Reed lifted his tall form and glared threateningly at his party associates, none dared to break that pledge. Mills was not a great orator; but in his quiet

---

[1] Taussig, 353 ff.
[2] See *Public Opinion,* March 10, 1888.

way, speaking for two hours, he made a powerful argument.[1] He began
by pointing out how, after the war, the taxes that bore upon the wealthy
were repealed, while those which rested upon the poor were retained.
The income tax of 1866 had brought the Treasury $72,000,000, paid by
some 460,000 well-to-do persons with net annual incomes aggregating
almost eight hundred million. Yet hardly had the guns grown cold when
the tax was declared odious, inquisitorial, and oppressive, and was swept
from the statute books. Taxes on insurance companies, express companies, banks, and other rich corporations were also abolished. Thus
while the nation still had a debt of more than two billions staring it in
the face, "they made haste to roll all the burden of taxation off the
shoulders of the wealthy and lay them upon the shoulders of the toilers."
But, continued Mills, unfair taxation was not the principal defect of the
existing tariff. The chief evil lay in its destruction of export values. Year
after year, more than three-fourths of the exports of the country were
agricultural products—cotton foremost, then breadstuffs, then pork,
beef, butter, cheese, and lard. When by high tariffs we limited importation, we automatically limited the ability of other countries to buy from
us. In a pungent passage he denied that it was the tariff which made
high wages:

> They say, as a matter of course, if you increase the value of the domestic
> product the manufacturer is able to pay higher wages. Unquestionably he is,
> but does he do it? No. Mr. Jay Gould, with his immense income from his
> railroad property, is able to pay his bootblack $500 a day, but does he do it?
> Oh, no, he pays the market price of the street. He gets his boots blacked and
> pays his nickel like a little man. (Laughter).

The Republican line of attack was ably indicated by the Ways and
Means minority.[2] On April 2 they submitted a report, written largely
by McKinley, which termed the Mills bill "a radical reversal of the
tariff policy of the government." More than a third of the new free list,
it declared, was made up of the products of the field, forest and mine,
and it would bear with special harshness on the American farmer, exposing him to the cruel competition of Canada. The wool-grower would
find his industry, one of the most valuable in the country, completely
broken down. The placing of tin-plate upon the free list had served
notice to the world that the Democratic party did not wish any of it

[1] *Cong. Rec.*, Apr. 17, 1888, vol. 18, p. 3057 ff.
[2] For Sherman's elaborate Senate speech see *Cong. Rec.*, Jan. 4, 1888, vol. 19, pp. 186–192.

made in this country; and the lowering of the duty on steel rails to $11 would insure the surrender of our rail market to England. Already, they argued, the supply of steel rails to the Pacific coast was in the hands of foreigners, the existing duty of $17 a ton not being sufficient to compensate Eastern mills for the transcontinental freight charges. "The minority regard this bill," they declared, "not as a revenue reduction measure, but as a direct attempt to fasten upon this country the British policy of free foreign trade."

The "historic" discussion (though history has somehow paid slight attention to it) came to a climax on May 19, after two days of oratory in which the best gladiators of the House participated. Carlisle, William C. P. Breckinridge, Randall, Reed, and McKinley all spoke. The galleries were filled, and the rule which prohibited the spectators from applauding was practically suspended.

The contrasts between the various combatants lent interest to the scene. Breckinridge was the orator, Reed the humorist; Randall and McKinley were the skilful wranglers; and Carlisle was the man who struck down to firm underlying principles. When Breckinridge arose the throng applauded so heartily that it was some time before he could be heard. He came of a family of speakers, for his father had been one of the most celebrated of Kentucky preachers, and his grandfather a Senator. Standing erect, a boutonnière in his coat, he indulged in a Southern profusion of rhetorical figures. Tom Reed, with his ponderous frame and slow drawl, was eagerly heard by the galleries for his biting wit. McKinley, looking like a taller Napoleon, spoke in his usual quick, energetic fashion, and since he was a master of detailed information upon the industries of the country and details of the tariff, really threw light upon his subject. One of his characteristic strokes attracted the attention of an amused public. Mills had said that the workman or farmer, because of the wicked tariff, could not buy an all-wool suit of clothes in the United States for $10. McKinley had recently visited Boston and at the store of Leopold Morse, a Democratic Representative, had bought for $10 a suit which the bill described as "all wool," and which he suddenly displayed to the gaze of Morse and the delighted galleries. Later Morse, who had a keen eye to business, made a good thing of advertising "McKinley suits."

But the best speech of the whole debate was not made by any of these veterans. It had been made a fortnight earlier by an almost unknown

member, William L. Wilson of West Virginia.[1] He had entered Congress
five years earlier looking like a boy, though actually thirty-nine and a
veteran of the Confederate armies. He was a true scholar in politics,
having been successively lawyer, college professor, and president of his
State University. The slight, studious-looking man with the blonde
mustache and mild blue eyes had till now failed to attract general attention, though intimates knew how keen was his mind and how firm
were his convictions. When he appeared in Washington the feud between
Carlisle and Randall was at its fiercest, and it was assumed that members from West Virginia, as a protectionist State, would support the
latter. Wilson instead voted for Carlisle, and induced his delegation to
follow him. He did more—against intense pressure from the protected
interests of his State, he voted for the first Morrison bill; and in 1884
he fought out the tariff issue to a triumphant conclusion in his own district. Now his speech suddenly made him famous. The happiest of its
many hits was at the expense of Henry Cabot Lodge, then a newly-
elected Representative. Wilson suddenly confronted the cultured Bos-
tonian with a quotation from his recent life of Alexander Hamilton.
Lodge had incautiously asserted his belief that Hamilton, if living in the
eighties, "would probably be foremost in urging a revision of the tariff,"
and that he certainly "would not be one of those who support heavy
duties in order to furnish to industries already firmly established a
protection which accrues solely to the benefit of the manufacturer, and
no one else." In reply Lodge tried a bit of characteristic fencing. Elicit-
ing from Wilson the fact that the book was copyrighted in 1882, he declared, "That was before the revision of 1883." The revision of 1883 was
a revision upward! Wilson had him on the hip, and immediately retorted: "When that was written, the average tariff in this country was
42.65 per cent, and now it is 47.1 per cent." [2]

In June and early July debate flagged while determined efforts were
made to line up all Democrats behind the bill. When the measure had
been first reported the Washington correspondent of the *Courier-Journal*
had estimated that it would immediately muster 142 Democrat, five
Republican, and four Independent votes, a total of 151. In the full
House ten more votes would be required, and they had to be secured

[1] *Cong. Rec.*, May 3, 1888, vol. 19, Appendix, p. 47.
[2] See N. Y. *Herald*, May 4, 1888; *Harper's Weekly*, May 13, for comment on Wilson's
speech.

among the 19 Randall Democrats. They were secured. Randall had fought behind the Republican breastworks all spring. In an effort to get rid of the surplus and so dispose of that argument for tariff reduction, he and the Republicans had joined hands behind a bill for refunding the direct tax levied upon the States in 1861. By this refund, twenty-eight Northern States would receive approximately $15,000,000 from the Treasury. The measure would never have been taken from the calendar had not Randall boldly joined Cannon and Reed of the rules committee in getting it reported for debate by special order. A voracious lobby swooped down upon Washington to support it, for many States had placed the collection of the direct tax in the hands of agents working on a percentage basis. In itself the $15,000,000 was a trifle, but the plot went deeper. It was proposed by protectionists that, when passed, it should be followed by a bill refunding to both the Northern and Southern States the tax laid on raw cotton during the war—and this refund would have reached $69,000,000.[1] Fortunately, a filibuster defeated the direct-tax scheme. Randall then introduced a separate tariff bill, which attacked the internal revenue taxes and raised some duties to a prohibitive level while lowering others—a last defiant gesture.[2]

On July 21, after a final speech by Mills, the House came to a vote. Mrs. Cleveland was in the gallery, and the President waited impatiently for the news. Randall, attacked by his old ailment of rectal cancer, lay stricken in the shabby little house on Capitol Hill, worth perhaps $5,000, which represented the savings of his life-time.[3] As the yeas and nays were ordered a fellow-Pennsylvanian obtained unanimous consent to read the letter in which he paired his vote against the bill. Amid cheers the measure then passed, 162 to 149. Four Democrats voted no, but their opposition was more than offset by the yeas of three Republicans, including Knute Nelson, and three Independents. The Randallite bloc, two years earlier 35 strong, had been wiped out. Next day, E. L. Godkin exultantly wrote for the *Evening Post*:

The vote on the Mills bill in the House will serve as the historical record of the transformation of the Democratic party which President Cleveland has accomplished. There could be no more forcible illustration of the value of civic courage to a nation than has been afforded by him since December last.

[1] For this plot, see N. Y. *Herald,* April 8–11, 1888.
[2] McKinley, in his speech of May 18, charged Cleveland with using the patronage to force the bill through.
[3] N. Y. *Herald,* July 12, 1888.

At that time his tariff-reform message, by its boldness and utter disregard of political expediency, filled his own party with consternation and his opponents with delight. But the step, having once been taken, could not be retraced. . . . Slowly but surely the Democratic leaders have pulled themselves up to the President's advanced position; and after less than eight months of argument and agitation the vote is taken which shows that the party is practically a unit behind the first leader which it has had for a quarter of a century.

IV

Meanwhile, the Presidential campaign was opening; for as the debate on the Mills bill raged, steps were being taken to select the two national tickets.

Cleveland's renomination was a foregone conclusion. An attempt by the Democratic politicians to substitute any other leader would have meant quick and complete party defeat. The disgruntled machines—the Tammany men, the Gorman men, the Harrison-MacDonald men in Chicago—hated him and caught eagerly at efforts by the *Sun* to boom Randall, and at the *World's* praise of Hill. Early in April, 1887, a significant indication of this enmity had appeared at a great Democratic meeting in Uhlich's Hall in Chicago. An Administration supporter introduced a resolution endorsing Cleveland's policies, and the gang element in Chicago politics rose as one man to howl it down. For a moment all that was mean and disreputable in the Chicago Democracy stood and shouted profane abuse. It was an exhibition of disappointed rage which citizens of the West interpreted as a high tribute to the President.[1] But in their hearts the politicians knew that they could not do without Cleveland.

Eighteen months before the national convention, the St. Louis *Globe-Democrat* interviewed every member of the Missouri Democratic Convention on his choice for President. Of 348 who expressed themselves, 326 were for Cleveland; only half a dozen mentioned Hill, the others advocating Morrison or some other Westerner favorable to silver. This was in spite of the opinion of many Missourians that "Cleveland doesn't turn the Republicans out fast enough," that "he caters to the Mugwump element entirely too much."[2] In New York many of the old Tilden following were distinctly hostile to Cleveland. Yet when Manning had

[1] Chicago *Daily News*, April 4, 1887.
[2] *Nation*, Sept. 2, 1886.

talked with Hill in the fall of 1886 he strongly advised him to avoid rivalry with the President. "Look here, Hill," he said, "you have no show in 1888 and you might as well give up the idea. We have got to stick to Cleveland. It won't do for the New York delegation to go to the convention split on Cleveland's renomination, and then have him crowded down our throat by other delegations. The South and West will be for Cleveland. These States don't like New York and will be only too glad to force us into line. There's no sense in riding for a fall." [1]

Among Republicans it was universally believed at the beginning of the year that Blaine, still in Europe, would be nominated. There persisted a stern opposition to him on the part of such moralists as Senator Edmunds, who declared that if the Republicans "would go to the West and select some good, clean, upright man," sound on the currency, they would have seven chances in ten of success. But the heart of the party remained with the fascinating Blaine. As the very embodiment of high-tariff doctrine he enjoyed the favor of manufacturers, while his prestige with the Irish voters was undiminished. There is evidence that John Sherman had actually sent word to him in 1887 that if he were to be a candidate for the nomination, Sherman would not stand in his way. But suddenly in the Republican camp a bolt descended from the blue.

On February 12, Chairman B. F. Jones of the Republican National Committee published a letter written him by Blaine from northern Italy, asserting that his name would not be presented at the Republican national convention. His declination, he said, was for "considerations entirely personal to myself." [2] This statement he compressed into a single brief paragraph. The remainder of the letter conveyed a message of encouragement to the party, thanking his supporters for their former loyalty. Many were incredulous. The New York *Tribune* maintained that those who accepted the letter as final were "unspeakable donkeys" and "snivelling idiots." But a fortnight later Blaine confirmed his withdrawal in an interview with a correspondent of the *World* in Florence, and gave two reasons for it:

I do not wish to make new affirmations upon the subject. I have said all I wish to say upon this subject in that letter. That letter, as you must know, was not a haphazard, offhand affair. It was the result of much deliberation and careful thought. I hold that I have no right to be a candidate again. A

[1] See the *World's* interview with Manning recorded in *Public Opinion*, May 28, 1887.
[2] Gail Hamilton, *James G. Blaine*, 604.

man who has once been the candidate of his party, and defeated, owes it to his party to withdraw, and not be a candidate a second time. More than this. . . . I could not go through the burden and fatigue of another Presidential canvass—such a one as the canvass of the last campaign.

We now know that Blaine was a hypochondriac, and his Italian physician, Dr. Fornoni, later told E. P. Mitchell of the *Sun* that at this very moment he was inexplicably depressed by a temporary ailment.[1] In coming down into Italy from the St. Gothard, he had stood without an overcoat on the rear platform of his train, had caught a chill, and was deeply pessimistic about his health when he reached Milan, taking to his bed at the Hotel Cavour. His gesture of refusal temporarily stunned his party friends. Yet despite the emphatic nature of the *World* interview, many Republicans refused to accept his statement as final. They pointed out that his original message was ambiguous: he had said that his name would not be presented, but he did not say that he would reject the nomination if it were tendered to him. Within a few weeks his more ardent supporters were declaring that while he was not an active candidate, he was "subject to conscription" by his party. They asserted, like Coolidge's admirers after his declaration that "I do not choose to run," that he *must* run. His own State shortly elected delegates pledged to him, and others followed. By the first of June, 377 Blaine delegates had been chosen to the Republican convention, many under positive instructions.[2] All this was done without a word of protest from him. On May 3 the *Nation* had said that nobody could avoid "the conclusion that the Republican party wants Blaine for the candidate, and means to have him."

The *Nation* also gave the principal reason: "Three out of four of the party 'workers' throughout the country prefer him to any and all other men." It was a remarkable fact that without power or patronage, while in a far-distant land, and after withdrawing his name from consideration, he remained the unrivalled choice of a great majority of his party. But Blaine ruthlessly cut short the swelling new demand for his renomination. In a letter from Paris on May 17 to Whitelaw Reid he made his refusal final. "Assuming that the Presidential nomination could by any possible chance be offered to me," he wrote, "I could not accept it without leaving in the minds of thousands of these men the impression

[1] E. P. Mitchell, *Memoirs of an Editor*, 316.
[2] Philadelphia *Press*, June 2–7, 1888.

Benjamin Harrison   James G. Blaine   Henry Cabot Lodge

CLEVELAND'S TWO OPPONENTS FOR THE PRESIDENCY

(A photograph taken at the Blaine residence at Bar Harbor, Me.)

that I had not been free from indirection, and therefore I could not accept it at all." [1]

When the Republican convention met in Chicago on June 19, John Sherman, the candidate with the strongest following, had approximately 250 delegates out of the 830. But he was too cold and austere to arouse enthusiasm, many Blaine men had learned to dislike him as Blaine's principal rival, and he did not come from a doubtful State. Since the critical areas would be New York and Indiana, Republican eyes naturally turned in their direction. The one New Yorker proposed, Chauncey M. Depew, was hopeless in view of his record as a corporation attorney; to nominate him would simply invite a repetition of the exposures of 1884, with the New York Central in the stead of the Little Rock & Fort Smith. He would be brilliant, theatrical, and utterly unsafe. [2] Indiana presented two able men who regarded each other with intense antagonism, Benjamin Harrison and Walter Q. Gresham, both veterans of the war and both prominent in law and politics. Of the two Gresham, recently in Arthur's Cabinet and now a Federal judge, was the more enlightened and independent. He believed in civil service reform, in a moderate reduction of the tariff, and in a "progressive" policy to meet economic maladjustments and social unrest. Though he had lost the Indiana delegates to his rival, those of Illinois and Minnesota supported him. But being a reformer, he had no more real chance than Bristow had possessed in 1876 and Edmunds in 1884. The Blaine men, and above all the highly-protected manufacturers, would have died in the last ditch to defeat him. The convention quickly made its decision. After many of the Southern delegates who had been instructed for Sherman were openly bought up by Alger of Michigan, [3] and amid circumstantial reports of a corrupt bargain between Harrison's supporters and Tom Platt, Harrison won. The vice presidential nomination went to Levi P. Morton.

The frigid and intellectual Harrison was well understood to be a representative of the ultra-protectionist element, and as such required a strong protectionist platform. When the Chicago *Tribune* had lifted its voice in favor of Gresham because he believed in compromise, the

---

[1] Gail Hamilton, *James G. Blaine*, 606.
[2] Cf. *Public Opinion*, April 14, 1888.
[3] John Sherman, *Recollections*, II, 1029. Alger was credited with buying fifty negro delegates for $7500 and expenses; see Cincinnati *Enquirer*, July 1, N. Y. *Herald*, July 3, 6, 1888, for details.

American Iron and Steel Association replied by demanding an aggressive campaign. "If the choice for the presidency next fall," said its *Bulletin*,[1] "is to be between Mr. Cleveland and a half-hearted, milk-and-water 'revenue reform' Republican, who is acceptable to the free trade element in the Republican party, Mr. Cleveland will be elected. If the Republican party is to be restored to power next fall, it must be upon an out-and-out platform of protection." Actually, the platform was amazing in its boldness. Turning its back on the declaration of four years earlier, which had generally been interpreted as meaning revision downward, the convention declared that "we favor the entire repeal of internal taxes, rather than the surrender of any part of our protective system." This was the result in part of a determined drive by manufacturing interests, and in part of a recent State election in Oregon where, the two great products being lumber and wool, something like a tariff panic had arisen. The Northwest was ruthlessly overridden. The *Nation* wrote of the plank: [2]

It is so at variance with all former deliverances of the party, with scores of resolutions of State Legislatures under Republican control, with hundreds of speeches and votes of Republican statesmen now living, with the report of the Republican tariff commission only five years ago, and with the recommendations of successive Republican Presidents and Secretaries of the Treasury, that the party can be likened only to the man who made a monster of which he became the unhappy victim. Protection is the Frankenstein of the Republican party.

V

Meanwhile, at St. Louis Cleveland had been quietly and cordially renominated. The collapse of all opposition was so utter that it surprised most observers. All winter and spring Hill and his Tammany allies had continued their underground machinations, and had aroused the indignation first of the President's friends and then of Cleveland himself. The legislative session at Albany was full of plottings, schemings, and petty insults to Cleveland. In January, for example, the party caucus gave vent to its spite by nominating Charles A. Dana, whose abuse of

[1] March, 1888.
[2] *Nation*, June 28, 1888. "Pig-Iron" Kelly, on reading the plank, remarked: "Lord, now lettest thou thy servant depart in peace, for mine eyes have seen the glory of the Republican party." *Public Opinion*, June 30, 1888.

the President had broken almost all records for journalistic foulness, for Regent of the University of the State of New York. "It means," wrote Eugene Chamberlain,[1] "it was meant to mean and I know whereof I speak—a deliberate insult to President Cleveland, and a demonstration to the country that Hill is the boss of New York State, and is against Cleveland." Bissell sent the President an account of Billy Sheehan's open enmity in Buffalo, and George Raines described similar operations in and about Rochester. All these reports stirred Cleveland's ire, and he wrote Bissell in January:[2]

I am quite fully convinced that schemes are on foot for an anti-Administration control in New York. Every day brings confirmation of that belief. I suppose you have your full share of it in your locality. It extends further than the State of New York, but you know my feeling well enough to be satisfied that it will not keep me awake at all.

I do think, however, that a move ought to be made towards organization for the sake of the best interests of the party—whatever they are.

To a letter from James Shanahan on the efforts of the Hill group to subsidize enough newspapers in different States to create a boom for the governor,[3] Cleveland replied more vigorously. He wrote that he would be glad to retire to private life, but that men declared the party and the country needed him. "Occupying the position I do on this subject, willing to obey the command of the party and by my own act being in no man's way, I confess I cannot quite keep my temper when I learn of the mean and low attempts which are made by underhand means to endanger the results to which I am devoted. And when I see such good staunch friends as you with their coats off and their sleeves rolled up, I feel like taking a hand with them." His friends all over the State had awakened to the danger, he added, and were taking every necessary precaution. "There has been enough lying since the meeting of the State Committee to damn the world; and it had amused us a good deal here to see certain people protesting either that they had nothing to do with some queer transactions or that they didn't mean anything. Ex-Mayor Grace was here and said to me, 'Don't let them give you any sleeping doses'—and I have not. I think I know a man who will before a great while be asking such men as you for the nomination for Governor and

[1] Albany, Jan. 23, 1888. Cleveland Papers.
[2] Jan. 13, 1888. Cleveland Papers.
[3] Shanahan to Cleveland, Albany, Feb. 5, 1888.

will be protesting that all his manipulation was for the general good and for the purpose of keeping certain discontented persons in line, etc., etc." [1]

While this friction between Cleveland and Hill augured badly for the fall campaign, the measures taken were quite sufficient to check all the disturbing manoeuvres. When the State Convention met in New York city in the spring it adopted an endorsement of the Administration written by Cleveland himself.[2] With the President's adherents in full control, a unanimous Cleveland delegation was chosen to the national convention, and Hill himself was significantly refused the position of delegate-at-large. The only dispute was whether Tammany or the Brooklyn organization should have the honor of presenting Cleveland's name in St. Louis, and on this no agreement was reached. As late as June 4, the second day of the national convention, both Alfred C. Chapin of Brooklyn and an eloquent Tammany leader named Daniel Dougherty were prepared with speeches! [3] Dougherty, in the interests of party harmony, was finally given the floor.

The St. Louis convention proved interesting chiefly for its action on the vice-presidency and the platform. In dealing with the former it made a grave error. Governor Gray of Indiana, Commissioner Black of Illinois, and Thurman of Ohio were the principal aspirants, and with Cleveland's acquiescence Thurman was named. He was loved as perhaps no other man in the party, while his long public service, high abilities, unspotted integrity, and ripe experience made him universally respected. But he was nevertheless a weak candidate. He was seventy-five years of age, infirm of health, and in nearly all his political convictions opposed to Cleveland's views. After long giving his support to the greenback cause, he had latterly become a silverite; he had wavered from side to side on the tariff; and he was a spoilsman of the old Marcy stripe. Riddleberger of Virginia, asked what he thought of the "bandanna" nomination, ejaculated: "Think? Why I think you have nominated a pocket handkerchief!" [4]

The tariff plank in the platform precipitated a shrewd and hard-fought battle between radicals and conservatives. Cleveland had been

---

[1] McElroy, *Grover Cleveland*, I, 281, 282.
[2] Text in McElroy, *Grover Cleveland*, I, 283–285.
[3] Richard Croker sent Lamont an anxious telegram. Cleveland Papers.
[4] Peck, *Twenty Years of the Republic*, 156.

anxious, for tactical reasons, that the convention should not go to extreme lengths. He had discussed the wording at length with party leaders, and Gorman had gone to St. Louis with a draft which the President had written in such moderate language that it would give the Republicans no opportunity to charge the Democratic party with free trade principles. But when the convention opened the enthusiastic low-tariff men could not be restrained. The platform sub-committee, almost evenly divided between a group under Gorman which wished to do little more than reaffirm the colorless tariff plank of 1884, and a group headed by Watterson which demanded a stand for drastic revision downward, met at dusk in a hot room of the Southern Hotel and began a fight which lasted practically all night. Reporters crowded about the closed door and wrote hourly bulletins for the Eastern newspapers.[1] Through the panels they could hear Watterson speaking again and again, his voice vibrating with earnestness as he pleaded against any sacrifice of principle to expediency. He was ready to make minor concessions for the sake of party unity, but not to let the Democracy go before the nation with an equivocal declaration upon the burning question of the hour. In the end he won the essentials for which he contended. There was a "compromise," but it was all in his favor.[2]

Watterson, erect and soldierly in his frock coat, his yellow mustache contrasting with his dark, closely-cropped hair, presented the platform at the final session of June 7. "Thanks to Grover Cleveland," he said, "the attention of the country, wooed by others so long in vain, is fixed at last upon a remedy for the real instead of the imaginary evils arising out of the late war, and henceforward the Democratic party, which has been the voice, will be the hand of the people." He did not mention the word tariff. Introducing Gorman at the close of his speech, he remarked that two good Democrats "can only understand one another thoroughly and love one another entirely when they have had some fun together." Gorman also refused to mention the word tariff. "Differ as you will about the phrases," he said, "we have presented a platform in strict accord with all the Democratic declarations that have preceded us. And if in the discussion of the great questions where local

[1] N. Y. *Herald, World,* June 6, 7, 1888.
[2] The sub-committee of 11 members could not agree, and the final decision was made by the committee of 42 members. N. Y. *World, Herald,* June 6, 7.

interests play so sharp a part there is during the campaign and during future campaigns some difference, there will be the same spirit of toleration." [1] The platform not only reaffirmed the tariff plank adopted in 1884, but approved of Cleveland's latest annual message as a correct interpretation of Democratic doctrines. Moreover, by a separate resolution the convention endorsed the Mills Bill.

The President had awaited the news of his renomination and the formal opening of the battle without anxiety. His friends were jubilant. St. Clair McKelway wrote Lamont that the spontaneous nature of the action at St. Louis was a reason for believing in principle, courage, and the people.[2] "How inadequate were even the most sanguine estimates in 1882 of the capabilities of the man then nominated for Governor! How the result in 1888 shows the appreciation of character by the people and the growth in ethics of the Democracy!" But Cleveland was imperturbable. Lamont, bearing the St. Louis telegram, found him in the White House library looking over a set of textbooks for Indian children. He glanced at the message, and turned again to his textbooks. A few days later he imparted his inner feelings, as usual, to Bissell: [3]

It seems quite a long time since I have written to you, and on this hot Sunday morning I have seated myself at Oak View to drop you a line.

The political turmoil has not fairly begun yet. In point of fact, the campaign thus far as I see it is very quiet. I sometimes think that perhaps more enthusiasm would have been created if somebody else had been nominated after a lively scrimmage at St. Louis. I mean to be as good a candidate as I can and after the people have done their voting I shall be content and doubly so in case of success because my reluctance to again take on the burden has been fully considered, discounted, and dismissed, and because I am sure in being a candidate again I am but answering the demands of public and political duty. These feelings can and do exist without the least lack of appreciation of the honor and satisfaction which a nomination tendered in the way mine had been should occasion.

The first important questions to be settled are the selection of the leader of the National Committee and your State Executive Committee. If anyone has any very clear ideas on these subjects I am not aware of it. . . . It is possible that I shall go to Ohio in September. If I do I have promised to go to Kentucky on the trip.

My wife sits by me and bids me send to you her affectionate regards. I

[1] N. Y. *Herald*, June 8.
[2] June 8, 1888. Cleveland Papers.
[3] June 17, 1888. Cleveland Papers.

tell you, Bissell, I am sure of one thing. I have in her something better than the presidency for life—though the Republican party and papers do say I beat and abuse her. I absolutely long to be able to live with her as other people do with their wives. Well! Perhaps I can after the 4th of next March.

JUNE of 1888 had witnessed the national conventions; July had brought the passage of the Mills Bill in the House and the commencement of the campaign; but in August public attention was suddenly diverted to foreign affairs. Visitors to Oak View during the late summer found Cleveland preoccupied with the Canadian fisheries problem; and well he might be, for the long-smouldering dispute with Ottawa and London upon the subject now flared up in a disturbing fashion.

Cleveland and Bayard had made it clear from the beginning that they planned a quiet and unadventurous foreign policy; there were to be no expansionist strokes like Grant's in San Domingo and no alarms and excursions in the Latin-American field like Blaine's. If Cleveland detested anything he detested jingoism and imperialism, for he was a thorough Jeffersonian in his ideas of war, peace, and external growth and adjustment. The work he did in 1885–89 to blight imperialist tendencies in the bud has seldom been recognized at its true value. Under Secretaries Blaine and Frelinghuysen, the State Department had made steady progress toward a protectorate of Nicaragua, as a concomitant of which we were to build a trans-isthmian canal. Had Cleveland accepted the Frelinghuysen-Zavala treaty of 1884 and pushed forward the whole grandiose undertaking, the Caribbean might rapidly have become an American lake, the new American navy might have been used to overawe Latin-America, and annexations and dollar diplomacy have been forced into early bloom. But Cleveland declared in his first annual message that any Isthmian canal "must be for the world's benefit—a trust for mankind, to be removed from the chance of domination by any single power, nor become a point of invitation for hostilities or a prize for warlike ambition." [1] His withdrawal of the treaty, his rigid hands-off policy with regard to weaker nations, his refusal to encourage foreign investments, and above all, his and Bayard's stern tendency to view foreign questions in a moral light, strengthened a national psychology quite inimical to imperialist tendencies. Only one foreign collision marked the first Administration—that with Canada.

There was no more picturesque industry in the world than that which,

---

[1] Richardson, *Messages and Papers*, VIII, 327.

celebrated by Winslow Homer's brush and Kipling's pen, was followed by the Gloucester fishermen in Canadian waters. The earlier race of Yankee seamen, whose pursuit of the whale had won the admiration of Burke, who had manned the privateers and frigates of 1812, and who in the clipper ships of the forties had shown the world a streak of foam, had passed away. But they had worthy successors in men who put off in schooners all along the coast from Salem to Penobscot, and wrung from the dangerous northern waters a scanty livelihood—so scanty that $300 a year was said to be the average return. There were some 14,000 or 15,000 of these hardy seamen, including many Canadians, Scandinavians, and Portuguese, but chiefly native Americans, and they manned more than 400 vessels out of Gloucester, more than 100 out of Portland, and many from smaller ports.[1] In general they were not paid wages, but invested their time and labor for one-half the catch, the other half going to the owner of the vessel and its gear. Most of the vessels were small, ranging from 80 to 125 tons, and ten men was a fair crew; many were owned by corporations, though it was not unusual to find thrifty fishermen who had placed the savings of a lifetime in a $10,000 boat. A large fish-packing industry had been built up in New England by their labors. For both financial and sentimental reasons Massachusetts and Maine regarded the fishermen fondly, and cherished the delusion that they offered a valuable recruiting-ground for the navy.

By the reckless action of Congress two years before Cleveland became President the fishing clauses of the Treaty of Washington, which guaranteed American fishermen valuable rights as to inshore fishing, bait-purchasing, and transshipment of cargoes within Canadian waters, had been abrogated as of July 1, 1885.[2] One motive for this abrogation lay in resentment over a high monetary compensation for the inshore rights which had been fixed by arbitrators in the seventies; another motive was the wish to stop the free admission of Canadian fish into American markets, guaranteed by the treaty. Naturally Canadian resentment was aroused. The Dominion authorities, in retaliation, fell back upon a strict and illiberal interpretation of the old treaty of 1818, which would now govern the fisheries.

[1] See the excellent articles on the fishing industry in N. Y. *Herald,* April 21–29, 1886; also the report by Dr. Spencer F. Baird of the Smithsonian Institution to the Secretary of the Treasury in Senate Misc. Docs., 2d Sess., 49th Cong., vol. 4.
[2] John Bassett Moore, *International Arbitrations,* I, 725–753.

Cleveland and Bayard in 1885 had been much alarmed. They had taken up the subject in haste with that curious creature the British Minister, Sir Lionel Sackville-West—a man of middle height, insignificant features, a pair of large, sad blue eyes, and a look of patient ennui. The only friends he made were among the duller Congressmen, and the alert young secretary of legation, Cecil Spring-Rice, concluded that he got on well with them because he was on their precise intellectual level. "They have a common taste for whiskey, poker, and business, and a common hatred for female society." [1] It was difficult to deal with this uninspiring diplomatist, but the Administration succeeded in arranging a provisional extension of the Treaty of Washington for six months. When this lapsed, Canadian cruisers shortly began arresting American schooners for violations of the law, and the situation grew dangerous. [2]

II

Cleveland found that he had a difficult problem on his hands. His aims, as always, were simple, clear, and based on what he believed the absolute equities of the situation. From beginning to end he had three great objects in view: First, by persuasion and argument to induce Canada to take a milder attitude toward the New England fishermen in her waters; second, to negotiate a treaty which would permanently settle the question; and third, if reason and negotiation failed, and it became necessary to retaliate against Canada, to place this retaliation on an unselfish and national plane instead of on selfish and sectional grounds. The third of these objects deserves emphasis, for it has seldom been understood and it explains one of the most dramatic acts of his first Administration. He did not find the Canadians unreasonable in the matter of the treaty—they were willing to make a new one. The puzzled British authorities were even more conciliatory. But a formidable obstacle to a fair and friendly settlement was presented by the New England leaders in the Senate, who insisted upon obtaining tariff protection for American-caught fish, who were willing to defeat any treaty simply in order to make trouble for a Democratic Administration, and who, when retaliation was considered, wanted it to be of a kind to benefit New England.

[1] *Letters and Friendships of Sir Cecil Spring-Rice,* I, 56.
[2] John Bassett Moore, *Digest of International Law,* I, 809 ff.

By assiduous effort Cleveland and Bayard succeeded in 1887 in restricting, though not wholly avoiding, the vexatious clashes in Canadian waters that had marked the fishing season of 1886. Bayard had directed Minister Phelps in London to bring pressure on the British Government to stop the boarding and seizure of Yankee schooners, which threatened, he wrote, "the peace of two kindred and friendly nations." [1] The State Department set forth in detail its objections to the Canadian port regulations, and the action of Canadian naval officers and courts. The Conservative Government of Lord Salisbury, which had come into power in 1886 and in which Salisbury himself was now handling foreign affairs, tactfully intervened at Ottawa; and it found the veteran Canadian prime minister, Sir John MacDonald, ready to respond. In May, 1887, MacDonald sent his minister of finance, Sir Charles Tupper, to Washington for conferences. Bayard frankly told the envoy that the two countries had come to the parting of the ways, and that the future threatened "embittered rivalries staining our long frontier with the hues of hostility." At first the Canadian cruisers again showed a disposition to behave arrogantly, but this soon stopped and the summer passed with little friction.[2]

While the northern waters were thus becoming calmer, Cleveland pushed forward his plan for a new treaty.[3] The Republicans refused to assist or even acquiesce in this undertaking. The Senate Committee on Foreign Relations, with Frye of Maine as chairman, brought in a resolution declaring that the selection of American commissioners to negotiate an agreement, as recommended by Cleveland, "ought not to be provided for by Congress." Gorman and some other Eastern Democrats actually voted for this resolution. But if the Senate had its own opinion, so did Cleveland. He felt himself bound in honor by the promises accompanying the provisional extension of the old treaty to negotiate a new one, while he was irritated by the effort of Edmunds, Hoar, and Frye to place a preposterously narrow construction upon his treaty-making powers. Hoar early in 1887 even offered a resolution declaring that "it is the judgment of the Senate that under present circumstances no negotiation should be undertaken with Great Britain in regard to existing difficulties with her province of Canada which has for its object the

[1] State Department, *Foreign Relations*, 1887, 425.
[2] For the "outrages" see Senate Exec. Docs., 50th Cong., 1st Sess., No. 113; for the State Department's efforts, *Foreign Relations*, 1886, 340 ff., 1887, 424 ff.
[3] Cf. Samuel Flagg Bemis, ed., *American Secretaries of State*, VIII, 58 ff.

reduction, change, or abolition of any of our present duties on imports." [1]
Bayard denounced this as an unprecedented attempt to interfere with
the President, and he and Cleveland went ahead in their own fashion.
They arranged with Great Britain for a joint commission to prepare the
draft of a new treaty, and able men were appointed on both sides.

Queen Victoria named Joseph Chamberlain, one of the most distinguished of British leaders, a consummate orator, who had recently
been one of Gladstone's strongest lieutenants but had quarreled with
him on Irish Home Rule; Sackville-West and Sir Charles Tupper, who
had been prominent in effecting Canadian confederation, and who as
a Nova Scotian was close to the fisheries problem. Cleveland named
Secretary Bayard; William L. Putnam, a Portland lawyer intimately
conversant with the fisheries dispute and known as one of our foremost
experts on international law; and President James B. Angell of the
University of Michigan. The arrival of Chamberlain in New York early
in November attracted much attention. A self-made man, he possessed
qualities which the American people could well appreciate. Everyone
knew that he came of plain business stock, and had made a fortune in
Birmingham before he was forty; that as mayor of that city his slum-
clearances, his model housing schemes, his establishment of parks,
libraries, an art-gallery, and schools, had given an impetus to municipal
improvements throughout Great Britain; that in Gladstone's Cabinet
he had stood for radical social reforms; and that he had sympathized
with Ireland, but had recoiled from Home Rule in the belief that it
would mean ultimate separation. Reporters who interviewed him were
obviously impressed by his spare figure, intellectual features, and quiet,
cool speech.

After Cleveland had formally received Chamberlain and Tupper at
the White House, the six commissioners began their labors. At first
little progress was made. The Anglo-Canadian representatives demanded
that the negotiations be given the broadest scope, including not only
the fisheries but the sealing question and the American tariff on fish;
while Bayard and his colleagues tried to restrict the discussions to the
Canadian legislation upon our inshore fishing privileges, which they
contended was unjustifiably severe, if not a direct violation of the
treaty of 1818. Just before Christmas there appeared danger that the
conference would break up. Fortunately Tupper and Chamberlain re-

[1] *Cong. Rec.*, vol. 18, p. 2191. Bayard to Senator Morgan, Bayard Papers, Feb. 26, 1887.

ceded from their extreme stand, and by a hasty trip to Ottawa induced the Canadian Government to agree to concessions. After Christmas the negotiations were resumed in a better atmosphere. They were facilitated by the brilliant entertainments given at the British legation, by Chamberlain's charm of manner, and above all by the statesmanlike attitude of Bayard toward the issues.

Bayard "was so magnanimous to his opponents," President Angell later wrote, "that to a certain degree his generosity unfitted him to negotiate with so keen a man as Chamberlain. He was tempted to concede too much. He was gifted with wit which was never ungenerous or bitter, but always most enjoyable." [1] Sackville-West, during the three months of discussion, never opened his lips except to move to adjourn. Once Angell asked Bayard if the British Minister had ever said anything on any subject. "No," replied Bayard, "he simply communicates the messages from Lord Salisbury, and acknowledges my replies: I can hardly understand why the British Government keeps a minister at a salary of $25,000, and then reduces him to the function of a postage stamp." Chamberlain pressed hard to gain what advantage he could for the Canadians, and Tupper, himself highly pertinacious, later testified that no man could have given more energetic support to the contentions of the Dominion. But if ever Bayard threatened to yield too much, Cleveland stood behind him to hold him firm. Angell declares:

I saw not a little of President Cleveland. I was impressed with the readiness with which he apprehended all the bearings of the discussions which we reported to him, and the promptness and soundness of his conclusions. I remember being in his office once at midnight, when he had a great pile of papers before him. He said he must go through them all before he slept. His capacity for work was prodigious.

By February 15, 1888, the draft of the treaty was concluded—a treaty eminently fair to both sides.[2] It provided that a mixed commission should delimit the territorial rights of American fishermen in Canadian waters, so long disputed under the treaty of 1818. It established the Canadian contention that while in drawing the three-mile line the sinuosities of the shore should be followed, the Dominion Government should exercise full jurisdiction over estuaries and bays

[1] *Reminiscences of James B. Angell,* 174, 175.
[2] Senate Exec. Docs., 50th Cong., 1st Sess. no. 176, gives the treaty and Cleveland's accompanying message.

which were entered by inlets not more than six miles wide. This was simply good international law and good common sense. But it secured to the United States the free navigation of the Strait of Canso, which separates Cape Breton Island from Nova Scotia. American fishing vessels were also guaranteed the right to purchase supplies on their homeward voyages, and ships in distress were given liberty to unload and sell their cargoes of fish. Finally, it was provided that if the duties on fish should thereafter be removed by the United States, the Canadians should permit American vessels touching their ports to purchase bait and fishing tackle, to transship their catch, and to hire men for their crews. Each side gained substantial advantages, and had every reason to accept the treaty.

III

Meanwhile, Cleveland had been handling to the best of his ability the vexatious question of retaliation against the Canadians for their harsh treatment of our fishermen. From New England there came a clamorous demand that since our ships and fish were excluded from Dominion ports, appropriate penalties should be imposed upon the Canadians. Cleveland realized that some legislation authorizing the President to retaliate would have to go on the statute books, and his determination that it should be fair legislation, of truly national scope, brought him into immediate conflict with the Senate.

The New England Senators, led by Frye and Edmunds, held that the object of retaliation would be best accomplished by prohibiting the entry of Canadian vessels and Canadian-caught fish into our ports. In other words, the proper reply to Canadian insults and injuries would be to give the Gloucester, Portland, and Boston shipowners a monopoly of the American fish-market! With this view Cleveland had no patience. He maintained that if we went in for non-intercourse, it must be complete non-intercourse, applying to railroads as well as ships. He had made this clear in a letter of April 7, 1887, to George Steele, president of the American Fishing Union [1]—a forcible if courteous missive, which flatly contradicted Steele's statement of the proper steps to be taken against Canada. Retaliation, wrote Cleveland, "is to be enforced, not to protect solely any particular interest, however meritorious or valua-

[1] N. Y. *Herald,* April 9, 1887.

ble, but to maintain the national honor and thus protect all our people." Sectional measures would not do. "Its effectiveness and value may well depend upon the thoroughness and extent of its application, and in the performance of international duties, the enforcement of international rights, and the protection of our citizens this government and the people of the United States must act as a unit—all intent upon attaining the best result of retaliation upon the basis of a maintenance of national honor and duty."

Cleveland's views were translated, early in 1887, into a House bill. The chairman of the Foreign Affairs Committee was young Perry Belmont, a son of August Belmont and an energetic New York attorney, who had been elected to Congress in 1880 and was an enthusiast for all Cleveland's policies. He drew up the measure Cleveland wanted, giving the President discretionary power to close our ports to Canadian vessels, suspend the transportation of Canadian merchandise in bond across our territory, and stop the transit of all Canadian cars and locomotives in the United States. This drastic bill took some members of the Committee aback. They doubted if Cleveland really desired such "war powers." "I went to see him," writes Belmont,[1] "to ask if he would receive our committee at the White House and express his opinion of the utility of such legislation. I remember distinctly this unusual incident of a full committee of Congress seated at a round table with the President, who soon convinced them that he would make good use of the power and that it would be good policy to pass the measure." On January 18, 1887, the bill was reported with a statement which laid emphasis on its railroad provisions.

On February 23 a retaliatory bill passed the House with but one dissenting vote. A similar measure was introduced in the Senate by Gorman, authorizing Cleveland at any time to suspend the passage of all "engines, goods, or vessels" to or from Canada. But the Republican Senators objected. Total non-intercourse would injure our border cities and northern railroads too heavily. They had already committed themselves to a bill introduced by Edmunds, which simply authorized the President to exclude Canadian vessels from our waters and stop the importation of Canadian fish or other goods. The result was that legislation on this limited plan passed, and Cleveland reluctantly signed it, though with no intention of putting it into effect.

[1] Perry Belmont to author, Dec. 30, 1930.

Then in 1888 occurred a dramatic series of events. The Chamberlain-Bayard Treaty went to the Senate as preparations were being made for the Presidential campaign. It was hopeless to expect fair treatment for it. A Republican Senator told Sir Charles Tupper that "We cannot allow the Democrats to take credit for settling so important a dispute." The Foreign Relations Committee brought in an adverse report, the Senate chamber resounded with Republican speeches attacking Canada and England, and when Blaine returned from Europe he told his welcomers in Portland that the treaty was "a complete abandonment of the whole fishing interests of the United States." The Democratic Senators tried to postpone a vote until after the election. But in vain; on August 21 the treaty was rejected by 27 yeas to 30 nays. The practical result was not disastrous, for the treaty had been accompanied by a *modus vivendi* which gave the United States most of its advantages and which remained in force. But the rejection had no little effect among the Irish-Americans. Godkin correctly declared that the whole business was more a bid for the Anglophobe vote than anything else. During his sojourn in Washington Chamberlain, a widower, had become engaged to Secretary Endicott's charming daughter. Because of the fear of the Irish vote, announcement of the engagement was held back until just after election day!

Cleveland had long foreseen the Senate's action, and was prepared for an instant counter-blow. Two days after the rejection he sent Congress a message in which he returned to his demand for sweeping retaliation. He began with a few severe words upon the refusal of the Senate to cooperate in making a satisfactory treaty. "I recommend," he went on, "immediate legislative action conferring upon the Executive the power to suspend by proclamation the operation of all laws and regulations permitting the transit of goods, wares, and merchandise in bond across or over the territory of the United States to or from Canada." This message threw the Senate into confusion. Edmunds forced a hasty adjournment, and some observers found the Republican leaders "completely dazed." It was indeed a stunning stroke. Nominally, it was aimed at Canada. Actually, it was aimed at the Senate. Cleveland had simply followed the bluster of that body to its logical conclusion. The Senators had talked bravely of a mock-retaliation that would merely enrich certain Yankee fishing interests. But here was retaliation in earnest, and they drew back. Portland was aghast, for under it she would lose her rich winter transshipment trade with Canada. New England railways which carried Canadian freight protested vigorously. Buffalo declared that the measure would destroy an immense import trade in Canadian goods. Many Detroit business men asserted that they would face actual ruin. From Minneapolis came a loud outcry, for the Twin Cities would lose a large Canadian business and be placed at the mercy of the American trunk-lines. A host of American investors in border and Canadian railroads protested.

In the House Cleveland's message was referred to committee, a Retaliation bill was whipped into shape, and it was promptly passed. But no one expected the Senate to follow suit, and it did not. New England interests would have been too heavily hit. The President's proposals were meekly shelved. Blaine, in his Maine speeches, was still firing off epigrams upon the treaty. "England is unanimously Democratic, and I am inclined to think that Canada feels the same way," ran one. But they failed of their old effect. Cleveland had delivered a happy blow. He had shown that, in what slight concern he had with foreign policy at this time, he was determined to pursue a straightforward and broad-minded course. By a bold stroke he had taken command of a nasty situation—a fact which he perhaps remembered in the Venezuela affair seven years later. And by insisting that retaliation, if adopted, must be on a national scale, and compelling the Republicans to face the consequences of their irresponsible rejection of the treaty, he had won a marked tactical success.

Chapter XXIV   The Republican Revival: Cleveland's Defeat

CLEVELAND, always clear-headed and practical, realized the risks which he ran in making tariff-revision the issue of the campaign of 1888; and talking with Gorman just before the convention, he insisted upon the need for reassuring business and labor.[1] Yet he probably did not understand just how difficult his task was. With his simple honesty of outlook, he believed that he could maintain the discussion of the tariff upon the high plane of his message of 1887, that the issue would be debated upon its merits, and that in a campaign of education the best side would win. He had too complete a trust in democracy to realize the ease with which dust could be thrown in the eyes of the voters and confusing prejudices aroused. Sometimes a campaign of education is real, as in 1896; sometimes it is false and deceptive, as in 1920. Moreover, Cleveland apparently did not comprehend in time the necessity for prompt and desperate efforts to bring his doctrines home to the voters. He did not at once perceive what an immense massed propaganda, supported by powerful economic interests, he had to face.

It is always a misfortune when an issue which demands calm study, like the tariff in 1888 or the League of Nations in 1920, becomes entangled with the heated complexities of a Presidential election. The two parties, in their eagerness for attack, are pushed into extreme positions. They are excited into repudiating the saner doctrines they had professed only a few months earlier. The victorious side is then certain to carry into practical legislation the unwise doctrines to which it has committed itself. Repeatedly it has been shown that no feature of American politics more effectually arouses passion and prevents compromise than the violent quadrennial collision, in a grim six-months battle, of the two parties. It is conceivable that under a parliamentary system and with no presidential election of 1860, the United States might have settled the slavery question in some more civilized way than by war, and that without the bitter election of 1920, it might have placed itself, with moderate reservations, in the League. The tariff question of the eighties should

---

[1] Just what was said in this Gorman-Cleveland interview is not known. Gorman later claimed that Cleveland had objected even to a convention endorsement of the Mills bill; but this was doubtless false. P. J. Smalley to Cleveland, Sept. 22, 1891; Cleveland Papers.

have been decided in Congress, not in the dusty, overheated arena of a Presidential contest; but to this arena it was now consigned.

History has long recorded, in its easy-going way, that Cleveland was defeated in 1888 upon the tariff question, and the Republican party eagerly acted upon this assumption two years later in passing the McKinley Act. But in reality there was no national decision against Cleveland's tariff policy. For one reason, he received a substantial majority of the popular vote; for another, various special factors played a decisive part in swinging the electoral vote against him.

II

The problem of organization in 1888 was of the sternest importance to the Democrats. The Republican plan of campaign was fairly obvious. Having behind them the industries which had grown rich upon high tariffs, and which under Arthur had refused to permit even a friendly tariff commission to make long-needed reductions, the party was sure to call upon the wealthy manufacturers for herculean efforts. Voters would be snowed under by pamphlets and speakers warning them of depression, wage-cutting, unemployment, and starvation. It was imperative that the Democrats choose managers who were heart and soul in the fight for tariff reform and who possessed all the resourcefulness that Whitney and Gorman had shown in 1884. It was equally important that they begin the contest the morning after the convention and leave nothing undone to show the voter the truth about a moderate revision.

Yet neither of these requirements was met. The campaign was placed in the hands of William H. Barnum of Connecticut and Calvin S. Brice of Ohio, whose interest in tariff reform was less than lukewarm. Barnum, the national chairman, owned large areas of iron ore in the upper peninsula of Michigan, would be heavily injured by free raw materials, and had long shown that his true affiliations were with the protectionists. We have seen how he had stamped out the tariff-reform movement in Connecticut in 1886. He was a member of the Iron and Steel Association, which was credited with wishing to put him back in the Senate; and there had been persistent reports early in 1888 that he was secretly opposed to Cleveland's renomination.[1] Brice, who was now made chairman of the executive committee, was a typical product of the big busi-

[1] For example, see N. Y. *Herald*, April 16, 1888.

ness of the period, and shared its protectionist leanings. A veteran of
the war, trained as a corporation lawyer in Cincinnati, he had shown all
the gifts of a great entrepreneur, and, turning to the financing and construction of railroads, had played a part in developing ten or eleven important routes.[1] It was he who did most to plan, build, and sell the
Nickel Plate line. Already very wealthy, he spent more of his time in
New York and Newport than in Ohio. He represented the cynical school
of politics, was chilly to Cleveland's ideas of reform, and was constantly
surrounded by protectionists. He was destined to enter the Senate a
few years later, and while there to assist in mutilating the Wilson Tariff
bill. Long after the campaign Cleveland's friend William B. Hornblower
wrote that "I do not think that he was heartbroken at the result of the
election." [2] It was absurd that such men as he and Barnum should hold
the positions of greatest power in a tariff reform campaign.

Cleveland cannot be exonerated from partial blame for the selection
of Brice, for he could have demanded a better man. But he was badly
advised by Thurman, who had been associated with Brice in railroad
affairs, and by Gorman, while an interview impressed him with the keen,
nervous, kindly charm of the Ohioan. Moreover, he thought that the selection of so moderate a leader would help exorcise the free-trade bogey.
Barnum held a semi-permanent position, and could not have been pried
out of it without trouble. The President was more fortunate in the manager of the New York State campaign, his friend William H. Murtha.
National headquarters were shortly opened at 10 West 29th Street, in
the fine old family mansion of Mynbert Roosevelt, while the State headquarters were at the Hoffman House. One of the most zealous of the
national committeemen, W. L. Scott, labored most of the summer in
New York, and Charles J. Canda made an efficient national treasurer.[3]

More than one friend had written to Cleveland urging haste in launching the national campaign. As early as June 15 Henry George had appealed to him.[4] "I know a good deal of the temper of that class of workingmen to whom in this campaign our opponents will address their most
frantic appeals," he wrote. "I know that they have courage; that they
are 'logical as children;' that within the last four years free trade ideas
have been making way among them, and a process of economic educa-

[1] *Dictionary Amer. Biog.,* III, 31.
[2] Memorandum by Wm. B. Hornblower, 1911. Cleveland Papers.
[3] See the interesting sketch of national headquarters in the N. Y. *Herald,* Sept. 2, 1888.
[4] Cleveland Papers.

tion has been going on. I have had a large experience in talking with and to them in various parts of the country, and I know that they will respond to an aggressive attack upon protection when they will turn away from a timid one. The only element of danger I see in the political situation is the half-hearted and treacherous timidity of Democratic politicians manifest in the doubtful States—the spirit manifest in the Tammany ratification meeting. No apologetic fight can stand the onslaught I look for." At the same time Eugene Chamberlain began pelting Cleveland with a series of almost frantic letters from the *Argus* office. He insisted that the work of educating voters should commence at once; that the Democrats should buy generous space in the labor press and cheap papers; and that circulars should be sent out in clouds. He burst out in denunciation of the Hillite mayor of Troy: [1]

Such time as Mayor Murphy can take from raising hell with Herrick he devotes to advocating the idea that the Democrats lay low until about two weeks before the election and then put in what money they have. Now, of course, if the men get the idea fixed that their wages will be reduced money enough could not be raised to do anything at all—laying aside the moral iniquity of bribery. Unless we get right among them with the truth, the struggle is useless.

Cleveland thoroughly shared this feeling. On June 17 he wrote Bissell expressing his delight that the situation in Buffalo looked more hopeful. "I approve fully of your plan of campaign," he added, "always supposing that you intend to circulate information to the people on the tariff question, as the main point of your efforts. The localities where this is done the most will be sure to show the best results." But Brice, Barnum, and Gorman cared little about tariff-reform propaganda. They planned an old-fashioned campaign, of the type waged in 1880 and 1884, and waited for strokes of luck that uniformly went to their more enterprising opponents.

For the Republican organization was a model of energy and shrewdness. The national chairman was Matthew S. Quay, who, elected Senator from Pennsylvania the previous year, was already a prominent representative of the alliance between big business and politics.[2] He had learned his politics in the Cameron machine, the most unscrupulous school in the country, in which he had been increasingly useful ever

[1] June 18, 1888, etc.; Cleveland Papers.
[2] On Quay's record see *Harper's Weekly*, Jan. 22, 1887.

since he had entered the legislature just after the war. The treasurer was
W. W. Dudley of Indiana, a Civil War veteran who had lost a leg at
Gettysburg, a second-rate lawyer hungry for the crumbs of office, and a
man who in politics believed the end justified the means.[1] He was an accomplished briber, and as former Pensions Commissioner knew how to
reach the veterans. Both men were expert in the process known, after a
phrase incautiously used by Quay, as "frying the fat" out of the business beneficiaries of the party. Quay shortly enlisted the aid of John
Wanamaker, who became head of a large committee of business men,
covering the whole country, with its own treasurer; while in the critical
States of Indiana and New York men of brains, experience and guile
were placed in charge. In the former State Harrison relied upon James
N. Huston, and in the latter upon Tom Platt, a master of political technique, and as president of an express company a friend of financial
kings.

III

The Republicans also possessed an immense advantage in the vigor
and astuteness of the high-tariff associations supporting them. There
were half a dozen of these bodies, all supported and largely officered by
the keenest business men of the period. The most important, as we have
said, was the American Iron and Steel Association, of which James M.
Swank of Pennsylvania was the leader. It had become a factor in politics
in the early seventies, and gradually extending its activities, now reached
into every Northern State. It made and unmade Congressmen, controlled Republican State committees, and lobbied in the halls of national conventions, while its spectacular success in retiring Morrison
had added greatly to its prestige. Its purse was almost bottomless, for
every ironmaster knew that the existing tariff schedules placed millions
if not tens of millions annually in the pockets of the mill-owners. Carnegie admitted this very spring that he had drawn as much as $1,500,000
out of the J. Edgar Thomson Steel Works in one year as his share of the

[1] Matilda Gresham, *Life of Walter Quinton Gresham*, II, 478. For Dudley's record of
bribery in Indiana in 1880 see the *Nation*, Nov. 8, 1888, which republishes Republican
evidence that he had then helped disburse $400,000 in the State in "buying votes, hiring
repeaters, bribing election officers to stuff ballot-boxes and falsify returns." At a banquet
at Delmonico's after the election of 1880 Arthur had cynically remarked that "Indiana was
really a Democratic State," but that it had been made Republican by a liberal use of "soap."

profits. Swank was a picturesque and able figure.[1] Reared in Johnstown, the seat of the Cambria Iron Works and other large iron and coal properties, he had graduated soon after the war from the editorship of a Whig newspaper to the position of clerk of the House Committee on Manufactures. In 1873 he became secretary of the Iron and Steel Association, and in 1885 its vice-president and general manager. A hardheaded, Calvinist-tempered man of Scotch-Irish blood, he made protection only less a gospel than the Bible of his Presbyterian ancestors. He could well boast that no other organization had ever distributed tariff propaganda so methodically and heavily as his. Now in 1888 the Association girded its loins for the fiercest struggle of its history. Within nine months after Cleveland's message it had scattered broadcast 1,-387,864 pamphlets,[2] paying special attention to the Northwest.

The Republicans had also the aid of the Protective Tariff League, organized several years earlier by such men as Cornelius N. Bliss and Levi P. Morton, and supported by the "One Thousand Defenders of American Industries," who each pledged a hundred dollars yearly and who included manufacturers all over the North.[3] It scattered protectionist documents like pollen on the wind, and sent its agents into Congressional districts, well armed with money. In 1886–88 one of its distinctive activities was the holding of prize contests among the seniors of numerous colleges for essays on protection. The Home Markets Clubs were a group of Eastern organizations founded by New England manufacturers, with headquarters in Boston and an active secretary named Herbert Radclyffe. We should also name the Industrial League, a Pennsylvania society in which such men as Daniel J. Morrell, Joseph Wharton, and Henry C. Lea had been prominent, and which distributed a monthly bulletin, a protectionist almanac, and huge numbers of reprinted speeches and articles.

The correspondence of such men as Wharton Barker, an able Philadelphia financier who had been an early advocate of Harrison's nomination and who supported a protectionist weekly called the *American,* shows that they were greatly alarmed by the Democratic threat. Assiduous attention was paid to the Middle West. Into Minnesota, for example, Swank's

[1] MS. sketch of Swank furnished the author by A. T. Volwiler; files of the Amer. Iron and Steel Assn. *Bulletin.*
[2] Amer. Iron and Steel Assn. *Bulletin,* Dec. 21, 1887, p. 351.
[3] Cf. article in N. Y. *Herald,* June 17, 1888, on the League.

organization mailed 125,519 pamphlets, while newspaper space was bought by the acre. Meanwhile, every effort was made to shake down wealthy manufacturers like Aladdin's jewelled trees. Mark Hanna, who was one of the numerous business men assigned special districts, canvassed Cleveland, Toledo, the Mahoning Valley, and the adjacent towns. Having given $5,000 himself, he was able to demand large subscriptions, and collected more than $100,000 for the National Committee.[1] In Indiana the Republican managers took a poll of the State early in September, and were aghast when it appeared that Cleveland would carry it by a large plurality. They sent a hurried demand to Quay for funds, and the chairman replied that the money must be raised in the West. The State leaders instantly began a canvass of Chicago manufacturers and bankers, and Chicago, as Walter Q. Gresham's biographer dryly remarks, "gave Huston all the money he asked for."[2] No one knows just how great were the sums raised in Pennsylvania, for Quay and Wanamaker prudently destroyed their campaign records.

IV

Compared with the realistic business men on the Republican side, the reformers who aided the Democrats seemed amateurs. It was impossible for such publicists as George W. Curtis and William Graham Sumner to play the rôles taken by Swank and Wharton Barker. The American Free Trade League, with David A. Wells as president, distributed tariff reform documents, but its activities were feeble beside those of the Iron and Steel Association. The most effective organizations were regional rather than national. In New England a good deal was done by the Massachusetts Tariff Reform League, which had been established as a direct result of Cleveland's ringing tariff message. In New York city the Reform Club was indefatigable.[3] Its guiding leaders, who included Secretary Fairchild, Charles R. Miller, editor of the *Times*, John De Witt Warner, a brilliant lawyer who had graduated in the first class of Cornell University, Everett P. Wheeler, and R. R. Bowker, were men of brains and influence. A tall, thin young North Carolinian with bright protruding eyes and humorous mouth, Walter Hines Page, early enlisted in it, while Godkin, Gilder, and Curtis, an impressive editorial

[1] Herbert Croly, *Mark Hanna*, 149.
[2] Gresham, *Gresham*, II, 603.
[3] See sketch in Burton J. Hendrick, *The Training of an American*, 198 ff.

triumvirate, were often seen in its rooms. By August, when it had attained a membership of twelve hundred, it was doing yeoman work and its headquarters at 12 East 33rd Street were a beehive of activity. Tens of thousands of carefully written documents were sent out. Speakers were recruited and trained. One member wrote to Lamont: [1]

> You know what important work the Reform Club is doing. Among other things, they are sending weekly to eight hundred newspapers matter for publication, and they are now compiling a list of all the manufacturing establishments in this State and getting together a great mass of data in regard to the material used in these industries and the conditions under which they are carried on. The Club . . . guarantees to hold at least one public gathering in every town and village in the State with a view to discussing particularly the bearings of the tariff and of the Mills bill upon its home industry.

In the Northwest there was one deceptively imposing organization—the American Tariff Reform League, incorporated in September, 1887, with headquarters in Chicago. Growing slowly at first, it received an impetus from Cleveland's message and by midsummer of 1888 claimed 60,000 members.[2] Its president was John A. King, a millionaire dealer in drugs; its vice-president was Franklin MacVeagh, a wealthy wholesale grocer and a brother of Wayne MacVeagh. On the executive committee were Charles W. Deering, head of a great farm implement factory, and A. C. McClurg, the bookseller. The members included such well known business men as Marshall Field, Philip D. Armour, John Cudahy, Potter Palmer, Cyrus McCormick, and Charles R. Crane. But this organization was all façade, for it did nothing to raise campaign funds, sent out few pamphlets, and aroused little attention. There was more real substance in the Iroquois Club, which had been firmly attached to tariff before Cleveland appeared as paladin of the cause. The Northwest, a good region in which to recruit low-tariff votes, was treated with singular apathy.

In short, the flabbiness of the Democratic organization and the weakness of their auxiliaries soon left them far behind. They possessed the best independent newspapers of the country. While some Mugwump dailies, like the Boston *Transcript,* went over to Harrison, the Springfield *Republican,* New York *Evening Post, Times, Nation,* and *Harper's*

---

[1] George P. Sawyer to Lamont, Aug. 29, 1888. Cleveland Papers.
[2] See sketch, N. Y. *Herald,* Aug. 12, 1888.

Weekly were all on their side. A monthly, *Belford's Magazine,* was established by Don Piatt early in 1888 to aid them. When a really able campaign manager, Abram S. Hewitt, had conducted Tilden's canvass in 1876, he had distributed documents on an unprecedented scale—more than 27,000,000 pieces. In 1888 the Democratic party should have far surpassed such figures, yet Cleveland's papers show that the hunger for pamphlets in the West was never satisfied. George F. Parker wrote early in September of "such unprecedented demand for speeches that it seems impossible to stop the printing presses. We had only the other day a requisition from Illinois for something like 500,000 in a single order. Of course we could not fill it and perhaps will not, but a certain proportion will be sent." [1] Chairman Brice reported that by the middle of September he had printed and distributed between eight and ten million documents, a grossly inadequate number. [2]

As the summer wore on Cleveland, with Congress still "on his hands," received warnings that his forces were fighting badly and that the Republicans were showing better discipline. News came from Indiana that Dudley and Huston were far more systematic in enrolling voters than the Democratic leaders. Alton B. Parker, after a visit of inspection to the Wabash, wrote Cleveland that the party must wake up there; that it must appeal to the State pride in the memory of Hendricks; and that it must obtain more stump orators of the right sort—"Indianians dearly love a speech, but it must be bright and sparkling, not too deep, or abstruse, or technical." [3] In New York city on August 9 Fifth Avenue resounded to the bands of a Harrison procession. There were only 15,000 men in line, many of them from Brooklyn, and they showed but moderate enthusiasm. "These people, however," wrote William B. Ivins to Lamont, "have got a complete start of us in our campaign. It is perfectly useless for our managers to rely on either Tammany Hall or the County Democracy conducting a national canvass and educating the people in this city. They are going to respectively conduct each its own canvass, and in the meantime the work of the Republican propaganda is not being counterbalanced by any work on our side so far as New York is concerned." He added the significant words: [4]

[1] Parker to Lamont, Aug. 18, Sept. 2, 1888. Cleveland Papers.
[2] Brice to Lamont, Sept. 11, 1888. Cleveland Papers.
[3] June 26, 1888. Cleveland Papers.
[4] Cleveland Papers.

As it stands today, the Republicans have got us on the run on the free trade issue. Their whole procession last night was an organized cry of "No, no, no free trade!"

Meanwhile, from city after city and State after State, convincing reports reached Cleveland that the heads of industrial plants were openly dragooning the labor vote. William F. Sheehan wrote from Buffalo that an organized propaganda in every iron mill was teaching the workingmen to regard the Mills bill with fear and trembling.[1] He asked if Randall, in whom most laboring men had warm confidence, could not be sent into the State to make speeches. Another Buffalo observer wrote that the Republicans "are working very hard, and have already commenced the old tactics of inducing manufacturers and large employers of labor to influence their men. Shoelkoff and Lautz Brothers have already had their men out on picnics and have got them labelled with Harrison badges." [2] Edward Murphy sent word from Troy that a director of the Albany Iron Works was pumping money out of the local business men with the threat that if Harrison were defeated, all iron works would shut down. He added that pay envelopes were being issued with printed threats of unemployment. "Enclosed you will find one of the envelopes used by Ives & Company, collar manufacturers of this city, to put the money wages of each of their employees (both males and females) in on Saturday last. The same kind of envelope has been used by every Republican collar manufacturer in this city, and I believe that these envelopes have been sent out to every Republican employer in the State, to be used for the same purpose." [3]

V

Among the causes of Democratic defeat, the intense hostility of the New York Mugwumps to Governor Hill, and the treachery of several small New York bosses, were destined to take an important rank. All the independent voters now distrusted and detested Hill. His veto in the spring of 1888 of a high-license bill had run counter to the best public sentiment of the State, which demanded that the number of saloons be sharply restricted.[4] The great Broadway Railroad franchise scandal, which grew out of the successful attempt of a traction boodler named

[1] Sheehan to Cleveland, Oct. 3, 1888. Cleveland Papers.
[2] S. S. Cary to Cleveland, Aug. 3, 1888. Cleveland Papers.
[3] Murphy to Lamont, Oct. 9, 1888. Cleveland Papers.
[4] See *Harper's Weekly*, April 23, 1887, for comment on Hill's veto.

Jake Sharp to corrupt the aldermen of the metropolis, bore indirectly upon him, for he was a close friend of Sharp. Worst of all was the scandal of the aqueduct contracts. Hill had entered into an arrangement to place the building of a new aqueduct for New York city under the direction of one Squire, a man whom he knew to be a characterless adventurer, and had then abetted various political workers in getting the contract for an important section of this aqueduct awarded to a man whose offer was $54,000 in excess of the lowest bid. Once the award was made, the contract was forthwith sold at a profit of $30,000. Of this sum $10,000 was employed by the treasurer of the State Committee to pay a campaign note signed by Governor Hill in 1885; and ex-Mayor Grace later testified that the note of $10,000 had been used for the governor's personal campaign expenses.[1] Other transactions had long since convinced observers that Hill was an unprincipled and slippery politician, unfit to rule over a great State.

As the time approached for making the Democratic nomination for governor, the opposition became portentous in volume. Curtis denounced Hill as "the special representative of debasing views of politics and public life." The *Times* and *Evening Post* declared that they would under no circumstances support him; the *Herald* asserted that the State would be safe for Cleveland only if Whitney or Hewitt were nominated, and that it was Hill's duty to step aside in favor of a better man.[2] The County Democracy, swayed by Hewitt, Edward Cooper, and Grace, was bitterly hostile to Hill, and ready to make any effort to destroy him. It is probable that the hue and cry against the governor would have been successful if it had been begun earlier, and if the opposition had been rallied about a single leader. But some demanded Hewitt, some Grace, some Roswell P. Flower, and some Smith M. Weed. While the disagreement continued, several leaders went to Cleveland and asked him to dictate the party's choice. It was one of Cleveland's fixed rules that no President should interfere in State politics. "To these overtures," said the *Herald* later, "it is absolutely true that Mr. Cleveland replied that under no circumstances would he interfere with the party management of the State. True to his principles, as in all things, the President kept his hands off." [3]

[1] *Nation*, Aug. 18, 1888.
[2] See *Public Opinion*, Sept. 22, 1888 for a summary of the independent press on Hill.
[3] N. Y. *Herald*, Sept. 13, 1888.

On September 7 there was a great anti-Hill mass-meeting at Cooper Institute. Every foot of the famous hall was occupied. Conspicuous on the stage were Henry George and Wheeler H. Peckham. John De Witt Warner read a long list of vice presidents and secretaries, including George Haven Putnam, Anson Phelps Stokes, Frederic R. Coudert, Montgomery Schuyler, and ex-Mayor Edson. Every mention of Hill's name was greeted with hisses and of Cleveland's with stormy applause. In a ringing speech Peckham rehearsed the history of the Aqueduct Commission, declaring that Hill stood in the some relation to the Democratic party in 1888 that Blaine had sustained to the Republicans in 1884—a campaign of apology would have to be made for him. Henry George asserted that for the very same reasons that he supported Cleveland "with an earnestness, an ardor, and a joy I never experienced in a national campaign since I cast my first vote for Abraham Lincoln," he would vote against Hill. A scathing address to the Democratic State Convention was adopted:

David B. Hill is not a Democrat. He had betrayed his trust to his party and his trust to the people. We charge him with having set the constitution of this State at defiance, and lost the Democratic party the control of the national and State legislatures—with the consequent loss of the Mills bill in the United States Senate. We charge him with having entered into nefarious deals with Republican partisans to rob the treasury of a great city. We charge him with having entered into deals with Republican partisans to give them control of the railway commissions in exchange for an office in the State prisons for one of his personal followers. We charge him with hypocrisy—that while pretending to be distinctly a Democrat he has nevertheless nominated to office more Republicans than were ever before nominated by any Democratic governor, and we ask you to compare his record in this regard with that of Governors Tilden, Robinson, and Cleveland. We charge him with being the avowed protector of the liquor interests.

But the renomination was successfully effected. In midsummer Hill had convoked a long-celebrated midnight conference at the Grand Hotel in Saratoga, where he, Edward Murphy, and William F. Sheehan laid plans to strengthen his lines all over the State; while Murphy came to New York city and obtained pledges of support from Richard Croker and the Tammany sachems. Now Hill showed increased defiance, declaring that he was like an Irish wolfhound, gentle when stroked but fierce when attacked. Alongside its description of the Cooper Union

meeting the *Herald* printed a column story on the obstinate preparations of the machine to nominate him. The State Convention met on
September 12 in Buffalo. The atmosphere of that city was far from
friendly to the governor. Cleveland's friends were surly, while the prohibitionists had just held a great rally in Music Hall, where several
thousands had cheered a neat speech by Frances E. Willard attacking
Hill and declaring that protection for pig-iron was not nearly so important as protection for the home. Yet outwardly all was harmony. Daniel
N. Lockwood nominated Hill, and his name was carried by acclamation.
The platform, carefully drawn under the supervision of D-Cady Herrick, represented Cleveland's views on the tariff, the fisheries question,
and other national issues. It was observed that Tammany and the
County Democracy bivouacked in the same hotel, and that there were
no fist-fights.[1]

Just how much Hill's candidacy cost Cleveland will never be known,
but it was a great deal. He supported the President loyally if coldly, and
in stumping the State gave earnest attention to the tariff and the Mills
bill. Personally likable, and altogether congenial to the rough-and-
tumble element in politics, he attracted two persons to his own support
for every one that he repelled. The difficulty, however, was that those
he attracted could by no means be counted upon to support Cleveland
as well; while many of those he repelled would certainly vote a straight
Republican ticket, dropping Cleveland along with Hill. This was why
the *Herald* spoke of his "almost incredible rashness" in imperilling the
national ticket. E. P. Wheeler, after a careful canvass of offices and
labor organizations in New York city, concluded that 20,000 business
men and 30,000 workmen would vote against Hill.[2] Soon afterward the
San Francisco *Examiner* printed an interesting interview between Hill
and Senator George Hearst. In this Hill made the conventional statements that New York would give a large majority for the national ticket,
that his own nomination had united the warring factions, and that all
looked rosy. But he also dropped several admissions that he and Cleveland fought at the head of different armies, and that there was an essential antagonism between their forces. Thus he referred angrily to the
attacks upon him by the *Times* and *Evening Post*. "I'll speak plainly,"
he said. "There are some people in the rank and file who don't think it

[1] Buffalo *Courier*, Sept. 12, 13, 14, 1888.
[2] N. Y. *Herald*, Sept. 8, 1888.

is quite the right thing that these two papers should attack me so seriously when I'm doing all I can to win for Cleveland. They think that the national leaders ought to squelch these newspapers which are endeavoring to make their little circle and Mr. Cleveland believe that he is above his party." And a moment later he made the significant remark: "There are many persons, to be sure, who will vote for him and not vote for me, *but this loss will be compensated to me.*" [1]

Despite intense pressure, Cleveland stubbornly refused to write a letter endorsing Hill. Chairman Brice went to the White House to plead for an endorsement, saying that the State Brewers' Association would deliver 25,000 votes to Cleveland if he only stood squarely by the governor. Cleveland said no. Brice reminded him that he had once written a letter in behalf of John R. Fellows. "Yes," said Cleveland, "and I was a fool for doing it." "But," persisted Brice, "Governor Hill is as much a Democratic nominee as you are yourself." To which Cleveland replied with heat, "I don't care a damn if he is—each tub must stand on its own bottom." [2]

In the end, Hill's candidacy cost Cleveland three groups of voters. It cost him many former Mugwumps who voted a straight Republican ticket; many prohibitionists; and most important of all, many shifty and calculating machine men. To this last-named element Hill's candidacy held up an irresistible temptation to play a double game. If Cleveland were to carry New York while Warner Miller, the Republican candidate for Governor, defeated Hill, then Hill would be a dead cock in the pit. But if Cleveland were defeated while Hill triumphantly carried the State, many would regard Cleveland's race as run and Hill as the rising luminary. Under such circumstances, thousands of machine men were sure to vote for Hill and Harrison. Richard Croker went to Washington for a much-discussed interview with Cleveland. "You understand, Mr. Croker," were Cleveland's parting words, "I ask no pledge, but trust entirely to the loyalty of Tammany Hall." "Mr. President," Croker replied, "you will never regret that trust." [3] The Tammany leaders made an earnest effort to keep the faith, and dinned the word loyalty into the ears of the district chiefs and ward officers. But as we shall see, in the end important machine groups sold out.

[1] Sept. 21, 1888.
[2] Henry Watterson in Louisville *Courier-Journal,* April 11, 1904.
[3] N. Y. *Herald,* Sept. 27, 1888.

VI

The principal hope of many Republicans in their long bedevilment of the fisheries question had been to arouse the latent Irish and New England prejudice against Great Britain, and thus injure the Administration politically. Selfish partisanship has seldom entered into our diplomatic relations in a more sinister way. It was very easy to inflame the Irish against Bayard, a lover of peace, and against Phelps, who had said that every American was at home in England, for he had changed his skies but not the hearts of the people about him. It was easy to buy up Irish-American agitators. O'Donovan Rossa, editor of the *United Irishman,* who supported Cleveland, wrote that a number of them were patriots for revenue only. It was also easy to paint the rejection of Cleveland's treaty as a vindication of national rights. But in August the President threw his enemies into confusion by his sudden demand for a retaliatory law.

The effect of this demand was to undo much of the political mischief already wrought. The Irish-Americans rose in jubilant applause. In Cleveland's papers are sheafs of hundreds of telegrams, all dated August 24–28, 1888, congratulating him fervently. Most of them bear Irish names—Kelly, Healy, McGuire, Ryan, Murphy, and so on. "God bless you for your devotion to old Erin," telegraphed one. From Odessa, Russia, came "Congratulations. Heenan." Manton Marble sent "cordial congratulations;" Henry Watterson telegraphed, "As John Kemble said when he gave the beggar a sovereign, 'It is not often that I do these things, but when I do them I do them handsomely;' " and William R. Grace wired, "My firm is likely to be a large sufferer by a policy of retaliation against Canada, and yet I feel constrained to heartily applaud your course." [1] Tammany men wrote or telegraphed by the score. The Irish and Catholic press was enthusiastic. It is certain that Cleveland, despite Senator Cullom's immediate accusation, thought little of political considerations when drafting his message. But it is equally certain that the act was decidedly to his political advantage.

Unfortunately his message had an unexpected sequel. It was read in Pomona, Cal., by a Republican named George Osgoodby, who interpreted it as an electioneering device to pull the wool over Irish eyes. It occurred to him that the best way to learn if the message was not essen-

[1] Cleveland Papers.

tially a trick, framed in collusion with British leaders, was to write to the British minister, Sackville-West. Adopting what his son euphemistically calls the device of a detective, he sent the Minister an adroit letter,[1] in which he represented himself as one Murchison, born an Englishman but now naturalized. He made an artful inquiry:

I am unable to understand for whom I should cast my ballot, when, but one month ago, I was sure Mr. Cleveland was the man. If Cleveland was pursuing a new policy toward Canada, temporarily only and for the sake of obtaining popularity and the continuation of his office for four years more, but intends to cease his policy when his reëlection in November is secured, and again favor England's interests, then I should have no further doubt, but go forward and vote for him. I know of no one better able to direct me, sir, and most respectfully ask your advice in the matter.. . . As you . . . know whether Mr. Cleveland's policy is temporary only and whether he will, as soon as he secures another four years in the presidency, suspend it for one of friendship and free trade, I apply to you privately and confidentially for information which shall in turn be treated as entirely secret.[2]

The alert Spring-Rice, having spent more than a year in Washington cracking jokes with John Hay, exchanging opinions with Roosevelt, learning from Henry Adams who were the originals of the characters in *Democracy*, and concluding that nowhere in the world was there so base a system of politics and politicians, had just gone back from the British legation to the Foreign Office. Sackville-West scrutinized the Murchison letter with his large, sad blue eyes, and wearily wrote an answer. He fell squarely into the trap. Pointing out that any party which openly favored the mother country would lose votes, and that the Democrats knew this, he announced, in effect, that he still thought Cleveland the best choice; for after the election he would be reasonable:

The party, however, is, I believe, still desirous of maintaining friendly relations with Great Britain, and still desirous of settling all questions with Canada which have been, unfortunately, reopened since the rejection by the Republican majority in the Senate and by the President's message to which you allude. All allowances must, therefore, be made for the political situation as regards the presidential election thus created. It is, however, impossible to predict the course which President Cleveland may pursue in the matter of retaliation should he be elected; but there is every reason to believe that, while upholding

---

[1] This story is now first told in full; see the letter of Charles A. Osgoodby to the Library of Congress, Feb. 13, 1931.

[2] N. Y. *Times, Herald, World*, Oct. 25, 1888.

the position he has taken, he will manifest a spirit of conciliation in dealing with the question involved in his message.

This letter, dated September 13 and marked "Private," was turned over to the Republican managers. They held it back till October 24. The Republican press commented upon it with gleeful acrimony, while Blaine made it the text for resounding appeals to the Irish vote. At last, cackled a thousand voices, the Administration had been caught in its "truckling" to Great Britain. From the Democratic leaders came an instant demand that Sackville-West be dismissed. It did not matter whether he was a fool or a knave, remarked the New York *Times;* he should go. A. K. McClure wrote Cleveland: "Now kick out Lord Sackville with your biggest boot of best leather, and you've got 'em. *Hesitation is death.*" [1]

For one day, October 25, Cleveland waited while Sackville-West called on Bayard and made a lame explanation, which utterly failed to mollify the President. Next day the *Tribune* printed an interview with the British Minister in which he spoke resentfully of American political tricks and the action of Congress, and by implication impugned the good faith of the President. That closed the case. Sackville-West called again at the State Department, and when Bayard expressed his amazement, explained that the reporter had garbled his remarks.[2] But it was too late. Cleveland had given Bayard his instructions, and that very afternoon the latter cabled London that the usefulness of Sackville-West had ended. When Lord Salisbury refused to call him home, he was dismissed.

In this Cleveland did right; for Sackville-West had committed a blunder so offensive that he deserved summary treatment. No intelligent tyro in politics could have read the Murchison letter without seeing that it was a trap. "Many English citizens," ran the third sentence, "have for years refrained from being naturalized as they thought no good would accrue from the act, but Mr. Cleveland's Administration has been so favorable and friendly toward England, so kind in not enforcing the retaliation act passed by Congress, so sound on free trade questions, and so hostile to the dynamite school of Ireland, that by the hundreds— yes, by the thousands—they have become naturalized for the express

[1] Oct. 27, 1888. Cleveland Papers.
[2] See Bayard's long dispatches to Phelps, Oct. 25, 26. Henry White Papers.

purpose of helping elect him over again, the one above all of American politicians they consider their own and their country's best friend." This was obviously for Republican publication. The minister's reply was censurable on two points. It virtually advised Murchison to vote for Cleveland, and this was interference in our domestic affairs. The letter by construction also accused Cleveland of acting hypocritically in an effort to delude the voters. He wished to settle all difficulties in "a spirit of conciliation;" but he knew that any party which favored the mother country "would lose popularity;" and "allowances must therefore be made" for his course just before election. This insult stung the President.

But the dismissal of Lord Sackville did not restore to Cleveland the ballots that had been lost by a mean and petty fraud, and a still meaner clamor. Irish-American feeling had just been exacerbated by the failure of Home Rule, the fall of Gladstone, and the severe measures of Arthur Balfour in Ireland. It was easy for men like Blaine to make Cleveland's whole policy, including his action on the tariff, seem unduly favorable to England. John Sherman told audiences that the Administration had always been pro-British, and now it had been found out. "They have given Sir Sackville the shake, and now all that remains for you to do is to give Mr. Cleveland the sack." [1]

VII

In the closing weeks of the campaign both sides exploited the tariff issue to the utmost. Blaine arrived home from Europe by the new steamship *City of New York* on August 10. This vessel, the pride of the Inman Line, and referred to by enthusiastic reporters as a "leviathan," had made a record maiden trip, but Blaine robbed the boat of all attention. Excursion boats thrashed down the harbor, with bands and hurrahing crowds, to greet him; private yachts plowed past; Murat Halstead, Whitelaw Reid, and William Walter Phelps scrambled upon the bridge to wring his hand.[2] He was hurried ashore, that night addressed a huge crowd from a grand-stand in Madison Square, and then, setting out for Maine, began discussing the tariff in speech after speech.

The Republicans shrewdly presented a double front on the tariff ques-

[1] New York *Herald*, Nov. 12, 1888.
[2] N. Y. *Herald*, Aug. 11, 1888.

tion. For the benefit of conservatives they offered the Allison bill in the Senate, a thoroughly moderate measure. A good many Senators had at first opposed showing their hand on the issue. Sherman, Cullom, and Platt of Connecticut argued that they ran a needless risk in offering a substitute for the Mills bill and that they would be wiser in simply standing for the principle of protection in general terms. But Chairman Allison of the Finance Committee replied that the party could not afford to evade the tariff issue, or pose as the opponents of all tariff reduction, and that they must do something about the surplus. At an informal caucus in Senator Evarts' breezy parlors on the night of July 25 he and Aldrich carried the day.[1] When Blaine came back he showed great discontent with this decision. He sent word by Senator Hale that the Republicans were foolish to attempt a bill, and that even yet they would do well to drop it; but Allison and his friends proved adamant.[2]

It was the discontented Northwest of which Allison was thinking. He knew how warmly the farmers of Illinois, Iowa, Nebraska, and Minnesota resented the Republican platform and the high-protectionist speeches that Harrison was making. Their indignation must be allayed. Moreover, Allison and Aldrich feared that if the Senate took a do-nothing attitude, defeated the Mills bill, and went home, Cleveland would summon an extra session in September and repeat his solemn warning about the danger of surplus taxation. This apprehension was well grounded and had great effect. Every Republican Senator could conjure up a vision of Cleveland, like some grim policeman, dragging the members back to their duty.[3] Congress remained in session until October 20. Through the hot days Allison, Aldrich, and Hiscock labored away till on September 25 their work was done, and the main provisions of the Allison bill were made public. This bill was much better than the Republican platform, and in the Northwest was rapidly made a substitute for it. The sugar duties were to be halved, the tobacco tax abolished, and the free list increased by various articles not produced in the United States—all this promising a lowering of the troublesome revenues by nearly $70,000,000.

But in the manufacturing East the platform was cried up and the Allison bill forgotten. Mill towns were plastered with protectionist tracts;

[1] Washington correspondence. N. Y. *Herald,* July 6, 26, 1888.
[2] N. Y. *Herald,* Aug. 18, 1888.
[3] N. Y. *Herald,* July 27, 1888.

petitions against the Mills bill were sent to shops and factories, superintendents were asked to obtain signatures, and work was suspended while the hands were called up to declare themselves against "free trade." Workingmen in some New Jersey cities reacted against this coercion.[1] Blaine's speeches implied that protection could hardly be high enough, and he and Ben Butler decried the idea that tariffs had anything to do with the trusts. A similar emphasis was laid upon high protection by Harrison himself, who in brief, pithy, and genuinely thoughtful discourses to the delegations that visited him in Indianapolis—ninety-four speeches in all—made his voice count in no uncertain fashion. The effect of Henry George's numerous speeches to Eastern workingmen was impaired by his emphasis on actual free trade, so that some thought he did more harm than good; and it was offset also by the protectionist assertions of Terence V. Powderly, head of the Knights of Labor.[2]

Cleveland was unfortunate in having no speakers who attracted nation-wide attention in the way that Blaine and Harrison did. The President was kept hard at work in Washington by the protracted Congressional session. Harried as always, he wrote Bissell that "I am beginning to feel very much indeed the want of rest and freedom from the terrible nagging I have to submit to here. The work I could get along with and be quite content and comfortable; but I am not permitted to work until other people are abed and asleep."[3] He was also estopped from speechmaking by his feeling for the dignity of his office, and he insisted that his Cabinet stick to their desks. His one appeal to the public was in his letter of acceptance, issued on September 10. Writing this with laborious care, he submitted it for criticism to a special meeting of the Cabinet, Carlisle, W. L. Scott, and Lamont. He came very near imitating his December message by dealing with the tariff alone, barely mentioning civil service reform and the currency. His paragraphs on the menace of the surplus, excessive duties, and the trusts were for once lit up by an attempt at epigram. "Unnecessary taxation is unjust taxation," he wrote. Again, "Our people ask relief from the undue and unnecessary burden of taxation now resting upon them. They are offered instead—free tobacco and free whiskey." He emphasized the fact that his party was embarking upon no free-trade crusade, but the quintes-

[1] N. Y. *Herald*, July 3; *Nation*, Oct. 18, 1888.
[2] Henry George, jr., *Life of Henry George*, 511: N. Y. *Herald*, Aug. 10, 1888.
[3] July 22, 1888. Cleveland Papers.

sence of his letter was an unflinching restatement of the principles he had laid down nine months earlier. Two days later Harrison replied in a letter that was equally unflinching and epigrammatic. The Democrats, he wrote, "are students of maxims, and not of the markets." [1]

Particularly unhappy was the attempt of Allen G. Thurman to join Carlisle, Mills, and the other Democratic speakers on the stump. He suffered from neuralgia. When an Indiana delegation waited on him at Columbus, O., he untied a handkerchief from his face. "God knows," he said, "that I would rather be at home with my dear old wife than in any office in the world." Early in September, amid carefully manufactured enthusiasm, he was brought to New York to address a meeting in Madison Square Garden. A crowd of twenty thousand filled the hall, and as many surged about it. Hill, Brice, Grace, and others filed upon the stage; but where was Thurman? Then came a thunder of applause; the old Roman, white-haired, rugged-faced, stood before them.[2] He began in a low voice: "Mr. President, ladies and gentlemen, Democrats of the city of New York. I have heard it said since I was nominated for the Vice Presidency of the United States that Allen G. Thurman is an old, weak, broken-down man. I don't know what to reply to this. It seems to me, though, that I am not quite as well as I ought to be, and I am in no condition to speak to an immense audience like this tonight. I want to speak. But I am too unwell. . . ." At this point he broke down; his face grew white, he turned from the audience, tottered, and was assisted to his chair. Then, amid sympathetic cheers, he was led from the hall while it was explained that he was suffering from cholera morbus.

As the summer closed Cleveland was frankly told by many friends that he was losing the fight. The *Herald* in August snorted its disgust over Barnum's silly claim that the prohibitionist votes were not really slipping to Harrison, a lifelong temperance advocate.[3] "The Democratic organization is weak. The Republicans began with an aggressive campaign and are forcing the fighting in every State. . . . While the Republican canvass shows animation the Democratic canvass droops and hangs." One prominent Congressman, not named, returned to the House from New York that same month "disgusted and made heartily sick by the apathy and indolence manifest" at Democratic headquarters.[4] The

[1] For sane comment, see Springfield *Republican*, Sept. 12, 1888.
[2] N. Y. *World, Times*, Sept. 7, 1888.
[3] Aug. 10, 1888.
[4] N. Y. *Herald*, Aug. 10, 13, 14, 1888.

shrewd Bissell entertained no illusions as to Brice's zeal and capacity. Following a visit to New York, he wrote Lamont in early October that the managers pretended to be working hard, "but there seemed a sort of amateurish air, and I gained the impression that they have washed fully as much as they will hang out." [1]

By frequent letters to Brice and Barnum, and above all by exhortations conveyed through Lamont, Cleveland did what he could to stiffen the party lines. Lamont unquestionably furnished no small share of what brains were actually used in the canvass. It was he who directed State Chairman Murtha in October to ignore the large cities and concentrate his attention on the interior towns of New York. While the Administration gave its principal attention to the Empire State, Cleveland by no means neglected Indiana. As apprehensive reports came from that quarter, he addressed Governor Gray a letter of warning, written with a tact that makes it of unusual interest: [2]

I have been hoping that some errand would bring you in this direction and that I might be thus afforded a personal interview touching Indiana politics. Since, however, all reports from there represent you as very actively at work in the canvass, I am satisfied that you are employed to the best possible advantage at home.

Our Indiana friends are nearly unanimous in their expressions of the utmost confidence in the result in their State; and I am sure I ought not to distrust their judgement. I have occasionally feared, however, that they were relying too much upon surface indications and were somewhat influenced by the enthusiasm of the campaign.

One or two quite shrewd Indianians have informed me lately that though they did not contemplate defeat in their State, the organization of the party there was not as close and complete as it ought to be.

But these reports have caused me no uneasiness since I have been assured that you have undertaken to look to this matter. I only want to remind you that there will be, later in the campaign, an attack made upon your forces, that will be exceedingly dangerous unless all our men are in line, and touching elbows.

VIII

One error, and only one, was made by the Republican managers; and it was made, naturally enough, in Indiana. The campaign in that State attained a fervor that amounted almost to frenzy. Harrison had pledged

[1] Oct. 3, 1888. Cleveland Papers.
[2] Sept. 29, 1888. Cleveland Papers.

his party that he would carry it and the initial evidence that it would go Democratic stung his associates to desperate exertions. Both parties kept the countrysides seething with rallies, political picnics, processions, and barbecues. Allen W. Thurman, son of the vice-presidential candidate, wrote Cleveland that the people there had become daft; he thought that he had seen political excitement before, but it was a mistake. To Lamont he sent a longer description of the uproar: [1]

I never in my life saw anything like it. Men, women, and children, boys and girls, have all gone crazy on the subject of politics. We saw not less than twenty "Frankie Cleveland Clubs," all dressed in red bandannas. These girls marched in the procession through the mud and rain at Shelbyville and Peru like the boys. At Brazil there was a company of about a hundred on horseback dressed in navy blue riding-habits, with bandanna vest fronts and vests of same, blue racing caps, and bandanna trimmings. They rode splendidly and presented one of the prettiest sights I have ever seen.

In their anxiety the Indiana Republicans finally overreached themselves in a way which, if the Democratic managers had been alert, would have cost them the election. On October 31, the Indianapolis *Sentinel* published the famous blocks-of-five circular sent out by the Republican national treasurer, W. W. Dudley, just a week earlier. Written on National Committee stationery, and addressed to local leaders throughout Indiana, it declared that he expected them to hold enough "floaters" and doubtful voters to give Harrison a plurality of 10,000. They would "certainly receive from Chairman Huston the assistance necessary"— i. e., the money. "Divide the floaters into blocks of five and put a trusted man with necessary funds in charge of these five and make him responsible that none get away and that all vote our ticket." [2] This was an incitement to wholesale bribery. The letter was unquestionably authentic. It had come to light through a Democratic mail agent on the Ohio & Mississippi Railroad, whose curiosity had been aroused by the large number of Republican missives suddenly sent to Indiana addresses, and who had opened one. It was immediately accepted by Lucius B. Swift and other impartial Indianians.

For a moment Quay and his associates were stunned; and then they resolved to brazen the matter out. With the aid of a Treasury secret-agent, Quay ascertained the mail clerk's name. He warned this man and

[1] Thurman to Cleveland and Lamont, Oct. 22, 1888. Cleveland Papers.
[2] See Gresham, *Gresham,* 602 ff., for a history of this incident.

the Democratic organization that as soon as he found time there would be a prosecution for theft from the Federal mails. Meanwhile, he declared the publication another Democratic lie. Dudley unblushingly denounced it as a forgery, and instituted face-saving suits, subsequently dropped, against the New York *World, Evening Post, Times,* and *Commercial Advertiser.* By this exhibition of nerve the Republican managers saved their party from the worst consequences of Dudley's act. It was easy for them to shout "roorback" and to recall the forged Morey letter of 1880. Though they deserved to lose Indiana on the issue raised by this letter, they carried it by a narrow margin of 2300 votes. If Brice and Barnum had possessed half the energy shown by Gorman in 1884, they would have used the incident to bury this plurality out of sight.

The final factor in Cleveland's defeat was the use of bribery in New York and Indiana. Many of the Democratic charges of fraud were doubtless mere froth and sputter, but some were well sustained. There is evidence that Quay transported a considerable number of Pennsylvanians to New York to register and vote. Singerly, the editor of the Philadelphia *Record,* learned that he was sending over gangs of two or three hundred at a time.[1] Godkin wrote just after the election that the quotations on New York voters had shown a marked appreciation. He knew of a village near the metropolis where seventy-five colored voters had always hitherto disposed of their votes for two dollars apiece; this year they insisted on five dollars apiece, and got it. They felt the buoyancy in the market almost as soon as the canvass opened.[2] Much more striking were the disclosures made shortly after the election by the *Mail and Express,* a Republican evening newspaper whose editor, Col. E. F. Shepard, was on the inside of politics. A detailed news-story laid bare the relations between the Republican managers and some local Democratic leaders. On the Saturday before election the National Committee paid through a State leader $150,000 for bribery. It was all used for the purchase of three "movements"—the James O'Brien movement, estimated at 10,000 votes; the Coogan movement, estimated at 30,000; and the John J. O'Brien or Eighth District movement, an unknown quantity. The *Mail and Express* declared that the Coogan movement promised Harrison and Miller 20,000 more votes than it really polled; the James O'Brien movement 10,000 more than it polled; and that the John J.

[1] See William M. Singerly to Cleveland, Oct. 18, 1888. Cleveland Papers.
[2] *Nation,* Nov. 22, 1888.

O'Brien movement kept its word pretty well for Harrison, but miserably for Miller. In other words, the *Mail and Express* was angry because a costly attempt to buy votes in New York city had broken down—only half of them had stayed bought! [1]

In Indiana the proofs of corruption were overwhelming. Immediately after the election the Democrats and the Assistant Federal Attorney in Indianapolis gathered much evidence; and a *World* reporter who interviewed Judge Gresham in Indianapolis found him shocked. He declared that the arm of the law should reach the central organizers. "You may convict a hundred—yes, even a thousand—obscure voters for bribery but the effect upon the community would be as nothing compared to that which would follow the conviction of one prominent man." This was obviously a reference to Dudley. By now the authenticity of the blocks-of-five letter was clear, and reports were circulated that the Republican national committee intended to make him a scapegoat for its sins. Dudley served notice through the press that if anything of the kind were attempted, he would "explode a lot of dynamite," and expose the entire inner workings of the Republican campaign. His threat was effective.[2] In the end all the efforts to prosecute him failed. The Federal district judge in Indianapolis, William A. Woods, repeatedly delayed action and finally, in January, 1889, addressed the grand jury in terms which made it impossible to indict the Republican treasurer; and it was later charged that he did so under pressure from men close to Harrison and high in Republican councils.[3]

Meanwhile, a hundred pens described the disgraceful scenes which had taken place. At Bloomington, under the shadow of the State University, Republican workers spent the day before election collecting the floaters. By nightfall more than a hundred had been impounded in the G.A.R. Hall, a Republican newspaper office, and other buildings. A woman who tried on election day to buy butter was told that it had all gone to make sandwiches for the blocks of five. Spectators at the Bloomington polls were scandalized by the open parade of bribed voters. A worker would drive up with two or three disreputable negroes, place ballots in their hands, and watch as they deposited the slips. The ruling

---

[1] N. Y. *Mail and Express*, Nov. 22, 1888; *Nation*, Nov. 29, 1888. Wanamaker was accused of raising an emergency fund of $400,000 in the last days of the campaign, but declared there was no last-minute appeal and the amount was less, though "more than $200,000." H. A. Gibbons, *John Wanamaker*, I, 253 ff.

[2] Gresham, *Gresham*, 608 ff.

[3] Indianapolis *Sentinel*, Jan. 17, 1889; Gresham, *Gresham, ut supra.*

price was $15 a vote, paid in five-dollar gold-pieces, and shopkeepers later reported that many of the glittering pieces were handed them for supplies.[1]

IX

Cleveland awaited the returns in the White House library with his wife and a few friends. At midnight Secretary Whitney, crossing from the telegraph room down the second-floor corridor, announced, "Well, it's all up." [2] Yet the Republicans had won the narrowest of victories. Of 401 electoral votes Harrison received 233, and Cleveland 168. But in Indiana the Republican plurality was only 2,348; in Rhode Island, 4,438; in New York, 13,002; and in Ohio, 19,599. In the total popular vote Cleveland had a plurality, according to one computation, of 100,-476, and by another, of 115,534.[3] A slight shift in the distribution of this popular plurality would have given him what all political wiseacres would have called a "sweeping" victory. Hill carried New York by a comfortable margin.

For two reasons Cleveland accepted defeat philosophically. At four o'clock on election day he had written his friend Dr. Ward that on private grounds he would welcome a return to private life. "You know how I feel in the matter and how great will be the *personal* compensations of defeat. I am very sure that any desire I may have for success rests upon the conviction that the triumph of my party at this time means the good and the prosperity of the country. You see I am in a good mood to receive the returns whatever they may be." On public grounds, he felt that defeat was in part really a victory—that from it, at any rate, victory would ultimately spring. A few days after the election he told a friend that the time had come when the issue between the two parties had to be made and the Democrats had made it. "I don't regret it. It is better to be defeated battling for an honest principle than to win by a cowardly subterfuge. Some of my friends say we ought to have gone before the country on the clean administration we have given. I differ with them. We were defeated, it is true, but the principles of tariff reform will surely win in the end." [4]

[1] *Nation*, Nov. 22, 1888.
[2] McElroy, *Grover Cleveland*, I, 298.
[3] *Appleton's Annual Cyclopedia* gives the former figure; *McPherson's Handbook* the latter.
[4] N. Y. *Herald*, Nov. 15, 1888.

This was the view of his friends and admirers. Horace White wrote him that the election vindicated his message, for he had done away with a mistaken timidity. "It was a perilous and paralyzing superstition to suppose that a party which should boldly attack the protective tariff would be necessarily overwhelmed in the first succeeding election. I confess that I shared this superstition myself to a large extent. So did Schurz and Wells. We all thought that no less than four years time would suffice to educate the people so as to avoid a paralyzing blow in the first round. You have dissipated this misconception from the mind's eye of any man who thought himself especially wise on this subject. From henceforth we have plain sailing, no fogs, no false lights. And for this we are indebted to nobody but yourself. If my advice had been asked about your message of last December I should have advised against it, and *I should have been wrong.*" [1] The Springfield *Republican* held that reform was sure to come, and that, as so often before, the principles of the defeated party might triumph through their opponents. Greeley had been beaten in 1872, but his contest drove the Republicans to concede amnesty to the Confederate leaders; Tilden was beaten in 1876, but Hayes freed the South; the Tories carried Parliament on the corn laws, but Peel found it necessary to abolish the grain duties. A young Western attorney named W. J. Bryan wrote [2] from Lincoln that "we would rather fall with you fighting on and for a principal (*sic*) than succeed with the party representing nothing but an organized appetite;" that " your position was so wisely and bravely taken that I believe the party will look back to you in after years with gratitude and not with reproach;" and that "if you would only move to Nebraska and run in '92 as a Western man with the friends you have in the East, we can elect you. Why not come to Omaha or Lincoln?" Harold Frederic assured him [3] that victory could not add anything to the grandeur of his moral position. But the best statement of the ground won was contained in a letter which Vilas wrote to Endicott: [4]

The same rampant sectionalism and corruption which, in reality, accomplished the end, would not have been stayed by any servile and time-serving avoidance of the obligation. But none can affirm that if, in such case, he had not been reëlected, we should not be a mere opposition, not a party, now;

[1] New York, Nov. 10, 1888. Cleveland Papers.
[2] Nov. 21, 1888. Cleveland Papers.
[3] London, Dec. 8, 1888. Cleveland Papers.
[4] Madison, May 10, 1891. Cleveland Papers.

carping at our adversaries, picking flaws to excite popular feeling, but not at all, as now, a great, united, cohering body aligned on well-defined principles, moving to ends as just, and as justly awakening popular support, as any that have ever gratified a triumphant political organization.

Even without taking account of the bribery in New York and Indiana, the election was perfectly negative on the tariff. The manufacturing State of New Jersey was carried by Cleveland with a higher plurality than in 1884. He carried the manufacturing State of Connecticut, though by a reduced plurality. In the principal manufacturing strongholds of these States—Newark, Paterson, Bridgeport, Waterbury—the free-trade scare did not work, and the Democrats gained ground. Nor did it work in Rhode Island; in Providence, in Pawtucket, and in the State as a whole, Harrison had a much smaller plurality than Blaine.[1] In the manufacturing city of Philadelphia Blaine's plurality in 1884 had been 30,000, and Harrison's was cut to 18,000. The principal wool-growing States of the North were Ohio and California. In both the Democrats, despite the clamor over the wool schedules, gained ground as compared with 1884. In Saginaw, Michigan, the large lumber and salt interests made special efforts to influence the workmen, and yet the Democratic plurality in that county was double what it had been in 1884.[2] Michigan, in fact, gave Harrison a plurality of only 23,000 as against Blaine's plurality of 43,000. Several distinctively manufacturing communities in Ohio, like Piqua, responded to the protectionist appeal by an increased Democratic vote.[3]

At first glance it seems a pity that, with the result so close, the additional effort was not made to turn the balance in the right direction. If Cleveland had presented his great tariff message a year or six months earlier; if he and his aides had organized the campaign more energetically; if a real manager had been chosen instead of the apathetic Brice—then the result might have been different. The country might have been spared all that the Harrison Administration gave it—the greed and folly of the McKinley Tariff; the reckless agitation of Lodge's Force Bill;

---

[1] Stanwood, *History of the Presidency*, 483 ff.
[2] *Nation*, Nov. 15, 22, 29, etc., 1888.
[3] The N. Y. *World* reproached Cleveland bitterly for loss of the election, declaring he should have done more to placate machine Democrats in New York State, and should have written his tariff message in 1886 or even 1885. The *Herald* said the party had sprung an issue upon the people without preparation, and had "to drill their recruits in the face of the enemy." N. Y. *Herald*, Nov. 8, 1888. But Whitney thought prohibition responsible, and Lamar denied that the tariff was the reason.

the wasteful Dependent Pensions Act; the dangerous Sherman Silver-Purchase Act.

But perhaps it was not a pity after all. A portentous storm was steadily brewing in the West. The clouds were piling higher and higher, but the tempest was not to burst until the years 1893–96. When it did burst a statesman was needed in the White House—not a Harrison, not a McKinley, but a leader of unyielding courage and rocklike principle. The country could well do without Cleveland in the next four years in order to have his strength and bravery available in the fearful crisis that was coming.

CLEVELAND, as his letters inform us, looked forward to his release from the presidency like a schoolboy looking forward to vacation. One element in his feeling was his resentment of the scandalous abuse to which he and his wife had been subjected during the previous year. A series of stories had been started before and during the campaign to counteract the obvious effect upon the public mind of his marriage to a charming woman; stories which went so far as to picture a drunken President driving his wretched wife out into the snow. A melancholy fact was that, as in 1884, a minister assumed the lead in retailing these scandals. This was the Rev. C. H. Pendleton, a Baptist of Worcester, Mass., who had attended a church conference in the capital and had brought home the fables about Cleveland's brutality and his bride's sufferings. He was promptly crushed by a letter which Mrs. Cleveland wrote for publication,[1] but the whispering campaign continued. In one instance the scandal was carried from house to house by a female colporteur who wept in telling it![2] Another element in Cleveland's repugnance to office was his simple weariness of its burdens; and a third factor was his belief that his principal work, that of departmental reform, was after all fully accomplished.

For a few weeks Cleveland was troubled by the problem of finding a home and an occupation; for he emphatically refused to think of Buffalo, and he knew that Washington, with the Republicans in power, would be uncongenial. But he received numerous offers of positions, and shortly acceded to the proposal of Francis Lynde Stetson that he form a connection with the law firm of Bangs, Stetson, Tracy, and MacVeagh. In their office he could do as much or little as he liked, and accept a type of work that would seldom take him into the courts; while in New York he could sink back into an inconspicuous position and 'live with his wife as other men do' more easily than elsewhere. The next few years reveal him in a new rôle, delighting in family and friends and in the first broad margin of leisure since boyhood.

---

[1] To Mrs. Maggie Nicodemus, June 3, 1888; Cleveland Papers. Mrs. Cleveland wrote that she could wish the women of America no greater blessing than that their homes might be as happy, and their husbands as kind, attentive, and considerate, as hers.
[2] *Nation,* June 14, 1888.

His last months in the White House were pleasantly free from for-midable cares. The annual message which he sent to Congress in Decem-ber, though full of detailed recommendations for legislation, was notable chiefly for his attack on trusts, for his reiteration that the tariff should be revised downward, and for some remarkably sharp words on the inequalities of wealth in America. It contained sentences so radical in tone that they might have been written by Henry George. One could search the messages of previous Presidents in vain for a parallel to the paragraphs in which he spoke of cities where "wealth and luxury" jostled with "poverty and wretchedness and unremunerative toil," and of the long-suffering farmers who were revolting against "the impover-ishment of rural sections." One hundred years after Washington, he de-clared, "The gulf between employers and the employed is constantly widening, and classes are rapidly forming, one comprising the very rich and powerful, while in another are found the toiling poor." The rich boasted of the achievements of aggregated capital, "while the citizen is struggling far in the rear or is trampled to death beneath an iron heel." Corporations which should be the creatures of the law and the servants of the public "are fast becoming the people's masters." Cleveland, for all his caution and his restriction of view, had reached a point where he was ready to demand stringent curbs upon wealth:[1]

Communism is a hateful thing and a menace to peace and organized govern-ment; but the communism of combined wealth and capital, the outgrowth of overweening cupidity and selfishness, which insidiously undermines the justice and integrity of free institutions, is not less dangerous than the com-munism of oppressed poverty and toil, which, exasperated by injustice and discontent, attacks with wild disorder the citadel of rule.

He was disturbed, as the year closed, by the predicament of Minister Phelps in London. Rightly or wrongly, Phelps concluded that since the Sackville-West affair Salisbury had decided not to send a new Minister to Washington while Cleveland remained in power, but was deliberately keeping his decision secret in order to humiliate the United States by placing her in a false position. There would be an American Minister in London but no British envoy in Washington. Phelps wished to come home but the magnanimous Bayard demurred; he could not believe that

[1] Richardson, *Messages and Papers*, VIII, 774–775.

the British Government was actuated by such base motives. When Phelps appealed to Endicott, declaring that the honor of the United States was at stake,[1] Endicott laid the situation before Cleveland. The President immediately granted a leave of absence, and the indignant Vermonter shook the soil of England from his feet. Henry White, the competent first secretary, took his place as chargé.

Another foreign problem was offered by Samoa, where Cleveland and Bayard had been laboring to preserve the autonomy of the islands. For years the United States, Great Britain, and Germany had possessed important treaty rights in Samoa; but the German residents were the most numerous, aggressive, and unscrupulous. The German Government was eager to establish its sovereignty over all or most of the archipelago, and late in 1888 its agents forcibly exiled the Samoan king, Malietoa, establishing their own puppet in his place. Their acts were so brutal that they excited the indignation of the American vice-consul and naval officers on the spot. Cleveland was aroused. He wrote with his own hand [2] the orders to Rear-Admiral Kimberly, who was hurried to Apia with the warships *Trenton* and *Vandalia,* equipped for action. On January 16, 1889, he sent Congress a sober exposition of his efforts to protect American interests in Samoa and save the islands from foreign seizure; but his feelings were not sober. A few weeks later he wrote another message to Congress, denouncing the conduct of the Germans, and declaring that from beginning to end their secret purpose had been to subvert Samoan freedom. Had this message been sent, it would almost certainly have caused a rupture of relations between the United States and Germany, but on second thought Cleveland withheld it. When his term ended, British and American warships lay at Apia frowning at German warships, and hostilities seemed imminent. Then burst the March hurricane which sank every vessel save the British cruiser *Calliope,* and dramatically averted the threatened war.

At home Cleveland had the satisfaction during the winter of seeing his friend Melville W. Fuller take charge of the Supreme Court. Chief Justice Morrison R. Waite had died on March 23, 1888. Cleveland had given prolonged thought to the position, considering many names. Minister Phelps received widespread support for the nomination, and

[1] Phelps to Endicott, Dec. 22, 1888. Endicott Papers.
[2] Jan. 10, 1889. Cleveland Papers.

Cleveland was the last man in the world to be intimidated by the Irish opposition to him.[1] Francis Lynde Stetson suggested James C. Carter, a Tilden Democrat and one of the good constitutional lawyers of the day.[2] John G. Carlisle was also strongly urged. When Senator Blackburn was expatiating upon his qualifications, Cleveland looked him in the eye and ripped out loudly: "Blackburn, you tell only part of the truth. You know why I won't appoint him. I won't appoint a man to be Chief Justice of the United States who might be picked up in the street some morning." [3] Among other men seriously considered were Frederic R. Coudert of New York and George Gray of Delaware, and Cleveland would have nominated the latter if only the party leaders of his State had agreed to reëlect Bayard to the Senate in his stead; but they refused.[4]

On April 30 Cleveland announced the nomination of Fuller, a New Englander by birth, a Chicagoan by residence, and a Douglas Democrat by political faith. Though he held an eminent place at the Illinois bar, he had seen almost no public service, and the Philadelphia *Press* truly remarked that he was the most obscure man ever appointed Chief Justice. It quickly became known, however, that he was one of the most versatile attorneys in the country, a lover of legal studies, a man of wide scholarship, and the possessor of a character of singular purity.[5] The only fact found to his discredit was that following the death of Grant he had written a remarkably bad poem on the general, which hostile journals printed in full. Cleveland had met him on his western tour, when he headed a reception committee, and had been impressed by his urbanity and cultivation.[6] Their acquaintance had been ripened into friendship by frequent letters, and thrice Fuller had refused offices tendered him by the President. For a time it seemed that the Senate might defeat the nomination. It delayed action for nearly three months while the rancorous Edmunds, as chairman of the Judiciary Committee, went over Fuller's Civil War record with a microscope. According to a

[1] Don Piatt wrote Dickinson: "I hope to God the President won't appoint Phelps Chief Justice. What a howl would go up from the Irish—we can't afford it now." April 20, 1888; Cleveland Papers. Patrick Collins called to protest against Phelps. But Cleveland later wrote that he had never even considered the Irish protests.
[2] March 23, 1888. Cleveland Papers.
[3] A. W. Greely, *Reminiscences*, 254, 255.
[4] Garland, April 14, 1888, made a long report to Cleveland on the Chief Justiceship, now in the Cleveland Papers. He favored Solicitor-General Jenks.
[5] Public Opinion, May 5, 1888.
[6] John Barton Payne to the author, April 2, 1931.

report of one of his speeches in secret session, Edmunds believed that no Democrat could possibly interpret the Constitution "in the light that has been thrown upon it by loyal men in the last quarter of a century;" but some of his Republican colleagues thought that he was resentful that Phelps had not been named.[1] Early in the summer Fuller was confirmed, 41 to 20, eleven Republican Senators, including those from Illinois and Maine, voting for him.

During the winter the character of the choice became clearer. Fuller's ability was never questioned, he made the best business manager the Supreme Court ever had, and he inspired a remarkable affection on the part of his colleagues at the bar. But he was emphatically a conservative, resolute in his strict construction of the powers of the government as against the political and economic liberty of the individual, hostile to all attempts to regulate corporations severely or impair property rights, and though never quite a reactionary, always opposed to constitutional innovations.[2] He gave the Supreme Court a flavour of oldtime individualism, and it was not until after his death that it began a swift retreat from the principles of property and contractual freedom which he had held sacred. He reflected Cleveland's former conservatism, now partly breaking up, and in that sense belonged distinctly to the Cleveland Era.

One of Cleveland's last official acts was to dismiss A. P. Edgerton, the senior Civil Service Commissioner, who had spoken of reform in insulting terms and had proved generally incompetent. The President gave his last official entertainment—a dinner to the Supreme Court, with fifty-four covers laid on tables which were arranged in the shape of the letter I. The last presidential interview appeared—a careful statement to the principal Washington correspondents, explaining in detail what he regarded as the chief results of his Administration, and paying a warm tribute to his Cabinet officers.[3] Though he recited a long list of accomplishments under such heads as Army and Navy, Public Lands, Foreign Policy, and Postal Service, and spoke with pride of his tariff battle, he again made it clear that his special attention had been to governmental efficiency:

The animating spirit of the Administration was administrative reform. Not exclusive attention to any one phase of improvement in the service, but a

[1] *Harper's Weekly*, Aug. 4, 1888; Cullom, *Fifty Years*, 239.
[2] See *Maine Law Review*, Jan., 1917; *Univ. of Pa. Law Review*, Oct., 1910, for analyses of Fuller's opinions.
[3] N. Y. *Times*, Baltimore *Sun*, etc., Feb. 23, 1889.

wholesale ventilation and stirring up of all the branches of that service, the lopping off of useless limbs, the removal of dead wood, and such a renewal of activity by the introduction of new blood as the necessities of the service should demand.

Mrs. Cleveland supervised the clearance of the White House attic, a jungle of gifts. The President had at first tried to return all presents of value, and had sharply rebuked manufacturers who sent him their wares, but the tide had proved irresistible. There were scores of photographs of presidential namesakes, gallons of patent medicines and mineral waters, bushels of rabbits' feet and luck-stones, and bundles of canes; fishing tackle, firearms, hunting-stools, and game-baskets; oil paintings, art albums, and a bust of Garfield done in soap. The Ancient and Honorable Artillery Company of Boston had sent a wicker-covered flask that had once belonged to Daniel Webster, well-filled.[1] It proved more difficult to dispose of the treasures at Oak View. Here were the pets—foxes, a dachshund, a French poodle, and a St. Bernard—together with farm animals and implements. Cleveland's seal-brown team was left to be sold. All the furniture, silverware, books, and other belongings had to be crated and sent off in great White House vans. Four years earlier the crowds on inauguration day had been amused to see a variety of trunks and valises marked G. C. rattle past Lafayette Square to the front portico of the White House; now, with augmented possessions, the owner was going back.

Mrs. Cleveland departed defiantly. As she bade goodbye to the servants on March 4 she said to the old colored servant, Jerry Smith: "Now, Jerry, I want you to take good care of all the furniture and ornaments in the house, for I want to find everything just as it is now when we come back again." As Jerry gasped, she added: "We are coming back just four years from today." [2] But Cleveland, who sometimes said later that he had always felt a "prisoner" in the White House, was heartily glad to leave, and in a few days was writing Bissell from New York: [3]

You cannot imagine the relief which has come to me with the termination of my official term. There is a good deal yet which seems to result from the Presidency and the kindness of people in a social way which keeps me in

[1] McElroy, *Grover Cleveland*, I, 304, 305; Cleveland Papers, *passim*.

"Woodley" in Washington
"Westland" at Princeton

The 816 Madison Avenue House

THREE OF CLEVELAND'S HOMES

remembrance of Washington life, but I feel that I am fast taking the place which I desire to reach—the place of a respectable private citizen.

I am overwhelmed with offers of houses to live in, but I am so comfortably treated at the Victoria that I can well take my time in selecting a permanent abiding place.

"The way I am pelted by real estate men puts me in mind a little of office-seeking four years ago," he shortly wrote Vilas.[1] "The Bar and all others have been very kind and courteous. Mr. Choate gives a dinner to me next Friday night where I shall meet thirty or forty of the best of my legal brethren; and as far as social attention is concerned, we have had a surfeit of it. And still the question, 'What shall be done with our ex-Presidents?' is not laid at rest; and I sometimes think Watterson's solution of it, 'Take them out and shoot them,' is worthy of attention. One thing I cling to with especial pleasure—the memory or rather the contemplation of the course of the last Administration and the assurance that after all we were able to do something for our country. And with this comes the thought of the devotion and affection of the men, good and true, who stood about us, and I ask myself, 'Is not this after all enough for one life?' "

II

From the Victoria Hotel the Clevelands soon went to a house at 816 Madison Avenue, near Sixty-eighth Street. It was a dignified four-story residence of red brick and brownstone, given a certain distinction by its fine windows, the curved arch of the doorway, and a square turret projecting from the two upper stories. Inside there was a good deal of handsome oak panelling. The furnishings were simple. The drawing room presented cheerful rugs and walls, old mahogany, an exquisite life-sized marble bust of Mrs. Cleveland on a black pedestal, a handsome onyx clock on the mantelpiece, and good pictures. The faithful William Sinclair served as butler. In the privacy of his home Cleveland took profound comfort. While he encouraged political or business friends to come to his office, he frankly discouraged callers at his house; he accepted few invitations to dinner, and entertained in but a quiet way. Late in 1892 he removed to 12 West 51st Street, next door to his friend E. C. Benedict.

[1] April 19, 1889. Cleveland Papers.

It was in the Madison Avenue house that the first Cleveland baby, Ruth, was born. "A few minutes after midnight," wrote Cleveland to Parker on October 3, 1891, "a little strong, healthy girl arrived at our home." [1] He begged that the news be imparted to the dignified *Evening Post* so that their announcement on Saturday afternoon would "serve to embarrass such Sunday morning papers as might contemplate making an exclusive sensation of it." The baby gave him an entirely new happiness in life. To Bissell, who was also expecting his first child, he poured out his emotions. "I feel an impulse to write you," he declared. "And I feel, too, that unless I make an effort, I shall write in a strange fashion to you. I who have just entered the real world, and see in a small child more of value than I have ever called my own before; who puts aside as hardly worth a thought, all that has gone before—fame, honor, place, everything—reach out my hand to you and fervently express the wish—the best my great friendship for you yields—that in safety and joy you may soon reach my estate." [2]

At the office of Bangs, Stetson, Tracy, and MacVeagh, located first at 15 Broad Street and later at 45 William Street, Cleveland held a peculiar position. He was not a partner, and had no share of the firm's business, but he was "of counsel." [3] He was given one of the best rooms in the firm's suite. He had the use of the library, law clerks, and stenographic staff, and like the full partners paid one-tenth of his fees toward the office expenses. Frequently he was called into consultation with the firm, and on several occasions wrote a brief for it, though he never represented it in the courts. At no time, as he later told William L. Wilson, was his income as a lawyer large. [4] The greater part of the work which came to him was that of a referee appointed by the courts, and this work he did entirely in the office, hearing evidence behind closed doors and writing the decisions with his own hand. For the time being he was virtually a judge—a judge in complex business disputes, where all his shrewdness, grasp, and keen sense of equity were required. He so arranged his cases that the work was done during the same months that the courts were sitting, leaving his summers free. Fortunately he did not feel pressed for money, the sale of Oak View to a real estate syndicate

[1] *Saturday Evening Post*, April 20, 1920.
[2] Oct. 21, 1891. Cleveland Papers.
[3] Conversations of author with Mr. Bruder and Mr. Gardiner, of the former Bangs, Tracy office, Oct. 31, 1931.
[4] W. L. Wilson, MS. Diary.

for approximately $140,000 having given him a profit of almost $100,000 on that property.[1]

It was a congenial situation, particularly as Cleveland was on terms of close friendship with Francis Lynde Stetson, the head of the firm. Stetson was one of the most cultivated attorneys in the city, a graduate of Williams College, a lifelong student, an omnivorous reader, and a man of exquisite courtesy and social grace. He was also one of the shrewdest corporation lawyers of his day. After the death of his partner Tracy, who had been a brother-in-law of J. P. Morgan, he had inherited the legal work of the Morgan house, which he handled with conspicuous success. In the troubled years just after the panic of 1893 he was to prove particularly happy in helping the monarch of Wall Street reorganize a great variety of shattered railway systems, Morgan looking after the business aspect of reconstruction and Stetson the legal aspects.[2] Cleveland liked to talk with him of politics and business, for he understood both.

It is still recalled in the office how often Stetson and Cleveland were seen chatting together, and how also hour after hour, day after day, Cleveland was busy writing, writing, with his own hand. He never dictated a letter, and seldom had one copied by a typist. Nor was he accustomed to call upon the law clerks for assistance, but did his own legal research. Callers, particularly politicians, came in shoals, but he never let them interfere with his cases. His health was robust, and he impressed everyone by his alertness and powers of endurance, which never flinched at long hours of night labor. He was kindly and democratic in his attitude toward the juniors, and never showed irritation except with the telephone. There were then two telephones in the office, both cumbrous instruments placed in the hall; one belonging to the Bell Company, and the other to the Law Company, a small system connecting the courts and principal law offices. At noon the ex-President went to the Downtown Association for lunch. Mornings and evenings he rode on the Sixth Avenue Elevated, though occasionally in fine weather he would walk part or all of the way uptown.

Cleveland cared little for a large circle of acquaintances, and much for a small circle of friends. The men closest to him in these years were Stetson, Fairchild, Richard Watson Gilder, Joseph Jefferson, Oscar

---

[1] N. Y. *World,* Feb. 28, 1890.
[2] Cf. Lewis Corey, *The House of Morgan,* 383 ff.

Straus, and E. C. Benedict; and of them all the most intimate was Gilder. The editor had first met Cleveland in 1887, when he had spent a week-end at the White House and talked with the President of international copyright. It was he who induced the Clevelands to make their summer home on Buzzards Bay. In July, 1888,[1] Mrs. Cleveland had gone to spend some days with the Gilders at their Marion cottage, on Sippican Harbor, and had returned with glowing reports of the region. Shortly after settling in New York, Cleveland turned to Gilder with the demand, "Are there any fish up around Marion?" The question was referred to Joe Jefferson, who called to tell Cleveland of the blue-fish and sea-bass which disported themselves in Buzzards Bay.[2] As a consequence, the early summer of 1889 found the ex-President experimentally occupying a small cottage near the Gilders.

Next year the Clevelands again went to Marion, taking a larger house. That fall they left for a sojourn in the Adirondacks, Dr. Ward of Albany again making the preparations. Cleveland took his favorite rifle, Death and Destruction; he secured his best guide, Dick Derby; and with Mr. and Mrs. Robert W. Chapin of New York as companions, he and Mrs. Cleveland enjoyed their last trip in the North Woods. Before the summer of 1891 they bought a cottage with several acres of land near Joe Jefferson's on Monument Point, between Cedar Pond Creek and Uncle Bill's Cove. "Gray Gables," as they called it, picturesquely placed on a long peninsula, with vistas over Monument River and Cohasset Narrows, was a homelike, clapboarded structure of two stories and many angles, secluded from public view. Congenial neighbors were scattered about the countryside. One was John M. Forbes, the railroad builder, to whose versatile brilliancy Emerson had paid high tribute, and who lived on the island of Naushon, at the entrance to the bay; he had been a leading Mugwump in 1884. Another was the publisher William W. Appleton of New York, and a third was Moses Williams of Boston.[3] Richard Olney had a place at Falmouth.

All this region was much wilder and lovelier then than now. There was at first no railroad station near Gray Gables, the only approaches being by sea or by a six-mile carriage drive. Untouched woods and fields stretched inland, while the placid waters of Buzzards Bay were

[1] N. Y. *Herald,* July 28, 1888.
[2] R. W. Gilder, *Grover Cleveland,* 53.
[3] Cf. Francis Wilson, *Joseph Jefferson,* 54 ff.; Rosamond Gilder, ed., *Letters of R. W. Gilder,* 139 ff.

untroubled by pleasure-seekers. Cleveland and Gilder would sometimes fish from his own catboat, the *Ruth,* and sometimes from Captain Ryder's large sailboat. Occasionally, with the Jeffersons, they would drive down through Sandwich to the Indian village Mashpee on Cape Cod. Here were two little lakes, Mashpee and Wakeby Ponds, in the latter of which Jefferson's son Charles had bought three islands. In imitation of such Indian names as Cotuit and Waquoit, they named the islets Cometoit, Getoffit, and Stayonit. Here the families would put up at a country hotel, and spend the days in long excursions—the ladies being left behind when serious fishing was in hand.

It is probable that Cleveland spent the happiest days of his life at Gray Gables. He went to Buzzards Bay each summer with the eagerness of a city-jaded boy escaping to the woods. Yet he took his pleasures, like everything else, conscientiously. Gilder, an insouciant amateur in fishing, marvelled at the grim application which kept him hard at work on the water. When Gilder's artistic eye roamed idly over wood and water, his reverie would be interrupted by Cleveland's warning growl: "If you want to catch fish, attend strictly to business." However early on the water, he was so loath to leave it that when he knew, like a truant youngster, that he would be late for dinner, he would plead as they started for home for "one more turn," and Captain Ryder would obediently bring the *Allie* about to afford one more cast for bluefish. The effulgent heat of early afternoon, driving Joe Jefferson to the shade, found Cleveland patiently fishing under the shelter of his flopping straw hat; and he angled through many a lively storm, pulling up bass while the thunder rumbled on the hills around Mashpee. Once he stuck to his boat during the fiercest hailstorm that Gilder ever witnessed. He himself wrote Gilder a jocular letter on his assiduity: [1]

I started the fishing branch of the firm business today and am glad to report that the season promises well. I found here a feeling of depression in the trade and on every side there seemed to be the greatest apprehension for the future. I determined to test the condition and am entirely satisfied that if the industry is properly cared for and prosecuted with zeal, industry, and intelligence, satisfactory returns may confidently be relied upon.

I caught twenty-five fish with my own rod and line, averaging larger than any lot we caught last season, about equally divided between bass and tautogs. We did not forget to send a wee mess to the Gilder mansion.

[1] June 9, 1890. Cleveland Papers.

At Gray Gables, as in New York, Cleveland insisted upon a rigid privacy. Governor W. E. Russell in 1892, after spending some days with the ex-President, was asked by the editor of the *New England Magazine* to supply a photograph of the interior of the house. He wrote that none existed. "Mr. Cleveland was very particular that no photographs should be taken of his family or of the interior of his home, and his wishes were observed by all who came there." [1] The same feeling led him, that year, to deny the request of a New York woman who wished to form a "Frances Cleveland Influence Club." "We trust," he wrote, "you will not undervalue our objection, because it rests upon the sentiment that the name now sacred in the home circle as wife and mother may well be spared in the organization and operation of clubs created to exert political influence." [2] And yet he could jest to his intimates on family events. Thus he wrote Vilas on the occasion of Mrs. Folsom's marriage to Henry E. Perrine of Buffalo: [3]

I am entirely alone tonight and that leads me to say that this condition comes from the marriage of Mrs. Folsom, which I expect took place tonight. It came off a little sooner than we expected it would. She had our consent to be married in June, but she went to Jackson, Mich., with the man there and the young things got in a hurry. Things are getting into a pretty tough condition when a man can't keep his mother-in-law in the traces. Mrs. Cleveland started last night to see the show. . . . And she will live in Buffalo—the place I hate above all others.

Among close friends he unbent completely. There were many gay evenings on his own narrow piazzas, or before the big fireplace in Mrs. Gilder's studio in the woods, or on the lawn before Joe Jefferson's house. Impromptu dramatics were gotten up. Once when Marion was celebrating its annual festival of Marigold Day, Cleveland suggested an acrostic contest to raise money for the community fund. The word Marion was the subject, and the rules, drawn up by Gilder, provided that the worst acrostic should be the winner, and that its author should subscribe a certain sum to the festival treasury and leave town forthwith. A crowd gathered in Mrs. Gilder's studio to see the contest decided. The editor presided; the committee of award, including Congressman

---

[1] July 9, 1892. Russell Papers.
[2] N. Y. *Press*, July 10, 1892.
[3] May 20, 1889. Cleveland Papers.

Burnett, sat in judgment; and it emerged that Cleveland's six-line acrostic was the worst. Only one line, descriptive of the task of portraying Marion's glories, has been preserved:

Rip ope thy cans of frenzied fire!

Gilder pronounced sentence with the severity of a Judge Jeffries. He was interrupted by a sudden burst of eloquence from Cleveland, who denounced in fiery terms the conspiracy against his property and his sacred liberty. He grew so vehement that a young woman whispered, "He's angry!" Others joined the debate. When Gilder handed a piece of silver to Charles W. Bangs, thus retaining the services of Cleveland's own firm, Cleveland suddenly changed sides completely, and made a ringing speech in defence of the chairman.[1]

With friends he liked Cleveland could be an excellent conversationalist. Gilder's statement that he was "one of the very raciest of talkers and raconteurs" is perhaps exaggerated, but as Oscar S. Straus says, he could be highly amusing with funny stories and with mimicry. He would give imitations of some political figures; for example, "Tim" Campbell, who had taken S. S. Cox's seat in Congress, and who at the White House had been wont to point to Cleveland's room and gaily ask the clerk, "Is his Royal Nibs in?"[2] With a stranger or a man in whom he lacked confidence he became reticent, while shyness made him uncommunicative whenever he met someone to whom he attributed superior learning or cultivation. Among literary men and scholars he felt a distinct uneasiness which sprang from a real modesty. Once he remarked wistfully to Gilder: "If I only knew as much as Abram S. Hewitt, I might amount to something." Like Grant, he always showed a scrupulous delicacy in conversation. Henry Holt writes:[3]

One haunting recollection of Cleveland: One night at the Century, which club his intimate friend Richard Gilder made specially attractive to him, he had legitimate occasion to tell our group something bordering on coarseness, where even an average member of that club would naturally have used a good many coarse words. Cleveland, whose origin was somewhat rough and tumble you know, steered around them as carefully as would a refined lady.

[1] Gilder, *Grover Cleveland*, 83.
[2] Straus, *Under Four Administrations*, 115 ff.
[3] Holt, *Garrulities of an Octogenarian Editor*, 224.

III

As in his earliest days, he showed a predilection for the society of children and of those Frederic Remington called "men with the bark on." At Gray Gables he would spend hours repairing a whirling-sailor weathervane or some like apparatus for the neighboring youngsters. He accomplished such manual tasks with surprising dexterity, and even succeeded once, after much tinkering, in converting a defective multiplying reel into a very effective plain reel. It was delightful, when he talked with children, to hear his grave frankness as he met them on their own level. Once in the summer of 1890 a small boy who had heard him addressed as President, and who had come to pay his respects, spoke to him as if he were still the Chief Executive. Cleveland saw that the lad was under a misapprehension. He explained that he had been defeated in the recent election. Exclaiming, "O, I had not heard of that, sir!" the boy added lively expressions of sympathy. Cleveland betrayed no inner amusement, and the conversation was as serious as if it had taken place in the Blue Room between the President and a foreign ambassador. After receiving a gift from one of Gilder's sons, Cleveland sent the father an appreciative note. "I flatter myself," he wrote, "it takes a pretty good man to gain and keep the good opinion of such a boy." [1]

Buzzards Bay possessed fishermen and longshoremen of salt individuality, and Cleveland grew friendly with the villagers of Marion and Mashpee. Within two years he was a loyal citizen of the Cape, speaking of it with the pride of an old resident. On July 25, 1891, he made a felicitous speech before a gathering of neighbors at Sandwich. It was strange, he said, that the entire United States did not flock to this district and take possession in Oklahoma style. "Let us look for a moment at some of our suburbs and surroundings. We have located Boston just far enough to be a convenient trading place, and yet not near enough to annoy us with its noise and dirt, nor to permit its children to damage our cranberry bogs. Though we know that the Pilgrims landed in Barnstable County, we see fit to maintain Plymouth Rock just far enough outside to serve as a stimulus without being bothered by the strangers who visit the spot. We keep the waters of Buzzards Bay clean and pure for fishing purposes, and do not propose to have our

[1] Gilder, *op. cit.*, 92.

reserve stirred up and contaminated by the inflow of other waters through the Cape Cod Canal." [1] For Captain Ryder, tall, weather-beaten, and solemn, Cleveland had a special regard. The skipper figures in an anecdote related by Dr. Bryant: [2]

All day long on Buzzards Bay we sailed and fished. The wind was blowing freshly and the boat bounded over the waves for twenty miles or more down the bay. We were sailing on a broad reach and the freshness of the breeze brought a touch of color into the strong face which was ludicrously hidden under the big straw hat with wide rim, around which he had tied a scarf which, passing under his chin, had given his hat the shape of an old-fashioned poke-bonnet. He laughed himself at the picture which we made, and as we held the lines, now and then drawing in a glorious bluefish, he talked almost uninter-ruptedly with the gaiety of a boy in his 'teens. The day wore on until it had become four o'clock and no word had been said about the luncheon reposing in the lockers until the friend, half-starved, called attention to it. Then the dinner in the home with a feast upon the fish which came from the day's catch. "Doctor," said the President, "it has been a wonderful day. We have not caught many fish, it is true, but did you notice my cross-eyed skipper with the face of a graven image? I have tried my best all summer long to break that man up. I have told him every funny story I could think of, but never a smile crossed his countenance. I think he is perhaps afraid of me. But today I caught him several times smiling, and once laughing outright at your stories. Yes, it has been a day of great success."

In these years he might have travelled widely, but he showed no de-sire to do so. His friends sometimes mentioned Europe. He would have liked, he said later, to see two European leaders—Salisbury and Bis-marck; [3] strong, rugged men like himself. But travel as a recreation or a means to education never appealed to him. He went as far afield as Ann Arbor and Boston, but merely to make speeches.

One of his short journeys was to Buffalo in the summer of 1891, where he saw all his old acquaintances and made two speeches. His friends in the city understood why he had grown chilly toward it, and tried to give him a pleasanter impression. He, Dr. Bryant, and the editor of the New York *Staats-Zeitung* were met at the station by Bissell and others, and taken to a new hotel, the Iroquois. In the after-noon he drove about to call on a few old intimates—Lewis F. Allen's family, Mrs. Bissell, and Mrs. F. L. Hayward; while he had a good

---

[1] MS. of speech in Cleveland Papers.
[2] Undated memorandum by Dr. Bryant in Cleveland Papers.
[3] Gertrude Allen to author, Aug. 6, 1931.

talk with such friends as Charles Bishop and Gustav Scheu, and learned all about William F. Sheehan's ambitions to be mayor. In the evening there was a dinner at the Iroquois. The next day receptions were held at the mayor's office and at the new clubhouse of the Buffalo Democracy; and he delivered an address before the German Y. M. A., which was celebrating its fiftieth anniversary. His "powerful speech," the *Courier* said, was heard "with breathless attention." [1] Cleveland was touched by the numerous manifestations of regard, and in a letter to Bissell afterwards spoke of the occasion in heartfelt terms. [2] Peace had been made between him and the city in which he had spent so many years, and thereafter there was cordiality on both sides.

He kept up a large correspondence, replying to all letters promptly, but almost never keeping a copy of what he wrote. When his friends expostulated with him upon his careless practise, he assured them that precautions were unnecessary. Perhaps they were—but many of his letters have been lost to history. It would be interesting, for example, to know what he replied to Harold Frederic when the latter begged him to read his newest book, one of the best of American historical novels. Frederic wrote him from London late in 1889: [3]

It occurs to me to beg you to try to see something at least of the story of mine now running in *Scribner's* called *In the Valley.* It is a close study of the rural part of our State during the Revolutionary period, full of patriotic color and impulse, and I am convinced that you would get a good deal of satisfaction out of it. I myself have so great a liking for the political side that if I could be sure that every young man in the United States would read it, I should feel like working day and night to provide every one of them with a free copy. I know that you don't read novels—but this is grave enough to be something else, and I shall doubt the wisdom of ever having written it if you don't read it.

These, Gilder wrote later of the "interregnum," were the golden years of a golden circle of friends, and undoubtedly Cleveland himself thought so. It meant much to his growth as well as pleasure to be in constant association with such men as he knew best. Joe Jefferson, who in his long half-century on the stage had given the American theatre some of its most picturesque characterizations—Caleb Plummer in *The Cricket on the Hearth,* Bob Acres in *The Rivals,* and Rip Van Winkle

---

[1] Buffalo *Courier,* May 11–13, 1891.
[2] New York, May 16, 1891. Cleveland Papers.
[3] Nov. 13, 1889. Cleveland Papers.

—and who was a wit and raconteur; Gilder, who, becoming editor of the *Century* before Cleveland was elected mayor of Buffalo, had done more than any other man living to revolutionize magazine management, and who was one of America's tenderest versifiers; L. Clarke Davis, the informed and alert editor of the *Public Ledger*, husband of the novelist Rebecca Harding Davis and father of Richard Harding Davis; and Benedict, a man of broad culture as well as wealth—these were a remarkable group. All of them found Cleveland, as Lowell had said, very *simpatico,* and Cleveland found in them a broadening and mellowing influence. Meanwhile, the carefully-guarded domestic life in which he took such delight also contributed to his emotional development. "His nearest friends," wrote Dr. Bryant later,[1] "have seen him deeply touched at the christening of his children, in the services of the church, and in many a home experience where the growing sweetness of his character was ever leaping to new expressions. Few men have ripened more in spiritual apprehension and real beauty of character than this man did."

[1] Undated Memorandum. Cleveland Papers.

FROM Gilder's notes on Cleveland's conversations, it is evident that even in his hours of relaxation his thoughts ran largely on public affairs. With his inborn taste for the application of ethics to government, he liked to talk of his past battles, his ideas of duty, and the public response to his acts. He believed in the people. He felt that they usually decided right. His own experience, he repeatedly said, was that whenever he had steeled himself to some difficult duty, believing that it would make him unpopular, he had been surprised by the general applause. Now and then he spoke indignantly of the misrepresentation he had suffered, especially in the camp of his friends. "They say I have gone back on every civil service pledge. I should like to know what pledge I have broken!" But while he thought the reformers hypercritical, he trusted the intelligent electorate. "Mr. Cleveland always insisted upon this—that if right political policies were simply and clearly put before the American people, they would generally make a wise and honest decision. He was sometimes discouraged; but I do not think he was ever fundamentally shaken in his belief." [1]

In these years the Harrison Administration was making what to Cleveland seemed one dangerous blunder after another. The Force Bill, the McKinley Tariff, the Sherman Silver-Purchase Act, the expenditures of a billion-dollar Congress ruled with a rod of iron by Thomas B. Reed, and the aggressive policy of Blaine in the State Department—all this struck Cleveland as a record in which perversity and weakness were equally mingled. He had a warm respect for Harrison's intellectual abilities and honesty of purpose. But it appeared to him that the predatory elements in the Republican party—the old soldiers who got their dependent pensions act, the manufacturers who got a protected market, the trading and investing interests which got support in their overseas adventures—were too strong for Harrison and his associates. They were perverting the government to the benefit of special privilege.[2]

[1] Gilder's Memorandum; McElroy MSS.
[2] For Cleveland's high opinion of Harrison see Parker, *Grover Cleveland*, 246.

For a year after leaving office Cleveland was loath to concern himself with politics in any form. He did not believe that it befitted a former President to speak *ex cathedra* upon every passing topic, and felt that he would only injure himself and his party if he interfered with Democratic affairs in any State. Yet when he made his first public address early in December, 1889, to the Merchants' Association of Boston on ballot reform, pleading for political honesty in the highest sense, the ovation he received led more than one editor to point out that his defeat the previous year had not left him a whit less important as a public figure.[1] Governor Ames and Andrew Carnegie, both Republicans, paid tribute to him; but what pleased Cleveland most were the verses that James Russell Lowell sent with his regrets for non-attendance:

> Let who has felt compute the strain
> Of struggle with abuses strong,
> The doubtful course, the helpless pain
> Of seeing best intents go wrong;
> We, who look on with critic eyes
> Exempt from action's crucial test,
> Human ourselves, at least are wise
> In honoring one who did his best.

A few days later Cleveland was mentioned before two hundred and fifty literary men at a breakfast given the Comte de Keratry by the American Copyright League. His name "was greeted with such prolonged and vigorous cheering that it seemed almost to put a slight by contrast on the guest and on the orators of the day; it was tribute, in fact, such as no other American could count on from such an audience."[2] He was encouraged to appear more frequently, and early in 1889 made a series of short addresses—one at the centenary celebration of the Supreme Court, a Washington's birthday address, a speech on the New York Circulating Library, and so on. He continued, however, to steer clear of all political complications. For example, he wrote a friend with genuine anger in the fall of 1889[3] repelling "the accusation that I have interfered or desired to interfere with or in any way influence the action of the Democracy of Ohio in the matter of United States Senator; it amounts to an impeachment of my common sense and

---

[1] For example, *Harper's Weekly*, Dec. 21, 1889.
[2] N. Y. *Evening Post*, Dec. 13, 1889.
[3] Nov. 29, 1889. Cleveland Papers.

is as foreign to my nature as possible." And he told Chauncey F. Black that he could not possibly make a political speech in Philadelphia: [1]

There is no mistake about one thing: duty and inclination dictate that I should, as much as possible, assume a modest position, free from any imputation of arrogating to myself special influence or control. There is a great deal in this which might be amplified, but which I hope will occur to you without amplification.

But the course of events rendered it impossible for Cleveland to sit aloof in his law office. During 1890 his profound indignation was aroused by the slow passage of the McKinley tariff to enactment, dragging over five months. Early in the spring it was reported that the Democratic members of the Ways and Means Committee intended to present a counter measure, and Cleveland sent an emphatic protest to Carlisle: [2]

I do not assume to obtrude my advice upon those who are upon the spot and whose judgments are so much better than mine, but I cannot help feeling some apprehension on that subject. I have thought as I have seen the Republicans getting deeper and deeper into the mire that our policy should be to let them flounder. I suppose that the bill which would be presented by us would not be exactly the Mills Bill. If it is not the cry will be raised that the passage and then the abandonment of that bill for something else shows that we do not know from one session to another what the country needs.

A bill presented by us (the Mills Bill or any other) will give the enemy what I should think they would want: an opportunity to attack this measure instead of defending their own. In that way they can shift ground and throw more dirt in the eyes of the public.

Is there not danger that it will be impossible to rally all our people in favor of a really good bill, with such promptness and unanimity as will make a good showing before the country? Won't you get into all sorts of tangles among the private and local interests in our party and won't this rob us of the advantage we are now gaining from the alarming and disgusting selfish grabbing going on among our opponents? Of course I take it for granted that nothing really good coming from our side would go through. I mean something fully up to our line all the way through. If this can be done it should be for the country's good and without counting policy, for I do not think we would get any credit for it with the masses of the people or that it would add a bit to the advantage that we now hold, in a pure partisan sense.

[1] Sept. 26, 1889. Jeremiah S. Black Papers.
[2] New York, April 7, 1890. Cleveland Papers.

As the McKinley Act became law, the Congressional elections were only a month distant, while in New York city the reformers, with Fairchild active as a leader, were attempting to oust the corrupt Tammany government of Mayor Grant, and elect Francis M. Scott in his stead. Cleveland was besought on every hand to speak up—to denounce the McKinley Act, to appeal for a Democratic Congress, and to assail Grant and Croker. He still objected. But when Lamont joined those who asked that he make a speech or give out an interview, he showed that he was weakening.

"The fact is, Colonel," he wrote,[1] "that the inclination is growing on me, daily, to permit things other than politics to claim the greatest share of my attention, and if I had my way, and regarded personal considerations exclusively, I would now put a stop, if I could, to the mention of my name in connection with any political office. Besides my personal repugnance to the atmosphere of politics in their present phase, as a question of good judgment I am nearly convinced that my nomination again for the Presidency would result in party defeat. I do not think there is any use in mincing matters. Mr. Hill and his friends would never permit me to carry the State of New York. But with all this, I am far from believing that I have a right to set up my own judgment and wishes against those of personal and political friends, and if an interview such as you suggest would in their opinion be useful to our cause I ought to be willing to consider the subject."

The memorable election of 1890, in which disapproval of the McKinley Act and general discontent swept 235 Democratic members into the House and all but 86 Republicans out of it, completed Cleveland's conversion to an active rôle. A week afterward he journeyed to Columbus, O., to attend a Thurman birthday banquet. Here he made a speech of a new kind—a fighting speech in denunciation of the McKinley Tariff. He particularly attacked McKinley's sneering phrases about "cheap and nasty goods," and "a cheap coat making a cheap man," as an insult to multitudes of plain-living Americans. The following month the jubilant Reform Club crowded into Madison Square Garden to celebrate the victory. Cleveland, in the centre of the row of speakers, dominated the gathering. When he rose to respond to the toast, "The Campaign of Education: Its Result is a Signal Tribute to the Judgment of the American People," he received an ovation. Again he de-

[1] Saranac Inn, Sept. 13, 1890. Cleveland Papers.

livered a ringing speech, but this time it was a paean of joy.

The public uprising against the new tariff was as much an act of petulance as of true indignation—as much a demonstration against the increased prices attributed to the law as against its principle. But it might well stir Cleveland's heart. The Middle West underwent a shore-changing political revolution. From Indiana westward to Minnesota, Nebraska, and Kansas, old landmarks went down beneath a Democratic flood. In Massachusetts, for the first time since the Civil War, the people elected both a majority of Democratic Congressmen and a Democratic Governor—the gallant young William E. Russell, recently mayor of Cambridge. He was one of the finest examples of the rising Democratic leaders who bore Cleveland's reform stamp on their foreheads. This Bay State election took place after a spirited agitation of the tariff question and a campaign directed chiefly against the McKinley Bill, and Russell's plurality of 9,000 was a decisive verdict.[1] To Cleveland it seemed that the tariff ought to be, and would be, the principal issue in the coming national campaign.

On Jackson Day, January 8, 1891, the Young Men's Democratic Association of Philadelphia held a banquet at which Cleveland spoke on "The Principles of True Democracy." It was one of the ablest addresses of his career, animated throughout by characteristic moral fervor. In an opening sentence he laid down a dozen general principles of Democracy, from State Rights to economy in government. Turning to the history of each, he argued that the Democratic party had in general supported them, while the Republicans had allowed them to be undermined, and as a consequence were now harkening "for the footsteps of that death which destroys parties false to their trust." He again paid his respects to the McKinley Act—"an unjust tariff which banishes from many humble homes the comforts of life, in order that in the palaces of wealth luxury may more abound." He also attacked the Reed rules and the Billion Dollar Congress, saying that it was important our Government should be the instrument of the people, and that its cost should be kept within the limits of strict economy. In crisp sentences he defined the objects of a truly patriotic Administration. "It is right that the influence of the Government should be known in every humble home as the guardian of frugal comfort and content,

[1] See Russell's article, "Significance of the Massachusetts Election," *Forum*, January, 1891.

and a defense against unjust exactions, and the unearned tribute persistently coveted by the selfish and designing. It is right that efficiency and honesty in public service should not be sacrificed to partisan greed; and it is right that the suffrage of our people should be pure and free."

II

Tariff reform, civil service reform, ballot reform, governmental economy—each was important; but another issue was destined to eclipse them all. The rattle of thunder from the silverite cloud in 1885-6 had died away as quickly as it came. Sunshine and calm had possessed the skies again. But now in the West was rising a far darker tempest, which threatened the republic with violent change and commotion.

The Republicans had made the error, in their platform of 1888, of denouncing Cleveland's opposition to silver coinage as an attempt to demonetize silver, and declaring in favor of the use of both gold and silver as money. Harrison had no sooner become President than insistent demands were made that the party redeem its pledge. In November, 1889, a great silver convention met in St. Louis. A. J. Warner of Ohio was chairman. Thirty States and territories were represented, and the delegates from the broad farming areas between Ohio and Kansas were even more impassioned in their pleas for silver than those from the mining States. Bland made a fiery speech. So did Stewart of Nevada, declaring that the capitalists of the world never wearied in their attempt to make money costlier. They had tried in the fifties, when California and Australia were producing huge quantities of gold, to demonetize it; in the seventies they had tried again, and successfully, to demonetize silver; if they were allowed to go on, they would hold the credit of the globe at their mercy. Europe, with its poverty and its enormous standing armies, was helpless against the money-power; but the free American people could spring to the rescue. The platform, which Bland wrote and the delegates adopted with wild cheers, demanded that the Fifty-first Congress open the mints to the free and unlimited coinage of silver, to be a legal tender for all debts.[1]

When the new Congress gathered in December, the Harrison Administration acknowledged that the situation was grave and that a free-coinage bill might be passed. The Northwest had just been strengthened

[1] *Public Opinion*, Nov. 30, 1889.

by the admission of six new States. A clumsy and abortive though sincere effort was made by Secretary Windom to avert radical legislation by a complex scheme for the larger use of silver for monetary purposes. Congress would have none of it, and after much discussion between the two houses, a compromise measure was finally drawn up which required the government to purchase each month 4,500,000 ounces of silver, and issue notes based thereon, which were to be a legal tender for debts. Senator Sherman, though detesting it, gave it his name and a reluctant support for fear that if it failed worse would come.[1] There was some hope in sound-money circles that Harrison would veto the bill, but with deplorable lack of courage in July, 1890, he signed it.

The Sherman Silver-Purchase Act was a Republican Act; it passed both houses by a strict party vote. But the attitude of the Democratic party toward silver was highly alarming to Cleveland. When a free coinage bill came up in the Senate on June 17, 1890, it was passed by a vote of 28 Democrats and 15 Republicans against 3 Democrats and 21 Republicans. In the House a free coinage amendment came within an inch of success. It was beaten by the desperate efforts of Tom Reed, who stubbornly invoked the powers of the Speaker, and one of the principal supporters was no less a Democrat than Mills of Texas. Every vote taken in the House and Senate proved that the free silver virus had more deeply infected the Democratic than the Republican party, and that it was almost as powerful in the South as in the West. In the summer of 1890 Democratic conventions in nearly all the greater States west of New York, from the headwaters of the Ohio to the Pacific coast, voted in favor of a return to free and unlimited silver coinage—twenty-one conventions thus going on record.

This was the situation which evoked one of the most dramatic and fearless acts of Cleveland's career, his memorable silver letter of February, 1891. The party was stirring restlessly and moving, herdlike, toward the Gadarene steep. One leader after another—Mills, Vest, Voorhees, Morgan, Beck—was declaring in favor of free silver. As the year closed reports were set afloat that Cleveland himself was becoming neutral if not actually favorable. The Boston *Journal* began asserting with malicious insolence that he was a convert to the silver cause.[2] A

---

[1] Theodore Burton, *John Sherman,* 371 ff. The Dakotas, Washington, and Montana were admitted in 1889; Idaho and Wyoming in 1890. All were silverite.
[2] The Cleveland Papers are full of clippings on this subject.

rumor was started that Don M. Dickinson had received a letter from Cleveland declaring for free coinage, and that Senator Vest had a similar epistle. Dickinson made a categorical denial, saying that all his efforts had failed to budge Cleveland. Vest was less candid; in an interview he threw dust in the air by saying that Cleveland was ready to admit that there were *plausible* if not valid arguments for free silver, and that there were honest Democrats who believed in it. These rumors were probably set afloat by Eastern Republicans eager to embarrass Cleveland. If he kept silence he would give color to the reports; if he spoke out he would divide the party and, so his enemies hoped, ruin his chances for the nomination.[1]

In January, 1891, the silver tide sent up another angry wave. A free coinage bill passed the Senate by a vote of 39 to 27. Once more the Democratic Senators gave the majority its principal strength. Every Democrat in the chamber voted or was paired for it except Gray of Delaware. Many of Cleveland's advisers told him that if he spoke out publicly against silver as he had been speaking privately, he would destroy his political future. "I am supposed to be a leader in my party," he replied. "If any word of mine can check these dangerous fallacies, it is my duty to give that word, whatever the cost may be to me." On February 10 he received an invitation from E. Ellery Anderson of the Reform Club, inviting him to a dinner-meeting to protest against free coinage. He sat down immediately and replied:

Dear Sir:—I have this afternoon received your note inviting me to attend tomorrow evening the meeting called for the purpose of voicing the opposition of the business men of our city to "the free coinage of silver in the United States."

I shall not be able to attend and address the meeting as you request, but I am glad that the business interests of New York are at last to be heard on this subject. It surely cannot be necessary for me to make a formal expression of my agreement with those who believe that the greatest peril would be invited by the adoption of the scheme, embraced in the measure now pending in Congress, for the unlimited coinage of silver at our mints.

If we have developed an unexpected capacity for the assimilation of a largely increased volume of this currency, and even if we have demonstrated the usefulness of such an increase, these conditions fall far short of insuring us against

---

[1] On the alleged Republican plot, see news stories in the N. Y. *Commercial Advertiser* and Boston *Post*, January and February, 891; and C. A. Conant's letter to Cleveland, Feb. 13, 1891; Cleveland Papers.

disaster if, in the present situation, we enter upon the dangerous and reckless experiment of free, unlimited, and independent silver coinage.

That was all. And that was enough. The veteran Democratic marshals professed despair. "Again," Godkin wrote, "the shrewd politicians sat down on the party stoop and wept, and prepared sorrowfully to nominate a first-class juggler in the person of David B. Hill, who was to show the wretched Mugwumps how much better it was to be able to keep six balls in the air than to be able to show the absurdity of a fluctuating medium." [1] Dana was in ecstasies over Cleveland's supposed downfall. The great majority of Southern and Western newspapers exploded in contemptuous wrath. Even Lamont, who knew Cleveland so well and respected him so completely, was at first aghast. Several months later, still depressed by Cleveland's indifference to political expediency, he wrote imploring his chief to send a new letter to the Ohio Democratic convention, smoothing over his rough attack on "the dangerous and reckless experiment" of free silver: [2]

The trouble with that is that your letter was so turned as to make you the representative of the ultra anti-silver sentiment and to create the impression with the masses that that is your situation. I have always thought that if you had had more time you would have written a letter that would have been differently received and yet expressed your views on the question. My idea now is that at the very outset in your letter you can in three or four sentences set the silver position aside as one on which neither party is united; perhaps state your opposition briefly to the ultra silver proposition and then take in the tariff question as the issue on which the parties divide, and give them something on that that could be used as a campaign leaflet. . . .

Some such letter would set the party back on the tariff question and away from the silver issue.

To Cleveland the immediate clamor against his letter meant nothing. As Gilder said, he was never happier than when he had just "thrown the presidency away." He wrote Bissell that he felt better than at any previous time since leaving Washington, "and it seems to me that a weight has been lifted off and a cloud removed. At any rate, no one can doubt where I stand." When someone later remarked upon his courage, he replied that this particular act had been far less difficult than his veto of the five-cent-fare bill in Albany, which he felt at the

[1] *Nation*, Nov. 10, 1892.
[2] Sorrento, Me., July 27, 1891. Cleveland Papers.

time had driven the last nail into his political coffin. Years of practise had made unrecking adherence to principle easier, and had taught him that sooner or later the public would respond to it.

And the response came—quickly at first from the East, slowly from even the semi-hostile West. Vilas dined the evening after the letter appeared with President Eliot of Harvard, who was visiting the University of Wisconsin. Eliot eagerly inquired its contents. "When I told him . . . he said with an unction that would have pleased you, 'Good! So say we all of us!' " Vilas himself was deeply gratified. "I felt better when I read it," he wrote. "Let the fools have it direct. . . . And I think the letter *great, big, sound, wise politics!*" [1] Charles A. Conant, Washington correspondent of the Boston *Post,* wrote Cleveland that he also regarded it as shrewd tactics. The farming States might be resentful, but they would realize before the next national campaign that the party could not afford to throw away the Eastern States for the shadowy chance of carrying the West. So thought Robert R. Roosevelt, president of the Holland Trust Company, writing that "the party had but one chance of defeat in the next election, and but for your timely intervention might have taken it." [2] Governor Russell sent his congratulations.[3] At the same time he wrote William L. Wilson that the letter had been a happy stroke: [4]

I think a wise party policy will look to Democratic support from New Hampshire, Connecticut, Rhode Island, Massachusetts, and New York, rather than to Iowa, Kansas, and the Western States. We can afford to let those States be Republican provided that we hold our own in the East and South. The only danger we now see is free coinage. I am sure that if the Democratic party stands united for that measure it is going to drive off from us the independent support that we have won here in the East.

Fortunately, after Cleveland's letter there came a lull. The unlimited coinage bill against which his statement had been directed failed in the House. For the time being the silver men were satisfied with what the Sherman Silver-Purchase Act had won them; to buy 4,500,000 ounces of silver monthly meant absorbing almost the entire output of the American mines. The silver tide paused for a moment, lapping omi-

[1] Madison, Feb. 15, 1891. Cleveland Papers.
[2] Feb. 14, 1891. Russell Papers.
[3] Feb. 16, 17, 19, 1891. Cleveland Papers.
[4] April 10, 1891. Russell Papers.

nously but harmlessly at the remaining dikes thrown up by the sound-money forces. Cleveland, in happier mood, wrote Gilder late in the summer that "I have frequently noticed lately the tendency to make less of the silver issue in the Southern papers, as well as in some of those published in the West. I am confidently looking for a return to common sense and conservative ideas in certain quarters." [1] So marked was the quiescence into which the movement fell that the issue played but a minor part in the campaign of 1892. Yet the storm was steadily coming nearer, and Cleveland was an Ajax whose defiance had marked him as its principal object.

III

As men began to talk of the Democratic nomination for 1892, their discussion constantly turned upon the ambition of Governor Hill to upset Cleveland. This ambition was patent. It was supported by the Hill machine, by Tammany, and by protectionist interests scattered over the East and South. It was emphatically not countenanced by the rank and file of Democrats, who believed that the man who had twice won a plurality of the popular vote should have a third chance. In February and March, 1890, Henry Watterson went on a long lecture-tour. "I have been much over the country," he wrote Cleveland on his return,[2] "and among Democrats, have heard no other name than yours seriously considered. . . . There is not a doubt that you are stronger today than ever before." But while "Governor Hill is out of the question —not to be thought of for a moment," he warned Cleveland that "he may so muddy the stream as to put you at a disadvantage," and that Cleveland should take steps to rally his friends. In fighting Hill, he would need them. "The man never lived who can afford, in the long run, to stand wholly aloof and alone. I have always thought, and regretted, that you do not give the personal aspects of life their sufficient position."

Cleveland had attempted to keep on terms of amity with Hill. He had discouraged the gossip in reform circles that Hill had knifed the Cleveland-Thurman ticket. After the legislative session of 1889 he had even written the Governor a cordial note on some of his veto messages,

---

[1] Aug. 18, 1891. Cleveland Papers.
[2] Louisville, March 9, 1890. Watterson Papers.

saying that " 'It's mighty good reading' and must produce good results." [1] But he did not need Watterson's kindly message to warn him that Hill intended to get the nomination by hook or crook. Just after election day in 1890 he wrote Bissell that of all the New York Democrats Hill was the least friendly to the low-tariff principle for which they were fighting; that he had made hollow noises in opposition to the McKinley Act, but his heart was not in the fight. He admitted that Hill had treated him very kindly, but insisted that the shiftiness of the man was almost incredible. No one knew yet just whom he wished elected Senator that next spring; no one knew whether he might not take the Senatorship himself. Cleveland went on: [2]

. . . The prospect is that a man will be elected subject to the objections which you suggest and with the distinct expectation in Albany that service shall be rendered in aid of the Governor's aspirations, or that the scheme will fail in a first-class row with much bitterness and recrimination. I believe that it is quite possibly felt that the credit for a majority in the Assembly is due to the Governor, and I think if he would take the place everyone would be content. But I am satisfied he will not do this—first because he would be accused of treachery, and second and chiefly, because he has other ambitions.

Of one thing you may be entirely certain. Hill and his friends are bent on his nomination for the Presidency, and failing in that they are determined that it shall not come towards me. You know how I feel about this matter as a personal question, but if I have pulled any chestnuts out of the fire I want them out. I ask them to keep a civil tongue in their heads, and further than this, I don't want to see my hard work wasted and the party fall back to shiftiness and cheap expediency. One other thing I want to say: This Hill movement is much more extended and has penetrated more quarters than many expect. . . .

Subsequent letters showed that he was watchful of the boiling political pot in New York. Prior to the elections of 1890 Hill had been inclined to thrust the Senatorship toward Smith M. Weed. But the sweeping Democratic majorities in New York and throughout the country gave new fire to his ambition for the Presidency. The prize now seemed within the grasp of whatever Democrat was nominated, and the possibility of obtaining it dazzled Hill. The Senatorship appealed to him as a stepping-stone, and he turned his back on Weed, Bourke Cockran, and the other aspirants. Some of his friends advised him to be cautious,

[1] New York, June 19, 1889. Cleveland Papers.
[2] New York, Nov. 8, 1890. Cleveland Papers.

saying that as a new member he might be lost in the Senate; but the New York *World* asserted that this objection was nonsense. Once more, as in 1886, Pulitzer was toying with the idea that Hill might make a better President than Cleveland. On November 7 the *World* declared that "the idea that election to and service in the Senate would injure him as a possible Presidential candidate is wholly fallacious. Governor Hill would go to the Senate as the most conspicuous representative and leader of the great political revolution of 1890, and the national fame which he would thus advance could not fail to promote rather than to hinder any natural ambition which he may cherish for a higher place." For a time the Governor still hesitated, and if his trusted friend Alton B. Parker would have accepted the seat, using it to work for Hill's nomination as President, he would have welcomed the arrangement. But Parker refused. Finally there was a conference between Hill, Sheehan, and Murphy. As they were leaving Hill, Murphy said: "I believe the old man wants it himself!" [1]

He did want it and he got it. In January, 1891, he was elected Senator on the first joint ballot of the two houses, and the chagrined Smith Weed became his bitter enemy. His election also shattered a faint hope which Cleveland had begun to cherish that Bissell might be elected— for Cleveland had sent Bissell a letter virtually pledging his influence to help "swing it in your direction." [2]

Meanwhile, Cleveland was continuing his correspondence with Watterson upon Hill's machinations. The Kentuckian had written on November 21, 1890, that he was worried about national party harmony. "I regard your nomination as indispensable; but union in New York seems equally so." In his uneasiness, he had addressed Hill a letter which he hoped Cleveland would approve his sending—a long letter, pleading in effect that Hill step aside gracefully in favor of Cleveland, and implying grave threats if he did not. [3] In all his rollicking, headlong career Watterson never wrote a bolder letter than this. He took leave to address the Governor, he began, as one of millions of Democrats who were deeply concerned over the party's welfare, and who believed that Hill held the key to it: [4]

[1] D. S. Alexander, *Four Great New Yorkers*, 144 ff.
[2] New York, Nov. 17, 1890. Cleveland Papers.
[3] Louisville, Nov. 21, 1890. Watterson Papers.
[4] New York, Nov. 24, 1890. Cleveland Papers.

Outside the State of New York there is a well-nigh unanimous demand among the rank and file of Democrats for the nomination of Mr. Cleveland. This is too strong for the party leaders and managers to resist. I think I have some influence in Kentucky. But, on that point, I should be overwhelmed in a State convention. If you should come to a national convention with a New York delegation solid against it, you would be overwhelmed. You are powerless to prevent it. But you can defeat the election of the ticket. . . .

My judgment is clear that, if you could reconcile it with your judgment and feeling to make peace with Mr. Cleveland, and to take a delegation to the national convention in 1892 to put him in nomination, you will save the party and place yourself upon an elevation you can never attain if you fail to do it. You would be received by the country with enthusiasm; be accepted at once as a Warwick; and I do not see how you could be kept out of the succession. On the other hand, even if you succeed in defeating the nomination of Mr. Cleveland, you will stand upon sinister and dangerous ground, with a stormy future before you.

These are plain words; . . . but they are true words; and I claim the right of a Democrat who has some knowledge of the country at large and has given some proof of intelligent devotion to the party interest, to ignore ceremony and send them to you.

Cleveland welcomed Watterson's intervention, and decided at once that the letter ought to be sent. It was a difficult task to say so modestly. The situation was almost a "stumper" to him, he wrote Watterson; he didn't know what to think about it, and shrunk from endorsing action that looked toward his nomination in 1892; but he thought the letter sound and useful. Watterson mailed it, but it produced no effect on Hill.

IV

During 1891 Cleveland watched with disgust the devious manoeuvres by which Hill sought to advance his siege-lines upon the Presidential nomination. He had seized the senatorship, but he was still reluctant to drop the governorship. He could not enter the Senate until December, 1891, and until that time he coveted all the temporalities of his position in Albany. To most citizens the idea that any man should for ten months hold both a high Federal position and the highest State position seemed almost indecent. The constitutions or laws of many States, indeed, forbade any such duplication of office, and precedent had established the same principle in New York. Some of Hill's best friends, including William F. Sheehan, advised him to drop the governorship, but he refused. "We do not hesitate to say," declared the *Tribune*, "that no other man in public life today would be guilty of such misconduct and continue to hold up his head." [1]

Cleveland was eager that the State Convention in 1891 should choose independent and high-minded candidates, and adopt a sound platform, and he watched resentfully as the machine elements tightened their grip. In March he was hopeful that a rebellion might be organized, while in June he urged his friends to place D-Cady Herrick, a friendly Albany lawyer, in charge of the movement. A revolt in Buffalo against the Sheehan organization momentarily heartened him. "The fact is," he wrote Bissell, "that it is getting very hard to endure and submit to a continuance of the prevailing bossism, and look honest men in the face. Such men as you and I, and the thousands of other good Democrats who believe that the principles of our party mean the good of the people and honesty and fidelity in public place, cannot afford to be traded off and misrepresented by those who are in politics for what can be out of it; and it is a disgrace for us to allow ourselves to be used to further their purposes." [2] But the revolt proved ineffective.

When the Democratic convention met at Saratoga in September, Hill was forced into the background; but leaders of a similar character were in full control—Sheehan of Buffalo, who had captured the Erie County delegation and defeated would-be delegates friendly to Cleveland; Edward Murphy of Troy; and Croker of New York city. They nominated for governor the wealthy, commonplace Roswell P. Flower, whom Cleveland found tolerable, but their nominee for lieutenant-governor was no less distasteful a person than Sheehan himself. [3] Ever since Cleveland had refused to run for mayor on the same ticket with Sheehan's elder brother, there had been bad blood between him and the Sheehan clan. The very worst had been feared of the platform. It omitted any explicit approval of Cleveland's tariff views. But on the currency question, thanks to Oscar S. Straus and others, a silverite pronouncement was avoided and the plank was faulty only in its vagueness. After condemning monometallism, the Sherman Silver-Purchase Act, and the coinage of any dollar which was not of the intrinsic value of

[1] N. Y. *Tribune*, March 31, 1891.

[2] Cleveland to Bissell, March 5, June 30, 1891; to Lamont, June 9, 1891. Cleveland Papers.

[3] Alexander, *Four Famous New Yorkers*, 152 ff.

every other dollar, it called for "free bimetallic coinage," a phrase it did not interpret. Cleveland wrote a few words of thanks to Straus.[1] But Hill, at a Democratic ratification meeting in Cooper Institute on October 8, promptly gave the plank an interpretation hostile to Cleveland by remarking: [2]

Thus we have taken impregnable ground in favor of honest money. Those who would have switched us off the bimetallic track have had their hands tied. *Those who would have run us into collision with our fellow-Democrats in other States, and thereby wrecked Democratic chances for success in 1892, have had their plans frustrated.* Our platform unites all Democrats upon the common ground of honest, bimetallic coinage. Whatever method, if any, for attaining perfect bimetallism the leaders of the party in their wisdom may decide to recommend in our national platform next year, conditions will then determine, and we may safely leave the matter to their judgment. . . .

It soon became evident that Hill's mystic scheme of "bimetallic coinage," with its "method, if any" to be worked out at some later date, was above all a scheme for capturing silver delegates in the West. The fall campaign, thanks to the folly of Platt and the Republicans in nominating J. Sloat Fassett for governor, ended in a victory for the Flower-Sheehan ticket. The result was decidedly uneven; Flower's plurality of almost 50,000 stood in marked contrast with Sheehan's of a little less than 35,000, the disparity indicating that many voters shared Cleveland's feelings toward the latter. But the verdict as a whole was accepted as a new triumph for Governor Hill, who had taken the centre of the stage, delivered many speeches, and given the public the impression that he was the very backbone of Democratic strength in New York.

Even before election Hill had made a tour to Atlanta, ostensibly to unveil a statue of Henry W. Grady but really to enlist the support of Georgia silverites and protectionists. Cleveland's friends wrote him that the "hippodrome" was badly managed, that Hill made a poor speech, and that he was coldly received by the Southern people,[3] but the *Constitution* told a different story; it spoke of widespread enthusiasm, and of a cordial reception. Hill's friends in New Jersey were active. In Chicago Carter H. Harrison, who had now been four times mayor of the city—a magnetic figure, of fine Virginia stock, a graduate of Yale, widely

---

[1] Sept. 27, 1891. Cleveland Papers.
[2] N. Y. *Times, World,* Oct. 9, 1891. Italics are mine.
[3] Wm. H. Black, Atlanta, Oct. 30, 1891, to Cleveland. Cleveland Papers.

read and travelled, but allied with the worst political gangsters of the city—purchased in the fall of 1891 the Chicago *Times*, a Democratic newspaper famous since Civil War days. He made it clear that on the two paramount issues he opposed Cleveland, for he believed in protection, taking pride in the views of a Henry Clay Whig, and stood for free silver. He demanded the nomination of some Western man, and failing a Westerner, preferred Hill.[1] Meanwhile, in September a party composed of Senator Faulkner of West Virginia, Representative Bynum of Indiana, Senator Beck of Kentucky, and others was travelling through the Northwest to the Pacific, avowedly to advance Democratic principles but actually to arouse sentiment against Cleveland and in favor of Hill or Gorman. A cloud of detraction floated back over their trail.[2]

Cleveland read of all this, and read also Hill's call to his gathering cohorts in a widely-bruited speech at Elmira on December 4 upon "The Issues for 1892." Adroit, full of simulated fervor, and containing many deft appeals to the prejudices of old-fashioned Democrats, this production lacked just one essential quality—the ring of sincerity. Hill proposed to fight the coming campaign upon the issues presented by the acts of the Billion Dollar Congress; but by this he meant something very different from what Cleveland would have implied by a similar statement. He wished the Democrats to demand the repeal of the McKinley Act, and a return to the tariff of 1883; Cleveland wished a repeal of the McKinley Act and an entirely new tariff closely akin to the Mills bill. Hill wanted the Sherman Silver-Purchase Act repealed, but asserted emphatically that silver coinage should be continued. Cleveland of course wanted the Sherman law repealed, and silver coinage stopped entirely. So hostile had Hill now become that he went out of his way to attack the ex-President, condemning his efforts in 1885–89 to repeal the Bland-Allison Act and commit the country to "gold monometallism." Speaking of the Republicans who were getting up public meetings in Eastern cities to go into fits of fright over free coinage, he flung another gibe at Cleveland by remarking scornfully that "of course they enticed a few unwary Democrats to appear as convulsionists at their scarecrow festivals." [3]

[1] W. J. Abbot, *Carter Henry Harrison: A Memoir*, 199, 200.
[2] P. J. Smalley, St. Paul, Sept. 22, 1891, to Cleveland. Cleveland Papers.
[3] D. B. Hill, *The Issues for 1892*, pamphlet reprint, Manton Marble Papers, University of London.

V

Cleveland realized that Hill's nomination would mean the defeat of the central principles of sound money, tariff reform, civil service reform, and departmental efficiency for which he had so long contended. Little by little he was aroused to a fighting temper. His growing belligerence may be traced in his letters to Bissell and Lamont. In midsummer of 1891 he had written the latter [1] that "we are great fools if we allow ourselves to be hauled about by Hill and his gang. I know that I, who am doing next to nothing to prevent such a condition, ought not to expect others to inordinately exert themselves; but I do hope the thing will not be neglected so long that the pins will be fixed fast and strong against us." He added that he was willing to take his discharge papers and be obedient and faithful "except in one contingency"—that contingency obviously being the nomination of Hill or his like on a silver platform. Wishing the party in the State drastically reformed, he was anxious "that no decent honest man shall . . . be left out of the fellowship of those who come to the front. I am satisfied that policy, as well as honesty, is on the side of becoming identified with the movement for a change." [2] He wrote bitterly to Gilder of the efforts to set him aside in the party. "A great deal is going on among machine politicians; and plans are on foot to rid the Democratic party of the *incubus* which in the seclusion of Buzzards Bay ought, according to their usual calculations, to be counted as perfectly harmless. If there were not features and incidents connected with all this which are exasperating and shamefully beastly, the entire manifestation would be only ludicrous." [3]

His hat was not yet in the ring, but his friends were eager to toss it there. As October closed Cleveland travelled to a Boston rally in Tremont Temple in behalf of Governor Russell, now running for reëlection. He, Russell, Patrick Collins, and others were to speak. One fact in particular made it a dramatic occasion. The Republicans and the Hill forces had spread a report that Collins was on bad terms with Cleveland, and would oppose his renomination. In his speech Cleveland eulogized Massachusetts and reviewed her contributions of brains and character to the nation. When Collins was introduced, everyone knew that

[1] July 3, 1891. Cleveland Papers.
[2] To Bissell, June 30, 1891. Cleveland Papers.
[3] Aug. 18, 1891. Cleveland Papers.

a frank intimation of his real position would be blurted forth, for he
was too honest to assume a false cordiality for the sake of harmony. He
settled all doubts in one crisp sentence: "This is not the first time I
have followed Grover Cleveland—and it may not be the last." The
words gave the signal for a wild burst of applause. Collins went on to
say that he was independent of faction, section, clique, or man. "I am no
man's man," he shouted. "I yield my homage to no human individual,
but [turning to Cleveland] I honor manliness, principle, courage, and
justice wherever I find it." And he added: "I salute the Democrat who
led, for the first time in four and twenty years, the Democratic host to
victory; I salute the Democrat who stood at the head of absolutely the
best Administration of the Federal government that this century has
seen." [1]

By the time of Hill's preposterous address at Elmira on "The Issues
of 1892" Cleveland's exasperation had reached the boiling point. On
that very day he had written Bissell calling his attention to Hill's performances in Albany, the attempt of the silverite Charles F. Crisp to
capture the speakership in Washington, and the general recklessness of
the party everywhere. "I don't think there ever was a more discouraged
and disgusted Democrat than I am today," he declared. "Was it for
this that we braved temporary defeat in order that we might stand on
principle?" [2] He was ready now to fight, and a week later gave the signal for organizing his forces in another angry letter to Bissell: [3]

Occupying the position I do in my personal relations to political affairs, and
in my complete lack of political ambition, I do not think that I ought to bother
you or my other friends with my views on the situation. And yet it is hard to
refrain from doing so occasionally, in view of the fact that I have every possible desire to see our party succeed in decent and honest views, and have a
strong disinclination to being exhibited at the tail end of a procession which
means the betrayal of the principles we profess and the deception of the people.
It seems very ridiculous for the State of New York to claim any sympathy
with the professed aims of the National Democracy and still be content to
follow the lead of Hill, Murphy & Co.

Sheehan has been boasting in Washington of the unanimity of New York
for Hill. Governor Francis of Missouri told me day before yesterday that
Sheehan told him that Hill would have every delegate with possibly the exception of six. . . . It seems to me that the only way for a decent Democrat

[1] M. P. Curran, *Life of Patrick A. Collins*, 111–113.
[2] Dec. 4, 1891. Cleveland Papers.
[3] Lakewood, N. J., Dec. 12, 1891. Cleveland Papers.

to live in New York and to maintain his self-respect and at the same time stand by his party is to break this thing up. I believe it could be done by coming to an understanding between the districts outside of New York City and the Kings County Democracy. This is of course for you alone at present.

The great pre-convention battle of 1892 was about to begin.

THE year 1892 rang up the curtain on the now embittered struggle between East and West, between debtor and creditor, between adherents of the gold standard and the silverite forces. This struggle was to fill the next quadrennium with noise and confusion. From it, despite Bryan's defeat, was to be liberated an irresistible new wave of progressivism, in time carrying all the truly important principles of the West—stricter control of business, fairer taxation, a quicker responsiveness of government to the popular will—to victory. For half a dozen years the conflict had been clearly foreshadowed. But the sudden ebullition of social discontent, of agrarian resentment and even despair, which in 1892 gave the Populist ticket under James B. Weaver its impressive total of 1,041,-000 votes, was the signal that the battle had actually commenced. It could no longer be repressed by the discipline of the old parties or evaded by the inertia of timid leaders.

The conservative Easterners who rallied about Cleveland in January, 1892, were conscious of the threat which was rising beyond the Alleghenies. Their zeal in supporting him was doubled by their confidence that he would stand like a rock against financial vagaries to which Hill would weakly yield. Foremost among these men were Fairchild and Whitney, the one a master of political preparation and the other of political management. It was Fairchild, with his urbane personality and gifted pen, who laid plans, enlisted State leaders, and gave quiet impetus to the movement for Cleveland's nomination. It was Whitney who a little later, surveying the battlefield like Marlborough in Addison's "Campaign," furnished instant decisions, aroused men to unrecking effort by his captivating personality, and dazed the enemy by his brilliant strokes. Fairchild was valuable in Cleveland's contest for delegates; Whitney was invaluable in the hurly-burly of the Chicago convention. These two men had energetic aides. One was George F. Parker, who since 1890 had been devotedly promoting Cleveland's candidacy. With meagre funds, from his little downtown office he had seen that copies of all Cleveland's speeches went to the newspapers and had interviewed editors, written letters all over the country, and buttonholed politicians.[1]

---

[1] Parker, *Cleveland*, 132 ff.

Among other active workers were Oscar S. Straus, Edward M. Shepard, Henry Villard, Vilas, Dickinson, and Russell.

Cleveland's first candidacy had been based upon a demand for administrative honesty; his second candidacy upon administrative honesty joined with tariff reform; and now his third candidacy represented a combination of both with the principle of unyielding conservatism in all that affected finance and business. He still held the loyalty of the reformers. But far more than ever before he was gaining the allegiance of frightened Eastern capitalism. Behind Fairchild stood the great banking interests; behind Whitney, who had recently doubled his fortune by reorganizing the surface transit-system of New York city, stood a large part of Wall Street; and the Straus brothers represented rich mercantile interests. Henry Villard, one of the principal railway builders of the eighties, tells us that, disgusted by Harrison's approval of the McKinley Tariff and Sherman Silver Act, apprehensive of the Western revolt, and believing that there was not the remotest chance of salvation from the Republicans, he decided that Cleveland was the only statesman who could meet the emergency. Early in 1892 Villard called on Cleveland, and secured his reluctant consent to the promotion of his candidacy. Going to Washington, Villard then consulted with Carlisle and William L. Wilson. They called a meeting of leading Democratic Senators and Representatives at Carlisle's house, where the three men argued that Cleveland could best meet the problems of the day, and that he alone could be elected. When the Congressmen demurred that Hill would be presented in the convention as New York's candidate, Villard announced that Cleveland would have the support of a powerful block of New York Democrats and Independents, and would be nominated—an assertion received "with smiles." [1]

II

Hill's candidacy in fact proved a mere rocket, brilliant and alarming for a moment but fading into blackness so suddenly that men rubbed their eyes to see it gone. His plan of campaign embraced an attempt, as soon as Congress opened, to enlist the influence of many members; a new tour of the South to rally support in that quarter; the capture of the New York delegates; a drive for delegates in New England and New

[1] Henry Villard, *Memoirs*, II, 361, 362. The Villard Papers at Harvard throw further light on his useful activities.

Jersey; and systematic efforts to cajole the Western silverites. It was a clever scheme—but in part quite too clever.

When Congress met in December, 1891, Hill's entrance into the Senate was accompanied with much trumpeting of his virtues. He quickly established his natural kinship with such associates as Brice and Gorman. In the House his friends, including the Tammany members, helped to elect Crisp of Georgia as Speaker over Mills and McMillin, thus striking a blow at Cleveland and opening a Pandora's box of evils. Crisp was a man of picturesque antecedents. His parents had been roving English actors, who had often played Shakespearean parts in such ante-bellum playhouses as the old Decatur Street Theatre in Atlanta; he had enlisted in the Confederate Army at sixteen and had fought for three years; and studying for the bar, he had begun practice in Americus, Ga., not far from the boyhood home of the Straus brothers. He was both able and attractive. But as Wilson wrote Cleveland, his selection as Speaker involved the House in endless "blundering and helplessness." [1] He placed Springer, who had decided protectionist leanings, at the head of the Ways and Means Committee, and deliberately minimized the tariff issue. In its stead he brought forward the silver issue, appointing Bland head of the Committee on Banking and encouraging him to report a free coinage bill, partly in the hope that it would embarrass Cleveland. It was finally killed by a filibuster, but not until a record vote had shown 130 Democrats supporting it and only 80 opposed.

Meanwhile, Hill in March had set forth on what the Atlanta *Journal* called another "Southern vote-begging junket." [2] He spoke at Roanoke, Knoxville, Meridian, and Jackson, addressing in the last-named city not only a massmeeting but the Mississippi House. Bands and cheering crowds greeted him everywhere; he was introduced as the great and wise leader under whom the Democratic hosts would march to victory in November. The Hill forces simultaneously organized a demonstration in Atlanta, where Senator Colquitt and General Sickles made speeches and General Longstreet sat on the platform. The Atlanta *Constitution* was beating the big drum for Hill's nomination, and all over Georgia the poor farmers were assured that when he sat in the White House and signed a free silver act, mortgages, low prices, and all the grinding hard-

[1] March 15, 1892. Wilson Papers.
[2] Atlanta *Journal*, March 14, 1892.

ships of life would disappear like a bad dream. By now Hill had many personal friends all over the central South.[1] With cotton prices again at a low ebb, the poverty of hundreds of thousands of small croppers had become appalling, and the news that Cleveland had taken a stand against the one measure on which they counted for relief, free coinage, had saddened their hearts. Justice Lamar had his ear to the ground, and he wrote Cleveland early in April: [2]

In the States of Georgia, Alabama, Mississippi, and Virginia, there has been unquestionably a skilfully planned movement organized by able, adroit, and ambitious men who have felt your character and career to be a reproach to their public conduct and methods, to secure for Senator Hill the delegates to the Chicago Convention, in their respective States, by the same methods that had been employed in his own State. These movements were seconded by men from whom better things might have been expected, but who yielded from a want of firmness to stand against what seemed to them to be the greater force. The minuteness with which the scheme was elaborated, going to the extent of providing for Cabinet Officers and Foreign Ministers, I should not have credited if I had not direct and unanswerable evidence of it.

But in New York the Hill forces sadly overreached themselves. Late in January the national committee announced the date for the national convention—June 21. Immediately thereafter the State committee, with Edward Murphy as chairman, called a convention to assemble in Albany on February 22 to elect delegates-at-large. Not once in the past twenty years had such a convention been held earlier than April 20! The motive for this flagrant violation of party usage was twofold. Men would be chosen to the "snap convention" by caucuses meeting while the roads were choked with snow, when few farmers up-State could attend and when little cliques of town politicians allied with Hill could dominate the situation. Moreover, the early action of the New York convention would impress other States and give impetus to the Hill boom. Hill himself seems to have preferred a later convention. If so, he was wiser than his State committee. No sooner had this body made its announcement than it was smitten with a storm of indignation unprecedented in the party history of the State.

"An act of midwinter folly," declared the *World;* "illogical, unfair, undemocratic, and unwise." Almost every Democratic newspaper of

[1] Clark Howell to author, May 29, 1931.
[2] April 3, 1892. Cleveland Papers.

character in the State and nation took the same position. Everyone who loved fair play and detested sharp practise reacted against the step. Justice Lamar wrote Cleveland that the effect on the South was to arouse an "insuperable repugnance" to Hill's methods. There and in the West men saw that if such practises were generally introduced the Chicago convention would be an assemblage of manipulated politicians instead of a great representative body. In New York city Fairchild, ex-Mayor Grace, Curtis, Coudert, and other Cleveland men convoked a mass-meeting in Cooper Union on February 11. Resolutions were adopted calling upon the State committee to rescind its action, and a Committee of Fifty was appointed to take such steps as were necessary to secure a proper representation for New York at the national convention. Plans were soon on foot for a great gathering of anti-snappers in Syracuse. Cleveland was meanwhile interviewed by the reporters as he returned from a hunting trip to Joe Jefferson's plantation in Louisiana, where he had seen no newspapers. They found him breakfasting on a Pullman at Baltimore. He was in good spirits as he asked how the Hill leaders explained the early call: [1]

"Well, Murphy says" (remarked the reporter), "he is glad of the early convention, because he wants to go away on a vacation sometime in March or April, and it might not be possible for him to attend the convention if the event were not fixed for this month."

Mr. Cleveland's eyes sparkled and he broke into a hearty laugh, finally adding: "What's the matter with May? State conventions have been held even as late as May." And, with a broad smile, the ex-President continued: "What you tell me is quite interesting. You see I know so very little about the matter."

"And Mr. Croker—"

"Yes, what does he say?"

"He thinks it is all right. He believes in young men, in innovations, and may want to run over to Europe and back before June 1."

Again Mr. Cleveland's face was the picture of innocent merriment, but he only remarked in a very general way that he was glad to hear of men in public life who did not allow politics to interfere with their personal affairs. The utmost good humor was apparent in every muscle of his face.

Asked to make a statement for quotation, Mr. Cleveland said in the drollest possible manner: "The State committee has selected a historic day. I hope the weather will be fine."

The snap convention duly instructed the entire New York delegation for Hill and bound them by the unit rule. Simultaneously Hill's sup-

[1] N. Y. *World*, April 2, 1892.

porters throughout the country staged celebrations. The Atlanta *Constitution* predicted his nomination on an early ballot; Watterson wrote that "Mr. Cleveland is no longer a possibility," that his selection would be "deliberate suicide," and that the Democrats of the Union should meet New York "in setting Mr. Cleveland aside and advancing Mr. Hill to the party leadership." [1] Some of Cleveland's friends were momentarily alarmed; Governor Russell, fearing late in February that he might withdraw, made a trip to Lakewood to insist that he must not—that he held overwhelming allegiance of the Democratic masses. But Cleveland had never felt more belligerent. On the day of the snap convention he was in Ann Arbor, delivering an address at the University of Michigan. A tremendous burst of applause came when, near the close of his speech —which for once he read from manuscript—he said: "Interest yourself in public affairs as a duty of citizenship, but do not surrender your faith to those who discredit and debase politics by scoffing at sentiment and principle, and whose political activity consists in attempts to gain popular support by cunning devices and shrewd manipulation." Soon afterward he told a caller that although he did not believe he could live out the trials of a second term [2] he would fight Hill to the bitter end, and on May 1 he wrote Lamar: [3]

I have within the last few months passed through much that is trying and perplexing to me. The office of President has not, to me personally, a single allurement. I shrink from everything which another canvass and its result involve. I know what another election means, and I know as well the dark depth that yawns at the foot of another defeat. I would avoid either if I would consult alone my comfort, my peace, or my desire. My discomfort arises from a sense of duty to honest people and devoted friends. . . . One thing I know. Forces are at work which certainly mean the complete turning back of the hands on the dial of Democracy and the destruction of party hopes. Is it ordained that I am to be the instrument through which Democratic principles can be saved—whether party supremacy immediately awaits us or not? If folly is to defeat us in any event, ought I to be called upon to place myself under the falling timbers? This last consideration smacks a little of care for myself, which perhaps ought to be discarded.

You shall know, my dear friend, my inmost thoughts. I shall be obedient to the cause of the country and of my party. Whatever happens, no one shall say that I refused to serve in time of peril or abandoned those whom I have been

[1] Louisville *Courier-Journal*, Feb. 23, 1892.
[2] C. S. Hamlin, MS *Diary*, Feb. 26, 1892.
[3] Thomas F. Madigan, *Catalogue*, 1931.

instrumental in calling to the field where is waged the battle of Democratic principles.

It quickly became evident that there was no national response to the action of the snap convention, and that in reality it had injured Hill. The *World* remarked that the Presidential election would not be confined to New York, and that forty-three other States would take part. With unquenchable enthusiasm the anti-snappers set to work all over the State. Cleveland, who had thought for a short time that his adherents were inert and had written a friend that they seemed "dazed," soon found them difficult to hold in rein. Men were enlisted in every county, money was raised, and meetings were addressed. As May ended an imposing convention, literally thousands being present with bands and banners, was held in Syracuse. Franklin D. Locke headed a thousand men from Buffalo. The convention adopted resolutions and chose a group to go to Chicago. It had no chance of being seated, but it would impress the country with the anti-Hill sentiment, and in the end it acted as an effective army of observation. This anti-snap movement was actually of immeasurable importance, for as Godkin wrote later,[1] Cleveland's nomination might well have proved impossible except for its demonstration that after all he could probably carry New York.

By the beginning of May the Hill boom had completely collapsed. Rhode Island in March held the second State convention. Hill and his aides made earnest efforts to carry it, and opened negotiations with Rhode Island leaders, but all in vain—the State chose delegates pledged to Cleveland. The Massachusetts convention immediately followed. Governor Russell and his friends had set an early date for the express purpose of influencing other commonwealths, being confident, since Patrick Collins had declared his intentions, that it would support Cleveland; and the result justified them. Massachusetts elected Cleveland delegates, and passed resolutions endorsing Cleveland's candidacy. Even where Hill had been strongest it became evident that he could not win. Threats that he would be repudiated poured in upon the party leaders. His position became still worse when Governor Flower and the Democratic legislature, who were popularly supposed to be under his control, enacted an election-inspectors bill which placed full control of the counting of votes in New York city in Tammany hands. The *World* gagged

[1] N. Y. *Evening Post*, Dec. 31, 1892.

over this law, declaring it a blunder as well as a wrong. "What universal dismay," exclaimed *Harper's Weekly*, "would not be produced by the prospect of the transfer to Washington . . . of the Democratic power which has been supreme at Albany during the last winter, which began the session with the theft of a legislature, and ended with the placing in the hands of Tammany Hall the control of the election in this city . . ." [1]

The death knell of Hill's hopes was rung by the Georgia Convention. Here, despite all the efforts of Speaker Crisp, Senator Colquitt, Clark Howell, the oldtime Randallite Democrats, the silverites, and the men who believe that Hill would resist a Force bill more aggressively than Cleveland, the latter won a decisive victory. Hoke Smith and John B. Gordon rallied Cleveland's forces. On May 14, at a massmeeting in the basement of the courthouse in Atlanta, they obtained a large majority and captured the Fulton County delegates. [2] Four days later the State convention was called to order in the capitol. The applause which followed the mention of tariff reform and Cleveland "fairly lifted the roof;" a Cleveland adherent was elected chairman, and a delegation of which all but a few men were for Cleveland was sent to Chicago. Hoke Smith's *Journal* was jubilant. Georgia had been noisily advertised as the strongest Hill State in the South, and the prostration of his boom there showed how utterly he was beaten. [3]

III

The Republican National Convention met first. It was to sit on June 7. As the month opened Harrison had almost a majority of the delegates, but many of Blaine's admirers declared that the frigid President would never gain a majority. The movement to nominate Blaine instead had gained steadily in momentum. All the Secretary's friends—Whitelaw Reid, Elkins, Henry Cabot Lodge, Cushman K. Davis, Senator Hale, and others—were ready to fight for him till hope expired. He could count upon the principal State bosses—Quay and Cameron of Pennsylvania, Platt and Fassett of New York, and Foraker of Ohio. His magnetism was as great as ever, and his hold upon the rank and file of the party so complete that the mere mention of his name produced an

[1] *Harper's Weekly*, May 14, 1892.
[2] Atlanta *Journal*, May 14, 1892.
[3] *Ibid.*, May 19, 1892.

enthusiasm which Harrison could never arouse. But if Blaine desired the nomination, he waited until too late. On June 4, within seventy-two hours of the convention, he treated the country to a sensation by his sudden resignation of the State Department. He gave no explanation. His friends varyingly attributed the act to ill-health, to fatigue, or to friction with Harrison. There can be no question that his relations with the President, and still more his wife's, had long been strained almost to the breaking-point; nor is it easy to avoid the conclusion that his sudden step, if not actuated by a desire to seize the nomination for himself, was intended to prevent Harrison from having it. If this was true, he miscalculated. The instructions of the delegates could not be altered, and at Minneapolis Harrison was easily nominated on the first ballot.

A party cannot repudiate a President after his first term without incurring grave dangers, and Harrison had fully earned his renomination. Henry Adams went hardly too far when he said that "Mr. Harrison was an excellent President, a man of ability and force; perhaps the best President the Republican party had put forward since Lincoln's death." [1] Hayes had unquestionably made a better Executive. Yet the principal weakness of Harrison's candidacy lay not in his record but his personality. He could address an audience of ten thousand, and captivate every auditor, but in meeting a roomful of men he froze them all into enmity. Particularly was he detested by Quay and Platt. The New York boss wrote in after years that "Harrison's renomination caused a chattering of the teeth among the warm-blooded Republicans of the East. When there was added to it the choice of Whitelaw Reid, a persistent assailant of the New York organization, many of the New York delegates, including myself, wrapped ourselves in overcoats and earmuffs, hurried from the convention hall, and took the first train to New York." [2]

By this time on the Democratic side it was obviously Cleveland against the field, with Hill quite out of the race; and the field included no stronger men than Gray of Indiana, Palmer of Illinois, Boies of Iowa, and Carlisle. The Boies candidacy was a curious sign of the times. As recently as 1884 he had been a Blaine Republican, but he had been swept into the Democratic camp by the rising Farmers' Alliance movement. Cleveland's principal opponents kept up a desultory but ineffective

---

[1] *Education of Henry Adams*, 320. Adams added that he preferred Cleveland.
[2] Thomas C. Platt, *Autobiography*, 246, 247.

fire. Watterson on June 12 had penned a warning against taking him or anyone else from New York, declaring that "If we go there for a nominee, we shall walk through a slaughter-house into an open grave." Tammany filled the air with muttered threats. When State Chairman Murphy reached Chicago, he gave out a denunciatory interview, asserting that Cleveland's nomination would mean the destruction of the regular organization in all the important cities of New York and in the State itself. Feeling against Cleveland "is growing very bitter," he said, "and we sincerely trust that the Democracy of other States will not humiliate the Democracy of New York by nominating a man who we are positive could not be elected." [1] But the confidence of Whitney and Parker rose day by day.

It was a confidence founded on consummate preparations. State after State had declared for the ex-President, an imposing list. Conventions all over the West had adopted resolutions sustaining the principles he had declared vital. On June 9 Whitney brought together at his house in New York an important "Conference" of national leaders, comprising a dozen representatives from ten States.[2] Under his leadership this body selected in advance the principal committees of the convention, those on credentials, resolutions, and organization, and decided upon the temporary and permanent chairmen. Arrangements were made for further meetings in Chicago. Cleveland knew of this "Conference," and indeed helped arrange it. One of the members was S. E. Morss, editor and owner of the Indianapolis *Sentinel,* whose name had been given Cleveland weeks earlier by D. S. Alexander, and whom the ex-President had promptly called to New York for a talk.[3]

The story of the convention has often been told: how Whitney, opening spacious headquarters at the Palmer House in Chicago, held the fate of the gathering in his hand, smoothing the temper of the ruffled Hillites, employing conciliatory tactics to win over Gorman and Brice, sternly breaking up an attempted coalition of silver delegates led by Montana, and gathering votes from every quarter. Since he was not a delegate, and had kept himself clear of factional quarrels in New York, he could appear as the *deus ex machina* of the convention. Suave,

[1] N. Y. *Times, World,* June 17, 1892. (A. P. interview).
[2] The conferees included Harrity of Pennsylvania, Morss of Indiana, Dickinson of Michigan, Vilas of Wisconsin, Wilson of West Virginia, Stetson of New York, Josiah Quincy of Massachusetts, and less notable representatives of Illinois, Rhode Island, and Vermont. Parker, *Grover Cleveland,* 156.
[3] Memorandum by D. S. Alexander; McElroy MSS.

cool, and indomitable, he had one unanswerable argument—that Cleveland could be elected, and nobody else could. Above everything, the party wanted to win. He was assisted by Bissell, Parker, D-Cady Herrick, and F. L. Stetson, all as indefatigable as himself. Repeated meetings of the enlarged "Conference" at the Hotel Richelieu planned nearly every step of the convention, from the choice of William L. Wilson as permanent chairman to the final vote.

One dramatic incident is among the legends of party history. The final session, just before the balloting, began at five o'clock on the afternoon of June 22. Hour after hour of oratory passed. After two o'clock in the morning the crowd of fifteen thousand became so restless that several speakers were heard practically in pantomime. Eager for a vote, it howled down Virginia's best orator. A terrific rainstorm had broken, and the peals of thunder mingled with the general uproar. At that moment the burly figure of Bourke Cockran was seen slouching toward the platform. Tammany, silent the whole evening, was sending in its Old Guard. Cockran was a tired man, suffering from a cold and neuralgia, and before mounting the platform moved for a recess until ten o'clock the next day; he wanted a fresh throat and a fresh audience. Dickinson, floor leader of the Cleveland forces, shook his head sullenly. Rousing himself for a tremendous effort, Cockran launched into his speech quietly, his mellow, penetrating voice, a slight Milesian accent agreeably enriching its flavor, reaching every part of the hall. He indulged in no rhetoric and no affectation; his manner and diction were perfect, and every sentence fell into place with the precision of a cut and polished block. For three quarters of an hour he held his exhausted audience in absorbed attention.[1] Then the spell broke. Tammany's thunderbolt had been launched, and the Cleveland ranks had not lost a single adherent.

A delegate rose to move the call of the States, and without a word of dissent the voting began. Alabama gave Cleveland fourteen votes and Hill two. Arkansas gave Cleveland sixteen and Hill none; California followed by giving Cleveland eighteen. Georgia gave Cleveland seventeen and Hill five. Swiftly the Cleveland column, as Illinois and Indiana fell into line, grew impressive. When New Jersey was reached not one

---

[1] Henry Cabot Lodge wrote Cockran June 27: "Now that you have emerged from the dust and heat, just a word to say how very fine I thought your speech—as a speech; strong, conclusive, dignified as it seemed to me, and yet despite the place and the excitement, entirely restrained and quiet." Bourke Cockran Papers.

voice was raised for Hill. The entire delegation had been switched to Cleveland by a dashing young leader of the Essex County machine, James Smith, Jr., a close friend of Whitney, who years later became one of the important figures in the making of Woodrow Wilson.[1] Pennsylvania was called, and Hill received not one of its sixty-four delegates. "It is a funeral!" exclaimed John R. Fellows. With 607 votes necessary to a choice, the ballot gave Cleveland 617⅓, Hill 114, and Boies 103.

Cleveland heard the returns by a special wire in the gun-room at Gray Gables. Besides Mrs. Cleveland and her mother, he had with him Governor Russell, Mrs. Russell, and Joseph Jefferson. Young Charles Jefferson kept tally of the balloting. As he later wrote, they were anxious over Cockran's speech and did not know what its effect would be. "All were bending over my shoulder watching the figures when the spell was broken by Mr. Cleveland remarking in a startled tone: 'I forgot to dry my lines today.' At the critical moment when New York was about to cast her vote and the danger of a break was greatest, Mr. Cleveland arose and went out and hung up his lines as unconcernedly as though the convention were of no interest to him." [2] As the last States were reached Mrs. Cleveland, glancing outside, saw that the sunrise was faintly gilding the lawn. And just as it was announced that Cleveland was nominated, the first ray of the morning flashed through the window and rested upon his head.

Once more, as in 1888, there was a prolonged struggle in the platform committee over the tariff plank. Cleveland favored a moderate pronouncement. Whitney and Vilas brought forward the same plank that had been presented in 1884 by the reformer Morrison, declaring for a revision of the tariff laws to remove their inequalities, lighten their oppressions, and put them on a fair basis; but it did not satisfy men like Watterson and Tom L. Johnson. Defeated in committee, these radicals carried the fight to the floor, and by a vote of 564 to 342 substituted a plank which denounced Republican protection in general as fraud and robbery, called the McKinley Act "the culminating atrocity of class legislation," and declared high tariff-taxation unconstitutional. Cleveland resented this plank, which John Hay said was worth thousands of votes to the Republicans, and for a time threatened to repudiate it in his letter of acceptance. Some correspondence ensued

---

[1] Cf. James Kerney, *Political Education of Woodrow Wilson*, 20.
[2] Undated Memorandum. Cleveland Papers.

between him and Watterson, marked on the editor's part by asperity and on Cleveland's by mildness culminating in exasperation. In explaining his wish for caution, Cleveland ventured on a prophecy. "If we are defeated this year, I predict a Democratic wandering in the dark wilds of discouragement for twenty-five years. I do not purpose to be at all responsible for such a result. I hope all others upon whom rests the least responsibility will fully appreciate it." Let us both, he concluded, be just, amiable, and modest. Watterson replied in an exceedingly unamiable tone, and Cleveland retorted with an angry letter which Watterson carefully suppressed in his autobiography, and which has apparently been lost. "Thus ended my personal relations with Mr. Cleveland," wrote the editor. "Thereafter we did not speak as we passed by." [1] Cleveland's own version of the incident, as related in Charles S. Hamlin's diary, is worth quoting: [2]

August 1, 1892. C. S. H. has interview with Cleveland at Gray Gables. Mr. O'Brien met him at station and they walked over together. Cleveland talked confidently as to the election. Favored tax to abolish ten per cent tax on State bank notes. Indicated he would refer to it in letter of acceptance. Said he had not heard from David B. Hill since the convention. Seemed surprised at this. Said none of the leading politicians had congratulated him or had written in any way. Said he had received long, egotistic letters from Henry Watterson as to the tariff plan, etc. Said that finally he wrote Watterson a rather sharp letter and thought he would not trouble him further. Said his letter to Watterson was scathing and he was only too glad to be rid of him.

Years later Cleveland and Watterson attended together the funeral of Mrs. John G. Carlisle. They did not meet. After the service all those present went upstairs for their hats and wraps. Anxious friends of the two men, seeing Watterson start toward one staircase, hastily tried to guide Cleveland to another. He saw their manoeuvre. "I will go up *that* staircase!" he ejaculated loudly, and stalked up the same steps as Watterson, never deigning a look at him.

An effort in the convention to declare for free coinage of both gold and silver was lost without a roll-call. But as a sop to the silverites, Adlai E. Stevenson of Illinois was nominated for Vice-President. The plank on coinage, like that inserted in the Republican platform, was a

---

[1] Watterson, *Marse Henry*, II, 132 ff.
[2] Hamlin Papers. Hill was credited with the wrathful statement that "the tariff plank in the Democratic platform has converted every workshop in the United States into a Republican campaign headquarters." N. Y. *Press*, Sept. 21, 1892.

declaration in favor of bimetallism under such conditions as would maintain the parity of the two metals; international agreement or special safeguards of legislation being both mentioned.

IV

When the conventions broke up, an undercurrent for Cleveland was already running with a force that was destined to sweep all the doubtful States into his following. But at first no one perceived it. The press predicted a hard battle. Many Republican organs declared that Cleveland was woefully weak; he had been beaten before, he was the sworn enemy of the Populists, his tariff record was unpopular in manufacturing districts, and the Hill-Tammany group would knife him.[1] The New York *Times*, while delighted by his nomination, feared that Democratic dissensions might defeat him. The *Sun*, making an absurd flop over the fence to Cleveland's side, announced with all Dana's usual magnanimity that it did so only because it would be better for the republic to elect the devil than reëlect Harrison. *Harper's Weekly*, again on the Democratic side, declared that "whether Mr. Cleveland or Mr. Harrison can carry New York is a purely speculative question." The significant fact was forgotten (till the day after election) that New York had virtually repudiated Hill, that the South was staunchly loyal, and that Cleveland had already shown a surprising strength in the West.

This time Cleveland made no error in his choice of a campaign executive. "I do think—indeed I know," he wrote Bissell, "that Whitney should nominally if not really and actively be at the head of the committee to manage the national campaign. I have regarded it as exceedingly desirable on my own judgment, and the letters I have received within a few days, and the expressions I have heard made, convince me that it is more essential and vital to success than any one thing."[2] Pressure was needed to induce Whitney to serve. Cleveland had Bissell, Vilas, Dickinson, and others write him pleading letters. But once he accepted, he threw himself into the contest with his usual headlong energy. "He could accomplish more in one day than any other man I ever saw could do in ten," Cleveland once said. "Every power of his mind would be concentrated upon the present duty. Social life, personal

[1] For example, N. Y. *Tribune,* June 27, 1892.
[2] Gray Gables, June 30, 1892. Cleveland Papers.

business—all were sacrificed, so that he would be fully ready. I have never known anything approaching this power of absorption. . . ." [1] And in this instance his energy was needed. The campaign organization was smaller than usual, and at the party headquarters in Fifth Avenue only seventy-five or eighty men were busy. Moreover, the State Committee was an uncertain factor, and contained men, notably Chairman Murphy and William F. Sheehan, whose treachery he and Cleveland feared.

The weak link in the Democratic chain was once more New York, where Hill sulked and many of the Tammany leaders were openly hostile. Whitney was eager to close up the ranks. In August he attempted to persuade Cleveland to write a conciliatory letter to Murphy, who had just lost a daughter. Indeed, he went so far as to send Cleveland a draft. "You may think it cheeky, my suggesting it," he wrote, "but it is to get the tone in which I hope you will write him." [2] This draft letter was a curious production:

Dear Murphy:
As I am the candidate and you are the State Chairman can't you come into the harbor some day and pay me a visit? Whitney will manage to bring you, I imagine, if you can come.

I regret very much to hear that your other daughter's health is requiring your attention. I hope it is nothing that will cause you anxiety. We are entering upon a campaign which in my honest judgment is full of the gravest consequences to the people of the country. I cannot feel that it is personal to me. It is for or against the triumph of Democratic principles that we are enlisting. Let us all sink our personal feelings in the greater interests involved. I shall hereafter look for my friends irrespective of differences of opinion heretofore held. It shall never prejudice a man in my mind hereafter that he opposed my nomination if he stands by the party in its principles and works for success in this fight.

If we all do the same and present a united front to the foe we can win easily in my judgment.

I shall rely upon you to second my efforts in this behalf.

Harrison wrote a much humbler letter than this to the disaffected Tom Platt. But to Whitney's draft Cleveland reacted with a cold fury. Opening it in the presence of his confidential secretary, Robert L.

---

[1] Alexander, *Four Famous New Yorkers*, 172. The nominal head was William F. Harrity of Pennsylvania.
[2] Aug. 11, 1892. Cleveland Papers.

O'Brien, he abruptly tossed it aside, saying: "I'll be d—d if I'll sign it!" [1] He wrote Bissell that he would see the whole outfit to the devil before he would mail such an abject letter, and that he was glad he was not to see Whitney for several days, "for I don't believe I could hold myself in." [2]

He and Whitney, indeed, took fundamentally opposing views of the strategy which the campaign in New York required. Cleveland wished to defy and ignore the Democratic malcontents; Whitney wished to conciliate them. Late in July the candidate, going to the palatial house of Commodore Benedict at Greenwich, Conn., had set forth on a cruise in Benedict's yacht *Oneida*. "We lingered on the way to fish a little and spent last night at New London," he wrote Bissell. "But fishing or eating, reading or drinking, asleep or awake, my mind has been on one thing constantly, and that is the situation politically in the city, county, and State of New York. *The thing is not right*—that is, in my judgment. I believe there is a lot of lying and cheating going on and unless the complexion changes we shall wake up I think the morning after election and find that we have been fooled by as base a set of cutthroats as ever scuttled a ship." [3] In fine, Cleveland believed that to try to compromise and coöperate with Murphy, Sheehan, and Tammany would be to invite betrayal; they could not be trusted. On the other hand, Whitney declared that compromise was essential, and that Murphy, Sheehan, and Tammany must be brought into line in an effort to isolate the unforgiving Hill. He wrote Cleveland on August 22: [4]

Hill has declined to go on the advisory committee. But I think we have all the rest of them—his friends from end to end—and I shall lay down on them pretty soon and either bring about a breach between them and Hill or bring Hill into line. If you hear from Murphy I wish you would let me know what he says and keep me posted generally on their movements so far as you see them.

The policy of getting everybody upon whom Hill relies and nullifying him is the true policy both for now and for the future. It is no use to say not trust any of them. We have got to trust them. They have the organization and the power and by trusting them we can make them pull straight.

Yours, W. C. Whitney.

[1] Robert L. O'Brien to author, June 4, 1929.
[2] McElroy, *Grover Cleveland*, I, 349.
[3] July 24, 1892. Cleveland Papers.
[4] Cleveland Papers.

I wish you would do as much reconciling of recalcitrants as you see your way to do. You can do much more with a word than I can do with a speech.

A few days later he wrote more peremptorily. Cleveland was making a great and "perhaps a fatal" error; "you do not realize that you were nominated against the united voice of your State organization;" and unless their irritation is quickly removed "you cannot carry this State." [1] To this Cleveland's answer was that if strenuous efforts were made in the West he could lose New York and by carrying Illinois and Wisconsin still win the day.

Whitney's insistence upon a policy of conciliation finally bore fruit in the famous Victoria Hotel conference in New York City in September. To the last minute Cleveland hung back. His political instincts were nearly always fundamentally sound, and there was much to be said for his position; if the national leaders truckled to Tammany, they would repel a host of Mugwumps and anti-Tammany Democrats not only in New York but all over the country. Moreover, he did not wish to turn his back on his anti-snapper friends. But there was also much to be said for Whitney's contentions, and they were supported by such men as D-Cady Herrick. Grumbling, reluctant, deeply troubled, Cleveland finally told Whitney on September 3 at Gray Gables that he would visit New York, talk with the recalcitrant machine leaders, and be as agreeable as he could. But, he wrote Bissell, I told him "I would not pledge myself to do their bidding in case of success." [2] When he arrived in New York, his perplexity and depression were extreme. Herrick, who had been called down from Albany for the occasion, found him laboring under intense and for him wholly preternatural excitement. He talked of withdrawing from the race. If his friends insisted that he must make extreme concessions to win the support of Tammany, he would drop the nomination; but if his friends would stand by him in his chosen policy, he would defy Tammany, call meetings in every county in the State, and inform the country that the regular Democratic organization had refused to support the regular candidate. [3]

In this mood he went to the dinner. He was accompanied by Whitney, Don M. Dickinson, and Robert L. O'Brien, Herrick refusing to go along for fear his presence would offend Sheehan. Before they started,

Cleveland remarked to O'Brien: "My boy, this is one of the most important dinners you will ever attend." The organization leaders present were Sheehan, Croker, and Edward Murphy, Jr. Dinner was served in a private room. Whitney, who had the tastes of a gourmet, had prepared a superb menu. During the meal the conversation was on general topics and not unfriendly. Then over the coffee and cigars Cleveland brought up the political situation by asking how the campaign was going. "Not very well," replied Sheehan, and began to explain why.

It at once became evident that Sheehan was truculent and embittered, that Chairman Murphy shared his feelings and supported his views, and that these two men and Cleveland could be restrained from an open rupture only with the greatest difficulty. Sheehan assumed the offensive with a series of complaints.[1] Their gravamen was that Cleveland was allowing his Mugwump allies, and particularly the editors of the *Evening Post, Times,* and *Harper's Weekly,* to attack him and the Tammany leaders on both public and private grounds in terms that were intolerable. It transpired that Sheehan had been particularly stung by some of Godkin's epithets, the *Evening Post* always calling his brother "Sheehan the Defaulter." He demanded that Cleveland do something to halt these reform attacks; and he also declared that if Cleveland were elected, he must grant the Tammany organization more patronage than in his first Administration. According to one version,[2] he asserted: "We want pledges from you. We want to know what you are going to do if you are elected. We want you to give us promises that will satisfy us that the organization will be properly recognized if you become President again." To which Cleveland replied, smiting the table with his huge fist: "Gentlemen, I will not go into the White House pledged to you or to anyone else. I will make no secret promises. I'll be damned if I will"—and thwacked the table again. Mr. O'Brien's more accurate recollection is that Sheehan's demand for recognition was made in urbane and tactful fashion, and that Cleveland rejected it by two quiet words: "No promises."

As Sheehan made his points, Edward Murphy kept up a rumble of supporting growls in the background. Cleveland's temper finally rose. At the critical moment he got to his feet and declared that sooner than

---

[1] Robert L. O'Brien to author, June 4, 1929; see his article in the Boston *Evening Transcript,* June 27, 1908. The date of the dinner was Sept. 8.

[2] McElroy, *Grover Cleveland,* I, 353 ff.

make improper concessions to win Tammany's support, he would withdraw from the race. Though it has been said that this statement was
coupled with the threat of a public appeal against Tammany, Mr.
O'Brien's recollection is that it stood alone, and no such threat was
made.[1] At every stage of the conversation Croker exerted himself for
peace. He and Whitney together pleaded for conciliation and mutual
forbearance, and in the end had their way. The conference broke up
without any definite decision, or explicit understanding; but not before Croker declared that Cleveland was quite right in not making any
pledges, and that it was improper to ask for them. The atmosphere was
cleared. From that moment the campaign proceeded in New York with
the support of Tammany. Whitney wrote in jubilant terms to Cleveland
just after the conference: [2]

Your last visit did a world of good. But for it we should be in bad shape
now.
Hill is thoroughly mad now. Madder at his own people than at us.
They are pressing him on all sides and telling him he can't play fast and
loose, etc. He has declined to see me. I hadn't asked him, but he sent that word
to me. I have warned Sheehan [that I wish] to see his speech before it is
delivered and he intends to let me.
I do not doubt now but we shall have the full organization strength on
election day. That is the way it is working now. Hill can't do much if he should
feel inclined.

And on September 19 even Hill, crushed, humiliated, sore, accepted
the inevitable. He appeared that day in Brooklyn, and in a sportsman-
like speech swept away whatever doubt had existed as to his loyalty
to the party and to Cleveland. Reminding his audience of the famous
assertion, "I am a Democrat," made there in 1885, he declared: "I was
a Democrat before the Chicago convention, and I am a Democrat still."

v

The campaign of 1892 was the cleanest, quietest, and most creditable
in the memory of the post-war generation. Not merely was there almost
no abuse of either nominee, and almost no waving of the bloody shirt;
there was an unprecedented calmness in facing the issues. Many speakers on both sides frankly confessed that the opposing candidate would

[1] Robert L. O'Brien to author, June 4, 1929.
[2] New York, Sept. 15, 1892. Cleveland Papers.

fill the presidency with credit. Travellers on long journeys told astonishing stories of never having heard a single reference to the election on trains or in the streets. The childish spectacularity of previous campaigns, the brass bands, the rallies, the torchlight processions, the caparisoned marching clubs, were largely discarded.[1]

The Republicans were handicapped by an uninspiring candidate and the necessity, particularly with the tariff, of fighting on the defensive. The McKinley Act, after two years, was still desperately unpopular. Nelson W. Aldrich and his colleagues of the Senate Finance Committee had been making an investigation of prices and wages for the preceding half-century, and he presented some of the most favorable statistics of their still unpublished report in the *Forum* for October in an effort to demonstrate that prices had been falling and wages rising. He had no difficulty in showing that real wages had risen decidedly more than in Great Britain, that prices of manufactured goods had steadily dropped, and that the nation was enormously richer than it had been under the Walker Tariff of 1846. But to show that these consequences of a hundred factors, and above all of our rich national resources, constituted an argument for the McKinley schedules—that was obviously absurd. Other Republicans pointed to the reciprocity arrangements just made; but William L. Wilson, in the same issue of the *Forum*, proved that reciprocity had done practically nothing to increase our trade. All that has been gained, he wrote, "belongs to the *de minimis."* Carlisle's speeches on the tariff were particularly effective.[2]

On July 5 the country was startled to learn that a bloody labor war had broken out at the Carnegie steel works near Pittsburgh. As the morning mists had risen on the Monongahela, a body of some 270 heavily-armed Pinkerton guards had moved up the stream from Pittsburgh to the Homestead works, which had been closed on July 1 in a lockout, and were to be reopened with strikebreakers the following day. The manager, Henry Clay Frick—Carnegie being at Braemar in Scotland—knew that this little private army, which had been recruited in New York, Philadelphia, and Chicago at $15 a week,[3] might be needed to protect the plant against the desperate men from whom he was taking their bread. He did not know their very approach would be a signal

---

[1] See review in N. Y. *Evening Post*, Nov. 7, 1892.
[2] *Public Opinion*, Aug. 6, 1892.
[3] *Harper's Weekly*, July 16, 1892. The men had not been told of the exact use to be made of them.

for battle, that the loss of life would stagger the country, and that the episode would be an important factor in the Presidential election. A mob of 5000 was waiting and the Pinkerton men were received with shots. They instantly replied. A pitched battle ensued, the workers firing from entrenchments protected by pig-iron and iron plates, and the Pinkerton men remaining under cover in their thick-walled barges. Both sides were determined to kill. Whenever a head appeared above the workers' parapets the Pinkerton men aimed at it; and in retaliation, the barges were sprayed with bullets by sharp-shooters, machine oil was pumped upon the water in a vain effort to set them on fire, sticks of dynamite were thrown from the banks, and two small cannon were brought into play. Once the detectives tried to hoist a white flag, but it was riddled amid cries of "no quarter." Finally they surrendered, and were allowed to march away—but not until ten men had been slain, and more than sixty wounded.[1]

The contest thus savagely begun was in the last analysis a struggle not over wages, hours, or working conditions, but for supremacy. The Amalgamated Association of Iron and Steel Workers had built up a powerful organization at Homestead, and had successfully introduced the principle of collective bargaining. It had obtained in 1889 a wage settlement satisfactory to itself, and intended to maintain its scale. Mr. Frick had become equally determined to stamp out the union.[2] The country in general perceived that Frick intended to destroy one of the few really powerful labor unions in the country, and to reduce the men at Homestead to the status of Carnegie's employees at the Edgar Thomson, Duquesne, and other works. Wages would then be dictated by the owners to suit their financial interests. Indeed, before leaving for Scotland in April Carnegie himself had placed in Frick's hands, for use at discretion, a notice declaring that "there has been forced upon this Firm the question Whether its Works are to be run 'Union' or 'Non-Union,' " and that the firm had decided that they "will be necessarily Non-Union after the expiration of the present agreement." [3] The country also perceived that in hiring a private army of nearly 300 men Frick had taken an intolerable step. Public opinion sternly disapproved the violence used by the strikers; it realized that the governor of Penn-

[1] George Harvey, *Henry Clay Frick the Man*, 118 ff.
[2] Cf. Rhodes, *The United States from Hayes to McKinley*, 386.
[3] Harvey, *Frick*, 165.

sylvania acted correctly when he called out 8,000 militia, under whose protection the Carnegie Company threw in non-union workmen and broke down the strike. But its sympathies were with the principle of collective bargaining, and it reacted vigorously against Frick.

From the outset it was obvious that the outbreak would cost the Republicans votes. The union leaders immediately pointed out that the protective tariff was involved. They issued an address in which they claimed that both the employees and public had distinct rights in the policies of the Carnegie mills, for the simple reason that the national government had fostered these mills by public taxation. No one could deny that the tariff on steel billets was a prohibitive tariff, that Carnegie and his associates had been carefully consulted when the steel schedules in the McKinley Act were framed, and that for years they had been piling up great fortunes behind the tariff wall. Indeed, Carnegie had succeeded in 1890 in persuading Representative McKinley to change the tariff on steel billets from the ad valorem to the specific basis, in order that as lower manufacturing costs the world over forced prices downward the tariff would constantly increase.[1]

Cleveland was scathing in his references to the Homestead affair. In his carefully prepared acceptance speech he referred to the crushing of the union as "the tender mercy the workingman receives from those made selfish and sordid by unjust governmental favoritism." He spoke of the hardships of the laboring masses under "the exactions wrung from them to build up and increase the fortunes of those for whose benefit" the laws furnished special subsidies. When a fanatical New York printer of anarchistic views, Alexander Berkman, attempted to assassinate Frick in his Pittsburgh office, part of the Republican press accused Cleveland of inciting the deed. It was noticeable that the Democratic press and leaders took a position much more sympathetic toward the strikers than that of the Republicans. Senator Palmer of Illinois immediately shocked his conservative colleagues by a speech embodying some decidedly radical opinions. He sharply condemned the use of the Pinkerton men; he spoke scathingly of the effrontery shown by great steel magnates in cutting wages after they had begged for tariff protection as a means of keeping wages high; and he declared that workingmen who had spent the best part of their lives in the service of a particular firm "have the right to insist on the permanency of their

[1] *Public Opinion*, July 30, 1892.

employment." The Republican leaders felt a vivid apprehension of the political consequences of wage-cutting in the country's largest steel works during a period of industrial prosperity. Whitelaw Reid, by a cipher dispatch through the State Department to Carnegie in Scotland, appealed for continued recognition of the union at Homestead. At the same time the Republican National Committee secretly sent John E. Milholland to Pittsburgh to interview Frick, who was in bed with his face and head swathed in bandages. The result was a rebuff. Carnegie, after first taking a favorable attitude, turned squarely about and cabled Frick that "probably the proposition is not worthy of consideration." [1] It was Frick who held the power of decision anyway, and he proved totally unwilling to give the Amalgamated Association—which was soon defeated—another day of life.

The unrest among laboring men the country over was increased by a series of events in the South and West. Late in August there occurred a distressing struggle between the miners of Eastern Tennessee and the State authorities. Partly because it had no fit prison and partly in order to make money, Tennessee regularly leased many convicts to work the mines of the Tennessee Coal, Iron, and Railroad Company, receiving a paltry $100,000 a year from the contract. The miners rose against this competition, burned or broke down a number of convict stockades, and gave way only when Governor Buchanan used the militia with an iron hand. In the Coeur d'Alene district in Idaho, meanwhile, occurred another desperate labor struggle.[2] A rich silver mine there, owned by Eastern capitalists, had cut wages again and again until the miners finally rebelled. They were numerous and well-armed, and after bloody fighting in July seized the property and drove the strikebreakers out. The governor thereupon asked President Harrison for aid, Federal troops were ordered to Coeur d'Alene, and the strike was crushed.[3] In August a switchmen's strike in the Buffalo yards was—after the intervention of several thousand State militia—similarly defeated. It was natural for many workingmen, frightened by the tremendous fighting power of the modern corporation, and resenting the obvious influence of the capitalist classes over the State and Federal Governments, to express their anger by voting the Democratic or Populist tickets.

[1] Harvey, *Frick*, 148 ff.
[2] See Mary Hallock Foote's interesting labor novel, *Coeur d'Alene*.
[3] John R. Commons and Associates, *History of Labor in America*, II, 497 ff.

Few events of the summer pleased Cleveland more than the defeat in the Democratic House, on July 13, of the Stewart Free Coinage bill which had passed the Republican Senate a fortnight earlier. This removed a dangerous question from the campaign in a way superficially flattering to Democratic pride. There was a good deal of rejoicing among Eastern Democrats. Those who scrutinized the figures closely, however, realized that this exultation was ill-founded, and that the Democratic party continued sicker under the free silver contagion than the Republicans. A few statistics made this as clear as a peal of thunder. Had the Stewart bill been left to the votes of Democratic members alone, it would have passed the Senate by a margin of 20 votes and the House by a margin of 23, while if it had been left to the Republicans alone it would have been defeated in the Senate by 17 votes and in the House by 51. It was patent that the Democratic party was perilously honeycombed. There was just one consolation: the negative votes of 94 House Democrats gave promise that Cleveland's tremendous influence, exerted with his unflinching courage, might well prove able to keep the party on the true and narrow road.

Cleveland made but one public appearance of any note in the campaign, his response before 20,000 people in Madison Square Garden to the notification of his nomination. For one reason, he was often tortured by the gout. Dr. Bryant wrote Lamont in midsummer [1] that he had just gone to see the ex-President about his foot, and "found him grunting as you know full well, suffering from an excess of medicine rather than the lack of it. He always believes that if a little will do some good, a bottle full must be of great advantage indeed." Moreover, during the summer Mrs. Harrison fell ill and died, and Cleveland—to the warm approval of the public—gave this "afflictive dispensation of Providence" as a reason why he should not attend the dedication of the World's Fair in Chicago or take the stump.[2] Most of the summer he spent quietly at Gray Gables.

Yet there was little time for fishing, for his correspondence was enormous, and party workers came in unending procession. In August occurred the famous murder of Lizzie Borden's father and stepmother in Fall River, and a host of politicians seized the opportunity to visit the scene of the crime and pay their respects to Mr. Cleveland in the

[1] July 7, 1892. Cleveland Papers.
[2] Rhodes, *The United States from Hayes to McKinley*, 394.

same week-end. Communication between Whitney's headquarters in New York and Buzzards Bay was made pleasant by Benedict's yacht *Oneida*, which on several Sundays dropped anchor off Gray Gables. Whitney repeatedly appealed to Cleveland to come to New York or Lakewood to make himself more easily available, and late in August he was in town for a time. Oscar S. Straus wrote Bayard that the visit had been valuable: [1]

At Mr. Cleveland's request I remained with him pretty much the entire time he was here to assist him in receiving the Democratic representatives and turning away "softly" the cranks. It was a most interesting experience and valuable political training. I can truthfully say the nearer one gets to Mr. Cleveland the more we must honor and love him for his simple sterling self. The situation here looks most encouraging, following, to use your well-chosen words, "the moral revolt that is going on in the minds of patriotic citizens all over the land."

The almost passive mood in which Cleveland went through the campaign of 1888 had now been replaced by a vital desire to succeed. He penned letters inciting party leaders all over the country to greater effort. Carter H. Harrison in Chicago, so recently an enemy, received one, and Lambert Tree wrote Cleveland that it had "captured him completely." [2] Both he and his Chicago *Times* plunged into the battle without reserve. Another letter went from Gray Gables to Senator Voorhees. Cleveland recalled how the two had used to talk together in the White House, how "I said once to you that I was willing 'to do the ploughing' and make way for another to harvest," and "how earnestly and with your big-hearted and peculiar generosity you antagonized the idea." For once Cleveland was more than tactful! "I am extremely anxious to be elected," he continued. "I want to carry Indiana. I do not for a moment suppose I can do this without your help. I hope that you will give the ticket the benefit of your experience and familiarity with Indiana politics. I say I 'hope' you will do this. That is not the word I should have used. I ought to have said 'I know' you will." [3] His alert eye seized upon points of special peril. Thus ten days before election he sent for Parker, and telling him that Adlai E. Stevenson had not yet written any letter of acceptance, and that the Republicans were about

---

[1] N. Y. Oct. 7, 1892. Bayard Papers.
[2] Chicago, Sept. 15, 1892. Cleveland Papers.
[3] Utica *Observer*, July 1, 1908; no date for the letter given.

to come out with a lurid exposure of Stevenson's record as a green-
backer, he proposed a plan for spiking the enemy's guns. Parker was
hurried off to meet Stevenson in West Virginia, and at Cleveland's suggestion handed him a tentative letter of acceptance which he consented
to use—a letter double-riveted in its treatment of sound money.[1]

The moral fervor of which Straus and Bayard had spoken was not
absent; but whereas eight years earlier it had been the fervor of men
fired by a vision of crusading reform, now it was that of men who felt
that the times, big with danger, needed a man of dauntless courage.
This feeling was keenest in intellectual circles. Of the thirty-three professors teaching at Amherst College, in the very centre of New England Republicanism, twenty-three were for Cleveland. They signed a
testimonial [2] declaring that "We admire his courage, his constancy, his
public spirit, his studious neglect of his merely personal interests where
they conflict with the calls of public duty. We remember his tariff message, his pension vetoes, and his letter against free silver as conspicuous
instances of disregarding personal considerations for the public good.
We therefore urge all our fellow citizens to give Mr. Cleveland their
hearty support." Cleveland's courage appealed also to James Schouler,
who wrote in the *Forum:* [3] "So far as 'free silver' may be considered at
this time a national issue, I trust most a President who is fearless and outspoken and whose words carry popular weight." Wayne MacVeagh,
T. M. Cooley, Seth Low, and Walter Q. Gresham were among the prominent Republicans who came over to his side.

VI

As summer ended, the omens began to look more favorable. The
September elections in Vermont and Maine showed a slump in the
Republican majorities amounting—as compared with 1888—to between fifteen and twenty per cent. Elections in the South immediately
afterward demonstrated that the Democrats there were holding firm.
A cunning scheme for combining the Populist and Republican vote in
Arkansas, Florida, Alabama, and Georgia had broken down because
there were fewer disaffected white men than were supposed, and because the negroes held aloof. Weaver had boasted that the Populists

[1] Parker, *Grover Cleveland,* 169–171.
[2] N. Y. *Evening Post,* Oct. 24, 1892.
[3] *Forum,* November, 1892.

would carry the State elections in Florida and Georgia, which came early, but he met a Waterloo in both. In Georgia, despite months of agitation, despite an impassioned tour by Weaver and Mrs. Lease, despite the poverty and ignorance of the rural population, the Democratic majority was 81,000.[1] Every Congressional district, even Tom Watson's, proved safe. Cleveland felt relieved, for Whitney had written him on August 30: [2] "In the South the impression of you got by the people is that you do not appreciate their suffering and poverty (and these are the real causes of the Alliance movement) and have your ideas formed by Eastern money power, etc., etc.—the usual twaddle. I think having this in view you might write on the tariff and on silver in a mood sympathetic to them and make a great change in the South. As you said to me, it is unaccountable what ideas they get and where they get them." The advice was good, and then and later a few expressions of sympathy for the West and South would have been to Cleveland's advantage.

"Weaver," wailed the Cleveland *Leader*,[3] "is useless south of Mason and Dixon's line." In the Middle West, however, the Populist strength was manifestly great and was certain to cut into the electoral vote of the Republicans. It was admitted by Harrison's managers that Weaver would win at least four electors in Colorado, three in Nevada, and ten in Kansas. Naturally the Populists had little liking for Cleveland. "It is universally known," said the Populist organ, the *National Economist*,[4] "that the entire body of economic legislation enacted by the Republican party during the period of its ascendency had been dictated or inspired by interests localized within the plutocratic circle which comprises New York, New Jersey, and Pennsylvania. It has not perhaps been so generally recognized that the species of Democracy known as Clevelandism seeks to go beyond the Republicans in the direction of compliance with the grasping demands of the moneyed and monopolistic interests of the same circumscribed section." But Populism drew most of its votes from Cleveland's opponents for the simple reason that most of the discontented Western farmers had been Republicans.

[1] See long explanatory article in Washington *Post*, Oct. 11, 1892.
[2] New York, Aug. 30, 1892. Cleveland Papers.
[3] Oct. 10, 1892.
[4] May 14, 1892.

To the last day the contest was regarded as close. Seldom has an election been so confused by a third party as was this one. In five Western States which the Democrats could never expect to carry—Colorado, Idaho, Kansas, North Dakota, Wyoming—they nominated no electors and threw their strength to the Populists as the best means of defeating the Republicans. In other States there was a partial fusion of the same kind. At the South the position was reversed—the Republicans voted for Populist electors.[1] In the last week of the campaign Republican confidence rose, partly because of favorable registration figures in up-State New York. Betting at first favored the Republicans, and Whitney asked Croker to join a pool to use half a million dollars in changing the odds at the Fifth Avenue Hotel. When Croker objected that he had no money, Whitney rejoined, "I'll put you in for a hundred thousand dollars"—and later handed him that sum as his share of the profits.[2] But there were Republican observers who knew that defeat lay ahead. Blaine's friend, Rowland B. Mahany, of the *Catholic Union and Times,* wrote him in September that "the ground swell is in favor of Democracy." [3]

Yet the magnitude of Cleveland's victory astonished everyone, for it was the most decisive since the reëlection of Lincoln in 1864. No one was surprised to find the doubtful States—New York, New Jersey, Connecticut, Indiana—slip into his column. But that he should sweep Illinois, Wisconsin, and California was extraordinary; no Republican had believed these States in danger and no Democrat had seriously predicted their conquest. Ohio, for the first time since the birth of the Republican party, was so closely divided that one Democratic elector slipped in. A shift of 750 votes would have given Cleveland all of them. In Michigan five electors went into the Cleveland column. With 277 electoral votes against Harrison's 145, he could have won even without New York. It was a landslide which left the Republican party more humiliated than in 1890.[4] Years later Senator Allison, looking back over national history, remarked: "It was God's mercy to this country that Grover Cleveland, and not Harrison, was elected President." [5] It

[1] Stanwood, I.
[2] Alexander, *Four Famous New Yorkers,* 191.
[3] Buffalo, Sept. 20, 1892. Blaine MSS.
[4] Stanwood, I, 517. Cleveland's popular vote was 5,556,000; Harrison's 5,175,000.
[5] N. Y. *Evening Post,* June 24, 1908.

was not providence, but the saving sense of the American electorate. Once more Godkin wrote the most fitting comment on the event:

Mr. Cleveland's triumph today has been largely due to the young voters who have come on the stage since the reign of passion and prejudice came to an end, and the era of discussion has opened. If the past canvass has consisted largely of appeals to reason, to facts, to the lessons of human experience, it is to Mr. Cleveland, let us tell them, that they owe it. But they are indebted to him for something far more valuable than this—for an example of Roman constancy under defeat, and of patient reliance on the power of deliberation and persuasion on the American people. Nothing is more important, in these days of boodle, of cheap bellicose patriotism, than that this confidence in the might of common sense and sound doctrine and free speech should be kept alive.

Something like this was shortly said to Cleveland's face by Carl Schurz, at a brilliant dinner tendered the President-elect by the Reform Club on December 10. One humorous fact made this dinner memorable. Speaker Crisp was invited, he supposed that he would be asked to speak, and preparing his address in advance, he gave it out to the press. Unfortunately there were so many other speakers that Crisp was not asked to rise. Highly dramatic was the spectacle of Carl Schurz, who had campaigned for Frémont and Lincoln and served in Hayes' Cabinet, addressing Cleveland directly, and paying him a remarkable tribute as a leader who had drawn to his side those who loved justice and courage. The next Administration, he predicted, would be one "born of the best impulses of the American people." The atmosphere of this gathering was one of unrestrained jubilance. But Cleveland himself struck a more sober note. One of his best friends has recorded that on election night, when his house on West Fifty-first Street was crowded with friends and until three o'clock in the morning all was bustle, happiness, and celebration, he had been grave, thoughtful, and silent. He was turning over in his mind the idea he had so often expressed: "Sir, it is a solemn thing to be President of the United States." Now, looking about the familiar clubroom crowded with his friends, he declared:

While we find in our triumph a result of popular intelligence which we have aroused, and a consequence of popular vigilance which we have stimulated, let us not for a moment forget that our accession to power will find neither this intelligence nor this vigilance dead or slumbering. We are thus brought face to face with the reflection that if we are not to be tormented by the spirits which we have ourselves called up, we must hear, above victorious shouts, the call of our fellow countrymen to public duty, and must put on a garb befitting public servants.

It was not an unworthy mood for one approaching four of the most troubled years in all our history.

LATE in February Dr. Wilton M. Smith went down to the cottage which Cleveland occupied at Lakewood—the so-called "little White House," beloved by the President-elect because it reminded him of his father's Fayetteville parsonage—to bid him godspeed. It was a cold and blustery evening. After dinner Cleveland remarked, "Come into my den, I want to read you my inaugural speech." The address deeply impressed Dr. Smith, and he said so. In reading it Cleveland had wrought himself to a high pitch of emotion. With heavy step, he paced up and down the floor, and then turning, faced Smith with words of fierce intensity, which fastened themselves upon the doctor's memory. "Doctor," he exclaimed, "I suppose at times you won't approve of many things I do, but I want you to know that I am trying to do what is right. I have a hungry party behind me and they say I am not grateful. Sometimes the pressure is most overwhelming, and a President cannot always get at the exact truth; but I want you to know that I am trying to do what is right. *I am trying to do what is right.*" The tears stood in his eyes as he began pacing up and down the room again, and blew his nose hard to conceal the tide surging in his breast.[1]

When he said this—when he penned the closing sentence of his inaugural, declaring that "I know there is a Supreme Being who rules the affairs of men and whose goodness and mercy have always followed the American people, and I know he will not turn from us now if we humbly and reverently seek his powerful aid"—Cleveland realized that the clouds were thickening about his Administration. Already there were portents of a great financial storm. A few far-sighted men, like Henry Villard, had grasped the dangers presented by the operation of the Sherman Silver-Purchase Act, and Villard was busily warning his German friends to keep their investments in the United States in liquid form.[2] The worldwide shock produced by the suspension of Baring Brothers in 1890 had quickly passed in the United States, and prosperity had apparently returned, but with the balance of trade becoming adverse, it was on an insecure footing. Within the Democratic party the

---

[1] Undated memorandum by Dr. Smith in the Cleveland Papers.
[2] Villard, *Memoirs*, II, 357 ff.

recent victory could not obscure a steadily widening schism. In a dozen Western States the party organization was already in the hands of the silver men, and in the South they were making steady progress. The new President needed all his strength and all his reliance on providence.

"I am dreadfully perplexed and bothered," wrote Cleveland to L. Clarke Davis in January. "I cannot get the men I want to help me." [1] As before, his Cabinet was not completed until late in February, and contained some distinct surprises. The chief was the nomination of a lifelong Republican, Walter Q. Gresham, to be Secretary of State. Cleveland had again offered the place to Bayard, who refused because he dreaded the high expense and preferred to be our first ambassador to Great Britain. Mr. Robert L. O'Brien, Cleveland's confidential secretary, believes that he also offered it to others, and even thought of drafting Melville W. Fuller for the post.[2] The choice, said the *Nation*, would give the whole reform wing of the Republican party new confidence in the President's independence and patriotism. But Gresham, while the most lovable of men, was not a conspicuous success as head of the State Department. With excellent intentions, a lofty ideal of foreign policy, and generally sound judgment, he acted in entire harmony with Cleveland in shaping our external relations. But his appointment angered a large element in the Democratic party. Moreover, his poor health and his tactlessness proved a handicap; members of the Senate kept away from him, and after he had offended Chairman Morgan of the Foreign Relations Committee by sending an Administration bill to another Senator for introduction, Morgan did everything he could to annoy and harass him. His absent-mindedness sometimes led him into ludicrous blunders. Once, leaving the White House after a late supper, he made a great pother over his lost overshoes, the servants looking everywhere till they were found on his own feet; and details of business often escaped him.[3]

For the Treasury, Cleveland desired Fairchild again, but he refused. As second choice the President-elect turned to John G. Carlisle. His expertness upon finance and taxation, his great influence as a party leader, his long friendship with Cleveland, and above all, his intellectual power, commended him.[4] He was the most brilliant man in the new

[1] Jan. 25, 1893. Cleveland Papers.
[2] Robert L. O'Brien to author, June 3, 1929.
[3] Hamlin, *MS Diary*, Index, I, 229.
[4] James A. Barnes, *John G. Carlisle*, 513 ff.

Cabinet; indeed, Charles S. Hamlin has declared him the most brilliant man he ever met, and Cleveland once pronounced him the ablest man in American public life. Hewitt had said that, given any set of premises, his mind would flash to the correct conclusion with the absolute precision of a machine.[1] His power of lucid statement was unrivalled, and like Gladstone, he could make a budget fascinating. Gifted, witty, and amiable, he possessed an army of friends, and his influence in Congress was expected to be valuable. His antecedents, character, and locality were such that nobody could accuse him of being a tool of Wall Street. It was true that he had certain weaknesses. While in Congress he had gone on periodical sprees, every few months disappearing for several days; the failing was pathological, and he told his intimates that these uncontrollable seizures came on him suddenly, liquor at all other times being repugnant to him. But after he entered the Cabinet he trod a straight path. He was also somewhat too pliable. As one politician remarked, the trouble with Carlisle was that he knew too many people who called him John; and his change of front on the silver question caused him much embarrassment. But Cleveland could supply what strength was needed. The President summed up their relations in a sentence when he said, "He knows all that I ought to know, and I can bear all that he needs to bear."[2]

The most picturesque Cabinet member was the Attorney-General, Richard Olney of Massachusetts, who accepted the place after George Gray had refused it. So little was this hardworking luminary of the Boston bar known in public life that he was not even mentioned by leading Democrats when Cleveland asked for lists of Cabinet suggestions. Nevertheless, he had twice refused a place on the Supreme Court of his own State. He was a man of masterful temper, renowned in his own circle for stubbornness and pugnacity.[3] In these qualities, as in his granite honesty, he resembled Cleveland. He came, like the President, of a Yankee preaching and fighting stock, was a graduate of Brown University and the Harvard Law School, and had been an attorney for large corporations and trust estates. His deep and accurate knowledge of the law, and his pertinacity in applying it, became noted. Indifferent to public office, he had never held any save those of selectman in West Roxbury and representative for one term in the Massachusetts legislature. He had a

[1] Memorandum by Erskine Hewitt, Feb. 11, 1932.
[2] McElroy, *Grover Cleveland*, II, 6.
[3] Cf. the anonymous article on Olney in the *Atlantic Monthly*, May, 1896.

hot temper and a vein of harsh eccentricity, illustrated by more than one unpleasant incident. For example, when a well-loved daughter married an unexceptionable young man of whom he had not disapproved, in a fit of angry pique he suddenly forbade her to enter his house again and kept his door always barred against her.[1] His appointment offended liberals like Pulitzer, who disliked his corporation record and demanded an independent-minded Attorney-General to enforce the anti-trust laws. As we shall see, his influence was destined to affect profoundly and unhappily Cleveland's treatment of one great internal and one great foreign crisis.

In making Bissell his Postmaster-General and Lamont his Secretary of War, Cleveland chose two old friends who had never held important public office and who possessed no political following whatever. The corpulent Bissell was known for little besides Cleveland's manifest affection, but he was a very able attorney. Lamont was an experienced politician, and in four years of rapid money-making in New York under Whitney's tutelage had also shown himself a good administrator. At first Cleveland had hoped that the latter would again become his private secretary, but Lamont now thought this position *infra dig*. Once more he was fated to be, in political affairs, the very efficient "assistant President." Bissell's handling of the postoffice department was dominated by a belief that almost everything John Wanamaker had done there was wrong, and since Wanamaker had introduced many department-store methods and had tried hard to advertise himself, this was not wholly an error.[2] But Bissell also showed great general capacity and stood loyally by civil service reform. He could sit sturdily in his office and repel the assaults of the politicians day after day, and when several candidates appeared for any postoffice, he was already ready to decide in favor of the best man.

The most obscure member was the Secretary of the Interior, Hoke Smith, who was known only in the South as a leading lawyer and as owner and editor of the Atlanta *Journal*, a paper devoted to tariff reform and sound money. As writer and speaker he had led the defense in Georgia against Weaver and the Populists, and had done much to stamp out the Hill infection. The son of a New England educator who had drifted South and married a daughter of the prominent Hoke family, he pos-

---

[1] Henry James, *Richard Olney,* 19.
[2] W. L. Wilson, *MS Diary.*

sessed marked ability. To obtain this appointment he had assiduously pulled strings all over his section, begging editors, Congressmen, and prominent citizens to urge his name upon Mills, upon Whitney, upon everybody with influence.[1] The news of his selection leaked out in a curious way. Mrs. Carlisle one day emerged from her husband's office, buttonholed a newspaper man, and demanded, "Who is Hoke Smith?" A great light dawned on the reporter, and next day his journal announced that Smith was slated for a place in the Cabinet. A burly giant with a chubby face and resonant voice, Smith lent himself to humor, and he was made a butt by Dana's *Sun*, where a special column of "Hokeiana" occasionally tickled the ribs of Republicans. But he proved an excellent Cabinet officer, for he was ceaselessly vigilant against the interests trying to exploit the government lands, the forests, and the Indians.

Hilary A. Herbert of Alabama, a Confederate veteran, wounded at the Wilderness, and long a member of Congress, became a competent head of the Navy Department. He represented the old South as Smith did the new. The Secretaryship of Agriculture went to a more picturesque person, J. Sterling Morton of Nebraska, a man of much charm and oratorical power. A free-trader of the Cobdenite school and a sound-money man, he had attracted Cleveland's attention when he had stood immovable in 1892 against the efforts of free-silver Democrats to effect an alliance in Nebraska with the Populists. He had grown up with the West, and his nostalgia on the bare Nebraska plains for the Eastern woodlands had given the nation Arbor Day. In Olney's unpublished autobiographical fragment there is a remarkable tribute to him.[2] Once satisfied he was right, says Olney, Morton's loyalty to his convictions knew no bounds, and he was rigid in his opinions to the point of severity; while it would be difficult to speak too highly of his work in the Agricultural Department. "He not only brought to his post uncommon intelligence and skill, but he applied himself to its duties with a zeal and assiduity from which every idea of selfish interest or partisanship was excluded. He rectified abuses, instituted reforms, abolished sinecures, and cut down useless expenditures without fear or favor. What resulted, and as Morton well knew would result, was protest and imputation of base motive from those personally interested, and inappreciation on

---

[1] Hoke Smith Papers. Cleveland, before making the appointment, requested Smith to submit a long memorandum on his political views and those of the New South.
[2] Olney Papers.

the part of the public." Like Hoke Smith, Morton was to suffer cruelly when his own State turned to Bryan and the free-silver cause.

Cleveland delivered his second inaugural address before a shivering audience standing on ground white with snow. It was brief and to the point. He promised that the tariff would be reformed in the interests of the people. Trusts and combines, he declared, would be curbed in so far as the Federal power could reach them. The standard of value of the currency would be maintained against any debasement or depreciation, and to that end he would use all the powers confided to him by law; but in his efforts to remedy the embarrassing financial situation he pledged himself to avoid intolerance. He made vigorous utterances in favor of economy and civil service reform.

II

Once more the pressure upon Cleveland for office was almost unendurable. Early in April a friend of Godkin who was in a position to know wrote him from Washington that he did not believe that either the President or Secretary Carlisle had been able to give a moment's thought, since taking office, to either the tariff or the silver question, because of the offices and office-seekers, and that Carlisle looked as if he were about to break down under the strain. Cleveland had even paid a brief visit to Bayard in Wilmington to gain a respite. Every Cabinet member was in a state of siege. Whenever Lamont made a trip to New York, a small army of office-hunters piled aboard his train to buttonhole him— on one journey thirty were counted. The President met the assault by issuing a series of "rules" intended to rid him of his persecutors in successive blocks. One rule was to appoint nobody who had held office in his first Administration, for he wished to avoid raising up an officeholding class—and when this was announced, "unusual crowds began to be observed on outgoing trains." Another rule excluded newspapermen from appointments, and it was followed by a second exodus. Finally, he called attention to the standing rule that extreme partisan activity was far from a recommendation for office.[1]

But these regulations did not suffice to meet the situation, and finally Cleveland revolted. In a statement published on May 8, 1893, he declared that all the efforts to guard his time had failed, and that the

[1] N. Y. *Evening Post*, March 13, 1893.

periods set apart for receiving Congressmen had been "almost entirely spent in listening to applications for office, which have been bewildering in volume, perplexing and exhausting in their iteration, and impossible of remembrance." Public duty and "an observance of the limitations placed upon human endurance" obliged him to refuse thereafter all personal interviews regarding office except those which he himself invited. He earnestly requested Senators and Representatives to cease escorting office-hunters into the Executive Mansion during the hours given to Congressmen; and he warned applicants that they would only prejudice their prospects by lingering in Washington. It was an extreme step, but public sentiment approved it—and it cleared Washington of the crowds.[1]

The worst pressure came not from individuals, but from organized groups. Many Congressional delegations had organized themselves in behalf of the office-hunters, those from Missouri, for example, setting up a Board of Patronage under Senators Vest and Cockrell which held several meetings to divide the offices. Congressmen of other States held caucuses for the same purpose.[2] Cleveland met these moves by announcing in the middle of March that he would not recognize such self-constituted patronage boards. Tammany Hall, through Richard Croker, tried hard to obtain some substantial appointments from Cleveland—a Federal marshalship, the customs collectorship and so on; but Croker's visit to Washington and his interviews with Lamont proved unavailing. It was not until 1894, after Hugh Grant had succeeded Croker as head of the wigwam, that Cleveland appointed a Tammany man as Federal marshal.[3]

From reformers came the inevitable complaints that after all Cleveland was yielding too much to the spoilsmen. His record was unquestionably uneven. In the Treasury and the State Department Democratic partisanship seemed to rule almost supreme, while in the Postoffice Department careful regard was shown to reform principles. "Cleveland," said the Springfield *Republican*, "ignores and angers the dominant Illinois political ring in the choice of a Chicago postmaster, and kneels with amazing subserviency to the ten times worse Voorhees gang in Indiana." Public attention was particularly drawn to the con-

---

[1] Cf. *Public Opinion*, May 13, 1893.
[2] Cleveland Papers.
[3] N. Y. *World*, July 13, 1894.

sulships and secretaryships of legation. Gresham had stipulated at the outset that he should be relieved of making appointments, alleging his former Republicanism and his ignorance of the Democratic leaders throughout the country. To free him from this labor, Josiah Quincy, member of a distinguished Boston family and for years known as a civil service reformer, became Assistant Secretary on the understanding that he was to hold office only until the more urgent appointments had been made.[1]

It was an unhappy position in which Quincy was thus placed. He received a vast amount of blame which should rightfully have fallen upon Cleveland, Gresham, and the spoilsmen of Congress. By August, out of 317 consular officials, 117 had been changed, and many of the dismissals were for purely political reasons. Quincy admitted as much when, clashing with Moorfield Storey at a dinner of the Massachusetts Reform Club in October, he declared that he had tried to insist on certain qualifications, such as the ability to speak the language of the country to which a man was sent, but that the consulates had generally been apportioned according to the demands of Congressmen.[2] The orders for this came from above. Indeed, in Cleveland's papers there is a letter from Quincy showing that after one error, he had decided to make no appointments without specific instructions from either Cleveland or Gresham.[3] He had nothing to do with such blunders as the dismissal of the expert Henry White, over Godkin's protest, from the first secretaryship in London.

The State Department was poorly prepared to meet criticism of its minor appointees for the simple reason that the major appointees were also a deplorably weak list of men. Cleveland grievously disappointed the Independents in New York by failing to select Frederic R. Coudert as minister to France. Instead, he showed a misplaced magnanimity by appointing ex-Senator James B. Eustis of Louisiana, who had attacked him so vehemently eight years before, and whose chief qualification was that he needed the job.[4] The new minister to Germany, Theodore Runyon, a former chancellor of New Jersey, was a somewhat better man. Hannis Taylor of Alabama was sent to Madrid, a position which proved more responsible and difficult than anyone expected or than he

[1] Statement in Olney's autobiographical fragment. Olney MSS.
[2] *Public Opinion*, Oct. 26, 1893; *Nation*, Oct. 12, 1893.
[3] "Saturday Evening," 1893. Cleveland Papers.
[4] *Nation*, March 23, 1893.

could well fill. At St. Petersburg Cleveland had the wisdom to retain Andrew D. White until nearly two years later he insisted on resigning. He and Bayard were the only men in the whole foreign service, with the exception of Patrick Collins, the new consul-general in London, who possessed any intellectual distinction. And while at the moment Bayard seemed an ideal choice for ambassador to Great Britain, in the end his record there was disappointing.

The appointment which received the most criticism, however, was that of James J. Van Alen. He was a wealthy citizen of Rhode Island who, having made a contribution of almost $50,000 to the Democratic campaign fund, was appointed—after Edward Cooper had refused the place—as minister to Italy. Gilder at once wrote Cleveland that he was unfit, while Godkin burst out in denunciation of what he regarded as the almost open purchase of an office. It was Whitney who had received the campaign contribution, and Whitney who had most vigorously urged the appointment. On careful inquiry, it turned out that Van Alen was a gentleman of education, linguistic training, and some real qualification for the place; quite as much as that of his rich predecessor, William Waldorf Astor. Aldrich was eloquent in his behalf, and ten other Republican Senators assisted in confirming him. But when he had received this partial vindication he resigned on November 20, though Cleveland, in a letter bitterly attacking the "malignant criticism," the "noise and clamor," urged him to stay.[1]

Some humorous and picturesque incidents, as always, enlivened the drab and sorry history of the patronage. It is interesting to find William Jennings Bryan appearing as a suppliant for postmasterships, and conservative Nebraska Democrats warning Cleveland that he would use them merely "to manipulate State conventions and beat down sound money men." [2] Vice President Stevenson once called at the Treasury to protest against an appointment, and was shown that he had written a letter endorsing the man. He thereupon told the Treasury heads to pay no attention to his written endorsements, for if he actually favored any one he would call and say so! In the fall of 1893 Cleveland suggested to C. S. Hamlin, Assistant Secretary of the Treasury, that a certain pay-inspector be transferred from the Portsmouth Navy Yard to that in Boston. Secretary Herbert told Hamlin that he was sorry, but he had

---

[1] Cleveland Papers, Oct.–Nov., 1893; cf. *Public Opinion,* Dec. 7, 1893.
[2] For example, G. L. Miller, Deerfield, Neb., March 20, 1893. Cleveland Papers.

promised the Boston place to Henry Cabot Lodge. Knowing that Lodge a few days earlier had bitterly attacked Cleveland on the floor of Congress, and that the President was wont to refer to him contemptuously as "that scholar in politics," Hamlin reported to the White House just what Herbert had said. Cleveland, who "almost turned blue in the face," wrote a note reading: "To the Secretary of the Navy: You will assign Paymaster May of Portsmouth to the paymastership in the Boston Navy Yard *immediately*"—and that was that.[1] In Cleveland's letters there is a protest against giving a man named Phillips, strongly recommended by some Democrats, any place in the State Department. "I learn that he is a good deal of a club man," wrote Cleveland, "and what is a settler with me, that his close associates are John Hay, Henry Adams, Henry Cabot Lodge, and such."[2]

Cleveland's interest in civil service reform never lagged. Roosevelt had thought it was walrus-and-carpenter work choosing between the record of the first Cleveland Administration and the Harrison Administration. In the fall of 1893, however, he wrote that the second Administration showed a slight improvement. "The Treasury Department is very much worse managed than it was under Harrison. Young Carlisle [Logan Carlisle was Appointments Clerk] had been a curse, and he has acted with the full approval of his father. The Interior Department is certainly no better than it was, and Joe Quincy has out-heroded Herod as a spoilsman among the consuls, but the postoffice department is very much better managed than it was under Wanamaker, and of course this is the department with which we really have most to do."[3] And immediately thereafter Cleveland began to take vigorous action. Order followed order, expanding the classified service by covering into it the lighthouse keepers, pensions clerks, and others, and culminating in the regulation of May 6, 1896, which simplified and improved the whole system and added 29,339 officers to those in the system. When Cleveland left office the classified service included more than 85,000 employees out of a total of about 205,000—a striking advance.[4] Cleveland wisely asked Roosevelt to remain as Civil Service commissioner, and to the jubilance of reformers, he did so until the spring of 1895. The chairman of the Commission was J. R. Procter of Kentucky, who was

[1] C. S. Hamlin, *MS Diary*, Index, I, 72 ff.
[2] Cleveland to Olney, Sept. 12, 1895. Olney Papers.
[3] Roosevelt to W. D. Foulke, Oct. 19, 1893. Foulke Papers.
[4] Carl Russell Fish, *Civil Service and the Patronage*, 225.

an ideal head. In courage, integrity, and capacity to do this very work, Roosevelt wrote the President, he could not be surpassed.[1]

Cleveland regretted the impossibility of inducing numerous men who were quite fit for Cabinet posts, but for various reasons could not be given one, to accept important subordinate positions. "Now if I were only free," he used to say, "to tender the Commissionership of Pensions or of Patents, or any important independent office, to this man." He did not always feel that he was doing friends a real favor when he appointed them to office. George F. Parker was pleased to receive the consulship in Birmingham, while Eugene T. Chamberlain, who resigned from the Albany *Argus* in 1893, was appointed Commissioner of Navigation. But Cleveland told Parker, with characteristic bluntness, that he had not agreed with Lamont when the latter insisted on the offer. "You know my attachment to you, but I do think it a shame that you should be asked to take an office. The pay is inadequate, the tenure uncertain, and the effect often hurtful to the appointee. Men like you and John P. Irish ought to be editing Democratic newspapers at salaries of $10,000 and $15,000 a year." [2] As before, sterling men were found for some of the secondary executive posts. One was W. W. Rockhill of Maryland, who became Assistant Secretary of State. In the Treasury Department W. E. Curtis appeared as Assistant Secretary, and with Gov. William E. Russell's young protégé, Hamlin, he proved invaluable to Carlisle.

In the appointment of a private secretary Cleveland fared less happily than in his first term. Henry T. Thurber, chosen at the suggestion of Don M. Dickinson, was a good fellow, a cultivated gentleman, and the possessor of independent means. But he was innocent of political knowledge and incapable of giving Cleveland the advice he needed. Moreover, he frequently handled small emergencies ineptly. Once a noted American died while Cleveland was absent on a fishing trip. The President had given orders that his departure was not to be disclosed. Thurber received the newspapermen who called, tiptoed into the executive office, remained a few minutes as if talking with Cleveland, and emerged to say that the President was deeply grieved, that he had seldom seen him show more emotion, and that he had said the nation had suffered a loss of the most deplorable kind. All this appeared next day

[1] April 23, 1895. Roosevelt Papers.
[2] Parker, *Grover Cleveland*, 187.

Lamont   Francis   Wilson   Herbert   Morton

      Olney   Cleveland   Carlisle   Harmon

CLEVELAND'S SECOND CABINET

side by side with dispatches reporting that the President had passed through Virginia on his way home! When Coxey's Army descended upon Washington and an extra guard was placed at the White House, the temporary shelter erected for it at the corner of the White House grounds was dubbed Fort Thurber.[1] Lamont, as Cleveland's constant political adviser, was assisted by Bissell and Dickinson. His duties as Secretary of War were light, and he was the one person whom the President was never too busy to see.

III

Once more the country had a hard-working Administration. Cleveland's desk-lamps on the second floor of the White House again burned night after night till two or three o'clock. Gresham and Carlisle never dropped their burden for an instant, and to both men it shortly became crushing. Hoke Smith, ponderous, slow, and sure, plodded month after month through mountains of paper, often laboring till midnight.[2] Morton by assiduous effort managed greatly to develop the scientific work of his department, and yet to cut down its expenses. The Cabinet member who relaxed most easily and regularly was Olney. He was not the kind of man who went home late with a green bag of papers under his arm. He left the office at five, took a long walk or played tennis on his own court, for he was adept at the game, and in summer was frequently seen in the baseball bleachers.[3]

The Clevelands settled into the old White House life with great content. Once more William Sinclair served as steward of the mansion, directing the small force of servants—only seven in all, including chef and nurse. They missed Oak View, and the President for a time thought of using the house of Admiral Porter at 1710 H Street as a quiet resting place for his family. Not long afterward he leased an attractive place not far from Oak View—Woodley. When in May, 1893, the World's Fair at Chicago was opened, the President and most of the Cabinet were in attendance; and en route they stopped in New York to witness from the deck of the *Dolphin* a great international naval review in the Hudson. Early in June the Infanta Eulalia visited Washington, and as a member of the reigning family of Spain, was entertained and fêted

[1] Robert L. O'Brien to author, Nov. 8, 1930.
[2] John S. Cohen to author, May 28, 1931.
[3] Article on Olney, *Atlantic Monthly*, May, 1896.

by the President and other officials. Cleveland, indeed, specially asked the families of his Cabinet to be present at the various functions, and Mrs. Olney, for one, came to the capital for that purpose.[1] The ordinary life of the White House went on with no changes except those resulting from the presence of the baby. In the early summer of 1893 little Ruth was wont to be taken out on sunny afternoons to play on the south lawns. The public soon learned of the fact, and fond ladies planted themselves in the shrubbery to pounce upon the baby and embrace her. Mrs. Cleveland then ordered the White House gates at the south end of the grounds locked. Every Saturday this summer the Marine Band under Fanciulli played on the lower grounds to thousands seated on the grass—making sufficient concession to the popular taste to include "Tarara-Boom-De-Ay" in nearly every programme.

One domestic event at the end of the summer attracted nationwide attention. On Friday, September 1, after long weeks at Gray Gables, the President, Mrs. Cleveland, and Baby Ruth returned to the White House in the midst of a rain. Eight days later Dr. Bryant ushered into the world the second Cleveland child, another daughter—the first child of a President ever born in the White House. Flowers and gifts poured in, and Cabinet members and their wives called to congratulate the President.[2] The country showed disappointment in the sex of the child, but those most concerned did not share it. "She is a sweet baby," wrote Mrs. Cleveland's mother to Mrs. Manning, "looking much as Ruth did at her age, with dark eyes and hair. All here are pleased that she is a girl, however disappointed the nation may be." [3]

But by the time this happy event occurred, the storm so long impending had burst with unexampled violence upon the Cleveland Administration. The hard-pressed and frequently despondent President was battling with an almost overwhelming combination of misfortunes—with industrial and agricultural depression, financial panic, foreign embarrassments, and a fierce political revolt in his own party.

[1] Autobiographical fragment, Olney papers.
[2] Washington *Post*. Sept. 2, Sept. 10, 1893.
[3] Washington, Sept. 28, 1893. Manning Papers.

Chapter XXIX   A First Victory: Repeal of the
                                Silver-Purchase Act

TEN days before Cleveland was inaugurated readers of the morning
papers saw in quiet but none the less startling headlines the news that
the Philadelphia & Reading Railroad, with debts of more than $125,-
000,000, had gone bankrupt. It was an ominous event. For months
prices of most staples, and notably breadstuffs, cotton, and iron, had
been declining. Gold had been going steadily out of the country until
the loss for the year 1892 had exceeded fifty million dollars. Violent
fluctuations in the price of securities gave evidence of increasing uneasiness over the condition of business. The European stock and money
markets were in an abnormal state, and governments and banks alike
were industriously searching the world over for gold; while Australia
was suffering from a terrific economic crisis. In the Treasury, where the
Harrison Administration was about to hand over the reins to Carlisle,
intense anxiety prevailed regarding the hundred-million-dollar gold reserve, which was so manifestly in peril that it was safeguarded only by
an emergency loan of six millions from New York bankers. Orders
were actually given to prepare plates for an issue of bonds.[1]

Throughout the winter Cleveland had been urged by many advisers
to call a special session immediately after March 4, 1893, for the repeal
of the Sherman Silver-Purchase Act. A movement in Congress for such
repeal had already been begun under the leadership of Carlisle. Don M.
Dickinson, Edward M. Shepard, and Henry Villard were active in pressing this counsel upon him; and they were supported by such politicians
as Vilas, Michael D. Harter of Ohio, and Hill, and such financiers as
August Belmont, James Stillman, and J. P. Morgan.[2] Villard argued
that a panic was coming, that if it burst without an effort by the new
Administration to prevent it Cleveland would be held largely responsible, and that as it grew intense nothing could save his policies from
failure. For a time Cleveland seemed about to yield. One February
morning Dickinson burst into Villard's office with a beaming counte-

---

[1] A. Barton Hepburn, *History of Currency in the United States*, 348, 349.
[2] Cleveland Papers, Jan.–March, 1893.

nance, and waving a piece of paper, exclaimed, "We are all right now!" He had spent the night at Lakewood, and prevailing after a fierce argument, had obtained from Cleveland a written announcement that there would be an immediate extra session to deal with the silver-purchase law, and that Congressmen should take notice that no appointments would be considered until they had done their duty in repealing the injurious statute. The announcement was to be published that afternoon. Villard jubilantly telephoned the news to a number of friends. But a few hours later he recalled it when Dickinson came back with a statement that Cleveland had changed his mind and would do nothing before March 4.[1]

In this decision Cleveland was governed partly by a dislike of seeming to yield to Wall Street pressure, partly by the advice of Carlisle, Gresham, and Lamont to wait, and most of all by his wise belief that the time was not yet ripe for repeal and that public sentiment must be allowed to mature. Villard and Dickinson did prevail upon him to write several leading Democrats in Congress, asking them to join with the Republicans in repealing the silver clauses before the old Congress expired. But though the two men went to Washington and lobbied diligently, nothing could be effected. Just before the inauguration Cleveland also permitted Villard to meet all the members of his Cabinet, Olney excepted, in the parlors of the Arlington, and to repeat his arguments. Villard pleaded earnestly, but only J. Sterling Morton agreed with him. When Hill, who wanted both the currency and tariff taken up before the patronage had been distributed and party differences had widened, saw Cleveland about this time, the latter spoke of calling an extra session in September.

II

But it quickly became evident that so long a delay might be disastrous. In the first week of May the great panic of 1893 was fairly upon the country. The causes of this panic, as complex as they were interesting, have not yet received the study they deserve, but their identity is fairly clear. The basic factors were several. In addition to the international disturbances of the time (for the "Baring Panic" had been severely felt), and the operation of the economic cycle, a heavy rôle

---

[1] Henry Villard, *Memoirs*, II, 363, 364; Villard Papers, Jan., Feb., 1893.

was played by the erratic financial practises of the whole period since the Civil War. A difficult situation had been made worse by the unwise legislation of the Harrison Administration, the extravagant appropriations by Congress, and excessive expenditures by the Federal Departments. The Silver Purchase Act was inflating the currency by about fifty millions annually, and this had helped bring about a marked expulsion of gold from the country. At the same time, the steady increase in Populist and free silver sentiment aroused fears of Western dominance and of destruction of the gold standard. The immediate causes were also several. Among the precipitating events in 1893 were the continued loss of gold to Europe—the net drain in the fiscal year ending June 30 amounted to $87,500,000; uneasiness over the bad situation of many banks and railroads; the prospect of tariff revision; and the apprehension of a crisis in the Treasury, which was receiving a dangerously small part of its revenue in gold, and which had always to be ready to redeem both greenbacks and the new silver certificates in that metal.

Immediately on entering office Cleveland and Carlisle had made desperate efforts to augment the gold reserve without an issue of bonds. Carlisle had requested banks in different cities to exchange part of their gold coin for other forms of currency held by the government, and he had so far succeeded that by March 25 the Treasury reserve reached $107,000,000. But immediately thereafter it fell alarmingly. On April 22, for the first time since its establishment, it went below the hundred-million mark, which as Cleveland said, was popularly regarded "with a sort of sentimental solicitude." Carlisle's ambiguous statement two days earlier that he would pay demands on the government in gold "as long as it has gold lawfully available for the purpose" had aroused a widespread fear that the Treasury might begin redeeming the Sherman Act notes in silver. Legally it had the right to do so, but such a step would have been equivalent to abandonment of the gold standard. Men remembered that Carlisle had voted for the Bland-Allison silver-coinage bill, and shivered. A flood of protests poured in upon Cleveland. He forthwith made an emphatic declaration that gold payments would be unflinchingly maintained. A host of relieved men wrote him that, as Carnegie put it, his statement had "saved this country from panic and entire confusion in its industrial interests." [1] But on May 4 the National Cordage Company, an inflated enterprise which in January

[1] April 22, 1893. Cleveland Papers.

had paid a 100-per cent dividend, went down. The stock market sank, rallied feebly, and sank again in irretrievable collapse.

As the panic thus came in April and May Cleveland was deluged with letters, resolutions, and editorials pleading for a special session. James J. Hill wrote him long descriptions of the acute economic and financial situation in the Northwest, which other Western industrialists corroborated. One after another the principal chambers of commerce, led by that of Cincinnati, voted resolutions demanding immediate repeal, while the entreaties from brokers and bankers became urgent in tone. Banks and commercial houses began distributing circulars in large numbers. Harvey Fisk and Company, in one such document, declared that the intrinsic value of the silver dollar was now but fifty-three cents and diminishing every day; and that nevertheless the nation was obliged to submit to the continued coinage of these dollars and the imminent threat of a drop to a strict silver basis, simply because its representatives were not called together, in accordance with the authority vested in its Chief Executive, and forced to remove from the statute books the law which was eating away the vitals of American honesty. Carlisle, changing his mind, told Schurz early in May that he was strongly inclined to favor the early convocation of Congress.[1]

Meanwhile, popular education was making progress. The one compensation for the suffering which the panic brought upon the country was that, as Cleveland had hoped, its rapid spread westward soon brought many districts in which free silver sentiment was strong to a more reasonable frame of mind. They had previously been adamant against any repeal of the silver purchase clauses, but now their determination was shaken. During May and June the refusal of New York banks to rediscount the notes of Western and Southern institutions forced many of the latter to close their doors, and gave the agricultural sections a taste of acute hardship. Though this refusal arose from sheer inability, many Easterners rejoiced in its results. So sober a newspaper as the Springfield *Republican* found a golden lining to the cloud in its "instructional possibilities," and declared that as the West had sown the wind in the silver-purchase law, so now it should taste the whirlwind.[2] Simultaneously the mountain States sustained a severe blow when news came that India had closed her mints to private

[1] Schurz to Cleveland, May 3, 1893. Cleveland Papers.
[2] Springfield *Republican*, April 29, 1893.

stocks of silver. Mines and smelters by the score were shut down, and Colorado, with 30,000 men out of work, was so hard hit that half her industries came to a standstill.[1]

On June 30, a month earlier than he had originally intended, Cleveland issued a call for an extra session to meet on August 7. He gave his reasons succinctly. Distrust and apprehension concerning the financial situation, he wrote, had already caused great losses and damage, and the crisis was largely the result of "a financial policy which the Executive branch of the government finds embodied in unwise laws which must be executed until repealed by Congress." To this decision he had been gradually tending ever since June 4, when he had hinted to a United Press correspondent that Congress would shortly be called together.

The comments of the press and of public men upon the announcement showed that a grim battle was at hand.[2] In the East the agencies of public opinion were united in approval of the call; for the Republican and Democratic newspapers alike, all business men, and all professional men desired an instant repeal of the silver-purchase clauses. In the West it was generally agreed that, with the financial crisis steadily devastating the country, Congress ought to be in session. Some previously hostile communities were ready to acquiesce in repeal, and others wavered. Nevertheless, beyond the Mississippi the general view was that the cause of free silver could never be given up, and that the currency must not be contracted. Senator Voorhees declared that he would vote to repeal the Sherman Act, but that he would not abate by one jot or tittle his opinions on silver. Richard Bland announced that the battle of the standards was on, and that he would fight to the bitter end; and the Denver *Republican* predicted[3] that Congress would never repeal the Sherman Act outright, though it might limit the monthly purchase of bullion by the Treasury Department to the production of the mines located within the United States. In the South the great mass of small farmers were against repeal, though the planters and merchants urged it; and the Atlanta *Constitution* asserted that Southern representatives would consent to no legislation that would not expand the currency.[4]

[1] See *Harper's Weekly*, July 29, 1893, for Colorado's plight.
[2] See *Public Opinion*, July 8, 1893, for summary.
[3] July 1, 1893.
[4] July 3, 1893.

Hard upon the heels of Cleveland's announcement came another silver convention at Denver, representing all the mountain area. The silver-mining States, as the delegates declared in an impassioned address, would gladly repeal the Sherman Act, for which they had never possessed any great enthusiasm, if they could obtain something better —the free and unlimited coinage of silver. The convention charged that a gigantic international plot had now been perfected by the world's capitalists to demonetize silver everywhere—in Germany, the Latin Union, India, and the United States—and thus drive upward the value of money. It begged the nation to pause before it committed itself to the final establishment in this country of the single gold standard of values, and thus at one stroke changed all debts to gold debts, and inaugurated a never-ending rise of gold and a continued corresponding fall in the price of every commodity.[1] The cross of gold!—and already a great part of the Western population believed that they, if not the whole world, were being crucified upon it.

III

At this moment, when the curtain was about to rise upon a battle royal in Congress, there occurred one of the dramatic minor episodes of American history. The whole strength of the assault upon the Sherman silver-purchase clauses lay, as everyone realized, in the grim determination of Cleveland's purpose. His weight of character could force enough members of his party into line, and nothing else could. Even temporary incapacitation might be fatal to his aims, while if any accident suddenly removed him from the scene, all would be lost; for the Vice President, Adlai E. Stevenson, would infallibly bring the nation to the silver standard. An unhappier time for the development of a dangerous malady was hardly conceivable. Yet on May 5 Cleveland noticed a rough spot on the roof of his mouth. It gave him increasing discomfort, and on June 18 he had it examined by the White House physician, Dr. O'Reilly. The latter found a malignant growth as large as a quarter of a dollar, extending from the molar teeth to within a third of an inch of the middle line, encroaching on the soft palate, and accompanied by some diseased bone.[2]

[1] *Public Opinion*, July 22, 1893.
[2] W. W. Keen, *The Surgical Operations on President Cleveland*, passim.

In alarm, O'Reilly called Dr. Bryant into consultation, while parts of the tissue were sent to Dr. William H. Welch of Johns Hopkins. They confirmed the diagnosis. "Were it in my mouth," Bryant told the anxious President, "I would have it removed at once." An immediate operation was imperative. Yet it had to be kept a complete secret, for the knowledge that Cleveland's life was in danger would have precipitated a new and far greater panic. The most urgent work on the President's desk was hastily dispatched. Dr. Bryant took complete charge of the case, writing Lamont that he could not assume the responsibility for any delay until even August 1st if the growth progressed as it commonly did in such cases.

A series of notes which he exchanged with the Secretary of War record the progress of his preparations.[1] On June 20 he wrote that he had obtained the services of Dr. W. W. Keen of Philadelphia, one of the most distinguished medical men in the United States—a surgeon in the Civil War, who had studied abroad, and who had collaborated with Dr. S. Weir Mitchell in various medical writings. On June 26 he added that Commodore Benedict's yacht *Oneida* would be at the disposal of the President on Wednesday or Thursday of the next week, and "I think our friend should go aboard on Friday night or at all events early Saturday." A general physician, Dr. E. G. Janeway, and an expert dentist, Dr. Ferdinand Hasbrouck, both of New York, had been included in the group. Cleveland was anxious to know whether he could see officers of the government shortly after the operation without revealing what he had been through, and on June 27 Bryant wrote that his appearance would not be abnormal, but that there would be a defect in his speech. The next day he wrote again to insist that "our friend should have a night's rest before the step is taken, and should secure it in the place best intended for the purpose"; and he urged that a Cabinet officer be present at the operation. His anxiety lest something go amiss appears in another note: [2]

Now, Colonel, if you do not intend that Dr. O'Reilly go along, for politic or other reasons, then you should let me know at once, for I must then find someone else. It is my intention to give the anaesthetic myself until time to begin the operation. I do this because I can thus set the example and also the patient will perhaps regard it with some degree of satisfaction. However, someone

[1] Letters in the possession of Miss Lamont.
[2] June 20, 1893. Miss Lamont's Letters.

must begin when I leave off, and I had assigned Dr. O'Reilly to this duty, as I cannot expect either of the other gentlemen to do this for many good reasons. Telegraph me when you leave.

Do you not think there should be a cipher code, which can be used? It seems to me that this will be especially important in case anything unfavorable happens. If anything "springs a leak" it may not be amiss. . . . Benedict is entering into this matter with earnest and well-directed zeal. Does the wife know about it? I ask because she may write me and I wish to know what to say. Give my regards to the President.

On the rough draft of Cleveland's message summoning the special session is a note in Lamont's hand: "Written the day the President left Washington on account of illness. Mrs. Lamont and I accompanied him to New York in Mr. Frank Thompson's car. The operation was the next day." [1] Cleveland, the Lamonts, and Dr. Bryant arrived in New York late in the evening of June 30, and drove openly to Pier A, where he was taken aboard Commodore Benedict's yacht *Oneida*. Here he found Drs. O'Reilly, Janeway, and Hasbrouck, and Bryant's assistant, Dr. John F. Erdmann. The President seated himself in a deck chair, lit a cigar, and chatted until nearly midnight. Once he burst out, "Oh, Dr. Keen, those office-seekers! Those office-seekers! They haunt me in my dreams!" The yacht was kept anchored all night in Bellevue Bay, and Cleveland slept without sedatives. [2] Dr. Bryant warned the medical staff to keep out of sight, lest they be recognized by the internes at Bellevue Hospital.

Next morning newspapers were taken aboard and there was a leisurely breakfast. Meanwhile, the saloon was cleared of everything but the organ, which was fastened down, and the yacht began steaming at half speed up the East River. The anxious Dr. Bryant told the captain, "If you hit a rock, hit it good and hard, so that we'll all go to the bottom!" [3] Cleveland was propped up in a chair against the mast, and the anaesthetic—first nitrous oxide gas, then ether—was given, difficulty being experienced in rendering him unconscious. Though Dr. Janeway's physical examination had revealed nothing wrong, and Cleveland had a strong pulse and little arteriosclerosis, it was the effect of the anaesthetic which Drs. Bryant and Keen chiefly feared. The President was fifty-six years old, very corpulent, with a short, thick neck,

---

[1] Cleveland Papers.
[2] Keen, *The Surgical Operations on President Cleveland*, passim.
[3] Dr. Erdmann furnished the author with many details, Nov. 14, 16, 1931.

and of just the build and age for a stroke of apoplexy; while he was worn out physically and mentally by four months of exhausting labor and of fighting with office-seekers.

Dr. Hasbrouck first extracted the two left upper bicuspid teeth, Dr. Bryant then made the necessary incisions in the roof of the mouth, and the operation began. Dr. Bryant, holding the knife, worked at top speed, and only thirty-one minutes elapsed after the administration of the ether before they had concluded their task. In that time they removed the entire left upper jaw from the first bicuspid tooth to just beyond the last molar, and took out a part of the palate; this extensive operation being necessary, writes Dr. Keen, "because we found that the antrum—the large hollow cavity in the upper jaw—was partly filled with a gelatinous mass, evidently a sarcoma." [1] Actually, states Dr. Erdmann, it was a carcinoma. No external incision was required, and it was not necessary to touch the orbit or skull-cavity containing the eye-ball; and as a result Cleveland was left with the advantage of a perfectly normal appearance of the eye and the absence of any external scar—a fact which aided greatly in keeping the operation secret. Throughout the operation Cleveland, as Dr. Erdmann states, was kept seated in the chair.

At 1:55 P. M. the operation was completed. "What a sigh of intense relief we surgeons breathed," writes Dr. Keen, "when the patient was once more safe in bed can hardly be imagined!" A small hypodermic injection of morphine was soon afterward administered. Dr. Erdmann was watching over Cleveland when he woke up. With his mouth filled with cotton, the President dazedly demanded, "Who the hell are you?" Dr. Erdmann satisfied him as to his identity and business, and on being asked where he came from, answered "Chillicothe." "Oh," said Cleveland, "do you know Mr. Nibge there?" "Yes, he's the druggist." "Well, is he so poor that he needs a job from me?" "No," said Dr. Erdmann. "Then he won't get one," growled Cleveland.[2]

The operation was completely successful. On July 3 Cleveland was up and about; and when on July 5 the *Oneida*, after five days of cruising, dropped anchor in Buzzards Bay, he was able to walk from the launch to Gray Gables with little apparent effort. On July 17 there was a second brief operation to remove some suspicious tissue, from which

---

[1] Keen, *The Surgical Operations on President Cleveland.*
[2] Dr. Erdmann to author, Nov. 14, 16, 1931.

Cleveland quickly recovered. Dr. Keen pronounced him the most docile and courageous patient he ever had the pleasure of attending. So well was the secret kept that for almost two months no outsider learned what had occurred. Charles S. Hamlin went to Gray Gables on July 23 to deliver Cleveland some statistics which Carlisle had prepared on the silver question. "Secretary Lamont and Dr. Bryant were there," he wrote in his diary.[1] "Cleveland appeared not well at all. Had his mouth packed with some kind of bandage. Could not speak distinctly. C. S. H. thinks he had some serious trouble with his mouth. Cleveland looked thoroughly tired out. C. S. H. had a long talk with him on financial subjects." A little earlier Attorney-General Olney had called at Gray Gables on business. He and the other Cabinet members except Lamont knew nothing of the real situation. Cleveland, as he states in his unpublished autobiography, had changed a good deal in appearance and lost much flesh, and his mouth was so stuffed with antiseptic wads that he could hardly enunciate. The first utterance Olney understood was something like "My God, Olney, they nearly killed me!" He talked little, was greatly depressed, and in Olney's opinion behaved and felt as if he would never recover.[2] But his constitution came magnificently to his rescue. Within a short time his wife was complaining to Mrs. Joseph Jefferson that she could do nothing with him—that he overworked on his correspondence, and "this morning when no one noticed he got a peach and ate it. Wouldn't you think a child would have more sense after the narrow escape he had?" On September 1 Dr. Bryant's notes recorded. "All healed."

Yet the operation left its mark upon him. Not externally, for when Dr. Kasson C. Gibson of New York fitted him with an artificial jaw of vulcanized rubber, his face appeared normal and his speech was unimpaired.[3] But thereafter he was thinner; he could no longer labor for twenty-four hours without showing fatigue; and his even temper more frequently betrayed acerbity. The country gradually learned something of the ordeal he had been through. On August 29 "Holland" (E. J. Edwards) published in the Philadelphia *Press* a circumstantial account of the removal of part of Cleveland's jaw. It was received with general

[1] Hamlin, MS. Diary.
[2] Olney Papers.
[3] A cast showing the exact nature of the work done is in the library of the New York Academy of Medicine.

incredulity [1] and denied by men close to Cleveland. At this period, says Dr. Erdmann, he did more lying than in all the rest of his life put together. L. Clarke Davis wrote the press from Marion, Mass., that the story "has a real basis of a toothache," but if it had any other "Mr. Cleveland's closest friends do not know it." He added that "I have seen the President at intervals since he first came to Buzzards Bay this summer, passing hours and days in his company and in the boat fishing with him. I passed all of last Monday with him, fishing, and I have never seen him in better health—never stronger, physically or mentally, and I consider him in both respects the healthiest man I know." [2] Not for almost a quarter century did all the chief facts become known.

IV

Meanwhile, on August 7 Congress had opened. Cleveland, when Olney had first met him, was struggling with his special message, but had written only twenty or thirty lines—the first two paragraphs—and Olney undertook to finish it for him. The belligerent Attorney-General was needlessly offensive in some of his references to the silver men, and unwisely extreme in urging Congress not only to repeal the silver-purchase clauses, but to provide that all outstanding obligations of the government should be payable in gold coin.[3] Cleveland struck out these expressions, and the message in its final form was a notably tactful and moderate document. It had to be, for unless he won a number of silver men temporarily to his side the repeal of the objectionable clauses would be impossible. He began by reviewing briefly the painful business situation, showing that "suddenly financial distrust and fear have sprung up on every side," and declaring that all this was principally chargeable to the silver-purchase legislation. Since the passage of this legislation the government had bought more than $147,000,000 worth of silver; many of the notes used in its purchase had been paid in gold; and the prospect loomed up of the entire substitution of silver for the gold in the Treasury. If this happened, the United States would sink

[1] See N. Y. *Times*, Sept. 1, 1893 Dr. Erdmann states that Dr. Bryant believed Dr. Hasbrouck responsible for the leak, and that it completely ruptured a close friendship between them. He would never speak to Dr. Hasbrouck again, or write him, and sent him his $250 fee by messenger.
[2] Philadelphia *Public Ledger*, Aug. 31, 1893.
[3] James, *Olney*, 32–35.

to the silver standard, and could no longer claim a place among the nations of the first class. In astonishingly mild and even vague language, he recommended, beyond the repeal of the purchase clauses, "that other legislative action may put beyond all doubt or mistake the intention and the ability of the government to fulfill its pecuniary obligations in money universally recognized by all civilized countries." The word gold, with all its hateful associations to the West, was not mentioned. If Cleveland could do it by temperate language, the road to sound money would be made smooth and easy.

But a new spirit was abroad in the land. The first signs of the fierce frenzy of class and sectional hatred which was to fill the middle nineties were appearing. The poverty of the Western farmer, the sufferings of millions of men, women, and children under the merciless pressure of glutted world markets, financial stringency, and heavy debts, were impelling the prairies to the fiercest revolt of their history. An undeniable element in the agony of the period was the increasing value of money, which made it necessary for the debtor everywhere to pay his obligations in a far dearer dollar than he had received, and which gave the Western producer a diminishing return for his products. Already men were beginning to personify gold and silver, to ascribe all virtues to the one and all dangers and wickedness to the other; to treat one as the salvation of humanity and the other as its destruction. The West and South were being set ablaze by men of utter sincerity and of an ability that deserved respect: Jeremiah Simpson, William A. Peffer, Henry M. Teller, William Jennings Bryan, Ben Tillman, Horace Boies, and James B. Weaver. They set forth many errors and half-truths, but they also stated many truths. Throughout the disaffected sections all party lines were giving way. Six months before Cleveland was nominated the Birmingham *Age-Herald* [1] had declared that his selection "would promote and accelerate the division already taking place among Southern Democrats"; that there was imminent a "sundering of old party ties"; and that "the division among our people will be stronger under the irritation of a Cleveland-gold-Wall Street triumph than under any other leader that could possibly have been named." It was a true prophecy.

The Republicans suffered only less than the Democratic organization. Just before Congress met in special session, news-stands were

[1] May 14, 1892.

selling an issue of the *Arena* [1] which contained a vehement argument by the Republican attorney-general of North Dakota, W. H. Standish:

Unless we have silver coinage, our wheat, cotton, and other products will become so cheap that we shall be ruined. Forty years ago, when silver was a standard of money, the gold coinage of the world amounted to about $220,-000,000 annually. Notwithstanding increased population and accumulating business, adverse legislation has destroyed silver as a standard of money, and the coinage of gold has decreased until the annual production is less than three-fifths of the former amount, that of 1890 being only $116,000,000 for the entire world. . . . The change made relative to silver coinage has already lowered prices thirty per cent in all countries, thereby increasing the value of every dollar in money, every mortgage bond note, and all State, national, city, and county debts by that much. Thirty per cent is not only added to private debts, but to taxation to discharge all public ones. . . . The legislation enacted against silver years ago compels us to send to Europe annually $102,857,600 more in value than would otherwise be needed to meet annual interest on debts that we owe there. A still greater advantage is now obtained by New England and the Middle States from the debtors and producers of this country, especially from the entire West and the entire South, as those States receive more interest and more produce from the West and South than our total exportations.

During this summer of 1893 a 42-year-old lawyer and journalist named William H. Harvey, who had been born in West Virginia, had practised in Montana, and had wandered back to Chicago, began the publication of a cheaply-illustrated but vividly-written paper called *Coin*, devoted to the free silver cause. Stump orators were making the West ring against repeal. Badly-spelled petitions were being signed in pencil by thousands. A week before Congress met a national convention of the American Bimetallic League was held in Chicago, with 800 delegates present from 42 States and Territories. Allen W. Thurman was president. The Chicago *Herald*, a Cleveland organ, characterized the body as a conglomerate crowd of silver-mining millionaires, would-be repudiators, and wild-eyed money maniacs; [2] but actually it contained many able and well-informed men, capably representing majority sentiment in the trans-Mississippi area. By unanimous vote, they adopted a platform declaring that since the industrial depression was as acute in gold-standard countries as in the United States, it was folly

[1] August, 1893.
[2] Aug. 4, 1893.

to blame it upon the Sherman Act; that an unconditional repeal of the gold-purchase clauses in an attempt to bring about gold monometallism was a flat violation of the last national platforms of both great political parties; and that there must be no pausing in the fight until the American mints were open to gold and silver on equal terms at the old ratio of sixteen to one.[1] This convention obviously represented an effort to stiffen the silver lines in Congress as the fight began.

Under circumstances less critical and appalling than those of midsummer in 1893 the silver lines would have held firm; but as the country reached the very nadir of financial distress, some members of Congress were shaken in their convictions. The abandonment of free coinage in India had resulted in an instant fall in the American price of silver to 77 cents an ounce. The Indian government had acted only after an exhaustive inquiry, and there seemed no chance that it would reverse its action. Austria-Hungary had taken a similar step only a short time before. The hope that silver might be sustained by an international agreement was thus destroyed, and it seemed obvious folly for the United States to try to raise its value by purchasing 4,500,000 ounces each month. During July numerous financial houses were still failing, mines and factories were closing, unemployment was increasing, and the money stringency was growing. On August 1 the savings banks of the country announced they would require sixty days' notice from depositors desiring to withdraw money. Banks in New York City declined, as a rule, to cash checks except for very small amounts, offering instead certified checks payable through the Clearing House. Tom L. Johnson of Cleveland, who was a member of Congress, travelled to the extra session by way of New York. A rich man, he kept an average deposit of $20,000 in one of the city banks, and was astonished when told that he could have only $50 on his check for $200; the teller was adamant, and it was not until he saw the president that he secured the money.[2] A currency famine set in, and men began hoarding not only gold but silver and greenbacks. At the West the tightness was so serious that the Pillsbury flour-mills were buying wheat with scrip; at the South many farmers were unable to sell cotton because money was unavailable.

[1] *Public Opinion,* Aug. 12, 1893.
[2] Washington *Post,* Aug. 23, 1893.

V

In an atmosphere charged with suspense, William L. Wilson rose in the House on August 11 and opened the debate on the Administration bill for the repeal of the silver-purchase clauses. This measure was almost identical with a bill which Sherman himself had offered in the preceding Congress. The West Virginia member shortly made a prolonged and able argument for it. When he sat down he was exhausted; he was pale and his hands trembled so violently that after vainly trying to still them he clasped them tight and held them between his knees.[1] Thus commenced one of the most dramatic of all the discussions that the House witnessed between the Civil War and Spanish War. Just fifteen days later ex-Speaker Reed closed the debate for the forces of repeal.[2] Between these two men all the best orators of the House had poured out their views, in the stifling August heat, to crowded galleries and benches of scribbling reporters.

The fight was admirably managed by the Administration forces. Led by Wilson and Bourke Cockran, they appointed two hard-working committees—a recording committee to keep track of all votes and expressions of sentiment, and a proselytizing committee to gain new adherents.[3] Both labored systematically, and the second used much personal interviewing and pressure. Amos J. Cummings of New York alone buttonholed every member. The silverites, by contrast, had enthusiasm but no organization. In Cleveland's papers there is an undated tabulation of the House membership at the beginning of the struggle, prepared by his secretary, Thurber, in which 114 Representatives are listed as silver men, 173 as anti-silver men, and 69 as doubtful. Sectional lines, according to this tabulation, were distinctly marked, the Far West and most of the South being a unit against the East. Even in Virginia all the Representatives were placed in the silver column, though Henry St. George Tucker and one or two others did not really belong there; while in New York all were listed as sound money men but three, who were classified as doubtful. On the whole, the tabulation proved remarkably correct. When on August 9 the free-silver Repre-

[1] *Ibid.*, Aug. 12, 1893.
[2] Robinson, *Reed*, 288 ff.
[3] Washington *Post*, Aug. 31, 1893.

sentatives held a caucus in the hall of the House, the clerk recorded 93
men as present, and Bland declared there were more than 100. The
caucus went on record for free and unlimited coinage, but did not try
to fix the ratio, Bland declaring that they would contend at the outset
for free coinage at 16 to 1, and compromise on a ratio of 20 to 1 if necessary. Actually the market price of silver at this time would have required a ratio of about 27 to 1 for parity with gold.[1]

Four great speeches marked the half-month of House debate, and
three of them—by Wilson, Bourke Cockran, and Reed—were made on
the sound money side; the silverites were outfought, and only two
young newcomers, Bryan of Nebraska and Joseph W. Bailey of Texas,
who had both arrived in 1891, gave eloquent voice to the West. Wilson,
who spoke repeatedly, prepared his speeches with meticulous care and
committed them to memory. Marked by close reasoning, fine diction,
and a delicate wit, and yet fresh enough not to smell of the lamp, they
read better than any others of the day. Bourke Cockran, who spoke
extemporaneously, loved a fight against odds, as at the Chicago convention. In his hour and a half speech on August 26 he was in his best
mood, quoting from Locke and Mill, citing many historical instances,
and closing with a magniloquent peroration of the sort then fashionable.
Tom Reed, clad in tow-colored linen, "rolled through the lobby like a
swell in Casco bay" to deliver a witty speech to which the galleries
listened with rapt attention. The demonetization of silver, he said, had
nothing to do with the current depression; after a period of inflation
and speculation the clock had simply struck in the United States for
the time of settlement, and "we are on the down grade to that period
of recuperation, economy, and self-denial which will cause grave suffering, especially to the poor." No single nation, he argued, could maintain bimetallism unaided, and even the silverites were coming to recognize realities [2] by admitting that 16 to 1 was not a heaven-appointed
ratio raised up by the Almighty and by consenting even to discuss market values.

Yet the greatest single triumph of the debate was Bryan's. On August
16, a drowsy summer afternoon, he rose to make an address for which
he had been preparing for months. He had attended the Bimetallic
League convention in Chicago, obtaining the statistics and arguments

[1] *Harper's Weekly*, Sept. 2, 1893.
[2] Robinson, *Reed*, 288 ff.

of the ablest members; he had gone to Springfield to talk with John P. Altgeld; he had spent endless hours over government documents, his pretty young wife—who, to be of more assistance to him, had studied law and been admitted to the bar—laboring by his side.[1] An expectant murmur came from the Westerners who had flocked to the galleries. Bryan's masterful pose, his air of a child of fortune, his handsome face and fine square jaw, inspired confidence. He recalled to the older members the early appearance of Samuel J. Randall, though he was taller than Randall. On his desk lay the proofs of the speech he had composed, and by it stood a glass of malted extract of beef to fortify his strength. Suddenly, as he looked about him, he decided that his prepared address would not do, turned his notes face downward, and began a wholly new speech. The first ringing tones brought members flocking from the lobbies as if by magic. Tom Reed, moving restlessly on the Republican side, sat down and gazed intently at the speaker. John C. Black of Illinois sat passively under Bryan's waving left arm. Senators came in groups from the other chamber, and, rarest compliment of all, the press gallery remained full.[2]

Bryan, intending to speak for one hour, actually spoke three. His manner, his voice, and his handsome presence were almost perfect, yet the success of his speech rested still more upon his lucid reasoning, his effective display of argument, and his restrained phrasing. There was rhetoric in his speech, but it was never, like Bourke Cockran's, ostentatious or forced. It lent literary finish to his successive paragraphs, it glinted in his marshalling of facts and statistics, and it adroitly persuaded the hearer against his own better judgment. His argument followed the familiar lines. He contended that there was neither gold enough nor silver enough to form the exclusive basis of the world's supply of specie; that to drive either out of circulation was to contract the currency all over the globe; and that such contraction, in the demonetization of silver, had resulted in augmenting the value of gold, increasing the burden of fixed debts, and lowering the price of the commodities produced by the debtor class. Even Blaine, he recalled, had categorically asserted all this in the House in 1878. Bryan maintained that if the United States would but keep its courage, it could preserve the parity of gold and silver dollars at the old ratio of 16 to 1.

[1] Paxton Hibben, *The Peerless Leader: William Jennings Bryan*, p. 53.
[2] Washington *Post*, Aug. 17, 1893.

It was foolish, he continued, to say that the Treasury or Sherman notes were the sole cause of the depletion of the Treasury's stock of gold; for if the Treasury notes were all destroyed, there would remain $346,000,000 in greenbacks which could be used for the continued withdrawal of gold. What was most needed was a firm assertion of national purpose. But this, he said, ran counter to the schemes of the capitalist classes and creditors:

> On the one side stand the corporate interests of the United States, the moneyed interests, aggregated wealth and capital, imperious, arrogant, compassionless. . . . On the other side stand an unnumbered throng, those who gave to the Democratic party a name and for whom it has assumed to speak. Work-worn and dust-begrimed, they make their mute appeal, and too often find their cry for help beat in vain against the outer walls, while others, less deserving, gain ready access to legislative halls.

Compared with Bryan's effort, Richard P. Bland's speech a few days later was a pathetic anti-climax. By that time it was known that repeal would pass by a heavy vote. The old Missourian, broken in health, behind him a lifetime of devotion to the free silver cause, before him certain defeat, stood talking to thinning galleries and empty chairs on a floor that more eloquent men had recently filled to overflowing. By force of honesty, pertinacity, and expert knowledge of his subject he had gained the respect of the House, but he was vanquished.[1]

Cleveland was pleased, when the vote was taken on August 28, by the decisiveness of his victory. The Wilson repeal bill passed the House 239 to 108. The silverites had at first predicted that repeal was impossible; later they had refused to concede a majority of more than 25 or 30; and now they were beaten by a margin of 131. But once more the showing was ominous for the internal harmony of the Democratic party. On the adoption of a free coinage amendment, the Democrats had mustered 104 ayes, against 114 nays; the Republicans 12 ayes against 113 nays; and the Populists 8 ayes. On the final passage of the repeal measure, the Democrats voted 138 ayes and 78 noes; the Republicans 101 ayes and 22 noes; and the Populists 8 noes. In other words, while about four-fifths of the Republican vote was steadily cast for sound money, the Democratic vote on free-coinage showed almost an even division.

[1] Washington *Post*, Aug. 29, 1893.

Meanwhile, a repeal bill had been introduced in the Senate—where the fight would be grim and close—under encouraging auspices. To Cleveland's displeasure, it contained a declaratory paragraph in favor of bimetallism, but otherwise it was sound. It was favorably reported by the Finance Committee, the affirmative being taken by Voorhees (the chairman), McPherson, Morrill, Sherman, Allison, and Aldrich, and the negative by Harris, Vance, Vest, Jones of Arkansas, and Jones of Nevada. But for the unexpected vote of the tall "sycamore of the Wabash" it would have been reported unfavorably. Behind his action lay a striking story.

Voorhees, whose long service and sixty-six years alone gave him some title to rank with the sages of the Senate, had fought to the last ditch in opposition to Cleveland's renomination. For nearly two decades he had been an inflationist; his florid eloquence had always been at the service of the silver cause, and this fact was well known when he became head of the Senate Finance Committee early in 1893. Two influences brought about a change of heart. One was the evidence that most Indianians joined with the East in demanding repeal, and the other was Cleveland's use of patronage. Nearly every President for two generations had at some time employed the patronage to reward his supporters or punish his opponents. Pierce, Buchanan, and Lincoln had all done so; Johnson had used it for his Reconstruction measures; and Grant had unblushingly thrust an able man out of his Cabinet in order to use the appointment of a successor to buy votes for his Santo Domingo policy. Most examples of these tactics were unhappy, for they had usually proved ineffective, had demoralized the public service, and had deepened the dissensions within the party. But in 1893 the crisis was great, and Cleveland remarked sardonically that "a man had never yet been hung for breaking the spirit of the law." He no sooner took office than he came to an arrangement with Voorhees, the nature of which is patent from Cleveland's papers. On March 21 an Indianapolis politician, Samuel N. Gold, wrote the President that he was puzzled to know why it was that Voorhees, although recently an anti-Cleveland man, seemed to have complete control of the offices in Indiana. The important appointments had all been of men who were close personal friends of the senior Senator.[1] Two days later a Democratic leader in Fort Wayne wrote to make the same perplexed inquiry. And, dated March 20, there came a significant note from Voorhees himself: [2]

My dear Mr. President:
I do not feel that the sun ought to go down before I convey to you my earnest and grateful appreciation of your kindness and courtesy today in the appointment of Mr. Bisley. I thank you most sincerely not only for the appointment itself, but also for the exceedingly kind and handsome manner in which it has been made. You have indeed made me very deeply and permanently your debtor, and it will be one of the principal pleasures and purpose of my life, and at every opportunity, to recognize and justify, as far as may be in my power, the generous confidence and friendly regard you have extended to me. Permit me to subscribe myself with the highest respect and esteem, yours faithfully, your friend, D. W. Voorhees.

A pledge of support could go no further! And this support was carefully nursed. Hoke Smith's papers contain two subsequent requests from Voorhees for the appointment of friends to office, and both are endorsed by Cleveland as deserving favorable consideration.[3] Cleveland also used the patronage, though less conspicuously, with other Senators. Before the inauguration he had written Carlisle that he would not "turn the other cheek" by making appointments for his opponents. The invaluable diary of Charles S. Hamlin records that when he took internal revenue papers to Gray Gables in August, Cleveland talked with him of the financial situation, showing anger toward the silver men and especially the Senators. "He said that if they wanted a fight, he would give them one. Senator Vilas had written him suggesting that he should hold back appointments. He said he should telegraph Vilas that his idea was a good one and that he had better suggest it to the Cabinet officers." [4]

At the beginning of September Cleveland was back in Washington watching the progress of the Senate debate. He was in an exasperated mood. The two captains of the silver forces, Isham G. Harris of Tennessee and Henry M. Teller of Colorado, marshalled the Democrats and Republicans respectively; discussion dragged on through the hot September days and into October; finally in desperation, on October

[1] Cleveland Papers.
[2] Ibid.
[3] One dated Sept. 4, 1893, the other undated. Hoke Smith Papers.
[4] Aug. 18, 1893.

11 cloture was invoked, and a continuous session began which lasted thirty-eight hours, the defiant silverites then defeating it by forcing an adjournment; and not until October 30 was a final vote reached, and the repeal bill passed.

Wearisome as the two months were, they contained much tense and engrossing drama. The emotions and resentments which the struggle engendered had not been equalled since the angry days of reconstruction. Repeatedly opposing Senators came near to blows. Once, Teller, drawn into a debate with Hawley, of Connecticut, began picturing the misery into which the people of Colorado would sink if the repeal passed, and wrought himself to such a pitch that he burst into tears, sank down at his desk, and buried his face in his hands. Even the placid Senator Morgan, who took the silverite side, was provoked to an outburst. Speaking of the union of sound money Democrats and Republicans, he remarked that "they stick as close and affectionately to each other as a stamp sticks to a love letter." The Senate sat up in surprise. But a greater shock followed when he launched into an attack on the Democrats who followed Cleveland through thick and thin: "The trumpet had sounded, the forces were marshalled, the clock had struck at the White House, and the cuckoos here all put their heads out of their boxes and responded to inform us of the time of day." Thereafter to the silver men Cleveland's followers were the "cuckoos"— though Jerry Simpson called them "pie-bellied hypocrites." In reply, the Easterners taunted Senators Jones and Stewart of Nevada with their personal ownership of silver mines.[1] Once during the continuous session Hoar, rubbing his sleepy eyes, interrupted Allen. "The Senator from Nebraska," he interjected, "said a while ago that there was no overproduction. Does he not regard his speech as an instance of overproduction?" There was an instant of surprised silence, for Hoar was always benign. "The question is too insulting for me to answer!" blazed Allen, and Hoar, moving toward the cloakroom, snapped back, "Don't answer it then!"[2]

More than once men desponded of passing the repeal. Obstruction has seldom been carried further than it was by the silverite minority. Colorado and Nevada combined had a population of less than half a million, and yet they were ready to filibuster to the end. Jones of Nevada

[1] *Harper's Weekly*, Aug. 26, 1893.
[2] Washington *Post*, Oct. 12, 1893.

made a speech filling a hundred pages of the *Congressional Record.* Senator Stewart droned on for hours, his clerk feeding him a continuous array of press clippings. On October 7 Senator Sherman, whose aid had been invaluable to the Administration,[1] surprised the nation by giving the Cincinnati *Enquirer* an interview in which he declared that unconditional repeal was impossible, that if Cleveland persisted he would only destroy his party, and that the two sides might well compromise by reducing the monthly purchases of bullion from four and a half to two and a half million ounces. This display of defeatism did not help the forces of repeal. Cleveland himself sometimes almost despaired. On October 9 he wrote thanking Don M. Dickinson for some words of comfort. "I am very much depressed," he added. "I find that I am looking full in the face a loss of popular faith in the Democratic party which means its relegation to the rear again for many years if not its destruction. I am feeling too the punishment of again occupying the office of President without the previous advice and consent of the United States Senate."[2] The attempt to make cloture effective was widely regarded as a last weapon. Against it the silver men gathered all their resources, and Allen of Nebraska spoke continuously for fifteen hours. When finally they broke the cloture the fact was announced in the Washington *Post,* a sound money organ, under the headline, "Death Blow to Repeal."

The tense feeling found one expression on the silverite side in denunciation of Cleveland—especially after he published a letter on September 25 to Governor W. J. Northen of Georgia—for interference with the legislative branch. Actually this letter was conciliatory in tone. He wrote that he wanted a sound currency, one that would maintain our currency abroad, and one that would be "so safe and reassuring that those who have money will spend and invest it"; but that within these limits, "I am a friend of silver." The feeling found expression among the repealers in attacks upon their Far Western opponents as unpatriotic obstructionists. *Harper's Weekly* could not recall an exhibition of more glaring private selfishness than that of the silver magnates and their attorneys; the *World* said that it was preposterous to suppose that one-sixtieth of the population could defeat the will of fifty-nine sixtieths. In the Senate the bitterness seemed to reach a climax on October 17,

---

[1] See *Harper's Weekly,* Feb. 10, 1894, for a tribute to his work.
[2] Cleveland Papers.

when Harris and Morgan, Gray and Hill, exchanged cutting personalities.[1] John Sherman made an eloquent appeal for action, and the chamber listened in silence as his speech came to its climax:

Why do we sit here without a single vote upon any question? If we will try it tomorrow, after all the long debate which has been had, and if we dispose of the question as we think best for the people of the United States, we will gladden the hearts of millions of laboring men who are now being deprived of employment; we will relieve the business care of thousands of men whose fortunes are embarked in trade; we will relieve the farmer and facilitate the transportation of his products to foreign countries, which is now clogged by the want of money. There is no money to buy cotton and corn and wheat for foreign consumption. Break down this barrier now maintained by the Senate of the United States, break up this filibustering and obstruction to the will of the majority; give the Senate force and power to pass this bill, and in ten days the skies will brighten, business will resume its ordinary course, "and all the clouds which lowered upon our house shall be in the deep bosom of the ocean buried."

VII

At the last moment there occurred one of those crises which so often tested the courage and resolution of Cleveland—and which always found his strength equal to the tension. On October 20 there arose among the Democratic Senators an irresistible movement to end the fight by compromise. Next day, Saturday the 21st, a letter was addressed to Voorhees, signed by 37 of the 44 Democrats in the Senate, outlining a compromise plan. This letter was in the handwriting of Gorman, who had constantly held out hopes of compromise to the silver men. According to his scheme, the operation of the Sherman Act purchasing clauses should be extended to July 1, 1894; the seigniorage of all bullion in the Treasury up to that date should be coined; and there should be no further issue of notes of a smaller denomination than $10.[2] Simultaneously the Republicans took action to encourage these compromise proposals. Senator Quay introduced an amendment to repeal the purchasing clauses as of January 1, 1896, and Senator Sherman gave warning that if the delay continued, the Republicans would prepare a bill of their own to meet the situation. The Washington *Post* lent prominence to an announcement that the Administration was yielding, its Capitol reporter categorically asserting that President Cleve-

---

[1] Washington *Post*, Oct. 18, 1893.
[2] *Ibid.*, Oct. 22, 1893.

land had abandoned his original determination to secure unconditional repeal and was willing to accept repeal to take effect on July 1, 1894.

Once more Cleveland was in a position where a man of ordinary strength would have bent to what seemed the inevitable, and accepted half a loaf as better than no bread. But what made him a statesman among politicians was the fact that his strength went far beyond ordinary limits. When Carlisle on Saturday afternoon took the compromise letter out to Woodley, Cleveland's anger was intense. At a Cabinet meeting on Monday, October 23, he smote the table with his fist and declared that he would not yield an inch. Before the gathering broke up Carlisle penned a statement which was at once given to the press associations. "The President," it declared, "adheres to the position that the purchasing clause of the Sherman silver law should be unconditionally repealed. . . . It is not true that Secretary Carlisle is, or has been, in favor of the compromise which was subscribed to by a number of the Senators on Saturday. He and the other members of the Cabinet are opposed to the measure." This statement knocked the compromise scheme into smithereens, and the Administration steering committee, still led by Voorhees, prepared for another determined effort.[1] Voorhees wrote Cleveland jubilantly on the 24th: "The unfortunate effects of Saturday's misunderstanding are disappearing and unconditional repeal, in my judgment, is near at hand. There is no wavering in our lines."[2] From the press of the country—even from organs which were none too friendly toward repeal but which recognized a man when they saw one—came a confused noise of cheering.

The wave of public sentiment which rose to greet the President's action, and the clear evidence that he would fight it out on his own line if it took all winter, at last broke the opposition. On October 24 it became evident that the silverite lines were wavering. The Western Senators still held firm, but those of the South and Southwest were yielding. Cockrell of Missouri, declaring he was ready to give up the filibuster, persuaded Harris of Tennessee and others to follow. The Washington *Post* on October 25, five days after it had hoisted the white flag, declared: "The outcome of the fight is a great personal victory for President Cleveland. This expression was on every lip at the Capitol yesterday as soon as it was thoroughly understood that unconditional repeal

[1] Washington *Post,* Oct. 22, 1893; see also Louisville *Courier-Journal,* Oct. 23, 24.
[2] Cleveland Papers.

was on the road to a vote. Against the most formidable obstacles and in the face of an opposition in his own party which was as large numerically as his own adherence, he has brought the entire Senate to his feet. 'Great is Grover Cleveland,' said Senator Manderson yesterday, 'and the Democratic Senate is his prophet.' " Sherman had said that unconditional repeal was impossible; the Washington *Post* had said it; Democrat after Democrat had said it; but Cleveland had proved that it was not so.

The great day came on October 30. The Senate met at 11 A. M. The galleries were jammed and long lines of spectators waited in the lobbies to watch the Senators arrive—Gorman with his clean-shaven face and Prince Albert coat; Teller with his look of a Methodist elder; Peffer with his long whiskers and white chrysanthemum; the venerable Morrill; the resplendently-dressed Wolcott. Senator Cameron, with the courage of his Covenanter ancestors, read a speech vigorously demanding free coinage, for he dared to stand against Pennsylvania sentiment on the subject. Morgan rose for a prolonged discourse, during the final hour of which he trembled painfully from fatigue. One after another the silverites, Vest, Wolcott, Jones, Dubois, Stewart, and others, fired their last shots; but their animation was gone, for they were pronouncing funeral orations. Peffer alone showed his usual fire in denouncing "the crowning infamy of the century." The roll was called in impressive silence. The clerk announced that the yeas were 43, the nays 32. Including pairs, the vote was 48 to 37. A moment later the Senate stood adjourned. A few spectators gathered about Voorhees to congratulate him, a knot of employees with mops and brooms took possession of the vacant chamber, and the great silver battle of 1893 had passed into history.[1]

The staunch adherents of the President deserved a share of the credit. At their head stood, in the House, William L. Wilson and Bourke Cockran, and in the Senate, the blustering Voorhees and the businesslike McPherson. Warm commendation had been earned by Mills of Texas, now a Senator, White and Caffery of Louisiana, and John M. Palmer of Illinois.[2] The Republicans had given indispensable if some-

---

[1] Washington *Post*, Oct. 31, 1893.
[2] Cleveland never forgave Gorman for his attempts to arrange a compromise, and privately denounced him as a traitor. He felt only less scorn for Senator Gray of Delaware, who had been willing to yield to the scheme. C. S. Hamlin, MS Diary, Index, Feb., 1893, May 24, 1894.

what grudging assistance. A number of newspapers also deserved credit for able and insistent pressure; Watterson, in the heart of the silver country, had hammered away as fiercely as the New York *World*, *Herald,* and *Times.* But the best laurels had been fairly won, on the ground both of sagacity and stubborn courage, by Cleveland. "Praise is due first," said the *World*, "to the Administration of Grover Cleveland, which has stood like a rock for unconditional repeal." The *Times* predicted that history, in regarding the crisis of 1893, would record that "at that moment, as often before, between the lasting interests of the nation and the cowardice of some, the craft of others, in his own party, the sole barrier was the enlightened conscience and the iron firmness of Mr. Cleveland."

In the White House, as the Senators left Washington, Cleveland was struggling with two other problems, the Hawaiian question and the tariff, to which we must now turn in rapid succession.

EARLY in 1893, while Cleveland was preparing for his return to the White House, the United States was suddenly confronted with a choice not less momentous than that which the Roman Senate had to make when the Mamertines invited it to occupy part of Sicily, and thus abandon the policy of isolation which had hitherto confined Roman expansion to the peninsula.[1] As the Roman power, according to Polybius, long hesitated to commit itself to so fateful an intervention, so the American Government was now to hesitate for half a dozen years before embarking upon a definite course of expansion. A revolutionary government in Hawaii was asking for annexation. President Harrison decided in favor of the step; Cleveland forthwith reversed the decision. The attempted acquisition of Hawaii in 1893 and its defeat by Cleveland constitute one of the most unjustly neglected episodes in American diplomatic history. All writers on the foreign record of the second Administration have centred their attention on the Venezuelan boundary dispute, when actually the Hawaiian affair was the more important. It brought out in sharp relief the conflict between Cleveland's foreign outlook and the expansionist tendencies fostered by Blaine. It furnished the first great debate in American history over the merits of imperialism. It illustrated the growing identity of interests between the United States and Great Britain, and in it can be detected the first tokens of the Anglo-American understanding that was to become so important after 1898. Finally, it revealed the force of the economic and nationalist impulses that were pressing for expansion overseas.

The fact must be kept clearly in mind that Cleveland from 1885 to 1897 had a consistent foreign policy, radically different from the Republican policy of Seward, Blaine, and Hay—a policy of unyielding opposition to imperialist tendencies, Latin-American or Pacific adventures, and overseas entanglements in general. Both his first and second elections brought a sense of marked relief to the Hispanic-American nations which had feared Blaine's romanticism in foreign affairs. The Chilian Government in 1893, recalling what it had just suffered from the Harrison régime, sent Cleveland a message declar-

[1] Cf. A. T. Mahan, "Hawaii and our Future Sea-Power," *Forum,* March, 1893.

ing that his restoration was a pledge that the United States would preserve the tranquillity and well-being of all nations upon the American continent.[1] Cleveland wrote Bayard in 1895 that he took pleasure in recalling how considerately the latter had treated the people and governments of South America, and how attached they had become to the first Administration. "Very few incidents attended my last coming to Washington more pleasing than the heartiness with which the representatives of Central and South America welcomed me." [2] Indeed, his reversal of our policy toward Latin-America in 1885 and again in 1893 was as striking as Wilson's rejection of Taft's dollar-diplomacy in 1913.

The new attitude embraced Hawaii, which to many Americans seemed important as a naval base for protecting the Pacific coast and a future Isthmian canal. As early as President Arthur's day there had been serious talk of annexation. But when Cleveland had taken office in 1885, this talk abruptly ended. In Sackville-West's dispatches to the British Foreign Office in the fall of that year is an account of a conversation with the Hawaiian Minister in Washington upon the subject: [3]

Mr. Carter, the Hawaiian Minister here, has stated to me that . . . personally he, Mr. Carter, is convinced that the question of the annexation of the islands to the United States would never be entertained by this Government, and he mentioned that an avowed annexationist named Spalding had been lately sent here in order to sound the United States Government on the subject, but had left much disconcerted at the reception he had met with. Mr. Carter proceeded to say that the reciprocity treaty which had created the commerce with California and thus opened the islands to American commercial enterprise by no means involved the ultimate loss of their independence, but on the contrary, in the present temper of the United States Government, was the means of preserving it.

Cleveland and Bayard had taken steps in 1887 to obtain a grant of Pearl Harbor, near Honolulu, as an exclusive naval base for the United States, and in the same year had opposed a suggested British loan of $2,000,000 to the Hawaiian Government upon a pledge of its revenues in security. They made it clear that Hawaii was within the American sphere of influence, but that they were against acquiring the islands.

Early in 1893 the reigning queen of Hawaii, Liliuokalani, was sud-

[1] *Nation,* March 9, 1893.
[2] McElroy, *Grover Cleveland,* II, 192, 193.
[3] Foreign Office, 5, 1905; Sackville-West to Lord Salisbury, Nov. 7, 1885.

denly dethroned by a revolution. The movement behind the revolt had long been gathering strength, and an overturn of some kind was inevitable. The queen had certain virtues—she was a poet, a composer, and interested in humanitarian work; but her government had been an unsatisfactory compound of dynastic autocracy and modern constitutionalism, and she had recently attempted to wipe out its constitutional features. Under evil advice, she had been seized with the idea of abolishing foreign influences and returning to pure native rule; and she had announced her determination to set up an absolute government and disfranchise all white men except those married to native women. That is, in the struggle for political supremacy between the whites and the colored races, she decided not for a working compromise but for colored supremacy. To turn the clock back in this way was intolerable. Though the islands had a weirdly polyglot population, comprising approximately 40,000 Hawaiians and half-castes, nearly 30,000 Chinese and Japanese, 9,000 Portuguese, and almost 2,000 Americans, it was the Americans, with their huge property interests, who were economically dominant. What civilization existed there was Anglo-American in origin. There was genuine need for less absolutism, more constitutionalism, and more business efficiency in the government.[1]

Unfortunately, the revolution was accompanied by serious and highly improper interference on the part of American officers. The American Minister, John Stevens, a close friend of Blaine's, believed stoutly in annexation.[2] When the revolt broke out he and his invalid daughter had just left Honolulu on the American warship *Boston* for a brief cruise to Hilo. They returned immediately, and marines were landed (January 14, 1893) and so manoeuvred as to intimidate all opponents of the revolutionary committee of safety. As soon as the coup had partially succeeded, and while the queen still occupied her palace, Stevens recognized the provisional government. Still more improperly, he shortly followed this (February 1) by proclaiming an American protectorate, and had the American flag raised over the government building. His recognition was granted before the people of Oahu had signified their acceptance of the government, before the other islands had even learned of its existence, and before it had demonstrated its capacity to keep order. Harrison's Secretary of State dis-

---

[1] W. D. Alexander, *Last Years of the Hawaiian Monarchy.*
[2] See Commissioner Blount's report in *Foreign Relations,* 1894, Appendix II, 481 ff.

avowed the protectorate, but the American flag continued to fly over the official buildings in Honolulu.[1]

There was also an indecent haste in the proceedings in Washington. Within five days after the original outbreak, commissioners representing the revolutionary government were on their way to the United States. They reached San Francisco on January 28, and the capital on February 3. Secretary Foster received them cordially, and he and they negotiated a treaty of annexation in the surprising time of eleven days. Harrison sped it to the Senate on February 15 with a message urging immediate action. His and Secretary Foster's motives were doubtless proper and patriotic; for disorder threatened in the islands, they feared that Britain or Japan would step in, and the whole American policy for four years had looked to just such an acquisition. Public sentiment seemed to favor it, and a little jingle about

> . . . Liliuokalani
> Give us your little brown hannie!

swept the country. Cleveland naturally, but unjustly, thought that Harrison was trying to present him with a *fait accompli*.

II

Even before he became President, Cleveland had called Gresham, Carlisle, and Lamont into conference at Lakewood to decide on his first steps. On March 9, five days after his inauguration, he recalled the treaty from the Senate. The New York *Times, World,* and other papers were already clamoring for an investigation, and Cleveland immediately appointed a special agent, James H. Blount of Georgia—a veteran Congressman, just retired, and recently chairman of the Foreign Affairs Committee—to undertake it. Blount was a man of ability, and though he had always opposed a large navy, and had been against the American construction of an isthmian canal, such a pronounced supporter of annexation as Albert Shaw endorsed his "judgment and discernment" in the *Review of Reviews.*[2] In Washington before leaving he talked with both Cleveland and Gresham, was instructed to obtain trustworthy information regarding the causes of the revolution, and

[1] *Idem,* 387 ff.
[2] *Review of Reviews,* April, 1893.

found that the President held no preconceived ideas regarding the problem.[1] What Cleveland had in mind was simply, as he put it later, an inquiry to ascertain the truth and to vindicate "national honor, conscience, and love of justice." [2] While Gresham held the same objects in view, his judicial training gave him a somewhat legalistic attitude toward the revolution, and he was not wholly uninfluenced by his inveterate dislike for Harrison. Cleveland thought primarily of the Hawaiian people, for his work in protecting the Indians had taught him how easily a simple race is despoiled, and he insisted that Blount distinguish carefully between the government in Honolulu and the masses in the islands. Gresham seems to have felt in addition a romantic throb for the defenceless queen—somewhat like Burke's emotion over Marie Antoinette!

Naturally a few of the many advocates of annexation raged over the withdrawal of the treaty and the appointment of Blount. Even so sober an organ as the New York *Commercial Advertiser* could declare: [3]

In ordering Old Glory pulled down at Honolulu, President Cleveland turned back the hands on the dial of civilization. Native rule, ignorant, naked, heathen, is reëstablished; and the dream of an American republic at the crossroads of the Pacific—a dream which Seward and Marcy and Blaine indulged, and the fulfillment of which the more enlightened of our 65,000,000 people awaited with glad anticipation—has been shattered by Grover Cleveland, the Buffalo lilliputian! He has ordered his man Blount, a Southern reactionary, to allow the gathering fabric of a stable government at Honolulu and of nobler things to fall to pieces. He has declared that the superstitious orgies of the heathen queen and her wild-eyed Kanakas may be resumed; that American property interests may no longer have the abiding protection that such men as Dole and Armstrong and Bishop declare is essential; that the Hawaiian islands shall be tossed a prize into the arena of international strife, for which the Japanese, the English, and heaven knows who else may scramble and quarrel.

Yet this was not the general attitude of the Republican press; for most observers supposed—a fact which has been usually overlooked—that the withdrawal of the treaty was but temporary. The President did it, said his opponents, to prevent Harrison from getting all the credit. Blount would gather a few facts, the Democrats would refurbish the treaty, and it would be resubmitted. The Washington correspond-

[1] See Blount's testimony in Senate Reports, 53rd Cong., 2d Sess., vol. 2.
[2] Cleveland to Mills, Dec. 13, 1893. Cleveland Papers.
[3] April 14, 1893.

ent of the *Tribune* said categorically that Cleveland and Gresham were in favor of absorbing the islands. Meanwhile, as Blount departed, a strident debate on imperialism—on the wisdom of acquiring territory outside the continent, inhabited by an alien race—broke out in Congress and the press. In such articles as Carl Schurz soon published in *Harper's Monthly*,[1] and in such speeches as Mills made in the Senate, few of the arguments later used against the acquisition of the Philippines were left untouched. The prevailing Democratic sentiment was against annexation; but some leaders recalled the party's glorious record of expansion in the days of Jefferson and Polk, and Senator Morgan strongly favored taking the islands because of his interest in a Nicaraguan canal.

While harshly criticized at the time and later by advocates of annexation, Blount—soon nicknamed "Paramount" Blount because his commission gave him paramount authority over American diplomatic and naval officers in the islands—proved an independent and judicious investigator. On arriving in Honolulu he found a virtual protectorate still in full operation, with the United States forces performing police duty for the provisional government; and he instantly put a stop to it, ordering the withdrawal of the flag and the marines. He refused a house proffered by wealthy supporters of the annexationist cause, and took up his quarters in a hotel. During the spring and summer he sent voluminous letters from Honolulu, for there was no cable, to Gresham.[2] He shortly concluded that Minister Stevens had let his sympathies lure him into such active coöperation with the revolution as to implicate the United States in the overthrow of the queen. Blount condemned his use of the marines, and still more sharply, his proclamation of the protectorate. It was revealed that Stevens had long urged the wisdom of an early annexation of the islands, and that on the very day the marines landed he had written the State Department: "The Hawaiian pear is now fully ripe, and this is the golden hour for the United States to pluck it." Most important of all, Blount found that the majority of the people did not favor annexation; that the natives who signed petitions for it did so under pressure from the sugar planters; and that there was not an annexationist who would dare to submit the question to a popular vote.

[1] October, 1893.
[2] Blount's dispatches may be followed in *Foreign Relations*, 1894, II, 421 ff.

After nearly four months of careful inquiry Blount wrote a long final report, dated July 11, which was sent to the State Department for Cleveland's consideration.[1] This report, kept secret until a leak in the department compelled its premature publication late in November, left no doubt whatever that on moral and legal grounds the treaty of annexation was unjustified, and Cleveland accepted it as final. The able journalist Charles Nordhoff, who had made an inquiry of his own for the *Herald*, pronounced it impregnable, for the points were all, so far as he knew, established on provisional government testimony.[2]

Both Blount's report and Nordhoff's series of articles brought out the fact that economic motives were the strongest single element in the movement for annexation, and that the Hawaiian "sugar barons" and their allies in the United States had played a dominant rôle.[3] Till twenty years previously, the production of sugar in Hawaii had been mainly a home industry. The plantations were of moderate size, held by many small individual owners, and worked by native labor. But in 1875 a treaty had been made admitting Hawaiian sugar into the United States duty-free, and thus giving the islanders an advantage of nearly two cents a pound over other foreign producers. As a consequence, American speculators were attracted, great corporations were formed, thousands of Chinese and Japanese were imported, and the character of the industry was radically changed. The acreage planted to sugar soon doubled, and most of it passed into the hands of stock companies, capitalized and managed abroad. Profits were large, and the absentee owners were rejoicing in dividends of from 20 to 80 per cent when suddenly the McKinley Act placed foreign sugar on the free list and gave a bounty to home producers. This deprived the holders of Hawaiian estates of the rich advantage they had enjoyed, and in the fall of 1892 Minister Stevens had estimated the loss to that date at twelve millions, much of it falling on Americans in the islands and in California.[4]

These Americans had resolved to rescue themselves by annexing the islands to the United States and thus obtaining the sugar bounty. They had stood in the background pulling some of the chief strings that moved the whole puppet-drama. The largest single insular producer had been Claus Spreckels, who developed great plantations and shipped

[1] Sen. Exec. Doc. No. 76, 52d Cong., 2d session.
[2] To Gresham, Dec. 9, 1893. Gresham Papers.
[3] See articles in N. Y. *Herald*, April, May, 1893.
[4] *Foreign Relations*, 1894, Appendix II, 382.

the sugar to his San Francisco refineries. Early in the nineties the Sugar Trust effected a consolidation with the Spreckels interests, and then made a contract with the Hawaiian planters that if at any time they should receive the benefits of the bounty offered by the McKinley Act, the trust was to get half of it. When the planters protested, the trust told them that "If you don't like these terms, eat your sugar." Large shipping interests also shared the annexationist designs of the sugar investors.[1]

Even after receiving Blount's report Cleveland moved slowly, and a definite policy on Hawaii was not formulated for more than two months. Late in September a new Minister to Hawaii was confirmed in the person of Albert S. Willis. But not until October 18 did Gresham present Cleveland and the Cabinet with a memorandum dealing fully with the subject and laying down a plan of action.[2] This memorandum summarized the essential conclusions of the Blount report, emphasized the fact that the queen had surrendered her authority in deference to American influence, throwing herself upon our sense of justice, and declared that a great wrong had been done her. So far, so good; but Gresham unfortunately went much further. He declared that the wrong ought now to be undone by restoring the legitimate government. "Anything short of that will not, I respectfully submit, satisfy the demands of justice." In the Cabinet discussion this impetuous moral view was criticized by the more hard-headed and practical Olney and Carlisle. The former, indeed, had already written a letter or memorandum of his own on the subject, which both Cleveland and Gresham had seen. In this he admitted that beyond question a great injustice had been inflicted upon the Hawaiians under the auspices of Minister Stevens, and that if possible it should be rectified. The queen's government was overthrown by an exhibition of force—if it could be reinstated by a like exhibition of force without any actual resort to it, there was not any real ground for hesitation. But the existing situation, he thought, was not really so simple.

Mr. Dole's government had now been in power, with our acquiescence, for many months, and there seemed to Olney a strong probability that it could not be ousted without fighting.[3] To the use of force

[1] See Consular Reports, 1892–94.
[2] Gresham, *Life of Gresham*, II, Appendix.
[3] Henry James, *Richard Olney*, 92 ff.

he believed there were formidable objections. One was that it would clearly be an act of war, and was hence beyond the President's constitutional power; another, that to hand over a devastated country to the Queen would be a poor act of reparation; and a third, that many Hawaiians were now apparently attached to the progressive administration just set up. "In my judgment," Olney shrewdly wrote, "the honor of the United States is hardly less concerned in securing justice and fair play for the Stevens government and its members and adherents than in the restoring to power of the queen's constitutional government." He arrived at three practical conclusions: that all the resources of diplomacy should be exhausted to restore the *status quo ante* without use of force; that nothing should be done to replace the queen until she promised fair treatment of the insurgents; and that if in the last resort force was found to be necessary, the issue must be submitted to Congress.

On the same day as the Cabinet meeting, the instructions [1] to Minister Willis were hastily—too hastily—drafted on the basis of Gresham's idea of repairing the queen's wrongs, and Olney's idea of first exacting assurances from her that she would not maltreat the revolutionists. Willis was directed to proceed to Honolulu and present his credentials to the provisional government. He was then to call on the queen and inform her of the President's desire to restore her authority if only she would promise to show clemency toward her opponents and recognize their acts while in power. If she should assent to this, the Minister was to request the provisional government to abdicate in favor of the queen. If either party refused, he was then to refer the matter to the State Department and await further instructions. Obviously Gresham and Cleveland had not thought the problem through beyond a possible refusal—and in this lay the great weakness of their policy.

III

The fact was that the course planned by Gresham was absurdly impractical. Everyone familiar with Hawaii knew that the queen's fall was final and complete, and that except by an American army, she could no more be restored than Humpty-Dumpty. The wealthy and well-organized Americans who supported Dole would never tolerate her return to power. As for using American bayonets to replace her, neither

[1] Text in *Foreign Relations, ut supra.* 459 ff.

Congress nor public opinion would ever permit it.

The moment it became known that Cleveland had resolved to eject the Dole Government, large sections of public opinion in the United States protested in violent terms. Most church sentiment, strongly sympathetic with the "sons of the missionaries," opposed the policy. The Republican leaders broke into fresh attacks. Ex-President Harrison declared that the queen could not resume her throne without bloodshed, and that "if Cleveland's policy suits him, mine suits me." Former Minister Stevens asserted that Gresham was committing a public crime, for he was trying to overthrow a government which embodied all that American piety, American benevolence, American schools, and American patriotism had accomplished in Hawaii in the past seventy years.[1] So good a Democratic organ as the *World* asserted that our true policy in Hawaii was to keep our hands off, and that we were under no obligation to replace a highly oppressive throne. "The Democratic party," remarked the Atlanta *Constitution* indignantly, "has not been in the habit of restoring monarchies anywhere"; and the Springfield *Republican* asserted that to interfere again in Hawaii would be to risk doing far more harm than good.[2]

Almost immediately, the Cleveland-Gresham policy encountered insurmountable obstacles in the islands. Indeed, an *opera bouffe* situation developed as soon as Minister Willis arrived. Between the bloody-minded Queen Liliuokalani, burning for revenge upon her enemies, and the stubborn President Dole, he found that nothing could be done. On November 13th he met the queen for a secret interview at the American legation, and when he announced that she must grant amnesty to the revolutionists, she tossed her head and replied: [3] "There are certain laws of my government by which I shall abide. My decisions would be as the law directs, that such persons should be beheaded and their property confiscated." Willis agitatedly informed the State Department that "Views of first party so extreme as to require further instructions," received a peppery answer from Gresham that "the brevity and uncertainty of your telegrams are embarrassing," with orders to stand firm for amnesty and recognition of the obligations of the provisional government, and after a delay of a month, on December 16th had another

[1] Kennebec *Journal,* Nov. 13, 1893.
[2] *Public Opinion,* Nov. 16, 1893.
[3] *Foreign Relations, ut supra,* 1241 ff.

interview with the dusky monarch. This time she gave up the behead-
ings, but talked of exile for the rebels instead. She had also made it
clear that if she came back into power her government would be extremely reactionary and anti-American, for in surrounding herself with
advisers she had ignored Americans, and given other nationalities, particularly the English, a prominent place. It was only by the severest
pressure that, just before Christmas, Willis extracted a written pledge
from her that if restored she would grant amnesty, sustain the constitution of 1887, and assume the obligations entered into by the provisional
government—these being Cleveland's conditions.[1]

Willis then called upon President Dole and suggested that he abdi- •
cate. By an emphatic written reply four days later Dole, with equal po-
liteness, invited Willis to go to Halifax. He argued that the provisional
government had now been fully recognized by the United States, denied
that Cleveland had any right to interfere in the internal affairs of
Hawaii, and expressed the hope that annexation would yet be achieved.
Huge annexationist massmeetings of protest had been held in Hawaii,
and white leaders had talked wildly of the impeachment of Cleveland
by Congress. The provisional government had prepared to defend itself
by placing sandbags about its buildings, and by a general issuance of
arms to its supporters.[2] Plainly it could not be ejected by force without
much bloodshed.

Cleveland had no sooner read Willis's detailed report of his first
interview with the queen than he had realized that he faced an impasse.
For some days he was in a state of great perplexity, and in the intervals
of other duties anxiously paced the White House library. At a Cabinet
meeting on December 7 he and his associates resolved to lay the whole
matter on the doorstep of Congress,[3] and he asked both Carlisle and
Olney to prepare drafts of a message for him.[4] It is clear that he had no
desire to await the complete demonstration of the ineffectiveness of
Gresham's policy. Even if he had, the popular clamor against this policy and the secrecy with which it had been invested had reached such a
height as to make the continuance of executive control difficult. The result was his special Hawaiian message of December 18, a document of
six thousand words reviewing in impressive fashion the evidence for his

[1] *Foreign Relations, ut supra,* 1269 ff.
[2] *Ibid.,* 1246 ff.
[3] N. Y. *Times,* Dec. 8, 1893.
[4] James, *Olney,* 92.

conclusion that the Dole Government owed its existence to an armed invasion by the United States. The argumentative portions were largely from Olney's pen,[1] and were somewhat overdrawn in their assertion that the queen's government had been subverted by a process every step of which was directly traceable to the American Minister and naval officers. But the most significant part of the message was not its exaggerated historical analysis, but its revelation of the motives which actuated the President. He wrote the eloquent opening appeal to moral considerations:

I suppose that right and justice should determine the path to be followed in treating this subject. If national honesty is to be disregarded and a desire for territorial extension or dissatisfaction with a form of government not our own ought to regulate our conduct, I have entirely misapprehended the mission and character of our government and the behavior which the conscience of the people demands of their public servants.

In stinging words, he remarked of Harrison's treaty of annexation that "the control of both sides of a bargain acquired in such a manner is called by a familiar and unpleasant name when found in private transactions." The Dole Government, he explained, was a mere executive council or oligarchy, and not a true republican government resting on popular support. He further revealed his motives in writing that the treaty of annexation "contemplated a departure from *unbroken American tradition* in providing for the addition to our territory of islands of the sea more than two thousand miles removed from our nearest coast." In short, Cleveland rested his policy upon two basic pillars: the traditional isolationism of every generation since Washington, and above all, the necessity of placing national honor above motives of greed.[2]

He closed his message, after confessing that his plans had met with a check, by a gesture of abandonment. He was forced, he said, by unfortunate public misrepresentations and exaggerated statements of the sentiments of our people to refer the subject to "the extended powers and wide discretion of the Congress," promising to coöperate in any legislative solution "which is consistent with American honor, integrity, and morality." The President thus brought to a climax the great debate on imperialism that had been raging all autumn, and which had led

[1] James, *Olney*, 92.
[2] See *Foreign Relations, ut supra,* 445 ff. for full message.

men like Captain Mahan and Senator Sherman to develop in detail the idea of manifest destiny, while men like Schouler, Schurz, and Godkin combated it. This debate had extended to Great Britain, where prevailing opinion urged the United States to step into the arena of world affairs and to take up in Hawaii the white man's burden—and rewards.[1] Congress, after much futile talk, and after an extensive Senate investigation of the whole subject, did nothing whatever about Hawaii, and President Dole's government was left in full control. His government had of necessity to be fully recognized by the United States, and Cleveland and the State Department treated it with a magnanimous courtesy.

It is possible to take two views of Cleveland's later course. It may be said that he and Gresham, after beginning admirably in their treatment of the Hawaiian affair, had impaired the fine effect of their general policy by an impotent conclusion. The President had been constrained to admit partial failure and bewilderment. He had been compelled, by a decided humiliation of the executive power, to ask Congress to furnish the leadership in solving a problem in foreign relations. To a limited extent this is true, and the two leaders must incur a certain amount of censure from history for their failure to think their problem through at the outset, and to foresee all its conclusions. But in a truer light Cleveland's final policy deserves not blame, but praise. He acted, from the moral point of view, with wisdom and courage. Though he did not foresee all the implications of his course, he did see in advance that it was well-nigh hopeless; he knew that his enemies would seize eagerly upon its "failure" and that it would expose him to criticism and villification. He nevertheless pushed forward. What he did was not worldly-wise and not the shrewdest kind of diplomacy; but it exhibited the highest aims and most honorable motives, and it vindicated the good name of the republic as a calculating policy could never have done.

This central achievement, the defence of the cardinal principles of justice in our foreign relations, was secure, and it deserves the heartiest praise. In an era of international land-grabbing Cleveland, despite angry sneers, had insisted that the United States should meet the loftiest obligations of honesty and unselfishness; in an era when the rights of small nations were almost universally trampled on, he had displayed a sensitive consideration for one of the weakest of them all. That his acts touched a responsive chord was proved by the letters which he received

[1] See files of the London *Times*, *Spectator*, and *Saturday Review* for 1893.

from many of the finest spirits in American life.[1] J. L. M. Curry stated that he had read his special message with patriotic pride and unalloyed pleasure, and that Cleveland was a modern Aristides in declaring: "It is not expedient because it is not just." Oscar S. Straus assured him: "Your clear and forcible exposition of the gospel of international morality, with its fitting application, will ever redound to our glory as a free and just people." And Charles Francis Adams, Jr., representative of a family that for a century had stood for the highest ideals of public life, wrote:

I wish to express the deep sense of respect, not to use a stronger term, I feel for the position the Administration has taken on the Hawaiian question. Of the right and the wrong of the question I know little; I do know that it requires courage in a public man to do what he is persuaded is right, when so doing is tantamount to a defiance of jingoism. I remember no stand taken by a government so morally sound and dignified as that now taken by Secretary Gresham and your Administration, since the similar stand taken some years ago by Mr. Gladstone toward the victorious African Boers. It is not easy to see how the United States can protest against the policy of force pursued by England and France in their dealings with semi-civilized natives and races if we ourselves are quite unable to resist the temptation to have an occasional hack at them on our own account.

[1] Cleveland Papers, Dec. 19–24, 1893.

IN JANUARY of 1893 Rutherford B. Hayes died amid the snows of Fremont, O. Cleveland went out from Lakewood to attend the funeral. "He was coming to see me," he told his wife, "but he is dead now, and I will go to him." As the train rolled through upper New York politicians climbed aboard at one station and dropped off at the next, shaking Cleveland's hand and exchanging ideas. Reporters came and went as well. One Democrat angered Cleveland by demanding loudly, "What's the matter with Edward Murphy, anyhow?" But a newspaper cub gave him an opportunity to score when he inquired if there would be a tariff revision. "What were we elected for? What were we elected for?" growled Cleveland—and the ejaculation promptly went the circuit of the country.[1] There were, in fact, two unescapable reasons for tariff revision. One was that the Administration was absolutely pledged to it, and the other was that the McKinley Act had proved totally unable, under the trade conditions of the time, to supply adequate government revenue.[2] This latter fact has been too often overlooked.

The history of the Wilson tariff is a distressing tale of the final defeat of long-deferred hopes. The Sisyphean burden, laboriously rolled half way up the hill in the first Administration, was now brought to the very crest—and then it rolled back again. Cleveland, loyal as ever to the principle of free raw materials and moderate reductions on manufactured goods, bided his time during 1893. Henry George and other radicals were disgusted because there was no immediate session for lowering the tariff,[3] but he wished to deal with silver first. When he was ready the bill was introduced. The events which followed may be briefly summarized. The House, under strong leadership, fell into line behind the measure Cleveland wanted. The Senate, where selfish economic interests were well entrenched and where there was no aggressive leadership, refused to do so. Cleveland yielded at first to vital amendments in the upper chamber because he believed that when the bill went into conference committee most of the lost ground could be regained.

[1] R. L. O'Brien to author, Nov. 8, 1930.
[2] *Report*, Secretary of the Treasury, 1893, p. lxix.
[3] George, *Life of Henry George*, 576.

When he found that this was not true and that the Senate was adamant, he exploded wrathfully; and at the end he hesitated whether to sign or veto the bill. But to explain just why this chapter of misfortunes occurred, and just what was Cleveland's rôle, is not a simple task.

II

The President was fortunate in his House leadership on the tariff. William L. Wilson had been appointed chairman of the Ways and Means Committee during the special session, with five Southern and five Northern Democrats under him.[1] As soon as the silver repeal had passed the House the committee began holding daily sessions. Everything possible was done to speed up its work; Reed and the other Republican members were allowed no share in its proceedings, and public hearings were cut off sharply on September 20. Under Cleveland's prodding, the Wilson bill was thus practically ready by November 27, 1893, when its details were revealed to the public. Soon after Congress met in regular session it was introduced (December 19) with an elaborate report, and was pushed forward in the House with little delay. The entire record thus far was one of creditable expedition.

This was well, for the time could hardly have been more inauspicious for a general tariff revision. Senator Cullom had declared that it was folly to try to reduce duties when "the year 1893 closed with the prices of most products at the lowest level ever known, with many workers seeking in vain for work, and with charity laboring to keep back the suffering and starvation in all our cities."[2] Andrew Carnegie had remarked that he hoped the President would decide that, under existing conditions, the nation as a patient was not ready for a surgical operation.[3] The fact was that neither Cleveland nor Wilson had really intended a surgical operation at any time. Their bill was exceedingly conservative; for while it placed important raw materials on the free list, this feature being described by Wilson as its boldest innovation, the reductions in the duties on manufactures were moderate. To be sure, the protectionist organs indulged in an instant and raucous outcry, the New York *Tribune* declaring that the bill meant hauling down the American flag, and the Philadelphia *Public Ledger* that it would prac-

---

[1] Bryan and Bourke Cockran were on the committee; N. Y. *World*, Aug. 14, 1893.
[2] Cullom, *Fifty Years*, 264.
[3] Letter in N. Y. *Tribune*, Jan. 3, 1894.

tically revolutionize our whole economic system. But the extreme free trade organs were equally critical, Watterson's *Courier-Journal* attacking the measure as feeble and inadequate.[1] The truth about its conservative character was well stated by the New York *Journal of Commerce:*[2]

> The reductions of duty are much more moderate than has generally been expected. As a rule, the existing duties leave such a wide margin of difference between the prices at which home goods can be profitably made and those at which like foreign articles can be imported, that the tariff goes far beyond all requirements for protective effort. The proposed new duties do not, for the most part, even approximately wipe out the surplusage of duty. Beyond this, most of the leading branches of industry will be benefited either by an entire exemption of raw materials from duty or by reductions of duty upon articles partly manufactured and which become the raw materials of other products. . . . The spectacle of an industrial revolution which has created such an incontinent scare all over the country is therefore dispelled. Those who had hoped for a fundamentally non-protective tariff find a tariff still more highly protective than that of any other country.

There was never any doubt that the bill would pass the House quickly and easily. While Speaker Crisp was so unwilling to play the part of Czar Reed that of the 352 Representatives, 265 participated in the debate, and while there was a sudden and alarming recrudescence of Randallism among the Democrats, Wilson kept the situation closely in hand. Black of Georgia said that he would vote for the bill only under protest, and Warner of New York that its defects were very serious; Oates of Alabama and Washington of Tennessee inveighed against free iron ore; McKaig of Maryland and Wise of Virginia pleaded for a duty on coal; and Blanchard of Louisiana argued for a tariff on sugar. But with the caucus in full control, nearly all attempts to amend the bill failed, and of the few which succeeded only one, the inclusion of an income tax provision, was important. This clause, under Western pressure, was written into the bill late in January by a vote of 182 to 48.[3] An interesting feature of the public discussion accompanying the House debates was a letter which Carnegie, then and later an admirer of Cleveland, published in the New York *Tribune* on January 8. The ironmaster, declaring that he favored passage of the bill

<hr>

[1] *Public Opinion,* Nov. 30, 1893.
[2] Nov. 29, 1893.
[3] Bryan was an early advocate of the income tax. Bryan Papers, Jan.–May, 1893.

with a few modifications, wrote that he hoped all moderate Democrats and moderate Republicans would unite upon a program of mutual concessions. It was important to get the vexatious question settled upon a basis of fair permanence and stability, and "I for one am quite ready to accept greatly reduced duties, judiciously framed, to accomplish this result."

The Democratic caucus had fixed upon February 1 as the date for the final vote on the bill, and as noon approached the halls and galleries became thronged to suffocation. Once more Tom Reed, received with gusty cheering which lasted for five minutes, led the protectionist forces. His address, contrary to his usual custom, had been carefully written out, but he delivered its 15,000 words with extemporaneous fire. Analytical in tone, it attacked the Wilson bill as badly planned, satisfactory to neither side, and certain to aggravate the business depression, while flashes of wit lit up his argument. He fired a shot at Bourke Cockran in speaking of "our wiseacres who are reading British books of forty years ago with the emotions of great discoverers;" and in replying to the contention that American efficiency should not be afraid to meet foreign competition, for the ablest would survive, he used a long-remembered illustration. Survival all depended on circumstance and environment, he said. "Compare the strong bull of Bashan with a salt-water smelt. Who doubts the superiority of the bull? Yet, if you drop them both into the Atlantic Ocean, I will take my chances with the smelt." [1] Speaker Crisp followed. Then, in mid-afternoon, William L. Wilson stood up to close the debate.

There was something indescribably dramatic in the spectacle of the frail, stooping Confederate veteran and former college professor, in rusty clothing, who came forward to lead the final onset of the tariff reformers. A man who sometimes met his monthly bills with difficulty, he was in charge of a measure which vitally affected the business of the whole nation and which meant a change of scores of millions in the annual revenues of the Treasury. His knowledge, his conscience, his acuteness of mind, made him one of the true leaders of the time. There was no one in Congress whom Cleveland trusted so implicitly. Everybody in Washington knew the Spartan simplicity of his life, the ideal goodness and purity of his character. He had married the daughter of a professor of Greek in Columbian College; he lived in an unpreten-

[1] Robinson, *Reed*, 308.

tious little cottage on N Street, near 11th, next door to his father-in-law; and the two families took their meals together. At a time when Capitol Hill was swarming with lobbyists flushed with money, a friend took dinner at this crowded board, the professor saying grace. "The patriarchal simplicity of the whole scene, the august demeanor of the old man, the homely dignity of the little N street household, were in striking contrast with the sordid magnificence of the elements that entered into the tariff issue." [1]

Wilson in an earlier speech had remarked that there were certain to be deserters. "We know from all experience of the past that not all who march bravely in the parade are found in the line when the musketry begins to rattle. . . . Reform is beautiful upon the mountain top or in the clouds, but ofttimes very unwelcome as it approaches our own threshold." Now he defended the general tenor of the bill and in especial the income tax provision. New England had said that it was sectional in character, "but her great economists, her Sumner, and Walker, and Perry," had themselves for a generation preached the wisdom and equity of the income tax. He closed with an eloquent appeal for party unity: "This is a roll of honor. This is a roll of freedom, and in the name of honor and in the name of freedom, I summon every Democratic member of this House to inscribe his name upon it." [2] Amid a storm of applause Bryan, John Sharp Williams, and others carried him from the scene on their shoulders. It was the crowning moment of Wilson's Congressional career.

A few minutes later the bill passed by a vote of 204 to 140. There were 194 Democrats and 10 Populists who heeded Wilson's call, and 18 Democrats who refused. The size of this dissenting group, New York furnishing nine votes, Louisiana three, Pennsylvania two, and New Jersey, Connecticut, Rhode Island, and Nebraska one each, was ominous. Party unity was still far from perfect.

III

The first obstacles had been passed, but by far the most difficult lay ahead. The Senate was closely divided, there being 44 Democrats, 38 Republicans, 3 Populists, and 3 vacancies. Two Populists, Allen and Kyle, were counted in advance for the bill, and one, Peffer, against it. [3]

[1] Fabian Franklin to author, July 30, 1931.
[2] *Cong. Rec.*, Jan. 8 and 9, 1894, vol. 26, pt. 9 (Appendix), 193-201.
[3] *Harper's Weekly*, April 7, 1894.

For months the high-tariff lobbyists had been concentrating their pressure upon the Senators known to be doubtful. Before the debate began it was reported that at least six Democratic Senators were undependable, and actually this estimate was low. Hill was unalterably opposed to any bill which contained an income tax clause; both Louisiana Senators were against any bill which did not give sugar a heavy duty; Gorman of Maryland, Murphy of New York, Smith of New Jersey, and Brice of Ohio were all frankly hostile to the House measure. In addition, the West Virginia and Alabama Senators objected to the provisions for free coal and free iron ore. By February 25 Cleveland knew that the measure would be in grave danger from this insurgent group, and wrote L. Clarke Davis of the *Public Ledger:* [1]

> I still believe that the right will win, but I do not now believe that all the men who loudly proclaimed their desire for better things were in earnest. At any rate, not a few of them are doing excellent service in the cause of the worst possible political methods.

The difficulties were accentuated by the violent personal enmity which many Senators had developed against Cleveland. Morgan of Alabama, a silverite and a believer in Hawaiian annexation, declared that "I hate the ground that man walks on." [2] Murphy of New York felt that he had special reason for detesting the President. Immediately after the election of 1892 Hill and Croker had combined to elevate Murphy to the Senate, in the face of his obvious unfitness and his recent record of hostility to the President-elect. The anti-snappers and Independents, when the plan was first disclosed, had angrily protested. Cleveland, who felt outraged, told Murphy to his face that he was unqualified, and urged William C. Whitney to enter the contest.[3] As the clamor swelled, the President-elect finally allowed the New York newspapers on December 27 to publish an emphatic statement. "It ought not to be necessary to repeat for the public," he said,[4] "what I have so often expressed to so many in private conversation, among them Mr. Murphy himself, Mr. Croker, and gentlemen who have been prominent in the party from every part of the State. . . . The interests of the party and the State, it seems to me, demand the selection of a Senator

[1] Cleveland Papers.
[2] Memorandum by Wm. Hornblower. Cleveland Papers.
[3] Alexander, *Four Famous New Yorkers*, 195.
[4] N. Y. *Times, World*, Dec. 27, 1892.

who can not only defend the principles of our party, but who can originate and promote policies that may be presented for consideration in the Senate." While it would have been easy to make such a declaration if it had promised to effect Murphy's defeat, it took the true Cleveland courage to do it when his election was a foregone conclusion. Murphy was chosen early in 1893, and went to the Senate filled with resentment, which was all the more bitter because he actually proved, as Choate said, an illiterate nonentity.

While the Wilson bill was passing through the House the antagonism felt in the Senate was both revealed and accentuated by Cleveland's militant attempt to place on the Supreme Court bench a man personally repugnant to Hill. Following the death of Justice Samuel Blatchford in the summer of 1893, the President shortly nominated William B. Hornblower of New York city to his vacant seat. It was an exceptionally good appointment, for Hornblower, a graduate of Princeton, the head of an important law firm, and personal counsel for Joseph Pulitzer, had high ability. But it stung Hill to the heart, for he justly regarded Hornblower as his bitter enemy. Two years earlier one of Hill's friends, Isaac H. Maynard, as deputy attorney-general and acting counsel for the board of State canvassers, had committed a scandalous robbery of the public records in order to destroy an election return from Dutchess County, and thus make certain of Democratic control of the State Senate. The State Bar Association appointed a committee to investigate this outrageous occurrence, among its members being Hornblower, James C. Carter, Frederic R. Coudert, and Elihu Root. Its report was scathing.[1] It held both Hill and Maynard guilty of an utterly unjustifiable crime, and declared the latter's offence "one of the gravest known to the law." Largely because of the vigor with which it appealed to public sentiment, when Maynard was subsequently nominated for the Court of Appeals he was defeated by more than 100,000 plurality, a crushing rebuke to him and Hill. Now, in resentment, Hill rallied all his friends against Hornblower's nomination. He declared that he was too young, though Hornblower had reached an age when Napoleon had closed his career, and was older than either Curtis or Story had been when they ascended the bench.

Had Cleveland taken pains to talk to various Senators he might easily have carried the appointment. Pugh of Alabama, as Hornblower

---

[1] Dated March 22, 1892; published N. Y. *Tribune*, Oct. 7, 1893.

later wrote, was aggrieved because as chairman of the Judiciary Committee he "had not been sent for by the President and consulted as to the nomination either before or after it had been laid before the Senate. It was characteristic of Mr. Cleveland not only to disdain the arts of conciliation but also to ignore the personal elements in the political world." [1] Several silverite Senators would have yielded to a request from the President. Hornblower also suffered from the fact that the test came at a time in January, 1894, when some Senators had not returned from the holidays and there was a bare quorum; and he was defeated by a margin of six ballots. He and Hill, who later met more than once face to face, never again spoke to each other. The defeat was accepted by the press as a frank challenge to the President. In effect, Hill and Murphy had declared before the nation that no man who had ever opposed Maynard on account of an act which was branded as a felony by the laws should have a chance to sit in the Supreme Court; and further, that the Senate was bound by the rule of Senatorial courtesy to make good this proclamation. All independent newspapers termed this an outrage of the first order. [2] They called upon Cleveland to deny this impudent disqualification and to keep on denying it.

At first Cleveland did so. His next step was defiant. Hill had let it be known that he would welcome the nomination of Rufus W. Peckham, a brilliant attorney of Western origin who had been a justice of the Court of Appeals in New York, who was one of Manning's best friends, and whom the President knew well. Cleveland had often said to him, "We'll get you down to Washington yet, Rufus." [3] Such a nomination would have cut the knot. But Cleveland, determined to make no terms with Hill on an issue of principle, nominated Rufus's brother, Wheeler H. Peckham. He had been even more conspicuous than Hornblower in resisting Hill's attempt to elevate a thief to the highest tribunal of the State. As president of the Bar Association he had appointed the committee which investigated the charges against Judge Maynard, was ex-officio one of its members, and had concurred in its report. Moreover, in 1888 he had fought tooth and nail against both the nomination and election of Hill, whom he despised. Naturally the senior New York Senator was outraged, and prepared to contest this second nomination

---

[1] Hornblower's Memorandum. Cleveland Papers.
[2] *Harper's Weekly*, Feb. 10, 1894.
[3] Simon Rosendale to author, June 11, 1929.

with all his strength. He told the press that Wheeler Peckham was not a Democrat, that he was a man of violent prejudices, and that he was utterly without judicial temperament or experience.[1] To enlist Lodge and Hoar, who had voted for Hornblower's confirmation, he made a secret bargain with them by which he agreed to furnish Democratic votes for defeating the nomination of one of Lodge's enemies as consul at Sherbrooke, Quebec.[2] He pushed forward his intrigues with Southern and Western Senators, some of whom assumed that Cleveland had turned his back on them because of their position on the silver repeal bill. The result was that Peckham was defeated on February 16, 1894, by the emphatic vote of forty-one to thirty-two.

Once more the Independents called upon Cleveland to keep up the fight. They urged him to nominate Coudert. On the day before Peckham was defeated he had written Bissell [3] that he was heartsick over "the present danger that the Ship of Democracy which has weathered all storms will sink through the mutiny of those on board," and that "if the thing is saved at all it must be through a quick and radical change of direction." Carl Schurz believed that with public opinion behind the President, with the Tammany grafters on the run in New York city, where the astounding revelations by Dr. Parkhurst had resulted in the Lexow investigation, and with his moral position invulnerable, Cleveland needed only to continue the battle in order to win.[4] The President did indeed ask Coudert to accept a nomination, but for business reasons Coudert refused. Cleveland then gave up; and amid widespread disappointment on February 19 he nominated Senator Edward D. White of Louisiana. It was a clear surrender. Hill emphasized his triumph by ostentatiously seconding the motion for White's confirmation. "He is offensive to no one," he said. "He has not been involved in any factious dissensions. He has not antagonized any regular Democratic organizations." The Senate accepted the nomination unanimously. Cleveland had suddenly realized that a protracted contest with the Senate might result disastrously for the tariff bill, and indeed much damage had already been done. Moreover, he hoped that White's promotion would temporarily weaken the protectionists. His great error was not in giving up the fight, but in handling the original nomination

[1] N. Y. *Times,* Jan. 23, 1894.
[2] Josiah Quincy to Cleveland, Feb. 16, 1894. Cleveland Papers.
[3] Feb. 15, 1894. Cleveland Papers.
[4] *Harper's Weekly,* March 3, 1894.

of Hornblower so clumsily as to meet a needless defeat in the first round. "Oh," said Gresham when he heard the news, "if Mr. Cleveland had only allowed us from the beginning to go to Senators and mollify them, how much better it would have been!" [1]

It may be noted here that a year and a half later, when the death of Mr. Justice Jackson led to the publication of reports that Cleveland was about to nominate Hornblower once more, the latter wrote him a letter declaring that he did not wish to be considered.[2] Coudert also refused a nomination. Cleveland thereupon determined to appoint Rufus W. Peckham. In order to make sure that Hill would not object, on November 18, 1895, he actually went to the length of sending the Senator an exceedingly tactful letter of inquiry. Cleveland was anxious for an immediate confirmation, and of course Hill acquiesced. The whole affair was a signal victory for "Senatorial courtesy," and a signal defeat for Cleveland.

IV

The stormy five-months' career of the Wilson bill in the Senate had begun on February 2, when it was referred to the Finance Committee. Voorhees, as chairman, had nominal charge of the measure; but actually it passed into the hands of the committee's two tariff experts, Vest of Missouri and Jones of Arkansas, and of Isham G. Harris of Tennessee, the parliamentary floor leader.[3] The first step was to send it to a three-day caucus. Here the debate waxed acrimonious. The Louisiana Senators, and especially White, argued vehemently against free sugar and for a tariff of one and a half cents a pound or 45 per cent ad valorem upon the raw product. Pugh of Alabama gave defiant notice that he would oppose any bill which placed coal and iron ore on the free list, and others rose in rebellion. Though the Administration leaders, Voorhees, Vest, Jones, and Harris, argued hotly, they saw that compromise was unescapable. The upshot of the caucus was therefore the reference of the bill to a sub-committee comprising Vest, Jones, and Mills, with instructions to meet the objections which had been revealed; these instructions being equivalent to an order to place duties upon sugar, coal, and iron ore.[4] In obedience to this decree, the three men

---

[1] Simon Rosendale to author, June 11, 1929.
[2] Nov. 9, 1895. Cleveland Papers.
[3] N. Y. *Evening Post*, Feb. 21–28, 1894.
[4] Stealey, *Twenty Years*, 117 ff.

reported to the Senate on March 20 a bill laying a moderate tariff on all three commodities—and a few days of debate made it clear that such moderate duties would never be accepted. The Republicans, in high spirits, began to predict the defeat of all tariff legislation.

At this desperate juncture Senator Jones took the bill in personal charge. He knew that to pass the bill he had to have 43 of the 44 Democratic votes—and Hill's was already lost beyond recovery. Eight of the other 43, Caffery and White of Louisiana, White of California, Irby of South Carolina, Gorman, Brice, Smith, and Murphy, were against the mildly-amended bill. They demanded drastic amendments. Jones undertook to find out just what would satisfy them and make passage possible.

"These Senators," he wrote later in a secret memorandum for the New York *World*,[1] "had entered into a combination confined to themselves to stand by one another in their different demands. I resolved to go through the bill paragraph by paragraph with each of the dissatisfied Democrats, discuss each item fully, and keep a memorandum of the insurmountable obstacles. At last this task was finished, and I knew just what were the smallest possible changes in each paragraph that would secure sufficient Democratic support to pass the bill." The combination of which he speaks was organized and headed by Gorman. It was supported by some of the most powerful economic interests in the country. Behind Murphy stood the shirt and collar manufacturers of Troy, behind Gorman and Pugh the iron and coal interests of their States, and behind Smith the glass and pottery works of New Jersey.

Taking his amendments to Secretary Carlisle, Jones went into a conference with him which lasted from two to eleven P. M., explained each one in detail, and asked his opinion. Carlisle replied, according to Jones, that if the changes would secure 43 Democratic votes he would unhesitatingly approve them. "I next saw Mr. Cleveland," wrote Jones, "to whom the Secretary had submitted the matter. The President expressed himself with great earnestness in favor of accepting the propositions and passing the bill, saying at the same time that he hoped we could ultimately get free coal and free iron ore out of it." What this statement really means is that Cleveland endorsed Jones' work only in general terms, with great reluctance, and with the distinct expectation that free coal and iron ore would be restored in conference. This was on or about

[1] Dated Feb. 3, 1896; in author's possession.

May 1. Senate debate on the bill had been continuing since April 2, and Jones had worked out his amendments while friends and enemies were pounding away on the mildly-revised bill. Unquestionably many of the changes which the eight insurgents forced Jones to make were really dictated by Republican members, who brought their suggestions to Gorman, Brice, Smith, and others. Aldrich was particularly active during the whole five-week period of April and early May in worming the amendments he desired into the new version.[1]

On May 3 a fresh Democratic caucus, dominated by Jones and his allies, resolved by a vote of 39 to 1, Hill being the dissenter, to support the 408 new amendments proposed by the Finance Committee—that is, the Jones amendments. Three days later Jones reported these amendments to the Senate. "From May 7, when the amendments were offered, till July 3, when the bill finally passed the Senate," he later boasted, "the 43 Democrats stood together like a stone wall and redeemed their pledges like men. There was subsequently a single break, when unfortunately three Democrats voted with the Republicans to make the sugar schedule take effect immediately upon the passage of the bill rather than on January 1, 1895, immediate effect being in the interests of the sugar trust."[2] The debate went on, and fresh amendments, mostly unimportant, were offered by the dozen, one disgusted Congressman remarking that "this is a free-lunch counter—walk up and help yourself." In the end the Wilson bill had been amended more than 600 times.

Since Gorman was the ringleader of the insurgents and his influence was supposed to be all-important, the rewritten measure was promptly dubbed the Gorman bill. Actually we have the word of Senators Jones and Pugh that Gorman was hardly more of a sinner than several others.[3] The eight insurgent Senators all had a finger in the pie. In its new form the bill left the tariff reformers utterly disheartened. Farm products were taken from the free list; the duty on raw sugar was placed at 40 per cent ad valorem, and that on refined sugar at one-eighth of a cent a pound—rates eminently satisfactory to the Sugar Trust; and the House schedules on iron, glass, chemicals, and woolen and cotton goods were all revised upward. While the Democratic and

Mugwump press called the bill a disgraceful patchwork, the Republicans waxed derisive. A reporter early caught Tom Reed stretched on one of the lounges in the House reception-room. "I have just read the 400-odd Senate amendments," he said, puffing a complacent cloud of smoke into the air. "Good heavens! What a compliment to Wilson!" [1] But most of the tariff reformers were in sympathy with Mills, who said that while no one could torture him into admitting that the bill met the pledges of the Democratic platform he would, however disgustedly, vote for any measure which reduced the tariff burden by even five cents.

And what was Cleveland's precise position? His attitude was colored by the fact that he had just emerged from a battle over the silver issue in which his stubborn refusal to compromise had carried off the victory. Senator Jones exaggerated the degree to which he accepted the mutilations of the original Wilson bill. He was willing to consent to many if not most of the changes in order to get the bill through the Senate, but he trusted that later in conference much of the lost ground would be won back. When he told Jones that he hoped "we could ultimately get free coal and free iron ore," he meant just this. As a matter of fact, he was disgusted with the poor leadership given the measure in the upper chamber, and hoped to the last that a better fight would somehow be made there.

His letters show that he watched the debates of May and June with rising indignation at the inertia of some, the submissiveness of other Democratic Senators.[2] The withdrawal from the upper chamber of Carlisle, the natural leader on the tariff question, was severely felt. Voorhees, who was growing old and was tired after the long silver fight, sat for hours with his head thrown forward upon his breast, and when Hoar or Gallinger threw down some gauntlet, roused himself merely to write a letter. Vilas, Gray, and John M. Palmer of Illinois were too new to be effective. Senator Jones, the Confederate veteran from Arkansas who acted as corypheus, possessed certain qualifications. He was a sound lawyer, he had a clear head, his coolness never deserted him even before the rasping Lodge, and in the protracted debate his fine physique stood him in good stead. But he had not given the tariff long study, while he was too conciliatory, and yielded far too much to the blarney-

---

[1] Washington *Post*, May 9, 1894.
[2] See Washington *Post*, May 27, 1894, for comment on the Democratic leaders.

ing, beseeching, threatening Senators about him. Vest of Missouri was a combative man, noted for the blunt vigor of his language, fighting always with a bludgeon, and afraid of nobody; but he was not an impressive figure intellectually. Harris was the outstanding figure on the Democratic side of the debate.[1] A romantic figure, his life had been full of stormy conflict. Before the war he was one of the giants of the Tennessee hustings. A thoroughgoing secessionist, he had done more than anyone else to drag Tennessee into the Confederacy, and as war governor showed marvelous resourcefulness and energy; for despite the fact that a large part of the State was Unionist, he gave the South 100,000 well-armed men. Upon the fall of Nashville he fought with the Army of the Tennessee. Broken in fortune and with a price upon his head, after the war he became an exile in Mexico. It is a loss to history that his experiences there as head of a colony of fugitives, and his relations with the court of Maximilian and Carlotta and with the patriot leaders of Mexico, have never been printed. Now he was the leading parliamentary expert of the Senate, a man of ponderous dignity, save when he gave way to his violent temper, and a dogmatic, imperious leader. He spoke seldom, and with the manner of a heavy tragedian. He was respected, but like Vest, he had no gift for management and could do nothing to bring the insurgents into line.

With the most resourceful and aggressive Senators—Hoar, Sherman, Allison, Gorman, Hill—all ranged in the opposition, Cleveland was at a cruel disadvantage, and he knew it. The Republicans showed a galling insolence. Aldrich, a quiet, urbane man, with an infinite capacity for intrigue though little for debate, sat before a desk piled high with letters from manufacturers on every schedule, which he read with provoking slowness for the benefit of the Democrats. Hoar, hiding under his cherubic face the vigilant instincts of his Yankee ancestors, loved to make himself a thorn in the side of the majority. His wide reading, fine command of language, and innate Machiavellian vein enabled him to make searching attacks, and he whetted his satire as Shylock did his knife for the blood of Antonio. He reminded veteran spectators of Sumner, but with more urbanity, less narrowness, and less also of power. These two were supported by Allison, a big rumbling fellow, and Chandler, a thin-blooded politician who believed, like Reed, that all Democrats belonged to an inferior order of beings. Toward the muti-

[1] W. T. Hale and D. H. Merritt, *Tennessee and Tennesseans*, I-III.

lated bill they took an attitude of triumphant disdain that was infinitely irritating to Cleveland and his friends.

Cleveland's disgust and that of reformers generally was accentuated by the disclosure that a frolic of speculation had accompanied the debate on the sugar schedules.[1] At this time sugar refining was controlled by one of the largest corporations in the country. A former loose combination of manufacturers had, in order to escape the anti-trust act, consolidated themselves into a single company which was capitalized at eighty-five millions and was paying enormous dividends. It had excited universal resentment by driving up the price of sugar. Charges were made in May by the Washington correspondents of the Philadelphia *Press* and other Eastern newspapers that this American Sugar Company, controlling four-fifths of the industry, had played a part in writing the sugar schedules. In their original form, these allegations were that large contributions had been made to the Democratic campaign fund in 1892 by the trust, that the authors of the tariff bill had so arranged the rates as to reward the corporation, and that Secretary Carlisle himself had helped to carry out the bargain. An investigative committee, headed by Gray of Delaware, set to work. It was in an unhappy position, for if the members probed deep they would have to ask highly personal questions of their colleagues, while to be good-natured would expose them to a charge of whitewashing. One by one the Senators, with the officers of the trust, were called up. Henry O. Havemeyer, the hot-tempered president of the corporation, forty-six years old, gave some brazen testimony. He admitted that the American Sugar Company contributed to the campaign funds of both parties, but not impartially. In New York, where the Democrats normally had a majority, they received the contribution, while in Massachusetts the Republicans had obtained it; and in return the trust "got a good deal of protection." Then, said Senator Allen, "the sugar trust is a Democrat in a Democratic State, and a Republican in a Republican State?"; and Havemeyer assented. But he refused to open his books.[2]

The charges of a Democratic bargain with the trust were swept away like dirty cobwebs. Havemeyer disposed of one flagrant lie in the Philadelphia *Press* by testifying that he had never met either Cleveland or Commodore Benedict, and it was shown that Carlisle's admitted par-

---

[1] Stephenson, *Aldrich*, 111 ff.

[2] For the sugar trust investigation see Senate Report no. 606, 53rd Cong., 2d Sess.

ticipation in the writing of certain sugar rates was entirely innocent.[1]
Senator Brice also escaped scot-free, Havemeyer and he having quarrelled over some whiskey and apollinaris when Havemeyer complained
that he was not getting justice from the Senate. But the charges of
speculation by others on the basis of their inside knowledge proved to
have a certain color. Senator McPherson testified that late in 1893 he
had bought 300 shares of stock in the sugar trust, but had shortly transferred them to his son. In the following February he had purchased a
thousand additional shares, he said, by accident, first writing out a
telegram to his broker, then, after a talk with his son, deciding that it
was improper for either of them to invest, and after all, "either through
my carelessness or the carelessness of a servant," allowing the telegram
to be sent. Before he could sell the stock he had made $1500. Quay
gaily testified that he had been "very active" in sugar stocks, had
bought and sold them frequently over the past twenty months, and had
made his last sale on the very day fixed for the vote on the sugar schedule. "I do not feel that there is anything in my connection with the
Senate to interfere with my buying or selling the stock when I please,"
he asserted, "and I propose to do so."

Undoubtedly much of the speculation was never discovered. An
officer of the Interior Department told one newspaper man that, by
following Secretary Lamont's advice to buy and sell at certain figures,
he had made $34,000 on an investment of $5,000.[2] The majority of the
committee censured Havemeyer severely, and proposed to turn him
over to the Federal district attorney for possible prosecution; but Senator Quay received no castigation save that from general public opinion. Chairman Gray believed that Havemeyer had been justified in
withholding his books.

v

As July began and debate on the tariff was exhausted, everyone knew
that the Senate vote was near at hand; but nobody dared to predict its
result. It was evident that the income tax was actually a source of
strength, test votes showing that it was one of the most popular features
of the bill. If Hill had not possessed this excuse for voting against the

[1] Report, 312; cf. Barnes, Carlisle, 333 ff.
[2] Arthur Wallace Dunn, From Harrison to Harding, I, 127, 128.

measure, he would have found some other. To the very end the amending continued. Free wire fencing was stricken out, to the disgust of the Western farmers, by a vote of 38 to 32, Hill, Gorman, and Brice all opposing it. Free wool, the most important single feature of the bill, was retained by the narrow vote of 37 to 32, and free lumber was also kept in.[1] Though Kyle of South Dakota, a Populist, represented a wool-growing State, he courageously declared that he was willing to let the Western sheepherders face the competition of the world. As the final vote approached, grave danger appeared that some Administration Senators would refuse to accept the bill. Men like Vilas, Gray, and Gordon were outspoken in their denunciation of it. Uneasiness was also expressed regarding the Populists, for the defeat of free barbed wire and their silverite detestation of Cleveland's financial principles rendered their stand uncertain.

At the last moment, on the morning of July 3, there was an interview between Harris and Cleveland in the White House. Harris told the President that he and his friends in the Senate, particularly Vilas, must reconcile themselves to the bill as it stood, without the dotting of an i or the crossing of a t, or all hope for tariff legislation would sink in utter failure before twenty-four hours elapsed.[2] A motion was pending to postpone any further consideration of the bill indefinitely, and there was danger it would pass immediately. Cleveland again argued for free coal, free iron ore, and the adjustment of the sugar schedule downward. All these, Harris emphatically rejoined, were impossibilities. "To this ultimatum," wrote Jones later, "the President was apparently resigned, emphasizing his solicitude by asserting that since delay was dangerous it was better to accept what he could obtain than to hazard all by striving for the impossible, and his last admonition to the Senator on that day was that the bill as it stood—being the best they could get—would be acceptable to him as some measure of tariff reform." As he departed Harris suggested that Cleveland would do well to communicate with Vilas, Palmer, and the other tariff reformers, and make sure they would vote for the measure; and Cleveland did so.

Late that night, after the exhausted Senate had been in continuous session for nearly eleven hours, the test came. Seventy-seven of the eighty-five Senators were in their seats. Twelve of the Senators were

[1] *Cong. Rec.*, Vol. 26, pt. 7, p. 7115 ff.
[2] Jones' Memorandum.

paired. Hill, it was said, was confident till the very end that his "no" would defeat the bill; and he made a speech in which he said that "as between a Populistic income tax on the one hand and a Republican tariff law on the other, I choose the latter." A sigh of relief went up from the Democratic side as it was announced that the bill had passed by a vote of 39 to 34. Yet the escape from defeat was narrower than this margin would indicate.[1] Blanchard of Louisiana, who had just been promoted to the Senate, refused to vote, and his colleague Caffery voted no in protest against what he considered an injustice to the State. When the roll-call reached Irby of South Carolina, who was known to be hesitant, he voted aye—and Caffery was observed to start. A moment later both the South Dakota Populist, Kyle, and Edward Murphy, also voted aye. As the roll-call ended, Caffery changed his vote to the affirmative, and Blanchard voted aye. It was clear that if the Louisiana Senators had stood firm and had been joined by Irby and Kyle, the bill would have been lost beyond recovery. As it was, the victory had been won—but it was a hollow victory.

Cleveland had been urging the House leaders to show fight, and now they did so. A canvass by the *World* showed that 116 House Democrats were decidedly opposed to the amended bill, and that only two definitely favored it. William L. Wilson undertook an aggressive battle to force the Senate to recede. He whipped the Ways and Means Committee into line behind a resolution of nonconcurrence, made an impressive speech,[2] and carried it by a large vote. A conference committee was appointed with Senator Harris as chairman, and its Democratic members began holding secret sessions in one of the Senate committee rooms. The details of tariff bills have almost always been adjusted in such committees, and most people expected a compromise. But as these meetings dragged on Senator Hill, who casually inspected the lunch trays sent in, made the astute guess that the conferees were at a standstill. He explained that "Men who are in agreement and making progress never send for sweet milk and corn bread; when you see the trays carrying a decanter and a box of cigars, you can bet that an agreement has been reached."[3] Cleveland was urging the House members to in-

[1] See Washington *Post*, July 4, 5, 1894, for an acute analysis of the vote. *Cong. Rec.*, July 3, 1894; vol. 26, pt. 7, p. 7136.
[2] *Cong. Rec.*, July 7, 1894; vol. 26, pt. 7, p. 7191.
[3] N. Y. *World*, July 12, 1894.

sist on free coal and iron ore, if no more,[1] but the Senators were adamant. On July 15 Senator Brice, who knew the inside of the conferences, predicted a total deadlock, and three days later the committee voted itself unable to reach a decision.

At this juncture, with the Democrats in confusion, the country disgusted and the Republicans jubilant, William L. Wilson persuaded Cleveland to let him explode a petard under the Senate obstructionists. This was in the shape of a letter which Cleveland had written Wilson on July 2, just before the Senate bill passed, beginning with the words: "I hope no excuse is necessary for my earnest appeal to you that in this crisis you strenuously insist upon party honor." The President insisted upon the principle of free raw materials, though he was willing to concede a tariff upon sugar; and he declared that the numerous violations of this principle by the Senate were intolerable. "There is no excuse for mistaking or misapprehending the feeling and temper of the rank and file of the Democrats. . . . Every true Democrat and every sincere reformer knows that the bill in its present form and as it will be submitted to the conference falls far short of the consummation for which we have long labored. . . . Our abandonment of the cause or the principle upon which it rests means party perfidy and party dishonor." The letter caused little comment in the House, though Reed made a speech criticizing the intimate relations between Cleveland and the Ways and Means Committee.[2] But in the Senate it had all the effect of a brickbat thrown into a nest of hornets.

The scenes in the Senate during the next week were dramatic—and not at all pleasant to those who hoped for a peaceable adjustment. The barest corporal's guard of Senators stood by the President. Vilas was one, Gray another, and strangely enough, Hill a third.[3] Not only the eight or nine obstructionists, but the principal Senators who had acquiesced in the compromise, including Jones, Harris, and Vest, regarded the letter as an attack upon their personal and political integrity, and were aflame with resentment. On July 23 Gorman launched against Cleveland one of the bitterest attacks ever delivered by a responsible Senator upon a President of his own party.[4] He called the letter the

[1] Jones' Memorandum.
[2] Cong. Rec., July 19, 1894; vol. 26, pt. 8, p. 7713.
[3] Idem, July 20, 1894; vol. 26, pt. 8, p. 7733 ff.
[4] Cong. Rec., July 23, 1894; vol. 26, pt. 8, p. 7801 ff.

most extraordinary, unprovoked, and unwise communication ever penned by a Chief Magistrate. He added that it was more than that—it was the product of dishonesty and duplicity. The Senate, he explained, had been confronted with great difficulties; by hard work Jones and Vest had overcome them; and their changes had all been accepted by Cleveland and Carlisle. "Every prominent amendment was as well known to him (Cleveland) as to me. . . . While neither the President nor his Secretary were in love with all the provisions of these amendments, from no quarter, high or low, from the President through the Cabinet, or by any member of this body, was it ever suggested or intimated that there was any violation of Democratic principles." Pausing at this point, he called upon Vest, Jones, and Harris to corroborate him, and in varying but emphatic terms all three declared that he was right.

Gorman resumed his speech with increased vehemence. At first, while nervous, he had tried to keep himself in hand, but now he yielded to his emotions, paced up and down the aisle, and shouted his denunciation of Cleveland. He could not remain silent, he declared, under such an imputation as the President's letter contained, and he hurled it back. The Democratic ranks in the Senate were composed of honest men, who had fought for tariff reform when "cowards in high places dared not show their heads." He believed that no man could alter the Senate bill without defeating it, and that no one who was not consumed with vanity would now take the responsibility of altering it. He further accused the President of violating the spirit of the Constitution, and he had a fellow-Senator read the passage from Washington's Farewell Address which deals with the encroachments of the executive upon the powers of Congress. The applause which followed his speech was a ruffle of drums over the grave of party harmony.[1]

Cleveland's letter, essentially an appeal to public sentiment, had come, like his tariff message of 1887, just a little too late. It had all the desired effect in calling forth a burst of remonstrance against the Senate obstructionists, but the time had passed when such a demonstration could do any good. Democratic State conventions in Iowa, Indiana, Florida, and Massachusetts passed resolutions endorsing the letter; public meetings for that purpose were held in Maryland; and Governor Matthews of Indiana declared that nine-tenths of the Democrats of his

---

[1] While Senators Jones and Harris said little, both believed Cleveland guilty of bad faith toward them. Jones' Memorandum.

State preferred no bill at all to the Gorman bill. While the Baltimore *Sun* compared the letter to the pipes and bugles that announced the approach of the relief columns to Lucknow, the New York *Herald* likened it to Zachary Taylor's ringing voice at Buena Vista as he turned defeat into victory. If it had been written in May or early June, and above all, if its publication had been accompanied by a determined effort to stiffen party lines in the Senate and break down the obstructionists there, it might indeed have been almost as effective as Havelock's Highlanders or Old Rough and Ready's stern commands; it might have wrested a favorable compromise out of defeat.

In this tariff battle Cleveland had faced an almost impossible task. If he had bargained with the Western silverites, as the authors of the McKinley bill did in 1890, he might have won the kind of measure he desired. If he had even consented to deal with the tariff first in 1893, placing it ahead of the financial problem, a satisfactory bill might have been passed. But when he drove the repeal of the silver-purchase act through Congress, he knowingly imperilled the cause of tariff reform. He made enemies who fought him thereafter at every step. Years later he counted this deliberate choice among his principal achievements for the nation. When in 1903 the *Evening Post* defended his calling of the special session to take up the financial crisis first, even though it had postponed and injured the tariff bill, he wrote a pleased letter to the editors.[1] "I have always regarded this," he said, "as the most self-sacrificing and patriotic service I have been privileged to render my countrymen."

Nevertheless, he had also reduced the chances of his bill by maladroit tactics. They may readily be compared with the expert strategy used by Woodrow Wilson in 1913, when he forced the Underwood tariff through a Senate that was equally close and equally representative of selfish interests; and the comparison is not to Cleveland's advantage.[2] Wilson read his tariff message in person to Congress, thus breaking the precedent of a hundred years; before he would consent to let Simmons of North Carolina, who had a high-tariff record, become chairman of the Senate Finance Committee, he exacted a pledge of earnest fidelity to tariff reform; he built up an *esprit de corps* to hold the weaker members in line; he gave battle to the protectionist lobby by denunciatory

[1] To Richard W. Knott, July 4, 1903. Cleveland Papers.
[2] Ray Stannard Baker, *Woodrow Wilson*, IV, 93–131.

statements which resulted in an investigation and in the rout of these vermin; and he brought vigorous personal pressure to bear upon wavering Senators like Newlands of Nevada. Cleveland's heart was as earnestly in the battle as Wilson's and his labors were even more indefatigable; but he did not know how to strike at the weak joints in his opponents' armor, or how to enlist public sentiment in time and throw it effectively into the fray.

With business chafing over the delay, on July 28 the conference committee again began its effort to dispose of the bill.[1] It shortly became evident that the Senate Democrats, incensed by Cleveland's letter, would stand intractably against any substantial concessions; and a movement developed in the House, led by Springer of Illinois, whose De Kalb district contained important barbed-wire interests and hence favored protection, to accept the bill. For a time Wilson, Bourke Cockran, and others struggled on against the inevitable; but finally a caucus of the House Democrats on August 13, after one of the most turbulent sessions in years, broke into a stampede for surrender.[2] The reluctant Wilson, his bill dead, as Reed remarked, on the field of dishonor, was compelled three days later to move in the open House to recede from disagreement with the Senate. After another heated debate, with Bourke Cockran gallantly fighting to the last,[3] the motion was carried by a vote of 182 to 106, with 61 not voting. Only 12 of the House Democrats voted in the negative. The rout was complete.

Most of the Democratic and Independent commentators, though sick at heart, tried to place the best possible aspect on the matter.[4] The Springfield *Republican* was glad that the House had yielded and thus put an end to the disturbing controversy, and hoped that Cleveland would sign the bill at once. "It is a question," it said, "whether the fight has not continued long enough as it is to cost the Democracy its place for years as a majority party, if not the very life of the organization." The New York *Times,* grumbling that the party of tariff reform, after twenty years of waiting, "had come into a plundered inheritance," also hoped that the President would sign the bill. *Harper's Weekly*

---

[1] N. Y. *World,* July 29, 1894.
[2] Vest served notice that the Senate bill was the only bill that could pass; *Cong. Rec.,* Vol. 26, p. 8367.
[3] *Ibid.,* Aug. 13, 1894; vol. 26, p. 8478.
[4] See summary in *Public Opinion,* Aug. 28, Sept. 6, 1894.

GORMAN'S TRIUMPH OVER THE WILSON BILL

(A cartoon by W. A. Rogers in *Harper's Weekly*, Sept. 8, 1894.)

emphatically approved the bill as a whole, pointing out that it substantially cheapened many of the necessaries and comforts of life. Meanwhile the *World* was printing a series of letters on the measure. Wilson wrote that he would have continued to fight, but that his army had refused to follow him; Senator Jones that the House had secured no concessions because it had asked too many; Senator Hill that he hoped the President would veto the bill; Senator Brice that it was the best piece of tariff legislation ever passed by Congress; and Bourke Cockran that its passage was the most disgraceful chapter in American history.[1]

Cleveland was in a cruel predicament. It was difficult for him to sign the measure he had so scathingly denounced in his letter of July 2; it was equally difficult to veto it and thus make the professions of his party ridiculous. Falling ill of an attack of malarial fever just after the passage of the bill, he went to Gray Gables to recuperate, returning to Washington on the 22d. For more than a month he had been wrestling with the problem of his ultimate decision. As early as July 17, according to Senator Jones' memorandum, he was weighing the possibility of letting the measure become law without his signature. On that date Senator Harris had reported to the President that the long struggle in the conference committee was nearing a complete deadlock, and that the House would have to give way. According to Jones' memorandum:

The President then suggested that he could be placated with free iron and free coal if nothing better could be granted, and leave the remaining controverted schedules to be cared for in subsequent separate bills. When Senator Harris responded that such a compromise was impossible and that disagreement was inevitable, the President exhibited at once his despair, contempt, and inconsistency by asking:

"Harris, do you think the Senate could be kept in session ten days after the date on which the House recedes from its position and agrees to the Senate's amendments?"

Senator Harris was astounded at this proposition. . . .

Before he left for Gray Gables Cleveland had told the Washington correspondent of the Atlanta *Constitution* that he might well veto the bill.[2] But this impulse, if such it was, did not last long. The day after

[1] N. Y. *World,* Aug. 14, 1894.
[2] Sam Small to author, May 23, 1931.

his return he was besieged by associates imploring him to assent to the bill, Carlisle and Crisp being the foremost.[1] Representative Clarke of Alabama, Representative Catchings of Mississippi, and other tariff-reform Congressmen urged him to sign; while Senator John M. Palmer of Illinois wrote him that the bill was the best that "true friends" in Congress were able to obtain, and that if he let it become law without his signature, he abdicated the leadership of the Democratic party. "The commander of an army and the leader of a party must alike share the fortunes of their followers." Ex-Governor Russell added his voice to the list. But Wilson, who knew Cleveland's mind better than anyone, insisted from the outset that he would not sign—and he did not. The bill, copies of which had long since been sent to all customs officers, became law on August 28 without action by the President.

Cleveland defended his course in a long letter to Representative Catchings, which contained several really eloquent paragraphs. "I take my place," he wrote, "with the rank and file of the Democratic party who believe in tariff reform and who know what it is, who refuse to accept the results embodied in this bill as the close of the war, who are not blinded to the fact that the livery of Democratic tariff reform has been stolen and worn in the service of Republican protection, and who have marked the places where the deadly blight of treason has blasted the counsels of the brave in their hour of might." [2] One sentence was especially pregnant with meaning, and embodied another of his memorable phrases. "The trusts and combinations—*the communism of pelf* —whose machinations have prevented us from reaching the success we deserved, should not be forgotten nor forgiven. We shall recover from our astonishment at their exhibition of power, and if then the question is forced upon us whether they shall submit to the free legislative will of the people's representatives or shall dictate the laws which the people must obey, we will accept and settle that issue as one involving the integrity and safety of American institutions." This was a threat to carry to the people the question of trust control over the Senate.

Yet Cleveland was sorrowfully aware that the tariff battle begun in 1885 was now over so far as he was concerned. With his party grievously divided and weakened, with financial difficulties thickening fast

[1] N. Y. *Times, World, Herald,* Aug. 24, 25, 1894.
[2] McElroy, *Grover Cleveland,* II, 116, 117.

about the government, with business prostration growing, the fight could not be renewed during his Administration. The House Democrats, their defeat rankling, had already tried to pass a series of supplementary tariff bills placing coal, barbed wire, iron, and sugar on the free list; but these "popgun" measures died in the hostile Senate. Cleveland was perfectly justified, in his letter, in asserting that the Wilson-Gorman bill presented a vast improvement upon the McKinley Act, but he was also justified in writing that "it contains inconsistencies and crudities which ought not to appear in tariff laws or laws of any kind." He had met one of the most painful defeats of his whole career. It was difficult for him to take much comfort in such words of cheer as came from Wayne MacVeagh: [1]

And now for the first time in an entire generation—since 1861—you have turned a revision of the tariff away from higher to lower duties. For the first time in that long period trade is to be freer and the people's burdens less heavy.

If the bill was a defeat for Cleveland and the tariff reformers, it was a defeat also for the agrarian interests of the West. For a long generation farsighted men in the Middle States had been struggling to reduce the tariff burden on the farmers. The Wilson-Gorman Act, except for the removal of the duty on wool, made no striking change in the character of tariff legislation. Here and there a bit of the burden had been lifted, but the tariff was still at a high level. The Treasury during the debates furnished a comparison of the Wilson-Gorman schedules with those of the McKinley Act. In chemicals, the McKinley rates averaged 31.6 per cent, and the Wilson-Gorman rates 24.4; in earthenware and glassware they stood respectively at 51.2 per cent and 37.3 per cent; in metals at 58.4 and 34.2; in wood at 32.6 and 22.8. In not a few instances the duties, while lower than those of 1890, were higher than those of 1883. Senator Mills declared that there were probably not a thousand people in the United States who were satisfied with the completed measure, and certainly the farmers had no reason to regard it with tolerance. A really drastic lowering of the tariff might have contributed to the reduction of their discontent. When they saw the lobbyists of the great corporations stand triumphant in Washington, and still more, when they found that the income tax clause of the tariff bill

[1] *Ibid.*, II, 120.

was destroyed in the Supreme Court, their belief that the moneyed East was in the saddle, and that they were being forced to the level of an exploited class in order to support a greedy plutocracy, became more fixed than ever.

Chapter XXXII   The Western Revolt and the First Bond Issue

IT would be easy to place the political events of the early nineties against a background that is varied, interesting, and full of color. These were the years in which the first skyscrapers were lifting men's eyes above the dull street level; in which electric lights, as the system which Edison had introduced in New York in the early eighties was scattered broadcast, began twinkling from town to town all over the country; in which trolley cars became commonplaces. In 1893 Chicago drew together the artists who turned their dream into a brief but radiant reality, the White City which caught men's breath and then vanished. They were the years of marching men—the Pullman strikers in Chicago, the "army" that Coxey led out of Massillon, the insurrectos and Spanish regulars in Cuba. Kipling, Conan Doyle, and Stephen Crane were blazing new luminaries in the literary sky. The new magazine, in the hands of Munsey and McClure, and the new journalism in those of Pulitzer, were laying their impress on the public mind. The University of Chicago was being born; La Farge was exhibiting his pictures of the South Seas; Frohman and Belasco were beginning their careers; and Langley was toiling to construct his flying machine. All times are full of new beginnings and bright hopes, but the early nineties, far from being a *fin de siècle* epoch, were fuller of beginnings than most years.

Yet the true background of political events has no such color and movement. It is a background of drab poverty, hopelessness, and revolt. The business depression which followed the panic, beginning in the seaboard cities, rolled westward in a series of waves. When it crossed the Wabash and Ohio it met an agricultural depression which was already overpowering. Ten cent corn, six cent cotton, and ten per cent mortgages had taken the West and South in a merciless grip. Distinct areas of agrarian discontent could be marked out on the map of the United States: the Southern cotton lands, where the tenant croppers and small farmers had always been poor and were now on the brink of starvation; the corn country of Illinois and Iowa, where once-prosperous farmers saw themselves slipping into a bottomless pit; the semi-arid regions of western Kansas and Nebraska, where successive droughts drove thousands, their little all packed in dilapidated covered wagons, eastward in an hegira of despair. But in every area the spirit of revolt burnt with precisely the same flame; a flame once lambent in the non-political Farmers' Alliances, now roaring like a prairie fire in the Populist and free silver movements.

II

It is impossible to describe with statistics and graphs the nature of a movement rooted deep in human emotion. Probably never before or since in American history have the times been so completely out of joint for so many millions of producers. By hundreds of thousands, farmers had sweated in heat and cold, in hope and fear, and then had seen the sheriff come striding across their dooryard. They had turned in bitterness from wheat fields devoured by chinch-bugs or grass-hoppers; had watched the short-grass parch under sirocco winds while empty clouds drifted mockingly across the skies; had lifted the tail-boards and dumped their grain on the streets rather than take the elevator prices; had gathered in menacing clumps as neighbor after neighbor was sold out at auction. From thin Kansas houses they had watched the furious blizzard which froze their cattle to death, and listened to the icy wind whine across the plains to cut the vitality from their huddling children. In Southern cabins they had tossed through hot nights sick with worry, and risen to stare out at shrivelled cotton not worth the picking. There was no sugar on the table, no money to put the son in high school, no books or magazines; they creaked to town in decrepit wagons, ate from oilcloth, and wore denim and·calico.[1] But they were of the fighting Anglo-Saxon stock that never yet has been ground to the level of a peasantry. At first blindly, then with increasing purpose and organization, they joined hands in one of the most power-ful agrarian revolts the world has ever seen.[2]

It was more than a revolt—it was a crusade. They fought not only to redress their wrongs, but to usher in a nobler era of economic justice and social charity. All over the West and South arose rough, self-educated leaders to preach a fairer distribution of wealth, a purer

[1] Cf. William Allen White, *The Editor and His People*, 149 ff.
[2] John Hicks, *The Populist Revolt*.

THE WESTERN REVOLT 591

polity: the income tax, the direct election of Senators, the curbing of the trusts, the resort to free silver to stop deflation. Jerry Simpson, the Scotch-Canadian immigrant who by sheer ability fought his way from the deck of a Great Lakes freighter to Senate; Mary Ellen Lease, Wichita's gaunt, determined Cassandra of the plains; James B. Weaver, veteran in Iowa of the greenback movement; the captivating Bryan, and minor orators by hundreds, took the field.[1] The farmers flocked to picnics, political rallies and nightly meetings in the little white or red schoolhouses. Drums and fifes that had been carried in the Civil War rattled and shrilled; songs of hope rose and fell on the prairie breeze; sons of the soil forced their way into county caucuses and State conventions, and seized the granger banner where it had fallen in the seventies. The impulse that had risen behind Jefferson and Jackson was rising again with enhanced fervor—but this time against far stronger and better entrenched forces.

To state in simple terms the causes underlying the hardships of the farmer is to distort and misrepresent a situation complicated by a hundred disparate factors. Western demagogues and Eastern reactionaries alike tried to simplify the picture and alike drew it in false lines. The principal element, beyond doubt, lay simply in the fact that the rapid development of colonization, transportation, and agricultural machinery the world over had glutted all the food markets. Our own West had grown far too rapidly for its own good and the nation's health.[2] The whole broad area from Minnesota and the Dakotas down to Oklahoma and Texas had been brought under the plow with astonishing rapidity. In the twenty years following 1880 the land under cultivation in the United States increased by some 305 million acres, or more than 50 per cent, and the number of farms rose from 4,000,000 to 5,700,000. But the same forces were declaring themselves in other parts of the globe. The Canadian Pacific reached out from the Great Lakes to Vancouver in 1886, wrapping the wheatfields of Manitoba, Alberta, and Saskatchewan in its iron fingers. There arose in Argentina a progressive administrator named Roca, the railway mileage of that republic doubled in a few years, English capitalists began erecting great meat-packing plants and competing with Chicago, and after 1890 a growing stream

[1] T. A. McNeal, *When Kansas was Young*, 200.
[2] So James Bryce had pointed out in his *American Commonwealth*. Cf. Webb, *The Great Plains*.

of Argentine wheat poured into Liverpool. Simultaneously, the grain production of Russia and Australia was steadily increasing.

Farmers had pushed into the West with too little capital and too little caution. They had plunged heavily into debt for land and equipment, and when the overproduction of grain, beef, and pork forced prices down, they could not pay. An Eastern economist who made a careful study of a typical Nebraska township in 1892–93 found that the farmer tended to succeed in direct ratio to his capital,[1] business qualifications, and good luck—but above all, his capital. The mortgage burden in the West was intolerably heavy. When the year 1890 opened, there were 2,300,000 mortgages on American farms, aggregating roughly $2,210,000,000; and as mortgage rates ran from 8 to 12 and even 15 per cent a year, with outrageous commissions for renewals, it is safe to estimate that the annual interest charges rose well over $200,000,-000.[2] Foreclosures were frequent, converting the independent farmer overnight into a renter, and in some States, notably Kansas, whole counties seemed to pass through foreclosure. Multitudes of farmers had taken up land which in one year might make a good crop, and in others prove totally barren. In 1893–95 thousands of people in drought-stricken Kansas and Nebraska were so utterly destitute that the East was called upon for contributions of food and clothing.

Unquestionably the debtor West was hard hit by the deflation which followed the Civil War and by the persistent drop in prices. While it is possible to cite government tables which show that there was much less money per capita in circulation in 1890 than in 1865, and that the world's production of gold fell almost continuously in the seventies and eighties, their exact relevancy to the agrarian distress is disputable. What is indisputable is that farm prices steadily dropped. Statistics differ, but they all agree in showing a decline. In both 1893 and 1894 wheat prices, for the first time since the Civil War, went below 55 cents a bushel in the Chicago market, which meant 30 to 40 cents at the local elevator—and it cost not less than 50 cents to grow.[3] The government's estimates of the yearly value per acre of the ten leading crops combined show that, by five-year periods beginning with 1866–70 and closing with 1891–95, the farmer's return fell by a steady succession of steps—

[1] Arthur F. Bentley, *The Condition of the Western Farmer.* His township is Harrison, Hall County, Neb.
[2] Edward Atkinson, *Forum,* May, 1894.
[3] *World Almanac,* 1895, p. 190.

$14.70; $14.05; $11.89; $11.33; $9.97; and $9.71.[1] During 1894 corn sold in the central markets at from twenty to thirty cents a bushel, and cotton, which during the eighties had averaged 11 cents a pound, went below seven cents. Livestock of all kinds—cattle, hogs, sheep—became unprofitably cheap, and it was noted that trolley-cars had lowered the value even of horses. Gov. L. D. Lewelling of Kansas wrote at the close of the dark year 1894 that a quarter of a century earlier the Southern farmer had been able to buy nearly $500 worth of goods with one bale of cotton, while with two bushels of wheat a Northern farmer could buy $5 worth; but now it required seventeen bales of cotton and more than twelve bushels of wheat to command the same sum.[2] Senator Peffer published some equally discouraging figures. Eastern writers · attributed all this to overproduction and a decline in the world's purchasing power; the West attributed it to a monetary stringency deliberately promoted by creditor interests in Europe and the East.

But the farmer suffered from still other disabilities. He paid an excessive share of the taxes of both State and nation. Not only was all his property tangible and easily assessed, but when his equity in the land might be only one-half or two-thirds, he was not allowed to make any deduction for the mortgage. The Federal revenue was raised wholly by indirect taxes on articles of common consumption, the tariff producing roughly two-thirds and the internal revenue taxes one-third; and the farmer and workingman paid a disproportionate share. Moreover, partly because of the tariff and partly because of the trusts, commodity prices did not fall in the same degree as food prices. Clothing, farm implements, house furnishings, and articles of general convenience were not properly cheapened. Railway charges, again, showed no abatement. The powers of the Interstate Commerce Commission did not include rate-fixing. The average freight costs on grain shipped from the Middle West to the Atlantic Coast actually increased during the decade 1885–95. The usual summer charge in these years hovered between 10 and 12 cents a bushel, which was better than the old 20-cent charge of the early seventies, but far higher than the 5 or 6 cent rate after 1900. Great and menacing railroad combinations, in the hands of men like Morgan, Hill, and Gould, were increasing.[3] Altogether, the Western

---

[1] *Statistical Abstract of the U. S.*, 1924, p. 607.
[2] *North American Review*, January, 1895.
[3] John Moody, *The Railroad Builders;* William Larrabee, *The Railroad Question.*

farmers had legitimate grounds for complaint; and our history presents few spectacles more ironic than that of their Eastern creditors taunting them with dishonesty while insisting upon being repaid in a dollar far more valuable than had been lent.

The country suffered heavily in these years from the defects of the national banking system, and the farmers suffered along with other groups. The principal faults of the system were three: an inadequate concentration of banking reserves; a want of elasticity in the means of making banknote issues; and a lack of adequate facilities for expanding credit in periods of financial pressure through the rediscounting system used by European banks of issue. Nothing could be done in the emergency following the panic of 1893 to effect the needed changes. The labor of long years of inquiry and agitation was required before thorough-going currency reform could be effected in the first Wilson Administration by the Federal Reserve Act. Nor, in the crisis of 1893–96, could the national government do anything to alleviate unemployment and penury. All Cleveland's strength was required to maintain the national credit and the gold standard. No money was available for any but the barest government necessities. The house was on fire, and internal reforms and social aids were impossible till the conflagration was extinguished.

It was natural that Cleveland's repeal of the silver-purchase clauses should fall upon the great mass of agrarian debtors as evidence that he had gone over, heart and hand, to their capitalistic oppressors. Stewart of Nevada, in the debate on the repeal, had charged Cleveland with gaining the citadel of Washington by an ignoble Trojan-Horse stratagem. Beneath trappings of bimetallism, tariff reform, civil service reform, and State rights in 1892, he had concealed "the monometallic gun of concentrated money and bonds." Peffer had declared that the President would yet see "a mighty people rising." [1] A hundred silverite agitators, some sincere and some demagogues, hurled defiance at the immovable figure in the White House. Typical of the spoutings of the worst of them was a speech which Thomas E. Watson of Georgia had delivered in Atlanta a few months after the repeal bill passed. Watson, a voluble hothead who made political demagogy and the editorship of a Populist weekly pay well, had won his way into Congress, and had bought a new house in Washington near the Capitol. "And by no means

[1] *Cong. Rec.*, Oct. 30, 1893; vol. 25, pt. 3, p. 2956 ff.

was it a mere shack," his biographer boasts. "It was a splendid brick building of four stories, with eight large rooms besides baths, closets, kitchens, and extra rooms." [1] He appealed to his audience in this characteristic fashion: [2]

Mr. Farmer, have you let the dog-fennel and black-jacks and old field pines take your farm because you have got too many silver dollars? Has a single factory closed and thrown its laborers into the streets because it had so many silver dollars that the factory hands wouldn't take them? Have the colored people left the farms because they got sick of getting so much silver money? (Cries of no! no! from the audience.) Grover Cleveland says they did; virtually says so. He and Mr. Carlisle say you have got more money than you can use. . . . Think of the sarcasm of it! Think of the injustice of it! Think of the cruelty of it! Think of the financial veins, shrivelled and shrinking, because not filled with this life-giving thing called money; of his telling the people they have got too much money, and therefore they will close the mints to the coinage of money!

But while these assaults were being made, Cleveland was preparing to take steps which would add oil to the flames.

III

The first of these steps was the issue early in 1894 of $50,000,000 in five per cent bonds, sold to realize net proceeds of $58,661,000 for replenishing the stock of gold in the Treasury. The Treasury, suffering for lack of revenue in these months of adverse trade conditions, was finding it difficult to maintain parity between gold and silver. Month by month the gold reserve, which should have been kept at a minimum of $100,000,000, was forced below that level. Everyone was eager to obtain and to hoard gold. Men who had to pay their customs or internal revenue dues to the government paid in silver certificates, and kept their gold in their pockets. Silver certificates and greenbacks were collected and presented at the Treasury for redemption in gold; and if the gold standard were to be maintained, they had to be discharged in that medium, because the Sherman law provided that the two metals were to be kept at parity. Yet when these silver certificates came into the Treasury, they could not be destroyed. They had to be reissued by

[1] W. W. Brewton, *Life of Thomas E. Watson*, 229 ff. One of Watson's reckless assertions was that "the currency has been contracted until it is now but $5.75 per capita against more than $50 per capita thirty years ago." Brewton, 214.
[2] Atlanta *Constitution*, May 20, 1894.

the government, and thus became an "endless bucket" for dipping up gold from the Treasury reserve.

On the day that the silver purchase repeal passed the Senate, the gold reserve stood at $84,000,000; on December 30, 1893, it had dropped to $80,000,000; and on January 18, 1894, it had been reduced to $69,000.000. Some remedy had to be found. Under the resumption act of 1875, Secretary Carlisle possessed authority to sell certain kinds of bonds to provide gold for redeeming the greenbacks. But the prescribed terms of sale were onerous to the government, and in his annual report for 1893 he asked Congress for authority to dispose of bonds bearing a lower rate of interest, and running for a shorter term of years. Congress roughly refused. The silver party declared that they had made enough concessions, and that the government, if gold failed, should use silver to redeem the silver certificates presented to it. To do this would of course have meant forcing the finances of the country to a pure silver basis.

Cleveland had been giving the whole subject anxious thought since before his inauguration. In a conference at Lakewood in January, 1893, he, Carlisle, and Gresham had decided that at all costs the existing financial system must be maintained. The next month he learned that the $100,000,000 reserve might be trenched upon at any moment, and that Harrison's Secretary of the Treasury, Foster, was ordering the Bureau of Engraving and Printing to prepare plates for an emergency bond issue. It is evident that the Harrison Administration was in close touch with him. On the day before Foster signed his order, Cleveland directed Lamont to see what could be done to sell the bonds: [1]

I am trying very hard to keep cheerful and in a most irritating and perplexing situation. I am only partially successful, and I am constantly wondering why there are not, within the circle of my life, more Lamonts and Dickinsons.

And this reminds me of another confidential mission I want you to undertake for me.

Will you go to Belmont & Company and see if they can arrange for the purchase [i. e., the sale] abroad of say fifty millions of *caisse* bonds (but within the declaration of the Sherman Act of the intention of the government to maintain the parity between the two metals and undoubtedly as good as if formally payable in gold) with interest at 3 or 4 per cent? I want in the transaction the *actual gold* brought from abroad and put in our treasury and I want it done promptly, and in such manner that the par value of the bonds shall be forthcoming to us free from commissions. Of course we do not commit ourselves

[1] Feb. 19, 1893. Miss Lamont's MSS.

to the issuance of these bonds. We may be anticipated or the necessity for such action may be averted. I only want you to find out in the most confidential way possible what can be done if the contingency arises.

Lamont discovered in Wall Street that, in the opinion of the bankers, the situation would shortly be improved by a reversal of the gold flow from Europe to America. He wrote Cleveland: [1]

Mr. Morgan has asked me to meet him tomorrow afternoon. Stillman thinks he prevented a serious break last week by sending $2,000,000 in gold to Gage at Chicago. I enclose a letter from Dr. Warner which expresses the views of Stillman and others I have seen—that gold is likely to be imported soon and the change of trade conditions will produce a situation that will be used by the silver people to prevent a repeal of the Sherman Act.

But as we have seen, the situation, far from improving, grew steadily worse. The Administration during 1893 delayed making a bond issue for three reasons: to do so would give another shock to business, already at the last ebb of vitality; it would complicate the struggle for the repeal of the Sherman silver-purchase clauses; and Cleveland and Carlisle alike hoped that Congress might enact a new and better authority for an issue.[2] But in January of 1894 the crisis had to be met. During the first seventeen days of that month $11,000,000 in gold was drained from the Treasury. Until the middle of the month Carlisle still hoped that Congress might authorize the sale of three per cent bonds maturing in five years. At that time he published a letter, in an effort to prod Congress into action, estimating that the Treasury deficit for the current fiscal year would reach $78,000,000.[3] Then he and Cleveland lost patience.

A Cabinet meeting was held at which Richard Watson Gilder, who happened to be present, saw Cleveland strike the table in exasperation. "This don't help us," he burst out. "I believe in taking the bull by the horns and coming out with an issue of bonds." [4] The Administration accepted the inevitable, decided to go ahead under the old and imperfect law, and on January 17, sent out the circular announcing its first bond sale. There were to be $50,000,000 of bonds bearing 4 per cent interest, in denominations of fifty dollars and multiples thereof, and re-

[1] No date; about Feb. 22, 1893. Miss Lamont's MSS.
[2] Barnes, *Carlisle*, 287 ff.
[3] See *Public Opinion*, Jan. 25, 1894, for Carlisle's letter of appeal to Voorhees.
[4] Gilder, *Grover Cleveland*, 127.

deemable "in coin" after ten years; no bids were to be accepted at less than 117.223, which would place the bonds on a 3 per cent basis, and payment was to be made in gold or gold certificates. Cleveland desired a popular sale, and advertisements were placed in all the postoffices. The Eastern press, substantially without regard to party, sustained his decision.

For some days the fate of the bond issue trembled in the balance. A number of leading bankers doubted whether the authority to sell bonds under the Resumption Act was clear, and whether future question as to the use of the proceeds might not affect the legality of the bonds themselves; while other investors were suspicious of the clause making the bonds payable in "coin" rather than gold, and demanded clearer language. The officers of the Knights of Labor, allied with the silver movement, applied for an injunction to restrain Carlisle from issuing the bonds, and one morning a subpoena was actually served on him as he was setting forth for a Cabinet meeting.[1] Silverites of the House Judiciary Committee hurriedly reported out a resolution declaring that the proceeds of the issue could not lawfully be used for current expenses, or any other purpose than to maintain the gold reserve. All this was intended to produce distrust and ruin the prospects of the issue. Partly as a result popular subscriptions were disappointing, while a number of frightened bankers who had made bids cancelled them. As the deadline was neared with less than $5,000,000 subscribed, Cleveland sent Carlisle to New York to plead with the principal bankers. No one knows what Carlisle said, though one man long afterward recalled his threat that the President might have to sign a seigniorage bill if the bond issued failed.[2] But as Cleveland has written, the Secretary's appeals to the financiers "resulted in so arousing their patriotism, as well as their solicitude for the protection of the interests that they represented, that they effectively exerted themselves, barely in time to prevent a disastrous failure of the sale."[3] They took the bonds at a price on which they later lost money.

Thus at the last minute the issue was floated. Yet its success was only partial. In order to obtain gold to pay for their subscriptions, some of the bidders withdrew it from the Treasury by presenting legal-tender

[1] Barnes, 315 ff.
[2] Hepburn, *History of Currency*, 355.
[3] *Presidential Problems*, 140.

notes; and of the $58,661,000 received about $24,000,000 thus represented no actual gain. Cleveland and Carlisle had erred in not taking precautions against this, but they had been in no position to bargain. The drain on the gold reserve steadily continued, and everyone knew that it was only a matter of months until another bond issue would be required.

Meanwhile, this first issue had aroused the silverites of the West and South to a new sense of outrage and betrayal. Many of them had been willing to accept the repeal of the silver-purchase clause as necessitated by the financial anxiety of the time, and as a possible step toward a more secure form of bimetallism; but the bond issue seemed to them proof that Cleveland and Carlisle were firmly allied with the gold interests of the East and intent upon the destruction of silver money. Peffer of Kansas told the Senate that the government had entered into an open partnership with Wall Street and the bankers, brokers, and speculators generally. "And this," he added, "in the face of a clamoring multitude, in the face of men and women with poverty drawing dark lines over their pale faces. . . . In the face of idleness, destitution, hunger, and desperation in every State and in every city of the Union, and with $250,000,000 in the public Treasury, the President is compelled to sell the people's credit to appease the clamor of these misers of Wall Street." [1] A day of retribution, he warned, was coming in a wave of fire and blood. Senator Stewart of Nevada used similar language. The iron hand of contraction, he declared, was being wielded by Secretary Carlisle at the dictation of the British financiers, and the Treasury Department had sold the bonds in order to give the Eastern plutocracy a safe place to invest their money.

A deluge of letters fell upon Cleveland and Carlisle, denouncing them as traitors, Judases, tools of the bloated baronage of wealth, friends of financial bloodsuckers.[2] And these letters were written with flaming sincerity. Their authors believed that if the government only paid its debts in silver, and let the country have more and cheaper money, poverty and suffering would vanish as mists before a flaming white sun. They believed that a coalition with the great bankers to maintain the costly gold dollar was an alliance to crush the poor deeper into the mire. During the spring occurred another event to deepen their resentment.

[1] *Cong. Rec.*, 53d Cong. 2d session, p. 1176.
[2] Cleveland Papers.

IV

A month after the flotation of the gold loan, the House on March 1 passed the Bland bill for coining the silver seigniorage and other loose bullion in the Treasury. Seigniorage represents the gain which the government acquires when it purchases bullion at a price less than the value stamped on the metal when coined; it is the difference between a dollar's worth of raw silver, and a silver dollar. Enough metal had accumulated in the Treasury to coin about $55,150,000 in silver dollars. The House mustered a large majority in favor of the measure, the vote standing 168 to 129, with only 49 Democrats in the negative. It was argued that another 55,000,000 dollars meant little, for the country had 382,245,265 Bland-Allison dollars, coined between 1878 and 1890, and more than $150,000,000 in silver certificates. The Senate, as was expected, quickly passed the bill by a vote of 44 to 31, and it went to the President. He remarked, when its author called at the White House a few days later, "Well, Bland, you do give me more trouble than any good man in the country." [1]

Once more Cleveland faced, as so often before, the temptation to yield to expediency in order to secure what appeared large and glittering rewards. The drive to make him sign the Seigniorage bill was terrific. Cajolery, promises, and threats were all used. "Never before," said the Springfield *Republican*, "has such pressure been brought to bear upon the present executive to overlook for once a matter of principle, affecting the whole country, in favor of party unity and success." [2] Men told him that the sum would not greatly affect the currency; that the seigniorage was a governmental asset which could be disposed of as Congress saw fit—there would be no breach of trust in coining it; and that the step would calm the nerves of the West and benefit the nation's health. Some Democratic newspapers which had supported the repeal of the Sherman silver-purchase clauses advised him to yield, arguing that this small concession might fairly be granted the free silver element after their overwhelming defeat of the autumn, and that party and political expediency counselled it. David R. Francis of Missouri wrote a long and urgent letter in this vein. If the bill became law, he declared, it would settle the silver question for at least six years to come, within

---

[1] W. V. Byars, *An American Commoner: Richard P. Bland,* 295.
[2] March 30, 1894.

which time an international monetary conference might dispose of it for good.[1] The passage of the silver repeal bill had, as Bryan later said, marked the temporary division of the party into two hostile factions, and now Bland's bill seemed to many to offer a bright hope of reuniting them. "These are days," Cleveland wrote Don M. Dickinson on March 18, "of special perplexity and depression, and the path of public duty is unusually rugged."

But as always, Cleveland never thought of yielding on a question of principle. To sign the bill would not only add to the already excessive proportion of silver in the currency; it would reopen the whole broad question of silver policy which the banking and commercial interests had regarded as effectually settled by the repeal act. It was not in Cleveland's nature to take such a backward step.[2] Governor Russell wrote Olney that if the bill were approved it would redouble the fear throughout the North and East that the Democratic party was unsound on financial questions. "The one hope and pillar of strength of the Democracy in these matters has been the President, and his position on such questions both in and out of office, before the election, during the campaign, and since his inauguration, has been consistent, courageous, and definitely understood by everybody, friend or foe. If he yields the last prop is gone and I believe our party will find itself seriously and permanently injured."[3] The party-unity argument only angered Cleveland. When a deputation of Southern and Western Congressmen used it, he turned on them in indignation, declaring that the integrity of the national finances and the credit of the government were too important to be treated from that point of view. In scathing words, he expressed his contempt for men who pandered to the delusions of the people and voted for all sorts of legislation in order to keep themselves in office. One Congressman emerged saying rather limply, "I never had a man talk like that to me in my life."[4]

On March 29 Cleveland vetoed the bill with a message condemning it as both unwise and inopportune. He attempted to make his stroke tactful. While he was sorry to disagree with Bland and his associates, he wrote, enactment of their measure would be regarded as a retrogres-

[1] No date. Cleveland Papers.
[2] Hewitt spoke of the proposal as "coining a vacuum," for under the law of 1890 the Secretary was required to pay immediately into the Treasury the gain or seigniorage arising from silver coinage. *Harper's Weekly*, Feb. 24, 1894.
[3] Boston, March 15, 1894. Russell Papers.
[4] Chicago *Record*, March 26, 1894.

sion from the sound financial intentions announced by the silver-purchase repeal, and nothing should be done to check the financial recovery slowly getting under way. The rage of the silverite press was extreme, and the New Orleans *Times-Democrat* declared that the party was "booked for ruin." Yet he had done exactly right. An already redundant circulation was continuing to assist in the expulsion of gold to Europe. Despite the loud silverite talk of a deficiency of currency, the supply of it had been increasing more rapidly than in any previous period of American history. Never, indeed, had the nation's stock of money approached the volume shown in the Treasury estimates for February, 1894.[1] The veto was sheer common sense.

And Cleveland took pains to follow his veto with a shrewd precaution. Speaker Crisp then occupied a suite at the Metropolitan Hotel with Sam Small, Washington correspondent of the Atlanta *Constitution*. On the very evening after Cleveland's veto, and as a direct answer to it, Crisp was appointed Senator by Governor Northen of Georgia in succession to Colquitt, who had just died, but at once refused the office.[2] The veto was to come up in the House on April 4. On the preceding night Crisp and Small, after retiring, were aroused at midnight by a bellboy bearing two cards, those of Walter Q. Gresham and Isidor Straus.[3] They had brought an urgent request that Crisp come to the White House. The Speaker, desiring to have a witness, insisted that Small accompany him, and the Georgians were ushered together into the second-floor library where Cleveland did most of his work. The President at once cut to the heart of the matter. "Mr. Crisp," he said in effect, "I sent for you because my veto message is coming up tomorrow. I understand a number of Democrats have filed applications to be heard in an attack on the veto and on me. That will be very damaging to the party. This is a vicious and hurtful bill; my motives in trying to destroy it have been entirely patriotic; if it is passed over my veto, or if any considerable demonstration is made in favor of it, that will inflict great injury on the nation."

"But how can I do anything, Mr. President?" asked Crisp.

"We have counted noses," said Cleveland in his most impressive tones, "and we are satisfied we can command a majority if the question

[1] Noyes, *Forty Years of American Finance*, 230.
[2] N. Y. *World*, March 30, 1894.
[3] Sam Small to author, May 23, 1931.

is brought to an issue *immediately without further debate*. We have selected a man to move the previous question instantly. We want you to
recognize him. Debate will be cut off and the veto will be sustained."
Crisp demurred. Some of the most influential Democrats in the
House, he pointed out, had filed demands to be heard. If discussion
were smothered they would be outraged, and would vent their anger
on the Speaker. "Do you know what this means to me?" he demanded.
"My people in Georgia are for silver; my political career will be
ruined."

At this Cleveland roused himself like a lion. He looked Crisp in the
eye. "Mr. Speaker," he roared, "what is your political future weighed
in the balance against the fortunes of the country? Who are you and I
compared with the welfare of the whole American people?" Crisp
flinched. "Well," he said slowly, "if you put it that way—I'll consent."

In the cab on the way back to the Metropolitan Hotel he said gloom-
ily to Small, "Well, I'm a dead cock in the pit." The next afternoon
Bland called in the House for three days of discussion. But Crisp summarily blocked the debate, including a magnificent speech which Bryan
had bottled up for the occasion, and the veto was sustained.

V

The silver-purchase repeal, the first bond issue, the seigniorage veto
—by these three steps Cleveland earned the unalterable hostility of the
free silver forces. A sullen Congress, an unfriendly South, and a fiercely
hostile West confronted him. It is an invariable rule that in times of
depression the ill-feeling of the public is vented upon the President in
power. If times had turned sharply better in the spring of 1894, as
many believed they would, the antagonism to Cleveland in the agricultural regions and among workingmen might have slackened. Instead,
they grew worse, and the financial and industrial ills brought in their
train alarming labor outbreaks. Shortly after Cleveland's veto of the
seigniorage bill, on April 21, 1894, there began a great strike in the soft-
coal fields, President McBride of the United Mine Workers estimating
that 126,000 men had instantly laid down their tools. Within a few days
160,000 were on strike, and the disturbance covered the whole country, from Pennsylvania to Alabama and Colorado. The struggle dragged
on for weeks, until the men, their funds gone, their families destitute,

surrendered and once more accepted a wage which they had characterized as intolerable. Its total cost was estimated at more than twenty
millions.[1] The latter half of April witnessed a spasmodic strike on the
Great Northern, the 1900-mile line between Puget Sound and the Great
Lakes which James J. Hill had completed only the previous year. Here
the men were led by Eugene Debs and other officers of the American
Railway Union, a new labor organization of the industrial (that is, not
the crafts) type. Pressure upon Hill in the Twin Cities forced an agreement, and early in May the strikers went back to work, with most of
their demands granted, and the prestige of the union much enhanced.
The late summer witnessed savage labor troubles in the textile mills of
New England, where an overwhelming majority of the operatives were
now paid less than six dollars a week.

Far more dramatic was the march of Coxey's Army, which typified
as no other single incident the desperation of the unemployed at this
crisis, and the grotesque readiness of men to clutch at any remedy for
their sufferings. All over the country in 1893–94 the shutting down of
mills, factories, and mines had thrown multitudes out of work. Estimates of their number varied widely, but the statement of Samuel
Gompers of the American Federation of Labor that more than 3,000,000
wage-earners were idle when 1894 began was not wide of the mark.[2]
After the panic of 1873 the country had been astounded and alarmed
by the bands and even little armies of tramps which sprang up. Now
the phenomenon repeated itself. Tens of thousands of men roved from
State to State, some returning to their old homes, some looking vainly
for work, some mere professional vagabonds living off the country. By
a mysterious mode of communication, they conceived the idea that a
systematic display of squalor would better their lot. At first their demonstrations were small; from the West and South came news that troops
of ragged, hungry men, fierce of mien and uncontrollable in temper,
were terrorizing the countrysides. Then the country learned that a number of these bands had coalesced into three or four great armies, the
chief of which, Jacob Coxey's, set out from Massillon, O., on March
25—just before Cleveland's veto—to march on Washington and demand the issue of $500,000,000 in irredeemable paper money.

[1] See Washington *Post,* June 20, 1894 for charges that this strike was deliberately forced
by the operators to enable them to get rid of a surplus of coal.
[2] *Public Opinion,* Jan. 4, 1894.

Coxey's movement passed rapidly through the phases of a great radical crusade, an itinerant catchpenny show, and a fiasco. At its outset it was taken with portentous seriousness by social elements which might have been expected to ridicule or attack it. The high-protectionist Republicans, with the Wilson bill pending, pounced upon it as evidence that Cleveland's tariff policy had sown the wind. Ex-President Harrison announced to the Republican State Convention in Indiana that "The times are full of unrest, disaster, and apprehension. I believe today that all the tumult of this wild sea would be satisfied, as by the voice of Omnipotence, if the industrial and commercial classes of this country would know today that there would be no attempt to strike down protection in American legislation." [1] Gompers saw in the march of the army a proof that the government must provide work for all; Governor Lewelling saw in it the result of the crime of '73. For a short time newspaper correspondents trailed the column like camp-followers, and the public read with eager interest descriptions of one alarmed community after another passing the motley cohort on to its neighbor. Then suddenly the whole affair began to seem a joke. Most of the army dropped by the wayside. Just as Europe was preparing to accept the news of a bloody uprising in America, Coxey's followers straggled into Washington, a mere remnant of 300 men, and their leader was arrested for carrying a banner on the Capitol grounds and trampling on the grass.[2]

The other armies also dissolved amid laughter. When General Hogan's force of about 500 marchers captured a Northern Pacific train at Butte, Mon., and started eastward, and some Federal troops from Fort Keogh heroically stopped the train and recaptured it, the country looked on with a broad grin. Frye's and Kelly's armies faded away. The popular feeling underneath the amusement was that these supposed idlers and cranks deserved little sympathy. Senator Wolcott expressed this in a pungent speech in the Senate, saying that men in public life "ought to begin to cultivate more regard for the perpetuity of republican institutions and to pander less to that miscalled portion of the labor vote whose labor is always with their throats and never with their hands." From this point of view the demonstrations did Cleveland no harm. But they betokened a general poverty and restlessness which did react heavily and directly upon him and his policies.

[1] *Public Opinion.*
[2] D. L. McMurray, *Coxey's Army: A Story of Industrial Unrest, passim.*

The numerous strikes of 1893–94 and the failure of the Wilson bill accentuated the sentiment of unrest and resentment throughout the country. A new radicalism was in the air. In some of its manifestations it was unfortunate; in others it was salutary. Richard T. Ely's outspoken denunciation of trusts and monopolies at the University of Wisconsin was raising a storm about his head. Lyman Trumbull, Lincoln's old friend, now eighty-two years of age, startled the country in October by a speech at a Populist convention in Chicago. He eloquently charged that the money power, which for ages had controlled legislation in most of the world, was now seizing control of the government in free America. Referring to the growth of monopoly and privilege, he said: [1]

If the accumulation of fortunes goes on for another generation with the same accelerated rapidity as during the present, the wealth of this country will soon be consolidated in the hands of a few corporations and individuals to as great an extent as the landed interests of Great Britain now are. Neither strikes of the laboring classes, which array against them the money power and the governmental power which it controls, nor the governmental control of the great railroad and other corporations, will remove the existing conflict between labor and capital, which has its foundation in unjust laws, enabling the few to accumulate vast estates and live in luxurious ease, while the great masses are doomed to incessant toil, penury, and want.

With reference to the recent conspicuous use of court orders and injunctions in labor troubles, Trumbull struck also at the rapidly growing power of the Federal courts. "These Federal judges, like sappers and miners, have for years silently and steadily enlarged their jurisdiction, and unless checked by legislation they will soon undermine the very pillars of the Constitution and bury the liberties of the people underneath their ruin." Objecting particularly to the issue of injunctions without notice, he expressed the hope that Congress would place some restriction upon the activities of the courts in managing railways and punishing men for contempt. His speech, which was warmly applauded by the Populist and silverite press and was received with surprising respect by even conservative newspapers, was a striking symptom of the universal tension and discontent.

Another symptom lay in a sudden eruption of radical publications. This year 1894 witnessed the appearance of Henry Demarest Lloyd's *Wealth Against Commonwealth;* of W. D. Howells' *Traveller From*

[1] *Public Opinion,* Oct. 18, 1894.

Altruria; of several of the most mordant stories of Hamlin Garland; of Henry Champernowne's exposure of municipal misgovernment, *The Boss;* and of John Swinton's defence of labor, *Striking for Life. Wealth Against Commonwealth* was a searching exposure, amply buttressed by detail, of the iniquities of the trusts and of big business in general. Nothing escaped Lloyd's keen eye, and his book deserves to be called the parent of the muckraking literature which came into flower a decade later. The combination of the beef-packers to increase prices; the monopoly of the anthracite fields by a group of closely-associated railroads, and their oppression of miners and consumers alike; the activities of the sugar trust, which had collected $28,000,000 of profits in a single year; the secret control of the Union Stock Yards by interests profiteering on the farmer; the operations of the tobacco trust; the helplessness of the Interstate Commerce Commission in the face of flagrant stockwatering, rate-boosting, and rebate-making; above all, the history of the Standard Oil Company, and its sordid record of business piracy—all this was laid bare in more than five hundred calm, unemotional pages. Howells' *Traveller From Altruria* satirized the social injustices of American civilization, and dissected their unreason by a suave but biting description of a more ideal society. Garland, as staff-writer for a radical monthly called the *Arena,* had taken part in the meetings of rebellious farmers in bare-walled Kansas and Nebraska schoolhouses, and was flinging before the East pictures of life on the prairies at its worst.

Still another symptom, in its relation to human nature the most disturbing of all, lay in the sudden burst of jingoism which now manifested itself in the United States. It had various sources, but one was unquestionably a simple desire to escape from the sordid miseries of everyday life in dreams of battle and conquest. A belligerent attitude was manifested by the press toward all the principal powers of Europe. Germany came under attack, particularly in the Western press, for decrees which had partially excluded American meat products on the ground that they were diseased. A source of friction with Great Britain arose in Nicaaragua. In 1893 Jose Zelaya began his long dictatorial régime there, and on February 12, 1894, his agents, seizing Bluefields, treated both British and American citizens roughly. The British warship *Cleopatra,* arriving a fortnight later, landed a force of marines and Gatling guns. Though Cleveland and Gresham showed vigilance in making certain that there would be no permanent occupation, as the trouble dragged on the Republican press abused the President, prodded Great Britain, and sighed, "Oh, for one day of Blaine!" The worldwide surge of imperialism; the uneasiness produced by the shaky European balance of power; the defiant tone of Blaine's foreign policy—all had contributed to produce the new spirit. It was in this year that there began the clamor which Godkin described only a few months later:

The number of men and officials in this country who are now mad to fight somebody is appalling. Navy officers dream of war and talk and lecture about it incessantly. The Senate debates are filled with predictions of impending war and with talk of preparing for it at once. With the country under the necessity for the most stringent economy, appropriations of $12,000,000 for battleships are urged upon Congress, not because we need them now, but because we shall need them "in the next great war." Most truculent and bloodthirsty of all, the Jingo editors keep up a din day after day about the way we could cripple one country's fleet and destroy another's commerce, and fill the heads of boys and silly men with the idea that war is the normal state of a civilized country.

The silver movement and the jingo mania united in an unexpected fashion just after the veto of the seigniorage bill. On May 2 there opened in London an international bimetallic conference of an unofficial kind, with four hundred delegates present. Brooks Adams and Senator Wolcott of Colorado represented the United States. Among others present were the heads of the British and French Bimetallic Leagues, prominent Continental bankers, and some Australians. Arthur Balfour spoke, saying that the world was face to face with a great danger which could be averted only by international action to restore silver to its proper function. From Washington came a cablegram signed by fifteen Senators, including Sherman, Allison, Hoar, Gorman, Voorhees, Brice, and Aldrich, who declared: "We believe that the free coinage of both gold and silver by international agreement at a fixed ratio would secure to mankind the blessing of a sufficient volume of metallic money, and, what is hardly less important, secure to the world of trade immunity from violent exchange fluctuations."

Cleveland took only slight interest in this conference. But he was roused to indignant hostility when on May 9 Senator Lodge offered a proposal for a discriminating tariff against the British Empire if its government did not consent to a bimetallic plan. The Administration rallied its forces against the resolution and promptly laid it on the table by the votes of 31 Democrats and one Populist against 20 Republicans.[1] Conservative editors derided the proposal, pointing out that a tariff war with incomparably our best customer would hardly cure the depression. Yet Lodge found supporters. No less a person than Thomas B. Reed gave an interview to a representative of the *Fortnightly Review*, in which he asserted that since cheap silver stimulated Asiatic exports, it was necessary to consider silver and the tariff as one issue. High gold prices, he argued, injured the United States by increasing the burden of our gold obligations payable abroad; and cheap silver equally injured this country by increasing the flow of Asiatic wheat and cotton to Europe. If England would not toe the line, "there may come a time for the nations friendly to bimetallism to unite, not in a monetary union but a tariff union—reciprocity being the reward of free coinage of silver."[2] Eastern cynics regarded this as a bid for the Presidential nomination in 1896, while even the West was dubious, for it wanted no high tariff. Yet the Lodge-Reed proposal brought all the jingoes to their feet in applause. Murat Halstead wrote that it was "of greater magnitude than any idea that has touched the pride and policy of the American people since Mr. Blaine formed the union of the words 'protection' and 'reciprocity' and sought to enlarge the comity of the nations of our continent."

VI

Even had there been no single great industrial explosion in this dark year, it would have engendered a steady increase of social friction, distrust of the government, and bad temper generally. But as the long depression after the panic of 1873 finally produced an outburst of labor violence in the railway strike of 1877, so the discontent, the unemployment, and the poverty of 1894 suddenly engendered the Pullman strike. To that we shall now turn. It placed before Cleveland one of the sternest problems he ever had to encounter. It presented to the nation a startling illustration of the element of truth in William Dean Howells' depiction,

[1] *Public Opinion,* May 17, 1894.
[2] *Public Opinion,* June 7, 14, 1894. The Republican State Conventions of Maine and Ohio endorsed the Lodge-Reed proposal.

in his short poem entitled "Society," of American social inequality in these years: [1]

> I looked and saw a splendid pageantry
> Of beautiful women and of lordly men,
> Taking their pleasure in a flowery plain,
> Where poppies and the red anemone,
> And many another leaf of cramoisy,
> Flickered about their feet . . .
>
> I looked again, and saw that flowery space
> Stirring, as if alive, beneath the tread
> That rested now upon an old man's head,
> And now upon a baby's gasping face,
> Or mother's bosom, or the rounded grace
> Of a girl's throat; and what had seemed the red
> Of flowers was blood, in gouts and gushes shed
> From hearts that broke under that frolic pace,
> And now and then from out the dreadful floor
> An arm or brow was lifted from the rest,
> As if to strike in madness, or implore
> For mercy. . . .

[1] *Harper's Magazine,* March, 1895.

CLEVELAND's troubles never came as single spies but as battalions. In the very midst of his perplexities over the Wilson Tariff, he was forced to confront the gravest labor disturbance, with one possible exception, which the country had yet known. No event of his second presidency, not even the Venezuela affair, has provoked so much controversy as the government's intervention in the Pullman strike in Chicago. This intervention consisted of two distinct steps, the resort to an injunction and the use of Federal troops, and both seemed unprecedentedly bold. Court injunctions had been used before in labor troubles, but never in such sweeping form. Federal troops had been called out before to suppress violence on the part of railroad strikers, but President Hayes had not employed them in 1877 until requested to do so by State authorities, whereas Cleveland waited for no such invitation. The President's course has been the object of both violent applause and violent abuse. As perspective lengthens, each seems exaggerated. It is true that he acted with characteristic vigor and decisiveness, but the lines which his action followed had been artfully blocked out for him by Attorney-General Olney. He manifested all his characteristic common sense in acting upon the facts as they were presented to him, but unfortunately Olney's presentation left much, in respect of candor, caution, and impartiality, to be desired.

The events which produced the strike are a familiar story and need not long detain us. During the gloomy winter of 1893–94 the Pullman Palace Car Company, occupying a large area on the southern outskirts of Chicago, reduced wages in a series of cuts by about one-fourth. Many men were dismissed and many more were put on part time. The company pleaded that the decline of its business necessitated this action. Yet actually the corporation was rich: it held undivided surplus profits of about twenty-five millions, and in the previous fiscal year it had distributed more than two and half millions in dividends upon a capital of $36,000,000.[1] When George M. Pullman was later asked by Federal investigators whether it would not have been juster to divide with the

[1] United States Strike Commission Report, Sen. Exec. Doc. 7, 53rd Cong., 3rd sess., p. xxxiii–xxxv.

employees for a time so as to give them a fair living wage, he replied: "I do not. It would have amounted to a gift of money to these men; it was simply a matter of business." [1] Nor were rents in the "model town" of Pullman reduced, though they were from one-fifth to one-fourth higher than in Chicago and most adjacent suburbs. This pretty village, with its lakes, parks, and trim red-brick houses, had sometimes been praised by sociologists. In point of fact there fell over it such a shadow of corporate despotism that its residents spoke of the company much as a Russian mentioned the Czar, while practical business men referred to its pious pretences with contempt. Mark Hanna's remark about it was unprintable. [2]

The long winter brought suffering and rebellion among the people of Pullman, for many employees were on a starvation wage. One expert witness later declared that after the rent was paid, the typical family had about seventy-six cents a day left for food and clothing. [3] Early in May a deputation of employees called on Mr. Pullman and requested that either wages be raised, or rents be reduced. Not only were they refused, but three members of the deputation were immediately afterwards discharged. This may have been accidental, but the workers naturally interpreted it as a punishment for *lèse majesté*, and five-sixths of them indignantly went out on strike. The company thereupon laid off the faithful one-sixth and closed its shops.

Had the strike remained localized it would have attracted little at-attention, but it promptly involved two powerful railway organizations. About 4,000 of the Pullman employees were members of the American Railway Union. This was a radical body which had been founded in Chicago the previous year by men discontented with the railroad brotherhoods, and which under the dynamic leadership of Eugene V. Debs had swiftly reached a membership of 150,000 men, enrolled in 465 local unions. The national convention of the A. R. U. met early in June in Chicago, and taking up the Pullman dispute, pleaded for arbitration. When the company rebuffed them, they voted a boycott and strike against all Pullman cars, to begin on June 26. By this step the A. R. U. came into collision with the railways themselves. Eight years previously the heads of the twenty-four railroads which then centred

---

[1] Strike Report, 554; *Public Opinion*, Sept. 6, 1894.
[2] Thomas Beer, *Hanna*, 133.
[3] W. H. Cawardin, *History of the Pullman Strike*.

or terminated in Chicago had formed what was called the General Managers' Association to coördinate their activities in various fields. At first this Association had paid little attention to labor, but in 1893 it had fixed a "Chicago scale" for switchmen, and had aroused hostility by proposing a similar scale for other groups. It now took the side of the Pullman Company.

On June 26 there began a struggle to the death between the A. R. U. and the General Managers' Association. Almost overnight it attained menacing proportions, extending into twenty-seven States and Territories, and showed the grimmest temper. Federal investigators later declared that capital was "determined to crush the strike rather than accept any peaceable solution through conciliation, arbitration, or otherwise." [1]

Cleveland, who was in Washington alone—Mrs. Cleveland and the children having gone to Gray Gables—had just returned from a fishing trip with Dr. O'Reilly and Robley D. Evans to the capes of the Chesapeake.[2] On June 28 he read in the morning newspaper a Chicago dispatch saying that the strike "has assumed the proportions of the greatest battle between labor and capital that has ever been waged in the United States." In Chicago 20,000 men had quit or were quitting work, while Debs' headquarters estimated that 40,000 were on strike farther west. During the day the Postoffice Department reported that the mails were completely obstructed on the Southern Pacific lines connecting San Francisco with Portland, Ogden, and Los Angeles. Similar complaints began coming from other parts of the West. In the next three days the news became steadily more alarming. The boycott of Pullman cars proved remarkably effective. Whenever efforts were made to move them, the trainmen usually quit in a body. Cleveland had of course taken steps to keep the White House informed of every development. On the 29th he learned that freight traffic in and out of Chicago was half paralyzed; on the 30th that it was almost at a standstill. Debs had given strict orders against violence, and for a time it seemed that the Managers' Association might be defeated by an entirely peaceful uprising. But on the 29th a crowd of a thousand strikers and sympathizers stopped the New York Limited on the Chicago & Erie at Hammond, Ind., and compelled the crew to detach two Pullmans. On the 30th

[1] Strike Report, xix.
[2] Washington *Post*, June 15, 1894.

turbulent crowds in Chicago temporarily held up two express trains on the Illinois Central and Panhandle lines.[1]

Everyone knew that the World's Fair had drawn to Chicago a mass of floating labor, vagabonds, and lawless adventurers, which the depression had left stranded there; and an incendiary outbreak was feared. During the previous winter more than 100,000 desperate men had walked the streets looking for work, and in sheer humanity during many weeks the City Hall had been given up to them at night, and its halls and corridors filled with ragged, starving sleepers. Soup houses had fed tens of thousands daily. Many of these unemployed would be tinder for any spark.

By July 1 the reports of the stoppage of a great part of the freight traffic of the West, of the mass demonstrations in and near Chicago, and of the fears there of a reign of violence, had thrown the conservative press into an indignant frenzy. The Chicago *Tribune* gave many newspapers their cue. On June 28 its front page had borne the headline, "Debs is a Dictator;" on the 30th, "Mob is in Control;" and on July 1, "Mobs Bent on Ruin." These wild statements were actually quite baseless. As Governor Altgeld later wrote Cleveland, many of the news stories from beginning to end were hopelessly exaggerated and distorted. The strike from the outset had the sympathy of some of the most public-spirited Chicagoans, including Eugene Field and Jane Addams; and young Clarence Darrow resigned his legal position with a railroad to support it.[2] Yet the *Tribune's* news accounts and dispatches like them led an imposing array of newspapers to declare that the strikers were no longer battling against Pullman, but were taking the public itself by the throat.

II

The Administration plainly faced a critical situation. Cleveland knew that it had two plain duties—to secure the unobstructed movement of mails, and to maintain interstate commerce. The Constitution and statutes gave the Federal Government ample authority to meet both obligations. It was bound to enforce the postal laws, and it was equally bound to enforce the Interstate Commerce Act of 1887, which by im-

[1] Washington *Post*, Chicago *Tribune*, June 28–30, 1894.
[2] McAlister Coleman, *Eugene V. Debs*, 132.

plication guaranteed full and free interstate traffic. But how much right did the government have to interfere with the strikers? Obviously, it could deal severely with them if they indulged in lawless obstruction. But just what constituted lawless obstruction? A liberal observer might say that nothing short of violence and rioting met the definition; a reactionary observer might say that the mere inciting of men to strike was in effect obstruction. Olney took the illiberal view, and labored desperately to bring Cleveland to act in harmony with it.

There were several reasons why Olney was certain to feel a prejudice against the strike. His long career as an attorney for the New York Central, Santa Fé, Chicago, Burlington, & Quincy, and Boston & Maine could not but affect his attitude.[1] As late as 1889 he had been a director of the C. B. & Q., one of the members of the General Managers' Association; and he had represented New England interests on several Western roads. His natural bent had always been toward the defence of property rights, and particularly corporation rights. Moreover, all spring he had been struggling with disturbances caused on the Western railroads by the Coxeyites or commonwealers. He had been aroused to a high pitch of indignation by their tactics, and had perfected a technique for dealing with them. Throughout the Northwest, from Oregon to Minnesota, masses of half-starved and discontented men had set out for the East. Lacking money for railway transportation, they had organized bands and seized railroad trains. Most of the lines involved were in the hands of Federal receivers, and the courts could not look on without an effort to save their property. They had therefore issued orders to the Federal marshals to protect the railroads—orders which Olney had found were seldom effective because the marshals could not find enough deputies to enforce them. In these circumstances, Olney had instructed the judges and marshals to join in applications to the Department of Justice for help from the Federal army; and as he later wrote, "whenever the facts were clearly proved, the commanding officers of such troops of the United States as were in the vicinity of any disturbance were ordered to put in force the orders of the United States court."[2] He took pride in this summary method of handling the situation. Now his resentment against the western Coxeyites who had law-

---

[1] For this service see Boston *Transcript*, June 25, 1895; *Green Bag*, June, 1893; *Cong. Rec.*, July 16, 1894, vol. 26, p. 7544.

[2] Autobiographical fragment; Olney Papers.

lessly seized trains was suddenly transferred to the Chicago unionists who had quite lawfully quit work on trains. As he read the flaming newspapers in the last days of June, his naturally truculent temper rose. The man who barred his daughter from his home when she married a dentist, who later wrote the belligerent words of the Venezuela message, whose fits of anger often made his subordinates tremble, made up his mind to deal harshly with the disturbance.[1]

Left to himself, he would have been ready to send Federal troops into Chicago without delay or preliminaries. He later wrote that the President might have used the troops to prevent interference with the mails or interstate commerce *"without waiting for action by the courts and without justifying the proceeding as taken to enforce judicial decrees."* [2] Beyond doubt he hinted this to Cleveland. But Cleveland quite properly demurred. And when Olney became convinced that Cleveland could not be induced to move "except in support of the judicial tribunals," [3] he decided to resort to the procedure he had repeatedly used in the West. He would get the courts to issue an order or injunction; the Federal judge and the marshal would presently certify that the injunction could not be enforced; and he would then persuade Cleveland to send troops to the rescue of the courts. His first step was to appoint a special counsel to assist the Federal Attorney in Chicago. The extraordinary fact that in making this appointment he took the advice of the General Managers' Association has been strangely overlooked in all subsequent accounts. The Association met in the Rookery Building, telegraphed to Olney proposing Edwin Walker, attorney for the Chicago, Milwaukee & St. Paul, and within two hours he was appointed.[4] Then on June 30 Olney sent Walker a remarkable message of instructions: [5]

It has seemed to me that if the rights of the United States were vigorously asserted in Chicago, the origin and centre of the demonstration, the result would be to make it a failure everywhere else and to prevent its spread over the entire country. With yourself directing matters for the government, I am sure

[1] Olney's hostility to the strike appears in his subsequent statement that "it seemed clear that whatever was done should be done at Chicago because that was the centre and headquarters of the strike and that, *if smashed there,* it would collapse everywhere else." Autobiographical fragment; Olney Papers.
[2] Henry James, *Olney,* 203. Italics mine.
[3] *Ibid.,* 203.
[4] N. Y. *Times, Tribune,* July 2, 1894; cf. Clarence Darrow, *The Story of My Life,* 61.
[5] James, *Olney,* 47.

all legal remedies will be resorted to that the facts will warrant.

In this connection it has seemed to me advisable not merely to rely on warrants against persons actually guilty of the offence of obstructing United States mails, but to go into a court of equity and secure restraining orders which shall have the effect of preventing any attempt to commit the offence. With that view, I sent a telegram to Mr. Milchrist [the Federal Attorney] this morning citing some decisions, which I think may probably be availed of in the present exigency.

The Marshal and the District Attorney have wired me about the employment of fifty deputies. I authorized it, of course. But I feel that the true way of dealing with the matter is by a force which is overwhelming and prevents any attempt at resistance. In that particular, however, I must defer to the better judgment of one who is on the spot and familiar with all the facts of the situation.

Three facts stare the reader of this message in the face. First, Olney's wish as regards the strike was to "make it a failure everywhere." Second, he desired a drastic injunction, forbidding any attempt to interfere with the mails. And third, he believed that this injunction ought to be enforced "by a force which is overwhelming and prevents any attempt at resistance"—that is, by the Federal army.

At this point we may ask just what Olney believed to be the grounds for an injunction, and how far he thought it ought to extend. His answer was given in full in a subsequent letter to Walker, when the strike had ended but the Debs case was still pending in the courts. He then wrote, in a document that has never been quoted or summarized, that in his opinion there were two grounds for action.[1] One was the Sherman Anti-Trust Act, which made illegal any combination in restraint of interstate trade. He believed that this applied to combinations of labor as well as capital. His second ground lay in the thesis that "a court of equity has a right to enjoin a public nuisance when it clearly threatens a public injury," and here he indicated just how sweeping he thought the injunction should be. Under this thesis he laid down a series of six propositions. They were: (1) the obstruction of a public highway is the plainest example of a public nuisance; (2) a railroad is a public highway; (3) as an instrument of interstate commerce an interstate railroad is a Federal highway; (4) any obstruction of a Federal highway is enjoinable by a bill in equity brought under the direction of the Attorney-General; (5) such obstruction is presented by "the concerted, sudden,

[1] Sept. 24, 1894. Olney Papers.

and simultaneous withdrawal from service of the trained corps of expert employees necessary to the operation of such highways"; and (6) if the intent of a strike "be unlawful, so as to create a public nuisance, any act in furtherance of that intent, whether it be the quitting of work or a combination or agreement to quit work, *or any other*, becomes tortious, and may be restrained by a court of equity."

This, it is plain, was as sweeping a doctrine as any Attorney-General has ever enunciated. In Olney's eyes, it was tortious or criminal for a worker on an interstate railroad to quit his job, or to enter a combination to quit the job, or to do *any other act* in furtherance of a strike. If this were so, just how much freedom was left to railwaymen?

Cleveland reposed greater faith in Olney than in any other member of his second Cabinet. The rugged, rockhewn strength of the man, his complete honesty according to his own lights, his dogmatic common sense, appealed to the same qualities in Cleveland himself. He knew that Olney was one of the foremost lawyers of America. While temporarily rejecting his Attorney-General's views on the use of Federal troops, therefore, he accepted them on the propriety of obtaining an injunction. Probably the terms of the proposed injunction were not discussed before Cleveland. These opening days in July were witnessing the tariff crisis which evoked Cleveland's famous letter to Wilson on "party perfidy," and legal details in Chicago had to be left to other hands.

III

On July 2 the injunction against Debs and the strikers was duly issued. All the previous night District Attorney Milchrist had toiled over the preparation of a bill. Early in the morning he met Judges Grosscup and Woods in the Federal Building. By what seems an indefensible procedure, they temporarily abandoned their judicial position to assist him in revising the application, and then granted the injunction. The Managers' Association was jubilant, calling it "a gatling gun on paper." It was rather an entire battery. In sweeping terms, it ordered all persons "to refrain from interfering with or stopping any of the business of any of the railroads in Chicago engaged as common carriers," and defined interference to include a long series of acts, even to the "persuasion" of employees to stop work. "A veritable dragnet," said the

New York *Times*. Milchrist announced that publication of the writ was equivalent to personal service upon everyone. "Under this interpretation thousands of strikers might be arrested day after day and arraigned and summarily dealt with for contempt of court," reported the press, "and this is precisely the policy, according to the reports at the Government Building tonight, that it is intended to pursue."[1] Once the strikers were arrested, they would be liable to a peremptory sentence, without trial. The mere existence of such an injunction was a body-blow to the A. R. U. As Debs later said, it broke the back of the strike, for it put the strikers in the position of rioters wantonly violating the law.[2]

Olney had thus taken the first of his three steps. And for the railway managers it had come none too soon. On July 1 and 2 the movement of freight trains in and out of Chicago almost ceased, while traffic was disrupted all over the Northwest. The grain trade was paralyzed. The Chicago packing houses were preparing to close down, and livestock was being unloaded at junctions throughout the upper Mississippi Valley. Factories were shutting for lack of coal, and thousands were being thrown out of work. The hospitals were running short of ice. Governor Altgeld had ordered militia to Danville, Decatur, and Cairo to liberate Wabash, Chicago & Eastern Illinois, and Illinois Central trains.[3] In Colorado and New Mexico Federal troops were being employed for the same purpose. At Sacramento a crowd of 3,000 was stopping all railway traffic. Particularly in the region about Chicago the strike seemed to be approaching success. Passenger trains were few and often came in hours late, and suburban traffic was in great confusion.

As yet there was no violence whatever in Chicago. But on July 2, in the town of Blue Island, almost half way between Chicago and Joliet, a large mob gathered along the Rock Island tracks, and when Federal Marshal Arnold appeared with 125 deputies, defied him, tipped over cars, and otherwise impeded traffic. A deputy was stabbed, and Arnold in all his dignity was rolled in the dirt. "I am here at Blue Island," he immediately telegraphed Olney. "Have read the order of the court to the rioters here and they simply hoot at it. . . . We have had a desperate time here all day and our force is inadequate. In my judgment it is

---

[1] N. Y. *Times*, July 3, 1894.
[2] James, *Olney*, 202.
[3] Waldo R. Browne, *Altgeld of Illinois*, 133.

impossible to move trains without having the Fifteenth Infantry from Fort Sheridan moved here at once. There are 2,000 rioters here and more coming. Mail trains are in great danger." The next day, however, was generally peaceful both in Chicago and outside. "The strikers at Blue Island," reported the press, "refrained from violence during the day." This was partly due to the presence of deputy sheriffs and marshals, and partly to reports that troops were coming.[1] The chief of police in Chicago later testified that there had been no disturbance.[2] Mayor Hopkins also testified that he had been assured by the officials of the different railroads "that they received the most efficient protection they had ever received during similar troubles; *that condition of things lasted until July 5.*"[3] But Olney wished a stiffer demand for soldiers. He was dissatisfied with Arnold's telegram and wired an unmistakable hint to Milchrist for another:[4]

Congratulate you upon the legal situation, which is all that could be desired. Trust use of United States troops will not be necessary. If it becomes necessary, they will be used promptly and decisively upon the justifying facts being certified to me. In such case, if practicable, let Walker and Marshal and United States Judge join in statement as to the exigency.

Milchrist grasped this, and there immediately came back from Chicago the following dispatch signed by Marshal Arnold and formally endorsed by Milchrist, Walker, and Judge Grosscup:[5]

When the injunction was granted yesterday a mob of from two to three thousand held possession of a point in the city near the crossing of the Rock Island by other roads, where they had already ditched a mail train, and prevented the passing of any trains, whether mail or otherwise. I read the injunction writ to this mob and commanded them to disperse. The reading of the writ met with no response except hoots and jeers. Shortly after, the mob threw a number of baggage cars across the track, since when no mail trains have been able to move. I am unable to disperse the mob, clear the tracks, or arrest the men who were engaged in the acts named, and believe that no force less than the regular troops of the United States can procure the passage of the mail trains or enforce the orders of the Court. I believe people engaged in trades are quitting employment today, and in my opinion will be joining the

[1] This statement is based on study of a dozen New York, Washington, and Chicago newspapers.
[2] *Strike Report*, xliii.
[3] *Strike Report*, 344.
[4] *Report Attorney-General*, 1896, Appendix, p. 65.
[5] *Ibid.*, 1896, Appendix, p. 66.

mob tonight, and especially tomorrow, and it is my judgment that the troops should be here at the earliest possible moment. An emergency has arisen for their presence in the city.

It has never been pointed out that this dispatch, signed by four Federal officers, bristles with misleading points. First, it speaks of a mob "in the city" when it really refers to the Blue Island disorders well outside the city limits. Again, it speaks of disorders which, grave enough on July 2, are agreed by the press and chief of police to have subsided on July 3. In the third place, it asserts that nothing less than the regular troops could restore order, though State troops had not been tried and had proved effective at Danville, Cairo, and Decatur. Finally, it contained a hearsay statement that workers in the trades were quitting employment, which was untrue, and an opinion that they would at once join the mob, which was an unjustifiable inference anyhow. But Olney was eagerly awaiting the certification of an emergency, and when he got it on July 3 he immediately carried it to the White House.

Cleveland that day had already called the Cabinet together. All the members were present except Carlisle and Morton. Earlier in the day General Miles, commander of the Western department, was at the White House and said that in his opinion Federal troops ought not yet to be used in Chicago. Secretary Gresham, who had so long lived in Chicago, had shared this opinion; and Secretary Lamont had also heretofore opposed calling out the troops.[1] But when Olney waved his Chicago telegram opposition vanished. The Washington *Post* reported next day that "there was no disagreement with the Attorney-General and President in the legal steps which they have taken." [2] Lamont crossed to the War Department and at 3.30 P. M. telegraphed orders that all the troops at Fort Sheridan were to be thrown into Chicago.[3] Early on July 4, as holiday crowds poured into the streets and parks, Colonel Crofton moved his infantry, artillery, and cavalry to three points—the stockyards, Grand Crossing, and Blue Island; and the acting departmental commander telegraphed that the people of the city felt much safer.

Reporters who called at Olney's office that day observed that news of the arrival of the troops pleased him. He was busy telegraphing

[1] John M. Schofield, *Forty-Six Years*, 494; Gresham, *Walter Q. Gresham*, I, 416–419.
[2] Washington *Post*, July 4, 1894.
[3] See orders in Schofield, 496 ff.

Milchrist to have the grand jury convened as soon as possible to indict Debs and others, and in telling the correspondents this, he jerked out savagely: "we have been brought to the ragged edge of anarchy, and it is time to see whether the law is sufficiently strong to prevent this condition of affairs. If not, the sooner we know it the better, that it may be changed." [1] Cleveland, by the grim purpose and none too subtle manoeuvrings of his Attorney-General, had been induced to send in the troops without waiting for a State application. In his own story of the affair he makes it clear that he had hoped to avoid this extreme step. He thought for a time, he writes, that the injunction might produce such an effect "that this alternative might be avoided." His narrative, which is too formal and bare to be of much worth, also shows that he accepted at their face value the assertions of Olney's Chicago subordinates that the troops were needed at once.[2]

An anxious week followed for Cleveland and his Cabinet. On the very day the troops arrived mob violence began and the next morning it flamed forth in terrifying fashion. It was widely said at the time that this was partly the work of *agents provocateurs* acting for the railways. Undeniably the railroads had employed many queer characters. The Federal marshals had appointed some 3,600 deputies who were selected by the General Managers' Association, were armed and paid for by the railroads, and acted in the double capacity of railway employees and United States officers. The press described them as "toughs," and Marshal Donnelly as in part "worthless" and drunken.[3] It was universally agreed later that the strikers had furnished little of the violence—that it was offered by hoodlums, women, a low class of foreigners, and recruits from the criminal classes.[4] One marshal ascribed it mainly to youths. Whether any of it would have occurred but for the harsh terms of the injunction, the arrival of the troops, and the hatred of the deputies, is a question impossible to answer. Undoubtedly the troops were an irritant. Debs, temporarily losing his head, told a United Press reporter on July 4: [5]

The first shots fired by the regular soldiers at the mobs here will be the signal for a civil war. I believe this as firmly as I believe in the ultimate success

[1] Washington *Post*, July 5, 1894.
[2] Cleveland, *The Government and the Chicago Strike.*
[3] N. Y. *Times*, July 2, 1894; *Strike Report*, 341.
[4] *Strike Report*, xliv.
[5] Washington *Post*, July 5, 1894.

of our course. Bloodshed will follow, and ninety per cent of the people of the United States will be arrayed against the other ten per cent. And I would not care to be arrayed against the laboring people in the contest, or find myself out of the ranks of labor when the struggle ended.

For a week following the 4th Cleveland hardly slept. Regular Cabinet meetings were supplemented by prolonged sessions of an emergency group composed of Olney, Lamont, Bissell, and General Schofield. Sometimes Gresham joined the conferences. A direct telephone wire was established between General Miles's headquarters in Chicago and the White House, and Cleveland held long conversations with the general. Night after night the lamps burned in the White House library and men were ushered in and out till two or three o'clock in the morning. Lamont had taken up his quarters in the Executive Mansion.

At first, on the 5th, 6th, and 7th, the news was of the most alarming character.[1] Tracks were blockaded by the mob, passenger trains stopped, box cars burned in hundreds, switches smashed, and signalmen driven from their towers. Six large buildings of the World's Fair were destroyed by incendiaries. There was almost a reign of terror. Residents of the Hyde Park section, at the height of the disorders, stood on their housetops at night and saw the skies in one direction lit up by blazing railway property, and in the other reddened by the burning exposition structures. They saw quiet streets, at the report of a pistol, fill in five minutes with hundreds of desperate and dangerous rioters. Wild rumors flew about that the rich department stores and the homes of the millionaires were to be looted. Eastern newspapers bore such headlines as "Mob Rule Supreme," and "Fired by the Mob: Chicago at the Mercy of the Incendiary's Torch." Propertied Chicagoans felt that they were living over a social volcano.

In a few days the city filled with troops. On the 5th and 6th shots were exchanged and on the 7th the mob and the military forces came into bloody collision, seven men being killed outright.[2] Altgeld at noon of the 6th ordered militia to the city, and by sundown that day more than 5,000 were on duty there.[3] Cleveland on the 8th issued a proclamation ordering all unlawful assemblages to disperse before noon the next day, and gave warning that "There will be no vacillation in the

[1] Washington and N. Y. Press, July 5–12.
[2] Cleveland, *Chicago Strike*, 34.
[3] Browne, *Altgeld*, 136.

decisive punishment of the guilty." On the 10th Debs and others were indicted and arrested for obstructing the mails—the total Federal indictments reached 71—and the final collapse of the strike and disorders quickly followed.

IV

Cleveland would have taken the steps he did even if public opinion had been heavily against him, but as a matter of fact it gave him enthusiastic support. With a few exceptions the leading newspapers, Democratic, Republican, and Independent, applauded the use of Federal troops. Letters of commendation were showered upon him. Many State Executives in the East sent him messages of support, and the governor of Vermont offered him every available man. A Senate resolution endorsing his "prompt and vigorous measures" passed on the 11th with a ringing chorus of ayes from both sides of the chamber, Peffer alone voting no. When Cushman K. Davis eloquently denounced Debs, "this Masaniello of a day, drunk with power," many voices suggested the Minnesota Senator for President. A Kentucky Congressman wrote Thurber that "I think the only strike now on is the ten-strike made by President Cleveland." [1] Commercial interests agreed with the letter which James J. Hill of the Great Northern sent Secretary Lamont three days after the troops reached Chicago: [2]

The present labor strikes throughout the country have prostrated business beyond anything that has ever occurred. The panic of last year is nothing compared with the reign of terror that exists in the large centres. Business is at a standstill, and the people are becoming thoroughly aroused. Their feeling is finding expression about as it did during the War of the Rebellion. . . . The action of the governors of Illinois and Colorado is severely condemned, while the public, without reference to party lines, are unanimous in approving and supporting the action of the President.

But it is evident that this approval was based upon the rioting which occurred after the troops went in rather than upon the situation before Cleveland's order. The general public assumed that the rioting would have occurred anyway; that State militia had not been sent in because Governor Altgeld did not want them sent in; and that only Cleveland's

1 Asher G. Caruth, July 13, 1894. Cleveland Papers.
2 St. Paul, July 7, 1894. Cleveland Papers.

timely precautions saved Chicago from disaster. The first assumption may have been erroneous. The second assumption certainly was. Altgeld, who had used militia elsewhere in the State, was ready to respond instantly to any request from either railroad heads or Mayor Hopkins; and he assured friends that "if it becomes necessary I could and would put 100,000 men into the city of Chicago inside of five days. The whole State would answer to the call as one man." [1] Where Altgeld erred was in not making prompt and vigorous announcement of his readiness to act, and in not ordering a few regiments to stand in readiness by July 3. This would have reassured the city and made Olney's interference more difficult. One regiment, the First, was in Chicago, and needed but to be summoned to its armory. As it was, the public saw only the blazing freight cars and the rioting, and jumped to the conclusion that Cleveland's promptness had saved Chicago from a fearful catastrophe. In the city itself business and professional men felt an almost universal gratitude to the President. Dozens of the older residents, questioned by the writer of these pages, have replied that Cleveland saved the community "from chaos." [2]

Beneath the approval also lay a general feeling that Cleveland had grappled with anarchy itself. Olney in his statement to the press used the word "anarchy." Gilder wrote the President that "The nation does not exist if anarchy and destructive despotism take the place of law." Cushman K. Davis said that Debs had "called from the caves and dens of Chicago the professed criminal, the idly vicious, the anarchist. Everybody who is conspiring to put down modern civilization is now moving under the mask of this strike and taking knife and destroying property in its name." The *North American Review* for August contained an article by Nelson A. Miles treating the strike as "anarchistic," and the *Forum* blazed out with an essay by Henry Holt on anarchism. In part this readiness to view the strike in the most vicious light possible was due to the worldwide shock caused by an anarchist's assassination of President Sadi Carnot in France just as the strike began, in part to remembrance of the Haymarket affair, and in part to sheer prejudice against labor. Whatever its origins, it was unjust to the strikers.

Yet Cleveland's action was at once attacked from two different di-

---

[1] Caro Lloyd, *Life of Henry Demarest Lloyd*, I, 147 ff.
[2] John Barton Payne, John M. Stahl, and others; vigorously combated by Clarence Darrow, Edgar Lee Masters, Carl Sandburg, and others.

rections: by sympathizers with labor, and by defenders of State Rights. Altgeld, the "Eagle forgotten" of Vachel Lindsay's noble poem, who never failed to fight for the poor and oppressed, addressed a vigorous letter to the President while the strike still raged, criticizing him for acting too hastily and upon grossly exaggerated reports, and for not giving the State authorities a due opportunity to deal with the situation. Cleveland answered the second of these criticisms by replying that the general government did not need to wait for State requisitions in protecting the mails and interstate commerce.[1] In this Cleveland was entirely right. When Altgeld wrote a second letter in a more bitterly argumentative tone, Cleveland sent back a curt assertion that "While I am still persuaded that I have neither transcended my authority nor duty in the emergency that confronts us, it seems to me that in this hour of danger and public distress, discussion may well give way to active efforts on the part of all in authority to restore obedience to law and to protect life and property."

His retort failed to impress many Southerners who clung to the principle of State sovereignty, and Governor Hogg of Texas echoed Altgeld's protest. "The State of Texas," he telegraphed Cleveland on July 11, "is able to control the situation and to enforce the law and protect rights guaranteed by the State and Federal Constitutions and she will do it. You are notified that you may not feel called upon by the plea of any alarmist to use United States troops here unless requested by State authority." Meanwhile, the radical ranks of labor were indignant at Cleveland. A massmeeting of ten thousand men at Cooper Union on July 12 heard Henry George criticize the President. "I yield to nobody in my respect for the rights of property," he said, "yet I would rather see every locomotive in this land ditched, every car and every depot burned and every rail torn up, than to have them preserved by means of a Federal standing army. That is the order that reigned in Warsaw."[2]

Though majority opinion continued to approve Cleveland's acts, as time passed the volume of criticism increased. It was shown that Judge Woods had accepted such important favors at the hands of railway corporations that his impartiality was highly questionable. Cleveland appointed a commission to investigate the strike, and under Carroll D.

[1] This correspondence is given in Browne, *Altgeld,* 128 ff.
[2] N. Y. *Times,* July 13, 1894.

Wright it made an admirable report, exposing the policy of the Pullman Company and the railroads in its true character. It condemned the selfish paternalism of the Pullman system; characterized the General Managers' Association as "an illustration of the persistent and shrewdly devised plan of corporations to override their limitations and usurp indirectly powers and rights not contemplated by their charters"; and exculpated the officers of the American Railway Union from the charge of provoking violence. The strike had cost the railroads, workers, and government at least ten millions and had resulted in twelve deaths—a high bill to pay for George Pullman's Bourbon aims.[1] The real blame for the disorders, the report suggested, "rests with the people themselves and with the government for not adequately controlling monopolies and corporations, and for failing to reasonably protect the rights of labor and redress its wrongs." It recurred to Cleveland's former proposal of a permanent strike commission of three men. In the Debs Case in 1895 the Supreme Court, while sustaining Cleveland's emergency action in employing both military and civil forces to meet a grave crisis, by no means—contrary to what is often said—sustained the terms of the Chicago injunction, but avoided any explicit pronouncement on them.[2] Such an injunction would now be condemned by all liberal jurists.

Undoubtedly Cleveland did his duty as he saw it, or rather as Olney unhappily showed it to him. He acted with all his usual conscientiousness and courage. For his course really required courage: Governor Altgeld and Mayor Hopkins both opposed his use of troops, they were the Democratic leaders in Illinois, and they had done more than anyone else to help Cleveland carry the State in 1892. Hopkins, a local idol, had been born in Cleveland's ward in Buffalo and Cleveland had thought of him as a political protégé.[3] To affront these men was to disrupt the party in Illinois. But any observer who possesses a due sympathy for the rights of labor must feel that Cleveland was led sadly astray at several points by his impetuous and bellicose Attorney-General. He played a far less happy part in this strike than Roosevelt did in the anthracite troubles of 1902; for by stern pressure Roosevelt forced the unwilling operators to arbitrate, and held the scales even between capital and

---

[1] *Strike Report*, xlvi. It is a significant fact that while the city of Chicago was legally liable for damage by rioters, no claims were ever presented by the railroads.
[2] Charles Warren, *The Supreme Court in United States History*, 1926 ed., II, 701.
[3] *Harper's Weekly*, Jan. 6, 1894.

labor.

The injunction, while proper under the circumstances, was quite improperly drastic in its terms. It was right to outlaw physical obstruction and violence; it was not right to outlaw the strike. Again, the order to send the troops into Chicago was premature. Olney and Cleveland should have waited for at least another day. If then actual rioting had broken out, if State militia had not been on the spot, and if the Federal marshal and his thousands of deputies had been unable to clear the tracks, Cleveland would have had far better warrant for using the regulars than he actually possessed. Altgeld did not move fast enough; the President moved too fast. Since a train was waiting with steam up at Fort Sheridan and troops could be thrown into the city within two hours, no real danger would have been incurred by this delay. Violence in such strikes always flares up when they begin to fail. Had it not been for the excessively drastic terms of the injunction and the use of the troops this one might possibly have succeeded—and there would then have been no violence. While the probabilities are otherwise, for strikebreakers were rapidly being inported from the East, the Administration might well have let this possibility be tested.

But at bottom, two different philosophies were involved. Cleveland well expressed one when he said that "If it takes the entire army and navy of the United States to deliver a postal card in Chicago, that card will be delivered." Henry George expressed the other in declaring he would rather see every locomotive ditched and every rail torn up than to see them preserved by a Federal standing army. Somewhere between these two views lay the true course. If Cleveland had possessed a more sober, careful, and unprejudiced Attorney-General, he would probably have found it.

From Olney's unfortunate rôle in the Chicago strike we must turn to his equally unfortunate influence upon Cleveland in the Venezuela affair.

DR. BRYANT once remarked that Cleveland "was temperate in all things, unless unduly irritated by those who would annoy him persistently and selfishly—then appropriate and emphatic remarks were made." [1] Again and again he endured opposition or misrepresentation patiently for a long period, and then suddenly exploded with a force which astonished observers who had not noticed the tokens of rising internal wrath. His attack on Grady and the other Tammany senators in 1883, his frontal assault on the tariff in 1887, his "perfidy and dishonor" letter when the Wilson bill was betrayed, were all illustrations of his readiness to let long-bottled wrath escape, from time to time, with startling detonations. The one instance of this in his conduct of international relations, his Venezuelan message of 1895, took the English-speaking world aback and gave our diplomatic history one of its most striking episodes. In releasing Hawaii he had placed the United States on a high moral plane, and now he insisted upon holding Great Britain to the same severe standards of international ethics.

From the Civil War to the Spanish War, most of our important foreign disputes were with the British government; a fact quite natural, since Britain was the greatest of the Powers, the only strong nation except ourselves in the Western Hemisphere, and the possessor of territory marching for three thousand miles with our own. The fundamental fact to be noted with regard to these disputes is that, while they produced transient irritations, most of them were ultimately settled by arbitration and with mutual regard and respect. The *Alabama* claims were arbitrated at Geneva by the first great international tribunal of the kind in modern history. The controversy over the right of British vessels to kill fur seals in the Bering Sea was submitted to arbitrators who met in Paris in 1893, and who decided in favor of the principal British claims.[2] The Alaskan boundary was finally arbitrated. It is to be noted also that in other ways the two nations had shown an increasing amity, and that British friendliness had sometimes found striking ex-

[1] Speech at City College memorial meeting, March 17, 1912.
[2] Moore, *International Arbitrations*, I, 914–922.

pression. Everyone remembered the episode of the American filibustering vessel *Virginius*, captured by a Spanish gunboat off Cuba in 1873. The crew were lined up on shore at Santiago, half of them were shot, and the others were held to be executed the next day; but the British warship *Niobe* arrived, trained its guns on the city, and served notice that further bloodshed would be the signal for a bombardment. The executions stopped. Everyone remembered the scene at Apia in 1889, when American and British cruisers, confronting German warships, had been overtaken by a typhoon. As the British warship *Calliope* crowded on every ounce of steam and gallantly fought its way out of the harbor to safety, the American sailors lined the rail and cheered it to the echo.

When Cleveland first became President the unsettled boundary between British Guiana on the east and Venezuela on the west had already caused much uneasiness in Washington. It had been unsettled ever since the British had taken that part of Guiana over from the Dutch in 1814, and many American observers now believed that England wished to keep it unsettled. She was infinitely the more powerful nation. Some day when Venezuela was embroiled with a neighbor, or divided by civil war, or had a dictator who could easily be bought, England would obtain the boundary she wanted; and she seemed to want above everything else a line which would touch the mouth of the Orinoco. Venezuela year after year pressed for a final determination of the boundary, but the British were skeptical of the stability of the Venezuelan government, and delayed any definite action. They were ready to discuss a boundary only as it might lie west of a line drawn some fifty years earlier by a British engineer, Sir Robert Schomburgk; but this line Venezuela flatly refused to accept. In 1887 the United States took a direct hand, offering through Minister Phelps to assist the two countries in arbitrating the line. England refused, and in 1888 Secretary Bayard asked Phelps to present another and plainer offer, but Phelps failed to do so. During the next Administration the American minister discussed the subject with the British Foreign Office, which still delayed acting. Then Cleveland came in again, and after the crowding duties of 1893–94 were off his hands, turned in an impatient mood to this dragging question.[1]

He lost no time in indicating that he wished to take it up energeti-

[1] See dispatches in *Foreign Relations*, 1894, 803 ff.

cally. In his annual message to Congress at the close of 1894 he stated that he would renew his efforts to bring about an arbitration, adding that Great Britain had always conspicuously favored arbitration in principle. Simultaneously he prodded Ambassador Bayard into action. On January 23, 1895, our envoy interviewed the British Foreign Secretary, Lord Kimberley, conveying the strong and friendly desire of the American Government to see the boundary settled; and on February 20 he had another interview. Early in April he wrote home a long and discouraging dispatch, showing that no progress had been made.[1] Lord Kimberley had been very cool indeed. In spite of the fact that Bayard had spoken of the "anxiety" of our government for a settlement, he had again refused to arbitrate anything east of the Schomburgk line, or any area long settled by the British. Moreover, he had said something much more disquieting: he had given at least a strong hint that Great Britain would insist on holding territory at the mouth of the Orinoco. It is evident that Cleveland's patience was now rapidly giving way to irritation.

Late in April Don M. Dickinson visited Cleveland in the White House —an episode that has been strangely overlooked.[2] The President read him Bayard's dispatch, emphasizing a paragraph in which Bayard wrote that Lord Kimberley had shown him a map of British Guiana "on which were delineated, in different colors, the three lines of delimitation. The line colored in pink was the Schomburgk line, one of the terminal points of which was a short distance inside the Orinoco, and which his lordship stated was conclusively proven and established as a British possession, and would not be submitted to arbitration, but that the ownership of the territory intersected by the other two lines, they would be willing to submit to arbitration." While it is true that the greatest extent of the Schomburgk line did just touch one mouth of the Orinoco, Great Britain had never made any formal claim to a boundary which reached that river. The news that Kimberley was asserting an informal claim was profoundly alarming. If Great Britain perched on that huge waterway, she would be in a position to control much of the internal trade of a vast region.

As luck would have it, at this moment in late April occurred another disquieting rupture of relations between Nicaragua and Great Britain.

[1] State Department Archives, Dispatch No. 404, April 5, 1895.
[2] Dickinson's visit is treated in the press; see Washington *Post.*

Several Britons, including a vice-consul, had been arrested and expelled from the country in 1894, and Lord Kimberley demanded the payment of £75,000 in damages. On April 22 three British warships arrived at Corinto to enforce the demands of London upon the Nicaraguan government; and five days later, payment having been refused, four hundred English marines and sailors seized the custom-house. Rioting followed and the president of Nicaragua at once protested to Cleveland. It was evident that the British had not overstepped the bounds of international law, and indeed had simply followed the course which the United States had proposed to take in Chile several years earlier. The affair ended when Nicaragua paid the indemnity.[1] But Cleveland was disturbed by the incident and expressed his feelings warmly before Dickinson.

When Dickinson returned to Detroit he seized an early opportunity to make a speech in which he hotly denounced British policy—a speech that the press called jingoist. He spoke of the British movements in Nicaragua and the strengthening of British fortifications in the West Indies. But he mentioned more particularly the boundary dispute in Venezuela and England's apparent designs on Venezuelan territory. "In the present conditions," he said with reference to Bayard's Anglophile speeches, "we may indulge in a reciprocity of polite phrasing and post-prandial exuberance, if our alert watchmen will meantime keep an eye upon our good friends across the Atlantic, especially when, having appropriated Africa, the islands and even the rocks of the sea, and wherever else force or intrigue may gain a footing, they begin to take an interest, not altogether born of curiosity or of a purely Christianizing spirit, in this hemisphere." His intimacy with the President was well known and the speech hence aroused unusual comment.[2]

Meanwhile, on May 9 Cleveland was posting Fairchild a significant letter. "I want to write you something quite confidentially," he began. "Affairs in Venezuela are liable to assume a position calling on our part for the greatest care and good management. Do you happen to recall anyone who would do well there as our representative in such a contingency? I think I ought to send someone there of a much higher grade than is usually thought good enough for such a situation. The salary is only $7500 and I believe Caracas is a fair capital to live in." [3]

[1] Appleton's Annual Cyclopaedia, 1895.
[2] Washington Post, May 11; Philadelphia Press, May 12, 1895.
[3] Fairchild Papers.

II

It is clear that Cleveland by the end of April, 1895, was greatly exasperated by the refusal of Great Britain to yield to the repeated suggestions that the long-standing boundary dispute be arbitrated. Quite naturally, he was always ready to suspect the Powers of willingness to rob weaker nations. What he had seen of the partitioning of Africa and the jealous greed of England and Germany over Samoa had left him no illusions. This very year France was engaged in gobbling Madagascar, the British *uitlander* agitation in the Transvaal was growing critical, and Japan was quietly mastering Korea. Cleveland knew well that the British navy was infinitely stronger than ours, and that British arrogance in dealing with little Nicaragua and Venezuela could not be checked by gentle words. In April, at his suggestion, Gresham began preparing an exhaustive report or note on the Venezuela question, and made frequent night visits to Woodley to talk on the subject with Cleveland.[1]

While engaged in this work Gresham took cold; acute pleurisy on May 1 was followed by pneumonia on May 25; and early on May 28 he died. Cleveland, like everyone else in the Cabinet, had developed the staunchest affection for Gresham. His frank and simple nature, his way of pouring out all his problems at Cabinet meetings, his warmth of heart, had made him more than an official partner—had made him a beloved friend, like Vilas in the first Cabinet. The funeral was held in the East Room. When the body was taken to Chicago for burial Cleveland accompanied it. On the train, after sitting plunged in melancholy thought for a long time, he asked one of the Cabinet to go with him to the baggage car where the coffin lay, and when there, requested to be left alone. An hour passed, and he had not returned. Two members of the Cabinet, fearing that some accident had occurred, went forward and found Cleveland on his knees by the bier of the dead Secretary, his arms on the coffin, his eyes blinded with tears. He had been oblivious of the passage of time. He was helped to his feet and led back to his stateroom, where he remained in seclusion till the end of the journey; and a servant who knocked at his door found him lying in his berth, his face buried in the pillows.[2]

[1] Gresham, *Gresham*, II, 795.
[2] McElroy, *Grover Cleveland*, II, 179, 180.

Olney had begun work on the Venezuelan problem during Gresham's illness, and, succeeding on June 10 to the Secretaryship of State, continued to drive forward the preparation of a dispatch to be sent to Bayard in London. He had, as his biographer says, a passion for disposing of any difficulty promptly, and he lent support to Cleveland's conviction that the matter had dragged on long enough. On July 2, his draft of a note finished, he carried it to Gray Gables.[1] Cleveland was somewhat preoccupied, for a few days later, as the President put it in a note to Olney, "our family was augmented by the addition of a strong plump loud-voiced little girl." At his home in Falmouth near by Olney waited in the greatest nervous suspense he had ever experienced for Cleveland's comments on the note.[2] When they came they were of unqualified approval. "It's the best thing of the kind I ever read," wrote Cleveland, "and it leads to a conclusion that one cannot escape if he tries—that is, if there is anything in the Monroe Doctrine at all. You show there is a great deal of that, and place it, I think on better and more defensible ground than any of your predecessors—or *mine*." [3] As Cleveland suggested, Olney took the document to Washington and read it to the four members of the Cabinet still there, Carlisle, Lamont, Herbert, and Harmon, after which it was dispatched.

This "twenty-inch gun" of Olney's, as Cleveland later christened it, was far more positive and belligerent in tone than any communication written by Gresham would have been, and showed in many passages the qualities of an aggressive lawyer.[4] It was based upon a broad construction of the Monroe Doctrine. The doctrine, wrote Olney, "has but a single purpose and object. It is that no European power or combination of European powers shall forcibly deprive an American state of the right and power of self-government and of shaping for itself its own political fortunes and destinies." The course pursued by Great Britain he regarded as an interference with these due rights and powers of Venezuela. It "in effect deprives Venezuela of her free agency and puts her under virtual duress"; for Great Britain had practically declared that Venezuela could get none of the debatable land by force, because she was not strong enough; none by treaty, because Great Britain would not agree; and none by arbitration unless she would

[1] James, *Olney*, 105.
[2] *Ibid.*, 110.
[3] July 7, 1895. Olney Papers.
[4] See text in *Foreign Relations*, 1895, I, 545.

first abandon to Great Britain such parts as the latter might designate. Olney also pointed out that the United States had now reached a position where she must demand a settlement:

By the frequent interposition of its good offices at the instance of Venezuela, by constantly urging and promoting the restoration of diplomatic relations between the two countries, by pressing for arbitration of the disputed boundary, by offering to act as arbitrator, by expressing its grave concern whenever new alleged instances of British aggression upon Venezuelan territory have been brought to its notice, the Government of the United States has made it clear to Great Britain and the world that the controversy is one in which both its honor and its interests are involved, and the continuance of which it cannot regard with indifference.

Thus far the note was excellent. But Olney included, and Cleveland strangely approved, certain obiter dicta which were totally unjustified by the facts of history or contemporary politics and which seriously weakened the communication. He wrote that three thousand miles of ocean "make any permanent political union between an European and an American state unnatural and inexpedient"; that "today the United States is practically sovereign on this continent, and its fiat is law upon the subjects to which it confines its interposition"; and that while the United States had thus far been spared great warlike establishments, "with the powers of Europe permanently encamped on American soil, the ideal conditions we have thus far enjoyed cannot be expected to continue." To this Lord Salisbury later found it easy to make a biting reply. He could assert that the union between Great Britain and Canada, or Jamaica, or Guiana, was both expedient and natural, and that the whole British Empire was prepared to maintain the fact. In Canada it was angrily denied that the fiat of the United States was law upon anything north of the Great Lakes.

While this note was being prepared and dispatched, Great Britain was passing from a Liberal to a Tory Government. On June 24, 1895, Rosebery's Ministry fell after its brief year of life, and the general elections in July brought Salisbury again into power. The change seemed to clear the air. Ambassador Bayard wrote Cleveland that "I am anticipating a much more satisfactory condition of things in the treatment and settlement of questions between the United States and Great Britain—as the present Government having a decided majority in Parliament will feel more secure and consequently able to be more definite in action." [1] The Cabinet itself, he added, would "have the great advantage of *united counsels,* and not be dependent upon groups of politicians discordant upon so many leading subjects, and with no distinct principle or purpose in view." Bayard, however, entertained the easy-going belief that it was not necessary to press our views sternly upon the British, and he deeply distrusted all such unstable nations as Venezuela. He warned Cleveland in this same letter that the character of her government "is difficult to comprehend and may always be considered unreliable," and that we should go slow—"if the United States are to have responsibility they must have conceded power and jurisdiction."

The dispute was now in the hands of four of the ablest, most determined, and most virile leaders who have ever controlled the great English-speaking nations. Cleveland had decided that here was a question which must be thrust into the open and *settled;* with bulldog combativeness and tenacity, Olney was supporting him. Lord Salisbury, since Bismarck's retirement the dominant figure among European statesmen, was an opponent worthy of their mettle. An aristocrat, a conservative, a man of blunt honesty tinged with cynicism, an immovable fighter for British interests, it was plain to anyone who looked at his huge shaggy head, sunk in broad shoulders, his heavy jaw, and his penetrating eye that he was not to be encountered lightly. He had beside him as Colonial Secretary a man of quicker parts but equal determination and force, Joseph Chamberlain. No one possessed more parliamentary skill or experience than Chamberlain, and no one was more passionately intent upon preserving and strengthening the Empire. When these four Anglo-Saxons came into collision the result was sure to be interesting. Cleveland and Salisbury were cautious men, and Olney and Chamberlain were devoted to the idea of Anglo-American friendship; but all four subordinated everything else to their convictions regarding national honor, security, and greatness.

III

The response of Lord Salisbury to Olney's note was inexcusably delayed. Bayard wrote Cleveland early in September that he had called the Prime Minister's attention "to your desire to have his reply as soon

---

[1] London, July 18, 1895. Cleveland Papers.

as possible"; and Olney had specifically requested a decision upon the question of arbitration before the President's message in December. But August, September, October passed—and still no reply. Twice the impatient Olney sent inquiries. Meanwhile, though the text of the "twenty-inch gun" had never been revealed, public restiveness was growing. Lodge published an article on Venezuela in the *North American Review* for June in which he used the word "fight" and said that the supremacy of the Monroe Doctrine must be established "at once—peaceably if we can, forcibly if we must." Senator Chandler brought out over his own signature in the Concord *Monitor* an editorial headed "Our Coming War With England—A Prediction," asserting that war was inevitable, and that we ought to begin it, if necessary, to save the mouth of the Orinoco.[1] Leaks from the State Department stimulated such utterances, and irritated Cleveland. "It is very provoking," he wrote Olney, "to have such matters as the Venezuela affair prematurely and blunderingly discussed in the newspapers. It would be easy I know from personal experience to so discourage the approach of newsgatherers and news harvesters as to be free from their vexatious intermeddling, but human nature and the desire to tell something is strong in official station as everywhere else." [2]

Salisbury's delay was not due, as Cleveland perhaps supposed, to discourtesy or any British desire to procrastinate the question. The Prime Minister was immersed in the Near Eastern problem, while his subordinates permitted him to make an error as to the date when Congress sat. His law-officers also wished ample time to compose a strong argument. Chamberlain particularly feared that if Great Britain once accepted the principle of arbitration the wideflung Empire would be whittled down all over the world by neighboring states which concocted boundary claims. Meanwhile, Bayard had totally failed to make it clear that Cleveland and Olney regarded this as an acute issue, which must be terminated at once. The grave, courteous Southern gentleman had been a peacemaker all his life, first in the Senate between North and South, then in the State Department between America and foreign nations; and his whole temperament and training inclined him to conciliation. On his visits to Salisbury he somehow diffused an impression that Olney's blunt note was not to be taken with complete

[1] See *Public Opinion*, Nov. 21, 1895.
[2] Oct. 6, 1895. Olney Papers.

seriousness. Henry White, a shrewd though prejudiced observer, thought him the least efficient of all our later ministers or ambassadors in London.[1] Olney also thought him a misfit, while Lord Salisbury confidentially spoke of him as an "amateur diplomat"; in growing irritation, Olney concluded during the summer that he ought to be removed and actually proposed the step to the President. But Cleveland, while admitting that Bayard had done badly, thought that it was too late to recall him and that it would do more harm than good. Olney's later distrust was undisguised.[2]

When on December 2 Cleveland sent his message to Congress there was still no British reply, and the President contented himself with briefly and emphatically stating his former views on Venezuela. He then departed on a duck-hunting trip. If the reply came, he told Olney, the latter should keep its contents secret and, if he had time, block out a message to be sent to Congress with it. "If I were here I should not be hurried in the matter even if the Congress should begin grinding again the resolution-of-inquiry mill."

On December 7 Sir Julian Pauncefote brought Salisbury's note to Olney at the latter's residence. It consisted of two sections, one dealing with the Monroe Doctrine and the other with the Venezuelan boundary. As for the former, Salisbury offered a strict-constructionist view, denying that Monroe's famous statement of principles justified our government in insisting, whenever a European nation had a frontier dispute in the Western Hemisphere, that it must refer the quarrel to arbitration. As for the latter, he maintained that Great Britain had made only the most conservative claims to territory; that Venezuela had for decades refused any reasonable settlement; and that the British ministers could never let her drag her more unreasonable pretensions before an international tribunal. They would arbitrate everything beyond the Schomburgk line. "But they cannot consent to entertain, nor to submit to the arbitration of another Power or of foreign jurists, however eminent, claims based on the extravagant pretensions of Spanish officials in the last century, and involving the transfer of large numbers of British subjects, who have for many years enjoyed the settled rule of a British colony, to a nation of different race or language." In short,

---

[1] Nevins, *Henry White*, 111 ff.
[2] For a tart summary by Olney of Bayard's course, see his letter of March 6, 1901, to Cleveland reviewing the whole affair; Cleveland Papers. Cf. C. S. Hamlin, MS Diary.

Salisbury would not budge.[1]

His note was not only positive and forcible, but in some degree provocative. It had an irritatingly didactic tone, which led Andrew D. White to remark that it was written in a cynical *Saturday Review* high-Tory style.[2] Asperity of phrasing particularly marked those passages which replied to Olney's remark that the union between Great Britain and her American colonies was inexpedient and unnatural; and the very fact that asperity was here justified probably angered Olney the more.

The result, as everyone knows, was Cleveland's special Venezuelan message of December 17. Few episodes in our diplomatic history have received so much study. We now know every factual detail: how Olney, with whom Cleveland had left instructions, wrote out the draft message to Congress, and had it copied by his Boston clerk on December 13; how Cleveland returned to the White House on Sunday afternoon, the 15th, and held a conference with Olney and Lamont; how he sat up all night rewriting Olney's document; and how when he finished at dawn, as he said later, he could not tell which sentences were Olney's and which his own. The message asked Congress to appropriate money for a commission to determine the true Venezuelan boundary, and declared that it would be the duty of the United States to maintain this boundary against any aggression. Congress received the document with lusty cheers. "Senator Lodge," cabled the London *Times'* correspondent, "is reported as saying, in answer to a question as to how he liked the message, that he was bubbling over with delight. There could not be a more sinister indication of the sense in which the message is understood."

The excessively sharp and even belligerent language of the message can be more readily explained than excused. Olney felt that nothing but a severe cut across Salisbury's knuckles would arrest his attention. He later apologized for his admittedly bumptious phrases by saying that "in English eyes the United States was then so completely a negligible quantity that it was believed only words the equivalent of blows would be really effective."[3] So far so good; but Olney's mere irascibility, his uncontrollable temper, also played a part in the phrasing. Cleveland

---

[1] For Salisbury's reply, see *Foreign Relations*, 1895, I, 563–576.
[2] White, *Autobiography*, II, 123.
[3] James, *Olney*, 140.

was in part thinking of peace. He believed, as Olney tells us, that if the dispute between England and Venezuela, which had already caused a rupture of diplomatic relations, ran on, the forces of the two nations would come into armed collision; Congress would then take the bit in its teeth; and we should be involved in the conflict.[1] He later told a friend that his aim was at one sharp stroke to bring the whole matter into his own hands, compel England to yield to arbitration, and put Congress in a position where it could not interfere; "my action, you see, has been in the interests of peace—permanent peace."[2] So far, again, so good; but Cleveland was also influenced by Olney's hot temper. With his usual lack of imagination, he did not foresee the effect that the more truculent passages would have on excitable people. Most of this truculent language was Olney's. As in dealing with the Chicago strike, the Secretary carried Cleveland further than he would have gone alone or should have gone. A comparison of the close of Olney's draft with Cleveland's final version shows this clearly:[3]

OLNEY	CLEVELAND
When such report is made and accepted, it will then be the duty of this government to communicate to Great Britain the boundary line thus ascertained, and to give notice that any appropriation of territory or exercise of jurisdiction by Great Britain beyond that line, except with the consent of Venezuela, will be regarded by this government as a wilful aggression upon rights and interests of the United States which this government cannot suffer to go undefended.	When such report is made and accepted, it will, in my opinion, be the duty of the United States to resist by every means in its power, as a wilful aggression upon its rights and interests, the appropriation by Great Britain of any lands or the exercise of governmental jurisdiction over any territory which after investigation we have determined of right belongs to Venezuela.
In making these recommendations I do not act without a keen sense of responsibility nor without a vivid realization of all possible consequences . . . I am nevertheless firm in the faith—in which I doubt not to have the hearty concurrence of all the American people—that of all the ca-	In making these recommendations I am fully alive to the responsibility incurred, and keenly realize all the consequences that may follow.
	I am, nevertheless, firm in my conviction that . . . there is no calamity which a great nation can invite which equals that which follows from a supine submission to wrong and injustice, and the consequent loss of na-

---

[1] *Ibid.*, 138.
[2] A. B. Farquhar, "Recollections of Grover Cleveland," *Harper's Weekly*, July 21, 1908.
[3] Texts in James, *Olney*, 120, 121.

lamities to which a great nation can subject itself none are more to be deprecated or more to be shunned than those which follow from a supine submission to wrong and injustice and the consequent loss of national honor and self-respect.

tional self-respect and honor, beneath which are shielded and defended a people's safety and greatness.

Cleveland might have restrained his phrasing if he had consulted other members of his Cabinet, but he did not. "Carlisle," writes C. S. Hamlin in his diary, "says that if Cleveland had taken his friends into his counsel he would never have put the threat of war into his message. Carlisle implied that Cleveland had not consulted at all with his Cabinet about the matter. Carlisle thought that, while Cleveland's position, both in the correspondence and message, was impregnable, the *form* of both was unfortunate, and could have been expressed in a more diplomatic manner with just as much force." [1] Secretary Morton also manifested displeasure. The truth is that an equally vigorous document might have been so written as to avoid what Carl Schurz well called "a grievous break in Mr. Cleveland's otherwise so dignified and statesmanlike foreign policy." The methods the President employed proved successful. But he had taken an unjustifiable risk of war. He had precipitated a break in the stock market, with a decided setback to economic recovery. And there were incidental consequences of a highly unfortunate character.

The worst of these consequences lay in two waves of feeling which swept the country—a primary wave of warlike enthusiasm, followed by a secondary and vaguer wave of imperialist sentiment. For three days the country seemed to rise in almost unanimous support of Cleveland. Congress instantly appropriated $100,000 for the boundary commission. Senators Lodge, Chandler, and Cushman K. Davis all indulged in bellicose outbursts. "War would be a good thing even if we get whipped," declared Senator Stewart, "for it would rid us of English bank rule." Dana's *Sun* and Watterson's *Courier-Journal* trumpeted joyously of a possible conflict, and the Washington *Post* burst out delightedly: "It is the call to arms; the jingoes were right after all, and it is not to be the fashion henceforth to sneer at patriots and soldiers." The Irish National Alliance issued a manifesto tendering the govern-

[1] MS Diary, Dec. 17, 1895; Jan. 5, 1896.

ment the services of 100,000 soldiers.[1] Thenceforward the change which
had been subtly declaring itself in the popular attitude toward foreign
embroilments and foreign expansion was accelerated.

IV

Fortunately, in the best circles an immediate current of counter-
feeling manifested itself. Pulitzer's *World* denounced the message as a
terrible blunder, and so did Godkin's *Evening Post*. The Springfield
Republican declared that while it was ready to support a stiff attitude
toward Great Britain, it could never endorse Cleveland's stand in asserting in advance that the findings of the commission must be given
armed support by the United States. A score of other newspapers were
strong in condemnation, and some accused Cleveland of striking for
a third term. Governor Russell of Massachusetts wrote the President
that "public opinion here is extremely strong and earnest in favor of
a peaceful and honorable solution of the difficulty"; [2] and Hewitt was
so amazed and indignant that he informed Lord Salisbury that Cleveland must have been drunk. John Bassett Moore, already the foremost American authority on international law, sent William L. Wilson
a vigorous letter of protest, which Wilson turned over to Cleveland.
Wrote Moore, in part:

> The whole system of arbitration presupposes that nations will be reasonable
> in their claims. The claim of Venezuela to all territory west of the Essequibo is
> not a scrupulous claim. The talk about Dutch usurpations is but an admission
> of English title.
> Instead of asserting that arbitration is the only satisfactory way of settling
> the question, I should say that it would be a very unsatisfactory way of at-
> tempting it; and in so saying I do not forget that Lord Granville once con-
> sented to lump boundary and all other questions in a general arbitration. We
> have arbitrated boundary disputes, and so has Great Britain, but never, so
> far as I am informed, where a line has not previously been agreed upon by
> direct negotiation. Governments are not in the habit of resigning their functions
> so completely into the hands of arbitrators as to say, "We have no boundaries;
> make some for us. . . ."
> Venezuela has represented again and again that the question of the mouth
> of the Orinoco is the "knot of the controversy"; and I observe that Mr. Ed-

---

[1] *Public Opinion*, Jan. 2, 1896. The Catholic press applauded the message; most Protestant organs bitterly assailed it.
[2] Dec. 23, 1895. Russell Papers.

munds, in a talk at Philadelphia the other evening, said he hoped that the President would not permit Venezuela to be "squeezed" out of the mouth of that river. Yet it is a fact that Great Britain has again and again offered to yield that point, if Venezuela would only settle. In 1890 Sir T. H. Sanderson, Under Secretary of State, acting for Lord Salisbury, offered to negotiate directly for a frontier of mutual convenience, following as far as possible all natural boundaries, and to that end to relinquish freely all territory adjacent to the Orinoco.

Cleveland quite properly made no public effort to amplify the reasons and arguments he had given in his message; but he did write a long explanatory letter to Ambassador Bayard.[1] After thanking him for a recent communication and the gift of a hunting stool, he remarked that "I am very sorry indeed that I cannot fully understand your very apparent thought and feeling on the Venezuelan question; and you must believe me to be entirely sincere when I say that I think my want of understanding on the subject is somehow my own fault." He recalled that in his first Administration he had steered clear of the Monroe Doctrine, which he imperfectly comprehended and knew to be "troublesome." Yet he had always been clear, he wrote, that the doctrine was not obsolete, but should be defended and maintained in any "state of facts" that required its use. In his opinion such a state of facts had now arisen. He did not see why the extensions of European systems and jurisdictions in the New World might not be effected as surely and unwarrantedly under the guise of boundary claims as by invasion. England since 1887 had been steadily if slowly enlarging her boundary claims, her refusal to let these expanding claims be examined by impartial arbiters had been "intensely disappointing," and he had acted to stop the absorption of Venezuelan territory. He added some words upon the British lack of generosity. "It would have been exceedingly gratifying and a very handsome thing to do, if, in the midst of all this Administration has had to do in attempts to stem the tide of 'jingoism,' she had yielded or rather conceded something (if she called it so, which I do not) for our sake." The United States did not threaten or invite war, he concluded, but simply declared that it would ascertain Venezuela's rights and protect them.

The effect of the message on Bayard had been, as we may imagine, profoundly depressing. He never lost his deep friendship and admira-

---

[1] McElroy, *Grover Cleveland*, II, 192 ff.

tion for Cleveland, but for the moment his faith in him was shaken. Yet in the private memorandum on the subject which he set down at Brancepeth Castle, Durham, he admitted in spite of himself that Cleveland's suspicions of England had much basis: [1]

I received Mr. Cleveland's letter yesterday, and carried it in my pocket to the shooting. It depressed me greatly, as it inclines me to the belief that his faculties have been unsettled and his comprehension of the condition of affairs is defective.

I fear he has made a gross and great error of judgment and has been too *precipitate*, for I do not see why he should abandon suddenly his attitude of conservatism and go apparently into the camp of aggressiveness. It is true that Great Britain has most unwisely disregarded the application so earnestly and frequently put forth by the United States to heal the Venezuelan sore, and relieve Venezuela and the United States of the fear that there was an indefinite plan of British occupation in the heart of America, involving a purpose of extensive domination originating in private possessions, and backed up by imperial force in the end. It certainly was in the power of Lord Salisbury to have disabused the public mind of any such intent, but several minor events have indicated a disposition to press forward without abatement the tentative lines of Great Britain. There is a profession of continuity of action in the succeeding administrations, but I fear it is only an *aggressive* continuity.

If Dr. Jameson had made a successful raid into Johannesburg, I can scarcely doubt that government would have sustained him—and yet his act would have been equally *without law*. Perhaps *now* more heed will be given to the remonstrance of the United States in the South American case. That I think should have been the course of the United States—earnestly and clearly to have stated the facts of the case, and then to have gravely protested against the refusal of Great Britain to submit her alarming and indefinite claims in the Orinoco region.

We have clear evidence that Cleveland was not affected by the hostile criticism of his message. On December 28 he saw Charles S. Hamlin. "Cleveland talked very freely over the Venezuelan boundary dispute," writes Hamlin in his diary, "showing the most intense interest in the matter. Cleveland said the honor of the country demanded that a firm stand be taken against infringement of the Monroe Doctrine. Said a great principle was at stake which the whole country would before long appreciate. Did not show the slightest sign of yielding to the clamor in New England and New York. Had evidently made up his mind cautiously and carefully and was firm as a rock in his conclusions.

[1] Jan. 10, 1896. Bayard Papers.

Said he had hoped to send Congress a much shorter message but he could not condense it further. Said he had received many letters from Boston, mentioning Moses Williams, Edward Atkinson, and Mr. Parkinson, his neighbor at Gray Gables. Said he had just answered Parkinson's letter. Was very much provoked at Atkinson; thought him almost insane. Showed great sorrow at speech of John E. Russell before New England Free Trade League; said he did not object to any opinion formed by him, but thought that, considering their intimate relations and the practical tokens of his confidence in Russell, he might at least have asked the League to suspend judgment until the evidence could be examined."

Meanwhile, he had been driving doggedly ahead with plans for the boundary commission, which he selected without consulting Olney.[1] Advice fell upon him in a steady shower. From Boston came a petition signed by Atkinson, Henry Lee Higginson, and others, asking that to ensure impartiality he appoint no one but foreigners; and many correspondents suggested that Gladstone be named. Cleveland had little difficulty in making up his list, though George L. Rives—who disapproved his message—declined. It included David J. Brewer, associate justice of the Supreme Court; Richard H. Alvey, chief justice of the court of appeals of the District of Columbia; Andrew D. White; Frederic R. Coudert, who had been one of the American counsel in the Bering Sea arbitration; and Daniel Coit Gilman. At its first meeting the commission elected Justice Brewer president.

The high character of the panel tended in some degree to reassure the public. Nevertheless, at a meeting of the Chamber of Commerce of the State of New York on January 2, 1896, Carl Schurz in an impassioned speech proposed that the President deviate from his course. While commending the commissioners, he pointed out that London might not accept their decision under a threat of war. He thought that Great Britain should be invited to appoint an equal number of commissioners to act with ours; that the two governments should agree upon some presiding officer of eminent character and ability; and that this joint commission should act simply as a board of inquiry or advisory council, to report to their respective governments. The Chamber fell enthusiastically into line behind the proposal, adopting a suitable resolu-

[1] C. S. Hamlin, MS Diary, Jan. 5, 1896. Cleveland told Carlisle that he would disregard Olney. Olney disapproved the selection of Judge Alvey.

tion and appointing an eminent committee—Hewitt, Schurz, John Bigelow, Oscar S. Straus, Seth Low, and others—to promote the plan. Of
course this came to nothing. But Cleveland watched such incidents
nervously, for he was fearful lest the negotiations be injuriously affected by them. In March he actually dispatched C. S. Hamlin to
Norwich, Conn., to ask David A. Wells not to publish an article he
had prepared attacking the position of the United States on the Venezuelan controversy. Hamlin brought proofsheets back to the White
House, and Cleveland made certain changes in the article, to which
Wells very amiably agreed.[1]

It is often said that the situation was saved by the Jameson Raid
and the Kaiser's telegram of January 2, 1896, to President Kruger of
the Transvaal. But actually it had been saved before. The Kaiser's
indiscretion simply dramatized the difference between the British attitude toward Germany and that toward the United States. After Cleveland's deliverance there had been a rush of peace messages in both
directions across the Atlantic; the Prince of Wales, Lord Rosebery,
and many others had hastened to pat the eagle's head, and the tone
of the press was conciliatory. After the Kaiser's step there were warlike preparations, shouts of defiance, and appeals to jingo sentiment.[2]
A squadron was mobilized to patrol the channel. For a time there was
a genuine war scare, for an Anglo-German collision would have meant
a general European conflict. Meanwhile, the expressions of Anglo-
American amity increased in number and cordiality. Wide publicity
was given to an article by James Bryce in the *North American Review*
for February, 1896, in which he explained that the British people had
not really known anything about the Venezuela question; adding in a
grieved way, that what most astonished the English "is the disclosure
of a hostility to Great Britain in considerable sections of the American people," for the British, liking America far better than any other
nation, had even indulged in the hope of a permanent alliance.

V

Observers could take satisfaction, within a month after the message,
in reflecting that it had actually and unexpectedly improved Anglo-

[1] MS Diary, March 16, 1896. Whitney had the historian John Bach McMaster write
an article supporting Cleveland in the N. Y. *Times.*
[2] Cf. *Public Opinion*, Jan. 16, 1896.

American relations. It had done this partly by ripping away a veil from English eyes, and partly by stimulating many Americans to send fervent expressions of cordiality in an effort to counteract Cleveland's brusqueness. Before 1896 was a year old there was a suggestion that the new cordiality might be seized upon as a basis for a general arbitration treaty between the two nations—a suggestion which Cleveland warmly approved. On January 15 Balfour told a Manchester audience that the time must come when some statesman of greater authority even than Monroe "will lay down the doctrine that between English-speaking peoples war is impossible." No one, it should be said, responded to such sentiments more cordially than Olney. Two years later he was uttering before a Harvard audience a striking prediction of 1917: [1]

There is a patriotism of race as well as of country—and the Anglo-American is as little likely to be indifferent to the one as to the other. Family quarrels there have been heretofore and doubtless will be again, and the two peoples, at the safe distance which the broad Atlantic interposes, take with each other liberties of speech which only the fondest and dearest relatives indulge in. Nevertheless, that they would be found standing together against any alien foe by whom either was menaced by destruction or irreparable calamity, it is not permissible to doubt. . . .

Cleveland could also feel happy that his message, however unfortunate in some of its expressions, really did promote a settlement. When Parliament met in February, 1896, Lord Salisbury declared that "from some points of view the mixture of the United States in this matter may conduce to results which will be satisfactory to us more rapidly than if the United States had not interfered." [2] This was a striking admission. After long months of negotiation, conducted chiefly in Washington, the boundary was referred to an arbitral tribunal of five, British settlements of fifty years' duration being excepted from the territory in dispute. The ultimate decision of this body, handed down in the autumn of 1899, upheld the principal British contentions, but at two points it gave Venezuela territory within the Schomburgk line.

To the deeper implications of this whole episode Cleveland was almost certainly oblivious. He was determined to get a prompt settlement of the question in harmony with his principles of justice and his in-

[1] Boston *Transcript*, March 2, 1898.
[2] A. L. P. Dennis, *Adventures in American Diplomacy*, 40, 41; *Hansard*, 4th series, vol. 37, c. 52, 53.

terpretation of the Monroe Doctrine, and by his smashing blow on the table he got it. That was all he wished, and with that he was satisfied. But he got very much more. Thereafter a broad interpretation of the Monroe Doctrine came into more general acceptance. American public opinion, suddenly awakening to the importance of the nation in world affairs, accepted a new bias toward vigorous action in foreign relations and the acceptance of overseas responsibilities—a bias thoroughly distasteful to Cleveland. Finally, the clearing of the atmosphere between Great Britain and the United States initiated a virtual *entente* that within a generation was to prove of the profoundest importance in world history.

Chapter XXXV   The Storm at Its Worst: The Morgan Bonds

FOR a week in the summer of 1894 the great majority of Americans had enthusiastically applauded Cleveland's course in the Chicago strike, and for half a week in 1895 almost the whole nation seemed to rise in praise of his Venezuela message. It is an ironic fact that while his finest displays of courage and sagacity brought him nothing but abuse, the two most vulnerable acts of his second Administration were cheered to the echo. The idea that Cleveland never cared for the sweets of popularity is a misconception. He often said that, amid the denunciation and misrepresentation which he continually encountered, he drew immense comfort from the occasional voices of confidence and appreciation that reached him. But by now he had steeled himself against a storm that seemed to come from every quarter and never to let up in its howling rage. Any reader of his private papers in these dark years must be struck by the evidence that as troubles thickened, he turned more and more to the simple religious faith of his fathers. "I know too there is a God," he wrote Richard Watson Gilder, "but I do not know his purposes, nor when their results will appear. I know the clouds will roll away, but I do not know who, before that time, will be drowned in their floods." [1]

There were periods when everything seemed to go wrong. The twelve-month from July 1, 1894, to July 1, 1895, might well be called the *année terrible* of American history between Reconstruction and the World War. On the heels of the Chicago strike and the failure of the Wilson bill came the disastrous elections of 1894, and their gloom had not lifted when the Supreme Court accentuated the class antagonism of the day by annulling the income tax enactment. The depression reached its very nadir in the winter of 1894–95, facing the government with the necessity of new bond issues. One was floated in the fall of 1894 and another early in 1895—both amid a clamor of billingsgate flung at the President, Secretary Carlisle, and the bankers. Meanwhile, Cleveland's political isolation was steadily growing clearer and icier. It is not strange that a note of desperation sometimes crept into his letters.

[1] Gilder, *Grover Cleveland*, 123.

"I have been dreadfully forlorn these many months, and sorely perplexed and tried," he wrote Bayard in the spring of 1895.[1] "Think of it! Not a man in the Senate with whom I can be on terms of absolute confidence." After speaking of the cowed and doubtful position of even Vilas and Gray, and of "the malevolent change in our public life since you and I worked together here," he went on: "I have at my side a Cabinet composed of pure-minded, patriotic, loyal men. I sometimes feel guilty when I recall the troubles I have induced them to share with me. In our hand to hand conflict our triumphs are many, but I am afraid as we triumph our party loses and the country does not gain as it should; and yet what would the condition be without us?" He struck again the religious note—he was "profoundly grateful for a guidance that has thus far kept me from pitfalls"; and he closed with a reference to his domestic consolations. "Mrs. Cleveland and the babies are well. God be praised for that! I often think that if things should go wrong at that end of the house, I should abandon the ship."

II

Tom Reed, taking the prophet's mantle, had remarked early in 1894 that "The Democratic mortality will be so great next fall that their dead will be buried in trenches and marked 'unknown.'" He added later, "till the supply of trenches gives out."[2] The party was now irremediably divided, and large elements were hopelessly discouraged and embittered. In Ohio hardly a single important Democratic newspaper was supporting Cleveland; the Cincinnati *Enquirer* viciously attacked him because its millionaire owner, John McLean, who lived in Washington, had a personal grudge, while the Cleveland *Plain Dealer* had broken with him over the Wilson tariff. Senator McPherson of New Jersey, rebuffed in a request for patronage, told Cleveland that he would make no more recommendations for appointments and never call again at the White House. "Suit yourself, Mr. McPherson, suit yourself," said Cleveland. "I can stand it if you can." Senator Cockrell of Missouri gave the same notice.[3] In Illinois Representative Fithian was declaring that the party had carried many a heavy load, "but it cannot carry Cleveland and win this fall." Bryan in August, after an-

[1] McElroy, *Grover Cleveland*, II, 89 ff.; Feb. 13, 1895.
[2] Robinson, *Reed*, 321.
[3] Cleveland to R. W. Gilder, July 27, 1902. Cleveland Papers.

nouncing his candidacy for the Senate on a platform which demanded free coinage, tariff reform, the income tax, popular election of Senators, government telegraphs, and stricter control of railroads, stumped Nebraska harshly assailing Cleveland at every opportunity. In the South Tom Watson and Ben Tillman vied with one another in venomous hostility.

Cleveland viewed the result of the election, which Champ Clark called the greatest slaughter of the innocents since Herod, with mixed feelings. The slain indeed lay in windrows. In place of the 219 Democrats and 127 Republicans in the old House there were 104 Democrats and 244 Republicans in the new, and both branches of Congress were now strongly opposed to the Administration. In New York Senator Hill, without resigning his office, had consented to run for governor, and despite a bold campaign, in which he sarcastically spoke of his audiences as "coming to see the man with hoofs and horns," was overwhelmed.[1] Such a Democratic humiliation was disheartening. Yet Cleveland found satisfaction in thinking that the party had been chastened for its sins on the tariff and the silver question. He was not grieved by the check administered to Hill. He was particularly pleased by the defeat of Bland, who in his famous "Parting of the Ways" speech of August 11, 1893, had served notice that the Western Democrats would place free silver above party loyalty, and who was now beaten by the loss of Cleveland votes and the nomination of a separate Populist candidate.[2]

The most ominous feature of the election was the polling of almost a million and a half of Populist votes. Their movement—the greatest third-party movement in its effect upon government that the country has ever seen—was a flood that was rapidly submerging most of the political landmarks between the Mississippi and the Rockies. They had held their first national convention in 1891, and that year had elected their first Senators, Peffer and Kyle. In 1892 they had carried a half dozen States, with twenty-two electoral votes, for General Weaver. Now in the fall of 1894 they polled a vote 42 per cent greater than in 1892, electing six United States Senators (though only four openly called themselves Populists), seven Representatives, twenty-one State executive officials, 150 State Senators, and 315 State Representatives.[3] What

---

[1] Alexander, *Four Famous New Yorkers*, 228.
[2] *Public Opinion*, Nov. 15, 1894; R. L. O'Brien to author, June 11, 1930.
[3] Hicks, *The Populist Revolt*, 238 ff.

would happen in 1896? The two old parties were rapidly being split in two by the silver issue. Even the Republicans were nervous. Jones of Nevada, who had sat in the Senate since 1873 as a staunch Republican, had now formally announced his withdrawal, declaring that "the great party which unflinchingly faced the slave power does not dare attack the money power"; and it seemed likely that before long Wolcott and Teller of Colorado, Dubois and Shoup of Idaho, and others would follow him. What would be the result if the Populists fused all the silver forces of the nation into one compact party? What would happen if the silverite element in either party, allying itself with the Populists, captured the old party organization and name?

This last question was one which the Democrats, with so much of their strength concentrated in the South and West, had to ask themselves with special uneasiness. Seymour, Tilden, and Manning had all been sound money men, and Cleveland, carrying forward their great tradition, had thus far held the party true to the gold standard. But he had done so only by pressure upon a hostile majority. In 1892 it had been estimated that three-fifths of the Democratic party was for free silver and two-fifths for the gold standard, and that in the Republican party the proportions were roughly reversed. Cleveland and the other Eastern leaders—Russell, Whitney, Carlisle, Fairchild—tried to regard the silver question as settled by the repeal of the silver-purchase law, but the West refused to accept that view. The succession of misfortunes which the Administration encountered in 1894–95 steadily weakened the conservative element in the party and strengthened the radicals. In the background all the great economic forces of the time appeared, for the moment, to be working for Bryan, Bland, and Tillman.

III

By election day in 1894 it was evident that a second bond issue to maintain the public credit was unescapable. The cash in the Treasury barely exceeded a hundred millions, and of this only some sixty-odd millions was in gold. Under the crushing weight of the depression the national revenues had fallen off heavily. The delay in passing the tariff bill, with other factors, had resulted in a decrease of imports for the first half of the year which broke all records in time of peace, and the returns under the Wilson-Gorman tariff proved disappointing. Gold was still exported steadily, no less than $73,700,000 being shipped abroad in the twelve months ending November 30, 1894. This was the consequence not of an adverse balance of trade, for it had now become favorable, but of foreign apprehensions of a financial collapse in the United States, and the consequent sale of American securities.[1] During the spring of 1894 Cleveland had hoped that the first bond issue would see the Treasury through. In an optimistic statement in June he had emphasized two great changes for the better in the situation: the favorable shift in foreign trade, and the fact that the government no longer had to buy silver bullion and issue gold obligations to pay for it. But the loss of revenue, the gold exports, and the destruction of public confidence made the first bond issue a mere stopgap. On November 14, 1894, with the gold reserve now down to $61,000,000, Carlisle issued a circular calling for bids on another $50,000,000 of five per cent ten-year bonds.

Cleveland and Carlisle had learned much from the first issue, and this time two precautions were taken [2]—one to make sure that the Treasury would not be again caught without subscriptions 48 hours before its books closed, and the second to make sure that the bankers would not simply draw gold out of one Treasury window to pay for bonds at another. The date set for the closing of the bids was November 24 at high noon. Nearly a week earlier Carlisle wrote all the important Eastern bankers asking their opinions upon the prospects for success. James Stillman and others responded that the loan was sure to be oversubscribed. Carlisle simultaneously took steps to prevent bidders from paying for their bonds by using legal tenders to withdraw gold from the Treasury. He not only induced the banks to refuse to aid customers in such transactions, but announced that he would publish the names of those who engaged in them. As a result a number of contemplated subscriptions, including one from Fairchild's bank, were withdrawn.

On the day appointed, in the presence of officers of the Treasury, J. P. Morgan, other New York financiers, and two newspapermen, Carlisle laid on the table of his office a black box containing the bids and opened it. The result was the award of the entire issue to a single syndicate of bankers. Altogether there were 486 bids, for a total of nearly $180,000,000. The syndicate had offered to take the whole of

[1] *Commercial and Financial Chronicle*, Jan. 5, 1895.
[2] Barnes, *Carlisle*, 358 ff.

the issue, but not any fraction, at 117.077. It was found that this would yield the Treasury almost $50,000 more than the aggregate of the other highest bids. Carlisle pointed out that there was also an important advantage in taking this bid in the fact that all the gold would be furnished outside and none drawn from the Treasury. "It is also more convenient and less expensive . . . to deal with one party rather than with many." Altogether, the government had made a fairly good bargain. Early in December the gold reserve rose to $111,000,000.[1] The syndicate did not come out so well. Its efforts to dispose of the bonds were impeded by the continued financial difficulties of the time, and in the end—though the West never believed this—it actually lost money.

Yet the success scored by the Administration was of brief duration. As A. D. Noyes says, while the first bond issue had sustained the Treasury for ten months, the second did so for only ten weeks.[2] As the winter of 1894–95 set in, times seemed as hard as ever. Unemployment, misery, and even starvation stalked in every large city. In financial circles confidence sank to a lower ebb than before as men perceived that the Congressional majority were still bent on free coinage, and as they heard the Western clamor for heavier greenback issues, repeal of the prohibitive tax on State banknotes, and other inflationist schemes. Bank failures continued numerous, and it was obvious that more and more people were hoarding gold. On December 15 Washington dispatches announced that legal tenders were again being presented in large numbers at the Treasury for gold, and that a third bond issue loomed up as inescapable. When December closed it was known that $31,000,000 in gold had been taken out that month, and that the reserve was again far under the hundred-million mark. A new wave of alarm possessed the East, withdrawals increased, and during January $45,000,000 more was taken from the Federal vaults. The Treasury was like a critical patient who, having received two hypodermic injections, lay at the point of collapse while his doctors frantically prepared a third.

Cleveland had watched the patient, as his papers show, in an agony of anxiety. In his December message he had lectured Congress vigorously and pledged himself to fight to the last for gold payments.[3] Noth-

[1] Barnes, *Carlisle*, 359.
[2] A. D. Noyes, *Forty Years of American Finance*.
[3] *Messages and Papers*, VIII, 786–788.

ing, he wrote, could be more senseless than the relation existing between the legal tenders, the gold reserve held to meet them, and the methods which had to be used to replenish this reserve. Even if the legal tenders could be cancelled on redemption, the reserve would be perilously small. "But these obligations when received and redeemed in gold are not cancelled, but reissued, and may do duty many times by way of drawing gold from the Treasury. Thus we have an endless chain in operation." Meanwhile, Congress would not permit bond issues except on the hard terms of the old act of 1875. Sardonically, Cleveland remarked that he could not believe that anybody wished the government to default or to go to a silver basis—for he knew well that the free silver men were praying daily that it might be forced to the silver standard. But he served warning that "as long as no better authority for bond issues is allowed than at present exists, such authority will be utilized whenever and as often as it becomes necessary to maintain a sufficient gold reserve, and in abundant time to save the credit of our country. . . ."

His anxiety increased as late in January more alarming news came from the Treasury: in nine days almost twenty millions in gold was withdrawn. Even large corporations began to join the ranks of the gold-hoarders. A feeling of panic was rising; "the banks are beginning a general run—I mean those who have heretofore abstained," wrote C. N. Jordan, who was in charge of the New York sub-treasury. Carlisle had just brought before Congress a currency reform plan on which he had been working for several years, and had hoped to press it, but now it had to be thrust aside. Cleveland on January 24 received a nervous letter from Isidor Straus: [1]

I had occasion to visit Wall Street yesterday, and finding a very grave feeling of apprehension, and talk of extraordinary heavy shipments of gold, some putting the figures as high as five million dollars this week, I took it upon myself to ascertain from different sources the immediate cause for so acute a condition.

There is no doubt that Europe is thoroughly aroused as to our inability to continue on a gold basis, and they are consequently selling their holdings in American investments as rapidly as the market will take them without inordinately depressing quotations. That naturally calls for heavy gold shipments, which nothing but a restoration of confidence in the stability of our currency can arrest.

[1] Cleveland Papers.

In my humble opinion Mr. Carlisle should give up all ideas of his bill for the present, and concentrate his influences on legislation that will authorize the issue of gold bonds—the retirement of the greenbacks and Treasury notes and the permission to national banks to issue currency up to the par value of the bonds.

This same day Cleveland spent several hours examining a "private and strictly confidential" memorandum from the Treasury on the government's financial condition.[1] It stated that the actual gold reserve was once more down to $68,000,000, and that withdrawals were rapidly continuing despite the existence of a large currency surplus, which in normal times would ensure an ample reserve. "This," wrote Cleveland on the margin, "negatives the assertion that larger revenues would cure our ills." The report further stated that a heavy mass of gold certificates was outstanding against the reserve, and that so much of the reserve was in bullion that the government had only $22,000,000 in gold coin to distribute among the Treasury, nine sub-treasuries, and three mints. "A sudden run upon the sub-treasury at New York—the banks of which hold upward of twenty millions of gold certificates—would precipitate disaster, and cause the government to suspend specie payments." Cleveland wrote in the margin, "except for a resort to our gold bullion in payment of certificates." The report went on to urge that Congress should immediately authorize Carlisle to procure enough gold to keep the reserve up to the hundred-million mark, and to obtain it either in the United States or abroad, to be deposited temporarily, if he liked, in England, France, or Germany. "The gold," wrote Cleveland, "ought to be in our own hands, and it would be very desirable to withdraw it from abroad."

Finally, stated the report, Congress should take such action that all the greenbacks and Sherman Act certificates "hereafter redeemed in gold when received should not be reissued except in return for a deposit in gold coin of equal value." And here Cleveland had written in positive strokes: "This or the retirement of them by the substitution of bonds is *the* important thing."

IV

It was clearly necessary to do something, and at once. Though efforts were made to get as much of the Treasury's scattered stock of gold coin

[1] Cleveland Papers.

into New York as possible, on January 28 the sub-treasury there had only $13,639,000 of it, a dangerously inadequate amount. On that day, by special message, Cleveland made a last appeal to Congress. After speaking of the recommendations in his annual message, he declared that "the situation has so changed and the emergency now appears so threatening" that different or additional legislation was required. He pleaded again that the Treasury be authorized to sell three per cent long-term bonds, in small denominations, payable in gold; these bonds to be made the basis for the issue of an equivalent amount of banknotes by national banks which held them. He asked also that the Treasury be authorized to redeem and cancel the greenbacks and the Sherman Act notes as fast as they came in, thus destroying the endless chain; and that the payment of all important duties be required in gold, to assure a constant gold flow into the Treasury. A measure embodying the main features of Cleveland's plan, the Springer bill, was at once reported favorably to the House. If it could have been passed, it would have placed the Treasury instantly on firm ground and dissipated all the black dread and uneasiness which pervaded financial circles. The Eastern press loudly applauded Cleveland's recommendations, and many commercial bodies and business men vehemently urged their Representatives to pass it.

But the West was obdurate. It was plain that the silver party, far from caring to relieve the embarrassments of the Treasury, wished to use them as a club to compel the passage of free silver legislation. A thousand clamoring voices showed that majority sentiment south of the Ohio and west of the Mississippi was in the ugliest of moods. "Outside the hotbeds of goldbuggery and Shylockism," exclaimed the Atlanta *Constitution*, "the people of this country do not care how soon gold payments are suspended." "Wheat is now worth but 50 cents a bushel in Chicago," observed the Topeka *State Capital*. "If the President's suggestion shall be enacted into law, we may look to see it come down to 25 cents a bushel." The Cincinnati *Enquirer* voiced a shrill defiance: "No gold bonds will be issued; no duties will be made payable in gold." Bryan's organ, the Omaha *World-Herald*, denouncing Cleveland's policy of "bonds, bankruptcy, and disaster," asserted that "civilization itself is at stake." Vest, Teller, and other Western Senators invited the Treasury to begin paying its obligations in silver coin, of which there was plenty. There was never the ghost of a chance for the Springer bill, and everyone knew it. Cleveland's message had done nothing except to show that never since Reconstruction had two sections and two bodies of sentiment been so angrily arrayed against each other.[1]

With the Congressional majority thus standing like a stone wall against financial reform, with the danger steadily growing that the government would be forced to a silver basis and the American dollar become worth sixty cents, Cleveland and Carlisle began planning hurriedly for a third bond issue under the unsatisfactory law of 1875. At all costs, the President would carry out his determination to replenish the gold reserve "whenever and as often as it becomes necessary." Not a day was to be lost. On January 31, 1895, the reserve touched a new low point, $45,000,000. On February 2 the amount of gold coin in the sub-treasury in New York fell below $9,000,000. A few weeks more and the government would default on its gold obligations.[2] It was Cleveland's conviction, which he had brought Carlisle to share, that this would mean sudden and catastrophic disaster. A generation later the world was to become used to the spectacle of nations, even Great Britain, going off the gold standard; but the position of the United States was isolated and peculiarly difficult. Another panic in the financial world, with fresh bankruptcies and industrial paralysis, would unquestionably have occurred.

The first question to be settled was whether the new bond issue could be floated by public subscription. Cleveland and Carlisle were reluctant to try any other method, but the best Eastern financial leaders advised them that with so little time available such a procedure would be hopeless. Night after night as February opened Cabinet meetings were held, and a smaller group—Cleveland, Carlisle, Lamont, and Olney—often remained in anxious discussion till the east paled and reddened.

If public subscription was impossible, the only alternative was to sell the bonds privately to some syndicate of financiers. As early as January 24 a syndicate of British bankers had offered to buy £20,000,000 worth, but in vague terms.[3] When August Belmont sounded European financial houses as to the possibility of selling United States bonds there, he found a general indisposition to have anything to do with our securities at that time. The Assistant Secretary of the Treasury, William E. Curtis,

---

[1] See *Public Opinion*, Feb. 7, 1895, for summaries of press.
[2] *Com. and Fin. Chron.*, Jan., Feb., 1895.
[3] Cleveland Papers.

was hurried off to New York to begin conversations with bankers and others there. In his first letter, penned late at night on January 30, he wrote that people seemed scared and panicky, and that the sub-treasury was praying that it might be able to keep up gold payments till the end of the week.[1] Next day he held a conference in the sub-treasury building with J. P. Morgan, August Belmont, and Assistant-Treasurer Jordan. Morgan, who had come on the invitation of both Curtis and Belmont, and who was easily the dominant figure in American finance, thenceforward assumed the active leadership in the bond negotiations. He agreed with Belmont that, in view of the critical state of the Treasury and the acute public anxiety, it would be impossible to obtain gold by general advertisement. While the prospects for selling a loan in Europe were dubious, it was certainly advisable to attempt negotiations to that end. Before the conference broke up, Morgan and Belmont had agreed with Curtis on some tentative provisions of a contract between the banking houses and the government for a bond sale of $100,000,000, the necessary gold to be brought from Europe; and Curtis left for Washington that night with this tentative scheme in his pocket.

Among adherents of the gold standard the mere news of this conference—for reporters had followed Curtis everywhere he went—produced elation and relief. In one day the demands for gold at the subtreasury fell off by more than a million dollars, and nine millions in gold which had been placed on shipboard for export were brought back during the night. But among the silverites the news caused an explosion of wrath. The Western and Southern press with almost one voice assailed the "dark-lantern financiering" of the government and the "conspiracy" between the Administration and Wall Street.[2] Carlisle, who had been still hesitant as to a private sale, drew back. He felt dissatisfied when a second conference between Curtis, Morgan, and Belmont in New York resulted in more detailed terms; for the bankers demanded bonds which would pay 3¾ per cent to the syndicate, they would take only $50,000,000 of them, and they would not promise to obtain more than half of the required gold in Europe. The Secretary wished to sell $100,000,000 in bonds, and he wished more generous terms. For a few days he and Cleveland, in great anxiety, debated the matter. Cleveland, always cautious, thought that a better bargain could

[1] Barnes, *Carlisle*, 373.
[2] *Public Opinion*, Feb. 14, 1895.

be made. Finally, on February 3 Carlisle wrote Morgan and Belmont rejecting their offer. The implication of his letter was that he would have recourse, after all, to a public issue.

When the letter reached New York on Monday morning, February 4, it was read with consternation, for Morgan and Belmont were more certain than ever that a public bond flotation was impossible. Most of the gold to buy it would necessarily have to come from the Treasury, and the announcement of a bond sale would shortly have been followed by announcement of government default.[1] Belmont started at once for Washington. That evening Morgan followed him in his private car with his counsel, Francis Lynde Stetson, and his junior partner, Robert Bacon.[2] "There may be papers to be drawn and I want you," Morgan told Stetson—but he also wanted Stetson for his influence over Cleveland.

The next morning witnessed a momentous conference in the White House. Cleveland presided, with Carlisle and Olney at his side, while American finance was represented by Morgan, Belmont, Bacon, and Stetson. One of the men who had thus far been most useful in the negotiations, Curtis, was conspicuous by his absence, but in a letter to his chief he had just ranged himself on the side of the bankers and against a public issue. "The difference in price between quotations for foreign bids and our views is nothing compared with panic and suspension," he wrote.[3] In the four-hour conference, the bankers explained their position. An immediate supply of gold coin from Europe was the only means of averting panic and disaster, declared Morgan, and this emergency purchase of gold need not interfere with a public sale of bonds later, when times became quieter. Cleveland and Carlisle, for their part, explained that they believed it unwise to close with the bankers until the pending Springer bill had been acted upon. Its defeat was certain within a few days. But "we had asked for legislation," said Carlisle later, "and we thought it was hardly respectful to Congress to undertake to negotiate a sale of bonds pending" the imminent disposal of the bill.[4]

Nothing was settled at this conference. But it was agreed that Morgan and Belmont were to return on Thursday or Friday, February 7 or

[1] Barnes, *Carlisle*, 383.
[2] Corey, *House of Morgan*, 187.
[3] Barnes, *Carlisle*, 380.
[4] Bond Sales Investigation; *Senate Exec. Docs. No. 5, 54th Cong. 2d. sess.*

8, and to see the President as soon as the Springer bill failed; and it was expected by the financiers that the syndicate contract would then be finally arranged and drawn up.

v

The close of the week therefore witnessed the dramatic final events in the history of the syndicate negotiations. At six o'clock on the evening of February 7 the Springer bill was defeated in the House. Three hours earlier Morgan, Bacon, and Francis Lynde Stetson had left for Washington in a private car attached to the Congressional Limited, and they reached the capital at about eight-thirty. Secretary Lamont was waiting at the station. He brought word that Cleveland was still uncertain as to his course and would not see Morgan that evening. The great "Pierpontifex Maximus" was disgusted, and talked of returning to New York at once and letting the government slide into bankruptcy. Lamont implored him to stay. "Do you remember," wrote Olney to Lamont years later,[1] "coming with Messrs. Morgan, Belmont, and Bacon to my house in the evening—when Morgan stated that they despaired of accomplishing anything in Washington and were going to return to New York that night and let things take their course? I think you and I persuaded them to hold on and try the result of an interview with Mr. Cleveland the next morning, which we felt certain we could bring about." Morgan yielded, went with his friends to the Arlington, and sat till far after midnight brooding over a game of solitaire.

An icy blizzard held the capital in its grip that night, and next morning the air was still darkened with snow as Morgan and Bacon skirted Lafayette Square to the White House. The press dispatches had told the country that the great banking magnate was in Washington and that the fate of the gold standard hung in the balance. In Eastern commercial centres men prayed for some action to relieve the tension; in the South and West many a poor farmer who had sold his cotton for six cents a pound or his wheat for thirty-five cents a bushel cursed the plutocracy which he believed had seized practical control of the government. Morgan, passing up the stairs to the library that was still the President's workroom, found Cleveland, Carlisle, Olney, and Lamont awaiting him.

---

[1] May 13, 1904; Miss Lamont's Papers.

The conference which followed was far more anxious and nerve-racking than that of the previous Tuesday. Cleveland was eager to make the best possible bargain for the government. He and Carlisle, still loath to abandon a public bond issue, had to be convinced by the financiers that this was impracticable. Morgan unconsciously ground his unlighted cigar into ashes as he talked.[1] At one point in the conference the telephone rang, and one of the Treasury officials was on the wire. He reported that there was now less than $9,000,000 in gold coin in the New York sub-treasury. Morgan broke the silence by remarking: "Mr. President, the Secretary of the Treasury knows of one check outstanding for $12,000,000. If that is presented today, all is over." [2] His statement was corroborated by Carlisle. Finally, since the crisis would admit of no further delay, Morgan carried his point and the idea of a public flotation was abandoned. It was then agreed, on the basis of the negotiations which Curtis had initiated late in January, that the best plan would be for the Treasury to issue bonds to the syndicate in payment for a large amount of gold, at least half of which was to be brought from Europe.

The question arose of the legality of such a contract. But that question had already been settled by the astute Curtis. He had some time previously discovered authority for such a transaction in a law of 1862 (Revised Statutes, Section 3700) and had brought it to the attention of Carlisle. "This was a proposition entirely new to me," Cleveland later wrote, and though some writers have tried to give Morgan the credit, it had also been entirely new to the financier.[3]

The final arrangement[4] was that the syndicate should furnish 3,500,000 ounces of gold, or about $65,000,000 worth, half or more of it to come from Europe, in exchange for $62,000,000 in four per cent bonds purchased at 104½, and should also do their utmost to protect the Treasury from gold withdrawals during the period of the loan. That is, it was to prevent gold exports by controlling the foreign exchange market. If Congress would within ten days substitute the words "gold bonds" for "coin bonds," the interest rate would be three per cent. A contract was at once drawn and signed at the Treasury. Cleveland that

---

[1] Corey, *House of Morgan*, 187.

[2] Carl Hovey, *Life of J. Pierpont Morgan*, 180. Hovey obtained his story of this conference from Bacon.

[3] See Horace White's letter, N. Y. *Evening Post*, July 8, 1908.

[4] Sen. Ex. Doc. No. 187 (1896), 9 ff. (Bond Sales Investigation).

same afternoon sent a message to Congress announcing that he had bought the gold, and that if it would agree to the phrase "gold bonds" it could save the nation $16,000,000 on the price. But Congress threw away the saving because a large majority would not tolerate the word "gold."

From the perspective of the present day we may pronounce the syndicate loan a decided success. The bond issue yielded $65,116,244 for the Treasury, and brought the gold reserve up above $107,550,000.[1] The export of gold to Europe was immediately stopped, and Morgan and Belmont, by hurried arrangements with the Rothschilds and by selling bills at a sacrifice in New York, held the exchange rate at a point which prevented further exports till they had completely fulfilled their bargain. In fine, they kept faith with the government. The bold action of Cleveland and Carlisle—a step which they knew would meet a storm of abuse—was thus justified by the result. "The crisis," Seth Low wrote the President, "was manifestly imminent, and those who criticize the action now seem to me to forget how much was imperilled for the moment, and how successfully the ship of state was guided out of the rapids into the comparatively smooth waters. . . . In my opinion history will accord to you a place in the struggle as significant as that of General Grant when he vetoed the inflation bill."[2]

Yet when the syndicate on February 20 disposed of the bonds at 112¼, amid a tremendous scramble of subscriptions, and their price in the open market shortly rose to 119, many Americans felt that the government had been grossly cheated. The *World* remarked next day that it had taken just twenty-two minutes for the syndicate to sell off its bond issue and to pocket profits of not less than five millions, a sum not earned by any service or risk; "it was gratuitously given to the syndicate in a secret conference, and will be paid out of the public treasury." Even the Springfield *Republican* grumbled:[3]

Why the government should have contracted to sell United States four per cent bonds at a 3¾ per cent rate, when the original 4 per cent bonds outstanding are selling in the open market at a 3 per cent rate, is a question we have already raised, and it is a pertinent one. . . . While the syndicate pays only 104½ for the new bonds, the old issue, right in the face of an impending output of a large quantity of new bonds of the same kind, are commanding

[1] Treasury Memorandum, Nov. 7, 1895. Cleveland Papers.
[2] Feb. 19, 1895. Cleveland Papers.
[3] Feb. 20, 1895.

above 110 in the open market, and would command nearly or quite 120 were they to run for as long a time as the new issue. The conclusion is inevitable that the government's credit in the open market is placed at a much higher point than the Morgan-Belmont syndicate places it.

A hard bargain had unquestionably been driven; but to all attacks upon the Administration the general answer, as the *Evening Post* said, lay in the emergency: [1]

How near the country was, the last week in January, to crashing down to a silver basis, may not be generally known. Bankers knew it, business men knew it, the President knew it. If he had not acted promptly the crash would have been on us before this. Gold was being drawn from the Treasury at the rate of $7,000,000 a week. The next week $10,000,000 would have gone; the week after, the last dollar. There was no time for prolonged negotiations. If bids had been invited for a further issue of 5 per cent bonds, the first danger would have been that the end of the Treasury gold would be in sight before any bids came in, the second danger would that been that no bids would come in. This last, in fact, was almost a certainty . . . Congress was standing there like a lot of boys playing with dynamite. No help was to be had from them. The bankers had got tired of flinging their gold into the bottomless pit. If ever there was an emergency in public finance, if ever extreme measures and great sacrifices were justifiable to save the public credit, the last week in January was the time. President Cleveland did just what any banker would have done in analogous circumstances in private business.

Criticism may justly fall upon Morgan and his associates, but it should not extend to Cleveland. Even the bankers were widely defended at the time. It was said that if Morgan and Belmont had not been able to inspire confidence in their ability to keep the nation on the gold standard, the bonds could not have been sold at even 100, and that they had a right to charge something for creating this confidence.[2] Various financiers pointed out the error in the popular impression that the syndicate, in buying the bonds at 104½ and selling them at 112¼, raked in the whole difference as a profit. The expenses of the transaction, including the maintenance of the exchange rate, probably reached 2 per cent; and 5 per cent was a customary bankers' commission for placing a large loan. But after all allowances are made, the profits must be pro-

[1] Feb. 21, 1895.
[2] See N. Y. newspapers, July 12, 1895, for reports of addresses before State Bankers Association.

nounced exorbitant. Morgan, when examined by a Congressional committee, flatly refused to reveal their amount.[1] But evidence was produced at the time that a net profit of 6⅝ per cent was realized, and Morgan's ablest biographer places it at not less than seven millions.[2] A conservative historian of American finance declares that the syndicate's terms "were extremely harsh," and that it "measured with little mercy the emergency of the government."[3] Cleveland undoubtedly thought so. But he fought to the last against selling to the syndicate at all, while he and Carlisle did their utmost to obtain moderate terms; and he cannot be held responsible for Morgan's selfishness in the transaction.

It was nevertheless inevitable that most Americans beyond the Alleghenies should believe, with Senators Morgan and Vest, that it was with Cleveland's tacit acquiescence that the selfish financiers had waited till the government was at their mercy, and then had seized it by the throat. There was no longer any common ground for understanding between the silver and gold forces; and the agrarian regions were suffering too keenly to reason calmly. Bryan, denouncing the sale in the House, had the clerk first read Shylock's bond. The *World* declared that the syndicate was composed of bloodsucking Jews and aliens. One of the organs of the Farmers' Alliance asserted that "the great bunco game played in Washington by which the people have been defrauded out of over $8,000,000, besides having another debt of $62,000,000 saddled on their backs," should arouse the masses to join the Populist party.[4] The taxpayers, it added, "will have to shoulder this additional burden as long as a set of vampires headed by a financial trust has control of our destiny. But a storm will come, it will sweep the scales from the eyes of the bonded people, and the clanking of the breaking chains will make merry music to the repudiation of these and other fraudulent bonds."

By hundreds of thousands, hard-handed Americans believed that Cleveland and Carlisle had sold the credit of the republic to the Morgans and Rothschilds, and had pocketed a share of the price. Their vituperative anger was additional evidence of a sectional and class

---

[1] Senate Exec. Doc. No. 187, p. 297.
[2] *Public Opinion*, Oct. 23, 1895; Corey, *Morgan*, 189.
[3] Noyes, *Forty Years of American Finance*, 234.
[4] *Industrial News* (Jackson, Mich.), March 9, 1895.

bitterness that now made even armed revolution seem far from impossible. But Cleveland, like Carlisle, was unmoved by abuse when he felt that he had done right. He would have written then, as he did in 1904: [1]

Without shame and without repentance, I confess my share of the guilt; and I refuse to shield my accomplices in this crime who, with me, held high places in that Administration.

VI

It was unfortunate that at just this juncture, when so much had occurred to arouse a sense of injustice and oppression among millions of Americans, a series of decisions by the Supreme Court—notably those in the income tax and the Debs cases—should add to the passions of the time. Of these the income tax decision unquestionably excited more feeling than any action by the Supreme Court since the Dred Scott opinion. It convinced many, especially in the West, that the tribunal was on the side of the capitalists and creditors, and reënforced their belief that the whole national government was conniving at a process by which one favored class and section exploited the others.

The demand for an income tax was a natural outgrowth of the struggle between the old agricultural America and the new industrial America. When the Civil War had revolutionized the financial system of the country, a high protective tariff and an income tax had been adopted as complementary measures of revenue. The latter, falling most heavily on the Eastern investing classes, had been a partial compensation for the burden which the tariff laid on Western consumers. In 1872, however, Congress had abolished the income tax, not because of its admitted crudities and defects—for these might easily have been repaired —but because of the growing hostility of the capitalist classes and because it was no longer needed for revenue.[2] The resulting unfairness of the national tax system did not escape the attention of the radical groups. In the seventies and eighties the Greenback Party repeatedly demanded the revival of the income tax, and the Farmers' Alliances and Populists took up the cry.[3] The Populist platform in 1892, declaring that "the fruits of the toil of millions are boldly stolen to build up

---

[1] *Presidential Problems.*
[2] E. R. A. Seligman, *The Income Tax*, Pt. 11, Ch. 3.
[3] Fred E. Haynes, *Third Party Movements,* 122 ff.

colossal fortunes for a few, unprecedented in the history of mankind,"
called for a tax on incomes as a means of reaching this swollen wealth.
Nearly all Western and Southern Democrats shared this feeling. In
England the tax, associated with the great names of Pitt and Peel, had
been continuously effective since 1842. When in 1893 the Ways and
Means Committee began work on the Wilson Tariff bill, eight of its
eleven Democratic members, brilliantly led by Benton McMillin and
Bryan, were in favor of including an income tax clause in the bill.[1]

Cleveland heartily believed in the justice of a general income tax,
though he feared that it was inexpedient to include the proposed clause
in the new tariff bill—that it would cost Eastern votes when every vote
was needed. At once it became evident that there was a marked division
in the party on the subject. Speaker Crisp, Tom L. Johnson, Senator
Voorhees, Assistant Secretary of the Treasury Wike, and many more
supported an income tax,[2] while most Eastern Democrats opposed it.
William L. Wilson, like Cleveland, approved the principle but believed
it was inexpedient to tack it to the tariff. But the Democratic party as a
whole leaned toward the income tax while the Republican party was
generally hostile. A partial poll of the House by the *World* as Congress
opened showed 61 Democratic Representatives for it and 18 against,
and 6 Republicans for it with 44 against. In the end, with some malicious aid from Tom Reed, who was anxious to divide the majority, the
clause was written into the bill.[3] The heaviest pressure was brought
upon Cleveland to come out publicly against it, but he stubbornly refused. Instead, he lent the movement support by declaring, in his
annual message in 1893, for a tax on all individual incomes derived
from corporations—a long step toward a general income tax.

When the Wilson bill passed there thus passed with it—despite the
opposition of Eastern Democrats like Hill and Eastern Republicans
like Hoar—a provision for taxing all annual incomes of $4,000 or more
by two per cent. Before the final House vote Wilson, speaking for
Cleveland as well as himself, argued vigorously in its behalf. He declared that it represented an honest initial effort to readjust the weight
of taxation in favor of the poor consumers who had previously borne it
all. It offered an important addition to the national revenues, equitably

---

[1] N. Y. *World*, Nov. 22, 24, 1893.
[2] N. Y. *World*, Nov. 10–13, 1893.
[3] *Ibid.*, Dec. 4, 1893; information of Benton McMillin to James A. Barnes.

collected. When, replying to Eastern critics, he declared that the greatest economists of that section had for a generation taught the desirability of the tax, he ranged the authority of every college and university on his side. In all his talk with Westerners and Southerners, he affirmed, he had met no one who supported the scheme in a sectional spirit. Yet the new law met the harshest denunciation in most Eastern circles. It was attacked as inquisitorial, as the use of wartime legislation in a period of complete peace, as a tax on thrift, and as an assault by rebel planters on Northern business men. Godkin, in his most sneering vein, remarked that it was "concocted without notice not so much to raise money as to punish certain people for being saving and successful and for holding odious views on the currency." *Harper's Weekly* declared that it was Socialistic in aim, that it would lead to confiscation, and that it was urged in the South and West "to plunder Eastern, and especially New York estates, and compel their property to pay nearly all Federal expense." [1] Millionaires who held large amounts of intangible and previously untaxed property prepared to attack it in the courts, and a test suit was soon brought (Pollock vs. Farmers' Loan and Trust Company).

The general opinion at first was that the suit would not succeed. It was brought primarily on the ground that the tax was a direct tax and hence unconstitutional; for a direct tax, unless based on population, can be levied only by the States and not by the Federal Government. But the Civil War tax had for a decade withstood all assaults. In 1880 the Supreme Court had decided, without any dissenting opinion, that an income tax on rents was not a direct tax but an excise tax and hence permissible. Several other court decisions had strengthened the view that income taxes were an excise, and that by implication Congress could constitutionally term a tax almost anything it pleased. The bar and public, moreover, were generally convinced that on broad grounds of national policy the Supreme Court should be very reluctant to disapprove any tax that Congress saw fit to enact, and that it was the responsibility of Congress to observe the constitutional limitations on its own powers.[2] If another war broke out, inability to resort to an income tax might be disastrous.

---

[1] Jan. 13, 1894.
[2] *Public Opinion*, April 18, 1895; C. T. Bullock, "Direct Taxes under the Constitution," *Political Science Quarterly*, XV (1900).

Yet the opponents of the tax gathered a brilliant group of Eastern attorneys, and left no implement or influence unused. Among the counsel entrusted with arguing the case were Joseph H. Choate and ex-Senator Edmunds, and behind them stood the Nestor of the New York bar, Charles F. Southmayd, who at seventy was too old to appear but who helped write the briefs and who was later credited by Choate with the principal part of the work.[1] "By this time," Choate writes with unconscious humor of Southmayd, "he had an ample income of his own which was affected, and he had a strong idea of the right of property being at the foundation of civilized government." The briefs and arguments of the attackers filled several large volumes. These arguments, Dr. E. R. A. Seligman tells us,[2] "abound in historical errors and economic inaccuracies." But such misstatements "pale into insignificance compared with the misinterpretation put upon the origin and purpose of the direct-tax clause—a misinterpretation which like most of the preceding mistakes was bodily adopted by the majority of the Court, who evidently found no time for an independent investigation of the subject." Choate in his speeches appealed unblushingly to class fears and prejudices. This first tax, he declared, was but the entering wedge, and if the law were sustained and "the communistic march" went on, a rate of 20 per cent might be imposed on large incomes. He appealed to the justices to declare the law invalid, and thus uphold civilization, without regard to "popular or Populistic wrath."

For a generation all histories have declared that the income tax was declared unconstitutional because Justice Shiras changed his mind; but this is almost certainly erroneous. On April 8 the court decided, six to two, that a tax on rents was unconstitutional,[3] but divided four to four on the more important question of the constitutionality of the tax on incomes from mortgages, interest, and personal property generally. Attorney-General Olney pressed for an immediate rehearing. Mr. Justice Jackson, who had been ill, meanwhile returned to the bench, and it was expected that his vote would break the tie and turn the second decision one way or the other. "The atmosphere here," Olney wrote on May 11 to his associate, James C. Carter,[4] "is all against the law and in favor of declaring it unconstitutional throughout. But what

[1] E. S. Martin, *Choate*, II, 15 ff.
[2] E. R. A. Seligman, *The Income Tax*.
[3] For the two decisions see 157 U. S. and 158 U. S.
[4] Olney Papers.

Mr. Justice Jackson thinks about it is no more known now than it was before he came to Washington." On May 20 the decision was announced. Jackson had voted for the constitutionality of the law—and if nothing had happened it would have been sustained, 5 to 4. But meanwhile one of the previous supporters of the law had changed his views, and though the vote was secret, the impression gained ground that it was Shiras. Actually there is full evidence that Shiras, who instantly became the target of unremitting attacks, was not guilty, and only less complete evidence that Mr. Justice Brewer was.[1] Brewer, a Kansan, was a conservative Republican whom Harrison had appointed to the bench in 1889, and who had already distinguished himself as a stern defender of property rights.

It was one of the unhappiest decisions in the history of the court. A writer in the *American Law Review* did not exaggerate in calling it "a wound inflicted on the rights of the American people." Two of the justices, Harlan and White, offered dissenting opinions through which their indignation could be seen to throb. It was a class decision, said Harlan in effect; the court had declared that men who held money derived from rents, stocks, or bonds, possessed privileges that could not be accorded to those who held money derived from manual or mental labor.[2] The London *Times* dryly remarked that under such a law and court Sir William Harcourt's budget would be unconstitutional. The most conservative Eastern newspapers were of course jubilant. "The fury of ignorant class hatred," said the *Tribune*, "has dashed itself in vain against the Constitution of the United States." Yet even in Eastern editorial offices there were numerous expressions of regret and resentment. The sober Springfield *Republican* declared the decision intolerable, and called for an amendment to the Constitution. The *World* spoke for the masses in the great Eastern cities when it asserted that "the overthrow of the income tax is the triumph of selfishness over patriotism. Great and rich corporations, by hiring the ablest lawyers in the land and fighting against a petty tax upon superfluity as other men have fought for their liberties and their lives, have secured the exemption of wealth from paying its just share toward the support of the government that protects it." [3]

---

[1] For this evidence, see Appendix II.
[2] Pollock vs. Farmers' Loan & Trust Co., 158 U. S. 601 ff.
[3] May 21, 1895.

In the West and South the note struck by Mr. Justice Harlan and the *World* was echoed and reëchoed. Bryan declared in his Omaha *World-Herald* that the court had taken its stand with the wealthy against the poor. Men concluded that the influences which had defeated Cleveland's effort at tariff reform, which had dealt so harshly with labor, which seemed intent upon making the dollar worth always more to the creditor and always less to the producer, had taken control of the highest tribunal in the land.

VII

This impression was accentuated by two other decisions of the Supreme Court. In January, by its decision in the case of the United States vs. the E. C. Knight Co., it had blocked the lackadaisical efforts of Olney to prosecute the trusts under the Sherman Act. This decision declared [1] that the corporations which had combined in the great sugar-refining trust were not guilty, so far as the evidence presented by the government showed, of a conspiracy in restraint of trade. Chief Justice Fuller, who delivered it, declared in effect that manufacturing is not commerce, and that the sugar-refining localized in Philadelphia in the Knight case was not an interstate transaction. The fact is that the case had been very badly prepared. The Attorney-General should have based his suit on the monopolistic selling in many States of the sugar manufactured in Pennsylvania and New York; instead, he based it on the manufacture of sugar in Pennsylvania! No direct evidence of the sale of sugar across State lines, and of the control of sales and prices, was presented, though it was easily procurable. Olney displayed no grief. "You will observe," he gaily wrote a friend,[2] "that the government has been defeated in the Supreme Court on the trust question. I always supposed it would be, and have taken the responsibility of not prosecuting under a law I believed to be no good—much to the rage of the New York *World*." One of the most greedy of American monopolies was thus cleared. As W. H. Taft later wrote, the effect upon the public and Congress "was to discourage hope that the statute could be used to accomplish its manifest purpose, and curb the great industrial trusts."

[1] 156 U. S. 1.
[2] To A. M. S., Jan. 22, 1895. Olney Papers.

And on May 27, just a week after the income tax case had been disposed of, the court had handed down its decision in the Debs case.[1] Written by Mr. Justice Brewer, its opinion upheld the injunction issued by the lower court to restrain Debs and his associates from obstructing trains engaged in interstate commerce or carrying the mails. In doing this it skirted the weak points of the injunction. It expressly refused to decide whether its terms were unconstitutional or illegal; it also refused to decide whether Debs had violated it. But in sweeping language, it sustained the writ on general grounds.[2] "The strong arm of the National Government," Brewer wrote, "may be put forth to brush away all obstructions to the freedom of interstate commerce or the transportation of the mails. If the emergency arises, the army of the nation, and all its militia are at the service of the nation to compel obedience to its laws." Always a staunch believer in injunctions, Brewer did not base his decision on the mere property right of the government in the obstructed mails. He declared that every government was entrusted by the very terms of its being with powers and duties for the general good, and that it had a right to apply to its own courts for any proper assistance in carrying them out.

This Debs case decision, a great landmark in American legal history, irritated labor as deeply as the income tax decision had irritated the overburdened farmers. Olney of course regarded it as a signal vindication of his policy. The conservative interests which had applauded Cleveland's use of the troops in Chicago welcomed it as a notable contribution to national stability and order. But the fact could not be overlooked, even by those who on the whole accepted the opinion as salutary, that it marked a long additional step in the centralization of authority. "Slowly but inevitably," wrote an observer,[3] "one after another of these State police powers is being brought within the limits of Federal jurisdiction." With the offended labor men, in this instance, agrarian interests were only too glad to stand. When the time came thirteen months later for the embattled Democracy of the West to write its platform in Chicago, it included a plank denouncing arbitrary interference by Federal authorities in local affairs as a violation of the Constitution and a crime against national freedom, and attacking government by injunction as a new and highly dangerous form of oppression.

[1] 158 U. S. 564.
[2] Warren, *Congress, the Constitution, and the Supreme Court*, 230, 231.
[3] Quoted in Warren, *Supreme Court in U. S. History*, 1926, II, 702.

Meanwhile, some Westerners even wished to overthrow the Supreme Court, and Governor Pennoyer of Oregon wrote: [1]

Our constitutional government has been supplanted by a judicial oligarchy. The time has now arrived when the government should be restored to its constitutional basis. The duty is plain and the road is clear. If Congress at the next session would impeach the nullifying judges for the usurpation of legislative power, remove them from office, and instruct the President to enforce the collection of the income tax, the Supreme Court of the United States would never hereafter presume to trench upon the exclusive powers of Congress. . . .

But naturally, if inexcusably, most of the ill-temper of the West was concentrated not upon the Supreme Court, the Senate, the Morgans, or the Rothschilds, but upon the devoted head of Cleveland. One incident after another had seemed to prove to the areas of discontent that he was allied with plutocracy and cared nothing for the plain people. The controversy over the so-called armor-plate frauds furnished an additional example. In the fall of 1893 Secretary Herbert had received information from an attorney representing certain employees in the Carnegie works that imperfect armor was being furnished for our warships. The charges were investigated and were found to have a certain measure of truth. The armor was not actually defective. Both Secretary Herbert and Capt. William T. Sampson, then Chief of the Bureau of Ordnance, declared that the plate received was somewhat better than the specifications called for. It was "at least five per cent better than the lowest limit of tolerance," said Herbert. But it was not as good as the best armor that Carnegie, Phipps & Co. were capable of making with their new and improved processes, and the government felt entitled to the best. Moreover, certain of the company employees had indulged in outright fraud in order to obtain premiums which the government had offered to Carnegie, Phipps & Co. in case the minimum requirements were materially exceeded. Specimen plates had been selected by naval officers at the mills and set aside to be tested at the proving grounds. At night the employees had secretly removed these plates and subjected them to additional "treatment" to increase their efficiency. Thus a higher rating was obtained for entire groups of plates than they deserved. Justly horrified at these practises, Secretary Herbert assessed upon the company a fine of 15 per cent of the value of all its armor plate already accepted by the government. The officers of the company were much agitated;

[1] *Amer. Law Review,* July 1895.

Carnegie and Frick made impassioned appeals to Cleveland from Herbert's decision; and they offered full evidence that the frauds had been practised without the intent or knowledge of any of the partners. Cleveland painstakingly investigated the subject, and against Herbert's protest, reduced the fine from 15 per cent to 10 per cent. This amounted to $140,000, which Carnegie, Phipps & Co. paid, one-fourth going to the informers. At once an indignant set of critics sprang up and accused the President of allowing a serious crime against the republic to go virtually unpunished. The House Committee on Naval Affairs made an exhaustive inquiry, and in August, 1894, gave the country a scathing report. It described the frauds in detail, exposed every deficiency in the armor, and asserted that "no fine or mere money compensation is an adequate atonement for such wrongs."

Part of the weight of this exaggerated report fell upon Cleveland. He had merely acted with his usual strict regard for equity, and his usual indifference to public clamor. He reduced the fine because he believed that the company as well as the government had been victimized by dishonest workers, and felt that its heads had been guilty not of bad faith but only of bad management. He did right by his own strict standards of justice. Yet it was easy to misrepresent his stand, and demagogues at once accused him of shielding Carnegie and Frick because they were rich and powerful capitalists. That accusation is not dead even today.[1]

As the months passed in 1895 he seemed more and more friendless. Always hated by most Republicans, abandoned now by the majority of his own party, he had only the sound-money Democrats and a handful of Mugwumps to stand by his side. Seldom did a member of Congress call on him. His mail shrank till it was less than that of an ordinary business man.[2] This was the year of two great literary sensations—Du Maurier's *Trilby*, and W. H. Harvey's little book *Coin's Financial School*, the most effective pamphlet published in America since Helper's *Impending Crisis*, if not since Thomas Paine's *Common Sense*. Word came from the West and South that people everywhere, in trains, in stores, in homes, were reading this homely narrative of how Coin, "a smooth little financier," established a school in the Art Institute of

---

[1] For the Cummings investigation see House Reports, 2d sess., 53rd Cong., No. 1468. For a typical attack on Carnegie see *Harper's Weekly*, Sept. 8, 1894. Mr. Burton J. Hendrick has furnished the author much material on this subject from his forthcoming life of Carnegie.

[2] R. L. O'Brien to author, May 10, 1931.

Chicago, and began to instruct editors, college professors, and even Senators in the elements of finance. Bryan had the effrontery to address an open letter to Cleveland calling his attention to the book as a plain and effective presentation of the free silver argument.[1] One of the woodcuts showed Cleveland and Sherman, looking like two desperadoes, undermining the silver foundations of the great temple of American prosperity. Millions of Americans actually thought of the President as a traitor to the masses.

At this time Congress had a little group of Democrats who called themselves "The Wild Horses." One of them, Sibley of Pennsylvania, distinguished himself by an atrocious tirade (January 8, 1895) in which he accused Cleveland of behaving like an autocrat, adding: "We have reached a time when the government of this people requires more than a combination of brains, belly, and brass." Even Hill could not resist girding at the President. Early in the year he had been invited, for the first time in the second Administration, to dinner at the White House. As he reached Cleveland in the receiving line the Marine Band, to the joy of the spectators, broke into "Love's Old Sweet Song." He and the President had chatted cordially, and the political correspondents had reported that the tomahawk had been buried. Yet in May, contributing to the *Times* his long review of Bigelow's *Tilden*, he filled it with cutting references to Cleveland.[2] "Tilden," he wrote, "never permitted the country to think or fancy that he was leading the Democratic party to act in behalf of selfish interests, whether Eastern manufacturers or speculators in Wall Street."

And that summer Ben Tillman, taking the South Carolina stump to campaign for the Senate, his one eye blazing, his hair tossing, yelled to delighted audiences: "Send me to Washington, and I'll tickle Cleveland's fat ribs with my pitchfork!"[3]

VIII

Cleveland, while deeply alarmed by the overwhelming drift of his party toward free silver and eager to combat it, cared little for this senseless abuse. He forebore to reply. But when in April, 1895, there once more came an opportunity to impress his sound money views upon

[1] W. J. Bryan, *The First Battle*, 160.
[2] N. Y. *Times*, May 5, 1895.
[3] Peck, *Twenty Years*, 459.

the country, he seized it. Chicago business men invited him to that city to address a gold-standard meeting, and, reluctantly refusing on grounds of official propriety, he wrote a long lecture on the currency.[1] Like so many of his papers, it was verbose and ponderous. He declared that it was time for the American people to reason together; that the farmer and wage-earner would suffer first and most heavily from a depreciated currency; that we could not treat our currency as isolated from that of all other nations; that it was shameful to libel the advocates of sound money by calling them rich parasites and enemies of the plain people; and that all Americans had a common interest in financial stability. There was not an eloquent word in the whole letter, and it produced no effect whatever on the silverites.

But from other quarters there came indications that it had served a much-needed purpose. Many industrial leaders, bankers, and editors all over the North were beginning to proclaim that they would support no man for President in 1896 who did not stand squarely for sound money. As yet on the Republican side neither McKinley, Harrison, nor Reed had dared come out in a flat declaration for the gold standard and against a bimetallic compromise. Their timidity suddenly appeared in sad contrast with Cleveland's boldness in declaring that "the line of battle is drawn between the forces of safe currency and those of silver monometallism." Both the old parties were split into irreconcilable factions by the money question. As by his tariff message in 1887 Cleveland had smoked out the compromisers and compelled them to fight under their true colors, so now he seemed to be smoking out the compromisers on the silver issue. Perhaps that was the purpose of his challenging letter.

[1] *Public Opinion*, April 25, 1895.

IN the spring of 1896 Walter Q. Gresham's body, at the desire of his widow, was returned from Chicago to Washington to be buried in Arlington Cemetery. After the funeral Gresham's son Otto, with his mother, went to Woodley. Cleveland took the young man into the library and talked long and feelingly of the money question and the plight of the party. They mentioned Indiana. Voorhees was for free silver. But his old law-partner, John E. Lamb, was for sound money, and this pleased Cleveland, who was pleased to learn also of the sound money views of such other Indianians as Tom Taggart and John W. Kern. Betraying great anxiety, Cleveland admitted to young Gresham that he had made mistakes in dealing with his' party men, but cautioned him against repeating the statement. He wished Gresham to take his coat off in the Middle West, and his parting words were, "Tell the boys that silver at 16 to 1 will not win." [1]

His anxiety for the nation in these years was always tempered by his knowledge that in the end, by virtue of its youthful vigor and enormous natural resources, it would emerge as strong as ever. Even stronger; for economic depressions are a disciplining process, purging business of its weak elements and constraining it to greater energy and efficiency. But his concern for the fate of the Democratic party had no such mitigation. In the fifties it had taken the wrong road on the slavery question, and the result had been three decades of discredit, inanition, and hopeless stumbling in the gloom. A few strong men, Cleveland himself the strongest, had rescued it and led it again to national power. But once more it was standing at the crossroads, and the desperate efforts of its ablest leaders to keep it on the straight course were of little avail against its wayward impulses. If it went wrong on the currency question, it might again wander for a generation in the wilderness. In a letter of April 26, 1895, to Gov. J. M. Stone of Mississippi, Cleveland embodied one of the most sagacious prophecies of his career.[2] He appealed to Democrats everywhere to look to the future. "They should deceive themselves no longer, nor longer refuse to look in the face the results that will follow

[1] Otto Gresham's Memorandum, Oct. 6, 1921. McElroy Papers.
[2] Printed in *Public Opinion*, May 9, 1895.

the defeat, if not the disintegration, of the Democratic party upon the issue which tempts them from their allegiance. If we should be forced away from our traditional doctrine of sound and safe money our old antagonist will take the field on the platform which we abandon, and neither the votes of reckless Democrats nor reckless Republicans will avail to stay their easy march to power."

II

Cleveland was often charged with being no political manager, and always accepted the charge lightly, for he had little desire to figure in that light. Yet in the spring of 1895 he took shrewd steps in an effort to hold the party in line. While it was obvious that most of the West was irretrievably lost, there was still hope for the sound money cause in the South. That section had maintained a loyal front against the Populist invasion in 1892. If it could be induced, even in part, to stand by the Administration in 1896, the silverite frenzy of the trans-Mississippi regions might yet be dammed back. Cleveland knew how desperately poor the South was, and what tinder for the flame of agitators the small farmers of that region presented. The political barometer there was the price of cotton. Beginning in 1891 prices had declined, the average New York rate that year being two and a half cents lower than in 1890. In 1892 occurred a further decline. There was a short crop in 1893, and despite the panic a reaction to higher levels. But in 1894 an enormous crop again surfeited the market, the world demand fell on account of the depression, and prices dropped sickeningly; while the next year the decline continued. In 1894 the New York market touched a low level of $6\frac{7}{8}$ cents a pound, and 1895 it actually fell to $4\frac{7}{8}$ cents.[1] One of Cleveland's friends sent him a little dialogue as reported by a student at the University of North Carolina: [2]

Stranger to farmer: "What do you-all live on down here?"
Farmer: "Mostly by barter."
Stranger: "Don't you ever see any money?"
Farmer: "Well, I have had as much as a half a dollar."
Farmer's Son: "You lie, dad, I never see you have more'n a quarter."

[1] J. L. Watkins, *Production and Prices of Cotton for One Hundred Years*, U. S. Dept. of Ag., 1895.
[2] Cleveland Papers.

And Tom Watson, the perfect type of the demagogue, was arousing Georgians in meeting after meeting with colloquies of the following kind: [1]

"Well, boys, I'm going to turn this gathering today into a school. . . . I'll start with the head pupil, who ought to know. Mr. Barnes [Watson's sound-money opponent], when a national bond is deposited, how much of its value does the government issue in money?"

No answer.

"Tell him, boys."

"Ninety per cent," roars a sea of voices.

"All right. Now, how much interest does the national banker pay on the money he gets on his bonds?"

"One per cent," the crowd yells in unison.

"All right. Now, how much interest do the farmers have to pay the banker every time they borrow a little money?"

"Eight per cent," the audience shouts.

"You bet they do. Then how much has the national banking system in Washington robbed the farmers of?"

"Seven per cent," roars the crowd.

"Yes, and then when the government goes and pays the banker four per cent on his bonds, his profit on his money becomes how much?"

"Eleven per cent," they shout.

"And what do you ever get?" Watson hurls at the crowd.

"Nothing!" they yell back.

Yet to Cleveland the South seemed worth fighting for. His letter to Governor Stone was part of a systematic campaign for that region. It embodied a direct argument to the cotton growers. They grew products which were exported for gold; yet they were willing to submit to all the loss which would arise from a fluctuating and depreciated silver currency, for buyers of cotton would have to insure themselves in every transaction against a sudden drop in silver, and the farmers would have to pay for this insurance. Cleveland declared that he simply could not understand their attitude. At the same time he began corresponding with such sound-money Southerners as Senator Caffery of Louisiana and Gov. C. O'Ferrall of Virginia.[2] When Representative Patterson of Tennessee made a sound-money speech in the House, Cleveland asked Fairchild if he could not distribute it broadcast in the Southern States. "I am entirely certain," he wrote,[3] "that section can be dislodged from

[1] Brewton, *Thomas E. Watson,* 220.
[2] Cleveland Papers, April, May, 1895.
[3] Feb. 16, 1895. Fairchild Papers.

their association with the West on the currency question. They have heard but one side and there is plenty of proof at hand that they will respond properly if the other side is made plain. A campaign of education such as was waged for tariff reform would produce quick and abundant results—in the South especially." He saw to it that sound-money Southerners were brought into close coöperation with the sound-money Democrats of Northern centres. For example, he introduced to Fairchild, by letter, the able Representative from the Mobile district, just reëlected on a gold platform: [1]

Mr. R. H. Clarke I understand will go to New York this evening to confer with certain parties there, in relation to an attempt to start an aggressive movement in the South on the subject of sound money. . . . I have no information concerning the details of his plan, but can do no less than to say to you that few if any men in Congress from the South (I think I may say no Representative from the South) has a better appreciation of public duty or sounder ideas on public questions. Without any prompting, and, so far as I have been able to see, without any reference to selfish interests, he has been faithful and sound among many faithless and unsound. There is no man in Congress whom I hold in higher esteem, and if anything is to be done to win his section back from error and misconception it must be done through just such men.

Most important of all, Cleveland arranged that Secretary Carlisle should make a tour of the border States in May, delivering sound-money speeches at Bowling Green, Covington, Louisville, and Memphis.[2] The Memphis speech was made at a much-advertised sound-money convention on May 23, before nearly seven hundred delegates representing every Southern State except Virginia and North Carolina. Never had Carlisle's lucidity of mind and expository charm appeared to better advantage than in these four discourses. Avoiding repetition, he linked the speeches into a matchless presentation, historical and economic, of the case for sound money. That the national financial system was unsound and needed reorganization he frankly admitted, and he gave his ideas upon this reorganization. But he exposed in masterly fashion the weakness of the chief free silver arguments. The market ratio of silver to gold was now 32 to 1; free coinage at 16 to 1 would halve the value of the dollar, and heavily reduce all wages; gold would be driven from circulation, and silver monometallism would mean a

[1] March 25, 1895. Fairchild Papers.
[2] Reprinted in pamphlet form, *The Free Coinage of Silver*, 1895.

contracted as well as depreciated and fluctuating currency. Mine-owners and those debtors who had not agreed to pay in gold might profit, but the great mass of workmen, merchants, and farmers would lose. The 21,000,000 Americans who had put money into savings banks, insurance companies, and building and loan associations would be re-paid in fifty-cent dollars. The Eastern press warmly praised Carlisle's speeches. So did the Memphis delegates, who were almost entirely busi-ness men, with few politicians, and who adopted resolutions praising "the unflagging courage and sturdy patriotism of President Cleveland."

Cleveland himself made a trip to the South in the autumn. On Oc-tober 24, with Vice-President Stevenson, Secretary Carlisle, and five other members of his Cabinet, he received a cordial reception at the Cotton States Exposition in Atlanta. After reviewing a military parade he made a speech to 50,000 people in which, while avoiding the cur-rency question, he decried all sectional and selfish interests in politics. Free-coinage and gold men alike could endorse his general attack on those who strove to gain some private advantage at the expense of their fellow-citizens; but what he specifically had in mind were the demands of mine-owners in the silver States.

III

Yet it proved impossible to raise money in New York or other cities for a systematic Southern campaign; and a succession of events in 1895 rendered it clear that Cleveland's struggle to hold that section was hopeless. The sound-money convention in Memphis was quickly followed, in June, by a silver convention in the same city; and a long list of political leaders were prominent among the thousand delegates. Senator Turpie of Indiana was made permanent chairman. Among those prominent on the floor were Senators Bate and Harris of Ten-nessee, Jones and Berry of Arkansas, George and Walthall of Missis-sippi, and Marion Butler of North Carolina. Tillman, the veteran Warner, and the youthful Bryan were all conspicuous. A number of Southern governors attended, the enthusiasm was marked, and many speakers favored placing the silver question above party allegiance.[1] During the summer one State convention after another went on record for free coinage. In a single week the Texas, Mississippi, and Missouri

[1] *Public Opinion*, June 20, 1895.

conventions declared for silver at 16 to 1, and adopted resolutions hostile to the financial policy of the government. Senator Morgan published in the *Arena* a long article on "Why Does the South Want Free Silver?"—reaching a new level of absurdity in such assertions as that "gold is the money of the speculator and miser, while silver fructifies industry as the rains do the earth." [1] Large silver conventions at Salt Lake City, Des Moines, and Springfield, Ill., encouraged the South.

The only important Southern election this year was in Mississippi, and in the struggle of the silver and gold forces the advantage lay wholly with the former. The Cleveland Democrats at first urged that the currency question, being a national and not a State issue, should be excluded from consideration; but a Senator was to be chosen, and the argument was rejected. Though the officeholding Democrats, with many local newspapers, fought gallantly, they were outnumbered. Governor Stone wrote Cleveland charging that Federal officials were being improperly used. The county conventions proved overwhelmingly for silver, and the State convention declared for free coinage and against bond issues.[2] The final election was simply a contest between the silver Democrats and Populists, the former of course winning, with no ticket for which gold Democrats could honestly vote. Autumn saw Speaker Crisp opening a senatorial campaign in Georgia on a 16-to-1 platform; Senator Harris announcing that the Democrats the next year must take up silver or accept defeat; and strong movements under way for electing silver delegations to the national convention. On August 14–15 a conference of free coinage Democrats met in Washington to effect an organization within the party strong enough to control the convention.[3] Among the leaders were Senator Jones, Harris, Jarvis of North Carolina, Call of Florida, and Daniel of Virginia; a group who denounced Cleveland and his "panic-breeding, corporation-credit currency," and appointed an executive committee to keep up the fight. The "Senatorial clique" of the Chicago convention was thus born.

In great parts of the Middle West the conflagration was now getting beyond control. The silverites were well organized, and thanks to the mine-owning interests of the mountain States, well financed. W. A. Clark and Marcus A. Daly of Montana had helped pay for the delivery

---

[1] November, 1895.
[2] *Appleton's Ann. Cyc.*, 1895, 497.
[3] *Public Opinion*, Aug. 22, 1895.

of the Omaha *World-Herald* to Bryan. Reprints of free-coinage speeches in Congress flooded the country, many pamphlets were sold or given away, and even books were distributed by the hundreds of thousands. The *National Bimetallist* and the *Arena* were gaining large circulations. *Coin's Financial School,* was followed by a plausible imitation—Ignatius Donnelly's *American People's Money,* which reported an imaginary conversation between a stupid banker and a brilliant farmer on a railroad journey.[1] The chairman of the Wisconsin Democratic Committee wrote Cleveland's secretary as early as April, 1895, that he was astonished to find so much growth in the silver movement.[2] "The difficulty in the nation is that the free silver advocates are active. They have been circulating literature rather freely and seem to have a fairly good organization throughout the country, while on the other hand those who believe in sound money and endorse Mr. Cleveland's views on the subject have apparently done very little systematic work." Teller, Weaver, Bland, Boies, Ebenezer Wakely, Sibley of Pennsylvania, and others were constantly active. Throughout 1895 Bryan was lecturing in the West and South, welcomed in many places, as the British journalist Sidney Brooks said, as almost a second Messiah; and as he travelled he wrote rough outlines for editorials on the backs of envelopes or torn bits of paper, and mailed them to the *World-Herald* office.[3] David F. Houston, who heard him at Fort Worth, discovered that a prairie schooner could be driven through any part of his argument, but he was unrivalled in winning adherents.

Here and there the Cleveland forces, like a besieged garrison, threw back the attackers. In Ohio, for example, Senator Brice took the field against Allen W. Thurman and the other free silver men, used his large fortune in the battle, and mustered 538 sound money delegates in the State convention of 808 men. The result was a conservative nominee for governor, and a platform which congratulated Cleveland on his policies.[4] But there was truth in the Chicago *Inter-Ocean's* remark that the victory was brought about by patronage and money; "Cleveland furnished one, Brice the other, and the hoops were knocked right off both barrels." And in general all the Western omens indicated that the national convention would be speedily captured by the silverites. In

[1] Hicks, *Populist Revolt,* 341.
[2] E. C. Wall to Thurber, April 19, 1895. Cleveland Papers.
[3] Hibben, *Bryan,* 169.
[4] Cf. Brice to Carlisle, May 11, 1895. Cleveland Papers.

Missouri a convention was called by special action, and with Bland as chairman proved overwhelmingly for free coinage. In Nebraska the Bryanites won an equally despotic control over the State convention. When some reckless delegate offered a resolution endorsing Cleveland and the national platform of 1892, the roof was lifted by a roar of protest, and order was not restored for ten minutes.

Congress met in December—now an overwhelmingly Republican Congress, but no more hostile than before—amid gossip that Cleveland, in a last effort to stem the tide, would enter the lists for a third term. This talk was taken seriously by men who ought to have known better. Cleveland really wanted Carlisle, or failing him, William E. Russell. Senator Gray of Delaware declared that the President would be the logical nominee the following year, and kindly explained that it would not really be a third term—only his second consecutive term. Chauncey Depew thought the nomination a certainty, and a good thing too, for like other railroad men, he remembered the defeat of the Chicago strike gratefully.[1] Even Roosevelt, writing his *fidus Achates*, Lodge, believed that Cleveland might be named. "I think we should beat him if he was; but I am by no means sure that he would not give us a good deal of a fight. People are crazy over him; though I think it is more our kind of people than the 'masses.' "[2] When the subject was first mentioned, Cleveland indulged only in indignant grunts. But as it grew irksome, he let the trusted correspondent of the *Evening Post* know that as soon as the third term business got beyond mere talk, he would put a stop to it.

IV

The thousand indications that the silver movement had completely escaped from control, that it was almost certain to capture the Democratic party, and that it would probably split the next Republican convention, greatly alarmed business and finance. Late in the summer the vigor which the Morgan-Belmont syndicate had imparted to the Treasury began to ebb. During August legal-tenders again began to be offered in large quantities at the Treasury for gold. Secretary Carlisle hurried back from a lighthouse-inspection trip he was making on the Great Lakes. In the uneasy state of the public mind the slightest indica-

[1] *Public Opinion*, Oct. 10, 1895.
[2] *Letters of T. R. and H. C. L.*, I, 156.

tion of another run on the Treasury gold was bound to cause anxiety and arouse discussion of a fourth bond issue. By September 14, 1895, the gold reserve had been reduced to $96,300,000, and was falling more than a million dollars a day. J. P. Morgan then announced that the syndicate would continue to aid the government and was constantly accumulating gold for the purpose, and this eased the tension. In October withdrawals almost ceased. But they recommenced in November, when $16,000,000 was taken out, and in December the situation became dangerous. The head of the New York sub-treasury wrote Carlisle in alarm on December 20.[1] " 'The Philistines are upon us'—in other words, private hoarding has begun—and we must stand both foreign and interior drains." He had lost more than $4,000,000 on that single day.

Once more, and again vainly, Cleveland asked Congress for helpful legislation. He mentioned the subject in his annual message, and on December 20 sent a special appeal. But it was generally agreed that no new legislation for a bond issue that would be acceptable to the House, or the Senate, or the President, would be approved by either of the other branches.[2] The silverites were as obstructive as ever, and the Republican majority in the House joyously took the position that the real trouble lay in the tariff—that if there were a higher tariff there would be more revenue, and more revenue was what the Treasury really needed. It was necessary to plan once more for a bond-sale under the old legislation. For a time in late December the conditions seemed highly unfavorable. Cleveland's message on Venezuela caused a disastrous flurry, sending rates for call money to 80 per cent, forcing several brokerage houses to suspend, and giving Carlisle sleepless nights.

The great question was how the bonds should be sold. For a few days, as 1895 closed and 1896 opened, it was generally believed that the fourth issue, like the third, would have to be disposed of by secret negotiation to a banking syndicate. No one believed this more strongly than J. P. Morgan. He took steps to form a great international syndicate, including other New York bankers, the Deutsche Bank of Berlin, and Morgan, Harjes Company of Paris, which was to purchase the bonds, retail them in America, Germany, France, and other countries,

[1] Barnes, *Carlisle*, 405.
[2] *Public Opinion*, Jan. 2, 1896.

and deliver gold coin to the Treasury in exchange.[1] Late in December he went to Washington and talked with Carlisle. On January 4, with the approval of the bankers associated with him, Morgan sent Cleveland a frank offer. He would buy from $100,000,000 to $200,000,000 of bonds on substantially the same terms as his purchase a year earlier, would furnish the Treasury an equivalent sum in gold coin, and would take steps to prevent gold exports. James Stillman of the City Bank vigorously supported the scheme, writing Cleveland that he could supply $22,000,000 in gold from the vaults of his own and one other bank, and could guarantee that the Deutsche Bank would furnish $25,-000,000 more. He and Morgan insisted that a sale to their syndicate would serve in every way the best interests of the people.[2]

Still another plan was suggested by Jacob H. Schiff, who opposed selling any bonds abroad.[3] He wrote the President that he should lose no time in asking the national banks to buy $100,000,000 worth of four per cent bonds, pledging their gold stocks in return but actually paying the gold only in instalments. This, he said, would give Americans the profit that foreigners would otherwise take, and would "prove our own strength in the face of the unparalleled crisis."

But Cleveland and Carlisle never intended to sell this fourth issue except by public offer; they were determined from the outset on a popular loan. They had disposed of the first two issues in this way; they had deeply regretted the exigency which made a public sale of the third issue impossible; and now they went back to their old method. Morgan was dimly aware of this purpose, and in making his offer of January 4, he wrote Cleveland that if he decided to sell the bonds to the public instead of the syndicate, then the House of Morgan would give the issue its fullest support and strive to make it a success. Yet, ignorant of the Administration's consistent intention of asking for public bids, Pulitzer and the *World* on December 26 launched a noisy campaign to force it to that course![4] The paper blazed forth with excited denunciation of "bond rings," of "greedy financiers" who "cornered" the government, of "credulous" public officials; it appealed to Cleveland in double-leaded editorials to avoid this "colossal scandal";

---

[1] Barnes, *Carlisle*, 413.
[2] Stillman to Lamont, Dec. 25, 1895. Miss Lamont's Papers. To Carlisle, same date. Cleveland Papers.
[3] Schiff to Cleveland, Dec. 22, 1895. Cleveland Papers.
[4] Cf. Don C. Seitz, *Joseph Pulitzer, His Life and Letters*, 208.

it inveighed against a government by syndicates for syndicates. This clamor was echoed in the halls of Congress.

On January 6 Cleveland and Carlisle quietly announced that the fourth bond issue of $100,000,000 would be sold by public subscription. The previous day Cleveland had written a letter to Senator Caffery in which he put the *World* and its Congressional allies right.[1] "The Secretary of the Treasury," he stated, "from the first moment that the necessity of another sale of bonds seemed to be approaching desired to offer them, if issued, to the people by public advertisement, if they could thus be successfully disposed of . . ." The mere fact that Morgan had formed a syndicate, he remarked, proved nothing. If Morgan was convinced that the government would be forced to sell its bonds again by private negotiation, he had a perfect right to put himself in a position to make a bid; indeed, he might regard it as a patriotic act. And there was a shot for the *World* in Cleveland's locker. "I am amazed," Cleveland wrote, "at the intolerance that leads even excited partisanship to adopt as a basis of attack the unfounded accusations and assertions of a maliciously mendacious and sensational newspaper." Yet Cleveland had made a mistake in not letting the public know in better time of his intentions. Because of this mistake, the absurd legend that the *World* had defeated another syndicate sale persisted for years.

Cleveland spent much thought on means of making this popular bond sale a success. By no means content to entrust all the details to Carlisle, he corresponded with Fairchild on the subject, and his letters —one of them beginning "It is horribly late and I am dreadfully tired"[2]—indicate that he was shaping various features of the loan himself. "I have already written one or two of our friends that the period between the instalments of gold (for payment) might be extended," he concluded, "and I have invited suggestions as to what extension should be made and intimated to Mr. Stewart that your knowledge of Treasury loans would make you a good man to advise with." After the period for subscriptions opened, he sat far into the night at his desk, writing friends and urging them to work for the loan. When the bids were unsealed at the Treasury on February 5, it was found there were 4,640 offers aggregating $568,269,000, most of them being at 110 to 112. The *World's* bid for a million dollars at 114 was the highest for any

[1] In *Public Opinion*, Jan. 16, 1896.
[2] Jan. 12, 1896. Fairchild Papers.

considerable amount. In the end, about $66,800,000 of the bonds went to 780 persons who had made subscriptions at various rates above 110.6877, and $33,179,250 went to Morgan at that figure. Cleveland was vastly pleased. As Robert L. O'Brien, who had now become Washington correspondent of the Boston *Transcript*, wrote that paper: [1]

"Seldom if ever have I taken so much interest in anything as I have in the success of this bond issue," said President Cleveland this morning. "Both Secretary Carlisle and myself have had it very much at heart." In response to a reference by your correspondent to the syndicate contract of last year, the President remarked that he had never had reason to question the wisdom of that arrangement under the conditions then existing. "That contract," he added, "helped us out at a time when 48 hours' delay might have produced serious results. I sympathize, nevertheless, with some of the objections made to that form of placing a loan. The difference between the price obtained by the syndicate and the price currently quoted can be twisted into an argument which will appeal to people who do not stop to calculate the actual cost to the syndicate of floating the loan at that time.

"My preference would have been to have the present loan much more popular than it appears on its face, but we have done the best we could. . . . If we could have sold them a three per cent gold bond at par I think it would have brought out a good deal of this gold, but the only bonds the law allows us have to be sold considerably above par in order to keep the net rate of interest within reasonable limits. But from such information as comes to me from various private sources I am convinced that more small holdings of gold will come into the Treasury by the present arrangement than appear on the surface. The small country banks, for instance, which are buying bonds for their customers, have made their bids through their New York and Boston correspondents, and this gives the loan the appearance of having been taken up by the big financial institutions at the money centres."

The issue quickly lifted the Treasury's gold reserve, which had fallen as low as $44,500,000, to a high point of $128,713,000. It was now permanently safe, and Cleveland might consider one of his greatest labors finally accomplished. Just what was the value of that labor no one can say, for no man knows what would have been the result if the country had suspended gold payments. But even if we appraise the service lightly—as few will—it is obvious that the struggle was heroic in character, and that Cleveland's courage and determination in the face of multiform obstacles and harsh abuse were never more worthy of honor from posterity.

[1] Boston *Transcript*, Feb. 6, 1896. The bonds were at 4 per cent.

V

The country could now quickly forget about the Treasury in the excitement of the opening presidential campaign; for the last act in that fateful drama, the rising of the West and South, was about to be enacted. The silver forces, frustrated in Washington, appealed to the court of last resort—the voters of the land. On January 16, while the bond issue was pending, the Democratic national committee met to select a convention city. The free coinage men demanded St. Louis, the gold men New York; and by a compromise which gave every advantage to the silverites, Chicago was chosen. A few days later another great conference of silver delegates was held at the capital. The Senate at the moment was whipping into shape a free coinage bill, which it passed on February 1 by a vote (counting pairs) of 48 to 41, the Democrats furnishing 24 yeas and only 15 nays. Cleveland watched with something like despair when a fortnight later the House defeated this bill by a vote to non-concur; for the defeat was accomplished by the Republicans, and the Democrats voted almost two to one—58 to 31—in favor of silver.[1] It was all too plain that these Democratic Congressmen represented the sentiment of the party.

The Democratic movement toward silver in the last six months before the Chicago convention was like an avalanche: a mere whisper at first, then a half-imperceptible shift in the landscape, and suddenly a roar, a crash, an irresistible cataclysm. During February and March there were no State conventions. The Administration forces, still cherishing a hope of saving some of the Middle Western States, made Chicago the centre of earnest activities. "Carlisle," wrote William L. Wilson in his diary for April 10, "read to us at Cabinet meeting today parts of the speech he is to make next Wednesday in Chicago on free silver as it affects the workingman. This, it seems to me, is one of the strongest arguments we have, but it has been very incompletely presented heretofore, and as in the beginning of the tariff fight, the workingmen, especially those in the protected industries, were against us, so now I believe the labor organizations of the country are largely for free silver, not understanding how disastrous its effect would be on the wage-earner."[2] Champ Clark called this address, given April 15, the

---

[1] See *Public Opinion*, Feb. 13, Feb. 27, for good analyses of the vote.
[2] MS Diary, April 10, 1896. Wilson, defeated in 1894 for Congress, had succeeded Bissell as Postmaster-General.

best single gold-standard speech ever delivered.[1] But it had little effect
on the silver men, and the Chicago *Record* described Carlisle as coming "fresh from the banquet table of Wall Street goldbugs to tell the
idle and starving workingmen" that robbery was no crime. In April,
moreover, disquieting news began to come in. The Missouri convention,
after riotous proceedings, overwhelmed the handful of gold delegates
from St. Louis and declared for free coinage. Mississippi went for
silver, and in Nebraska, where the two factions held separate conventions, the silver men were far stronger. In the East, Pennsylvania, which
endorsed Pattison for the nomination, and the Massachusetts and
Rhode Island conventions, which came out for William E. Russell,
adopted gold planks. But this had been discounted in advance.

Late in April Cleveland was particularly concerned over Michigan.
He had written several times to encourage Dickinson in the struggle.
The convention was held in Detroit on the 29th, and that night news
came that the gold men had carried their platform, and that 17 of the
28 delegates to Chicago would be for gold. "Light out of darkness!"
rejoiced Wilson, adding next day: [2] "The silver men seem dazed by the
victory of the Administration forces." Cleveland sent Dickinson a
heartfelt letter of thanks for the achievement. But their joy was short-
lived, for on May 7 the Tennessee convention voted for silver and there
came bad news from Illinois. Altgeld had seized control of the party
machinery and expected to carry the delegates for silver. "What ups
and downs we are having in this fight!" wrote Wilson.[3] "Before the
Michigan convention we were very blue. After that the fight seemed
won. With Illinois under Altgeld's control we may yet lose the convention."

Thereafter there were two defeats for every victory. In the last ten
days of May the Democrats of Iowa declared 675 to 270 for silver and
endorsed Boies for the nomination; the South Carolina Democrats,
with Tillman in control and only four dissenting votes, denounced the
Administration as tyrannical and un-Democratic; and Wyoming and
Oklahoma went overwhelmingly for silver. At the beginning of June
the Virginia convention, after instructing the 24 national delegates to
vote as a unit for free coinage, greeted Cleveland's name with hisses,

[1] Champ Clark, *My Quarter Century of American Politics*, I, 236.
[2] MS Diary, April 29, 30, 1896.
[3] Idem, May 8, 1896.

while the gathering in Kentucky hooted every mention of both Cleveland and Carlisle. "The sun of Austerlitz rises this morning," exclaimed Senator Blackburn to the Kentuckians. "Having captured the convention of Kentucky, we will go on and capture the convention of Chicago." Cleveland in Cabinet meeting sadly congratulated Carlisle that he had escaped humiliation by not attending.[1] Kansas on June 2, and North Dakota, Utah, and California soon afterward, all fell into line for silver.

Yet many conventions sat late, and hope was not completely given up to the very end. One of the worst blows to the gold forces occurred in Indiana. Here the fatal prostration of Voorhees, with the activity of the capable Tom Taggart, had seemed to open a roseate chance for success. But the county conventions went steadily against gold, and the State convention in Indianapolis on June 24 adopted a silver plank. The previous day 1065 delegates in Illinois had voted unanimously for free coinage. Kenesaw M. Landis wrote that "the God's truth is, the Democratic party in Indiana and Illinois is wildly insane on this subject of silver." [2] A little group of Northwestern States—Wisconsin, Minnesota, and North Dakota—gave partial aid to sound money. But the Democratic organization in New York, dominated by the jealous and indifferent Hill, once more struck Cleveland from the rear. The leaders should have imitated the Massachusetts Democrats by calling an early State convention, adopting a rigid sound-money plank, and commending the Administration. Instead, they did nothing to stem the silver tide and sat inactive until a few days before the Chicago convention was to assemble. On June 24 the convention met at Saratoga, with Hill, Whitney, and John Boyd Thacher in charge, and voted a platform which struck most gold men as weak and colorless. It called for international bimetallism along with the gold standard, and endorsed "gold and silver as the standard money of the country." In short, New York had faltered in the fight. Meanwhile, on June 23–25 Ohio (where Brice too was sulking), Texas, Georgia, and North Carolina all went into the silver column.

The silver men now possessed far more than a majority of the delegates, but they were not yet sure of two-thirds; they could write the platform, but it was not certain they could name the candidate.

[1] W. L. Wilson, MS Diary, June 1, 1896.
[2] Barnes, *Carlisle*, 452.

As the excitement mounted the rancors and passions of recent years all came frothily to the surface. The hotheaded Tillman had set an evil example in January by a speech to the Senate in which he arraigned Cleveland with the harshest epithets, calling him "bull-headed," "self-idolatrous," a "besotted tyrant," and an "arrogant and obstinate ruler," and going so far as to term Carlisle "this Judas from Kentucky." Worse still, he declared that "millions are on the march," and that unless speedy relief arrived they would "come to Washington with rifles in their hands to regain the liberties stolen from them." [1] The Eastern press gave back adjective for adjective, the New York *Times* calling Tillman a filthy baboon, and the *Mail and Express* describing him as a political ruffian. But the agarian Democrats rose behind him with loud cheers, and General Weaver wrote him to strike again: "Keep your whip in your hand; it is the same one twice used in the temple scene at Jerusalem, and you struck the same set of scalawags." It happened that in March Cleveland went to New York to attend a rally in Carnegie Hall in behalf of the home missions of the Presbyterian Church. In the course of his speech he referred to the lawlessness, the dramshops and gambling-dens, to be found on the frontier, and excited the wrath of a host of Westerners by adding: [2]

These conditions, if unchecked and uncorrected, fix upon the new community, by their growth and expansion, a character and disposition which, while dangerous to peace and order in the early stages of settlement, develop into badly regulated municipalities, corrupt and unsafe Territories, and undesirable States. . . . These churches and this religious teaching were never more needed than now on our distant frontiers, where the process of forming new States is going on so rapidly, and where newcomers who are to be the citizens of new States are so rapidly gathering together.

These words, which doubtless in part reflected Cleveland's irritation with the selfish silver-mining States, aroused an absurdly exaggerated storm. Senator Teller gathered bundles of statistics on the comparative number of jail inmates, paupers, prostitutes, and murderers in the East and West, and flung them at Cleveland's head. Senator Dubois accused him of ignorance, narrow-mindedness, and sectional pharisaism. According to Senator Vest, he had stood with the ghastly light of the hell-holes and rum-cellars of New York shining on his face and

[1] *Cong. Rec.*, Jan. 29, 1895.
[2] See *Public Opinion*, March 26, 1895.

had cantingly said that home missions must be used to civilize the heroic pioneers. Western nerves, it was clear, were badly on edge.

VI

In both West and South, indeed, more than one observer has described the temper of the hour as a veritable frenzy. Representative Henry St. George Tucker of Virginia, for standing loyally by Cleveland, was cut by old friends, and even feared physical violence as he went about his district. Former supporters shook their fists in his face.[1] In Georgia the general feeling among small farmers, small shopkeepers, and laborers was of sullen rage. Survivors of that era laugh at the idea that by any possible measures Cleveland could have checked the silver forces. "All hell," states Senator Cohen, "couldn't stop them." [2] When Hoke Smith in the spring of 1896 engaged in a series of joint debates with Crisp, his reception varied between icy coldness and almost mob-like hostility. William L. Wilson, hopelessly battling against the craze in his old West Virginia district, wrote that "I have never seen the masses of the people so wild over a question they know little or nothing about. To reason with them is as impossible as to talk down an angry cyclone, and they turn away from all those whom they have been wont to follow in public matters with contempt." [3] On the western plains men talked with confidence of what they would do to the bloated money-holders when they came into power. Multitudes were convinced that they were the victims of a gigantic conspiracy by the money interests of Wall Street and Lombard Street, and that only a sharp change in the standard of values could stop their exploitation.

During June Cleveland was besought on every hand to say something. The Chamber of Commerce of the State of New York, through its committee on financial legislation, urged him to address a letter to some prominent Westerner or Southerner, pointing out again the folly of debasing the currency. "We feel," they wrote, "that there is a great lack of leadership, political and national, for the sound money forces." [4] After much hesitation, Cleveland yielded to the pressure and on June 16 gave the country a statement through the New York *Herald*. De-

[1] Representative Tucker to author, June 6, 1931.
[2] Senator Cohen to author, May 29, 1931.
[3] MS Diary, May 27, 1896.
[4] J. C. Hendrix to Cleveland, June 3, 1896. Cleveland Papers.

claring that he did not wish to pose as a party dictator, he confessed that he could not forbear making a last appeal in behalf of the grand old organization, so rich in honorable traditions, so justly proud of its achievements, and so undaunted in its battles for the people's welfare:

> I have made no figures as to the probable action of delegates already chosen or to be chosen to the Democratic National Convention, but I refuse to believe that when the time arrives for deliberate action there will be engrafted upon our Democratic creed a demand for a free, unlimited, and independent coinage of silver. I cannot believe this, because I know the Democratic party is neither unpatriotic nor foolish, and because it seems so clear to me that such a course will inflict a very great injury upon every interest of our country, which it has been the mission of Democracy to advance, and will result in lasting disaster to our party organization. There is little hope that as a means of success this free silver proposition, after its thorough discussion during a political campaign, will attract a majority of the voters of the country. It must be that many of the illusions influencing those who are now relying upon this alleged panacea for their ills will be dispelled before the time comes for them to cast their ballots, which will express their sober second thoughts. The adoption by the Democracy of this proposition would, I believe, give to our opponents an advantage, both in the present and future, which they do not deserve. . . .
>
> In my opinion no effort should be spared to secure such action of the delegates as will avert party demoralization. It is a place for consultation and comparison of views, and those Democrats who believe in the cause of sound money should there be heard and should be constantly in evidence. A cause worth fighting for is worth fighting for to the end.

A chorus of commendation came from the conservative press. Most of the sound-money newspapers said yes, fight to the end, there was still hope. But others asserted that the cause of free coinage had gained such headway that little short of a miracle could stop it. Any chance that the statement would affect the Western Democrats had been destroyed by the systematic abuse of Cleveland there. "No President," as the Indianapolis *Sentinel* said,[1] "was ever so persistently and malignantly lied about as Grover Cleveland has been. The judgment of thousands of men has been warped by whispered stories that are too silly to discuss."

William C. Whitney had arranged to sail for Europe on June 17, but after consultation with Senators Hill and Gorman and other Democratic leaders, he cancelled his passage and announced that he would

[1] June 17, 1896.

go to Chicago and join others in a tremendous effort to insert a gold plank instead of a free coinage plank in the platform.[1] He would not be a delegate, but would simply use his personal influence. Various silver men instantly accused him of plotting to buy up Democratic delegates as Mark Hanna had been accused of buying up Republican delegates. But Whitney, who had recently spent several months in Europe studying the currency question, and who was a staunch believer in bimetallism by international agreement, issued a conciliatory statement. "I am not foolish enough," he said, "to suppose that any Eastern man could be nominated by this convention, much less that I could be. I sympathize thoroughly with the feeling in the South that has caused the uprising and that will find expression in Chicago; but as to the principles which the uprising has brought forth and the issues being framed, I entirely disagree." His appearance in the lists revived flagging hopes. William E. Russell, everywhere regarded in the East as the logical successor of Cleveland, wrote a friend on the 18th that "it is of the utmost importance that the Democratic Party should take an absolutely sound position on the money question, and I am hopeful of that result in Chicago, although I admit at present the chances seem against it." [2] Winslow Warren, in a sudden access of enthusiasm, thought that Whitney himself might be the Ney of this Friedland. "Only one man can have a chance of turning the tide back and that is Whitney. The saving of the party and the nation perhaps, seems to me to demand from him the sacrifice. If he would avow himself a candidate upon a good platform pledged to use his utmost efforts, if elected, for international bimetallism (whatever that may be) his wonderful popularity South and West might turn things yet." [3]

These momentary and delusive hopes gained a certain color from the result of the Republican convention which opened in St. Louis on the 16th. The rout there of the silver men, who fell far below the numbers with which they had been credited, was complete. Hanna, who had long before determined on a gold plank, sat in his rooms at the Southern Hotel inwardly chuckling as one Eastern leader after another—Platt, Lodge, Lauterbach—demanded that he accept such a plank. The gold standard sentence was actually in the platform by

[1] *Public Opinion,* June 26, 1896.
[2] Russell to John De Witt, June 18, 1896. Russell Papers.
[3] Warren to Russell, June 29, 1896. Russell Papers.

Friday night before the convention opened; these men, making their speeches to the omnipotent Hanna on Saturday and Sunday, went away afterwards bragging that they had forced his hand.[1] The actual writer of Hanna's plank was Melville E. Stone, head of the Associated Press, chosen because he was the only man present at the time who could spell "inviolable." When the platform was formally adopted the silver delegates, in one of the dramatic moments of Republican party history, formed behind Teller and Dubois and marched from the hall. "Go to Chicago!" shrieked the convention, and Hanna yelled "Go! Go!" with the rest.[2] The whole event, thought the New York *Times*, "increases immensely the probability of a like triumph for the gold standard at the Chicago convention." And, said the *World*, "McKinley's triumph is Democracy's opportunity. . . . Shall it be a campaign— or suicide?"

The gossip that Cleveland might yet be presented for a third term continued, and embarrassed him and his friends. William L. Wilson tells us in his unpublished diary that he and the President repeatedly talked the matter over. Cleveland said in April that he was getting scores of letters every day appealing to him to run, and that some public disclaimer seemed necessary from him, but he had never found the fitting time and person to make it. He did not like to speak when the prospects of the sound money wing were increasingly gloomy, and he thought it better to remain quiet for a time if his doing so inspired anyone to work who might otherwise become inactive.[3] Once he was about to make a flat announcement that he would under no circumstances be a candidate, but Justice Peckham dissuaded him. Just after the gold forces carried the Michigan convention William L. Wilson urged him to issue the statement, and again he almost made up his mind to do so; but this time Dickinson successfully intervened. He was the more easily persuaded because he felt that the idea of his running again was preposterous, and he was reluctant to dignify the rumors by noticing them.

Nevertheless, his failure to speak out was a great tactical blunder. It would have strengthened the gold forces if in April or early May he had said that he would refuse a nomination; for the third-term

[1] Beer, *Hanna*, 144.
[2] William Allen White, *Masks in a Pageant*, 214.
[3] MS Diary, April 17, 1896.

WILLIAM E. RUSSELL AS A FISHERMAN

(Governor Russell at the right, Mr. F. G. Webster at the left)

talk injured the sound money cause more in the South and West than it helped it in the East. It irritated Hill; it irritated Brice of Ohio. There was a dinner-table conference at Hill's home, Wolfert's Roost, in April, at which Hill, Brice, Gorman, Alton B. Parker, Adlai E. Stevenson, and John R. McLean all considered the possibility of stopping the silver movement. When McLean urged Brice to go to Chicago to help in the fight, Brice burst out explosively: "I don't propose to pull any more chestnuts out of the fire for Grover Cleveland. If you will get a statement from him that he will not be a candidate, I will do it." Late in June McLean came to Carlisle, and said: "There is yet a way for the President to smash free silver." "How is that?" asked Carlisle. "Well, I care nothing about silver, but I hate Cleveland. Let him say he is not a candidate, and the Ohio convention can be controlled." Carlisle told Cleveland of the conversation, the President pooh-poohed McLean's demand, and the Ohio convention declared for silver. It was Carlisle's own opinion that a timely utterance would have been of great benefit to the gold forces, and Wilson agreed.[1]

Cleveland simply did not realize how intense was now the hatred which many men had for him. An illustration of its violence was presented by an altercation this spring between Dickinson and Senator Pugh of Alabama. The scene was John Chamberlain's restaurant in Washington, where Dickinson was dining. Pugh was sitting at a table near by, and observing his presence, began a malignant and vile tirade against Cleveland for the purpose of offending him. As Dickinson rose at the close of his meal, Pugh's companion, Benton McMillin, who was half tipsy, dragged him over to be introduced to "my friend, Senator Pugh." Dickinson said, "I don't want to know the d—d old blatherskite!" Pugh retorted, "You are a scoundrel!" Dickinson came back with "You are a d—d old wart!" and as Pugh pretended to be drawing a weapon the former Postmaster-General shouted at him, with another epithet, "Sit down!" Pugh sat down.[2]

Yet Cleveland all through these stormy and disastrous weeks somehow maintained his spirits. Wilson wrote in his diary that he was much pleased by Whitney's decision to stay and fight it out. "He does not comprehend the madness of the free silverites nor the hopelessness of trying to accomplish anything by reason, appeal, or entreaty. Yet he

[1] Idem, July 30, 1896, quoting Carlisle at length; cf. G. S. Bixby, *Life of Hill.*
[2] Wilson, MS Diary, May 15, 1896.

is not specially hopeful of staying the lunacy of the convention." [1]
Particularly significant was a statement which he made at the beginning
of June. The President and Wilson were talking of the work the Administration had done. Their conversation was not cheerful, though
they felt they had performed their duty. "I told the President," writes
Wilson,[2] "that history would put in its true light his great but unpopular
fight for public credit. He answered jocularly and half seriously, 'I am
not concerning myself about what history will think, but contenting
myself with the approval of a fellow named Cleveland whom I have
found to be a pretty good sort of fellow.' "

Cleveland left for Gray Gables on the evening of June 29. At that
hour delegates were already beginning to gather in Chicago for the
convention, which was to open on July 7. Before the doors of the White
House closed behind him he had written a final appeal to the party—
a letter read at the Tammany celebration of the Fourth. Remarking
that the situation was one which invested the national celebration with
more than usual impressiveness, he added: "The high and firm financial ground which we have thus far been able to hold should not be
abandoned in the pursuit of a policy never attempted without national
injury, and whose bright promise of individual benefit has never been
fulfilled." Having penned this letter, he commended the fight at Chicago
into the hands of Whitney.

VII

Whitney's special train of three handsome parlor cars left New York
on Thursday afternoon, July 1, reaching Chicago at 4:40 P. M. the following day. He had made plans for the trip with his usual care. "Now is
the time," he had written Russell a fortnight earlier.[3] "Come with me
to Chicago and we will do one of two things—either beat down this
craze or save the *esprit de corps* of the Eastern Democracy by most
emphatic action. This last is probably all we can do, but there is more
duty in that at the present time than in anything else." Russell had
responded with equal enthusiasm—he would be heart and soul in the
battle at Chicago. But he had laid down one condition.[4] "I must go to
Chicago to aid in the fight for sound money with no idea in the public

1 MS Diary, June 20, 1896.
2 *Ibid.*, June 1, 1896.
3 June 18, 1896. Russell Papers.
4 June 19. Russell Papers.

mind that I am to have a personal interest in the success of the cause;
and therefore before going I shall disclaim any candidacy and announce that my name will not be presented to the convention as a candidate, otherwise it certainly would seem as if I were fighting for a
cause in the hope of some personal benefit out of its success. This I will
not do under any circumstances." To this Whitney, quite properly,
objected. He did not wish Russell to disclaim his candidacy, for the
sound money forces might find it necessary to centre their fight about
him.[1] And he insisted that Russell prepare a speech with the utmost
care. He had arranged a mass meeting in the Auditorium on the Saturday night before the convention opened, and "It will be the opportunity of your life. . . . You have beyond any man in this country the
ability to utilize this great occasion."

Plainly, Whitney hoped against hope not only for a sound money
platform, but for the nomination of Russell on it. The special train,
well stocked with comestibles and drinkables, carried a strange array
of men.[2] David B. Hill was there, for once reconciled with Cleveland's
best friends. So was "Blue-eyed Billy" Sheehan, chatting amiably with
Senator Gray of Delaware. Ex-Mayor Hughie Grant, leader of Tammany, and Charles R. Miller, editor of the *Times,* contrived to endure
each other. George Harvey and Senator Smith of New Jersey, two men
who were to help make Woodrow Wilson's career, fraternized with
Thomas Fortune Ryan and Smith M. Weed. At Detroit Don M. Dickinson, mutton-chop whiskers and all, climbed aboard. These men
cheered each other up wonderfully. "It was evident," wrote a reporter
for the Chicago *Tribune* who joined them at Jackson, Mich., "that they
hitherto had underestimated the strength of the silver element in the
West, and the fact that almost for the first time in the history of Democratic conventions New York and the East generally were to be systematically ignored."[3]

But this ignorance was quickly dissipated. The train rolled into the
station under the stares of a hostile crowd, and the little group emerged
upon streets alive with silver badges and gay with silver banners. Within
half an hour, they knew that their fight was utterly hopeless.[4] Whitney

[1] June 22; Russell Papers.
[2] Described for author by Charles Warren, aboard as Russell's private secretary; Nov.
10, 1931.
[3] Chicago *Tribune,* July 4, 1896.
[4] Charles Warren to author, Nov. 10, 1931.

had taken a suite in the Auditorium Hotel, and acting as chief of staff, ordered his associates to scatter and size up the situation. They came back profoundly impressed by the mad enthusiasm, the crusading energy, that swirled around them. One silver delegation after another was arriving with its supporters. Men bitter with a sense of injustice and burning with a desire for redress—not all politicians, but in part plain farmers, storekeepers, and labor representatives—were filling every lobby. "These men are mad," declared John R. Fellows. "We should get out a writ of *de lunatico inquirendo.*" And Warren remarked to Whitney: "For the first time I can understand the scenes of the French Revolution!"

Whitney, imitating his tactics of 1892, had quietly summoned a group of trustworthy leaders—Harrity of Pennsylvania, Everett of Massachusetts, Francis of Missouri, Faulkner of Georgia, and others—to Chicago. They held a secret meeting in the "hoodoo" room of the Auditorium, where four years earlier the Tammany delegates had drawn up a round-robin of protest and denunciation against Cleveland's nomination; but they were as dispirited as the silver leaders at their headquarters in the Sherman House were elated. On Saturday evening, July 3, the sound money forces held their rally in the Auditorium theatre. Franklin MacVeagh of Chicago presided. Russell spoke with fluent persuasiveness, and with all the irresistible personal charm which, as he moved about the lobbies and streets, led hostile Southerners and Westerners to say, "We'd like to vote for you, Governor, but not this year!" As a means of making converts to the gold standard, however, the meeting was a total failure. Meanwhile, few men mentioned Cleveland's name anywhere except to assail him. His portrait mysteriously disappeared from the New York headquarters, where it was replaced by pictures of Flower, Murphy, and Hill.[1]

On Sunday the 4th, amid exploding firecrackers, the trains poured fresh crowds into the city. Every few minutes a distant band would announce the approach of some new delegation or club. Among the first was the Bland Silver Club of St. Louis, five hundred men in linen suits. Then came the Blackburn Club of Lexington, the Matthews Club of Indiana, the Jacksonian Club of Omaha, and noisiest of all, the Bryan Club of Lincoln. At the Sherman House, under the portraits of

[1] Alexander, *Four Famous New Yorkers,* 265.

the four Western heroes, Bland, Boies, Blackburn, and Pennoyer, the silverites surged about the pale and taciturn Governor Altgeld, who might well have been nominated had not his foreign birth made him ineligible.[1] He supported the "Senatorial clique" which, led by Vest, Harris, and Tillman, had decided upon Bland as the nominee.

On Tuesday, a cool and cloudless day, the convention was called to order by National Chairman Harrity in a great hall of 20,000 seats. Senator Hill had been proposed by the national committee for temporary chairman, but he was now regarded as a gold man, and his name was the signal for an outbreak. "Will you turn down David B. Hill?" indignantly shouted Waller of Connecticut. "We will," shrieked the delegates—and by a vote of 556 to 349, they placed Senator Daniel, who with his air of courtesy and dignity looked like a second Edwin Booth, in the chair. It was evident that the silver wing still lacked the two-thirds vote necessary to control the nomination. On Wednesday, therefore, the silverite committee on credentials made sure of it by increasing the delegations from all the Territories, and ejecting a number of the gold delegates from Michigan and Nebraska. Hats, flags, and newspapers flew in the air as the newly-seated Nebraskans, headed by Bryan, marched in and took their places.

Thursday, again cool and clear, brought the crisis of the convention. As Senator Jones read the platform reported by the committee on resolutions, the planks which were aimed directly at Cleveland's policies—those condemning the bond issues, the "trafficking with banking syndicates," the use of injunctions, and Federal interference in local affairs—seemed to stun even many of the silver delegates. The party was not merely repudiating its President, but insulting him. Tillman took the floor in defence of the new doctrines. He declared that the Southern people were tired of being mere hewers of wood and drawers of water, while New York and the other great Eastern States were eating up their substance. "You ask us to endorse Cleveland's fidelity," he said. "In reply, I say he has been faithful unto death, the death of the Democratic party." As he closed, he read a set of resolutions which condemned the Cleveland Administration as "undemocratic and tyrannical," as abhorrent to liberty-loving Americans, and as one which had

---

[1] See the vivid description in Charles Warren, "The Manufacturer of History," *Stories From McClure's*, 11–56.

sought to plant a plutocratic despotism "on the ruins of the republic." Hill followed with an admirable defence of the Administration, tactful but emphatic. Vilas spoke. Then Russell, pale and worn, his fine voice choked with emotion, rose to make the last speech of his life—a speech pleading rather in sorrow than in anger against the destruction of the party to which he had devoted his brief and crowded career. And as he sat down there climbed the steps to the platform a tall, robust figure, with the elastic step of youth, and with a strikingly handsome head—William Jennings Bryan.

Tillman and Jones had treated Cleveland with contumely, but not a single hostile reference to the President marred the beauty of Bryan's discourse. Indeed, every reference to his opponents was courteous. "It is not a question of persons," he said: "it is a question of principle; and it is not with gladness that we find ourselves brought into conflict with those who are now arrayed upon the other side." We know now how assiduously Bryan had for years practised almost every passage of this speech; we know how carefully he had laid his plans to stake everything upon it and sweep the convention before him. But to nearly everyone in the huge hall it had the charm of novelty. He spoke with deliberation, with dignity, and with a sonorous eloquence that drove every word home. From the outset he held the attention of his hearers. The passage that first fired them to exultant enthusiasm was his rhetorical reference to McKinley: "Why, that man who used to boast that he looked like Napoleon, that man shudders today when he thinks that he was nominated on the anniversary of the battle of Waterloo!" Thereafter almost every sentence was followed by a burst of wild applause from twenty thousand throats. He spoke of the farms as the basis of American prosperity; of the way in which the petitions of the people had been scorned and their entreaties mocked; of the issue of 1776 and the new contest for national independence. Amid a painful silence, he came to his climax, delivered in tones of labored and solemn protest: "Having behind us the producing masses of the nation and the world, the laboring interests and the toilers everywhere, we will answer their demand for a gold standard by saying to them: 'You shall not press down upon the brow of labor this crown of thorns—you shall not crucify mankind upon a cross of gold!'"

The roar that followed these words was the signal that Cleveland was no longer the head of the party he had twice led to victory; that he was thrust aside and its future leadership lay with the young orator from Nebraska.

Cleveland's friend Otto Gresham, who was in the audience, has told us what ensued: [1] "State after State planted its banner alongside of the Nebraska standard until there were two-thirds of the convention represented. John E. Lamb with a drawn face stood holding to the Indiana banner while the other Indiana delegates sat mute in their places. Senator Voorhees was home sick and he died a few months later. 'He is nominated without a roll-call,' was the cry. To my mother and Mrs. Potter Palmer, who sat beside me, I said, 'Uncle Grover will pull the sound money men out before there is a roll-call. They will bolt as soon as they vote on the platform.' Whether Mr. Cleveland attempted to pull them out I never learned. But that night after the convention adjourned, I learned that Tammany was willing to go out but that the other New Yorkers and the New England men—men like William C. Whitney and Governor Russell of Massachusetts—were unwilling to go that far." This was correct. The gold men sat in sullen silence as pandemonium raged for thirty-five minutes after Bryan sat down. They sullenly answered to the roll-call as the platform was carried, 628 to 301, and the old Democratic party, the party of Tilden and Cleveland, passed out of existence.

That evening the nominating speeches began. Bryan's name was on every tongue; the animosity toward the Eastern delegates was such that the slightest incident might have produced an explosion. But no incident occurred, for again the gold delegates sat silent as the roll of the States was called, or stated in brief and bitter words why they had no candidates to offer. William F. Harrity alone presented Pattison of Pennsylvania. The next day the balloting began. Most of the gold leaders left early, and when on the fifth ballot Bryan was named for the presidency, they were at their hotels sadly packing up and making ready to catch the first train. But Otto Gresham remained, and as Bryan's nomination was announced he heard Senator Vest ejaculate triumphantly, "Now we are even with old Cleveland!"

And Cleveland? Nearly a thousand miles distant he was gazing out on the waters of Buzzards Bay, his heart filled with we know not what bitterness. We know only that he denied himself to most callers, and answered few letters; that when C. S. Hamlin, returning from the

[1] Memorandum dated Oct. 6, 1921. McElroy MSS.

convention, spoke of running up to Gray Gables, he was told he had better not go; and that he burst out in a letter to Dickinson, "If ever there was a penitentiary devoted to the incarceration of those who commit crimes against the Democratic party, how easily it could be filled just at this time!"

THE first question which Cleveland and his Cabinet had to face was whether they should bolt the Chicago nominations. Their decision was difficult to make. Almost every Democratic newspaper in the East sharply disavowed a candidate who was described by the *World* as the product of hysteria, and a platform that the *Evening Post* declared was baser than any adopted since slavery days. But considerations of party honor and loyalty made it difficult for the President to issue an open repudiation of the Democratic organization or to give even tacit support to McKinley and the Republicans. A third ticket was obviously required. Some of the sound money men before leaving Chicago agreed upon a statement rejecting Bryan and his doctrines and calling for a new convention, and this was published on July 14 over the signatures of Senator Palmer, Comptroller Eckels, two former Representatives from Illinois, Forman and Cable, and others. The Reform Club of New York gave Eastern leadership to the movement. On July 15 it was announced that Secretary Herbert had bolted and that Olney would not support Bryan. Postmaster-General Wilson and other Cabinet members were besieged by reporters demanding a statement of intentions. The newspapers were full of names of prominent Democrats in private life who turned their backs on Bryan, and full also of endorsements of the ticket by men who might have been thought hostile. Such leaders as Gorman and Hill proved more interested in keeping control of their State machines than in maintaining the former principles of the party. For a time some thought of Hill as a possible sound-money nominee. He retired to Wolfert's Roost and to silence, refusing to be interviewed. Then, having announced that "I am a Democrat still— very still," in August he gave a dinner for Bryan and his wife.[1]

II

Cleveland thought of Bryan as a Populist pure and simple,[2] without the remotest idea of true Democratic principles; but he exhibited his

[1] Alexander, *Four Famous New Yorkers*, 272.
[2] Parker, *Grover Cleveland*, 209.

usual caution. "I have an idea, quite fixed and definite," he wrote Lamont,[1] "that for the present at least we should none of us say anything. I have heard from Herbert today. He says he has declared he will not support the ticket. I am sorry he has done so. We have a right to be quiet—indeed I feel that I have been invited to that course. I am not fretting except about the future of the country and party . . ." The President, who felt hurt that Whitney had not consulted him just before leaving for Chicago, was not in communication with him or with many others. William L. Wilson agreed that Cleveland and the Cabinet would be wise to keep silent and act together, and wait and see if a sound money ticket was not later nominated which they could support.[2] Already a movement toward that end was on foot, for in accordance with the Palmer-Eckels call all national committeemen belonging to the gold wing of the party were being urged to meet in Indianapolis on August 7.

Meanwhile, Cleveland was called from Gray Gables to attend the funeral of William E. Russell in Boston. The Massachusetts leader, after days and nights of exhausting labor in Chicago, the first of Whitney's party to rise and the last to go to bed, had departed for a short vacation in the woods near Little Pabos, Quebec. For years he had overtaxed his frail body. On the morning of July 16 his friends at the fishing camp found him cold in bed, where he had died peacefully in his sleep. It was a loss that conservative Democracy could ill afford. As Charles Eliot Norton said, he was the most persuasive and effective of all the younger men in the party because his great abilities were matched by a complete sincerity.[3] He had written his wife from the convention on July 8 that "I had no idea how hard and distasteful this task would be. I have but one comfort in it: I have done my duty with fidelity"—and as the *Nation* remarked, this last phrase might be taken as the summary of his laborious life. To the newspaper men at the funeral Cleveland, carefully dressed in a long frock coat and silk hat, and tanned a brick red by the Cape Cod sun, looked worn and discouraged. "His face apparently was as full as ever, but there was a look of added age; the lines seemed harder and the gray mustache, for all its bristling, had less color than even a few months ago."[4]

[1] McElroy, *Grover Cleveland*, II, 226.
[2] MS Diary, July 15, 1896.
[3] *Harvard Graduate's Magazine*, December, 1896.
[4] Boston *Journal*, July 21, 1896.

The conference of Gold-Democratic committeemen in Indianapolis early in August resulted in the call for a national convention to be held in the same city on September 2. Palmer, Vilas, and Dickinson were the men most active in the movement, while the Louisville *Courier-Journal* office became a headquarters for the labor of bringing delegates together. It was an uphill task; but a fortnight before the convention met the principal owner of that newspaper, Walter N. Haldeman, wrote Watterson that, after much hard but effective work, the promise at last was for a large convention of first class men, the delegates representing every State and Territory in the American Union except possibly "three of the rotten boroughs of the West." For a time the leaders were in great perplexity as to whom they should nominate. Vilas and Bragg of Wisconsin were suggested; a small group favored Watterson, who was in Europe at the time, and another small group J. Sterling Morton; while there was an insistent demand from various quarters for William L. Wilson. When Oscar S. Straus told Wilson that Carl Schurz and others were vigorously recommending his nomination, Wilson demurred. He did not want the honor, others were willing and eager to grasp it, and he feared that he would be accused of using the patronage of the Postoffice Department to help his candidacy. "I shall do all I can to direct attention to Senator Palmer," he confided to his diary, "and in any event away from myself." [1]

Palmer, in the end, was the man. He was nominated on the first ballot by a huge majority over Bragg, and Gen. Simon B. Buckner of Kentucky, a Confederate veteran, was named for the vice presidency. Delegates from forty-one States and three Territories were present, and the name of National Democratic Party was adopted. Cleveland was pleased by the candidates and still more by the declaration of principles, for the convention praised his patriotism and courage in the heartiest terms, and denounced protection and free silver in the same plank as schemes to enrich a few at the expense of the masses. "I feel grateful," he wrote Vilas,[2] "to those who have relieved the political atmosphere with such a delicious infusion of fresh air. Every Democrat after reading the platform ought to thank God that the glorious principles of the party have found defenders who will not permit them to be polluted by impious hands." He could have had the nomination

[1] MS Diary, July 28, 1896.
[2] Sept. 5, 1896. Vilas Papers.

for himself by acclamation, but he had peremptorily refused it.

Everyone, including Cleveland, understood that the Palmer-Buckner ticket would not obtain a single electoral vote. The two old soldiers, invested with the pathetic nobility of the past, made a vigorous campaign and were a stirring sight as they appeared together on the platform; but they were sacrificial figures, whose real mission was to divert enough votes from the Bryan column to make certain of the election of McKinley.[1] Cleveland was quite willing that, in States like Kentucky, the Gold-Democratic ticket should throw the electors to McKinley. He never believed for an instant that the Chicago ticket was Democratic at all, and as between Bryan and McKinley he unquestionably preferred the latter. It was with some difficulty that he refrained from making a public attack on the silver candidates, and he wrote Lamont:

I am perplexed concerning the course I should pursue. My inclination, of course, is to join the chorus of denunciation, but I am doubtful as to the wisdom of such action, in the light of a chance that [it] might do more harm than good. My position cannot be misunderstood by any man, woman, or child in the country. I am President of all the people, good, bad, or indifferent, and as long as my opinions are known, ought perhaps to keep myself out of their squabbles. I must attempt to coöperate with Congress during another session in the interest of needed legislation, and perhaps ought not to unnecessarily further alienate that body and increase its hatred of me, and if I take an active and affirmatively aggressive position it may aid the cause we have *not* at heart, in increasing the effectiveness of the cry of presidential interference. In addition to all this, no one of weight or judgment in political matters has advised me to speak out—though I shall be surprised if Palmer does not urge it soon.

If you say anything, I do not care how plainly you present the inference that I am in accord with your views.

Yet very wisely, for in good taste he could pursue no other course, he avoided all active participation in the campaign. When the Gold-Democrats held their notification meeting at Louisville, he declined to attend. He merely permitted the publication of a letter to the national chairman, saying that as a Democrat devoted to the integrity of his party he should greatly have liked to be present and to mingle with those who insisted that its glorious standard should still be borne aloft as of old in faithful hands.[2] Late in October he went to Princeton,

---

[1] Cf. Isaac Marcosson, *Adventures in Interviewing*, 19.
[2] Sept. 10, 1896. Cleveland Papers.

where the college (just becoming a university) was holding its sesqui-centennial celebration. Here, in the presence of a large body of scholars and public men, he delivered one of the most carefully prepared addresses of his career. He spoke on the themes usual for such an occasion—the duty of educated men, the responsibility of institutions of learning to the state, and the dangers of public ignorance concerning the fundamental principles of economics and politics. Some of the passages of the address had a direct application to the campaign then approaching its close. It was as important, he said, for a nation to show honesty and fidelity to its obligations as for an individual to do so.[1] "Neither the glitter of its power, nor the tinsel of its commercial prosperity, nor the gaudy show of its people's wealth, can conceal the cankering rust of national dishonesty, and cover the meanness of national bad faith." A constant stream of thoughtful, informed men, he believed, should come from our colleges to preach national honor and integrity. And later in the address he touched on the perils which lurked in social or political intolerance. "When popular discontent and passion are stimulated by the art of designing partisans to a pitch perilously near to class hatred or sectional anger, I would have our universities and colleges sound the alarm in the name of American brotherhood and fraternal dependence." This speech, which received much commendation from the conservative Eastern press, both Democratic and Republican, brought Cleveland as near the verge of an actual political utterance as he came.

III

While he thus kept out of the campaign, he had to deal with what he regarded as the treachery of important Federal officeholders who got into it on the Bryan side. Of these there were many. He was disappointed, for example, by the course of Holmes Conrad, the Solicitor-General, who immediately espoused the silver ticket. Early in September Cleveland wrote Vilas that he was exceedingly angry and humiliated by the actions of these false Democrats, and was anxiously considering his duty in the matter.[2] He realized that many of the renegades—for so he thought of them—had powerful political sponsors, and that to

[1] Public Opinion, Oct. 29, 1896.
[2] Sept. 5, 1896. Cleveland Papers.

make many dismissals would accentuate the schism in the party. "I am hesitating," he concluded, "but it must not surprise some of these people if they run against unpleasantly sharp corners." In the end tolerance won the day, and he rejected a proscriptive policy.

A particularly difficult question, however, was presented by the defection of Secretary Hoke Smith. The able Georgian had, in the face of immense pressure, steadily supported the gold standard, arguing for it in many speeches in his native State and upholding it through his Atlanta *Journal*. But like other Southerners, he felt that to lead a revolt against his party would be to run the risk of a Republican victory and the restoration of negro rule—an intolerable prospect. Reluctantly, he fell into line behind Bryan; though he never accepted free silver, and during the late summer and fall repeatedly said so in public speeches.

Smith wrote frankly to Cleveland on July 20, explaining that he had promised the people of Georgia before the convention that he would support the nominee, and that the "local situation" made it necessary for him to do so.[1] At the same time he began to show constraint in his relations with the other Cabinet members. He had been wont to ride around nearly every evening on his bicycle to Carlisle's house for a chat, but now ceased doing so.[2] Cleveland sent him a rather tart reply, combining both rebuke and expostulation. He did not understand, he wrote, how Smith could accept the Chicago nominees and reject the platform—it was straining at a gnat and swallowing a camel; he did not see how he could take off his coat to help elect men whose nomination largely depended upon the virulence of their hatred of the Administration; and he was not impressed by Smith's argument on the local situation—"I suppose much was said about the 'local situation' in 1860." Though it was a natural position to take, it was not very considerate. Smith accepted the reference to 1860 in good part, writing Cleveland that while he was devoted to the nation, in the year named he would have gone with his State, and now he must stand by it. Other Cabinet members, and especially Carlisle and Wilson, hoped that he would not be forced out of the official family. As Carlisle well said, Smith had been an able Secretary; the Administration had but a few months to continue, and for the present was without organized support; his retirement would make an unpleasant stir in the country, and

[1] Hoke Smith Papers.
[2] Wilson's MS Diary, July 30, 1896.

give him the position of a man persecuted for party's sake—and then he was such a bluff, likable fellow!

But Cleveland was adamant, and Smith's resignation, offered on August 6, was accepted ten days later to take effect on September 1. In his place Cleveland named David R. Francis of Missouri. "I hope I need not say," he wrote Smith, "how deeply I regret your retirement, and how much I appreciate the devotion, industry, and ability which have characterized your discharge of duty as a member of my official family." [1] Wilson always thought that if Smith had gone to Gray Gables just after the convention, and explained how delicate was his position as a good Georgian and the editor of a daily newspaper, the difficulty might have been smoothed over without a rupture.[2] However, there was no ill feeling. Cleveland the next winter kindly invited Smith to attend the annual Cabinet dinner at the White House, and Smith accepted.

The result of the election was hardly in doubt after the middle of September. Lamont, who was in close touch with Hill and the situation in New York, told the Cabinet a fortnight later that the Bryan movement was on the wane, and that while the regulars and Tammany men made a great show of enthusiasm for the ticket, this was utterly hollow. Many who shouted the loudest in public for Bryan were saying in private that they would not vote for him. Cleveland returned to the White House on October 9, "looking thoroughly well and in excellent spirits, being fully convinced that there is no danger of Bryan's election." [3] In the last week of the canvass a certain undercurrent of uneasiness was visible among sound money people because of numerous reports that much of the labor vote was drifting to Bryan. There was a sharp squeeze for money on October 29, call rates in New York going to one hundred per cent; and withdrawals of gold took place in the metropolis and in San Francisco. But this flurry passed. On the evening of election day all the Cabinet officers who were in the capital met at eight o'clock at the White House to hear the returns. They soon came pouring in on a special wire, announcing immense Republican gains from the Northeast and Central West, and it was easy to discern that a great tidal wave was carrying McKinley to victory. Cleveland and his associates then fixed their attention particularly upon the re-

[1] Aug. 16, 1896. Hoke Smith Papers.
[2] Wilson's MS Diary, Oct. 2, 1896.
[3] *Ibid.*, Oct. 9, 1896

turns from the border States—Kentucky, in which Carlisle was interested, West Virginia, Wilson's State, and Maryland. While the evening was still young Maryland was pronounced safe. At one in the morning, when the gathering broke up, West Virginia as well was in the McKinley column, and it was all but certain that Kentucky was to be placed there.[1]

Cleveland could not but be pleased by the decisive nature of the result. In a total vote of almost fourteen million, McKinley had a plurality of 602,000 over Bryan. Though the Gold-Democratic ticket had polled only 135,000 votes, it had been the means of transferring many more to the McKinley column. In State after State in the South —Alabama, Georgia, Louisiana—Bryan's vote ran behind that of Cleveland in 1892. Cleveland was pleased even more by the fact that the verdict at the polls was quietly and peacefully accepted. The Bryan movement had represented an attempt on an unprecedented scale to array the poor, the neglected, the unemployed, and the discontented against the "plutocratic" elements in America; it had aroused a depth of sectional feeling unknown since Reconstruction days; and yet the decision was accepted without a ripple of protest. And what gratified the President most of all were the voices, not a few in number, which declared that the victory for sound money was rather his than Hanna's or McKinley's. Dr. Fabian Franklin wrote in the Baltimore *News:*

When the history of the present time comes to be seriously written, the name of the hero of this campaign will be that of a man who was not a candidate, not a manager, not an orator; the fight which has just been won was made possible by the noble service of one steadfast and heroic citizen, and the victory which was achieved yesterday must be set down as the crowning achievement of his great record. . . . It is impossible to overestimate the value of the service Grover Cleveland has done through his twelve years of unswerving fidelity to the cause of honest money.

[1] Wilson's MS Diary, Nov. 3, 1896.

Chapter XXXVIII   *The Last Months in the White House*

IN this narrative of the political events of 1896 we have been hurried past a series of current governmental problems which gave Cleveland much toil and anxiety. Chief among them was the Cuban problem, one of the most intricate and interesting of all his foreign difficulties. Half-unwittingly, the United States was fast approaching a great turning-point in its history, when it could no longer claim isolation in world affairs. This approach Cleveland did his utmost to retard; and the Cuban crisis illustrated better than any other phase of his second Administration his attachment both to the old ways and to the cause of international peace. His treatment of it, as of the Hawaiian question and the Nicaraguan treaty, showed how deeply he detested a meddling or expansionist foreign policy. And since the question had to be taken up by McKinley where he dropped it, his determined resistance to the interventionists presents certain instructive contrasts with McKinley's policy.

The final Cuban insurrection against Spanish misgovernment had broken out in February, 1895. The island at this time contained about 1,500,000 people. Roughly two-thirds of them were whites; one-third were negroes, mulattoes, or of Indian and white blood. They were for the most part illiterate, poverty-stricken, and superstitious, but they were not too degraded to rebel against the intolerable treatment given them by the Spanish government. Within a few months the revolt had become desperately serious to Spain, and almost equally serious to the United States—an inky cloud that overspread our whole southern horizon. In all its features it was calculated to embarrass and involve our government. It was openly directed and nourished by a Cuban junta in New York under the able Estrada Palma. It was assisted by filibustering expeditions joyously fitted out in the United States, more than two-score of which left our shores in the first two years of the revolt and fifteen of which successfully reached Cuba. From beginning to end it was encouraged by a violent jingo propaganda in this country, which in Hearst's *Journal* and Pulitzer's *World* became malignantly sensational.

Most telling of all, the economic interests of Americans were injuriously affected by the rebellion, while their sentiment for liberty was deeply touched. The war raged in every part of the island, and the rebels shortly adopted a systematic policy of destruction. If they ruined the industries and resources, they said, and reduced Cuba to a desert, the Spaniards would have to abandon it. Plantations were laid waste, with the result that the sugar crop, which the year before the revolt had been well above a million tons, fell in 1896 to barely 200,000 tons, while the tobacco crop in the same period dropped from 450,000 bales to 50,000 bales. American investors and importers suffered. Meanwhile, the harsh behavior of Spanish officials and troops excited indignation in the United States, where many people felt that we should show a fraternal regard to a body of devoted revolutionists striving to gain freedom from an old-world monarchy.[1]

Cleveland had acted promptly in defining the government's position. He issued the usual proclamation of neutrality, which did not recognize the belligerency of the Cubans but did acknowledge the existence of a state of rebellion; and he saw to it that the professions of neutrality were enforced. A strict watch was maintained against filibusterers, and though evasions were numerous, the American patrol of our own coast became more effective than the Spanish patrol of Cuban waters. Madrid was convinced, as Cleveland and Olney knew, that the insurrection would not have lasted a month but for the assistance that the Cubans obtained from America. The Administration therefore tried to leave no loophole for a charge that our governmment was negligent of its duty. At the same time, Olney intervened vigorously in behalf of American citizens, chiefly of Cuban birth or descent, who were arrested in Cuba, and he claimed compensation for injuries to American property. In this two-sided policy—maintenance of neutrality and insistence on recognized rights—iron rigor was shown and it met with success.

But it rapidly became necessary to do more—to urge Spain to remove the causes of this dangerous conflagration, and to resist the interventionist spirit which rapidly arose in Congress. The former undertaking proved fruitless. When Olney in the spring of 1896 sent a long note to Spain through her minister, Dupuy de Lome, urging concessions in the interests of peace, the head of the Spanish government, Canovas, sent back a virtual refusal. He was willing to make vague

[1] Charles E. Chapman, *A History of the Cuban Republic*, 73 ff.

promises to the insurgents, but nothing more. Cleveland and Olney had to retreat, the former writing his Secretary on July 13 that "I am thinking a great deal about Cuba, but am as far as ever from seeing the place where we can get in." [1] Since Spain remained immovable to the end of the Administration, there was no place whatever to "get in."

From the very beginning Congress had more than reflected the general sympathy with Cuba. Members of all parties, with the Presidential election approaching and with the popular dislike of Cleveland mounting in the South and West, were glad both to seek votes in warlike speeches and gestures, and to make trouble for the Administration. The Senate naturally assumed the lead in attempting to provoke a controversy with Spain. Its sessions in the spring of 1896 were enlivened by the bellicose antics of Lodge and Vest, and its proceedings were filled with speeches denouncing the Spanish "butcheries," with bills proposing the appropriation of millions for new battleships and fortifications, and with resolutions for an inquiry or for peaceful intervention. Even Sherman, the chairman of the Foreign Relations Committee, talked wildly of "crimes that are almost beyond description." In April the two houses passed a concurrent resolution recognizing Cuban belligerency, and proposing that the President should offer Spain our friendly offices to bring about peace on the basis of the independence of the island. As this was not a joint resolution, no presidential action upon it was necessary. The topic was nervously discussed in a Cabinet meeting,[2] where Olney suggested that the President might head off precipitate measures by sending a commission or an agent to Cuba to report on the conflict. This was an old idea of Olney's—he had previously proposed sending General Schofield to the island. The suggestion did not strike the others as feasible, and Cleveland let the matter drop. But a few days later he told William L. Wilson that if a joint resolution came to him "I have made up my mind how to deal with it, and if they try to play politics I am ready for them."

Some Congressmen even talked of forcing Cleveland to recognize Cuba, which would of course have meant war. "The Cabinet meeting today," Wilson wrote early in May,[3] "was largely given to foreign affairs, Olney reading a translation furnished by the Spanish Embassy of

[1] Olney Papers.
[2] Wilson's MS Diary, Feb. 28, 1896.
[3] *Ibid.*, May 12, 1896.

the speech with which the Queen Regent opened the Cortes yesterday. Some conversation ensued on the probability of the passage of the *joint* resolution offered by Senator Morgan, directing the recognition of the Cuban insurgents, and it was believed by all that there was a dangerous playing with politics in it. 'If it comes,' said the President, 'it will give me an opportunity to tell the American people some plain truths, and d—d if they don't get them!' " But the Congressional leaders were too wary to expose themselves to such a rebuke.

II

During all this time Cleveland was giving perplexed thought to the larger aspects of the Cuban problem. He wrote Olney after the national conventions that the plan of purchase was really worth considering, but that it would be absurd to spend perhaps a hundred million dollars in buying the island and present it to the inhabitants. On the other hand, he hesitated even to think of incorporating it into the United States as a territory, and he knew that many who talked loudest in favor of intervention, such as Sherman, were opposed to any form of annexation. He added that he did not like the way in which Consul-General Fitzhugh Lee in Havana was "rolling intervention like a sweet morsel under his tongue." Cleveland had been informed by Senator Call of Florida that in 1892 a group of London bankers had undertaken to form a syndicate to purchase the independence of the island for $100,000,000, that sum to be repaid them, with a profit, by the new Cuban government. According to Call, the Spanish Ministry at the time had been seriously considering the offer when it fell. This story is not very plausible. The ruling idea of the President, at all events, was that he must move cautiously and let events ripen. A friend who visited him that summer at Gray Gables writes: [1]

Monday night, the 3rd (of August), had an interesting talk, especially about Cuba. He told me of the visit of the sub-committee of the Senate Committee .on Foreign Relations. He asked them why they did not acknowledge the belligerency of the insurgents if they thought it wise; the Congress had the power to bring about war—it would be the duty of the Executive to obey. Oh, no, they did not wish that. Then he explained how the Executive had pushed the American demands as to damages, treatment of prisoners claiming American protection, etc. He thought they went away content, after seeing the actual difficulties, to let the matter remain in the hands of the Executive.

[1] Unsigned Memorandum. Cleveland Papers.

The President went on to tell me of the difficulties of the position. He was willing to go a great way in insisting upon humanity—in fact, he feared there were some outrages upon both sides, if the truth were known. But in a general way he felt it incumbent upon him to be extremely careful; as the public mind seemed to be in an inflammable state, and a spark might kindle a conflagration. He said there seemed to be an epidemic of insanity in the country just at this time.

The virtual repudiation of the Cleveland Administration by its own party in the summer of 1896, and the defeat of the Democrats in November, naturally made Cleveland and Olney more cautious than ever in their handling of Spanish relations. But it in no way impaired their courage, and in December they once more took a firm stand against the interventionist tendencies of Congress. Cleveland in his annual message dealt with the situation in a number of long paragraphs. Their tone was patient, but he said flatly that the Spanish demand for an unconditional surrender on the part of the insurgents appeared unreasonable; that it seemed that if Spain would offer the Cubans genuine home rule, peace might be effected on that basis; and that the United States could not let the insurrection drag on forever—there would come a time, if useless bloodshed continued, when our obligation to the government of Spain would be superseded by a higher obligation, which we could not hesitate to recognize and discharge. In effect, Cleveland was warning Spain to act. At the same time, he was pleading with Congress that she be given a little more time to come to her senses. Both pleas were made more striking by what immediately followed.

In December the Foreign Relations Committee at once took up the Cameron resolution for recognizing the independence of Cuba—that is, for war. It was introduced by Cameron on the 9th; the Administration indicated its stern opposition; and for a time it was supposed that the committee would stifle it. Olney was relieved when Chairman Sherman called on him and told him that he entirely agreed with his course in Cuban affairs. This was in accordance with a pronouncement by Hoar, who was against armed intervention and had said that Olney was a good square, clear-headed Yankee, who could be trusted with the diplomacy of the government. Yet on the very next day Sherman asked Olney to come to the committee's room, met him on the threshold with the announcement that they had decided to adopt resolutions on Cuban independence, and asked his advice on the phraseology! Olney felt betrayed, and his anger may be imagined. He forthwith gave the press a heated interview.

In this interview he said that there were likely to be serious misapprehensions both at home and abroad regarding the Cameron resolution recognizing Cuban independence, and that he wished to correct them.[1] It was his duty to point out that if Congress passed the resolution, it could be "regarded only as an expression of opinion by the eminent gentlemen who vote for it." The power to recognize the so-called republic of Cuba, he asserted, rested exclusively with the Executive. All that the resolution would accomplish would be to inflame popular passions in the United States and Spain, place in peril the lives and property of American citizens travelling abroad, and make the conduct of our foreign relations more difficult. At once there was a storm in the Senate. Cushman K. Davis asserted that if Congress should adopt a joint resolution requiring the President to recognize the Cuban Republic, and should pass it over Cleveland's veto, the President would have either to execute the law or submit himself to impeachment. Senator William E. Chandler frothed with anger, and said that to intimidate Congress the President was playing the rôle of Andrew Johnson. Evidently the constitutional problem involved was debatable. Various authorities took different sides. But Olney's sensible statement had done its work; almost the whole press attacked the resolution, and ex-Senator Edmunds declared that Olney had not only acted properly, but had performed a patriotic duty. There was a break in the stock market even before the resolution was reported. "Somebody at the Washington end," wrote R. L. O'Brien,[2] "was making money out of it before the committee had opened its doors." But amid general relief the resolution was put aside and left to gather dust on the Senate calendar.

In dealing with the Cuban troubles, Cleveland and Olney had accomplished several minor achievements and one of major importance. They had strictly enforced the neutrality laws, they had protected American rights, they had brought pressure on Spain to promise constitutional changes in Cuba, and above all, they had kept the peace. Cleveland's friend A. B. Farquhar more than a decade later described an interview between the President and some excited members of Congress who talked of an immediate declaration of war against Spain—

---

[1] *Public Opinion,* Dec. 24, 1896.
[2] See R. L. O'Brien's history of this whole episode in the Boston *Transcript,* March 18, 1897.

the date of the interview being given only as "one Sunday afternoon." [1]
The President, according to Farquhar, drew himself up and asserted
that if Congress declared war he, as commander-in-chief, would refuse
to mobilize the army. It is incredible that he ever made such a statement, and Farquhar doubtless exaggerated some simpler occurrence.
But till the very end Cleveland remained viligant. A week before he
left office he called Frederic R. Coudert to the White House, told him
that he feared war with Spain was imminent unless an adjustment
could be reached at once, confessed that he had lost all faith in Consul-
General Lee, and proposed that Coudert accept a special mission to the
Spanish authorities in Cuba. With his knowledge of Spanish and the
Latin peoples, he said, he might bring about an accommodation. But
Coudert refused. By their very coolness Cleveland and Olney in these
months did much to damp the jingoism raging about them. Within two
years McKinley was being wildly applauded as a war President; but
as our perspective lengthens, the rôle of Cleveland seems decidedly
the more creditable of the two.

III

A far happier chapter in our foreign affairs during the last year of
Cleveland's Administration had to do with the arbitration treaty with
Great Britain. Ever since he entered office Cleveland had been a stalwart friend of international arbitration. In the atmosphere of amity
which followed the Venezuelan agreement, the long-standing proposals
for a general treaty of arbitration between the two great English-
speaking Powers were rapidly brought to a head. With the cordial
approval of Lord Salisbury, Sir Julian Pauncefote and Olney during
1895 negotiated a compact. [2] It pledged the two nations, for a period
of five years, to submit to arbitration, under certain limitations, all
disputes which they might fail to adjust by diplomatic means, and
provided for the choosing of arbitrators. [3] Cleveland sent the treaty to
the Senate on January 11, 1897, with a warm message of approbation.
It might be of immeasurable benefit, he thought, not only to the two
nations signing it, but to the world at large. The lessons its successful
operation would teach "are sure to be felt and taken to heart by other

[1] *Harper's Weekly*, Aug. 1, 1908. McElroy accepts the story.
[2] R. B. Mowat, *Life of Lord Pauncefote*, 160 ff.
[3] The text of the treaty is in James, *Olney*, 280 ff.

nations, and will thus mark the beginning of a new epoch in civilization."
The treaty indeed embodied a far-reaching plan, in which everyone
concerned might take the greatest pride. Lord Salisbury deserves credit
for initiating the negotiations, and for "working like a nigger," as his
wife told Henry White, on the project.[1] Cleveland deserves credit for
instantly responding, in the spirit of a passage of his inaugural address
of 1893 advocating general arbitration treaties. Pauncefote is to be
credited with much tact and skill in the drafting the instrument. The
principal labor, however, was performed by Olney, who threw himself into the undertaking with characteristic impetuosity, insisted that
arbitration must be automatic instead of depending upon special agreements in each instance, and brought the British Government, against
its original intention, to include a limited arbitration of territorial
claims.[2] Though the world has since found that arbitration agreements
do not always work efficiently, this instrument was at least a fine gesture
of mutual trust and optimistic belief in reason by the two most powerful nations of the globe. Parliament ratified it without hesitation.

In the United States its reception was enthusiastic. The press, without regard to party, was almost a unit behind it.[3] Bryan's *World-Herald*
grew dithyrambic, saying that it was "one of the grandest triumphs
of humanity," "the supreme achievement of the nineteenth century."
Only a few journals, like Dana's *Sun*, opposed it. Carnegie was delighted. Carl Schurz sent Cleveland his congratulations couched in
extravagant terms. "It is a masterpiece in point of workmanship," he
wrote. "It sheds the brightest lustre upon the close of the nineteenth
century. It does infinite honor to the great American republic and to
the administration that bears your name."[4] A National Arbitration
Committee, headed by William E. Dodge, with John Bassett Moore for
secretary, and a list of eminent members—Taft, Schurz, Charles W.
Eliot, Nelson A. Miles, and many more—began a brisk propagandist
campaign. Many State legislatures passed resolutions in favor of the
treaty; petitions poured in upon the Senate from universities, chambers
of commerce, church congresses, and local massmeetings throughout
the country. "We sent out last week," Dodge wrote Cleveland early in

[1] Nevins, *Henry White*, 124.
[2] James, *Olney*, 147, 148.
[3] *Public Opinion*, Jan. 21, 1897.
[4] Jan. 13, 1897. Schurz Papers.

February,[1] "fifty thousand circular letters to ministers like the enclosed, endorsed by the heads of each denomination, and some three thousand letters to leading people. We have also sent to all the Senators and to editors the enclosed brief." An effort was made by a group including Alice Freeman Palmer, Maud Ballington Booth, Elizabeth Custer, and many more to enlist the women of the country.

Yet after all these efforts, the treaty failed in the Senate. The debate, beginning when it was favorably reported by the Foreign Relations Committee on February 2, ran into the new Administration, which favored it as warmly as Cleveland had done. On May 5 it fell short of a two-thirds majority, the vote being 43 yeas to 26 nays. Cleveland's disappointment was keen, and Olney's even keener. The latter soon afterward committed to paper an extended analysis of the reasons for the rejection, which he sent to London and which was circulated among the British Cabinet.[2] Olney wished it understood that the great mass of the American people loved peace and were attached to Great Britain, and asked the English leaders to ignore the "mouthings" of cheap politicians and the "lurid utterances of the political exiles and convicts who infest our large cities." He explained that the treaty had been defeated by individual jingoism; by partisan dislike of anything emanating from the Cleveland Administration; by a reaction against the gushingly Anglophile speeches of Ambassador Bayard; by the irritation of silverite Senators against Great Britain as the most prominent and powerful supporter of the gold standard; and by pressure from shipbuilding interests anxious for a large navy. But above all other reasons he placed the fact that the Senate was steadily asserting itself as the dominant power in the government; that it was aggressively encroaching on the other branches, and when it received a treaty, insisted that "it must be either altogether defeated or so altered as to bear the unmistakable Senate stamp—and thus be the means both of humiliating the executive and of showing to the world the greatness of the Senate."

It might be added, as another reason, that some Senators feared the treaty would result in an unfavorable arbitration of the Alaskan boundary, and cripple the United States in its efforts to have the Clayton-

---

[1] Feb. 10, 1897. Cleveland Papers.
[2] Nevins, *Henry White*, 125 ff.

Bulwer Treaty abrogated. It was evident that Cleveland and Olney had miscalculated the response of the Senate to a generous ideal and to public opinion. But the moral effect of their effort was great, and contributed much to the now rapid growth of cordiality between England and America.

IV

The closing months of Cleveland's Administration were marked also by renewed activity in the prosecution of the trusts under the Sherman Act of 1890. As Attorney-General, consciously or unconsciously biassed by his corporation leanings, Olney had shown a distinct lack of vigor in this field. He had been hampered by the attitude of the lower courts toward the anti-trust law, which received a stricter construction than its authors had ever expected or intended; but he had also allowed the government's cases to be carelessly prepared, and had acquiesced too readily in the assumed limitations on his powers. It was true that the Sherman Act, as the Federal courts interpreted it, contained at least four defects. It was based on the interstate commerce clause of the Constitution, forbidding any combination or conspiracy in restraint of trade or commerce; yet it did not prohibit interstate commerce in articles produced, owned, or controlled by monopolies. The general words and phrases which it contained, such as "monopolies" and "contracts, combinations and conspiracies in restraint of trade and commerce," were nowhere defined. It contained no provision, such as had been incorporated in the Interstate Commerce Act, to prevent the refusal of witnesses to testify on the ground of self-incrimination. Finally, there was no appropriation enabling the Department of Justice to accumulate evidence and investigate violations of the law. Experience during the Harrison Administration showed that no victories could be scored against the trusts under such a statute unless strong cases were prepared, with the indictments placed on the best possible ground and supported by a telling array of evidence. Yet Olney allowed the suit against the Sugar Trust to go to trial in deplorably weak form, with the result that, as we have seen, in January of 1895 the Supreme Court dismissed it.

His successor in the Attorney-Generalship, Judson Harmon, now proved that he could do better. He had not been in office eight months when he informed Congress (February 8, 1896) of the weaknesses of the Sherman Act, and requested some remedial legislation. Cleveland supported him in this demand, and in his long annual message of December, 1896, included a section on the trusts, which he vigorously condemned and for dealing with which he asked a new enactment. But while the Administration thus stamped the existing law as inadequate, it prepared for the first time to make the best possible use of it. Late in 1896 Harmon brought up in the Supreme Court the case of the United States vs. the Trans-Missouri Freight Association, a dangerous railroad pool.[1] He had briefs and evidence prepared with a thoroughness that Olney had never shown. The result was that on March 22, 1897, the Supreme Court, by a vote of five to four, reversed the decision of the lower courts and held the Sherman Act applicable to this monopolistic railway group. Harmon had appeared in person before the court, and had faced a group of the ablest attorneys in the United States, including James Carter, E. J. Phelps, W. F. Guthrie, and John F. Dillon. It was a signal victory and laid the foundation for the successful action under President Roosevelt and Attorney-General Knox against the Northern Securities merger. Meanwhile, Harmon had begun a new anti-trust suit, that against the cast-iron pipe monopoly (the Addyston Pipe & Steel Company) which eventually was also won by the government.[2]

It is evident to anyone who studies Cleveland's papers during these years that Olney constantly tried to induce him to take a more resigned attitude toward the difficulty of trust prosecutions than he wished to take. Cleveland was always loyal to his Cabinet, and usually gave them a large responsibility within their own spheres. When the *World* vociferously denounced Olney for neglect of duty, Cleveland wrote with his own hand two letters to the editor, trying to persuade him that his criticisms were founded upon a misunderstanding of the law.[3] But he never followed Olney to the extreme length of the latter's views upon the helplessness of the government. As late as December, 1896, Olney was still trying to influence the President, and in his papers there is a set of "suggestions" on the trust question which he prepared for Cleveland's message of that month. This remarkable document,[4] a

[1] 166 U. S., 290.
[2] 78 *Fed.*, 712.
[3] These letters, never published, are now apparently lost.
[4] Dated December, 1896. Olney Papers.

virtual hoisting of the white flag, is nowhere mentioned by his authorized biographer. Olney began by stating that the law had proved "almost wholly inoperative because of inherent difficulties surrounding the subject-matter and because of the complex character of our governmental system which, while making the Federal authority supreme within its sphere, has carefully limited that sphere by metes and bounds which cannot be transgressed." He went on to say that it had been tested in many courts in all parts of the Union, and had broken down; and that it had now received "its final and conclusive interpretation from the Supreme Court" (that is, in the Sugar Trust case). "The result seems to be that, unless transportation between States or between the United States and foreign countries are covered by it, the intended subjects-matter of the law are not within the scope of Federal jurisdiction." But, Olney concluded, that did not mean that there was no remedy for the evils of the trusts. That remedy "is to be sought in a different quarter, namely, in the powers vested in the several States. No reason is perceived why these powers are not ample for the correction of all the evils and abuses which are alleged." He forgot that the failure of the States in their anti-trust prosecutions had been a main reason for the passage of the Sherman Act.

But Cleveland refused to accept this doctrine. His message asked for increased Federal powers, and he supported Harmon in his prosecutions. Thanks to the increased aggressiveness of the Department of Justice in 1896–97, the Administration thus went out of office with a far more creditable record against the trusts than had seemed possible in 1895.

In the last week of his Administration Cleveland was compelled to take action upon the difficult question of immigration restriction, and in his veto of the Lodge bill for a literacy test he evinced a resolution that is easily underestimated. A movement of protest against unrestricted immigration had been gaining headway for a decade. As the tide of aliens rose during the eighties and its sources shifted to southern and eastern Europe, a feeling of uneasiness had grown into positive alarm. In 1882 the number of immigrants had reached 789,000; it had fallen in the next few years; and then it began to increase again, reaching 547,000 in 1888. The prospect of a continuous stream of more than half a million foreigners annually from Italy, Greece, Hungary, Poland, and the Slavic nations was alarming to conservative minds.

They believed that it threatened the essential character of the nation, and they connected it with the Haymarket massacre, the anarchist agitation, and the disorders of labor. From a multitude of lecture platforms, editorial offices, and labor headquarters poured forth demands for the restriction of immigration. We were getting the offscourings of Europe; [1] the moral fibre of the nation was being enfeebled by its absorption of the dregs of the Old World; [2] if there was not a stop, America would soon be dominated by foreign defectives and their descendants [3]—so the protests ran. The impulse was rising which a generation later, thrusting Presidents and liberals out of its way, was to bar the gates of the nation to all but a little rill of carefully apportioned immigrants.

Lodge's bill refused entry to any immigrant over sixteen who could not read and write either English or some other language; though it permitted persons over fifty, accompanying as parent or grandparent some qualified adult immigrant capable of supporting them, to enter even if illiterate. Northern Europe had little illiteracy, but the proposed law would fall hard on southern and eastern countries. The bill passed the House by a large majority, and the Senate by 34 to 31. There were many evidences that it had the general support of the public. Most Protestants were in favor of it, most labor leaders, especially outside the unions of skilled workers, and many social workers who were disturbed by problems of pauperism and social assimilation. If Cleveland had signed the bill he would have met with applause of the most fervent kind. In numerous issues of that convenient scrapbag, *Public Opinion*, from 1887 to 1897, we find restrictionist doctrines quoted from literally scores of important journals. The roster includes not only practically all Western and Southern newspapers, but the New York *Times*, the Philadelphia *Press*, the Baltimore *News*, the Chicago *Tribune*; such a progressive newspaper as the Springfield *Republican*; and even the *Jewish Messenger*.

But two days before he left office Cleveland vetoed the bill. He explained that it seemed to him unnecessarily harsh and oppressive, that the ability to read and write was a poor test of the qualities of a desirable citizen, and that there appeared no need for a reversal of the

[1] Philadelphia *Telegraph*, March 28, 1887.
[2] Chicago *Times*, March 27, 1887.
[3] Milwaukee *Journal*, March 27, 1887.

existing immigration policy. The Republican leaders who had pressed the measure (for the Senate vote had shown 26 Republican nays, 25 Democratic nays) were wroth, and Roosevelt wrote that "I took a kind of grim satisfaction in Cleveland's winding up his career by this action, so that his last stroke was given to injure his country as much as he possibly could." Lodge some years later heard that Cleveland then spoke of the veto with regret, and that he had been influenced by the misrepresentations of the German steamship offices in New York.[1] Upon the wisdom of the veto there may well be two opinions, but upon its courage there can be but one.

V

Late in 1896 Cleveland had began to make preparations for his retirement to private life. He would probably have decided to return to New York city had there not been three good reasons for preferring a place with more air, sunshine, and quiet—reasons named Ruth, Esther, and Marion. While still uncertain of his future place of residence, he had paid the visit to Princeton already noted. In this beautiful village, with its elm-shaded campus of two hundred acres, he had been entertained in a way which gave him some understanding of the social life of the faculty and townspeople. The students also had made him welcome in their own enthusiastic fashion. They had arranged a parade, and one of the transparencies they carried read, "Grover, send your boys to Princeton." At that moment there were only girls, but the invitation was all the more striking. Mrs. Cleveland, who had been to Westchester to look at houses, came down to breakfast one morning and said, "I have had an inspiration about our future home." "So have I," said Cleveland. Simultaneously they asked each other. "What is it?" And simultaneously each replied, "Princeton!"[2] Within a week after the election Cleveland had written Andrew F. West, professor of the classics, asking him for complete information about the town as a place to live;[3] and in his papers is still preserved the long reply which West sent under date of November 12. The final decision shortly followed.

In his last weeks in the White House Cleveland was beset by friends and others who wished his sanction in preparing magazine articles upon

---

[1] Letters of T. R. and H. C. L., I, 259–260.
[2] Mrs. Thomas J. Preston to author.
[3] Nov. 8, 1896. Cleveland Papers.

his Administration. As early as November 20 he wrote Gilder that "There are now three projects on foot to serve me up and help people to breast or dark meat, with or without stuffing." One of them was presented by no less a man than Carl Schurz. Cleveland was delighted, when the tall German-American appeared in Washington, to find that he had recovered from the Venezuelan affair and was satisfied with the civil service reform record. "He is a good and useful man and I am always pleased to have him friendly," wrote the President, "but as I told him once, he is a 'hard master.' " [1] Schurz's article, an admirable interpretation of the last four years, was published in *McClure's* for May, 1897. Another article, entitled "Mr. Cleveland as President," was prepared by Woodrow Wilson, and came out in the March *Atlantic*. Gilder himself for a time thought of a special essay, and Cleveland had spoken favorably of his doing something for "my poor old battered name"; but the undertaking was postponed and allowed to ripen into a series of intimate sketches which, after seeing the light in the *Century*, were finally published in book form in 1910.

A house was chosen in Princeton by Mrs. Cleveland—"Westland," a large colonial mansion of severely simple aspect, built of stone and covered with stucco, and surrounded by spacious grounds. Once more the effects of the family were packed and sent off. With characteristic modesty, Cleveland ordered his portrait by Eastman Johnson, which was White House property, taken down from the walls and placed in the attic. His wife and children departed for the new home. On the even of the inauguration McKinley, invited more than a month beforehand, came to dine at the White House, and the outgoing and incoming executives greeted each other with unaffected cordiality.[2] Next day they drove together to the Capitol, and Cleveland stood by his successor's side while Chief Justice Fuller administered the oath. Before they parted he warned McKinley of the danger of a war with Spain; but the subject on which he spoke to him with special earnestness was the preservation of a sound currency. The day might come again, he said in effect, when gold Democrats and gold Republicans would have to stand together against the silverites, and he hoped that McKinley would do nothing to make such a union difficult.

A southern excursion had been planned by Cleveland—a three weeks'

[1] McElroy, II, 241.
[2] Charles S. Olcott, *Life of William McKinley*, I, 341.

trip with Robley D. Evans, Leonard Wood, and Captain Lamberton on one of the lighthouse tenders, with fishing and shooting in the land-locked waters near Cape Hatteras. Years later Wood recalled in an address the beginning of that trip.[1] Cleveland came aboard the ship immediately after the inaugural parade, tired and worn from weeks of hard work. He sat down heavily. "I have had a long talk with President McKinley," he said. "He is an honest, sincere, and serious man. I feel that he is going to do his best to give the country a good administration. He impressed me as a man who will have the best interests of the country at stake." Cleveland paused. Then he went on, with a sigh. "I envy him today only one thing, and that was the presence of his own mother at the inauguration. I would have given anything in the world if my mother could have been at my inauguration."

Already the times were changing—in fact, they had changed. The election of 1896 seems, as we look back, to have ushered in a period of faster tempo in American life: a period of martial ardor, the Rough Riders, heavier gold production, unprecedented business prosperity, "A Hot Time in the Old Town," Mr. Dooley, bigger and more ruthless trusts, the first automobiles, the first movies, Stephen Crane, Frank Norris, the romantic novel of the *To Have and To Hold* type, more fashion, more travel, more education; a period of greater energy, variety, and exuberance. The clouds and gloom of the second Cleveland Administration rolled back; the sky seemed brighter, the air more sparkling, because of the storm that had passed. Cleveland was unfortunate in his era. The coming generation was to associate him with stagnation, poverty, and depression. He had held the craft on its course under a hurricane which had made the bravest cower and which all were glad to forget. Under a luckier commander the ship of state, the Union stronger and greater than ever, rode forth under blue skies and over gleaming waves. And yet he was not altogether unfortunate to have been tested as few Presidents have been. The day was to come when there was to seem something more heroic in the burly, silent figure who had held the wheel immovable under the blast than in most of the pilots who were favored by wind and tide.

[1] Cleveland Memorial Service, March 18, 1919.

Chief Justice Fuller   Mr. McKinley   Mr. Cleveland

MCKINLEY AND CLEVELAND ON MARCH 4, 1897

CLEVELAND in 1897 could not have found a more charming place of residence than Princeton. The pretty village retained an air of isolation, for it lay off the main railroad line and the automobile had not yet brought it close to New York and Philadelphia. It had a rural aspect and its life was simple, leisurely, and democratic. Yet the university relieved it from provincialism, gave it a touch of cosmopolitan culture, and by its now rapid growth made the place stir with life. Departments were steadily being added and the student body was increasing. Nevertheless, the old traditions were maintained. The Presbyterian flavor, so congenial to Cleveland, was still pervasively present; Greek letter fraternities were forbidden and the excesses of athletics frowned upon; and the faculty was not too large to possess a good deal of family spirit. Conservatism still ruled the university. Its president, Dr. Francis L. Patton, a former clergyman and professor of theology, was able and witty, but he believed in making progress by exceedingly slow and cautious stages.

The community in which the Clevelands took their place had not only many delightful people but a few men of distinction. Woodrow Wilson, coming in 1890 with his wife and three little girls, had conquered the initial distrust which some felt for him as a Southerner; William Milligan Sloane was at work on his large biography of Napoleon; Bliss Perry was teaching English literature; George McLean Harper, the future biographer of Wordsworth, was professor of Romance languages; and Andrew F. West, later dean of the graduate school, had charge of the instruction in Latin. Others of ability were to join the faculty within a few years. Paul Van Dyke was shortly to become professor of modern European history, and in 1900 his brother Henry Van Dyke was to leave the Brick Presbyterian Church in New York to teach literature; while in the same year John H. Finley was to drop the editorship of *Harper's Weekly* to occupy the chair of politics. Jesse Lynch Williams lived in Princeton for a time. With some of these men Cleveland had only a friendly acquaintanceship, but with others he reached a cordial intimacy. The closest to him were West, a huge rugged man, two hundred and forty pounds in weight, with a sea-captain's hearty voice and bearing and a blunt and stubborn character; and the athletic young Finley, still in his thirties when Cleveland met him.

Cleveland first saw "Westland," named in honor of the man who had brought him to Princeton, when on March 18, 1897, he returned from North Carolina amid a pouring rain. He was shortly writing West: "I have been here almost a week and have not seen you yet. How am I to get on in this way? Unless I see you within a very brief period I shall pull up stakes and clear out." He was elected to the Nassau Club, professors began to call, and as the noise of hammering ceased he wrote his old friends, Gilder, Benedict, and the rest, inviting them to Princeton. A study had been fitted up for him on the second floor. Troubled by the mass of presentation volumes which had accumulated during his presidency, he called upon the library to select any of the books he did not want. When the reference librarian, Varnum Lansing Collins, called, he reached into the pile, extricated a tome gorgeous in red leather and gilt, and remarked: "This is the Bible in the language of Borneo. I seldom read it. Could the library make use of that?" Before the end of March Benedict had arrived with some boxes of fine cigars and won $2 at cribbage. On April 2 occurred an event important to the Cleveland children. "We got the pony out of the cars and on to *terra firma* with some difficulty," wrote Cleveland,[1] "and today has been pony day here."

It was with surprising completeness that Cleveland identified himself with the Princeton community. The stiffness that had so often characterized his attitude in relation to learned men, the false modesty that had led him while President to refuse honorary degrees from Harvard and Princeton, the sternness that had marked him when public burdens lay heavy on his shoulders, all dissolved. In part this was due to the mellowness which advancing years and freedom from care brought him. In part it was due to the deference and cordiality—not unmingled with a little adulation—which members of the university showed him. In June he accepted the degree of doctor of laws, writing Gilder and Olney with humorous pride of his cap and gown and the faultless Latin of President Patton's speech of investiture. The little address with which he acknowledged the honor he felt in the new tie

[1] Cleveland Papers.

binding him to Princeton and "her glorious history, her venerable traditions, her bright trophies won on the field of higher education, and her sacred relation to the patriotic achievements which made us a nation," was admirably phrased. When in the summer of 1897 he went to Gray Gables, West came for a short visit. That fall, as the university reopened, he made a short speech to the faculty and students which attracted much attention and brought a pleased letter from W. L. Wilson.

His life in Princeton thereafter soon settled into a pleasant routine. He rose between seven and eight every morning; after breakfast he read the newspapers and dealt with his morning mail, to get which he sometimes strolled down the village street to the postoffice. It was only slowly and with reluctance that he was brought to accept the occasional help of a secretary, usually a student.[1] If improvements were going forward within his grounds he liked to superintend them. At some time during the day he usually went for a drive with his wife, for he had a handsome pair of horses in the stables and a coachman. When friends from out of town arrived he would drive to the station to meet them. Dinner was formal, and guests were more often present than not, but Cleveland cared little for dining out or for going to evening concerts or lectures. One of his first changes at "Westland" was an addition which afforded a billiard room downstairs and extra bedrooms upstairs. Another early experiment was the purchase of a rocky little farm about three miles from Princeton as a convenient stopping-place when out for a day's hunting; for he liked to shoot rabbits and quail across the snowy fields, and sometimes fished on Millstone River. This farm became a sore trial later, when he leased it to a young man who opened a farm-school there and tried to give others the misleading impression that it was under Cleveland's patronage.

At general university meetings Cleveland was often called into the chair. William L. Wilson describes in his diary for 1898 how he attended a Princeton-Yale debate as judge; Cleveland presided, there was a supper afterwards at the Nassau Club, and Cleveland, Patton, Woodrow Wilson, and others made speeches. At commencement Cleveland, in cap and gown, always headed the academic procession with the president of the university; and a peculiar interest attaches to photo-

---

[1] Andrew F. West, "Grover Cleveland, A Princeton Memory," *Scribner's Magazine*, January, 1909.

graphs which show him and Woodrow Wilson, the only two Democratic Presidents of their times, marching side by side. He maintained sympathetic relations with the 1200 or 1400 young men of Princeton, and their celebration of athletic triumphs was seldom complete without a noisy defile to his gate. He would come out on the porch, say a few pleasant sentences, and sometimes even lead them in the Princeton yell. At Brokaw Field two of the best seats were reserved for the Clevelands, for he liked athletic sports. Sometimes at a football game a tremendous uproar would break forth in the bleachers, the students hooting as if mad; alarmed strangers would demand what was the matter; and the indignant rejoinder would come—"Aw, a jay got into Grover's seat!" The students at once formed the custom of celebrating his birthday with a serenade, and when he reached seventy they presented him, through Professor John Grier Hibben, with a loving-cup. In reply, Cleveland remarked that "I feel young at seventy because I have here breathed the atmosphere of vigorous youth and of hopeful aspiring young manhood." When in the fall of 1897 his first son, Richard Folsom, was born, the students adopted the boy by posting on the bulletin-board a notice that he would enter Princeton with the class of 1919 and play centre-rush on the championship football teams of his four years.

On October 15, 1901, Cleveland became a trustee of the university, and till his death discharged the duties of the post with great earnestness. He was indefatigable in attending meetings, interested himself in all university details, from the library budget to examinations for the doctorate, and spoke frequently if modestly on these subjects. He used to rebuke idlers among the thirty-two trustees by quoting Moses Taylor Pyne: "Every man must pull his full weight in the boat!" His general attitude on university policy was highly conservative. When Woodrow Wilson was installed as president in 1902, Cleveland made the most important of his academic addresses, reviewing the historic obligations of Princeton and defining its obligations.[1] He declared against the elective system, saying that "We of Princeton are still willing to assert our belief that we are better able to determine than those who come to us for education what is their most advantageous course of instruction." Alluding to the confusion in current university aims, he added: "If false educational notions should prevail, Princeton will

[1] N. Y. *Times, Tribune,* Oct. 26, 1902.

bide her time till they are spent." A somewhat similar address came from him when the remodelled Nassau Hall was formally opened in 1906 as a meeting-place for the faculty.[1] The university must cling tightly to its heritage, he said. "The teachers that meet in this room for counsel may adopt improved methods of education; but they cannot without recreancy change the current or purpose of Princeton's teaching." His natural conservatism was deepened by his constant intercourse with West, who had a keen and lively mind, but who loved the past with the ardor of a classicist and who held decided ideas as to just how Princeton should grow.

In the same year that Cleveland became trustee West was chosen head of the graduate school; the next year Woodrow Wilson entered upon his presidency with a radical programme in mind; and in October, 1904, Cleveland became chairman of the trustees' standing committee on the graduate school. There shortly arose the dispute between President Wilson and Dean West over the new graduate college —that is, the halls to house the school. Wilson wished it placed "at the heart of Princeton," while West gradually formulated the plan of a college site outside of the central campus. Cleveland greatly respected Woodrow Wilson's abilities. Indeed, he made the motion in the board of trustees in 1902 which clothed Wilson with sweeping powers for reorganizing the university faculty.[2] But as the quarrel developed it was inevitable that the ex-President should align himself with West. His conservatism distrusted Wilson's vision of the rapid reorganization of Princeton. The dean was frequently at his home; they discussed in great detail the plans for the development of the graduate school; and Cleveland threw himself into the undertaking with characteristic thoroughness. In 1906 Dean West was offered the presidency of the Massachusetts Institute of Technology, and, feeling discouraged by the slow progress of his enterprise, thought of accepting. We are fortunate in having a statement by the dean which describes Cleveland's part in the sequel. He writes: [3]

A meeting of the trustees' committee was held. Mr. Cleveland presided and President Wilson was present. I told the committee in President Wilson's presence that I was discouraged by the failure to obtain the graduate college and by the increasingly unfriendly attitude of President Wilson toward me

[1] Varnum Lansing Collins, *Princeton*, 278.
[2] Ray Stannard Baker, *Woodrow Wilson*, II, 144.
[3] Memorandum for the author by Dean West.

personally. President Wilson then said, "I challenge you to give any instance of this." I detailed a number of instances and then asked him to say whether he thought anything I had said was unfair or untrue. His only reply was: "I must say you have a remarkable memory." I then said that as I now had an honorable opportunity to leave and undertake a new work, I was inclined to do so. I was asked to retire from the meeting until the committee had deliberated on the matter. When I returned Mr. Cleveland as chairman announced that, "speaking for everyone in this room," as he said, they strongly wished me to remain, and would pledge their active support in my efforts to obtain the graduate college. I thanked them, and asked President Wilson if he fully concurred in this. He replied: "Of course I do. How could you doubt it?" . . . Relying on this, I remained in Princeton.

In the following June (1907), President Wilson surprised and startled the board of trustees by proposing the adoption of his "Quad" plan calling for a sweeping rearrangement of the undergraduate residential life and necessitating a very large financial expenditure, thereby displacing the graduate college from its priority of opportunity and perhaps postponing it indefinitely. Mr. Cleveland strongly opposed the "Quad" plan, and told me that he had told President Wilson that it was not keeping faith with the assurances given to me. In October, 1907, the board of trustees requested President Wilson to withdraw the "Quad" plan. This was done.

Cleveland opposed the "Quad" plan not only because it seemed certain to delay the graduate college, but because he distrusted the principle involved. He did not think that this modification of the English plan of placing students in residential colleges under the guidance of tutors was likely to profit American boys, for he held that it savored of coddling when individualism and initiative should be encouraged. He wrote out a long argument against it. In the spring of 1908 an important vote was taken, in the trustees' committee on the graduate school, on the vital question whether the new graduate college should be placed on or off the campus. Cleveland concurred with West and Pyne in voting to place it slightly outside the old university grounds. When on his death-bed that spring he sent for West. "He reviewed the situation," writes Dean West, "telling me he had read my report on it again, that the plan was sound, and that I had done right at every step in my efforts. 'Hang on to it like a bulldog,' he said, 'no matter what is done to you. Your present outlook is very dark.' Then he went on to express his distrust of President Wilson at some length and in no uncertain terms." As everyone knows, in the end the ideas of Dean West and Cleveland on the graduate college completely triumphed.

President Wilson's authorized biographer takes the view that Cleveland, much shut in by bad health in his last years, was imperfectly informed upon Wilson's side of the dispute. That view is also taken by Cleveland's nephew, Mr. Cleveland Bacon.[1] But it is earnestly combated by those closest to Cleveland, who declare that he studied every side of the question with characteristic caution and thoroughness, and made up his mind only on the fullest evidence. However this may be, a regrettable bitterness grew out of the controversy. At one stage of it Cleveland announced to his wife: "President Wilson is coming to call on me this afternoon. I am going to talk United States to him on his foolish graduate college position." Wilson came and stayed for two hours. When he left Cleveland remarked to his family: "I guess he knows where I stand now. I was as emphatic to him as the English language permits." But that evening Professor John Grier Hibben dropped in. He had just seen Wilson. "Do you know what he said?" he asked Cleveland. "He said he had called on you this afternoon. 'And,' he said, 'I think I have virtually won Mr. Cleveland over to my side!'" Cleveland looked at Dr. Hibben a moment in consternation. Then he said slowly and emphatically: "It's a d—d lie!"[2] In the end he was convinced that Wilson had shown bad faith. Wilson, for his part, was convinced that Cleveland had failed him in a sound and progressive cause. Olney later repeated to a friend a remark that he had heard Wilson make: "I am prepared to believe that Cleveland was a better President of the United States than a trustee of Princeton." In the campaign of 1912 it was said by Wilson's enemies that Cleveland had written a letter denouncing Wilson, and phrases from this alleged letter were even quoted.[3] But Cleveland's immediate family do not believe that any such letter was ever penned.

Cleveland's interest in the graduate college has been commemorated by the imposing Cleveland tower erected by popular subscription as part of the graduate college building in 1911–12. In every possible way he labored for the university. He tried hard to induce Andrew Carnegie to contribute to the endowment. From a visit which Carnegie paid him at "Westland" was born the final plan for Lake Carnegie, created by

[1] Baker, *Woodrow Wilson*, II, 222 ff.; Cleveland Bacon to the author.
[2] Mrs. Thomas J. Preston to the author.
[3] William Allen White, *Woodrow Wilson*, 27; Robert L. O'Brien heard Olney's statement.

impounding the waters of Stony Brook near the lower campus.[1] Cleveland lent his shoulder to other plans for raising money. He gave warm support to the improvement of the faculty by the addition of able men, and had ideas of his own as to what constituted a good professor. He believed that every professor should as a matter of course be a scholar, but not that every scholar was fit to be a professor; for other qualities, and especially character, were requisite. To newcomers he helped extend a welcome. Since John Finley failed to find a suitable house, Cleveland built one for him in a corner of his grounds. It was an excellent house, but at first there was water in the cellar. When Finley hesitantly called one day and mentioned this water, Cleveland robustly demanded: "Well, my dear fellow, what did you expect—champagne?"[2]

In 1899 an alumnus who wished to utilize Cleveland's knowledge of politics for the students founded the Henry Stafford Little Lectureship on Public Affairs. Cleveland accepted it, and was expected to prepare one or two lectures a year. The first were delivered in 1900. On April 9 and 10 Alexander Hall was jammed to hear his two addresses on "The Independence of the Executive," a rehearsal of his struggle with the Senate over the Tenure of Office question. The next spring he lectured twice on the Venezula boundary question, and after an intermission of two years, in 1904 he read one lecture on the great Pullman Strike. The composition of these discourses cost him protracted anxiety and toil. He wrote for weeks; he besieged Olney, Carlisle, and others with demands for information and advice; and his letters just before his public appearances were filled with dark forebodings. All the lectures were heard with close attention and were reprinted. It may be said that all of them, and particularly that on the Venezuelan issue, contain materials of value. But they are nevertheless disappointing. He wrote not intimate personal narratives but formal historical discourses embodying numerous official documents; they contain all too little of what Cleveland alone could give, and all too much of what any competent annalist could supply by a little research.

[1] E. M. Norris, *Story of Princeton*, 247.
[2] John Finley, "Cleveland—Gentle But Inexorable," *Scribner's Magazine*, April, 1927.

II

Cleveland had retired with a moderate fortune. Daniel Lamont estimated it in 1897 at from $300,000 to $350,000—the savings from his law practise, his presidential salary, and the sale of Oak View. This afforded a competence, which Cleveland increased by prudent investments under the advice of Commodore Benedict. His letters show that at first he watched the market narrowly, investigated securities carefully before purchasing, and preferred to place his eggs in a few baskets—Southern Railroad preferred was one. But by 1900 he had learned that Benedict could make more money for him than he could alone, and trusted his surplus to the Commodore with little question. Sometimes he had a good deal at hand; for example, in 1899 we find him with $35,000 which he thought he had better keep in the bank a while to await developments. He took great comfort in the slow increase of his estate. In the last two years of his life he wrote again, and again, with wistful anxiety, of his desire to "make everything snug" for his family before he left them.[1]

While it was unnecessary for him to earn money, he would have found a life of idleness intolerable. At first his only employment was as an occasional consultant in legal cases for large corporations. But he soon began to write. In 1899 George Horace Lorimer, becoming editor of the *Saturday Evening Post,* began the regeneration of that venerable weekly. One of his first notable contributors was Cleveland, who between May, 1900, and December, 1906, furnished him eighteen articles. For some he was paid as much as $2500. At the same time he contributed to *Collier's,* the *Atlantic,* the *Century,* the *Youth's Companion,* the *Independent,* and the *Ladies' Home Journal;* and in 1906 some of his outdoor papers were brought out in book form by the Outing Company under the title of *Fishing and Shooting Sketches.* The most important of all his magazine articles, by far, was one of 10,000 words on "The Cleveland Bond Issues" in the *Saturday Evening Post* of May 7, 1904. This was included in his book published that year by the Century Company, *Presidential Problems,* which contained his accounts of the Venezuela affair, the struggle with the Senate over appointments, and the Chicago strike.

[1] Cleveland Papers.

None of his other magazine articles possessed qualities entitling them to remembrance. Those which were most clearly written *con amore* bore such titles as "The Serene Duck Hunter" and "The Mission of Fishing and Fishermen." They had a pleasant geniality and sometimes a dry humor, while they showed expertness in the craft of the sportsman; but they lacked keen observation of natural scenery and wild life, and there was no salt of originality in them. Another group of papers comprised admonitory lectures to the Democratic party: "The Plight of the Democracy," "Democracy's Opportunity," and so on, all inveighing against Bryanism. Still others discussed, with common sense and unfailing conservatism, some of the simpler questions of the day, such as civil service reform, the waste of public money, the duties of corporation directors, and woman's suffrage—which, like nearly all men at the time, he opposed. He was frequently importuned to write his autobiography, and the idea sometimes attracted him. "I honestly think," he wrote Gilder, "that there are things in my life and career that if set out, and *read* by the young men of our country, might be of benefit to a generation soon to have in their keeping the safety and mission of our nation. . . ."

But three facts prevented the execution of a book of reminiscences. In the first years after he left the presidency he was convinced that the nation in general was so bitterly hostile to him that an autobiography would merely invite abuse and ridicule. After that mood passed he feared that anything he wrote would be "out of tune with the vaudeville that attracts our people and wins their applause," meaning by this the current taste for Rooseveltian ideas. And finally, in his last few years he felt too old and tired for any sustained labor of the kind. When S. S. McClure and Ida Tarbell were urging him in 1905 to prepare twelve articles for *McClure's Magazine,* for which they offered to pay him $10,000, he went so far as to suggest that he might give a number of autobiographical interviews to some trained writer for publication. Unfortunately, this suggestion did not appeal to Mr. McClure. If it had been acted upon, a skilled interviewer might have elicited from Cleveland much confidential information regarding his public acts which he never put into his lectures or articles. This final discussion of a book elicited from Cleveland one of his rare expressions of sentiment. He wrote Gilder:

There is a circle of friends like you, who I hope will believe in me. I am happy in the conviction that they will continue in the faith whether an autobiography is written or not. I want my wife and children to love me now and hereafter to proudly honor my memory. They will have my autobiography written on their hearts where every day they may turn the pages and read it. In these days what else is there that is worth while to a man nearly sixty-eight years old?

In the intervals of writing, legal consultation, and public speaking, during the first years after he left the White House, Cleveland had ample time for sports and amusement. At Gray Gables every summer he angled for tautog and squeteague. He went trout-fishing with Joe Jefferson or Olney. Repeated winter trips, usually just before Christmas, were made to General Alexander's estate in South Carolina to hunt ducks. He more than once visited Jefferson and other friends in Florida. From April to October every year Benedict's yacht was almost always at his disposal. Once in a set of cribbage games Cleveland "won" the *Oneida* from its rash owner, but this exploit was really unnecessary. So great were the affection and confidence between the Commodore and "Admiral," that Cleveland never hesitated to say when he wished to use the vessel. "The truth is," we find him writing in the spring of 1897, for example, "I am not getting the rest and freedom I crave, and somehow my mental works and nerves are not in first-class condition. It would be very nice if after the Grant ceremonies you would take Olney, Carlisle, and me on board the *Oneida* for a trip to Gray Gables." Of course Benedict did so. Year after year the two took cruises together— once to Maine with Carlisle and William L. Wilson, several times to the South Carolina marshes with Robley D. Evans, and once to Bermuda.

Indoors Cleveland was devoted to billiards and cribbage. He and Benedict played for ten-cent stakes, using bright new dimes, and many are the references to "shiners" in their letters. Their assiduity may be inferred from one balance-sheet which shows that between March 31 and August 22, 1897, they played 527 games. "As we play about five games per hour," wrote Benedict to Cleveland,[1] "105 hours have been consumed, or ten and a half working days of ten hours per day; and I have only made a little less than $1.50 a day. I now look to you to raise my wages." Now and then he would travel to New York, staying with

[1] Aug. 25, 1897. Cleveland Papers.

Benedict or Oscar S. Straus, and would attend a play with Mrs. Cleveland and some friends. His preference for comedy was well understood. Straus tells how, when he came to the city in 1903 to deliver his speech at the Beecher memorial exercises, they went together to see Sothern in *If I Were King*, a play which did not greatly interest Cleveland; and a night or two later he led the party to Weber and Fields' Music Hall at Broadway and Twenty-ninth. This was the visit on which he accidentally met Charles F. Murphy of Tammany at Delmonico's, and after a chat with him, made the surprising remark: "He looks like a pretty clean fellow." But the occupation in which he most delighted, at Princeton or his summer home, was sitting on the piazza to watch his children at play. His second son and last child, Francis, was born in July, 1903, and was a new source of delight to him.

Little by little Cleveland's circle of friends was narrowed by death. Bayard died in 1898, having first paid Cleveland a visit at Princeton in which Venezuela was not mentioned; Endicott died in 1900; Bissell died in 1903, Cleveland and Carlisle going to Buffalo together to attend the funeral. In the summer of 1900 Cleveland was shocked by news of the dangerous illness of William L. Wilson, at that time the hard-working head of Washington and Lee University. Word came suddenly from Red Sulphur Springs that his physician had given him less than a year to live. "He is weak and despondent and cannot think and act for himself," wrote his son to Isidor Straus, begging that his friends help persuade him to go away to some sanitarium. Everyone loved Wilson; Straus wrote of the son's letter that "the contents of it so completely unnerved me that I could not summon sufficient courage to reply to it" for twenty-four hours. Everyone knew that after a self-sacrificing life he was very poor. It was necessary to raise money for him, and Cleveland and Isidor Straus took instant action. On their initiative, a small group arranged to place at Wilson's disposal a fund of $425 a month for a year or $5,000 in all, to enable him to go away to Arizona and, if his strength permitted, write a history of the second Cleveland Administration, a work that he had often spoken of wishing to accomplish.[1] But it was too late. Within a few months Wilson was dead, and Cleveland was helping to raise a fund of $100,000 to endow a memorial chair at Washington and Lee.

Death also entered Cleveland's own family. Few fathers have ever

[1] Cleveland Papers, Aug.–Sept., 1900.

loved children more tenderly; tears would often rise to his eyes as he watched them play, and his friends found that he could not attend the annual Christmas-carol service in Princeton, for the childish treble affected him too deeply. On January 2, 1904, his eldest daughter, Ruth, was taken sick with tonsilitis; on the 6th the doctor found that she had diphtheria; and early on the 7th she died. It was the heaviest blow that he had felt since the death of his mother twenty years earlier, and his diary shows that he reeled under it. On January 10 he wrote, "I had a season of great trouble in keeping out of my mind the idea that Ruth was in the cold, cheerless grave instead of in the arms of her Saviour." He added next day: "It seems to me I mourn our darling Ruth's death more and more. So much of the time I can only think of her as dead, not joyfully living in heaven." But on the 15th he declared: "God has come to my help and I am able to adjust my thought to dear Ruth's death with as much comfort as selfish humanity will permit. One thing I can say: Not for one moment since she left us has a rebellious thought entered my mind." And that spring he wrote his sister that "We still miss dreadfully our dear Ruth; but I believe there has been given to both Frank and me such confident faith that it is well with her, and such a feeling that we are the only losers, as seems to be of very great comfort to us." [1]

One result of this loss was the abandonment of Gray Gables. For several years Cleveland, fearing the threat that the Cape Cod Canal would be built past his door, had talked of selling the place. Now he and his family shrank from the anguish of going back to the familiar scene without Ruth. He leased the property for the summer of 1904, and they all went instead to the hills of New Hampshire. With the assistance of John Finley, who had a place there, a new home was ultimately found near Tamworth, within sight of Mt. Chocorua and Mt. Passonconway and not far from Lakes Ossipee and Winnipesaukee. Congenial neighbors, including Ferris Greenslet, helped make "Intermont," as they called the house, attractive. Cleveland liked the clear mountain air and varied scenery. Dean West, who visited him there, has recorded seeing him, as he fished on a lake one bright September day, the green forest all about splashed here and there by the gold and crimson of autumn, lift his face and gaze around with a look of rapture. He used to say of the more glorious manifestations of nature that "They are too

---

[1] To Mrs. Hoyt, April 27, 1904. Mrs. Yeomans' Papers.

good for us." Taking up fresh-water fishing in earnest, he found it more exciting than sea-fishing. He made many improvements—one a straighter road up Stevenson Hill, now, thanks to John Finley and others, the "Grover Cleveland Memorial Road." He liked the rural inhabitants and found humor in their talk. But every year, in a wistful fashion, he would try to steal a day or two of fishing on Buzzards Bay within sight of the familiar roofs of Gray Gables.

Cleveland's interests, upon his release from public labors, showed little broadening; but he did read more widely. His letters mention books with greater frequency. He praised Gilder's volume of poems, *For the Country*, with genuine appreciation. Lamont sent him a copy of *David Harum*, and he liked it so much—for it vividly recalled his boyhood in upper New York—that he mailed copies to Benedict and other friends.[1] He read history with interest. When Harry Thurston Peck's *Twenty Years of the Republic* appeared, Peck's errors of detail, his sharp condemnation of the course of the government in the Chicago strike, and his sympathy for the desperate farmers who espoused the free silver movement, excited Cleveland's wrath. "I don't care who he is," Cleveland wrote Gilder; [2] "it must be he is a lover of falsehood, who had rather, in the cloak of history writing, put down something new and striking, than tell the truth." The papers of the Fathers interested him, and he often expressed his admiration for the stylistic force of the *Federalist*. Now and then he reverted to poetry, and he particularly liked Byron and Macaulay's *Lays of Ancient Rome;* while Dean West remembered how often he quoted Matthew Arnold's *Palladium*. Once he heard Woodrow Wilson read Wordsworth's *Character of the Happy Warrior*, and it became a favorite poem.[3] At first he did little light reading. But in the almost constant illness and pain of his last two or three years he devoured fiction, and took especial delight in W. W. Jacobs' incomparable tales of the old salts of London River.

III

It is natural for a President to view with jaundiced eye the acts and policies of his successor; but Cleveland watched McKinley's Administration with more than the usual irritation. One of its principal acts he

---

[1] April 13, 1897. Cleveland Papers.
[2] *Ibid.*, Jan. 28, 1905.
[3] Baker, *Woodrow Wilson*, II, 385.

Esther   Francis   Mrs. Cleveland   Richard   Mr. Cleveland
Marion

THE CLEVELAND FAMILY AT PRINCETON

regarded as a piece of treachery. It had been elected by the assistance of the Gold Democrats—that is, it had been placed in power by a coalition of low-tariff and high-tariff men; and yet it promptly betrayed the former by passing the Dingley Tariff. He also regarded the foreign policy of McKinley and Day with distress. The revival of the treaty to annex Hawaii seemed to him a dangerous folly. "Did you ever see such a preposterous thing as this Hawaiian business?" he wrote Olney.[1] "The papers I read are most strongly opposed to it, and there ought to be soberness and decency enough in the Senate to save us from launching upon the dangerous policy. . . ; but I am prepared for almost anything." And as the Administration showed a want of firmness in dealing with the Cuban troubles he waxed even angrier.

A series of statements on our foreign relations drawn from his letters, chiefly unpublished, will indicate better than any summary his precise views. The first mentions a minister of his own who, returning from Madrid, had spoken insultingly of Spain:

(To Olney, Nov. 11, 1897). I am thoroughly disgusted with Hannis Taylor. I'd give a month's salary as President if I was in the White House and he was in Madrid. What a satisfaction it would be to bounce him! It is an aggravating thing to have to put up with his general inefficiency, and find out at last that he is not even a gentleman. Well! He is another of our Southern men of "high character" who if appointed "will reflect credit on the Administration." He wrote me that he intended to come to see me. I hope he will not come.

(To Olney, Feb. 16, 1898). It has undoubtedly occurred to you that popular sentiment seems to be vindicating our ideas on certain unfinished public business. All the influence of this Administration appears unable thus far to bring to a successful issue the Hawaiian monstrosity; the delectable Lodge is still howling, apparently to no purpose, for the passage of his immigration bill even in a modified form; if the President's backbone holds out our Cuban policy will, I believe, be fully justified; our treatment of Union Pacific affairs has been outdone, though in a very questionable way; and the idea seems to have entered many minds that there are pension frauds. As parties are now organized, however, neither side is inclined to even whisper approbation of our work.

(To Olney, March 27, 1898). I only yesterday had an opportunity to read your address. . . . The touch-up of Eliot on the Hawaiian business was perfectly neat, and the isolation of ridiculous tariff legislation and navigation laws was grandly instructive, and ought to be useful. . . . Notwithstanding

[1] *Ibid.*, June 17, 1897.

warlike indications, I cannot rid myself of the belief that war will be averted. There would be infinitely more credit and political capital in avoiding war when so imminent than in carrying it on even well. And then there is Spain's condition and the reflection that may come to her that "the game is not worth the candle."

(To Benedict, April 6, 1898). I wish the President would stand fast and persist in following the lead of his own good sense and conscience; but I am afraid he intends to defer and yield to Congress. I cannot yet make myself believe there will be war. If there is and it is based upon present conditions the time will not be long before there will be an earnest and not altogether successful search by our people for a justification.

(To Benedict, April 14, 1898). My judgment that we would have no war was predicated upon the anticipation that we would continue to hold a position from which we could honorably and consistently meet any conditions that gave the least promise of a successful outcome. It seems to me, however, that we have allowed ourselves to be crowded away from that position and that we face today a sad, afflictive war, that our people will look back upon as unprofitable and avoidable, and which in the sight of contemporaneous judgment and history alike may seem unjustifiable.

(To Judson Harmon, July 24, 1898). Olney . . . wrote me some time ago that imperialism had gone far in advance of what he said in his address at Harvard. This whole thing is very clear to me and very sad too. By the time disgust for the rascally Cubans becomes more general and death in battle and disease has made thousands of American households dark, I shall be prepared for a revulsion of feeling that will start the general and ominous inquiry as to the justification and necessity of this war and as to the consistency of its prosecution with its declared purpose.

His contempt for the jingo press was scorching. On February 27, 1898, William Randolph Hearst telegraphed Cleveland that Levi P. Morton, Nelson A. Miles, Rear-Admiral Selfridge, William C. Whitney, Chauncey M. Depew, fifteen governors, more than fifty mayors, and other prominent citizens had accepted membership upon his committee to erect a monument by popular subscription to the heroes of the *Maine;* and he asked permission to add Cleveland's name. Forthwith came back over the wires Cleveland's reply: "I decline to allow my sorrow for those who died on the *Maine* to be perverted into an advertising scheme for the New York *Journal.*"

The conflict proved brief; and imperialism as an issue was clearly placed before the nation when in October, 1898, McKinley instructed the peace commissioners in Paris that the United States must retain the whole Philippine Archipelago. Among those who instantly rallied against annexation, the old Mugwump element and the conservative Cleveland Democrats were most conspicuous. Such public men as Carl Schurz, Moorfield Storey, Charles W. Eliot, and Oscar S. Straus, and such editors as E. L. Godkin, Rollo Ogden, and Samuel Bowles led the attack. Fairchild, Dickinson, Vilas, and Olney were all outspoken in denouncing overseas expansion. Cleveland had seized an early opportunity of underlining his position. On January 24, 1898, when Senator Morgan had made some misleading statements regarding his attitude toward Hawaii, he had told the Associated Press that such annexations were "a perversion of our national mission. The mission of our nation is to build up and make a greater country out of what we have, instead of annexing islands."

If the silverite and gold wings of the Democratic party could have united in 1900 upon an anti-imperialist platform, they might have had some chance of success. Cleveland was always ready to hold out the olive branch to repentant free-silver men. He revised and approved a speech which Charles S. Hamlin delivered on Jackson Day, 1897, in Chicago.[1] It adverted sadly to the internecine divisions of the party, declared that the silverites "are still our brothers, united to us by bonds growing out of the real underlying principles of our political faith," and invited them to turn from the Populist will-of-the-wisp to "the sacred fires of Democracy which we have kept burning." A few weeks later the Reform Club gave a dinner in New York for the purpose of unifying the scattered elements of conservative Democracy. De Witt Warner presided and speeches were made by Cleveland, Carlisle, Caffery, and others. In his address Cleveland declared there could be no compromise on the currency question, but he repeated the invitation to the silver men to turn back from their delusive doctrine. Olney lent his support to these efforts. When late in 1897 Cleveland was invited to attend some exercises in memory of William E. Russell, Olney advised him to decline. The exercises, he said, were arranged by some Cambridge and Harvard doctrinaires whose utterances were likely to increase rather than lessen the party schism, and it would be a calamity if Cleveland abetted them in heightening the Democratic dissensions.[2] Cleveland did not go.

[1] Hamlin Papers.
[2] Dec. 6, 1897. Olney Papers.

The free-silver element, however, naturally refused to respond. Its leaders believed they were the true Democratic party and laughed at the weakness of the gold men. In 1897 the Gold Democrats courageously ran State tickets in several parts of the country where the silver forces were in the ascendancy. Watterson and the *Courier-Journal* supported one such ticket in Kentucky, ex-Secretary Morton another in Nebraska, and the Cleveland men a third in Iowa. They made a pitiful showing. In 1898, when the Republicans increased their majority in both houses of Congress, the Gold Democrats lost further ground. Bryan prepared to take full charge of the party fortunes in 1900 and to do it in his own way.

Cleveland hoped in 1899 for the defeat of the peace treaty by which we acquired Porto Rico and Cuba. He was disgusted when Bryan went to Washington and cajoled and prodded seventeen Democratic and Populist Senators into voting for the treaty, thus saving it by one vote. In the situation thus presented he had his own simple plan. George Boutwell sent him a memorandum which suggested that the United States might either turn the Philippines over to some other nation or to the Filipino people, and urged the latter course. Charles R. Codman also sent a memorandum, calling for withdrawal coupled with an agreement among the Powers for the neutralization of the islands.[1] Cleveland declared in favor of a brief occupation followed by friendly oversight. Tradition and principle alike, he wrote in an undated paper,[2] "demand that our occupation and control of the islands shall only be for the purpose of leading the inhabitants to the establishment of their own government; that these inhabitants shall be reassured and pacified by an immediate declaration of such purpose; and that when with our friendly aid such purpose is accomplished, our control and occupation of the islands shall cease, save only so far as they may be desired or be necessary for the maintenance of peace and order under the new government."

When the Democratic national convention which met in Kansas City on July 4, 1900, renominated Bryan and adopted a platform which declared again for free silver at 16 to 1, Cleveland's course was plain. He could never vote for Bryan. The platform, to be sure, declared imperialism the paramount issue, and Bryan emphasized it in his speeches. One sound-money Democrat after another wryly announced his acceptance of the ticket. Olney, writing Cleveland that "there can be no greater

[1] Cleveland Papers.
[2] *Ibid.*

national calamity than the reëlection of McKinley, with all that it means directly and indirectly," did so. Carlisle came out for Bryan. So did Watterson. J. Sterling Morton wrote his old leader before election day: [1] "It is a choice between evils, and I am going to shut my eyes, hold my nose, vote, go home, and disinfect myself." But Cleveland was adamant. His only public expression was to authorize Don M. Dickinson, on October 29, to republish his no-compromise speech at the Reform Club dinner in 1897 as a statement of the tenets which he still held.

But again Cleveland's feelings before and after the campaign may best be brought out by a series of excerpts from his manuscript letters:

(To Edward M. Shepard, Feb. 7, 1900). I am satisfied you are wrong in suggesting my presence at your meeting of conciliation. Thousands of those who have struggled to maintain the true Democratic faith may be forgiven by the apostles of the newly-invented Democracy; but it seems to me that I am as yet beyond the pale of honorable condonation. Prominent among your guests of honor will be those who lose no occasion, on the floors of Congress or elsewhere, to repudiate me as a Democrat and to swell the volume of "jeers" and "laughter" that greet the mention of my name in that connection. Perhaps they are justified; but if I have sinned against Democracy I am ignorant of my sin; and in any event, my love of country and party will not permit me to sue for forgiveness while being dragged behind the chariot of Bryanism.

(To Olney, June 25, 1900). I see Massachusetts' sweet-scented "scholar in politics" played true to his despicable nature at Philadelphia.[2] As for our own party, the old Adam occasionally dominates me to the extent of prompting me to second the suggestion of a queer old woman who said a few days ago, anent the *Herald's* suggestion that I run for President, "Let them that got into the scrape get out of it."

(To Judson Harmon, July 17, 1900). As between imperialism and a continued struggle against sound money, you and many other good and patriotic Democrats see more danger in the first. The latter and much more trouble we would surely get with Bryan. How certain can you be that he would save you from imperialism? What did he do toward that end when the treaty of peace was before the Senate; and how do you know what such an acrobat would do on that question if his personal ambition was in the balance?

My feeling is that the safety of the country is in the rehabilitation of the old Democratic party. It would be a difficult task to do this, at the end of four years of a Bryan Administration and its absurdities for which the Democratic

---

[1] *Ibid.*, Nov. 2, 1900.
[2] Lodge transferred New England's support from John D. Long for the Vice Presidency to Roosevelt.

party would be held responsible. With the defeat of Bryan and the sham Democratic organization gathered about him, and his and its disappearance in the darkness of accusing Democracy's scorn and contempt, the old guard, untainted with either Bryanism or McKinleyism, could gather together the forces checking . . . Republican excesses . . .

(To Bissell, Sept. 16, 1900). The pending campaign has brought me much unhappiness. First there came numerous letters from apparently honest Democrats in every part of the country, asking my advice as to how they should vote. These have been largely succeeded by persuasions and demands from self-styled rock-ribbed Democrats that I should publicly declare myself in favor of the ticket of the "party which has so greatly honored me"; and in many cases the insistence is made that a word from me would ensure the success of the ticket. . . . I cannot conceive that anything I might say would better conditions or change results. It would add to the volume of abuse which for a long time has been hurled at my defenceless head, and by a bare possibility destroy any opportunity for usefulness in the future. I have some idea that the party may before long be purged of Bryanism, and that the rank and file, surprised at their wanderings, and enraged at their false leaders, will be anxious to return to the old faith; and in their desire to reorganize under the old banners will welcome the counsel of those who have never yielded to disastrous heresy.

(To Hoke Smith, Jan. 20, 1901). You do not remember an expression in a letter I wrote to Lamar a little prior to the nomination of 1892, since published, in which I suggested a fear that the free silver vagary would come to be considered a Southern heresy, which if persisted in would awaken again the anti-Southern feeling in the North. I feel the same way now about Bryanism, which comprises more than free silver. . . . Of one thing I feel absolutely certain: none of the States lost to the ticket called Democratic last November will ever be regained upon the Chicago and Kansas City platforms. The redemption or continued failure of the Democratic party is in the hands of its Southern wing. And my belief is that the young Southern Democrats who have a future before them,[1] and who must have cast upon them the welfare of their section and the promotion of Democracy as an element in that welfare as well as in the safety of the country, must work out this salvation.

IV

In May, 1902, a strike began in the anthracite coal fields. John

---

[1] Woodrow Wilson, Oscar Underwood, Carter H. Glass, E. M. House, David S. Houston, Walter Hines Page, and others; a remarkable prophecy.

Mitchell, head of the United Mine Workers, led 140,000 miners in a struggle for fair pay and working conditions; George F. Baer led the operators in a refusal to make concessions. The struggle dragged through the summer. By October coal had reached famine prices, schools in New York city were closed, and suffering and riots lay just ahead. President Roosevelt on the 3rd of that month presided over a conference of operators and union leaders at the temporary White House. With Baer showing especial insolence, the operators refused to budge. Mitchell was willing to have the President appoint a commission to decide the issues, and pledged obedience to its findings, but Baer would listen to no such plan. The meeting broke up amid general antagonism.[1] Roosevelt was already meditating a drastic step: he would send in troops, take possession of the mines, and use soldiers to get out the fuel. In other words, he would act as if the country were in a state of war.[2] But of course he said nothing publicly of this. At the same time the President was under heavy pressure to follow just such a "constitutional" course as Olney had persuaded Cleveland to follow in the Chicago strike; that is, to use troops to preserve order and protect property while the operators brought in masses of strike-breakers.

On the morning of October 4 Cleveland, journeying home from Buzzards Bay, read press accounts of the President's conference and was aroused to wrath. The tone and substance of the operators' deliverances especially angered him. He sat down in Princeton and wrote Roosevelt a letter.[3] The suggestion it made was impractical. He proposed that the miners and operators be invited to call a truce for the public benefit, produce enough coal to meet emergency needs, and then, if they wished, take up the fight again where they had left off. "I know there would be nothing philosophical or consistent in all this," he wrote; "but my observation leads me to think that when quarreling parties are both in the wrong, and are assailed with blame so nearly universal, they will do strange things to save their faces."

This impractical plan was not important; the fact that Cleveland wrote the letter was. It gave Roosevelt a moral support that he badly needed.[4] Cleveland's letter expressing strong indignation at the operators, and proposing an entirely different course from that which

[1] Henry F. Pringle, Theodore Roosevelt, 264 ff.
[2] Roosevelt, Autobiography, 474.
[3] McElroy, Grover Cleveland, II, 305.
[4] Cf. Mark Sullivan, Our Times, II, 434.

the capitalists demanded, was invaluable to the President. It spiked all the appeals to the Chicago precedent. Moreover, Cleveland was still a power among many Democrats. If the President embarked on an aggressive course, the letter would help to answer Democratic criticism. Roosevelt at once replied to it. His plan now was to use troops to get out the coal, and while they did so to set up an investigating commission to inquire into the merits of the controversy; and he wrote Cleveland asking him to accept the chief place on this commission. Cleveland answered that he would do so. Armed with this reply, Roosevelt on October 9 had Secretary Root write a letter to J. Pierpont Morgan suggesting that a commission might be "appointed by the President or by you" to devise a solution. On October 11 Root and Morgan held a conference on the financier's yacht in the Hudson. Exactly what was said is not known. But it seems certain that Root used with effect the threat of working the mines with Federal troops while a commission under Cleveland investigated the whole problem.[1] As a consequence, Morgan brought pressure on the stupid operators and forced them to agree to arbitration.

As everyone knows, the operators haggled for days over the character of the arbitration board. With ineffable silliness, they objected to such a dangerous radical as Cleveland. When the final panel of seven was made up, he was hence omitted. Roosevelt wrote on the 16th that "I appreciated so deeply your being willing to accept that it was very hard for me to forego the chance of putting you on the commission." But as a matter of fact, Cleveland had never said that he was willing to go on an arbitration commission. His authorized biographer carelessly says that he had. Roosevelt, not so carelessly, said later that he had.[2] But actually he had consented only to serve on a commission of inquiry. When Roosevelt in the campaign of 1904 made unauthorized use of his first letter, adding this misstatement, Cleveland was angry. He wrote Lamont in heated terms:

> There were, I am quite sure, no letters or communications leading up to the "coal letter," as Mr. Roosevelt calls it. He had already inaugurated his interference with the coal situation, to no purpose; the operators (or at least one or more of them) had in his interview with them behaved very badly, as I thought; and I was deeply affected by the threatened distress among our people. . . . Thus influenced, I wrote the letter. I am not ashamed of it and I do not desire to retract one word of it. Of course Mr. Roosevelt's use of it and

[1] Pringle, *Roosevelt*, 274.
[2] McElroy, *Grover Cleveland*, II, 313; Roosevelt, *Autobiography*, 474.

the publicity he has given to a communication received in the circumstances existing at the time the letter was written, is a matter to be governed by the rules which should govern intercourse between gentlemen.

His conduct in this regard, however, can be better accounted for than his apparent determination to have it appear that I was willing to be one of the board of arbitrators afterwards created. Nothing would have induced me to accept such a position. He wrote me, after his failure to accomplish any result by his interview with the operators, that he had in mind the appointment of a sort of commission to inquire into the facts of the situation for *his own information and guidance*, and asked me if I would consent to act on such a commission. After serious thought and *because* the inquiry proposed could in no sense be called an arbitration, I thought I ought to consent—and I did so. Soon after an arbitration was agreed on, and I was relieved from further concern with the matter. After that Mr. Roosevelt (notably at the time the new Chamber of Commerce building was opened) tried to explain to me why I was not put on the *Board of Arbitration,* and I then distinctly told him that I would not have accepted the position.

Cleveland was willing to help ascertain the facts of the dispute. For some reason he was not willing to act as a judge in deciding upon hours and wages. He wished the distinction observed, and resented Roosevelt's misrepresentation. "I am amazed at Roosevelt," he wrote Gilder in 1904; and after some biting words on the President's lust for glorification, added that "there are some people in this country that need lessons in decency and good manners." [1] But by his unexpected and partial interposition—which cost him $2500 when he sold some stock in a coal-carrying railroad—he had helped Roosevelt greatly in finding a solution.

V

The result of the campaign of 1900 accelerated a change in the public attitude toward Cleveland which had been insensibly but steadily gaining ground. When he retired from the presidency he believed himself the most unpopular man in America. It is true that multitudes in the South and West hated him, and other multitudes in the East regarded him as a figure of the past. He declined many invitations to write or speak because he believed that he would meet only derision or abuse. When his friend Eugene Tyler Chamberlain compiled his *Public Papers* he hardly cared to see a copy. "There will be little need for unpacking

[1] March 11, 1904. Cleveland Papers.

them," he wrote Lamont of the package that reached him, "as but few people care for that sort of literature in these days." A year later he wrote Gilder that "no one wants to read anything from me." [1] This feeling played a part in his refusal to accept any public employment. He declined President Crespo's invitation to sit for Venezuela on the boundary arbitration commission chiefly because he feared that he would not be an impartial agent. He declined President McKinley's offer of appointment as one of the permanent arbitrators under the Hague agreement of 1900 chiefly because he believed that agreement futile. But he also felt in these refusals that he had been repudiated by his own countrymen and should remain in obscurity.

Little by little, however, the tide turned. After 1900 invitations to make speeches became not only more numerous but more pressing. He began to appear more frequently—at Founder's Day at Carnegie Institute in Pittsburgh, at the opening of the new Chamber of Commerce in New York, at the inauguration of President Finley at City College, at memorial meetings for Carl Schurz, Bayard, and J. Sterling Morton, at Old Home Week in Norwich, Conn. Tributes came from many quarters. He was pleased in spite of himself when Roosevelt wrote him late in 1900 [2] that "during the last campaign I grew more and more to realize the very great service you had rendered the whole country by what you did about free silver. As I said to a Republican audience in South Dakota, I think your letter on free silver prior to your third nomination was as bold a bit of honest writing as I have ever seen in American public life." He was pleased again when in 1902 Roosevelt wrote on the anniversary of his Venezuelan message to say that he had always been proud of supporting it.[3] In reform groups and among the Eastern conservatives Cleveland had always been highly regarded. Now an intelligent esteem for him began to reach wider circles. In 1903 a massmeeting was held in New York to protest against the pogrom in Kishinev. Cleveland stepped upon the stage while Mayor Seth Low was in the midst of his speech. The hall was full of plain New Yorkers, including many poor and radical Jews; but the moment Cleveland's portly figure was seen a deafening storm of handclapping arose. When he finished his short speech the applause was almost riotous, and at the close of the

---

[1] To Lamont, Aug. 1, 1897; to Gilder, June 20, 1898. Cleveland Papers.
[2] Nov. 22, 1900. Roosevelt Papers.
[3] Dec. 25, 1902. Roosevelt Papers.

meeting the crowd stormed the stage. To this audience the ex-President represented as no one else could have done the sober sense of the American people, its strength and its aroused purpose. In the same year John T. McCutcheon of the Chicago *Tribune* wrote Cleveland that he had been delivering some lectures on the work of a newspaper cartoonist in Iowa, Wisconsin, and Illinois.[1] During his talks he had drawn rapid sketches of several public men, and he had invariably found that Cleveland's picture received much more applause than any of the others, even Roosevelt's. "If this had occurred only once or twice I should not have remarked it, but as it has occurred at every one of twenty or more lectures I consider it a faithful barometer of the kindly feeling that people in the Middle West have for you."

It was in this year also that Cleveland went west to help dedicate the St. Louis Exposition, held in Bland's own State and in the heart of the free-silver territory. President Roosevelt was there. So was Mark Hanna. So were other powerful men. They marched together through the April sunshine to the platform. Machinery whirred and bands played. The President was greeted with warm applause. But when Cleveland rose he received an ovation which far overshadowed that given Roosevelt, a tumult of applause that continued minute after minute. The roar astounded observers. It was the apology of the West to a man of courage.

[1] Undated letter, 1903. Cleveland Papers.

THE Democratic forces entered upon the year 1904 with rising hopes of victory. A party dinner was held in New York on January 4, with Olney and Hill the principal speakers. Cleveland sent it a letter declaring that "the skies are bright with the promise of victory, if Democrats stoutly reaffirm old principles which the times demand." He criticized Roosevelt harshly, calling his seizure of Panama a disregard of "the territorial rights of another nation" which cast odium on "our national good faith." This criticism was echoed by Olney, who asserted: "We have had a surfeit of sensations and spectacles, and we need a rest. We need it to recover our equilibrium." Hill furnished a long and drastic review of Roosevelt's acts, saying "the people want a safe, consistent, level-headed, conservative Administration." The Eastern Democrats were making a new bid for party leadership.

From the beginning five men were most prominently mentioned for the nomination: Olney, Senator Gray of Delaware, Senator Cockrell of Missouri, Alton B. Parker, and William R. Hearst. To this list many added Cleveland's name. Those who supported him for a third term were for the most part conservative business men who were as much alarmed by Roosevelt's progressivism as by Bryan's Populistic ideas. Oscar and Nathan Straus were prominent in urging Cleveland to reenter politics, and early in 1904 James Stillman told a friend that if Cleveland were renominated he would personally guarantee a campaign fund larger than that which Hanna had raised for McKinley in 1896.[1] The Brooklyn *Eagle* and New York *Herald* had for some time been urging that Cleveland be drafted. Henry White wrote Roosevelt from London in June that he was talking with rich tourists.[2] "I have been struck by the fact that many of those who have affiliations with what I may describe as Wall Street, although not necessarily belonging to New York, say that they mean to vote for you 'unless Cleveland is nominated,' in which case they would without hesitation vote for him."

While Cleveland was pleased by the mention of his name for the

[1] McElroy, *Grover Cleveland*, II, 329.
[2] June 25, 1904. White Papers.

presidency, he knew it was preposterous. He was approaching seventy. His health was increasingly infirm. He suffered much from rheumatism and was sometimes in bed for weeks together. Thus in the winter of 1899–1900 a severe illness lasted six weeks, and on February 23 he wrote Benedict [1] that "excepting on our Southern trip I haven't been out of the house but five times (and then only to ride) since November 26." His digestion also became increasingly troublesome. After 1900 he kept a stomach-pump always at hand and not infrequently used it. Quite apart from his fixed disbelief in third terms, he simply did not have the strength for the presidency. It was with this in view that he published in the Brooklyn *Eagle* of November 27, 1903, a letter saying he could not "open my mind to the thought that in any circumstances or upon any consideration I would ever again become the nominee of my party for the presidency. My determination not to do so is unalterable and conclusive." He meant this to be final.

Yet he perceived early in 1904 that it was impolitic to repeat this statement. It was important to let his name be used to rally and unify the Eastern Democracy. The astute political leaders supporting Alton B. Parker, among them Hill and James Smith of New Jersey, wished to employ Cleveland as a dignified stalking-horse. As long as he was a potential candidate the Bryan and Hearst elements would concentrate much of their fire upon him. Adherents of Olney in Massachusetts shared this feeling, and so did the leaders of Tammany Hall, who hoped that they might bring forward George B. McClellan as the nominee. Indeed, Charles F. Murphy, Tammany's new head, went to Lamont's office in February and asked him to persuade Cleveland to "do no further declining now." He added: "Let's have the benefit of his name to round up a Cleveland party, and all will agree on a Cleveland candidate." Lamont approved the advice, and pronounced Murphy a man of sense.[2]

Partly because of this general desire, partly because it was unnecessary, Cleveland did no "further declining." His personal preference was for either Olney or Gray; but he quickly saw that the best chance for a union of the conservative Democrats was behind Parker. After all, Parker had made an excellent chief judge of the Court of Appeals; important Eastern papers, including the *Evening Post,* favored him; and he had such practical politicians as Hill and Tom Taggart with him. On

[1] Cleveland Papers.
[2] McElroy, *Grover Cleveland,* II, 330.

March 29 Cleveland advised William B. Hornblower, who possessed much influence among the Independents, to support Parker.[1] It was important to get the decent elements of the party together, and "Parker's candidacy had such a start and has so many elements ready to support it in the convention that he appears to present a better rallying point than anyone else." Hornblower at once gave out the desired endorsement.

By the time the convention met in St. Louis on July 6 Parker's lieutenants had the situation completely in hand. Hill and Taggart controlled so many delegates that it needed only the adherence of James Smith and a few other insiders to make the nomination certain.[2] Cleveland had given an interview in May to the Philadelphia *North American* advocating the selection of Parker. He had also supplied Smith with a letter requesting him to "prevent the use of my name" at the convention, adding that even if he received the nomination "I certainly could not accept it." At the proper moment Smith produced this letter from an inside pocket and placed the uninstructed Jersey delegates, some of them strong Cleveland men, on the Parker bandwagon. Hearst had spent large sums in gathering delegates, of whom he had 104 instructed for him, but he was an impossible candidate. As a desperate expedient, Bryan made an effort to stampede the convention to Cockrell, a man of deserved popularity, but in vain. On the first ballot Parker had almost the requisite two-thirds, and he was quickly nominated.

But what was more striking than the nomination was the fact that the convention was animated from beginning to end by enthusiasm for Cleveland's ideas. John Sharp Williams, the temporary chairman, declared that "the gold standard, established by the dogged persistency and indomitable will of Grover Cleveland in securing the repeal of the Republican silver-purchase law, is and is indefinitely to be the money standard of the country." This assertion evoked a wild demonstration. Throughout the sittings there were repeated calls of "three cheers for Grover Cleveland," and they always brought a ringing response. Never before, men remarked, had a political leader within eight years lost control of his party and then seen it return to his side, acknowledging that he had been right and it had been wrong. When Parker found that the platform was silent on the monetary issue, he sent the convention a telegram declaring that he regarded the gold standard as irrevocably

[1] *Ibid.*, 336.
[2] James Kerney, *Political Education of Woodrow Wilson*, 23 ff.

established, and by a decisive vote the delegates acquiesced. His firmness pleased Cleveland, who wrote to Hamlin: [1]

> I am very much pleased with the outcome of the convention. . . . I was so hard to please that I thought the gold standard declaration recommended by the [platform] sub-committee a rather poor thing, and when that was stricken out and nothing substituted my heart sank away down to my boots. I am quite happy now because I think Parker's telegram and the action of the convention thereon have made both the platform situation and the *candidate* situation better than they could have been made in any other way. Of course if the advantage is to continue and grow, Parker must not let down in any spot or place, but must keep alive and deepen the impression that he is in command.

Unfortunately, Parker proved a weak candidate. Cleveland, eager for victory, urged him to follow the aggressive line he had taken in his St. Louis telegram and make a series of determined utterances. "If we can only keep peanut methods out of our campaign management," he wrote Olney,[2] "I believe there is a good chance to rid the country of Rooseveltism and its entire brood of dangers and humiliations." He thought that the Gold Democrats and the business men of the country ought to exert every sinew. His attitude toward Roosevelt, indeed, was one of curious apprehension. "When I consider the alternative presented to our people in the pending campaign," he wrote Hamlin,[3] "and realize the consequences involved in their voting power, I am almost frightened." Cleveland was able to make only two speeches, one in New York and one in New Jersey; but he wrote campaign articles for *Collier's*, *McClure's Magazine*, and the *Saturday Evening Post*, and Parker sent him a heartfelt letter of thanks. He unquestionably did much to strengthen a hopeless candidacy.

The result of the election staggered him. The first reports on election night sufficed to disclose a Roosevelt landslide, and he went dejectedly to bed a little after ten o'clock. Roosevelt had carried every State outside the South. More than a month later Cleveland wrote that it was astounding, that he had hardly recovered his composure, and that he sometimes wondered if a change had not taken place in the character of the American people. In one sense the Cleveland doctrines had

---

[1] July 20, 1904. Hamlin Papers.
[2] Aug. 14, 1904. Cleveland Papers.
[3] Aug. 14, 1904. Hamlin Papers.

triumphed in the campaign; Democracy was purged forever of free silver ideas. In another sense the general conservatism now represented by Cleveland had been as badly beaten in 1904 as Bryanism had been in 1900. It was not until the two wings of the party were united under Woodrow Wilson in 1912 that it was to achieve success—and when that happened Cleveland was in his grave.

II

One final public service of importance remained for Cleveland—his work in helping to salvage and reorganize the Equitable Life Assurance Society.

The Equitable Life, the Mutual Life, and the New York Life were three great insurance companies supposedly conducted for the benefit of policy-holders alone. Actually they had become three huge reservoirs of surplus money used for the benefit of men floating securities, merging railroads, forming trusts, and engaged in other forms of financial promotion. They were supposedly conducted with strict honesty and conservatism. Actually they were the arena of outrageous corruption and theft.[1] The men who managed them played the game of high finance in its most reckless form. They used the money that rightly belonged to policy-holders to speculate in stocks, to underwrite financial schemes of all sorts in the hope of large profits, to subsidize trust companies in which they were interested, and to make improper "loans" to friends. They also indulged in or connived at direct stealing. They used company funds to pay huge salaries, to meet personal expenses, to support nepotism; they took graft in the erection of enormous company buildings; they protected themselves by giving company money to campaign funds and to powerful politicians employed as counsel at fat salaries. All this was done under a cloak of outward respectability. They were supposedly supervised by boards of directors chosen for their known ability, integrity, and disinterestedness. The directorates included men high in banking, business, and public life, and among them were former governors and Senators. In reality the members were for the most part mere dummies.

Early in 1905 an internal dispute over the management of the

[1] Cf. Report Joint Legislative Committee of the State of New York to Investigate Life Insurance, 1906.

Equitable came to a head. James W. Alexander and members of his family, long associated with the company, gave battle to young James Hazen Hyde, son of the founder, for its control. The directors of the Equitable broke up into warring groups. Rumors of the prevalent corruption and speculation reached the public. The *World* took them up. In April the State Insurance Department began an investigation. As the scandal grew worse a demand arose for a special session of the legislature; Governor Higgins called it to meet in June, the Armstrong Committee was appointed, and Charles E. Hughes soon began his famous inquiry.

Meanwhile, out of the mêlée of financiers seeking control of the Equitable and its surplus a victor had emerged. On May 5 Thomas Fortune Ryan, for $3,500,000, bought from young Hyde a controlling block of Equitable stock, 502 shares. His purpose, he said, was to avert a receivership that would result in "frightful losses" to not only the policyholders but the financial community at large, including himself. Whether this was the entire motive was perhaps doubtful.[1] Possession of the stock had in the past given enormous collateral advantages to those interested in financial operations. But it was no doubt the largest motive. In view of the vast suspicion the public felt for the old management of the Equitable and for all Wall Street operators who meddled with it, Ryan desired to make the grand gesture of putting his controlling stock in the hands of men whom everybody would trust. Who better than Grover Cleveland? On June 9, 1905, Ryan read to George F. Parker a letter inviting the ex-President to make one of a board of trustees with power to vote the stock in reorganizing the directors of the company. The other two members were to be Justice Morgan J. O'Brien and George Westinghouse, both large policy-holders. Parker next day took the letter to Princeton, explained the situation to Cleveland, and secured his consent.

The task which Cleveland thus undertook was important and laborious, but it was not complex. The Equitable had fifty-two directors. They had previously all been elected by the stockholders. The officers now proposed to mutualize the company by allowing the policy-holders to elect a majority, 28, of the board; and the State Superintendent of Insurance had approved this plan. Cleveland, Westinghouse, and Justice O'Brien would therefore themselves select twenty-four directors, and guide the policy-holders in choosing the others. They met within a week,

[1] Mark Sullivan, *Our Times*, II, 44.

accepted the deed of trust from Ryan, who never thereafter attended, and set to work.[1] At the same time Paul Morton, a son of J. Sterling Morton and recently Secretary of the Navy, was made president of the Equitable. Cleveland undertook to master as much as he could, within the short time available, of the business of life insurance and the special requirements of the Equitable. Among the dummy directors who had resigned from the company were Edward H. Harriman, James J. Hill, Henry C. Frick, Jacob H. Schiff, and August Belmont. He and his trustees desired to get men of similar ability and repute, but men who would take their duties seriously. Within a fortnight more than two hundred candidates had been presented by themselves or their friends. This list was supplemented by names of suitable men taken from the rolls of policy-holders and by names which occurred to Cleveland, O'Brien, and Westinghouse.

"It shall be our effort," Cleveland assured the policy-holders, "to . . . secure for directors from among policy-holders such persons as are imbued with conservative views of management, and who will regard as distinctly violative of duty the use of the funds of the Society directly or indirectly in the promotion, underwriting, or syndicating of new and uncertain enterprises, or the investment of such funds in speculative stocks and securities." The trustees refused to consider insurance agents, speculators, promoters, or members of stock exchanges. Cleveland rejected a man whom he admired greatly for business ability and integrity, and to whom he would have been willing to entrust every cent he had, because he had once done some underwriting, "and I feel that underwriting just at the present time is, or ought to be, a little out of fashion among directors of the Equitable Assurance Society." But appointments were steadily made and the board was kept at its legal strength. At the same time the work of enabling the policy-holders, more than 350,000 in number, to ballot for their own directors, was carried forward. Elaborate instructions were drawn up by Cleveland himself and sent out to every insured person, accompanied by blank ballots and proxies. The expected result occurred. When the polls closed more than 94 per cent of the policy-holders responding had sent proxies enabling the trustees to represent them—a token of their absolute confidence in Cleveland and his associates.[2]

[1] Parker, *Grover Cleveland,* 230 ff.
[2] *Ibid.,* 236.

Before the year ended the trustees' work was done. Meanwhile, from the beginning of September to the end of December, 1905, the Armstrong Committee had held nearly sixty public hearings, Hughes had mercilessly questioned a long list of prominent financial and political figures, and the evils which had sapped the Equitable, New York, Mutual, and Prudential companies had all been probed. The way was cleared for drastic reformative enactments by the next legislature. Humiliated and distrusted, the companies saw that they would benefit greatly if they continued and enlarged Cleveland's employment. He had been paid $12,000 a year as trustee; during December Paul Morton offered him, on behalf of the New York, Mutual, and Equitable companies, an additional $12,000 to serve as referee between the companies in disputes arising from the allowance by their respective agents of rebates on their premium commissions. Such rebates were an evil which Cleveland vigorously condemned. It was unlikely that the disputes would be numerous and they could usually be submitted to him at Princeton by letter; while he could help to stamp out the abuse. He therefore accepted. More than a year later, in 1907, a third place was offered him —the headship of a protective organization called The Association of Presidents of Life Insurance Companies. Its main object was to resist regulative legislation which insurance executives regarded as unnecessary or ill-advised. Cleveland hesitated to take the position, which virtually made him a public representative of the whole life insurance business, but finally did so, and made a number of effective statements and addresses on insurance affairs. The one legal brief of his which has ever been published was one brought out by the Association in 1907 in opposition to State laws limiting the compensation of life insurance officials.

The work which Cleveland did for honest insurance was considerable in both its direct and indirect results. Unquestionably the most important reforms sprang from Hughes' work and the efforts of new executives like Paul Morton. Yet Cleveland performed a valuable service in helping reorganize the rich company which was the centre of the scandal, and one still more valuable in helping promote an early return of confidence in all the companies. For this effort his name and character were worth more than those of anyone else in the country, and the fruits of his labors long outlasted his connection with the business.

III

Cleveland's last years were as bright and serene as his failing health permitted. He had everything to make him happy—young children, a devoted wife, work to do, boon friends, public honors—and he appreciated them. His letters show no trace of the querulousness which had occasionally crept out just after he left the presidency. He was often full of spontaneous humor. Now and then, his friends record, he indulged in a pun, as when he told John Finley, who had threatened him with a portrait-painter: [1] "I will not lend my countenance to the enterprise." He could write Benedict in high spirits even of a fire at Tamworth. It "destroyed the woodshed and ice-house in the immediate vicinity of the dwelling. Acts of tremendous heroism were frequent during its acute stage." [2] He commented on the Yankee haying which made it impossible for him to hire the help he wanted. "This word does not mean in these parts steady work in the field having for its object the speedy cutting of meadows and storing of hay. On the contrary, it means a sort of picnic season, or a continuous and long indulgence in a kind of hay-bee, with just enough work about it to give a slim pretext for the tiresome iteration, 'I'll see what I can do when I get through haying.' " Words of affection for his friends frequently crept into his correspondence. "The older I grow," he wrote of General Alexander, "the more near and dear such genuine and unaffected friends are to me." And when on his sixty-ninth birthday he received scores of messages conveying affection and praise, he wrote Gilder that as he read them he had struggled between smiles and tears.[3] "Somehow I am wondering why all this should be, since I have left many things undone I ought to have done in the realm of friendship, and since in the work of public duty and effort, God has never failed to clearly make known to me the path of duty." His only regrets were over the beloved Gray Gables. "It's a dreadful thing," he wrote in 1906, "the way we have turned our backs on that place, so wringing wet with good times."

As old political resentments were forgotten he had become a national figure, esteemed and praised by all. His seventieth birthday in 1907 was

[1] John Finley to author, March 12, 1932.
[2] Sept. 2, 1905. Cleveland Papers.
[3] *Ibid.*, March 18, 1906.

the occasion for an informal national celebration. For the first time in a half century the mayor of New York ordered flags raised in honor of a private citizen. Woodrow Wilson wrote an anniversary article for the New York *Times*. Three of his best friends, Dean West, Gilder, and John Finley, placed a bronze tablet in the room where he was born in Caldwell. A celebration had been planned in Princeton, but Cleveland vetoed it and went south on a gunning trip to escape any spontaneous observance. A year earlier Mark Twain had written him that his character had been placed upon a summit as high as Washington's, and Woodrow Wilson had sent him a note [1] to say "how specially strong the admiration and affection of those of us in Princeton who know you best have grown during the years when we have been privileged to be near you. It has been one of the best circumstances of my life that I have been closely associated with you in matters both large and small." Now similar messages came from every quarter.

He still found strength to make public appearances. In 1907 he delivered a Washington's birthday address before the Union League Club in Chicago. He still maintained a hopeful interest in party affairs. In March, 1908, he wrote an acquaintance that he saw a brightening light ahead for Democracy, that he felt that movements had been set in motion which would relieve the organization from its incubus, and that he hoped to see John A. Johnson of Minnesota nominated for President. He attended a committee meeting of the Princeton trustees as late as March 2, 1908, and the next month held a conference on the graduate school at his home. But his strength was now ebbing. He was in the grip of gastro-intestinal disease complicated by ailments of the heart and kidneys. Early in the spring he was prostrated by a painful attack, and went to Lakewood to recuperate. It was in a suite of the hotel there that, with his family about him, he celebrated his last birthday. As his strength sank he longed again for Princeton. With great secrecy, stretched on a mattress in a private automobile, he was brought back. William Sinclair was summoned to help nurse him. One attack followed another. On June 23 it was reported that he was better, but that night he sank and at 8:40 on the morning of June 24 he died.

In his last illness his innate religous feeling had come out more strongly than ever. He had sent to his old home for a copy of the hymnbook he had used as a boy. In a box by his bedside he kept a

[1] *Ibid.*, March 5, 1906.

printed copy of Whittier's beautiful religious poem, ''At Last.'' It had been given him by Bayard, with a letter explaining that the venerable Dean of Llandaff, lying on what he thought his deathbed, had found in it such consolation that when he unexpectedly recovered he had had copies printed for his friends; and Cleveland had always cherished it.

On Friday, June 26, he was buried. The press of the country was unrestrained in its eulogy. News came that South American republics, remembering the Venezuela message, had ordered their flags at half mast. To the services held at his Princeton home only a select number were invited. President Roosevelt was there; Chief Justice Fuller; others eminent in the government; six members of Cleveland's Cabinets; and intimate friends. Since the Presbyterian church has no ritual, only some simple passages of Scripture were read. But Dr. Henry Van Dyke closed the service with *The Happy Warrior,* the central lines of which fitted Cleveland so well:

> Who, if he rise to station of command,
> Rises by open means; and there will stand
> On honorable terms, or else retire,
> And in himself possess his own desire;
> Who comprehends his trust, and to the same
> Keeps faithful with a singleness of aim . . .
> Whom neither shape of danger can dismay,
> Nor thought of tender happiness betray.

IV

James Russell Lowell had called Cleveland the most typical American since Lincoln. Typical, perhaps, yet also unique; so limited in some directions and so powerful in others, so lacking in all that men call magnetism and yet so compelling. His must always seem an astonishing career; that of a man who might have seemed doomed to mediocrity, yet whose life became inextricably mingled with the dramatic occurrences of national history for a score of years. In some ways he was indeed a man of plain and simple talents. Yet so shrewd a judge as Lord Bryce found in him great powers, and his massive strength of character made these powers count with singular force in public affairs. He imposed himself upon his time in a way that no mediocre man could for a moment have done. He had also the good fortune of fitting the needs of his generation with a completeness that is true of few of our political leaders. He came upon the national stage at a moment when the country desperately needed some strong figure to rally and lead the forces of liberalism—the simple, basic liberalism expressed in honesty, economy, and efficient governmental service; and he performed his task so well that for his time and later times he became the very embodiment of Reform as Americans in the last quarter of the twentieth century interpreted that word.

His character is one upon which it will always be refreshing and inspiring to look back. Its fineness has been underestimated by those who associate his strength with coarseness of fibre. It was founded upon a simple, rocklike piety, a faith in the divine government of the universe and an unswerving belief in the necessity of making personal endeavor square with eternal principles. It was fed by a tenderness of sentiment that those who saw only his brusquer side seldom grasped, but which is illustrated by a thousand incidents. It was guided by a sense of rectitude that in the end became second nature to him, and which led him sometimes to remark deprecatingly to his intimates: "It is no credit to me to do right. I am never under any temptation to do wrong!" In its strength and integrity, it became a great national asset, and in time of crisis a pillar of national confidence. He belonged to the Anglo-Saxon race which values character above everything else; and his career shows why that valuation is a just one.

Intellectually, his chief characteristic was his powerful common sense; his mind was always vigorous, deliberate, and logical. But to say this is not to say enough. He had a highly individual method of attacking problems. He would assay every bit of evidence, step by step; when any part of the evidence was missing, he took careful note of it, and unlike many men, remembered the gap as he proceeded to study other aspects of the problem; and he would display the utmost caution in making up his mind. But once he reached a conclusion, no force could compel him to quit it. Most men are sometimes troubled, after fixing upon a decision, by qualms of uncertainty; they wonder if they were entirely right. Not so Cleveland. When by painstaking logic he had arrived at what he believed the correct position, neither friend nor foe, neither argument nor entreaty, could shake him. Both by initial caution and subsequent firmness he was thus admirably equipped for the work of an executive who acts under constant fire.

What did he accomplish for his time? Perhaps few men think of him as a great constructive force in American affairs. Yet four striking achievements must always be associated by history with his name. He restored honesty and impartiality to government at a time when the service had become indispensable to the health of the republic. He planted deep in the American mind the idea that the special privilege and the interference with free economic life which the bloated protective system represented ought to be abolished. That idea has been selfishly combated. But when the time comes, as come it will, when tariff walls the world over are lowered to a level consonant with common sense and with justice, the name of Grover Cleveland will be one of those most honored for the victory at last won. In a period of unparalleled stress and confusion, his invincible determination alone saved the nation from abandonment of the gold standard—an abandonment that would have meant heavy loss and perhaps economic chaos. Finally, by his treatment of the Nicaraguan, Hawaiian, and Venezuelan problems he taught the American people that in their handling of foreign affairs conscience ought always to be the one dominant force.

But he performed a greater service than any of these. He left to subsequent generations an example of the courage that never yields an inch in the cause of truth, and that never surrenders an iota of principle to expediency. Such courage is the very rarest element in the political life of modern democracies. We are surrounded on every hand by leaders who compromise here and waver there. Even the greatest among them are too often found to have a breaking-point, to be ready to surrender part of an eternal principle in order to obtain a temporary gain. From such leaders it is pleasant to turn to the memory of Cleveland and his tariff message of 1887, his silver letter of 1892, his refusal to accept a compromise on the repeal of the silver-purchase clause, his utter defiance of Tammany and all other unprincipled politicians, his scathing contempt of the jingoes who tried to exploit the Cuban rebellion. In future national crises men will long recur to the memory of the sorebeset President of the years 1893–97 who held the breach against financial error; who under the heaviest attacks and the wildest abuse, with few to aid or defend him, still smote the desk with his fist and cried "Never, never!" To have bequeathed a nation such an example of iron fortitude is better than to have swayed parliaments or to have won battles or to have annexed provinces.

Bibliography

MANUSCRIPT MATERIAL

Lewis F. Allen Papers. In possession of the family, Stockbridge, Mass. Contain some unique Cleveland items.

Jeremiah S. Black Papers. Library of Congress. Contain a few Cleveland letters, and many from Samuel J. Randall on politics and the tariff.

W. C. P. Breckinridge Papers. Library of Congress. Reflect the activities of the low-tariff element in Congress, with material also on silver.

William Jennings Bryan Papers. Library of Congress. A fragmentary collection, most of Bryan's papers being in the possession of Charles Bryan of Lincoln and closed to students. Indispensable for the silver contest in Congress and the schism of 1896.

Grover Cleveland Papers. Library of Congress. An enormous and invaluable collection of Cleveland's correspondence for the whole of his public life. Now (1932) being bound and placed in more usable form.

Bourke Cockran Papers. New York Public Library. A small collection, chiefly clippings.

Don M. Dickinson Papers. In family possession, Detroit, Mich. Of considerable value for political affairs.

Charles H. Fairchild Papers. New York Historical Society. A score of Cleveland's letters, some of them valuable.

Walter Q. Gresham Papers. Library of Congress. A small but valuable collection bearing on foreign affairs, Democratic party politics, and some of the domestic problems of the second Cleveland Administration.

Charles S. Hamlin Papers. In Mr. Hamlin's possession. An invaluable diary covering both Administrations, and many clippings, manuscripts, and papers bearing on Treasury affairs 1893–97. About 200 volumes.

Daniel S. Lamont Papers. Library of Congress. A large collection bearing on both Administrations, but particularly the second.

William R. Morrison Papers. Held by Carlisle B. Morrison, Waterloo, Ill. Contain press clippings only, some of them illuminating.

Justin S. Morrill Papers. Library of Congress. Present data on the Republican side of the tariff and currency questions, 1885–1897.

John T. Morgan Papers. Library of Congress. A voluminous collection; disappointing for the currency question, but of some value for foreign relations, Morgan in large part disagreeing with Cleveland.

Richard Olney Papers. Library of Congress. A considerable collection, by no means fully covered by the authorized biographer, and valuable for foreign affairs, the Chicago strike, and the anti-trust cases.

William Gorham Rice Papers. Partly in custody of Mr. Rice, partly in the

State Historical Library at Albany. A valuable collection for Cleveland's governorship in particular.

Theodore Roosevelt Papers. Library of Congress. Contain a few letters to and from Cleveland.

William E. Russell Papers. In the possession of Professor Philip Chase, Harvard University. Of great value for the years 1890–96.

John Sherman Papers. Library of Congress. One of the largest collections in Washington, and very full on the Republican attitude toward all Congressional questions.

Henry Villard Papers. Harvard University. Valuable for monetary questions, the campaign of 1892, and the demand for a special session in 1894.

William F. Vilas Papers. Wisconsin Historical Society. Contain a large number of Cleveland's letters, of which copies are also in Washington and at Columbia.

Henry Watterson Papers. Library of Congress. Though full of gaps, for Watterson was careless of his letters, contain some singularly outspoken comment on men and questions of the time.

Printed Material

(Necessarily a much abbreviated list.)

Abbot, Willis J. Carter Henry Harrison: A memoir. New York. 1895.

Adams, Henry. Education of Henry Adams. Boston. 1927.

Adler, Cyrus. Jacob H. Schiff, his life and letters. New York. 1929.

Alexander, D. S. A political history of the State of New York. New York. 1923.
—Four famous New Yorkers. New York. 1923.

Altgeld, John P. Live questions. Chicago. 1890.

Arnett, Alex M. The Populist movement in Georgia. New York. 1922.

Barnes, James A. John G. Carlisle: financial statesman. New York. 1931.

Barry, David S. Forty years in Washington. Boston. 1924.

Beard, Charles A. and Mary R. The rise of American civilization. New York. 1930.

Beer, Thomas. Hanna. New York. 1929.

Bigelow, John. Retrospections of an active life. New York. 1909.

Bishop, Joseph B. Presidential nominations and elections. New York. 1916.—Theodore Roosevelt and his times. New York. 1920.—Notes and anecdotes of many years. New York. 1925.

Bowers, Claude G. Life of John W. Kern. Indianapolis. 1918.

Brewton, William W. Life of Thomas E. Watson. Atlanta. 1926.

Browne, Waldo R. Altgeld of Illinois. New York. 1924.

Bryan, William Jennings. The first battle. Chicago. 1896.—The memoirs of William Jennings Bryan. Chicago. 1925.

Buck, Solon J. The agrarian crusade. New Haven. 1920.—The Granger movement. Cambridge. 1913.

Burr, Anna Robeson. The portrait of a banker, James Stillman. New York. 1927.

Busbey, L. White. Uncle Joe Cannon. New York. 1927.

Byars, William V. An American commoner: The life and times of Richard Parks Bland. Columbus, Mo. 1900.

Carnegie, Andrew. Autobiography. Boston. 1920.

Chadwick, French E. The relations of the United States and Spain. New York. 1911.

Clark, Champ. My quarter century of American politics. New York. 1921.

Cleveland, Grover. Fishing and shooting sketches. New York. 1906.—Presidential problems. New York. 1904.—Letters and addresses of Grover Cleveland, edited by Albert Ellery Bergh. New York. 1909.—Public papers of Grover Cleveland, twenty-second President of the United States, 1885–89. Washington, 1889.—Public papers of Grover Cleveland, twenty-fourth President of the United States, 1893–97. Washington, 1897.—Writings and speeches of Grover Cleveland, edited by George F. Parker. New York. 1892.

Coleman, McAlister. Eugene V. Debs, a man unafraid. New York. 1930.

Corey, Lewis. The house of Morgan. New York. 1930.

Cortissoz, Royal. The life of Whitelaw Reid. New York. 1921.

Croly, Herbert. Marcus Alonzo Hanna: His life and work.

Cullom, Shelby M. Fifty years of public service. Chicago. 1911.

Curtis, George W. Orations and addresses, edited by C. E. Norton. New York. 1894.

Darrow, Clarence. The story of my life. New York. 1932.

Depew, Chauncey M. My memories of eighty years. New York. 1922.

Dewey, Davis R. National problems, 1887–1897. New York. 1907.

Dorsheimer, William. Life and public services of Grover Cleveland. Philadelphia. 1888.

Dunn, Arthur Wallace. From Harrison to Harding. New York. 1922.

Eckenrode, H. J. Rutherford B. Hayes: statesman of reunion. New York. 1930.

Foraker, Joseph B. Notes of a busy life. Cincinnati. 1916.

Ford, Henry Jones. The Cleveland era. New Haven. 1921.

Ford, Worthington C. The letters of Henry Adams, 1858–1891. Boston. 1930.

Foulke, William Dudley. Fighting the spoilsmen. New York. 1919.—A Hoosier autobiography. New York. 1922.

Fuess, Claude M. Carl Schurz, reformer. New York. 1932.

Garland, Hamlin. Main-travelled roads. New York. 1899.

George, Henry, Jr. Life of Henry George. New York. 1900.

Gibbons, Herbert Adams, John Wanamaker. New York. 1926.

Gilder, Richard Watson. Grover Cleveland, a record of friendship. New York. 1920.

Gilder, Rosamond. The letters of Richard Watson Gilder. Boston. 1916.

Godkin, Edwin L. Reflections and comments. New York. 1895.

Gompers, Samuel. Seventy years of life and labor. New York. 1925.

Goodrich, Frederick E. Life and public services of Grover Cleveland. Boston. 1884.

Gosnell, Harold F. Boss Platt and his New York machine. Chicago. 1924.

Gresham, Matilda. Life of Walter Quinton Gresham. Chicago. 1919.

Griffin, Solomon B. People and politics. Boston. 1923.

Harvey, George. Henry Clay Frick, the man. New York. 1928.

Harvey, W. H. Coin's financial school. Chicago. 1894.

Hay, John. Letters and diaries. Privately printed.

Haynes, Fred E. James Baird Weaver. Iowa City. 1919.—Third party movements since the Civil War. Iowa City. 1916.

Hibben, Paxton. The peerless leader, William Jennings Bryan. New York. 1929.

Hicks, John D. The Populist revolt. Minneapolis. 1931.

Howe, M. A. de Wolfe. Moorfield Storey: the portrait of an independent. Boston. 1932.

Hoar, George F. Autobiography of seventy years. New York. 1903.

Houston, David. Eight years with Wilson's cabinet. Garden City. 1926.

Hovey, Carl. The life of J. Pierpont Morgan. New York. 1911.

Hudson, William C. Random recollections of an old political reporter. New York. 1911.

James, Henry. Richard Olney and his public service. Boston. 1923.

Kent, Frank R. The Democratic party, a history. New York. 1928.

Kinley, David. The Independent Treasury and its relation to the banks. Washington. 1910.

Krock, Arthur. The editorials of Henry Watterson. New York. 1923.

La Follette, Robert M. La Follette's autobiography: a personal narrative of political experience. Madison. 1911.

Lane, Franklin K. The letters of Franklin K. Lane. Boston. 1922.

Lauck, William Jett. The causes of the panic of 1893. New York. 1907.

Laughlin, J. Lawrence. The history of bimetallism in the United States. New York. 1896.

Lloyd, Caro. Henry Demarest Lloyd, a biography. New York. 1912.

Lloyd, Henry Demarest. Wealth against commonwealth. New York. 1894.

Lodge, Henry Cabot. Selections from the correspondence of Theodore Roosevelt and Henry Cabot Lodge, 1884–1918. New York. 1925.

Lynch, Denis T. Grover Cleveland: a man four-square. New York. 1932.

Mayes, Edward. Life of Lucius Q. C. Lamar. Nashville. 1896.

McCall, Samuel W. The Life of Thomas B. Reed. Boston. 1914.

McElroy, Robert. Grover Cleveland, the man and the statesman. New York. 1923.

McMurray, Donald L. Coxey's army. Boston. 1929.

Marcosson, Isaac F. Adventures in interviewing. New York. 1920.

Millis, Walter. Martial glory: the war with Spain. Boston. 1931.

Mitchell, Wesley Clair. Gold, prices, and wages. Berkeley. 1908.—A history of the greenbacks. Chicago. 1903.

Moore, John Bassett. History and digest of international arbitrations. Washington, 1898.—Principles of American diplomacy. New York. 1918.

Myers, William Starr. The Republican party, a history. New York. 1928.

Nevins, Allan. The emergence of modern America. New York. 1927.—The Evening Post: A century of journalism. New York. 1924.—Henry White: thirty years of American diplomacy. New York. 1930.

Newton, Lord. Lord Lansdowne, a biography. New York. 1930.

Noyes, Alexander Dana. Forty years of American finance. New York. 1907.

Parker, George F. Recollections of Grover Cleveland. New York. 1909.

Peck, Harry Thurston. Twenty years of the republic, 1885–1905. New York. 1906.

Paxson, Frederick L. Recent history of the United States. New York. 1928.

Pettigrew, R. F. Imperial Washington. Chicago. 1922.

Platt, Thomas C. The autobiography of Thomas Collier Platt. New York. 1910.

Pringle, Henry F. Theodore Roosevelt: a biography. New York. 1931.

Pyle, Joseph G. The life of James J. Hill. Garden City. 1917.

Ralph, Julian. Our great West. New York. 1913.

Ralphdon, Harold Fulton. Age of Cleveland. New York. 1888.

Rhodes, James Ford. History of the United States from Hayes to McKinley. New ed. New York. 1919.—The McKinley and Roosevelt Administrations. New York. 1927.

Richardson, James D. Messages and papers of the Presidents. Washington. 1897, 1909.

Ripley, William Z. Railroads: rates and regulation. New York. 1913.

Robinson, William A. Thomas B. Reed, parliamentarian. New York. 1930.

Roosevelt, Theodore. Autobiography. New York. 1912.

Schurz, Carl. Speeches, correspondence, and political papers. Edited by Frederic Bancroft. 6 vols. New York. 1913.

Seitz, Don C. Joseph Pulitzer, his life and letters. New York. 1924.

Smalley, George W. Anglo-American memories. New York. 1911.—Second series. New York. 1912.

Sprague, O. M. W. History of crises under the National Banking System. Washington. 1910.

Stanwood, Edward. James B. Blaine. Boston.—American tariff controversies in the nineteenth century. Boston. 1903.

Stealey, O. O. Twenty years in the press gallery. New York. 1906.

Steffens, Lincoln. The autobiography of Lincoln Steffens. New York. 1931.

Stephenson, Nathaniel Wright. Nelson W. Aldrich, a leader in American politics. New York. 1930.

Stewart, William M. Reminiscences. New York. 1908.

Stoddard, Henry L. As I knew them. New York. 1927.

Stoddard, William O. Grover Cleveland. New York. 1888.

Straus, Oscar. Under four administrations. Boston. 1922.

Sullivan, Mark. Our Times: The great adventure. New York. 1926.—Our Times: The turn of the century. New York. 1929.—Our Times: Pre-War America. New York. 1930.

Tarbell, Ida M. The tariff in our times. New York. 1911.

Taussig, F. W. The tariff history of the United States. New York. 1914.

Thayer, William Roscoe. Life and letters of John Hay. Boston. 1915.

Thomas, Harrison C. The return of the Democratic party to power in 1884. New York. 1919.

Thompson, Charles Willis. Presidents I've known and two near-Presidents. Indianapolis. 1929.

Villard, Oswald Garrison. Prophets true and false. New York. 1928.

Washington, Booker T. My larger education. Garden City. 1911.

Watterson, Henry. Marse Henry Watterson, an autobiography. New York. 1919.

Werner, Morris R. Bryan. New York. 1919.—Tammany Hall. New York. 1928.

Wheeler, Everett P. Sixty years of American life. New York. 1917.

White, Andrew D. Autobiography of Andrew D. White. New York. 1905.

White, William Allen. The real issue. New York. 1909.—Masks in a pageant. New York. 1928.

White, Horace. Life of Lyman Trumbull. Boston. 1913.

Whitlock, Brand. Forty years of it. New York. 1925.

Whittle, James Lowry. Grover Cleveland. London. 1896.

Wiley, Harvey W. Harvey W. Wiley, an autobiography. Indianapolis. 1930.

Winkler, John K. Hearst, an American phenomenon. New York. 1928.

Williams, Jesse Lynch. Mr. Cleveland, a personal interpretation. New York. 1910.

Wilson, Woodrow. Congressional government: a study in American politics. Boston. 1885.

Appendix I   Cleveland's Letters Regarding his Marriage, 1886

(These letters, all written to Cleveland's sister Mrs. Hoyt, are presented as throwing an interesting light upon his personality. At the time of the first the news of his engagement had just become public property. It leaked out in an interesting fashion. Miss Folsom wrote from Europe to a Buffalo friend announcing in confidence the approaching marriage, but neglected to place her injunction of secrecy in the first sentences of the letter. The friend read the letter aloud at the breakfast table, and thus let the cat out of the bag. Cleveland's worry over details makes his communications to his sister amusing, while his delicacy of feeling comes out clearly.)

Executive Mansion, Washington, March 21, 1886.

DEAR MARY:

. . . I expect to be married pretty early in June,—very soon after Frank returns. I think the quicker it can be done the better and she seems to think so too. You know she can hardly be said to have a home, and if the event was delayed long after her return the talk and gossip which would certainly be stirred up could not fail to be very embarrassing to her. I find it very hard to settle the question as to the manner in which the thing should be conducted. It will, I suppose, be impossible for me to go on a trip at that time or until Congress adjourns, which it seems to be the general impression will not take place until July or August.

I want my marriage to be a quiet one and am determined that the American Sovereigns shall not interfere with a thing so purely personal to me. And yet I don't want to be churlish and mean or peculiar for the sake of being peculiar. But if the example of the President is worth anything I want it in this matter to be in the direction of sense and proper decency. I have thought of having no one but the family, hers and mine, present at the ceremony; but maybe there are but few that would come. Hers is not large. Her mother has two sisters and two brothers and her mother. Then I have thought it might be well to have the Cabinet people at the ceremony. They have all been so devoted to me all through and on all occasions that it seems almost as though they should be with me there. As far as the ceremony proper is concerned I do not feel like extending the attendance beyond that above indicated. I have thought that after the ceremony and on the same evening I might have a card reception, or that might be postponed to an evening or two later, or it might be given up entirely. A more democratic and popular thing, and what I would like on some accounts better, would be a public reception; but it seems rather hard to subject Frank to such an ordeal at that time. I wish you'd think of all these things and let me know how they strike you. Of course I can't get along without you and I shall utterly refuse to go through the thing unless you are about. I have calculated that you would come to me not later than the first of May and stay through, and the sooner you can come the better.

I believe I shall buy or rent a house near here where I can go and be away from this cursed constant grind. I have thought it would be rather nice if Mrs. Folsom could live there and keep up the establishment, but I don't know as I could make that work.

It has occurred to me that it would be nice to have the little room adjoining mine which William occupies fixed up for a dressing room, etc., for Frank, or a place where she could sit and stay during the day.

You can see from all this that I have been pretty busily thinking though I have not settled on much. This is the first time I have suggested any of these things to a human being. I suppose my bridal present for my new wife is in process of manufacture. I am almost afraid I shall make a mistake there and have something too expensive. I have my heart set upon making Frank a sensible, domestic American wife, and I would be pleased now to hear her spoken of as "The First Lady of the Land" or "The Mistress of the White House." I want her to be happy and to possess all she can reasonably desire, but I should feel very much afflicted if she lets many notions in her head. But I think she is pretty level-headed.

Let me hear from you as soon and as fully as possible upon all the topics touched upon in this letter. . . .

Executive Mansion, Washington, April 14, 1886.

DEAR MARY:

I must before I go to bed write you a little letter and tell you that I received yours of a late date and how pleased I am at the prospect of your being here soon. I want to talk with you about the event which is soon to take place. You know as it draws near there are lots of little things which I begin to stew over a little, and I can't talk to anyone about them except the Colonel. He and I canvass the matter and I expect we could get it pretty nearly right, but probably there might be something in which you could help us.

It looks now as if Frank would reach New York about the 28th of May, stay there a few days, and then come here and be married the next day or the day of her arrival—say the 2nd or 3rd of June.

We have sort of planned the thing in this way: Have the ceremony at 7 o'clock, with no one present but the two families; have a dinner immediately after the ceremony; have the members of the Cabinet and their families come about 8:30 o'clock, and have a reception *by card* from 9 to 11.

I had a letter from Libbie tonight. . . . Let me know just as soon as you can when you will probably be here. . . .

Executive Mansion, Washington, April 19, 1886.

DEAR MARY:

. . . I have changed my ideas entirely in regard to the wedding. I am decidedly of the opinion now that the affair should be more quiet even than at first contemplated. The time when Frank [Miss Folsom] will arrive in this country is not entirely certain, and for that reason the day of the wedding cannot be fixed, with no chance of postponement, long enough in advance to permit of all arrangements on the part of the families to attend. If they should attend they would be subjected from the time of their arrival to the impudent inquisition of newspaper correspondents and if this latter dirty gang were not entirely satisfied, our friends would probably be dished up in a very mean way; and the newspapers and the people have acted in such a mean way that I don't care to gratify either of them.

My notion now is to have you and Libbie [Rose Elizabeth Cleveland] and Bissell (if he will come) and Miss Nelson on my side, and Frank's mother and perhaps one or two of her aunts and one or two others on her side, and be married by Dr. Sunderland with no reception the same night or any other time unless we choose—which we can decide when we get ready. I should like to have Col. Lamont at the ceremony, but am not strenuous about that. He and I have canvassed the whole matter and agree that the plan above outlined is the best that offers. I have written the whole scheme to Frank and from something she wrote in her last letter I think she will be pleased with it. If she is not I will accede to her wishes; but I am of the opinion that after she sees the newspaper clippings I sent her yesterday she will feel more than ever like falling in with my ideas.

The good people of the country will, I am sure, be satisfied to have their President behave on such an occasion like anyone else and dispense with all nonsense and flummery.

I want you to approve the manner in which I am inclined to have the thing arranged. It would be hard to do so with your preconceived notions, but you must put yourself in my place as nearly as you can and try to see how much that may be unpleasant will be avoided. I am very indignant at the way Frank has been treated and mean to give "the gang" as little chance at us hereafter as possible.

I believe I shall make no change in the house until she is here, when I expect I shall be better able to tell just what we want. So I don't want you to write to any members of the family about it—at any rate until I give you the word. . . .

Executive Mansion, Washington, April 26, 1886.

My Dear Sister:

. . . I have written to Frank more than a week ago giving her my new scheme and I am inclined to think she will agree to it. I have lately thought of adding to the very few family and intimate friends, the Cabinet, General Sheridan and wife, Admiral Porter and wife, Chief Justice Waite and wife and daughter, and such, making about fifty or more.

It would not do at all to invite all my family and omit her uncles and aunts. They are all the relatives she has and she has lived with them so much that they are precisely as near as her brothers and sisters. I would not propose making any distinction between them and my sisters and brothers. It will work out some way, but I would like to talk with you about it. I can't write all I want to say.

Do you happen to remember what was done with the key I had to cable messages? I can't find it. It's awkward fixing this business because it takes about a month to get an answer to a letter.

Let me hear from you again very soon. You see, Frank is entering a life where she can have all the excitement she wants, and she can afford better than a good many girls to have a quiet wedding.

Executive Mansion, Washington, May 5, 1886.

DEAR MARY:

I was pleased to hear from your last letter that you were to be with me next week. On the strength of your coming Libbie writes me that she will probably leave Holland Patent the last of next week and stay over Sunday in New York and arrive here probably the first of week after next.

She seems to think it too bad not to have all the brothers and sisters at the wedding, and yet she thinks I ought to go to Frank somewhere and be married and take my bride to the White House. If Frank would agree to it I think I would be quite willing to be married in New York with no one present but the witnesses. . . .

Executive Mansion, Washington, May 20, 1886.

DEAR MARY:

. . . I think I shall have very nice arrangements perfected for a short stay at Deer Park after the performance; but I don't know how all our plans may be changed by the death of Frank's grandfather Folsom yesterday. I should think the wedding might go on as planned very quietly. And an additional reason is afforded for quietness which may seem to cut off some guests which have heretofore been calculated upon—Miss Grigg, for instance.

The news from the ship office in New York is that the vessel will arrive not earlier than Tuesday afternoon nor later than Thursday. I have just received a letter from Mrs. Welch, the aunt, asking me what the arrangement now is by which, according to letters from the travelling party, they propose to circumvent people. I don't know what to write to her, and think I will put off a reply to such time as it will reach her just about as the ship arrives. . . .
Let me hear what effect you think Mr. Folsom's death will have on the plans and what Louise says.

Executive Mansion, Washington, May, 28, 1886.

DEAR SISTER:

. . . Mrs. Lamont was just here (9:15 A. M.) and says she has just received a dispatch from the Colonel that he is on his way from New York and will arrive at 10:40. I heard from him last night to the effect that at half-past five there was no news. I think now that the ship came in later. And just this very moment a dispatch is handed me from Ben dated this morning saying: "Arrived safe. All in good health." So that I guess now that the Colonel is hurrying home to complete arrangements for the wedding to take place at the time contemplated.

I think you may safely calculate on that.

Appendix II   Mr. Justice Shiras's Alleged Reversal of Opinion

(The information here presented is condensed from a memorandum prepared for the author by Mr. Sidney Ratner. A detailed study of the question, with many new facts, may be found in his doctoral dissertation now in preparation at Columbia University on *The Income Tax of 1894*.)

A long list of works, including such authoritative volumes as Charles Warren's *Supreme Court in United States History* and Louis B. Boudin's *Government by Judiciary*, assert that it was Mr. Justice Shiras who reversed his vote on the income tax of 1894. None of these works presents any evidence or cites any authority. The statement has been copied from one historical treatise to another, and yet it rests in the last analysis upon rumor and newspaper accounts.

Yet as early as March 2, 1897, the Hon. John Dalzell of Pennsylvania, a very close friend of Mr. Justice Shiras, denied the charge in the House of Representatives. (See *Cong. Rec.*, 54th Cong., 2d sess., vol. 29, p. 2653 ff.) Mr. Dalzell did not disclose which Justice had reversed the part of his first decision favoring the income tax. He probably kept silent because of the unwritten rule of the Supreme Court that all votes are to be held in confidence, except as they are disclosed in the public reports of decisions. Eight years later another intimate friend of Mr. Justice Shiras repudiated the charge. This was the Hon. Frank Warren Hackett, a noted lawyer who was Assistant Secretary of the Navy 1900–1901. He wrote a vigorous note correcting a contemporaneous statement regarding the income tax decision; and in this he not only forcibly denounced the accusation as unfounded, but declared that if necessary he could confirm his statement by information which he had received in 1900 from an authoritative source, in no wise connected with Justice Shiras. (See *Yale Law Journal*, June, 1915, vol. 24, pp. 661–662.) Mr. Chief Justice Hughes has more recently given what may be considered the *coup de grace* to the charge. In his volume of 1928 entitled *The Supreme Court of the United States*, he has authoritatively stated that "there is good reason to believe that the charge [against Justice Shiras] was without foundation, and that he was not the member of the court whose views were altered on the reargument." In a letter to the author of this biography he has reemphasized this statement.

Still further evidence is presented by Mr. George Shiras 3rd, son of Mr. Justice Shiras. In a letter to Mr. Ratner dated January 21, 1932, he states that from his father and other sources he obtained a distinct impression that his father had not changed his vote. He adds that his father had been disappointed in his hope that Chief Justice Fuller or Chief Justice White would make public the secret vote on the income tax.

The question then arises, Which of the justices, other than Shiras, reversed that part of his first decision which favored the income tax?

It is possible, by a careful study of the court reports, to narrow the choice to Justices Brewer and Gray. These reports show that, as everyone familiar with the case knows, Justices Harlan and White were consistent supporters of the income tax. Justice Field was consistently opposed. So, also, it would seem, was Chief Justice Fuller. In the Olney Papers is a eulogy of Mr. Fuller, written many years later by Mr. Olney, in which his vote against the constitutionality of the income tax, at a time when a vote in its favor would have been of great political benefit to the Administration, is cited as evidence of Mr. Fuller's courage. Moreover, Chief Justice Fuller consistently upheld the traditional rights of property against the progressive tendencies of his time. Justice Jackson was of course present only at the rehearing and cast only one vote. Justice Brown voted for the income tax on the rehearing.

The evidence that Brewer rather than Gray changed his vote now remains to be considered. Mr. Chauncey Hackett, son of the Hon. Frank Warren Hackett, writes Mr. Ratner that, according to his recollection, his father stated in private conversation that Brewer was the man. Moreover, if it was Brewer who reversed his vote, then the refusal of the Supreme Court to divulge the name of the justice who altered his opinion becomes easily understandable. For immediately after the income tax was pronounced unconstitutional, Mr. Justice Brewer handed down the noted and highly unfortunate Debs Case decision. He thus brought down upon his head—very deservedly—the wrath of the Western agrarians and the Eastern workingmen. If the Supreme Court had published the secret vote on the income tax, Brewer would have been exposed to a double storm of public indignation.

Another fact which renders plausible the opinion that Brewer changed his vote is that he was the nephew of Mr. Justice Field. The latter was a vehement opponent of the income tax. He might have succeeded in influencing his nephew to change his vote. Finally, it is to be noted that Brewer went out of his way to make a speech in defence of the final income tax decision at the University of Iowa on June 8, 1898. It seems possible that it was a change of vote which made him feel a special obligation thus to defend the income tax decision.

All in all, it is certain that Mr. Justice Shiras has borne obloquy for an act that he never committed; and it seems probable—though the evidence is not conclusive—that this obloquy should have been visited upon Mr. Justice Brewer.

Made in the USA
Coppell, TX
04 October 2021

63462563R00453